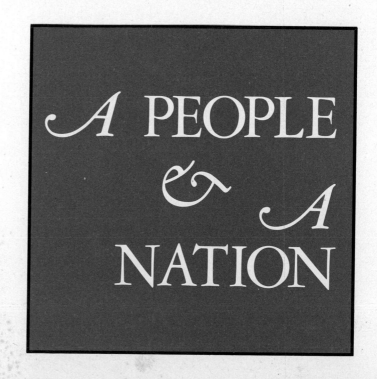

MARY BETH NORTON
Cornell University

DAVID M. KATZMAN
University of Kansas

PAUL D. ESCOTT
University of North Carolina, Charlotte

HOWARD P. CHUDACOFF
Brown University

THOMAS G. PATERSON
University of Connecticut

WILLIAM M. TUTTLE, JR.
University of Kansas

HOUGHTON MIFFLIN COMPANY   BOSTON

Dallas   Geneva, Illinois   Hopewell, New Jersey   Palo Alto   London

A PEOPLE
& A
NATION

A HISTORY OF
THE UNITED STATES   *Volume I: To 1877*

Printed in the U.S.A.

Library of Congress Catalog Card Number: 81-84809

ISBN: 0-395-29091-0

Cover photo: *The Residence of David Twining 1787.* Oil on canvas.
By Edward Hicks (1780–1849).
From the Abby Aldrich Rockefeller Folk Art Center, Williamsburg, Virginia.

Chapter Openers

Chapter 1
Tenochtitlan. The American Museum of Natural History.

Chapter 2
Indigo culture. William R. Perkins Library, Duke University.

Chapter 3
"The Fishing Lady." Museum of Fine Arts, Boston, Seth K. Sweetser Fund.

Chapter 4
British troops on the Boston Common, 1768. Boston Athenaeum.

Chapter 5
The Battle of Lexington. The Connecticut Historical Society.

Chapter 6
Washington presiding over debate at the Constitutional Convention. The Library Company of Philadelphia.

Chapter 7
Salute to General Washington in New York Harbor. National Gallery of Art, Gift of Edgar William and Bernice Chrysler Garbisch.

Chapter 8
Washington, D.C., in 1800. Library of Congress.

Chapter 9
The Erie Canal. The New-York Historical Society.

Chapter 10
Slaves returning from the fields. The New-York Historical Society.

Chapter 11
Farmers at Dennison Hill, Southbridge, Massachusetts (artist unknown). National Gallery of Art, Gift of Edgar William and Bernice Chrysler Garbisch.

Chapter 12
Antislavery rally (1841). Library of Congress.

Chapter 13
"The Eagle's Nest." The Connecticut Historical Society.

Chapter 14
Army of the Potomac. National Archives.

Chapter 15
Richmond, Virginia, following the Civil War. National Archives.

Map Credits

Page 62
Non-English White Settlements 1775, Black Population, c. 1775, in *Atlas of Early American History: The Revolutionary Era 1760–1790,* by Lester J. Cappon et al. (copyright © 1976 by Princeton University Press), published for the Newberry Library and the Institute of Early American History and Culture, pp. 24 and 25. Reprinted by permission of Princeton University Press.

Page 97
Stamp Act Crisis, in *Atlas of Early American History: The Revolutionary Era 1760–1790,* by Lester J. Cappon et al. (copyright © 1976 by Princeton University Press), published for the Newberry Library and the Institute of Early American History and Culture, p. 42. Reprinted by permission of Princeton University Press.

Page 147
Cession of Indian Lands to U.S., 1775–1790, in *Atlas of Early American History: The Revolutionary Era 1760–1790,* by Lester J. Cappon et al. (copyright © 1976 by Princeton University Press), published for the Newberry Library and the Institute of Early American History and Culture, p. 61. Reprinted by permission of Princeton University Press.

Page 188
1790 Black Population: Proportion of Total Population, in *Atlas of Early American History: The Revolutionary Era 1760–1790,* by Lester J. Cappon et al. (copyright © 1976 by Princeton University Press), published for the Newberry Library and the Institute of Early American History and Culture, p. 67. Reprinted by permission of Princeton University Press.

Page 371
The War in the West, 1861–July 1863, from *The Essentials of American History,* Second Edition, by Richard N. Current, T. Harry Williams and Frank Freidel. Copyright © 1976 by Alfred A. Knopf, Inc. Copyright © 1959, 1961, 1964, 1966, 1971, 1972 by Richard N. Current, T. Harry Williams and Frank Freidel. Reprinted by permission of Alfred A. Knopf, Inc.

CONTENTS

APPENDIX

INDEX

Maps and Charts

PREFACE

We are always recreating our past, rediscovering the personalities and events that have shaped us, inspired us, or bedeviled us. When we are buffeted by the erratic winds of current affairs, we look back for reassuring precedents. But we do not always find that history is comforting. The past holds much that is disturbing, for the story of a people or a nation—like any story—is never one of unbroken progress. As with our own personal experience, it is both triumphant and tragic, filled with injury as well as healing.

This volume is our recreation of the American past: our rediscovery of its people and of the nation they founded and sustained. Drawing on recent research as well as on seasoned, authoritative works, we have sought to offer a comprehensive book that tells the whole story of American history. Presidential and party politics, congressional legislation, Supreme Court decisions, diplomacy and treaties, wars and foreign interventions, economic patterns, and state and local politics have been the stuff of American history for generations. Into this traditional fabric we have woven social history, broadly defined. We have investigated the history of the majority of Americans—women—and of minorities. And we have sought to illuminate the private side of the American story: work and play; dress and diet; entertainment; family and home life; relationships between men and women; and race, ethnicity, and religion. From the ordinary to the exceptional—the steelworker, the office secretary, the plantation owner, the slave, the ward politician, the president's wife, the actress, the canal builder—Americans have had personal stories that have intersected with the public policies of their government. Whether victors or victims, dominant or dominated, all have been actors in their own right, with feelings, ideas, and aspirations that have fortified them in good times and bad. All are part of the American story.

Several questions guided our telling of this intricate narrative. On the official, or public, side of

| Major themes |

American history, we have sought to identify Americans' expectations of their government, to show who governs and how power is exercised, to explain the origins of reform movements, and to compare the everyday practice of government and politics with the egalitarian principles to which Americans theo-

retically subscribe. We have looked at the domestic sources of foreign policy and at the reasons why the United States has chosen to intervene abroad or to wage war. We have sought as well to capture the mood or mentality of an era, in which Americans reveal what they think about themselves and their public officials through their letters, music, and literature, their rallies and riots.

In the social and economic spheres, we have emphasized technological development and its effects on the worker and the workplace. We have traced major economic trends. And because geographic mobility is such a striking part of American history, we have given considerable attention to the questions of why people migrate and how they adapt to new environments. The interactions of racially and ethnically diverse people, the social divisions that have resulted and the efforts that have been made to heal them, are also, it seems to us, central to the study of the American past.

In the private domain of the family and the home, we have examined sex roles, childbearing and childrearing, diet and dress. We have attempted to show how public policy and technological development—war and mass production, for example—have forced change on these most basic institutions. Finally, we have asked how Americans have chosen to entertain themselves, as participants or spectators, with sports, music, the graphic arts, reading, theater, film, and television.

Our experience as teachers of American history has shown us that students not only need to address these questions, but can and want to address them. Unfortunately, dull, abstract writing often kills their natural curiosity. Thus we have taken pains to write in clear, concrete language and to include wherever possible the stories of real people, as told in their letters and diaries and in oral histories. We have tried to stimulate readers to think about the meaning of American history—not just to memorize it.

In planning the book, we decided to open each chapter with the true story of an American, ordinary

| Structure of the book |

or exceptional, whose experience was representative of the times. Following the story we devote a few paragraphs to placing it in historical perspective and introducing the major themes and events of the chapter. Students should find these introductory sections, which in effect provide an overview of the chapters, useful study guides.

We have used boxed glosses to highlight key persons, events, concepts, and trends. Our illustrations, maps, tables, and graphs are closely related to important points in the text. Similarly, the four full-color photographic studies of changing patterns in work and leisure are specifically related to the chapters in which they appear.

Most chapters close with a chronological list of important events, and all chapters end with a bibliography for follow-up reading. In the Appendix we have provided a bibliography of general reference books by subject; important documents; tables of election results, administrations (including Cabinet members), party strength in Congress, justices of the Supreme Court, and territorial acquisitions; and a statistical profile of the American people.

During the long and painstaking course of writing and revision the six of us read and reread one another's work and debated one another across note-strewn tables. In our effort to produce a unified and spirited book, we became friends and better scholars. Though each of us feels answerable for the whole, we take primary responsibility for particular chapters as follows: Mary Beth Norton, Chapters 1–7; David M. Katzman, Chapters 8–9, 11–12; Paul D. Escott, Chapters 10, 13–15; Howard P. Chudacoff, Chapters 16–21, 24; Thomas G. Paterson, Chapters 22–23, 25, 27–28, 32; and William M. Tuttle, Jr., Chapters 26, 29–31, and 33–34.

Acknowledgments We have been alert to the constructive suggestions of the many teachers and scholars who have read and criticized our manuscript in successive drafts. Their advice has been invaluable, and we are grateful for it:

Robert Abzug, *University of Texas, Austin*
Lois Banner, *George Washington University*
William Barney, *University of North Carolina, Chapel Hill*
Michael C. Batinski, *Southern Illinois University, Carbondale*
Susan Becker, *University of Tennessee, Knoxville*
Barton Bernstein, *Stanford University*
Stephen Botein, *Michigan State University*
Jonathan Chu, *University of Massachusetts, Boston*
Allen Davis, *Temple University*
Peter Filene, *University of North Carolina, Chapel Hill*
Lewis Gould, *University of Texas, Austin*

J. William Harris, *Committee on Degrees in History & Literature, Harvard University*
George Herring, *University of Kentucky, Lexington*
William Holmes, *University of Georgia, Athens*
Michael F. Holt, *University of Virginia, Charlottesville*
Nancy Jaffe, *Riverside City College, California*
Charles Johnson, *University of Tennessee, Knoxville*
Alice Kessler-Harris, *Hofstra University*
Richard Lowitt, *Iowa State University*
George Lubick, *Northern Arizona University*
John G. MacNaughton, *Monroe Community College, Rochester, New York*
Pauline Maier, *Massachusetts Institute of Technology*
Robert Martin, *St. Louis Community College at Florissant Valley*
Arthur F. McClure, *Central Missouri State University*
Russell Menard, *University of Minnesota, Minneapolis*
Eric Monkkonen, *University of California, Los Angeles*
Philip D. Morgan, *Institute of Early American History and Culture, Williamsburg, Virginia*
Jerome Mushkat, *University of Akron*
William O'Neill, *Rutgers The State University of New Jersey, New Brunswick*
George Pilcher, *University of Colorado, Boulder*
Jackson Putnam, *California State University, Fullerton*
Harvard Sitkoff, *University of New Hampshire, Durham*
James Smallwood, *Oklahoma State University*
Sue Taishoff, *University of South Florida, Tampa*
David Thelen, *University of Missouri, Columbia*
John Trickel, *Richland College, Dallas, Texas*
James Turner, *University of Massachusetts, Boston*
Ronald Walters, *Johns Hopkins University*
Darold Wax, *Oregon State University*
William Bruce Wheeler, *University of Tennessee, Knoxville*

We acknowledge with thanks the special contributions of Warren I. Cohen, Jeffrey Crow, Gregory DeLapp, Paul Dest, John Emond, Shirley Harmon, Pam Harrison, Chico Herbison, Sharyn A. Katzman, Jean Manter, Sally McMillen, Paula Oliver, Holly Izard Paterson, Roberta Rudgate, and Mary Erickson Tuttle. We also appreciate the guidance and generous assistance of the many members of the staff of Houghton Mifflin Company who worked on the book.

T.G.P.

ABOUT THE AUTHORS

Mary Beth Norton

Now a professor of history at Cornell University, Mary Beth Norton was born in Ann Arbor, Michigan, and received her B.A. from the University of Michigan (1964). Harvard University awarded her the Ph.D. in 1969, the year her dissertation won the Allan Nevins Prize. Her writing includes two books, *The British-Americans: The Loyalist Exiles in England, 1774–1789* (1972) and *Liberty's Daughters: The Revolutionary Experience of American Women, 1750–1800* (1980). With Carol Berkin she has edited a book of original essays, *Women of America: A History* (1979). Mary Beth's articles have appeared in the *William and Mary Quarterly* and in *Signs*. She has been active in the Organization of American Historians' Committee on the Status of Women and the executive committee of the Society of American Historians, and has served on the National Council of the Humanities.

David M. Katzman

David M. Katzman is a professor of history at the University of Kansas, where he directs the college honors program. Born in New York City, he attended Queens College (B.A., 1963) and the University of Michigan (Ph.D., 1969). David won the Philip Taft Labor History Prize for his book *Seven Days a Week: Women and Domestic Service in Industrializing America* (1978) and has received awards from the Guggenheim Foundation, the National Endowment for the Humanities, and the Ford Foundation. He is known for his book *Before the Ghetto: Black Detroit in the Nineteenth Century* (1973) and for his contribution to *Three Generations in Twentieth-Century America: Family, Community and Nation* (Second edition, 1981). With William M. Tuttle, Jr., David has edited *Plain Folk: The Life Stories of Undistinguished Americans* (1981). He has written articles for the *Dictionary of American Biography* and serves as the associate editor of the journal *American Studies*.

Paul D. Escott

A native of St. Louis, Missouri, Paul D. Escott earned his B.A. from Harvard College (1969) and his Ph.D. from Duke University (1974). Now an associate professor of history at the University of North Carolina, Charlotte, he has written two books: *After Secession: Jefferson Davis and the Failure of Confederate Nationalism* (1978) and *Slavery Remembered: A Record of Twentieth-Century Slave Narratives* (1979). Paul's articles have appeared in the *Georgia Historical Quarterly, Civil War History,* and the *Encyclopedia of Southern History* (1979). He is a recipient of the Whitney M. Young, Jr., academic fellowship and the Rockefeller Foundation fellowship.

Howard P. Chudacoff

Born in Omaha, Nebraska, Howard P. Chudacoff received his degrees from the University of Chicago (A.B., 1965; Ph.D., 1969). He is now a professor of history at Brown University, where he has co-chaired the American civilization program. Howard's many articles have appeared in the *Journal of American History* and the *Journal of Family History,* among others. He has published *Mobile Americans: Residential and Social Mobility in Omaha, 1880–1920* (1972) and *The Evolution of American Urban Society* (Second edition, 1981), and has won many awards, including grants from Brown University for curriculum enrichment.

Thomas G. Paterson

Born in Oregon City, Oregon, Thomas G. Paterson graduated from the University of New Hampshire in 1963 and received his Ph.D. from the University of California, Berkeley, in 1968. He is now a professor of history at the University of Connecticut, where he has served as a coordinator of undergraduate studies. His many books include *Soviet-American Confrontation* (1973), *On Every Front: The Making of the Cold War* (1979), and the bestselling textbook *American Foreign Policy: A History* (1977); his articles have appeared in the *American Historical Review, The Nation,* and the *Journal of American History.* Tom has served on the editorial board of the journal *Diplomatic History* and has been elected to the council of the Society for Historians of American Foreign Relations. Recently he has spent his summers directing a National Endowment for the Humanities summer seminar for college teachers.

William M. Tuttle, Jr.

William M. Tuttle, Jr., received his B.A. from Denison University in 1959 and his doctorate from the University of Wisconsin, Madison, in 1967. A native of Detroit, Michigan, he is now a professor of history at the University of Kansas. Bill has written *Race Riot: Chicago in the Red Summer of 1919* (1970) and with David M. Katzman has edited *Plain Folk* (1981). His numerous articles have appeared in the *Journal of Negro History, Labor History, Journal of American History, Phylon,* and *Technology and Culture,* and he has received research assistance from the Guggenheim Foundation, the National Endowment for the Humanities, the Charles Warren Center, and the Harry S Truman Library Institute.

A PEOPLE & A NATION

1 &

THE MEETING OF OLD WORLD AND NEW, 1492–1650

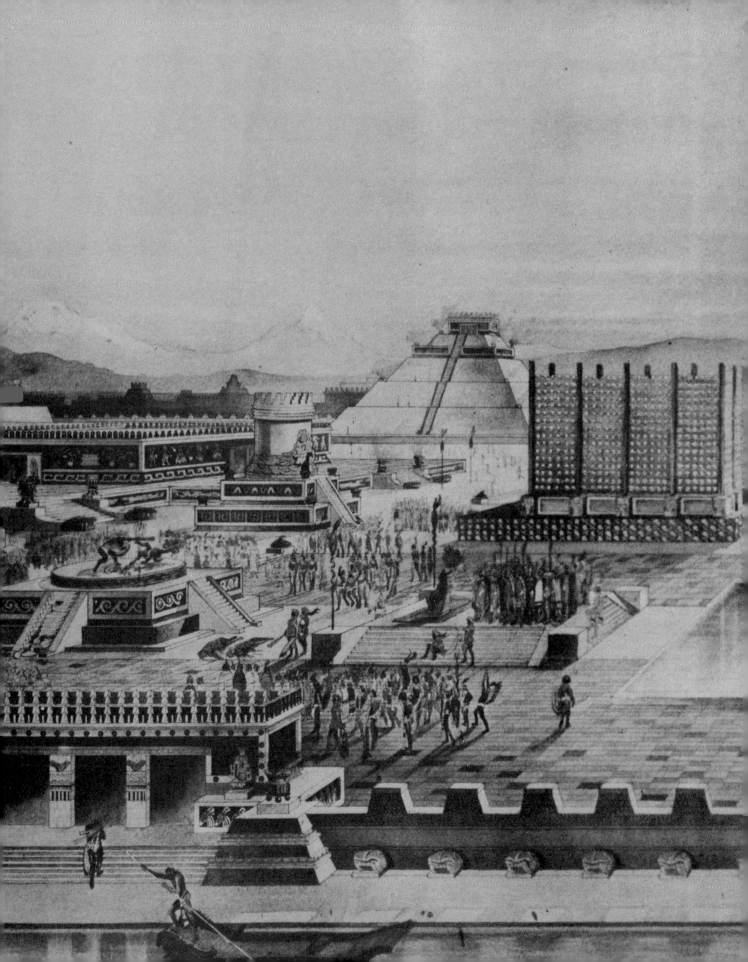

"It spread over the people as great destruction," the old man told the priest. "Some it quite covered [with pustules] on all parts—their faces, their heads, their breasts. . . . There was great havoc. Very many died of it. They could not stir; they could not change position, nor lie on one side, nor face down, nor on their backs. And if they stirred, much did they cry out. Great was its destruction. Covered, mantled with pustules, very many people died of them. And very many starved; there was death from hunger, [for] none could take care of [the sick]; nothing could be done for them."

It was, by European reckoning, September 1520. Spanish troops led by Hernando Cortés had abandoned the Aztec capital of Tenochtitlan after failing in their first attempt to gain control of the city. But they had unknowingly left behind the smallpox germs that would ensure their eventual triumph. By the time the Spaniards returned three months later, the great epidemic described above had fatally weakened Tenochtitlan's inhabitants. Even so, the city held out for months against the Spanish siege. But in the Aztec year Three House, on the day One Serpent (August 1521), Tenochtitlan finally surrendered. The Spaniards had conquered Mexico, and on the site of the Aztec capital they constructed what is now Mexico City.

After many millennia of separation, inhabitants of the Eastern Hemisphere—the so-called Old World—had encountered the residents of the Americas, with catastrophic results for the latter and untold benefits for the former. By the time Spanish troops occupied Tenochtitlan, the age of European expansion and colonization was already well under way. Over the next three hundred and fifty years, Europeans would spread their civilization across the globe. They would come to dominate native peoples in Asia and Africa as well as in the New World. The history of the thirteen tiny English colonies in North America that eventually became the United States must be seen in the broader context of worldwide exploration and exploitation.

Two themes pervade the early history of English settlement in America: the clash of divergent cultures—European and Indian—and the English settlers' adaptation to an alien environment. A latecomer to the New World, England hoped to copy Spanish successes and exploit the New World's rich resources of gold and silver. But the region colonized by the English, the North American coast, had few such resources. As a result, England soon shifted its focus and began to establish agricultural settlements. The colonists' attempts to transplant English ways of life to the New World led to repeated conflicts with the native peoples. For some years the Indians' determination to resist seizure of their lands, coupled with the Europeans' difficulties adjusting to the unfamiliar surroundings, called into question the ultimate survival of the settlements. But by the middle of the seventeenth century English colonies had taken firm root in American soil.

European exploration of America

October 12, 1492, is one of those historical rarities: a well-known date that deserves the significance attributed to it. On that day Christopher Columbus, a forty-one-year-old Genoese sea captain sailing under

| Christopher Columbus |

the flag of the Spanish monarchs Ferdinand and Isabella, landed on a Caribbean island he named San Salvador (one of the Bahamas). He and the three ships under his command—the *Pinta,* the *Niña,* and the *Santa Maria*—had sailed west from Palos, Spain, on August 3, in hopes of reaching China and the East Indies. Until the day he died in 1506, Columbus evidently persisted in believing that he had discovered a new route to the fabled wealth of the Indies. Others knew better even before his death. Columbus did not accomplish his goal, but he changed the dimensions of the known world.

In his own day, Columbus was regarded as something of a crackpot. Like other well-informed men of his time, especially other experienced navigators, Columbus believed the world to be round. (Only ignorant folk still thought it was flat.) Where he differed with most of his contemporaries was in his estimate of its size. Columbus thought that the distance from Portugal to Japan was less than 3,000 miles (it is actually 12,000 miles), and that no land mass lay in his path. Experts scoffed at both assumptions. Thus when Columbus approached the monarchs of France, Portugal, and England in search of support for his planned expedition to China, his proposal was rejected out of hand. But Columbus was obsessed with his idea and persisted in his quest for financial backing for more than a decade. Finally, Queen Isabella of Spain—who rather liked him in spite of his eccentric views—agreed to fund the voyage.

Why was Columbus so intent on finding a route to the East by sailing west? Why was Queen Isabella willing to support him? Most Europeans had lived for centuries in ignorance of the land beyond the western ocean. Only the Norsemen had ventured past Ireland, reaching Iceland (870 A.D.) and Greenland (c. 985 A.D.) and finally, in 1001, under the leadership of Leif Ericsson, encountering a wooded land they called Markland (present-day Labrador). The Norse adventurers established a permanent camp in a region they named Vinland (now identified as L'anse aux Meadows, Newfoundland). But after several attempts to colonize the area, they retreated to Greenland, frightened off by hostile natives. Aside from that single flurry of interest, lasting no more than two decades nearly five hundred years earlier, Europeans had failed to investigate whether there was any truth to the rumors of wealthy lands beyond the seas.

Early Norse explorers

But in the fifteenth century four new developments combined to propel Europeans like Columbus out into the unknown oceans. The first development was purely technical: the invention and refinement of navigational instruments such as the quadrant, which enabled sailors to determine their latitude by measuring the height of the sun and stars above the horizon. The new instruments allowed mariners to spend weeks and months out of sight of land and still have some rough idea of their location. The other three factors—political changes in Europe, the quest for scarce trade goods, and a desire to convert heathen peoples to Christianity—were more complex.

Throughout Europe, the fifteenth century witnessed the consolidation of power and authority in the hands of kings. These political changes were important preconditions for exploration. In England, Henry VII founded the Tudor dynasty and began uniting a land divided for generations by the Wars of the Roses between the houses of York and Lancaster. In France, Francis I similarly established a claim to unchallenged authority. In Spain, Ferdinand and Isabella, rulers of the independent states of Aragon and Castile, married and combined their kingdoms. In 1492, the year Columbus sailed westward, they defeated the Moors and expelled the Jews from their domain, which was now unified under Christian rule for the first time. Only such powerful monarchies could muster the resources necessary to support large-scale colonial enterprises.

The third factor impelling the westward thrust was greed—the desire to find an easy trade route to the East. For centuries Europeans had traded with the Orient via the ports of the eastern Mediterranean (especially Venice and Constantinople) and the long land route across Asia known as the Silk Road. They treasured the valuable and expensive items they obtained from the East: dyes, silk, perfumes, drugs, gold, jewels, and spices, particularly pepper, cinnamon, nutmeg, and cloves. In 1477 the publication of Marco Polo's *Travels*—which had circulated in manuscript for nearly two centuries—stimulated Europeans' interest in China, where Polo had lived for twenty-four years. His report that China was bordered by an ocean on the east helped to convince many, including Christopher Columbus, that that land of fabulous wealth could be reached by ship. It was in hopes of establishing a shorter trade route to China, Japan, and the Spice Islands (the Moluccas) that Columbus chose to sail west from Spain.

Search for a trade route to the East

He was not the first to cherish thoughts of tapping the riches of the Indies directly. During the first half of the fifteenth century, Prince Henry the Navigator, son of King John I of Portugal, had dispatched ship after ship southward along the coast of Africa in an attempt to discover a passage to the East. In 1488, long after Prince Henry's death, Bartholomew Dias first rounded the Cape of Good Hope, and a decade later Vasco da Gama reached India by sailing south around Africa. The Portuguese, then, found what Columbus did not: a usable oceanic trade route to the East.

But Columbus did not realize he had failed, especially on his first voyage. In his logbook and official reports he described the extraordinary beauty and fertility of the islands he had discovered, and commented on the friendliness and gentleness of most of their inhabitants. He insisted that the islands lay close to the Asian mainland and that he could have found vast stores of gold and spices had he had more time to explore. Columbus also expressed his belief that the Indians (as he called the natives, thinking them residents

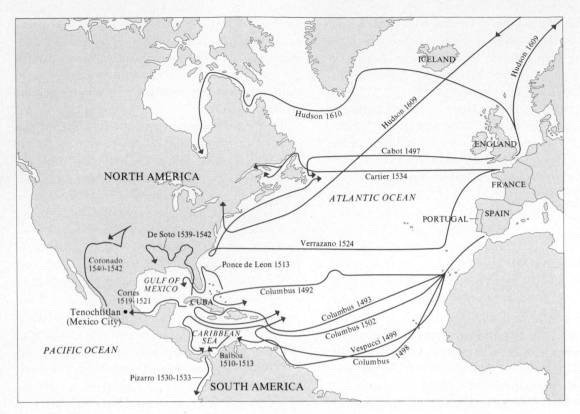

European explorations in America

of the Indies) could easily be converted to Christianity. They would, he predicted, readily become faithful subjects of the Spanish monarchs.

Columbus's prediction arose from the fourth major cause of the fifteenth-century impulse toward exploration: the desire to convert heathen peoples. This motive alone would not have impelled Europeans to sail in search of unknown lands, but it provided them with a spiritual justification for doing so. They were not necessarily being hypocritical. Fifteenth-century Europeans were convinced that Christianity was the only true religion and that it was their duty to spread Jesus Christ's message across the world. If they and their nations became wealthy in the process, so much the better. Most of them saw no conflict between their dual motives.

Columbus made four voyages to the Western Hemisphere, sailing along the coasts of Central and South America and further exploring the Caribbean (see map). In 1497 John Cabot, a Genoese backed by England, rediscovered Newfoundland, the Norse out-

post of five centuries earlier. Giovanni da Verrazano, a Florentine dispatched by Francis I, explored the North American coast in 1524. A decade later Jacques Cartier, also sailing for France, found the mouth of the St. Lawrence River and ventured inland as far as the first rapids. By then, everyone realized that a new world had been discovered. Because the first to reach that conclusion in print was Amerigo Vespucci, who had sailed along the coast of the southern continent in 1499, a mapmaker in 1507 labelled the new land *America*.

Most Europeans saw the Americas as a barrier on the route to the Indies, rather than a region to be exploited and colonized. Indeed, both Verrazano and Cartier were looking for the fabled Northwest Passage through the North American continent when they made their voyages of exploration. Long after Ferdinand Magellan (1521–1522) and Francis Drake (1577–1580) circumnavigated the globe, Europeans were still exploring America chiefly in the hope of finding an easy route to China and India.

Chapter 1: The meeting of Old World and New, 1492–1650

Only Spain, with its reinvigorated monarchy and belief in Columbus's prediction of vast wealth in the interior of the continent (even if the continent was America rather than Asia), immediately moved to take advantage of the discoveries. On his first voyage, Columbus had established a base on the island of Hispaniola. From there, Spanish explorers fanned out around the Caribbean basin: in 1513, Ponce de Leon reached Florida and Vasco Nuñez de Balboa crossed the Isthmus of Panama to find the Pacific Ocean. Less than ten years later, the Spaniards' dreams of wealth were realized when Cortés conquered the Aztec empire, killing its ruler, Moctezuma, and seizing a fabulous treasure of gold and silver.

| Conquistadores |

Venturing northward, conquistadores like Hernando de Soto (who discovered the Mississippi River) and Coronado (who explored the southwestern portion of what is now the United States) found little of value. By contrast, Francisco Pizarro, who explored south along the western coast of South America, conquered and enslaved the Incas in 1535, thus acquiring the richest silver mines in the world. Just half a century after Columbus's first voyage, the Spanish monarchs—who treated the American territories as their personal possessions—controlled the richest, most extensive empire Europe had known since ancient Rome.

The costs to the New World were extraordinarily high. The conquistadores destroyed sophisticated Indian civilizations that had built huge urban centers, developed a calendar more accurate than the Europeans' own, invented systems of writing and mathematics, and constructed roads, bridges, and irrigation canals. The Spaniards deliberately leveled Indian cities, building cathedrals and monasteries on sites once occupied by Aztec, Incan, and Mayan temples. Just as deliberately, they attempted to erase all vestiges of the great Indian cultures by burning whatever written records they found. As a result, present-day knowledge of the Aztec, Maya, and Inca civilizations rests almost entirely on architectural remains, pottery artifacts, and records left by some of the priests who accompanied the colonizers.

But the greatest destruction wrought by the Europeans—English and French as well as Spanish—was unintended. Diseases carried from the Old World to the New by the alien invaders killed hundreds of thousands, even millions, of native Americans, who had no immunity to germs that had infested Europe, Asia, and Africa for centuries. The greatest killer was smallpox, which was spread by direct human contact. The epidemic that hit Tenochtitlan in 1520 had begun in Hispaniola two years earlier and subsequently spread through Mexico, Central America, and South America. Indeed, the reason Pizarro conquered the Incas so easily was that their society had been devastated by the epidemic shortly before his arrival. Smallpox was not the only villain; influenza, measles, and other diseases added to the destruction.

| Effects of disease |

The statistics are staggering. When Columbus landed on Hispaniola in 1492, about one million Indians resided there. Fifty years later, only five hundred were still alive. According to the best current estimates, five to ten million Indians inhabited central Mexico before Cortés's invasion. By the end of the century, fewer than one million remained.

Even in the north, where smaller Indian populations encountered only a few European explorers, traders, and fishermen, disease ravaged the countryside. A Frenchman commented early in the seventeenth century that the Canadian Indians were "astonished and often complain that, since the French mingle with them and carry on trade with them, they are dying fast and the population is thinning out." In 1616–1617, four years before the Pilgrims landed at Plymouth to begin the first English settlement north of Virginia, the local tribes suffered greatly from an unknown malady brought by fishermen. One of the English witnesses later wrote that the Indians had "died on heapes, as they lay in their houses. . . . And the bones and skulls upon the severall places of their habitations made such a spectacle upon my coming into those partes, that, as I travailed in the Forrest nere the Massachusetts, it seemed to me a new found Golgotha." As one historian has observed, America was more a widowed land than a virgin one when the English finally settled there.

The Americans, though, took a revenge of sorts. They gave the Europeans a disease previously unknown in the Old World: syphilis. The first recorded case of syphilis in Europe occurred in Barcelona, Spain, in 1493, shortly after Columbus's return from the Caribbean. Although less deadly than smallpox,

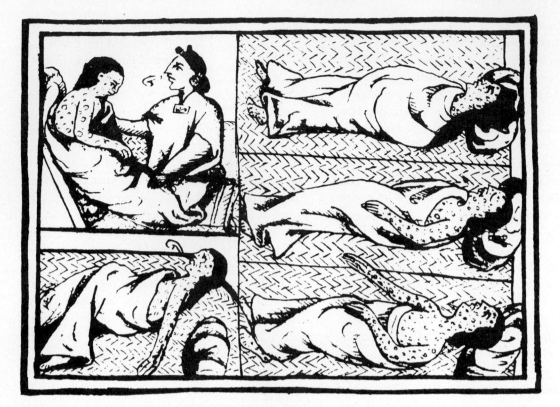

Aztec Indians suffering from smallpox during the Cortés invasion. From Fray Bernardo de Sahagun's *General History of the Things of New Spain (Historia de las Cosas de Nueva Espana)*, published in the sixteenth century. Biblioteca Medices Laurenziana.

syphilis was more virulent in sixteenth-century Europe than it is today, and doctors did not know how to treat it. It spread quickly through the Mediterranean, carried by sailors and prostitutes, reaching England by 1496, Russia by 1499, and China by 1505. Syphilis caused considerable havoc among the ruling houses of Europe. Most royal families of the day were infected with the disease, which interfered with the normal biological processes of conception and childbirth, and as a result they could not produce legitimate heirs.

The exchange of diseases was only part of a broader mutual transfer of plants and animals that resulted directly from Columbus's voyages. The two hemi-

Exchange of plants and animals

spheres had evolved separately over millions of years, developing widely different forms of life. Many large mammals were native to the connected continents of Europe, Asia, and Africa, but the Americas contained no domesticated

beasts larger than dogs and llamas. On the other hand, the vegetable crops of the New World—particularly corn, beans, squash, and potatoes—were more nutritious and produced higher yields than those of the Old, like wheat and rye. In time the Indians learned to raise and consume European domestic animals (cattle, pigs, and sheep) and the Europeans became accustomed to planting and eating American crops. As a result, the diets of both peoples were vastly enriched. One consequence was the doubling of the world's population over the next three hundred years, after centuries of stability.

The exchange of two other commodities significantly influenced the two civilizations. In America the Europeans discovered tobacco, and smoking and chewing the "Indian weed" quickly became a fad in the Old World. Tobacco cultivation was later to form the basis for the prosperity of the first successful English colonies in North America. Despite the efforts of such skeptics as King James I of England, who in

1604 pronounced smoking to be "loathsome to the eye, hatefull to the Nose, harmfull to the brain, [and] dangerous to the Lungs," tobacco's popularity has continued almost undiminished to the present day.

But more important than tobacco's influence on Europe was the impact of horses on certain native American cultures. The conquistadores brought with them the first horses Americans had ever seen. Inevitably, some escaped or were stolen by the natives; such horses were traded north through Mexico into the Great Plains, where tribes like the Apache, Comanche, Sioux, and Blackfeet eventually made the horse the focal point of their existence. They used horses for hunting and warfare, measured a man's wealth and status by how many horses he owned, and moved their camps frequently because their horses continually needed fresh pastures.

The first English outposts in America

During the sixteenth century, while Spain was expanding and consolidating its empire in Mexico, the Caribbean, and Central and South America, other European nations had only sporadic contacts with the New World. Fishermen from a number of countries discovered that the Newfoundland Banks, off the north coast of North America, offered an abundant supply of cod and other fish. They set up temporary summer camps on the American shore, where they dried and salted their catch to preserve it on the long voyage home. But each autumn the fishermen returned to Europe; none of them seem to have contemplated living permanently in America.

Other Europeans who sailed along the coast soon found that the American natives, who still used stone implements, were eager to trade for steel knives, brass kettles, and other metal goods, along with beads and cloth. In exchange, the Indians offered the Europeans
Early trading posts
furs. As the trade developed and Europe began to demand more pelts (especially beaver, which was used for making felt hats), some nations began to establish permanent trading posts on North American soil. In 1608 the French, led by the explorer Samuel de Champlain, founded Quebec on the site of some abandoned Indian villages on the St. Lawrence River.

Spaniards on horseback meet Aztec messengers. Although popular myth has it that the Indians were terrified by the strange four-legged creatures (and that that was a major reason for the Spanish triumph), these Aztec warriors do not seem overawed. Fray Bernardo de Sahagun, *Historia de las Cosas de Nueva Espana.*

Seventeen years later the Dutch built a trading post on Manhattan Island, at the mouth of the river Henry Hudson had discovered in 1609 and named for himself. And in 1638 Sweden sent a small number of traders to the Delaware River valley.

The French, Dutch, and Swedish settlements differed considerably from those of New Spain. The northern European colonists made no attempt to subject the Indians to European rule, although—particularly in New France—they did try to convert them to Christianity. Unlike the Spaniards, they viewed the Indians as trading partners rather than laborers, and did not try to enslave them or destroy their cultures. For the most part, they were also content to control only the land immediately surrounding their forts. The trading posts were permanent settlements, to be sure, but they were not intended as beachheads for large-scale European migration to the New World.

At first, English colonizers thought along the same lines as their northern European neighbors. In the

1580s, a group of West Countrymen, among them Sir Humphrey Gilbert and his younger half-brother Sir Walter Raleigh, hoped to establish American outposts that would trade with native peoples for gold and silver, serve as way-stations on the long sea routes to China and India, and bring the message of Christianity to heathen Americans. Their ambitions were fed by England's increasingly hostile relationship with Spain.

In 1533, when the English king Henry VIII divorced his Spanish queen Catherine of Aragon for failing to produce a male heir after twenty years of marriage, the once-cordial relationship between England and Spain had begun to crumble. The cracks widened when the pope refused to approve Henry's divorce. Henry left the Catholic Church, founded the Protestant Church of England, and proclaimed himself its head—a series of actions that appalled the orthodox Spanish Catholics. The marriage of Henry's Catholic daughter Mary (the child of Catherine) to Philip II of Spain was designed to cement the alliance once again. But when Queen Mary died childless in 1558, her Protestant half-sister Elizabeth I (Henry's daughter by his second marriage, to Anne Boleyn) ascended the throne. Thereafter England and Spain, though not always at war, were bitter enemies.

Accordingly, Gilbert and Raleigh pressed their case for English colonies in America by advancing a persuasive argument: such settlements would serve as excellent bases for attacks on New Spain, and especially on the Spanish treasure ships that carried the New World's wealth home to Europe. English "sea dogs" like John Hawkins and Francis Drake had proved in the 1560s and 1570s that well-executed raids on Spanish colonies and vessels could produce riches rarely dreamed of by previous English adventurers. Outposts in the New World appeared to hold enormous promise.

Queen Elizabeth agreed, and authorized Raleigh and Gilbert to colonize North America. Gilbert failed to plant a colony in Newfoundland, dying in the attempt, and Raleigh was only briefly more successful. After an exploring party reported favorably on the territory he named Virginia (for Elizabeth, the "Virgin Queen"), Raleigh in 1587 dispatched 117 colonists, including 17 women and 9 children, to Roanoke Island in what is now North Carolina. But

Founding of Roanoke tragedy struck. A supply ship destined for the colony was delayed by the Spanish Armada, Spain's aborted attempt to invade England in 1588. When the vessel finally arrived at Roanoke in 1590, the colonists had vanished without a trace. Among the missing were Eleanor Dare and her daughter Virginia, the first white child born in English America.

The failure of Raleigh's attempt to colonize Virginia ended English efforts at settlement for nearly two decades. Three years after Elizabeth's death in 1603, though, a group of West Countrymen interested in American ventures combined forces with a like-minded group of London merchants. Together they asked James I, Elizabeth's successor and the first Stuart monarch, to charter a joint-stock company that would again try to establish English colonies in the New World.

Joint-stock companies had been developed in England during the sixteenth century as a mechanism for *Joint-stock companies* pooling the resources of a large number of small investors. These forerunners of modern corporations were funded through the sale of stock. Since investors would receive returns only in proportion to their share of the whole enterprise, joint-stock companies did not hold forth the promise of immense wealth. But because they did not require individuals to put up large amounts of capital, they enabled merchants and members of the gentry to finance trading voyages without risking bankruptcy. Joint-stock companies thus had many benefits, but their drawbacks were to prove more decisive in the history of early colonization. Most investors wanted quick profits, which in the English colonies were rarely forthcoming. Many of the early colonization efforts thus suffered from a chronic lack of capital, causing dissent within the companies and conflicts with the settlers in America, who often accused the parent companies of failing to support them adequately.

The charter James I granted the Virginia Company in 1606 gave it the right "to digg, mine, and searche for all manner of mines of goulde, silver, and copper." It also required the company to pay one-fifth of all proceeds to the king. The company's West Country investors (the Virginia Company of Plymouth) tried and failed to plant a colony at Sagadahoc, in what is now Maine. Meanwhile the merchant group (the Virginia Company of London) turned its attention southward. Although the settlers it sent to America at first searched for the precious metals named in the charter, they soon realized that Virginia was not another Mexico. Within twenty years the Virginia settlement had taken an entirely new form.

English and Indians encounter each other

Human beings were not native to the Americas. The "Indian" peoples who inhabited the Americas when the Europeans arrived were descended from Asians. Their forebears had migrated in waves across a now-vanished land bridge that joined the Asian and North American continents at the site of the Bering Strait. The first migrants may have arrived 75,000 years ago; others may have come as recently as 12,000 years ago. (There is conflicting evidence and considerable disagreement about when the migration occurred.) The migrants, who were nomadic hunters of game and gatherers of wild plants, spread slowly throughout North and South America.

Early Indian peoples

About 4000 B.C. Indians living in central Mexico learned how to cultivate food crops deliberately, instead of relying on foraging for their grain supply. As knowledge of agricultural techniques spread, many Indian groups started to live a more settled existence. Many became entirely settled or only seminomadic (moving only two or three times a year, among fixed sites). The development of agriculture brought about population increases by improving the food supply. It also allowed for more leisure: people no longer had to devote all their time to subsistence activities. That, in turn, made possible the production of ornamental objects, accumulation of wealth, and the creation of elaborate rituals and ceremonies.

In the fifteenth century, when Europeans first came to the New World in large numbers, the most sophisticated Indian civilizations in the Western Hemisphere were located in Central and South America.

Pottery object created by the Mound Builders, Indian peoples who lived in the central and southeastern United States from around 1000 B.C. to 500 A.D. Unfortunately, we know little about the Mound Builders' civilization; they left no written records. But many of their huge mounds, some shaped like animals, still survive. Museum of the American Indian, Heye Foundation.

The Indian tribes living in what is now the United States varied dramatically in culture and lifestyle. The tribes along the Pacific coast lived largely by fishing, combined with some agriculture. While settled agriculture was the norm in the Southwest, tribes of nomadic hunters and gatherers roamed the Great Basin and the Great Plains. East of the Mississippi, most tribes lived a settled or seminomadic existence combining hunting, fishing, and agriculture. Their houses were made of bark, woven mats, or animal skins; they dressed largely in decorated skins and furs, and sometimes lived in extended family (or clan) groups. Most eastern coastal tribes spoke variants of Algonkian languages.

To an outside observer, had one existed, the cultures of seventeenth-century English and Algonkian peoples might have appeared similar at first glance. Both lived mainly in small villages, depending for subsistence chiefly on the cultivation of crops. Both supplemented a largely vegetable diet with meat and fish, although the Indians hunted meat and the English raised livestock. Both peoples were deeply religious, orienting their lives around festivals and rituals.

Both societies featured clear-cut social and political hierarchies; neither was egalitarian in the modern sense of the word. And finally, both cultures were characterized by sharply defined sex roles, with men and women occupying distinctly different spheres.

Such similarities were, however, outweighed by significant differences. The contrasts between the two ways of life were readily evident to both English and Indian witnesses. For example, Algonkian women bore the prime responsibility for cultivating crops.

| *Cultural differences between the Indians and the English* |

Once their husbands had felled trees and cleared the land, women handled the farming as well as cooking, making clothes, and raising children. In England, men worked in the fields while women cared for children and did the housework. Indian men thus regarded white males as effeminate because they did women's work, while white men described male Indians as lazy. Whites also considered Indian women oppressed, since they had to do heavy field labor.

Other differences between the two cultures caused serious misunderstandings. Although both societies were hierarchical, the nature of the hierarchies differed considerably. Among the east-coast Algonkian tribes, social and political standing were determined by a number of factors, including wealth, kinship, and talent. People were not born to automatic positions of leadership, nor were political power and social status necessarily inherited through the male line. A man's status might change several times, for better or worse, during the course of his life. English society was more rigid. A noticeable gap separated the gentry (who normally inherited their position from their fathers) from the common folk, even though successful individuals occasionally managed to rise into the gentry. English political and military leaders tended to rule autocratically; the authority of Indian leaders rested largely on a consensus they shared with their fellow tribesmen. Accustomed to the European concept of powerful kings, the English sought such figures within the tribes. If they found none, they created them. Often (for example, when negotiating treaties) they willfully overestimated the ability of chiefs to make independent decisions for their people.

Furthermore, the Indians and the English had very different notions of property ownership. In most eastern tribes, land was held communally by the entire group. The concept of absolute sale of property was utterly alien. The English, on the other hand, were accustomed to individual landholding. Perhaps more important, the English definition of entitlement to land excluded seminomadic tribes from consideration. Like other Europeans of the time, the English believed that nomadic peoples could not own land, properly speaking, since they had not placed it under intensive cultivation. They therefore paid little attention to tribal claims to traditional hunting territories and sites occupied only occasionally.

An aspect of the cultural clash that needs particular emphasis is the English settlers' unwavering belief in the superiority of their civilization. Although in the early years of colonization they often harbored thoughts of living peacefully alongside the Indians, they always assumed that they themselves would dictate the terms of such coexistence. They expected the Indians to adopt English customs and to convert to Christianity. When most tribes resisted, the English concluded that the Indians were irredeemable. Most colonists reached that conclusion quite early in the history of their settlements.

Ironically, the ethnocentric Englishmen dispatched by the Virginia Company settled in a region dominated by an equally ethnocentric coalition of Indian tribes, the so-called Powhatan Confederacy (see map, page 14).

| *Powhatan Confederacy* |

Powhatan, the chief of six allied tribes on the coast of what is now Virginia, was consolidating his control over about twenty-five other tribes in the area when the English colonists arrived. (His attempt to extend his power was unusual among Indians.) Fortunately for the Englishmen, Powhatan seems not to have viewed them as enemies but as potential allies in his struggle to establish uncontested authority over his Indian neighbors. Powhatan's confidence in his own strength apparently caused him to disregard the threat posed by the English colonists until it was too late.

Initially at least, Powhatan had good cause for self-assurance. The 104 men and boys who in May 1607 established the settlement called Jamestown, on a swampy peninsula in a river they also named for their

| *Founding of Jamestown* |

monarch, were indeed ill-equipped for survival. The colony was afflicted by dissension and disease; by January 1608 only 38 of the original colonists were

Chapter 1: The meeting of Old World and New, 1492–1650

Secota, an unfortified Indian village on the Carolina coast, as drawn by John White, an artist with Raleigh's 1585 expedition. Letters A, B, C, D, and K identify ritual sites and show the dancing and feasting that were an important part of the Indians' religion. The picture also shows the Indians' chief crops—tobacco (E), corn in two stages of growth (G and H), and pumpkins (I). The hut labeled F housed a watchman assigned to keep animals and birds away from the fields. The river (L) was the village's source of water. Note the hunters shooting deer at top left.   Rare Book Division, The New York Public Library, Astor, Lenox and Tilden Foundations.

English and Indians encounter each other

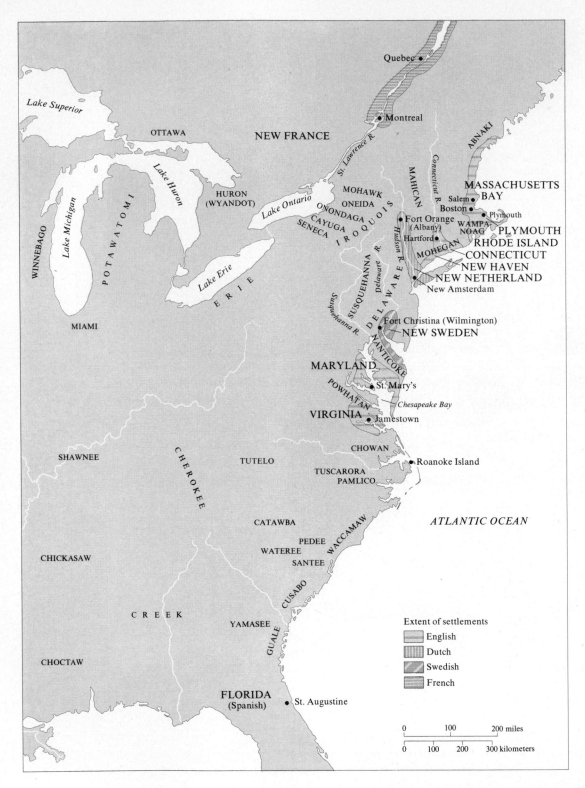

European settlements and Indian tribes in America, 1650. Source: Redrawn by permission of the Smithsonian Institution Press from B. A. E. Bulletin 145, *Indian Tribes of North America,* John Swanton, Smithsonian Institution, Washington, D.C., 1952.

Chapter 1: The meeting of Old World and New, 1492–1650

still alive. Many of the first immigrants were gentlemen unaccustomed to working with their hands and artisans with irrelevant skills like glassmaking. Having come to Virginia expecting to make easy fortunes, most could not adjust to the conditions they encountered. They resisted living "like savages," retaining English dress and casual work habits despite their desperate circumstances. Such attitudes, combined with the effects of chronic malnutrition and epidemic disease, took a terrible toll. During the notorious "starving time," the winter of 1609–1610, some colonists even resorted to cannibalism. As late as 1624, fewer than 1,300 of the more than 8,000 immigrants to Virginia had survived.

The one Englishman who fully understood the necessity of adapting to the realities of life in Virginia was Captain John Smith, a daring soldier of fortune and former prisoner of war among the Turks. Smith, a member of the first group of settlers, took charge of the colony in September 1608, after its original leaders had died. The year in which he governed almost singlehandedly was, by nearly all accounts, the most successful in Jamestown's early history. Smith imposed military discipline on the settlers, requiring everyone to work. Recognizing the prevalence of disease at the Jamestown site, he copied the Indians' seminomadic lifestyle and dispersed the colonists during the summer, the most unhealthy season. And Smith's previous experience with alien peoples gave him an understanding of Powhatan lacking in his fellow colonists. Powhatan and Smith respected and sparred with each other as equals. Though their relationship was never cordial, it was founded upon a kind of reluctant mutual admiration.

The early Virginia settlers had frequent contacts with the Indians. Powhatan's people found the English settlers an infallible source of such desirable goods as steel knives, hatchets, and guns. In exchange, they traded their excess corn to the starving colonists— without which the settlement could not have survived, despite all Smith's efforts. Englishmen often wandered into Indian villages and vice versa; there were some violent clashes, but the two races were chiefly preoccupied with learning from each other. One of the most frequent visitors to Jamestown was Powhatan's favorite daughter, Pocahontas, who greatly admired Smith. She may never have saved

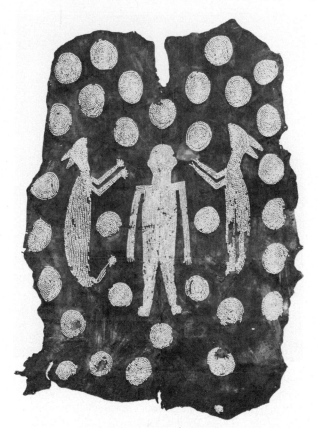

Powhatan's Mantle. This deerskin cloak, decorated with shells, may not have belonged to Powhatan, but it is one of the oldest known examples of North American Indian art. It was taken to England by early explorers returning from America.   Ashmolean Museum, Oxford, England.

him from execution at her father's hands (as Smith claimed in his memoirs), but on several occasions she warned Smith of Powhatan's plots against the colony.

Smith left Virginia forever in 1609. But Pocahontas continued to visit Jamestown, and in 1613 the Englishmen seized her as a hostage. In captivity she fell in love with a widowed planter, John Rolfe, and married him the following year. Her father approved the match, agreeing as well to a formal treaty with the colonists. Pocahontas's marriage linked Powhatan with the whites; the treaty cemented the alliance, strengthening his position with respect to the thirty tribes he had subjected to his rule. Powhatan had cleverly used the presence of the Englishmen for his own purposes. It must have seemed to him that his strategy had worked.

English and Indians encounter each other

Pocahontas (1595/96?–1617), here called Matoaka alias Rebecka, portrayed in Elizabethan dress. During her visit to England with her husband John Rolfe in 1616, the Indian princess became the toast of London society. She died the following year, just as she was leaving England to return to her homeland, and was buried in the parish church at Gravesend. National Portrait Gallery, Smithsonian Institution, Washington, D.C.

The peace established in 1614 lasted eight years, persisting beyond Pocahontas's death in 1617 and Powhatan's the next year. But even before 1614 the force that would eventually destroy the peace had been set in motion. That force was the spread of tobacco cultivation.

In tobacco the settlers and the Virginia Company found the saleable commodity for which they had been searching. The tobacco native to North America was harsh and unpleasant, but the climate was well suited to its cultivation. Thus John Rolfe imported the seeds of preferable varieties from South America, planting his first crop in 1611. By 1613 he shipped some home to England; in 1615 he and other Virginians exported 2,000 pounds of cured leaves. Just five years later their shipments reached 40,000 pounds, and by the end of the 1620s exports had jumped dramatically to 1.5 million pounds. The great

Tobacco economy

tobacco boom had begun, fueled by high prices and substantial profits for planters. The price later fell almost as sharply as it had risen, and fluctuated wildly from year to year in response to increasing supply and international competition. Nevertheless, tobacco became the foundation of Virginia's prosperity.

Successful tobacco cultivation required abundant land, since the crop quickly drained soil of nutrients. Planters soon learned that a field could produce only about three satisfactory crops before it had to lie fallow for several years to regain its fertility. Thus the once small English settlements began to expand rapidly: eager planters applied to the Virginia Company for large land grants on both sides of the James and its tributary streams. Lulled into a false sense of security by years of peace, the planters established farms at some distance from one another along the river banks—a settlement pattern convenient for tobacco cultivation but poorly designed for defense.

Opechancanough, Powhatan's brother and successor, watched the English colonists steadily encroaching on Indian lands and attempting to convert members of the tribes to Christianity. He recognized the danger his brother had overlooked. On March 22 (Good Friday), 1622, under his leadership, the confederacy launched coordinated attacks all along the river. By the end of the day 347 colonists (about one-third of the total) lay dead, and only a timely warning from two Christianized Indians saved Jamestown itself from destruction.

Opechanca-nough's attack

The Virginia colony reeled from the blow but did not collapse. Reinforced by new shipments of men and arms from England, the settlers struck back. Over the next few years, they repeatedly attacked Opechancanough's villages, burning houses and crops. An uneasy peace returned in the 1630s, but in April 1644 Opechancanough tried one last time to repel the invaders. Perhaps 500 colonists were killed in a widespread attack on outlying settlements, but the English population of Virginia was by then over 8,000. In the ensuing war, Opechancanough himself was captured and killed.

In 1646, the survivors of the Powhatan Confederacy accepted a treaty formally subordinating them to English authority. They thus became official "friendly" Indians, their choice of chiefs subject to approval by the colonists. After 1646, the locus of conflict between Indians and the English intruders in the Chesapeake area moved westward. The Powhatan Confederacy's efforts to resist the spread of white settlement had ended.

Life in the Chesapeake

The 1622 massacre that failed to destroy the Virginia colony did succeed in killing its parent company, which had never made any profits from the enterprise. In 1624 James I revoked the company's charter and made Virginia a royal colony, ruled by the king through appointed officials. Significantly, though, two company policies remained in effect under royal authority. In an attempt to attract settlers, the company had in 1617 promised a land grant of fifty acres, called a headright, for every new arrival. Persons who financed the passage of others received a proportional number of headrights from the company. James continued that practice. He was more reluctant to retain the second company policy, implemented in 1619, which allowed the men of the major Virginia settlements to elect representatives to a legislative body called the House of Burgesses. At first, James abolished the legislature, but the settlers protested so vigorously that by 1629 the assembly was functioning once again. At the local level, Virginians adapted the forms of English county government to suit their needs. Only a few decades after the first permanent English settlement took root in the New World, the colonists had evolved a system of representative government with considerable local autonomy—a pattern that has continued in the United States to the present day.

By the 1630s, tobacco was firmly established in Virginia as the staple crop and chief source of revenue. It quickly became just as important in the second English colony planted on Chesapeake Bay: the proprietorship of Maryland, chartered by the king in 1632. The Calvert family, who founded Maryland, intended

| Founding of Maryland |

the colony to serve as a haven for their fellow Roman Catholics, who were being persecuted in England. Cecilius Calvert, second Lord Baltimore, became the first colonizer to offer prospective settlers freedom of religion, as long as they were practicing Christians. In that respect Maryland differed from Virginia, where the Church of England was the only officially recognized religion. In other ways, however, the two Chesapeake colonies resembled each other. In Maryland as in Virginia, tobacco planters spread out along the river banks, establishing isolated farms instead of towns. The region's deep, wide rivers offered dependable water transportation in an age of few and inadequate roads. Each farm or group of farms had its own wharf, where oceangoing vessels could take on or discharge cargo.

Abundant land alone could not produce tobacco. As essential as acreage was labor, the second factor that shaped the Chesapeake. The planting, cultivation, and harvesting of tobacco had to be done by hand; these tasks did not take much skill, but they were repetitious and time-consuming. When the headright system was adopted in Maryland in 1640, a prospective tobacco planter anywhere in the Chesapeake could simultaneously obtain both land and the labor to work it. The more workers one brought into either colony, the more property one could acquire. Good management could make the process self-perpetuating: a planter could use his profits to pay for the passage of more workers, and thus gain title to more land. Under these circumstances, planters could accumulate substantial wealth rapidly.

There were two possible sources of laborers for the growing tobacco farms of the Chesapeake: Africa and England. In 1619, a Dutch privateer brought more than twenty blacks from the Spanish Caribbean islands to Virginia; they were the first known Negro inhabitants of the English colonies in North America. Nine years later, some natives of Africa were sold directly to Virginia settlers. Over the next few decades small numbers of blacks, mostly from the West Indies, were carried to the Chesapeake, but even as late as 1670 the black population of Virginia was at most 2,000 and probably no more than 1,500. Chesapeake tobacco planters first looked to England to supply their labor needs. And because they favored certain types of workers, the population of the Chesapeake soon became largely young and largely male. Such laborers migrated to America as indentured servants; that is, in return for their passage they contracted to work for planters for periods ranging from four to seven years.

Who were the thousands of English people who chose to emigrate to the Chesapeake as servants in the seventeenth century? Indentured servants accounted for 75 to 85 percent of the approximately 130,000 English immigrants to Virginia and Maryland during those years. Roughly three-quarters of them were men, mostly between the ages of fifteen and twenty-four. A majority had been farmers and laborers; though none were gentry, many had been skilled tradesmen and even clerks, teachers, and accountants. In other words, the servants did not represent the dregs of society. They were instead what their contemporaries called the "common" or "middling" sort. Judging by their youth, though, most had probably not yet established a firm foothold for themselves in England.

Immigrants to the Chesapeake

What motivated the servants to leave their homeland? Like later immigrants to America, they were probably influenced by a combination of push-and-pull factors. Many of the servants came from areas of England that were experiencing severe economic disruption. Some had already moved from their home districts to London or Bristol in search of work months or years before they decided to migrate to America. For such people the Chesapeake appeared to offer good prospects. Once they had fulfilled the terms of their indentures, servants were promised "freedom dues" consisting of clothes, tools, livestock, casks of corn and tobacco, and sometimes even land. From a distance at least, America seemed to hold out chances for advancement unavailable in England.

What did indentured servants actually find in Virginia and Maryland? Their lives were not easy. Servants typically worked six days a week, ten to fourteen hours a day, in a climate much warmer than they were accustomed to. Their masters could discipline or sell them, and they faced severe penalties for running away. Even so, they did have some rights enforceable in the courts. Their masters had to supply them with sufficient food, clothing, and shelter; they had to be allowed to rest on Sundays; and they could not be physically abused. Yet few seem to have been happy with their lot. Richard Frethorne, a Virginia servant, begged his parents in 1623 to purchase the time remaining on his indenture. Describing the hard work and poor food to which he was subjected, Fre-

Conditions of servitude

thorne pleaded, "Good father, do not forget me, but have mercy and pity my miserable case. I know if you did but see me, you would weep."

Servants also had to contend with epidemic disease. Although the extremely high mortality rates characteristic of the Jamestown colony had fallen as the Chesapeake population dispersed, death rates remained high in comparison to seventeenth-century England. Immigrants had first to survive the process the colonists called "seasoning"—a bout with disease (probably malaria) that usually occurred during a servant's initial summer in the Chesapeake. They then had to endure recurrences of malaria, along with dysentery, influenza, typhoid fever, and other diseases. As a result, approximately 40 percent of male servants did not survive long enough to become freedmen. Even young men of twenty-two who had successfully weathered their "seasoning" could expect to live only another twenty years at best.

For those who survived the term of their indentures, however, the opportunities for advancement were real. Until the last decades of the century, former servants were usually able to become independent planters ("freeholders") and to live a modest but comfortable existence. Some even assumed such positions of political prominence as justice of the peace, sheriff, militia officer, and member of the assembly. But in the 1670s tobacco prices entered a thirty-year period of stagnation and decline. At the same time, good land grew increasingly scarce and expensive. In 1681 Maryland dropped its legal requirement that servants receive land as part of their freedom dues, forcing large numbers of freed servants to live as wage laborers or tenant farmers instead of acquiring freeholder status. By 1700 the Chesapeake was no longer the land of opportunity it had once been.

Life in the seventeenth-century Chesapeake was hard for everyone, regardless of sex or status. Farmers (and sometimes their wives) toiled in the fields alongside the servants, laboriously clearing the land of trees, then planting and harvesting not only tobacco but also corn, wheat, and vegetables. Chesapeake households subsisted mainly on pork and corn, a filling but monotonous and not particularly nutritious diet. Thus the health problems caused by epidemic disease were magnified by diet deficiencies and the near-impossibility of preserving food for safe winter consumption. (Salting, drying, and smoking, the only methods the colonists knew, did not always prevent spoilage.) Few farm households had many material possessions. Among the settlers' most valuable property was their clothing, since cloth usually had to be imported from England. (Spinning and weaving were traditionally done by women, and the few women in the Chesapeake could not supply the needs of the entire colony.) Linen clothing was especially prized because of its fine quality and thinness. But woolen cloth was easier to make and thus used more widely, despite its unsuitability for the hot, humid summer climate.

The predominance of males, called a high sex ratio,[1] and the high mortality rates combined to produce unusual patterns of family life. Because there were so few women, many men were never able to marry. Meanwhile, nearly every adult free woman in the Chesapeake married, and widows remarried quickly. Servant women, though, usually remained single during their term of indenture, since most masters denied them permission to marry, fearing pregnancy would make them unable to work. The high death rates also produced many widows, widowers, and orphans. In one Maryland county, for example, only one-third of marriages lasted as long as a decade. In a Virginia county, more than three-quarters of the children had lost at least one parent by the time they married or reached the age of twenty-one. As a result, both Maryland and Virginia developed elaborate laws and systems of orphans' courts designed to protect children from greedy step-parents and distant relatives.

| Family life in the Chesapeake |

Family life in the seventeenth-century Chesapeake therefore differed considerably from family life at home in England. There, powerful husbands and fathers had controlled the lives of their wives and children (called a *patriarchal* system of family governance). In the early Chesapeake, few fathers—or mothers, for that matter—lived long enough to have much say in their children's lives. Thus Chesapeake youths, who in England would have needed their parents' approval of an intended spouse, typically chose their own mates. Moreover, few social norms re-

[1] When men are in the majority, a society is said to have a high sex ratio; when women outnumber men, a society has a low sex ratio.

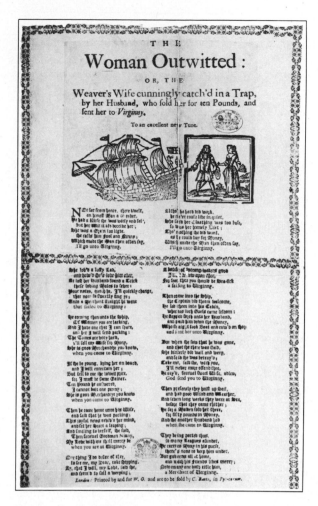

This popular English ballad drew its theme from the shortage of women in the Chesapeake. Contrary to its story, few white people seem to have been carried to the colonies against their will, except for convicted felons. And few married people of either sex immigrated to Virginia.   Rare Book Division, New York Public Library, Astor, Lenox, and Tilden Foundations.

stricted people's behavior in the fluid Chesapeake society. More than a third of immigrant brides in Somerset County, Maryland, were already pregnant at the time of their weddings.

Seventeenth-century Chesapeake families were relatively few, small, and short-lived. Servant status prevented most immigrant women from marrying until their mid-to-late twenties. They probably bore only one or two children who survived to maturity. By contrast, their American-born daughters tended, because of the scarcity of women, to marry shortly after puberty. In Somerset County, amazingly, the mean age of marriage for girls born in America before 1670 was sixteen-and-a-half. In the Chesapeake as a whole, most native-born women married before age twenty-one. They consequently bore more children than had their immigrant mothers—who had begun child-bearing later—and the Chesapeake population slowly began to grow by natural increase as well as immigration. Even so, not until after 1700 did native-born residents of the Chesapeake outnumber their immigrant compatriots.

The fact that the Chesapeake population was primarily immigrant until 1700, if not longer, had important implications for politics in Maryland and Virginia. Both Virginia's House of Burgesses and Maryland's House of Delegates (established in 1635) were composed almost entirely of immigrants until late in the seventeenth century. The same was true of the governors' councils in both colonies. (The councils acted in two capacities: as the upper house of the legislature and as executive advisor to the governor.) Such immigrants came from different parts of England and had few ties to each other or to their new colonial homes. They tended to look to England for

| Political instability |

solutions to their problems. Moreover, most of the elected representatives felt little need to be responsive to their constituents, about whom they knew very little. Their bitter and prolonged struggles for power and personal economic advantage often thwarted the colonial governments' ability to function effectively. As a result, the existence of representative institutions failed to lead to political stability— the people's willingness to work out disagreements within an agreed-upon framework, instead of resorting to plotting and violence. The Chesapeake paid a high political price for its unusual population patterns.

It is sometimes argued that the Chesapeake population's high sex ratio improved the status of women. Since men had to compete for the few available women, it is said, women were able to make better marital bargains. Yet it is difficult to see how conditions in the early Chesapeake worked to the benefit of women. Immigrant female servants could not marry until their mid-to-late twenties, and the fact that about one-third of them were pregnant at marriage does not suggest that they "shopped around" carefully for desirable husbands. Likewise, the fact that

their daughters married very young does not seem to indicate the exercise of great care in the choice of a spouse. In short, although the lives of women in the seventeenth-century Chesapeake certainly contrasted sharply with those of their English counterparts, there is little evidence that they were on the whole any better off. Indeed, since colonial women were probably at greater risk of death, they might even be said to have worsened their condition through immigration.

The pattern of life prevalent in the Chesapeake was not, however, characteristic of all the English settlements in North America. In New England, immigrants seeking freedom of worship established a very different society.

The founding of New England

England's Protestant Reformation, mentioned earlier in the chapter, began the chain of events that eventually brought thousands of English men and women to the northern portion of Virginia, otherwise known as New England. When in the 1530s Henry VIII rejected Roman Catholicism and established the Church of England in its place, he set in motion forces he and his successors on the throne could not entirely control. Under Henry and his daughter Elizabeth, the Anglican Church reformed both theology and church structure. But by the early seventeenth century many people in England believed that Henry's reformation had not gone far enough. Instead of merely simplifying the church hierarchy, they wanted to abolish it altogether. Instead of a church subordinated to the interests of the state, they wanted a church free from political interference. And instead of a church composed automatically of all members of society, they wanted church membership to be more restricted. Because such people hoped above all to *purify* the church of corrupt influences, they were called Puritans.

The Puritans were followers of John Calvin, a Swiss cleric who had revised and enlarged on the Protestant doctrines originally outlined by Martin Luther. Calvin stressed the omnipotence of God and people's power-

| Puritanism |

lessness to affect their ultimate fate. Reacting against the notion (common in the medieval Catholic Church) that people could, in effect, ensure their spiritual salvation by donating money to the Church or doing good works, Calvin declared that God predestines souls to heaven or hell before their births. Christians could consequently do nothing to change their destiny.

Within that doctrine lay the Calvinists' major conceptual problem. If people's fates were determined by God before they were born, why should they behave well on earth? Members of the elect would be saved regardless of their actions, and those who were damned to hell would continue to be damned no matter how many good works they performed. The Calvinists resolved this dilemma ingeniously. God, they reasoned, did not just save the elect. He also gave them the ability to accept their salvation and to lead a good life during their stay on earth. Therefore, although good works could not earn one a place in heaven, a person might take his or her ability to live according to God's commandments as an indication of salvation. The reward for good works, in other words, was not guaranteed entrance into heaven; it was the likelihood that one's good works were evidence of elect status.

Conscientious Puritans devoted themselves to self-examination and Bible study, since it was considered each person's solemn duty to attempt to determine the state of his or her soul. (One result of that doctrine was the spread of literacy: to understand the Bible, Puritans obviously had to know how to read.) Despite their emphasis on self-study, though, Puritans believed that even the most pious could never be absolutely certain they were numbered among the elect. Mortals simply could not comprehend God's mind, motives, or behavior. Thus devout Puritans were often filled with anxiety about their spiritual state, and they felt deeply their inability to affect their own ultimate fate. For example, one man declared that he "had no power to think one good thought [or] speak one good word." His only hope for salvation, he realized, came "from the Lord out of his free and abundant grace and mercy to me," for God alone could "pardon my sins, subdue my lusts, remove my temptations."

Some Puritans (called Congregationalists) wanted to reform the Anglican Church rather than abandon it. Another group, known as Separatists, believed the Church of England to be so corrupt it could not be salvaged. They wanted to establish their own religious bodies, with membership restricted to the elect (as nearly as they could be identified).

In 1609 a group of about 125 Separatists migrated from the village of Scrooby, Nottinghamshire, to Leyden, Holland. The Netherlands' tolerant attitude enabled them to practice their religion openly, as they could not do in England. But ironically, the same relaxed atmosphere posed a serious threat to their little congregation. As William Bradford, one of the Separatists' leaders, later wrote in his *Of Plymouth Plantation,* the adults discovered that their children were "drawn away by evil examples into extravagant and dangerous courses, getting the reins off their necks and departing from their parents." Consequently, Bradford recounted, the members of the congregation began to think about moving to America, where they could practice their religion without such worries.

In early 1620 the Separatists obtained permission to settle in the northern part of the territory controlled by the Virginia Company of Plymouth. A total of 101 men and women, some of them "strangers" (non-Separatists), set sail in September on the aged, crowded *Mayflower.* Two months later they sighted land—the tip of Cape Cod, which was outside the northern boundary of the company's territory. But by then it was too late in the fall to go elsewhere. The

| Founding of Plymouth |

Pilgrims located their settlement, named Plymouth after the English city from which they had sailed, on a fine harbor that had once been the site of an Indian village.

Though the weather that year was quite mild, the Pilgrims were ill prepared to survive the rigors of a New England winter. They were racked by disease and suffered seriously from malnutrition. When spring arrived, only half the *Mayflower*'s passengers were still alive. But spring also brought what Bradford termed "a special instrument sent of God for their good beyond their expectation" in the person of Squanto, a friendly Indian. Squanto had been kidnapped and carried to Europe in 1614 by an English sea captain who had hoped to sell him as a slave. Four years later he had escaped and made his way back to America, only to discover that his tribe had been wiped out in the great epidemic of 1616–1617. Squanto spoke good English and served as the Pilgrims' interpreter. In addition, Bradford noted, "he directed them how to set their corn, where to take fish, and to procure other commodities, and was also their pilot to bring them to unknown places for their profit, and never left them till he died."

Although the Pilgrims had to endure one year of a "starving time," they were far more fortunate than the Jamestown settlers. The northern climate was healthier than that of the Chesapeake, and the Pilgrims displayed a willingness to work uncharacteristic of the early Virginians. They also benefited from the seriously weakening effect the great epidemic had had on the tribes of the Cape Cod region. Massasoit, the chief of the Wampanoags, the strongest tribe in the immediate area, agreed to a peace with the Pilgrims during their first spring in America, and the treaty was observed by both sides for more than half a century.

The Pilgrim colony at Plymouth grew slowly, and was completely absorbed into the larger and more prosperous Massachusetts Bay colony in 1691. It is nonetheless famous for the so-called First Thanksgiving—when the settlers gave thanks to God for their first harvest in their new home—and for the Mayflower Compact. Because the Pilgrims landed outside the jurisdiction of the Virginia Company, some of the "strangers" questioned the authority of the colony's leaders. In response, the Compact, signed in November 1620 while everyone was still on board the *Mayflower*, established a "Civil Body Politic" and a rudimentary legal authority for the colony. The settlers elected a governor and at first made all decisions for the colony at town meetings. Later, after more towns had been founded and the population had increased, Plymouth, like Virginia and Maryland, created an assembly to which the male settlers elected representatives.

Before the 1620s had ended, another group of Puritans—this time Congregationalists, not Separatists—launched the colonial enterprise that would come to dominate New England. When Charles I, who was hostile to Puritan beliefs, succeeded his father James I in 1625, some non-Separatists began to think about settling in America. Under the auspices of the New England Company, which held a land grant from the Council for New England (the successor to the Virginia Company of Plymouth), a group of Congrega-

tionalist merchants sent out a body of settlers to Cape Ann, north of Cape Cod, in 1628. The following year the merchants obtained a royal charter, constituting themselves as the Massachusetts Bay Company.

Founding of Massachusetts Bay

The new company quickly attracted the attention of other Puritans of the "middling sort" who were becoming increasingly convinced that they would no longer be able to practice their religion freely in England. The Congregationalists who now looked to the Massachusetts Bay Company for a solution to their problems remained committed to the goal of reforming the Church of England. But prudence seemed to dictate that they pursue that aim in America rather than at home. In a dramatic move designed to further their purposes, the Congregationalist merchants boldly decided to transfer the headquarters of the Massachusetts Bay Company to New England. The settlers would then be answerable to no one in the mother country, and would be able to handle their affairs, secular and religious, as they pleased.

The most important recruit to the new venture was John Winthrop, a pious but practical landed gentleman from Suffolk and a justice of the peace. In October 1629, the members of the Massachusetts Bay Company elected the forty-one-year-old Winthrop as their governor. With the exception of only isolated years in the mid-1630s and early 1640s, he served in that post until his death in 1649. It thus fell to Winthrop to organize the initial segment of the great Puritan migration to America. In 1630 more than 1,000 English men and women were transported to Massachusetts—most of them to Boston, which soon became the largest town in North America. By 1643 nearly 20,000 compatriots had followed them.

Governor John Winthrop

On board the *Arbella,* en route to New England in 1630, John Winthrop preached a sermon, "A Modell of Christian Charity," laying out his expectations for the new colony. Above all, he stressed the communal nature of the endeavor on which he and his fellow settlers had embarked. God, he explained, "hath so disposed of the condition of mankind as in all times some must be rich, some poor, some high and eminent in power and dignity, others mean and in subjection." But differences in status did not imply differences in worth. On the contrary: God had planned

Chapter 1: The meeting of Old World and New, 1492–1650

the world so that "every man might have need of other, and from hence they might be all knit more nearly together in the bond of brotherly affection." The Puritans faced a "community of perils"; thus "the care of the public must oversway all private respects." In America, Winthrop asserted, "we shall be as a city upon a hill, the eyes of all people are upon us." If the Puritans failed to carry out their "special commission" from God, "the Lord will surely break out in wrath against us. . . . [and] we shall surely perish out of the good land whither we pass over this vast sea to possess it."

Winthrop's was a transcendent vision. The society he foresaw in Puritan America was a commonwealth in the true meaning of the word, a community in which each person put the good of the whole ahead of his or her private concerns. It was, furthermore, to be a society whose members all lived according to the precepts of Christian charity, loving and aiding friends and enemies alike. Of course, such an ideal was beyond human reach. Early New England had its share of bitter quarrels and unchristian behavior. What is remarkable is how long the ideal prevailed as a goal to be sought, if seldom or never attained.

The Puritans' communal ideal was expressed chiefly in the doctrine of the covenant. As Winthrop's words indicated, they believed God had made a cov-

| Ideal of the covenant |

enant—that is, an agreement or contract—with them when He chose them for the special mission to America. In turn they convenanted with each other, promising to work together toward their goals. The founders of churches and towns in the new land often drafted formal documents setting forth the principles on which such institutions would be based. The same thing was true of the colonial governments of New England. The Pilgrims' Mayflower Compact was a covenant; so too was the Fundamental Orders of Connecticut (1639), which laid down the basic law for the settlements established along the Connecticut River valley in 1636 and thereafter. The leaders of Massachusetts Bay likewise interpreted their original joint-stock company charter in ways that enabled them to establish a covenanted community based on mutual consent. They gradually transformed the General Court, officially merely the company's governing body, into a colonial legislature, and opened the status of "freeman," or voting member of the company, to

John Winthrop (1588–1649). His strength and determination are clearly shown in this portrait, painted before he immigrated to America.   Massachusetts Historial Society.

all adult male church members resident in Massachusetts. Less than two decades after the first large group of Puritans had arrived in Massachusetts Bay, the colony had a functioning system of self-government composed of a governor and a two-house legislature. The General Court also established a judicial system modeled on England's and in 1641 adopted a legal code, *The Laws and Liberties of Massachusetts,* spelling out crimes and their proper punishments.

The colony's method of distributing land helped to further the communal ideal. Unlike Virginia and Maryland, where individual applicants sought headrights for themselves and their servants, in Massachusetts groups of families—often from the same region of England—applied together to the General Court for grants of land on which to establish towns. The

| Town land grants |

founders of Dedham in 1636 came largely from Yorkshire and East Anglia; the town fathers of Sudbury were from Hampshire, Essex, and Suffolk; and

The figure of the Indians fort or Palizado in NEW ENGLAND And the maner of the destroying It by Captayne Vnderhill And Captayne Mason

Hear enttere Captayne Vnderhill

Their Streets

The Indians houses

Diagram of the attack on the Pequot fort at Mystic. The Puritans and their Narragansett allies surround the fort, shooting everyone who tries to escape the flames. Drawn by Captain John Underhill, who participated in the attack.   The Library Company of Philadelphia.

those who moved to Andover in 1646 came from Wiltshire, Hampshire, and Lincolnshire.

The men who received the original town grant had the sole authority to determine how the land would be distributed. Understandably, they copied the villages from which they came. First they laid out town lots for houses and a church. Then they gave each family parcels of land scattered around the town center: pasture here, a woodlot there, an arable field elsewhere. They also reserved the best and largest plots for the most distinguished among them (usually including the minister); people who had been low on the social scale in England received far smaller allotments. In Sudbury, for example, the clergyman was granted 112 acres in the original distribution, but the poorest of the settlers received just 7½ acres. Indentured servants commonly received nothing.

In their new towns, the Puritans quickly established diversified farming as the chief means of subsistence. The first settlements in New England thus bore little resemblance to those in the Chesapeake. The Puritans attempted to create in the New World an idealized version of the village life they had known in the Old. As more immigrants poured into Massachusetts than could be housed in the earliest towns, the process repeated itself. First the General Court and then the founders of each town kept a tight communal grip on the colony's land. The settlement of Massachusetts was orderly and controlled. Even when immigrants began to move beyond the territorial limits of the Bay Colony into Connecticut (1636), New Haven (1638), and New Hampshire (1638), the same pattern of town land grants was maintained in these areas as well.

Chapter 1: The meeting of Old World and New, 1492–1650

The migration to Connecticut ended the Puritans' relative freedom from clashes with neighboring Indian tribes. The first English settlers in the Connecticut River valley moved there from Newtown (Cambridge), under the direction of their minister, Thomas Hooker. Connecticut was fertile, though remote from the other English towns, and the wide river promised easy access to the ocean for purposes of trade. The site had just one problem: it fell within the territory controlled by the Pequot tribe.

The strong Pequots, themselves recent migrants from the upper Hudson valley, dominated the weaker tribes native to the region. The Puritans and the Pequots had concluded a peace treaty in 1634, but that was before English families began to move into northern Connecticut lands occupied by the Pequots' tributaries. (Some of the weaker tribes invited the Puritans into the area, hoping to counterbalance Pequot power.) After two incidents in which Indians (probably not Pequots) brutally killed white men, a

| Pequot War |

Massachusetts force in 1636 burned some Pequot villages and crops. The raid provoked the Pequots to attack the new English town of Wethersfield, on the Connecticut River. Nine settlers, six men and three women, were killed and two others captured in that attack in April 1637.

In retaliation, Massachusetts sent a force of about ninety Englishmen, accompanied by some Narragansett Indians, to attack one of the main Pequot villages on the Mystic River. The Puritans and their allies surrounded the fortified village at dawn on May 26, 1637, set it on fire, and slaughtered at least four hundred Pequots, many of them women and children. Of the English, only two were killed and twenty wounded. The power of the Pequots was broken. The few surviving members of the tribe, dispirited and despairing, were captured and enslaved by the colonists and their Indian allies. (Slavery was often the fate of Indians captured by the English colonists—see Chapter 2.)

In *Of Plymouth Plantation,* William Bradford described the Puritans' pleasure at their conquest. "It was a fearful sight to see them thus frying in the fire and the streams of blood quenching the same," he commented, adding that the settlers praised God for giving them "so speedy a victory over so proud and insulting an enemy." The Puritans had good reason to be thankful, for the Pequots had been the only tribe strong enough to oppose their rapid migration into the New England interior. Their victory in the short but bloody Pequot War had won the colonists forty years of peace in which to expand the area of English settlement.

Life in New England

Colonists in New England led lives dramatically different from those of their contemporaries in the Chesapeake. The chief differences lay in their patterns of settlement, in the relative importance of religion in the settlers' daily lives, and in their family organization and behavior.

Although religion seems to have played a minor role in the lives of seventeenth-century Chesapeake settlers (largely because it proved difficult to transfer the Church of England as an institution to the colonies), it was ever-present in the lives of New Englanders, even those who were not Puritans. The governments of Massachusetts Bay, Plymouth, Connecticut, and the other northern colonies were all controlled by Puritans. Congregationalism was the only officially recognized religion; members of other sects had no freedom of worship except in Rhode Island. Only male church members could legally vote in colony elections, although some non-Puritans appear to have voted in town meetings. All households were taxed to build meetinghouses and pay ministers' salaries. Massachusetts' *Body of Laws and Liberties* incorporated regulations drawn from Old Testament scriptures into the legal code of the colony. Moreover, penalties were prescribed for expressing contempt for ministers or their preaching, and for failing to attend church services regularly.

In the New England colonies, church and state were intertwined. Puritans objected to secular interference in religious affairs, but at the same time expected the church to influence the conduct of politics. They also believed that the state had an obligation to support and protect the one true church—theirs. As a result, though they came to America seeking freedom of worship, they saw no contradiction in their refusal to grant that freedom to others. Indeed, the two most significant divisions in early Massachusetts were caused by religious disputes, and by Massachusetts Bay's unwillingness to tolerate dissent.

Roger Williams, a Separatist, immigrated to Massachusetts Bay in 1631 and became assistant pastor at

Roger Williams

Salem. Williams was well liked but soon began to express eccentric opinions. Among them was the notion that the Massachusetts and Plymouth charters were both defective because the king of England had no right to give away land belonging to the Indians. Another was his insistence that church and state should be kept entirely separate. Furthermore, Williams argued, if Puritans could not be certain of their own salvation, they could hardly require others to conform to their religious beliefs. Banished from Massachusetts in 1635, Williams founded the town of Providence on Narragansett Bay. Because of his beliefs, Providence and other towns in what became the colony of Rhode Island adopted a policy of tolerating all religions, including Judaism.

The other dissenter, and an even greater challenge to Massachusetts Bay orthodoxy, was Anne Marbury Hutchinson, the pious daughter of an Anglican

Anne Hutchinson

clergyman with Puritan leanings. Anne Hutchinson had immigrated to Boston with her husband and family in 1634 in order to follow her pastor, John Cotton, who had moved to New England the previous year. Cotton's preaching particularly stressed God's free gift of salvation to unworthy human beings (the covenant of grace), whereas most Massachusetts clerics emphasized preparing oneself to receive God's grace through good works, study, and reflection. As a disciple of Cotton, Hutchinson too stressed the covenant of grace.

Anne Hutchinson quickly became well known in Boston as a skilled midwife. In 1636 she began to hold women's meetings in her home to discuss Cotton's sermons. Soon men started to attend as well. At first Hutchinson simply summarized Cotton's sermons, but eventually she began to express her own interpretations of his statements. In so doing, she emphasized the covenant of grace more heavily than did Cotton himself. Indeed, she went so far as to adopt the so-called Antinomian heresy—the belief that the elect can communicate directly with God and be assured of salvation. Such ideas had an immense in-

trinsic appeal for Puritans. Anne Hutchinson offered them certainty of salvation in exchange for the state of constant tension in which they otherwise had to live, never knowing whether they would be saved or damned for eternity.

Hutchinson's ideas were a dangerous challenge to Puritan orthodoxy, so in November 1637 she was brought before the General Court of Massachusetts. She was charged with having libeled the colony's clergymen by claiming that they preached salvation through works. For two days she defended herself cleverly against her accusers, matching scriptural references and wits with John Winthrop himself. Finally, in an unguarded moment late in the second day, Hutchinson declared that God had spoken to her "by an immediate revelation." That heretical assertion assured her banishment; she and her family, along with some faithful followers, were exiled to Rhode Island.

The authorities in Massachusetts Bay perceived Anne Hutchinson as doubly dangerous to the existing order: she threatened not only religious orthodoxy but also traditional sex roles. Puritans believed in the equality before God of all souls, including women, but they also considered women inferior to men, forever tainted by Eve's guilt. Christians had long followed St. Paul's dictum that women should keep silent in church and be submissive to their husbands. Anne Hutchinson did neither. The magistrates' comments during her trial make it clear that they were almost as outraged by her "masculine" behavior as by her religious beliefs. Winthrop charged her with having set wife against husband, since so many of her followers were women. Another of her judges told her bluntly: "You have stept out of your place, you have rather bine a Husband than a Wife and a preacher than a Hearer; and a Magistrate than a Subject."

The vehemence with which the General Court reacted to Anne Hutchinson's implicit challenge to customary gender roles indicates the extent to which traditional English family patterns had been duplicated in New England. The northern environment and the characteristics of the migrant population combined to make the familial experiences of Puritan New Englanders very different from those of residents of the Chesapeake.

In the first place, Puritans commonly migrated as families—sometimes even three-generation families—

Chapter 1: The meeting of Old World and New, 1492–1650

Important events

1001	Norse explorers reach Labrador
1477	Marco Polo's *Travels* published
1488	Bartholomew Dias rounds Cape of Good Hope
1492	Christopher Columbus discovers Bahama Islands
1493	Syphilis first recorded in Europe
1497	John Cabot charts coast of Newfoundland
1498	Vasco da Gama reaches India
1507	Western Hemisphere first called America
1513	Ponce de Leon explores Florida Vasco Nuñez de Balboa crosses Isthmus of Panama; discovers Pacific Ocean
1518–30	Smallpox pandemic decimates Indian population of New World
1521	Tenochtitlan surrenders to Cortés; Aztec empire falls to Spaniards
1521–22	Ferdinand Magellan circumnavigates the globe
1524	Giovanni da Verrazano explores North American coast
1533	Henry VIII divorces Catherine of Aragon
1535	Francisco Pizarro conquers Inca empire
1539–42	Hernando de Soto explores southeastern United States
1540–42	Francisco Vásquez de Coronado explores southwestern United States
1558	Elizabeth I becomes queen
1577–80	Sir Francis Drake circumnavigates the globe
1587–90	Sir Walter Raleigh's Roanoke colony fails
1603	James I becomes king
1606	Virginia Company chartered
1607	Jamestown founded
1608	Samuel de Champlain founds Quebec
1609	Henry Hudson explores Hudson River
1611	First Virginia tobacco crop
1619	First blacks arrive in Virginia
1620	Plymouth Colony founded
1622	Powhatan Confederacy attacks Virginia colony
1624	Dutch settlement on Manhattan Island Virginia Company charter revoked; Virginia becomes royal colony
1625	Charles I becomes king
1629	Massachusetts Bay Company chartered
1630	Massachusetts Bay Colony founded
1634	Maryland founded
1635	Roger Williams expelled from Massachusetts Bay; founds Providence, Rhode Island
1636	Connecticut founded
1637	Pequot War Anne Hutchinson expelled from Massachusetts Bay
1638	New Haven Colony founded New Hampshire founded Swedish outpost on Delaware River established
1640	Great Migration to New England ends

rather than as individuals. That meant that the age range of the immigrants was wider and the sex ratio more balanced, so that the population could immediately begin to reproduce itself. Second, New England's climate was much healthier than that of the Chesapeake. Once Puritan settlements had survived the difficult first two or three years and established self-sufficiency in foodstuffs, New England proved to be even healthier than the mother country. Though adult male migrants to the Chesapeake lost about ten years from their English life expectancy of fifty to fifty-five years, their Massachusetts counterparts gained about ten years.

Consequently, although Chesapeake population patterns made for families that were few in number, small in size, and transitory, the demographic characteristics of New England made families there numerous, large, and long-lived. In New England more men

| *Family life in New England* |

were able to marry, since there were more female migrants; immigrant women married earlier (at twenty, on the average); and marriages lasted longer and produced more children, who were more likely to live to maturity. If seventeenth-century Chesapeake women could expect to rear three healthy children, New England women could anticipate raising six to eight. Households were thus very crowded, since New England dwellings usually contained only four small rooms.

The nature of the population had other major implications for family life. New England in effect created grandparents, since in England people rarely lived long enough to know their children's children. And while seventeenth-century southern parents normally died before their children married, northern parents exercised a good deal of control even over their adult children. Young men could not marry without acreage to cultivate, and because of the communal land-grant system they were dependent on their fathers to supply them with that land. Daughters, too, needed the dowry of household goods their parents would give them when they married. Yet parents needed their children's labor on their farms, and were often reluctant to see them marry and start their own households. That at times led to considerable conflict between the generations. On the whole, though, children seem to have obeyed their parents' wishes. They had few alternatives. One indication of tighter paren-

tal control there than in the Chesapeake was New England's lower premarital pregnancy rate. Fewer than 20 percent of northern brides in one town were pregnant when they married, as opposed to more than 33 percent in a southern county.

In 1630 John Winthrop wrote to his wife Margaret, who was still in England, "my deare wife, we are heer in a paradise." He was, of course, exaggerating. In another letter he admitted that "our fare be but coarse in respect of what we formerly had (pease, pudding, & fishe, being our ordinary diet)" and detailed the many difficulties that beset the Puritan settlers, along with numerous deaths. Yet even though America was not a paradise, it was a place where English men and women could worship as they wished or attempt to better their economic circumstances. Many died, but those who lived laid the foundation for subsequent colonial prosperity. That they did so by dispossessing the Indians bothered few besides Roger Williams. By the middle of the seventeenth century, one fact was indisputable: English people had come to the New World to stay.

Suggestions for further reading

General

Charles M. Andrews, *The Colonial Period of American History: The Settlements,* 3 vols. (1934–1937); John E. Pomfret, *Founding the American Colonies, 1583–1660* (1970).

Indians

Harold E. Driver, *Indians of North America,* 2nd ed. (1969); George E. Hyde, *Indians of the Woodlands: From Prehistoric Times to 1725* (1962); Alvin Josephy, Jr., *The Indian Heritage of America* (1968); Smithsonian Institution, *Handbook of North American Indians,* 15: *The Northeast* (1978); Robert F. Spencer, Jesse D. Jennings, *et al., The Native Americans: Ethnology and Backgrounds of the North American Indians,* 2nd ed. (1977).

England

Carl Bridenbaugh, *Vexed and Troubled Englishmen, 1590–1642* (1967); Mildred Campbell, *The English Yeoman under Elizabeth and the Early Stuarts* (1942); G. R. Elton,

England under the Tudors (1955); Peter Laslett, *The World We Have Lost* (1965); Wallace Notestein, *The English People on the Eve of Colonization 1603-1630* (1954); Lawrence Stone, *The Crisis of the Aristocracy, 1558-1641* (1965); Michael Walzer, *The Revolution of the Saints* (1965).

Exploration and Discovery

Fredi Chiapelli, *et al.*, eds., *First Images of America: The Impact of the New World on the Old,* 2 vols. (1976); Alfred W. Crosby, Jr., *The Columbian Exchange: Biological and Cultural Consequences of 1492* (1972); J.H. Elliott, *The Old World and the New, 1492-1650* (1970); Charles Gibson, *Spain in America* (1966); James Lang, *Conquest and Commerce: Spain and England in the Americas* (1975); Samuel Eliot Morison, *Admiral of the Ocean Sea* (1942); Samuel Eliot Morison, *The European Discovery of America: The Northern Voyages, A.D. 1500-1600* (1971), *The Southern Voyages, A.D. 1492-1616* (1974); J.H. Parry, *The Age of Reconaissance* (1963); David B. Quinn, *North America from Earliest Discovery to First Settlements* (1977).

Early contact between whites and Indians

Wilbur R. Jacobs, *Dispossessing the American Indian: Indians and Whites on the Colonial Frontier* (1972); Francis Jennings, *The Invasion of America: Indians, Colonialism, and the Cant of Conquest* (1975); Nancy O. Lurie, "Indian Cultural Adjustment to European Civilization," in *Seventeenth-Century America: Essays in Colonial History,* ed. James M. Smith (1959); Calvin Martin, *Keepers of the Game: Indian-Animal Relationships and the Fur Trade* (1978); Frances Mossiker, *Pocahontas: The Life and the Legend* (1976); Alden T. Vaughan, *American Genesis: Captain John Smith and the Founding of Virginia* (1975); Alden T. Vaughan, *The New England Frontier: Puritans and Indians 1620-1675,* rev. ed. (1979).

New England

Ben Barker-Benfield, "Anne Hutchinson and the Puritan Attitude toward Women," *Feminist Studies,* I (1972), 65-96; Charles E. Clark, *The Eastern Frontier: The Settlement of Northern New England, 1610-1763* (1970); John Demos, *A Little Commonwealth: Family Life in Plymouth Colony* (1970); John Faragher, "Old Women and Old Men in Seventeenth-Century Wethersfield, Connecticut," *Women's Studies,* 4, No. 1 (Jan. 1976), 11-31; Philip J. Greven, Jr., *Four Generations: Population, Land, and Family in Colonial Andover, Massachusetts* (1970); Sydney V. James, *Colonial Rhode Island* (1975); Lyle Koehler, *A Search for Power: The 'Weaker Sex' in Seventeenth-Century New England* (1980); George Langdon, *Pilgrim Colony: A History of New Plymouth, 1620-1691* (1966); Kenneth A. Lockridge, *A New England Town: The First Hundred Years (Dedham, Massachusetts, 1636-1736)* (1970); Edmund S. Morgan, *The Puritan Dilemma: The Story of John Winthrop* (1958); Edmund S. Morgan, *The Puritan Family: Religion and Domestic Relations in Seventeenth-Century New England,* rev. ed. (1966); Edmund S. Morgan, *Visible Saints: The History of a Puritan Idea* (1963); Samuel Eliot Morison, *Builders of the Bay Colony* (1930); Sumner Chilton Powell, *Puritan Village: The Formation of a New England Town* (1963); Darrett Rutman, *American Puritanism: Faith and Practice* (1970); Darrett Rutman, *Winthrop's Boston: A Portrait of a Puritan Town, 1630-1649* (1965); Alan Simpson, *Puritanism in Old and New England* (1955).

Chesapeake

Lois Green Carr and Lorena Walsh, "The Planter's Wife: The Experience of White Women in Seventeenth-Century Maryland," *William and Mary Quarterly,* 3rd ser., 34 (1977), 542-571; Wesley Frank Craven, *The Southern Colonies in the Seventeenth Century, 1607-1689* (1949); Wesley Frank Craven, *White, Red, and Black: The Seventeenth Century Virginian* (1971); Karen O. Kupperman, "Apathy and Death in Early Jamestown," *Journal of American History,* 66 (1979), 24-40; Aubrey C. Land, Lois Green Carr, and Edward C. Papenfuse, eds., *Law, Society, and Politics in Early Maryland* (1977); Edmund S. Morgan, *American Slavery, American Freedom: The Ordeal of Colonial Virginia* (1975); Darrett Rutman and Anita Rutman, "Of Agues and Fevers: Malaria in the Early Chesapeake," *William and Mary Quarterly,* 3rd ser., 33 (1976), 31-60; Abbot E. Smith, *Colonists in Bondage: White Servitude and Convict Labor in America, 1607-1776* (1947); Thad W. Tate and David L. Ammerman, eds., *The Chesapeake in the Seventeenth Century: Essays on Anglo-American Society & Politics* (1979); *William and Mary Quarterly,* 3rd ser., 30, No. 1 (Jan. 1973): *Chesapeake Society.*

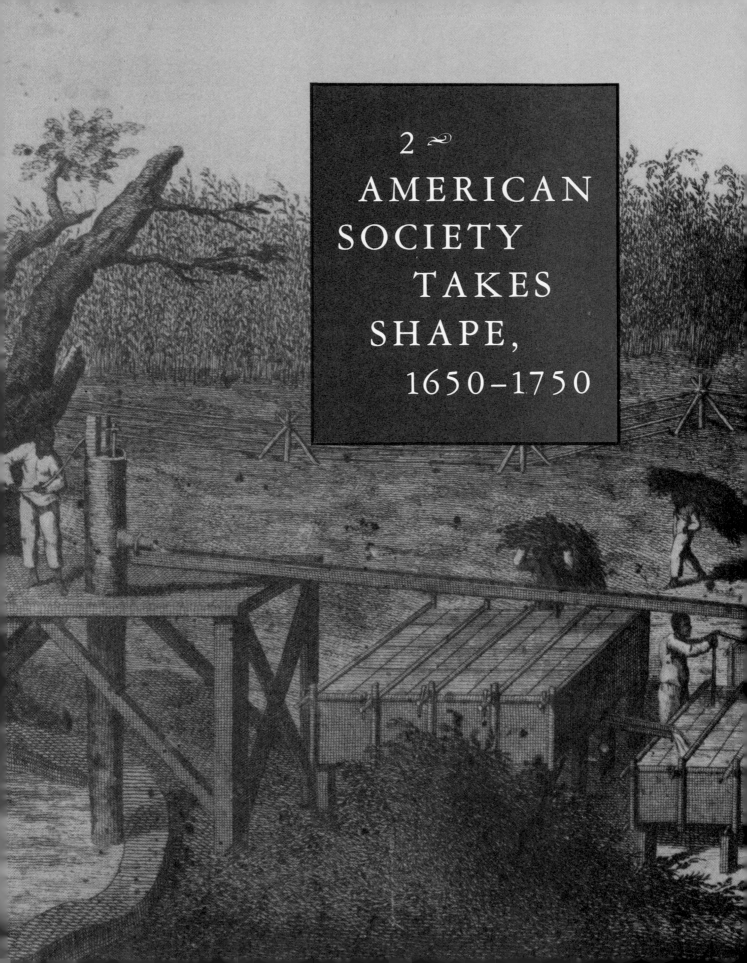

2 ~

AMERICAN SOCIETY TAKES SHAPE, 1650–1750

Olaudah Equiano was eleven years old in 1756 when black raiders in search of slaves kidnapped him and his younger sister from their village in what is now Nigeria. Until then, he had lived peacefully with his father and mother, his father's other wives, and his seven siblings and half-siblings in a mud-walled compound that itself resembled a small village. Equiano and other members of the Ibo tribe were, he later observed, "habituated to labour from our earliest years." Men, women, and children worked together to cultivate corn, yams, beans, cotton, tobacco, and plantains (a type of banana). They also raised cattle, poultry, and goats. Equiano's family, like others in the region, held prisoners of war as slaves. With what may have been idealized hindsight, he later recalled that the slaves did "no more work than other members of the community, even their master; their food, clothing, and lodging were nearly the same. . . . There was scarce any other difference between [masters and slaves] than a superior degree of importance which the head of a family possesses . . . and that authority which, as such, he exercises over every part of his household."

Equiano's experiences as a captive differed sharply from the life he had led as a child in his father's house. For months he was passed from master to master, finally arriving at the coast, where an English slave ship lay at anchor. Terrified by the light complexions, long hair, and strange language of the sailors, he was afraid that "I had gotten into a world of bad spirits and that they were going to kill me." Equiano was placed below decks, where "with the loathsomeness of the stench and crying together, I became so sick and low that I was not able to eat, nor had I the least desire to taste anything." The whites flogged him to make him eat, and he thought about jumping overboard but was so closely watched that his plan was foiled. At last some other Ibos told him that they were being taken to the whites' country to work. "I then was a little revived," Equiano remembered, "and thought if it were no worse than working, my situation was not so desperate."

After a long voyage during which many of the Africans died of disease caused by the cramped, unsanitary conditions and poor food, the ship arrived at Barbados, a British island in the West Indies. Equiano and his shipmates feared that "these ugly men" they saw there were cannibals, but experienced slaves were brought on board to assure them that they would not be eaten and that many blacks like themselves lived on the islands. "This report eased us much," Equiano recalled, "and sure enough soon after we landed there came to us Africans of all languages." Everything in Barbados was new and surprising, but Equiano later remarked particularly on two-storied buildings and horses, neither of which he had ever seen.

Because of his youth, Equiano was not purchased in the West Indies, and was instead carried to Virginia along with the other less-desirable slaves. There, on the plantation of his new owner, he was separated from the other Africans and put to work weeding and clearing rocks from the fields. "I was now exceedingly miserable and thought myself worse off than any of the rest of my companions," Equiano reported, "for they could talk to each other, but I had no person to speak to that I could understand. In this state I was constantly grieving and pining and wishing for death rather than anything else."

But Equiano did not remain in Virginia for long. Bought by a sea captain, Olaudah Equiano eventually became an experienced sailor. He learned to read and write English, purchased his freedom at the age of twenty-one, and later actively supported the English antislavery movement. In 1789 Equiano published *The Interesting Narrative of the Life of Olaudah Equiano . . . Written by Himself,* from which this account of his captivity is drawn. Until he was purchased by the sailor, Equiano's experiences differed very little from those of other Africans who were forced into slavery in the English colonies of the New World. Like him, many were kidnapped by black slavers and taken first to the West Indies, then to North America. His *Interesting Narrative,* one of a number of memoirs by former slaves, depicts the captives' terror powerfully and convincingly.

If the most important aspect of the first fifty years of English colonization was the meeting of European and Indian, the key occurrence of the next century was the importation of more than two hundred thousand Africans into North America. That massive influx of black slaves, and the geographic patterns it took, has dramatically influenced the shaping of American society ever since.

Many other major events also marked the years between 1650 and 1750. New colonies were founded, populating the gap between the widely separated

New England and Chesapeake settlements. England also took over the coastal outposts established by other European nations. As English settlements spread to the north, west, and south, they moved onto territory controlled by the powerful Indian tribes of the interior. After many years of peace, colonists and native Americans once again went to war. Furthermore, internal disputes within the colonies often resulted in open rebellions against established governments. Yet by the middle of the eighteenth century, stable political and social structures had evolved in all the colonies. After a century and a half of English colonization, the American provinces assumed a mature form.

The forced migration of Africans

Few Africans were imported into the English mainland colonies before the last quarter of the seventeenth century. This pattern was in sharp contrast to that of Britain's Caribbean colonies. The Caribbean islands were first settled in the 1620s and 1630s, and by the 1640s the white colonists had already begun to purchase large numbers of slaves to work in the production of sugar cane. As early as 1655, enslaved blacks nearly equalled whites in numbers on the island of Barbados, and by 1680 blacks outnumbered their white masters two-to-one. In the Leeward Islands (Nevis, St. Christopher, Antigua, and Montserrat), whites still made up a small majority in 1680, but thirty years later they comprised only one-quarter of the total population. What accounted for the difference between the island and mainland colonies with respect to black slavery? More important, since England itself had no tradition of slavery, why did English settlers in the New World begin to enslave Africans at all? The answers to both questions lie in the combined effects of economics and racial attitudes.

The English were an ethnocentric people. They believed firmly in the superiority of their values and civilization, especially when compared to the native cultures of Africa and North America. Furthermore, they believed that fair-skinned peoples like themselves were superior to the darker-skinned races. Those beliefs alone did not cause them to enslave Indians and

This bronze plaque from Benin, Nigeria, demonstrates the artistry of that sophisticated African civilization, and suggests the cultural loss Africans must have suffered when they were enslaved and carried to the Americas.   Museum für Völkerkunde, Staatliche Museen Preubischer Kulturbesitz, Berlin (West).

Africans, but the idea that other races were inferior to whites helped to justify slavery.

Moreover, although the English had not previously practiced slavery, other Europeans had. English people knew that Spanish and Portuguese Christians had enslaved Moorish prisoners of war (who were black and Moslem), and that Christian doctrine allowed the enslavement of heathen peoples. Thus when the English settlers in the New World needed laborers, almost without thinking they looked to dark-skinned non-Christians to supply those needs. In the Spanish colonies, the Catholic Church discouraged Indian slavery because it wanted to convert the native peoples rather than subjugate them. No such religious motive worked against Indian slavery in the English settlements, but there as elsewhere the native peoples' familiarity with the environment made them difficult to enslave. Often Indian captives were able to escape from their white masters.

Africans were a different story. Transported far from home and set down in alien surroundings, they were frequently unable—like Olaudah Equiano—to communicate with their fellow workers. They were also the darkest (and thus, to European eyes, the most inferior) of all peoples. Black Africans therefore seemed to be ideal candidates for perpetual servitude. By the time the English established settlements in the Caribbean and North America, Spanish colonists had already held Africans in slavery for over a century. The English newcomers to the New World, in other words, had a ready-made model to copy.

Nevertheless, a fully developed system of lifelong slavery did not emerge immediately in the English colonies. Lack of historical evidence makes it difficult to determine the legal status of blacks during the first two or three decades of English settlement, but at least a few of them seem to have been free. After 1640, on the other hand, some blacks were being perma-

Emergence of slavery

nently enslaved in each of the English colonies. Colonial assemblies started to pass laws specifically governing the behavior of blacks. Also, black servants began to command higher sale prices than their white counterparts, suggesting service for life rather than a fixed term of years. By the end of the century, the blacks' status was fixed. Barbados adopted a comprehensive slave code as early as 1661, and the mainland provinces soon did the same. In short, even before the extension of the direct African slave trade to North America, the English settlements there had established a clear legal basis for a slave system.

The question still remains: why did Chesapeake and Caribbean colonists differ at first in their choice of laborers, and why did the Chesapeake tobacco planters turn increasingly to blacks after 1675? Both supply and demand factors were influential.

In the West Indies, the environment was decisive. English people did not adapt easily to life in the tropics; they died in droves from epidemic diseases their doctors did not know how to treat. Potential servant migrants to the Caribbean may well have learned of the area's dangers and decided to go elsewhere. In any event, sugar planters soon came to prefer African laborers, who were accustomed to the tropical climate and resistant to the most serious of the diseases that

killed whites. (The inherited sickle-cell blood trait carried by many blacks helped to combat malaria, and exposure to yellow fever in Africa had immunized black immigrants to that disease.) Thus the black population of the Caribbean islands grew rapidly due to continuing importation.

The Chesapeake environment, though dangerous, was measurably less deadly to whites than the Caribbean, and tobacco planters relied almost exclusively on white indentured servants for fully half a century. But after about 1675 they could no longer obtain an adequate supply of white workers. A falling birth rate

Decline in white immigration

and improved economic conditions in England combined to decrease the number of possible migrants to the colonies. And by the end of the century many other English settlements in North America were competing with the Chesapeake for newcomers, both indentured and free. As a result, the number of servant migrants to the Chesapeake levelled off after 1665 and fell in the 1680s. After 1674, when the shortage of servants became acute, imports of Africans increased dramatically. As early as 1690, the Chesapeake colonies contained more black slaves than white indentured servants, and by 1710 one-fifth of the region's population was black. Slaves usually cost about two-and-a-half times as much as servants, but they repaid the greater investment by their lifetime of service.

Yet not all white planters could afford to devote so much money to purchasing workers. Accordingly, the transition from indentured to enslaved labor increased the social and economic distance between richer and poorer planters. Whites with enough money could acquire slaves and accumulate greater wealth, while less affluent whites could not even buy indentured servants, whose price had been driven up by scarcity. As time passed, white Chesapeake society thus became more and more stratified; that is, the gap between rich and poor steadily widened. The introduction of large numbers of Africans into the Chesapeake, in other words, had a significant impact on white society, in addition to reshaping the population as a whole.

The other southern colony founded in the seventeenth century was also dramatically affected by the institution of slavery and the presence of blacks. In 1669 King Charles II, grandson of James I, granted a

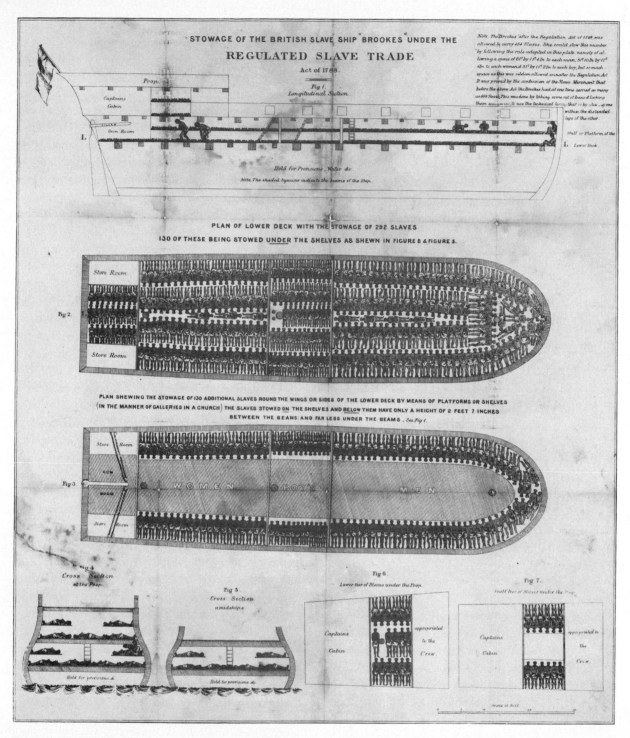

Eighteenth-century diagram of a slave ship, with its human cargo stowed according to British regulations. Many captains did not give slaves even this much room. On the assumption that a large number of Africans would die en route, shipmasters packed as many slaves as possible into the hold to increase their profit.   Library of Congress.

The forced migration of Africans

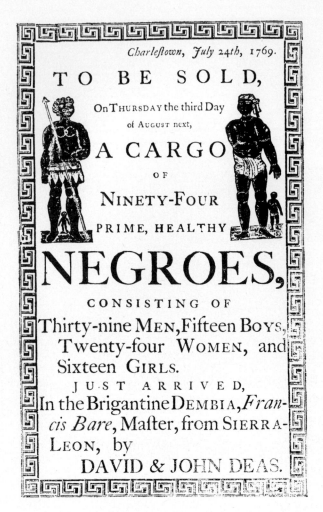

Charlestown, July 24th, 1769.

TO BE SOLD,

On THURSDAY the third Day
of AUGUST next,

A CARGO

OF

NINETY-FOUR

PRIME, HEALTHY

NEGROES,

CONSISTING OF

Thirty-nine MEN, Fifteen BOYS,
Twenty-four WOMEN, and
Sixteen GIRLS.

JUST ARRIVED,

In the Brigantine DEMBIA, Francis Bare, Master, from SIERRA-
LEON, by

DAVID & JOHN DEAS.

Slave traders announced their sales in newspaper advertisements and broadsides like this one, from South Carolina. Note the imbalanced sex ratio among the slaves in the cargo.   American Antiquarian Society.

two distinct population centers, which in 1730 split into separate colonies.

The Albemarle region that became North Carolina was first settled by Virginians. They established a society much like their own, with an economy based on tobacco cultivation and the export of such forest products as pitch, tar, and timber. Because North Carolina lacked a satisfactory harbor, its planters continued to rely on Virginia's ports and merchants to conduct their trade, and the two colonies remained tightly linked.

South Carolina developed quite differently. Its first settlers—who founded Charleston in 1670—came from Barbados, which was already overcrowded. With them they brought their slaves; perhaps one-quarter to one-third of the first residents of South Carolina were black, and of those three-fourths were male. The high proportion of Africans and Caribbean-born blacks in South Carolina's population from the very beginning inexorably shaped the colony's early history.

The Africans' familiarity with a semitropical environment was useful to white South Carolinians, who found the region alien and threatening. African-style dugout canoes became the chief means of transportation in the colony, which was crisscrossed by innumerable rivers. Fishing nets copied from African models proved to be more efficient than those of English origin. The baskets slaves wove and the gourds they hollowed out came into general use as containers for food and drink. Africans' skill at killing crocodiles equipped them to handle alligators as well. And, finally, slaves adapted African techniques of cattleherding for use in the American context. Since meat and hides were the colony's chief exports in its earliest years, blacks obviously contributed significantly to South Carolina's prosperity.

Their central position in the colony's economy was not established, however, until almost the end of the century. In the 1670s and 1680s, white Carolinians, like other English people in the New World, employed white indentured servants and Indian slaves as well as blacks. But in the last decade of the century South Carolinians developed a new staple crop: rice.

Introduction of rice and indigo Europeans knew little about techniques of cultivating and processing rice, but slaves from Africa's

group of his friends a tract of land stretching from the southern boundary of Virginia to Spanish Florida. The proprietors named their new province Carolina in honor of their king (whose name in Latin was Carolus), and planned to establish a colony governed by an

Founding of the Carolinas elaborate hierarchy of landholding aristocrats. The "Fundamental Constitutions of Carolina," written by the political philosopher John Locke, amounted to a blueprint for a utopian society with a carefully structured distribution of political and economic power. But Carolina failed to follow the course Locke had outlined for it. Instead it quickly developed

so-called Rice Coast (present-day Ghana and Sierra Leone) had spent their lives working in the rice fields. It may well have been their expertise that enabled their English masters to grow rice successfully. As the colony's commitment to rice cultivation grew, so did the demand for African workers (as opposed to workers of English or American origin). The Africans' relative immunity to malaria and yellow fever also prompted Carolina planters, like those in the West Indies, to prefer them to other laborers. As a result, by 1710 a majority of South Carolina's residents were black.

South Carolina developed a second staple crop in the 1740s, and it too made use of blacks' special skills. The crop was indigo, much prized in Europe as a blue dye for clothing. Carolinians had first tried unsuccessfully to grow indigo in the late seventeenth century. Then, in the early 1740s, Eliza Lucas, a young Antigua woman who was managing her father's South Carolina plantations, began to experiment with indigo cultivation. Drawing on the knowledge of an overseer from Montserrat and the experience of some West Indian blacks familiar with the crop, she developed the planting and processing techniques later adopted throughout the colony. Indigo was grown on high ground, and rice was planted in low-lying swampy areas; rice and indigo also had opposite growing seasons. Thus the two crops complemented each other perfectly. Although South Carolina indigo never matched the quality of that raised in the West Indies, the indigo industry flourished because Parliament offered Carolinians a bounty on every pound they exported to Great Britain.

After 1700 white southerners were irrevocably committed to Negro slavery as their chief source of labor. The same was not true of white northerners. Only a small proportion of the slaves brought to the English colonies in America went to the northern mainland provinces, and most of those who did worked as domestic servants. Lacking large-scale agricultural enterprises, the rural North did not demand many enslaved laborers. In northern urban areas, though, white domestic servants were hard to find and harder to keep (because higher wages were paid for other jobs in the labor-scarce economy), and blacks there filled an identifiable need. In some northern colonial cities (notably Newport, Rhode Island,

and New York City), black slaves accounted for more than 10 percent of the population.

Between 1492 and 1770 more Africans than Europeans came to the New World. But just 4.5 percent

Slave importation, 1492–1770	

of them (345,000 persons by 1861, or 275,000 during the eighteenth century) were imported into the region that later became the United States. By contrast, 42 percent of the approximately 9.5 million enslaved blacks were carried to the Caribbean, and 49 percent went to South America, mainly to the Portuguese colony of Brazil. At first, most of the slaves brought to the English mainland colonies arrived via the West Indies, but as time passed direct traffic from Africa increased. Overall, about 80 percent of the slaves imported into the colonies before the American Revolution had been born in Africa. Early in the century South Carolina and the Chesapeake imported roughly equal numbers of slaves, but by the 1760s the southern colony dominated the trade. Carolinians by then purchased three times as many blacks each year as did Virginians and Marylanders together.

When Africans arrived in the English colonies, what kind of life did they find? The conditions under which they labored varied considerably from place to place. In the West Indies, the unhealthy environment and rigorous work schedules on sugar plantations combined to produce appallingly high mortality rates. Also, planters there preferred male laborers, and bought few female slaves. Thus the black population could not reproduce itself, and planters had to continue to import large numbers of slaves from Africa simply to maintain their labor force at a constant level.

Among the mainland colonies, South Carolina most closely resembled the West Indies. Rice cultivation was difficult and unhealthful, partly because the rice swamps were ideal breeding-grounds for malaria-carrying mosquitoes. Furthermore, Carolina planters, like those of the islands, maintained a slave population with a high proportion of males to females (about two-to-one). During the mid-eighteenth century, therefore, South Carolina slaves barely managed to reproduce themselves, and the black population increased in size only because of massive imports of slaves from Africa.

In the Chesapeake, by contrast, imports accounted for black population growth only until about 1720. From 1740 on, the black population of Maryland and Virginia grew chiefly through natural increase. This

| Natural increase of the slave population |

significant change indicates that— against all the odds—Africans had been able to create families in the Chesapeake. Precisely how and why such a transition occurred is not yet clear. The more moderate climate and less demanding work routines in the Chesapeake probably contributed to greater survival rates among the immigrants. Moreover, by the middle of the eighteenth century some whites had begun to recognize the advantages of encouraging their slaves to marry and have children. As the Virginia slaveholder Thomas Jefferson put it some years later: "I consider a woman who brings a child every two years more profitable than the best man of the farm. What she produces is an addition to the capital, while his labors disappear in mere consumption."

Jefferson thus correctly identified one of the most important consequences of the fact that the black population of the Chesapeake had started to rise through natural increase. A planter who began with only a few slave families could watch the size of his labor force increase steadily over the years without making additional major investments in workers. It was no coincidence that the first truly large Chesapeake plantations appeared in the 1740s, when natural increase became the dominant factor in the growing slave population. The two developments went hand in hand. Greater concentrations of slaves and more balanced sex ratios (due to natural increase) meant a greater likelihood of marriage and childbearing among blacks. This in turn meant greater wealth for their owners. These changes affected the nature of both the plantations and the slave society in the Chesapeake.

By midcentury, then, the vast majority of slaves in the Chesapeake and a substantial proportion of those in South Carolina had formed persistent marital unions and had American-born children. A distinctive Afro-American society had begun to emerge out of the forced migration of thousands of blacks from different tribes and regions of Africa. That society will be described further in Chapter 3.

The secularization and commercialization of New England

In 1642 civil war broke out in England between Puritans led by Oliver Cromwell and Anglicans supporting Charles I, who in 1625 had succeeded his father James I. Charles not only persecuted Puritans but also ruled autocratically. The Puritans, who dominated Parliament, successfully overthrew him after several years of war and executed him in 1649. Cromwell then controlled the government (taking the title of Protector) until his own death in 1658. Two years later the Stuart family was peacefully restored to the throne in the person of Charles II, son of Charles I. Thus ended the tumultuous chapter in English history known as the Interregnum (Latin for "between reigns").

These events had profound consequences for the American colonies, especially New England. The Puritans' triumph at home eliminated their major incentive for immigration to America. The Puritan migration largely ceased, and some colonists even packed up and returned to the mother country. New England's population growth in the seventeenth century,

| Population growth and land use |

therefore, resulted almost entirely from natural increase. The first settlers' many children also produced many children, who tended to live longer, on the average, than their Chesapeake contemporaries. In 1700, therefore, when the Chesapeake population totaled no more than the number of immigrants to the region (perhaps 100,000), New England's population had already quadrupled its total immigration and had also reached approximately 100,000.

In New England, the area of settlement and the number of towns constantly expanded as members of each subsequent generation sought land on which to establish and support their families. This process was not always smooth, nor was there an infinite amount of land available for farming. As noted in Chapter 1, fathers often resisted giving sons their own independent allotments of land. Since sons (and occasionally daughters) usually shared equally in their father's property, the size of landholdings tended to decrease with each generation. The earliest settlers of some of the first Massachusetts towns, for example, eventually received land grants averaging about 150 acres during their lifetimes. By the third quarter of the eighteenth century, the average landholding in the same towns was only 30 to 50 acres.

Many of the acres in those first large farms went unused because the New Englanders did not have the manpower to cultivate them, nor would they have had a market for surplus crops in any case. The smaller eighteenth-century farms were still adequate to support a family, which was all that was necessary. But the comparison illustrates the pressures that the ever-increasing population placed on the supply of arable land. Members of the first American-born generation could usually farm in their home towns. But their children and grandchildren often had to migrate—north into New Hampshire or Maine, south to New York, westward beyond the Connecticut River valley—to find sufficient farm land. Alternatively, they could learn artisanal skills such as blacksmithing or carpentry and ply their trades in their home towns or in such seaports as Boston, Salem, New Haven, Newport, or Providence.

As the population increased, New England towns changed in shape and character. The settlement patterns established by the town founders, in which each family lived on a village lot and cultivated small scattered pieces of land, soon gave way to consolidated farms situated at some distance from the town center. When the population in an outlying area had reached a sufficient number, the farmers there commonly asked the town for permission to construct their own church, so they would not have to travel so far on Sundays. Often the next step was a formal division of the town.

The history of Dedham, Massachusetts, will serve to illustrate the process. The first settlers (about thirty families) received title in 1637 to more than 200 square miles of territory. Over the course of the next century, five more towns were carved out of the original grant. (Eventually another seven towns were created). Medfield (1651), Wrentham (1671), and Bellingham (1719), whose centers of settlement were located more than ten miles from Dedham village, seceded from Dedham with little difficulty. But Dedham strongly resisted the loss of the nearby areas that

became Needham (1711) and Walpole (1724). The struggle went on for years, causing angry disputes between townspeople eager to maintain Dedham's traditional character and outlying farmers who sought greater local control over churches, roads, schools, and other matters.

Just as inevitable as changes in the land-population ratio and alterations in town boundaries was the major religious crisis caused by a conflict between two basic tenets of New England Puritanism. The first was a belief in infant baptism for the children of all church members. The second was the requirement that potential church members prove to the congregation that they had experienced the gift of God's grace, or "saving faith," before they could be admitted to full membership. (That usually involved a searching examination into the state of their souls. It did not mean that applicants had to identify a single moment of conversion.)

The passage of time alone brought the requirements for church membership into conflict with the practice of infant baptism. By the 1650s, baptized American-born children of immigrant church members were themselves marrying and having children. But many of them had not applied for full church membership, since they had not experienced saving faith. What was to be done when such families presented their infants for baptism? A synod of Massachusetts ministers, convened in 1662 to consider the problem, responded by establishing a category of "halfway" membership in the church. In a statement that has become known as the Halfway Covenant, the

> Halfway
> Covenant

clergymen declared that adults who had been baptized as children but were not full church members could have their children baptized. In return, such parents would have to acknowledge the authority of the church and live according to moral precepts. They would not be allowed to vote in church affairs or take communion.

Local churches at first resisted the change, but were eventually forced to accept it in order to maintain adequate levels of membership. Understandably, American-born Puritans did not display the same religious fervor that had prompted their ancestors to cross the Atlantic. Their piety had not been strengthened by persecution; they were not dissenters but adherents of an orthodox religion. Though Puritan divines repeatedly scolded their congregations for lack of piety, using a standard sermon form known as the jeremiad, church records for the period show no decline in the total number of members. On the contrary, the Halfway Covenant brought into the church people who would otherwise have been outside its bounds, most notably third-generation Puritans who had had no direct experience of saving faith.

Studies of patterns of membership in Puritan churches after 1660 have yielded an important finding: ever-larger proportions of church members were women. In New England's early days men and women had joined the church in approximately equal numbers, but by the end of the seventeenth century women were in the majority in many congregations. It was probably in response to their increasingly female audiences that clerics such as Cotton Mather, the most prominent member of a family of distinguished ministers, began to preach sermons outlining woman's proper role in church and society. Mather's sermons were the first formal examination of that theme in American history. In "Ornaments for the Daughters of Zion," Mather instructed women to be submissive to their husbands, watchful of their children, and attentive to religious duty. The evidence from church membership rolls suggests a growing division between pious women and their more worldly husbands, a split that was to be enshrined in the ideology of "woman's place" in nineteenth-century America. It also reflects the significant economic changes occurring in New England during the latter half of the seventeenth century, which originated in the impact of the English Civil War.

Before 1640 the northern colonies had developed only one dependable export—furs—which they obtained by trading such items as knives, combs, scissors, and mirrors to local Indian tribes. Beaver pelts in particular commanded a premium price in Europe, and the New England colonies competed with each other for control of the major sources of supply. One measure of the importance of the fur trade to New England's economy was the colonies' adoption of wampum, the Indians' currency, as legal tender for payment of debts and taxes. Strings of wampum (polished beads made from seashells by the Narragansett tribe) were routinely used as money by both whites and Indians. The colonists began to produce their own coins in 1652, and though wampum ceased to be legal tender in the 1660s, it continued to be used in private transactions until the early eighteenth century.

Proceeds from furs alone were insufficient to purchase all the manufactured goods the settlers required. For one thing, New England's supply of pelts was limited because the region lacked rivers giving ready access to the interior of the continent. Furthermore, when the outbreak of the English Civil War virtually ended the flow of immigrants, it became apparent that the colonies' economy had depended heavily on a continuing influx of new settlers. New England farmers had been producing surplus crops—such as seed grains and cattle—which they sold to the newcomers, who in return supplied them with clothing, plows, and other such items. When there were no longer many newcomers, New England's first economic system collapsed.

The Puritans then began a search for new saleable crops and markets. They found such crops in the waters off the coast—fish—and on their own land—grain and wood products. By 1643 they had also found the necessary markets: first the Wine Islands (the Azores and Canaries) in the Atlantic, and then the new English colonies in the Caribbean, which were beginning to cultivate sugar intensively and to invest heavily in slaves. The islands lacked precisely the goods New England could produce in abundance: cheap food (corn and salted fish) to feed the slaves, and wood for barrels to transport wine (the Atlantic islands) and molasses (the Caribbean colonies).

Rise of a mercantile economy

Thus developed the series of transactions that has become known, inaccurately, as the triangular trade. Since New England's products duplicated England's, the northern colonists sold their goods in the West Indies and elsewhere to earn the money with which to purchase English products. (Southerners did not have the same problem. Their crops—tobacco, rice, and indigo—could be sold directly to England.) There soon grew up in New England's ports a cadre of merchants who acquired—usually through barter—cargoes of timber and foodstuffs, which they then dispatched to the West Indies for sale. In the Caribbean the ships sailed from island to island, exchanging fish, barrel staves, and grains for molasses, fruit, spices, and slaves.

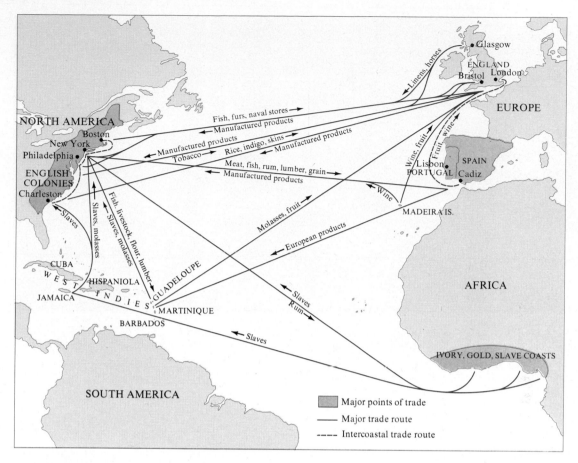

Map labels:
- Glasgow
- ENGLAND
- Bristol London
- EUROPE
- NORTH AMERICA
- Boston
- New York
- Philadelphia
- ENGLISH COLONIES
- Charleston
- Fish, furs, naval stores →
- Manufactured products
- ← Manufactured products
- Tobacco
- Rice, indigo, skins →
- Manufactured products
- Meat, fish, rum, lumber, grain →
- ← Manufactured products
- Linens, horses
- Wine, fruit
- Fruit, wine
- Lisbon
- PORTUGAL
- SPAIN
- Cadiz
- ← Wine
- MADEIRA IS.
- Molasses, fruit →
- European products →
- ← Slaves
- Fish, livestock, flour, lumber
- ← Slaves
- Slaves, molasses
- Slaves, molasses
- CUBA
- HISPANIOLA
- GUADELOUPE
- JAMAICA
- MARTINIQUE
- BARBADOS
- ← Slaves
- Rum
- WEST INDIES
- AFRICA
- IVORY, GOLD, SLAVE COASTS
- SOUTH AMERICA

Legend:
- ▬ Major points of trade
- —— Major trade route
- ----- Intercoastal trade route

Atlantic trade routes

Sometimes they would then sail to England, and occasionally to Africa for slaves to sell in South Carolina or the Chesapeake. Most often, though, they returned to Boston, Newport, or New Haven to dispose of their cargoes. Thus the trading pattern was not a neat triangle but a shifting set of irregular polygons (see map). Its sole constant was uncertainty, due to the weather, rapid changes of supply and demand in the small island markets, and the delicate system of credit on which the entire structure depended.

The network of seventeenth-century trade, which had achieved mature form by the 1660s, was fueled not by cash (no one had much of that) but by credit in the form of bills of exchange. These were, in effect, promissory notes in which one merchant pledged to pay another a certain sum on demand. Bills of exchange passed from hand to hand, circulating much as currency does today. Ultimately, though, their value rested on trust and the credit standing of the first mer-

chant in the chain. That was one of the major reasons why the seventeenth-century mercantile community was composed chiefly of men related to each other by blood or marriage. A Bostonian who needed a reliable representative in Barbados would send his brother-in-law, son, or cousin to handle his interests; a London merchant might dispatch a relative to Boston for the same reason.

The Puritan New Englanders who ventured into commerce were soon differentiated from their rural counterparts by their ties to a wider trans-Atlantic world and by their preoccupation with material endeavors. Moreover, as time passed, increasing numbers of Puritans became involved in trade. Small investors who owned shares of voyages soon dominated the field numerically if not monetarily. The gulf between commercial and farming interests widened after 1660, when—with the end of the Interregnum and the restoration of the Stuarts to the English throne—

Sea Captains Carousing in Surinam, a scene that could have occurred in any tavern in any Caribbean port. Several recognizable Rhode Island merchants are included among the merrymakers. Painted by John Greenwood (1758), a Bostonian who lived in Surinam (Dutch Guiana), on the northern coast of South America.   The St. Louis Art Museum.

Anglican merchants began to migrate to New England. Such men had little stake in the survival of Massachusetts Bay and Connecticut in their original form, and some were openly antagonistic to Puritan traditions. As non-Congregationalists they were denied the vote, and they could not freely practice their religion. They resented their exclusion from the governing elite, believing that their wealth and social status entitled them to political power. Congregationalist clergymen returned their hostility in full measure, and the jeremiads lamenting New England's fall from pristine piety also criticized its new commercial orientation. The Reverend Increase Mather (Cotton Mather's father) reminded his congregation in 1676 that *"Religion and not the World* was that which our Fathers came hither for."

A clash between the commercial community and Puritan political leaders was inevitable. In 1684, encouraged by the merchants and their allies, England revoked the Massachusetts Bay Colony's charter. After several years of experimentation with a combined government for all of the New England provinces (see page 54), a new charter making Massachusetts a royal colony was issued in 1691. Henceforth, its governors were to be appointed by the king, and church membership could no longer be a condition for voting. An Anglican parish was even established in the heart of Boston. It seemed that the "city upon a hill," at least as John Winthrop had envisioned it, was no more.

The extreme stress New England was undergoing as a result of upheavals in its religious life, social organization, and economic system gave rise in 1692 to accusations of witchcraft in Salem Village (now Danvers), Massachusetts. Like their

| Witchcraft in Salem Village |

contemporaries elsewhere, seventeenth-century New Englanders believed in and greatly feared witches, who appeared human but whose power, they thought, came from the devil. If New Englanders could not find rational explanations for their troubles, they tended to suspect they were being bewitched. Although such accusations occurred elsewhere, the tensions resulting from New England's commercialization and secularization exploded most dramatically in a little rural community adjoining the bustling port of Salem.

Chapter 2: American society takes shape, 1650–1750

The crisis began when a group of adolescent girls accused a number of older women—mostly outsiders of one sort or another—of having bewitched them. Before the hysteria spent itself ten months later, nineteen people (including several men, most of them related to accused female witches) had been hanged, another pressed to death by heavy stones, and more than one hundred others jailed. Historians have puzzled ever since about the origins of the witchcraft episode. It has been variously attributed to tension between mothers and daughters (with the witches serving as surrogate mothers), persistent antagonisms among the town's leading families, and even hallucinations arising from a form of food poisoning.

But the most plausible explanation may lie in the uncertainty of life in late seventeenth-century New England. Salem Village, a farming town on the edge of a commercial center, was torn between old and new styles of life. Some families were abandoning agriculture for trade, while others were struggling to maintain traditional ways. The villagers who exploited the new economic opportunities were improving their status relative to their neighbors. Most people were uncertain about their destiny, but none more so than adolescent girls. As children their fate lay in the hands of their parents, yet their ultimate destiny would depend on their husbands. But would their husbands be farmers or artisans or merchants? What would their future lives be like? No one knew. By lashing out and in effect seizing command of the entire town, the girls gave their lives a certainty previously lacking. At the same time, they afforded their fellow townspeople an opportunity to vent their frustrations at the unsettling changes in their lives. The accused witches were scapegoats for the shattered dream of an isolated Bible Commonwealth.

The founding of the middle colonies

New Netherland, founded in 1624, remained small in comparison to its English neighbors to the north and south. A trading outpost of the Dutch West India Company, New Netherland was neglected because the company's economic interests lay chiefly in

Founding of New Netherland

Africa and Brazil. And because the Dutch were not afflicted by the economic and religious pressures that caused English people to migrate to the New World, immigration remained sparse. Even a 1629 company policy promising a large land grant, or patroonship, to anyone who would bring fifty settlers to the province failed to attract takers. (Only one such tract—Rensselaerswyck, near today's Albany—was ever established.) In the 1660s, New Netherland still had only about 5,000 white and black inhabitants. Virginia's population had by then reached 40,000, and New England's 50,000.

New Netherland's chief export was furs, which the settlers obtained by trading with the Indians at Fort Orange (Albany) on the upper Hudson River. The Dutch presence at Fort Orange exerted a decisive influence on the balance of power among tribes in the area. Lured by European trade goods, the Mohawks, whose territory lay to the west, attacked the Mahicans, who lived in the vicinity of the fort, driving them east of the Hudson. By 1629 the Mohawks were the chief suppliers of furs to Dutch traders.

The powerful Mohawk tribe was the easternmost component of the Iroquois Confederacy, which also included the Seneca, Cayuga, Onondaga, and Oneida

Iroquois Confederacy

tribes. Under the terms of a defensive alliance forged in the sixteenth century, the key decisions of war and peace for the entire confederacy were made by a council composed of tribal representatives, although each tribe retained some autonomy. The Five Nations vigorously protected their territory against encroachments by whites and other Indians alike, and sought to destroy or subjugate potential rivals. Thus in the 1640s the Iroquois went to war against the Hurons, their major competitor for control of the European trade. Using guns supplied by their Dutch allies, the Iroquois practically exterminated the Huron tribe, forcing its tiny remnant to migrate south and west beyond the confederacy's reach. After the defeat of the Hurons, the Iroquois reigned supreme from the Great Lakes to the Hudson.

Because the Dutch traders and the Iroquois needed each other, their relationship was—if sometimes uneasy—generally cordial. But this was a matter of circumstance rather than principle. When Dutch colonists wanted land, not pelts, like the English they paid

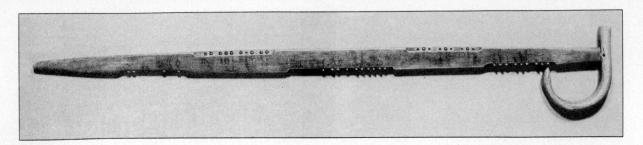

This notched staff recorded attendance at the Great Council of the Iroquois. Each row of notches corresponded to a particular tribe. The number of tribal representatives was indicated by the holes, and the pegs recorded which of them actually attended the meetings. *Cranbrook Institute of Science.*

little attention to Indian concepts of land ownership. The farmers of New Amsterdam, at the mouth of the Hudson, clashed repeatedly with neighboring tribes as they sought to expand their territory. (Among the dead in the bloody and costly warfare between 1641 and 1646 were Anne Hutchinson and her family, who had moved to New Netherland after seven years in Rhode Island.) In 1655, the Indians attacked New Amsterdam itself as a last gesture of defiance, but could not dislodge the Dutch.

The English were more successful in achieving that goal. As early as the 1640s Puritan New Englanders had begun to settle on Long Island, and New Netherland thus contained an appreciable English minority. Then in March 1664, in total disregard of Dutch claims to the area, Charles II gave the entire region between the Connecticut and Delaware rivers, including the Hudson valley, to his brother James, Duke of York. James immediately organized an invasion fleet. In late August the vessels anchored off the coast of New Netherland and demanded the colony's surrender. The Dutch complied without firing a

English conquest of New Netherland

shot. Although the Netherlands regained control of the colony in 1672, it permanently ceded the province two years later.

Thus James (and—after he became king in 1685—the English nation) acquired a tiny but heterogeneous possession. Together, the Dutch and the English accounted for the majority of the population. But New York, as it was now called, also included sizable numbers of Germans, French-speaking Walloons, Scandinavians (New Netherland had swallowed up Swedish settlements on the Delaware River in 1655), and Africans, as well as a smattering of other European peoples. Because the Dutch West India Company actively imported slaves into the colony after its efforts to attract white settlers had failed, almost one-fifth of New York City's approximately 1,500 inhabitants were black. Slaves thus comprised a higher proportion of New York's urban population than of the Chesapeake's in the early 1670s. One observer commented—probably exaggerating only slightly—that eighteen different languages could be heard in the colony.

Recognizing the diversity of the population, the Duke of York's representatives moved slowly and cautiously in their efforts to establish English authority. The Duke's Laws, a legal code proclaimed in March 1665, at first applied only to the Puritan settlements on Long Island; they were later extended to the rest of the colony. Dutch forms of local government were maintained and Dutch land titles confirmed. Religious toleration was guaranteed through a sort of multiple establishment: each town was permitted to decide which church to support with its tax revenues. Furthermore, the Dutch were allowed to maintain their customary legal practices. Until the 1690s, for example, many Dutch couples wrote joint wills, which were enforced in New York courts even though under English law married women could not draft wills. Much to the chagrin of English residents of the colony, the Duke's Laws made no provision for a representative assembly. Not until 1683 did the

Chapter 2: American society takes shape, 1650–1750

duke agree to the colonists' requests for an elected legislature. Before then, New York was ruled by an autocratic governor, as it had been under the Dutch.

The English takeover thus had little immediate effect on the colony. Its population grew slowly, barely reaching 18,000 by the time of the first English census in 1698. Until the second decade of the eighteenth century, New York City remained a commercial backwater within the orbit of Boston. The English renamed Fort Orange "Albany," but did not alter Dutch-Indian trade policies. Pelts obtained from the Mohawks continued to be the province's major export.

One of the chief reasons why the English conquest brought so little change to New York was that the Duke of York quickly regranted the land between the Hudson and Delaware rivers–New Jersey–to his friends Sir George Carteret and John Lord Berkeley.

| Founding of New Jersey |

That left his own colony confined between Connecticut to the east and New Jersey to the west, depriving it of much fertile land and hindering its economic growth. He also failed to promote immigration. Meanwhile the New Jersey proprietors acted rapidly to attract settlers, promising generous land grants, freedom of religion, and–without authorization from the crown–a representative assembly. In response, large numbers of Puritan New Englanders migrated southward to New Jersey, along with some Dutch New Yorkers and a contingent of families from Barbados.

Within twenty years, Berkeley and Carteret sold their interests in New Jersey to separate groups of investors. Because of the resulting large number of individual proprietary shares, and because the governor of New York had granted lands in New Jersey before learning that the duke had given it away, land titles in northern New Jersey were clouded for many years to come. Nevertheless, New Jersey grew quickly; at the time of its first census in 1726, it had 32,500 inhabitants, only 8,000 fewer than New York.

The purchasers of all of Carteret's share (West Jersey) and portions of Berkeley's East Jersey were Quakers seeking a refuge from persecution in England. The Quakers, formally known as the Society of Friends, denied the need for an intermediary between the individual and God. Anyone, they believed, could receive

In Quaker meetinghouses men and women sat separately, with their heads covered unless they were speaking. Note that among the meeting's leaders, seated on the raised platform, are two women.   Museum of Fine Arts, Boston, M. and M. Karolik Collection.

the "inner light" and be saved, and all were equal in God's sight. They had no formally trained clergy; any Quaker, male or female, who felt the call could become a "public Friend" and travel from meeting to meeting to discuss God's word. Moreover, any member of the Society could speak in meetings if he or she desired. In short, the Quakers were true religious radicals, Antinomians in the mold of Anne Hutchinson. (Indeed, Mary Dyer, who followed Hutchinson into exile, became a Quaker, returned to Boston as a missionary, and was hanged for her beliefs.)

The Quakers obtained a colony of their own in 1681, when Charles II granted the region between Maryland and New York to William Penn, one of the sect's most prominent members. The pious yet fun-loving Penn was then thirty-seven years old. Penn's

| Pennsylvania, a Quaker haven |

father, Admiral William Penn, had originally served Oliver Cromwell, but later joined forces with Charles II and even loaned the monarch a substantial sum of money. The younger Penn became a Quaker in the mid-1660s, much to his father's dismay. But despite Penn's radical political and religious beliefs, he and Charles II were close personal friends. Were it not for their friendship, the despised Quakers would never have won a charter for an American settlement. As it was, the publicly

Penn's Treaty with the Indians, by Benjamin West (1771), one of the first great American-born artists. A Pennsylvanian, West had been raised on stories of Penn's benevolent Indian policies. His painting of Penn's negotiations with the Delawares captured the spirit of the colony's founder.   Joseph and Sarah Harrison Collection, Pennsylvania Academy of the Fine Arts.

stated reason for the grant—repayment of the loan from Penn's father—was just that, a public rationalization for a private act.

William Penn held the colony as a personal proprietorship, and the vast property holdings earned profits for his descendants until the American Revolution. Even so, Penn, like the Roman Catholic Calverts of Maryland before him, saw the province not merely as a source of revenue but also as a haven for his persecuted co-religionists. Penn offered land to all comers on liberal terms, promised toleration for all religions (though only Christians were given the right to vote), guaranteed such English liberties as the right to bail and trial by jury, and pledged to establish a representative assembly. He also publicized the ready availability of land in Pennsylvania through promotional tracts published in German, French, and Dutch.

Penn's activities and the natural attraction of his lands for Quakers gave rise to a migration whose mag-

nitude was equalled only by the Puritan exodus to New England in the 1630s. By mid-1683, over 3,000 people—among them Welsh, Irish, Dutch, and Germans—had already moved to Pennsylvania, and within five years the population had reached 12,000. (By contrast, it took Virginia more than thirty years to achieve a comparable population.) Philadelphia, carefully planned to be the major city in the province, drew merchants and artisans from throughout the English-speaking world. From mainland and West Indian colonies alike came Quakers seeking religious freedom; they brought with them years of experience on American soil and well-established trading connections. Pennsylvania's lands were both plentiful and fertile, and the colony soon began exporting flour and other foodstuffs to the West Indies. Practically overnight Philadelphia acquired more than 2,000 citizens and began to challenge Boston's commercial preeminence.

A pacifist with egalitarian principles, Penn was determined to treat the Indians of Pennsylvania fairly. He carefully purchased tracts of land from the Delawares (or Lenni Lenape), the dominant tribe in the region, before selling them to settlers. Penn also established strict regulations for the Indian trade and forbade the sale of alcohol to tribesmen. In 1682 he visited a number of Lenni Lenape villages, after taking pains to learn the language. "I must say," Penn commented, "that I know not a language spoken in Europe that hath words of more sweetness in Accent and Emphasis, than theirs."

News of the Quakers' exemplary Indian policies spread to other tribes, some of whom decided to move to Pennsylvania. Several tribes from western Maryland, Virginia, and North Carolina came northward near the end of the seventeenth century to escape repeated clashes with white settlers. The most important of these were the Tuscaroras, whose experiences will be described later in this chapter. Likewise, the Shawnees and Miamis chose to move eastward from the Ohio valley. By a supreme irony, however, the same toleration that attracted Indians to Penn's domains also brought non-Quaker Europeans who showed little respect for Indian claims to the soil. In effect, Penn's policy was so successful that it caused its own downfall. The Scotch-Irish, Palatine Germans, and Swiss emigrants who settled in Pennsylvania in the first half of the eighteenth century clashed repeatedly over land with tribes that had also recently migrated to the colony.

Relations between whites and Indians

As the area of English settlement expanded after 1650, white colonists came into contact with increasing numbers of Indian tribes. By no means all of these contacts were peaceful; as will be seen, the years from 1670 to 1730 witnessed some of the fiercest Indian-white conflicts of the entire colonial period. But warfare was not the only way whites and Indians interacted.

Two circumstances helped to bring the races together. First, there was no clearly defined frontier: white settlements and Indian villages were often lo-cated near each other, and in many cases tribal lands were surrounded, rather than overrun, by whites. As a result, Indians were a common sight in many English towns, and white merchants frequently visited Indian villages. Second, the Indian trade contributed significantly to the colonial economies, especially in the earliest years of each settlement. Some time usually elapsed before English settlers were themselves able to produce surplus goods for sale elsewhere. In the meantime, they relied on trade with nearby tribes for saleable items to send to Europe in exchange for manufactured goods.

South Carolina is a case in point. The Barbadians who founded the colony were fortunate that the Carolina coast was inhabited by weak tribes who tended to welcome, rather than oppose, the newcomers. The whites quickly realized that they could reap substantial profits from trade with the coastal Indians and the stronger tribes of the interior (Cherokees, Creeks, and Choctaws). At first, the chief commodity obtained in trade was deerskins, which were almost as valuable as beaver pelts in European markets. During the first decade of the eighteenth century, South Carolina exported an average of 54,000 skins annually, and deerskin exports later reached a peak of 160,000.

A traffic in Indian slaves also enriched the pockets of white Carolina traders. The many local tribes were frequently at war, a fact that white Carolinians ex-

Indian slave trade

ploited by urging victorious tribes to sell their captives into slavery and even by fomenting wars. Initially the whites kept many such enslaved Indians within the colony; in 1708, for example, 14 percent of South Carolina's population was Indian slaves. But the Indians' ability to escape, coupled with fears of a general Indian uprising, soon caused the whites to export most enslaved Indians to the West Indies and New England. There are no reliable statistics on the extent of the trade in Indian slaves. Certainly, though, thousands of southern Indians and at least hundreds of northern ones (captured in such conflicts as the Pequot War) were sold into slavery, mostly far from their ancestral homes.

By contrast, whites captured by Indians were often adopted into the tribes as full members of Indian families. A number of such people (especially women captured when young) refused to return to white society when offered the chance to do so. One such captive was Mary Jemison, taken by the Senecas when she was only twelve. She married, bore children, and became a respected matron among the Iroquois. In her memoirs, written late in life, Jemison explained that she had stayed with the Indians not only because of her ties to her husband and children, but also because she preferred the work life of an Iroquois. Seneca women's work was "probably not harder than that of white women," she wrote, and their cares were "certainly . . . not half as numerous, nor as great." Women labored in the fields together, keeping their children with them, and, as Jemison remarked, "[we] had no master to oversee or drive us, so that we could work as leisurely as we pleased." Though the lives led by white captives of the Indians should not be romanticized, it is clear that some of them found a "savage" existence preferable to a "civilized" one. (To the colonists' dismay, few Indians were similarly attracted to white society.) The mere existence of such captives indicated, of course, that relations between Indians and whites were not always cordial. And after 1670, a new cycle of hostilities began as English colonists gradually moved beyond the territory of the coastal tribes they had already defeated.

The Spanish and the French also encountered serious difficulties in their efforts to expand their control into the American interior. The experience of the French resembled that of the Dutch in New Netherland. The French outposts along the St. Lawrence River valley (notably Montreal and Quebec) were primarily fur-trading centers rather than permanent agricultural settlements. Few French men and fewer women emigrated to the colonies; many of the fur traders (called *coureurs de bois*—literally, "woods runners") took Indian wives and lived among the tribes.

French-Indian relations

After the Iroquois victory over the Hurons, France's chief trading partner, in the 1640s, coureurs de bois ranged westward in search of new sources of pelts. Frenchmen like Louis Jolliet, Father Jacques Marquette, and the Chevalier de la Salle explored the Great Lakes and the Mississippi valley in the 1670s and 1680s, but not until the eighteenth century did France try to establish some control over that region. France then planned to construct a series of forts along the western rivers in order to surround the English settlements, a scheme vigorously resisted by the Natchez

tribe of the lower Mississippi. Only when the French enlisted the aid of the Choctaws in 1730 did they defeat the Natchez in a bloody conflict and finally implement their strategy.

The Spaniards also met with resistance from the local tribes as they spread northward from Mexico into what is now Texas, Arizona, and New Mexico, establishing a capital at Santa Fe. The Pueblo Indians, forced to pay heavy taxes and cultivate the land for their conquerors, grew restless under the heavy-handed rule of the autocratic Spanish governor. In August 1680, led by Popé, a respected medicine man, they rebelled and drove the Spaniards south to El Paso. For a time New Mexico remained solely in Indian hands, but after Popé's death in 1692 the Spaniards returned to re-establish their authority.

Just five years before Popé's uprising forced Europeans to leave New Mexico (if only temporarily), Metacomet—known to the English as King Philip—had set out to achieve a similar goal in New England. The son of Massasoit, who had signed the treaty with the Pilgrims in 1621, Metacomet was chief of the Wampanoags, whose lands on Narragansett Bay were now entirely surrounded by white settlements. Metacomet was concerned not only about white encroachments on his lands but also about the impact of European culture on his people. When a Plymouth

King Philip's War

colony court presumed to apply English law to three Wampanoags accused of killing another Wampanoag (they were hanged), Metacomet and his warriors took the act as a grievous insult. In late June 1675, they began to attack nearby white communities.

Soon two other local tribes, the Nipmucs and the Narragansetts, joined Metacomet's forces. In the fall, the three tribes jointly attacked settlements in the northern Connecticut River valley; in the winter and spring of 1676, they devastated such well-established villages as Sudbury and Andover and even attacked Plymouth and Providence. Altogether, the alliance totally destroyed twelve of the ninety Puritan towns and attacked forty others. A tenth of the able-bodied adult males in Massachusetts were captured or killed; proportional to population, it was the most costly war in American history. New England's very survival seemed to be at stake.

But the tide turned in the summer of 1676. The Indian coalition ran short of food and ammunition, and

Chapter 2: American society takes shape, 1650–1750

Captives of the Tuscaroras at a tribal dance in 1711. After their ransom, Count Christopher von Graffenried, founder of the Swiss-German settlement in North Carolina, sketched this picture showing himself, his surveyor, and his black servant being tortured.   Burgerbibliothek, Bern.

whites began to use Christianized tribesmen as guides and scouts. After Metacomet was killed in an ambush in August, the alliance crumbled. Many surviving Wampanoags, Nipmucs, and Narragansetts, including Metacomet's wife and son, were captured and sold into slavery in the West Indies. The power of New England's coastal tribes was broken.

It was more than coincidence that Virginia, the other original English mainland colony, was wracked by conflict with Indians at precisely the same time. In both areas the whites' earlier accommodation with the tribes—reached after the defeat of the Pequots in the north and the Powhatan Confederacy in the south—no longer satisfied both parties. In Virginia, though, it was the whites, rather than the Indians, who felt aggrieved.

By the early 1670s, whites were hungrily eyeing the rich lands north of the York River that had been reserved for the Indians under earlier treaties. Using as a pretext the July 1675 killing of a white servant by some Doeg Indians, they attacked not only the Doegs but also the Susquehannocks, a more important tribe. In retaliation, the Susquehannocks began to raid frontier plantations in the winter of 1676. The land-hungry whites rallied behind the leadership of Nathaniel Bacon, a planter who had arrived in the colony

only two years before. Bacon and his followers wanted, in his words, "to ruine and extirpate all Indians in generall." Governor William Berkeley, however, hoped to avoid setting off a major war like that raging in New England.

Berkeley and Bacon soon clashed. After Bacon forced the House of Burgesses to authorize him to attack the Indians, Berkeley declared Bacon and his men to be in rebellion. As the chaotic summer of 1676

| Bacon's Rebellion |

wore on, Bacon alternately pursued Indians and battled with the governor's supporters. In September he marched on Jamestown itself and burned the capital to the ground. But after Bacon died of dysentery the following month, the rebellion collapsed. A new Indian treaty signed in 1677 opened much of the disputed territory to whites, and thereafter only the Iroquois Confederacy stood in the path of English expansion north of the Carolinas.

In the Carolinas, on the other hand, whites were just beginning to gain a foothold along the coast. In 1709, a group of Swiss and German settlers expropriated without payment lands belonging to the Tuscarora tribe, an Iroquoian people who had migrated southward many years earlier. In 1711, the Tuscaroras and their allies struck back, initially killing more than

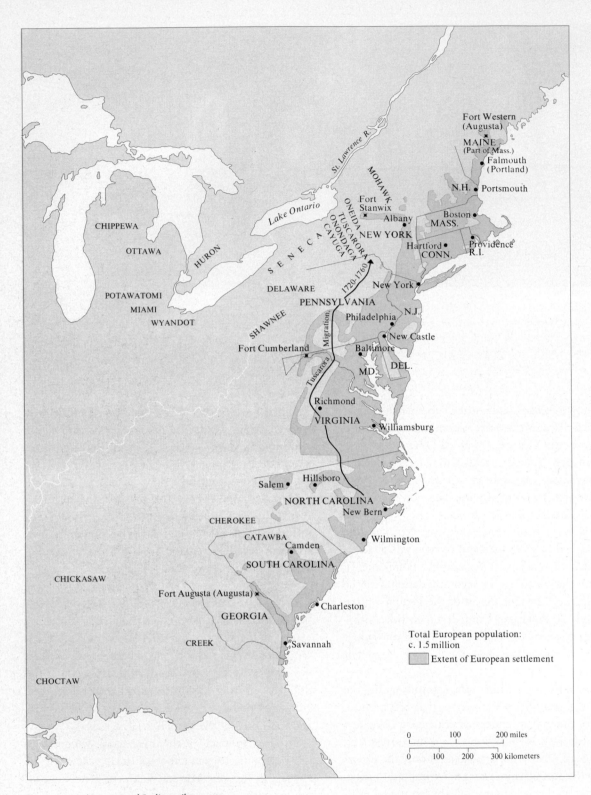

European settlements and Indian tribes, 1750

Chapter 2: American society takes shape, 1650–1750

one hundred whites, then conducting further raids

| Tuscarora and Yamasee wars | along the frontier. Since thinly populated North Carolina was incapable of raising a force large enough to oppose the Indians, South Carolina came to its aid in 1712 and again in 1713 with armies composed largely of tribesmen. The Tuscaroras, badly defeated in the second campaign, gradually began drifting northward to New York, where they became the sixth nation in the Iroquois Confederacy (see map).

Two years later the Yamasees, who had helped the South Carolina whites subdue the Tuscaroras, themselves rose against the English colonists. Their chief grievance was exploitation at the hands of Carolina traders, who regularly engaged in corrupt and deceptive practices. One contemporary observer reported that the traders "go to any of [the Yamasees'] plantations take what they pleas'd without Leave . . . and if the Indians grumbled or Seem Discontented threaten to beat them and very often did beat them Cruelly." He noted that the traders bragged openly about raping Yamasee women, and that he had himself witnessed such an incident. Furthermore, the traders overcharged the Yamasees, and then seized women and children to sell as slaves in payment of the Indians' "debts."

With the aid of the Creeks, the Yamasees began coordinated attacks on outlying white settlements on April 15 (Good Friday), 1715. As the raids continued through the summer, white refugees streamed into Charleston by the hundreds. At times the Creek-Yamasee offensive came close to driving the whites from the mainland altogether. (At Port Royal, for example, three hundred people were saved only because they crowded aboard a ship in the harbor while the Yamasees set fire to the town.) But the key to victory lay in the hands of the Cherokees. Wooed by both sides, they finally decided to align themselves with the whites against their ancient enemies, the Creeks. Their cause lost, the Yamasees moved south into Florida to seek the protection of the Spanish, and the Creeks retreated to their villages in the western highlands.

By the end of the first quarter of the eighteenth century, therefore, the colonists had effectively destroyed the power of all the Indian tribes east of the Appalachian mountains. The entire eastern seaboard, extending inland for over a hundred miles, was safe for settlement. The one dangerous gap—between the southern border of South Carolina and Spanish Florida—was plugged in 1732 with the chartering of Georgia, the last of the colonies that would become part of the United States. Intended as a haven for debtors by its founder James Oglethorpe, Georgia was specifically designed as a garrison province. Since all its landholders were expected to serve as militiamen to defend English settlements against the Spanish, the charter prohibited women from inheriting or purchasing land in the colony. That clause was soon altered, but it, and a similarly short-lived injunction against the introduction of slavery, revealed the founders' intention that Georgia should be peopled by sturdy yeoman farmers who could take up their weapons at a moment's notice.

Colonial political development and imperial reorganization

From the mid-1630s to the restoration of the Stuarts in 1660, England was too concerned with its own internal disputes to pay much attention to its New World possessions. The American provinces were thus left to develop political structures and practices largely on their own. The New England Puritans worked out their own governmental forms without outside interference, and in the Chesapeake neither the king (Virginia) nor the proprietor (Maryland) exercised heavy-handed executive authority.

In the absence of direct intervention from England, the colonists gradually evolved governments composed of a governor and a two-house legislature. In

| Colonial political structures | New England, the governors were elected by the people or the legislature; in the Chesapeake, they were appointed by the king or the proprietor. A council, elected in some colonies and appointed in others, advised the governor on matters of policy and sometimes served as the province's highest court. The council also had a legislative function: initially its members met jointly with representatives elected by their districts to debate and vote on laws affecting the colony. But as time passed, the fundamental differences between the two legislative groups'

purposes and constituencies led them to separate into two distinct houses. In Virginia, that important event occurred in 1663; in Massachusetts Bay it had happened earlier, in 1644. Thus developed the two-house legislature still used in almost all American states.

While provincial governments were taking shape, so too were local political institutions. In New England, elected selectmen governed the towns at first, but by the end of the century the town meeting, held at least annually and attended by most adult white townsmen, handled most matters of local concern. In the Chesapeake the same function was performed by the judges of the county court and by the parish vestry, a group of laymen charged with overseeing church affairs, whose power also encompassed secular concerns.

The English colonies established later in the century adopted similar political structures. Charles II, who authorized the new settlements, included in each charter (except that of New York) a provision requiring the inhabitants' consent to governmental measures. None of the charters specified the form such consent should take or defined the voting population; such questions were left in the hands of the proprietors. In the Carolinas, Pennsylvania, and even New Jersey (where the New York charter was at first the controlling document), representative assemblies were established as the means of obtaining consent. Pennsylvania's legislature had only one house, but the other colonies followed the two-house pattern. As already noted, an assembly was formed in New York in 1683 at the urging of the people.

By late in the seventeenth century, therefore, the American colonists were accustomed to exercising a considerable degree of local political autonomy. The tradition of consent was especially firmly established in New England. Massachusetts, Connecticut, and Rhode Island were, in effect, independent entities, subject neither to the direct authority of the king nor to a proprietor. In 1662 and 1663 respectively, Charles II confirmed the status of Connecticut and Rhode Island by granting them charters legitimizing the political systems evolved since their founding. In the colonies to the south, political structures were somewhat less stable and assemblies less powerful because the largely immigrant population prevented the development of coherent colonial interests and consistent leadership. The desire for local control was basically

identical in north and south, but greater continuity of officeholding in New England made for more political coherence and less instability throughout most of the seventeenth century. For example, at the end of the century all the major officeholders in Windsor, Connecticut, were descendants of leading early settlers; in Maryland in the same period, fewer than one-quarter of the officeholders had even been born in the province. Terms of service differed as well. Once elected, New Englanders usually continued to serve in some capacity for most of their lives. In Maryland, though, more than three-quarters of assembly members before 1715 served fewer than three terms in office.

The Stuart restoration ended England's neglect of its American colonies, and clashes between the mother country and its possessions became practically inevitable. Charles II (who reigned from 1660 to 1685) and his brother James II (1685 to 1688) both concerned themselves with colonial administration more directly than had any of their predecessors, including Oliver Cromwell. The trend continued even after the Catholic James II was ousted by Parliament in the bloodless rebellion known as the Glorious Revolution. His Protestant successors, the Dutch Prince William of Orange and his wife Mary (a Stuart), oversaw a major reorganization of colonial administration at the end of the century.

The chief reason for the unprecedented interest in America was economic. By 1660, it had become evident that the American colonies could make important contributions to England's economic well-being. Tobacco from the Chesapeake and sugar from the West Indies had obvious value, but other colonial products also had profitable potential. The new policies thus had two related goals. First, the Stuart monarchs wanted to ensure that colonial commerce would benefit England rather than competing with the mother country or aiding other nations. Second, as a means of achieving that end, they (particularly James II) wanted to tighten England's administrative controls over the colonies. England's pursuit of those goals aroused considerable opposition from the Americans, who had long been accustomed to substantial independence of action.

English administrators in the late seventeenth century based their commercial policy on a series of assumptions about the operations of the world's economic system. Collectively, these assumptions are usually called *mercantilism,* though neither the term itself nor a unified mercantilist theory was formulated until a century later. The economic world was seen as a collection of national states, each competing for shares of a finite amount of wealth. What one nation gained was automatically another nation's loss. Each nation's goal was to become as economically self-sufficient as possible while maintaining a favorable balance of trade with other countries (that is, exporting more than it imported). Colonies had an important role to play in such a scheme. They could supply the mother country with valuable raw materials to be consumed at home or sent abroad, and they could serve as a market for the mother country's manufactured goods.

Parliament applied that mercantilist theory to the American colonies in a series of laws known as the Navigation Acts. The major acts—passed in 1660,

| Navigation Acts |

1663, and 1673—established three main principles. First, only English or colonial merchants and ships could engage in trade in the colonies. Second, certain valuable American products could be sold only in the mother country. At first these "enumerated" goods were wool, sugar, tobacco, indigo, ginger, and dyes; later acts added rice, naval stores (masts, spars, pitch, tar, and turpentine), copper, and furs to the list. Third, all foreign goods destined for sale in the colonies had to be shipped via England and pay English import duties. Some years later, a new series of laws declared a fourth principle: the colonies could not make or export items that competed with English products (such as wool clothing, hats, and iron).

The intention of the Navigation Acts was clear: American trade was to center on England. The mother country was to benefit from colonial imports and exports both. England had first claim on the most valuable colonial exports, and all foreign imports into the colonies had to pass through England first, enriching its customs revenues in the process. Furthermore, English and colonial shippers were given a monopoly of the American trade. (It is important to note that the American provinces, especially those in the north, produced many goods that were not enumerated—such as fish, flour, and barrel staves. These products could be traded directly to foreign purchasers as long as they were carried in English or American ships.)

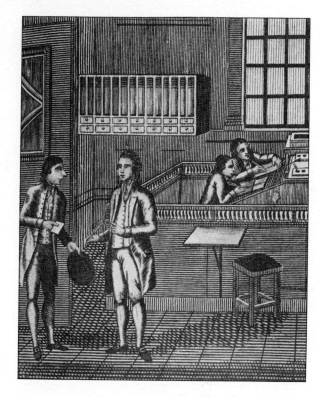

Northern merchants conducting business at their city offices, or counting houses. In the background, their clerks copy letters to overseas traders and maintain the elaborate credit accounts that underlay the merchants' transactions.   The Library Company of Philadelphia.

The English authorities soon learned that it was easier to write mercantilist legislation than to enforce it. The many harbors of the American coast provided ready havens for smugglers, and colonial officials often looked the other way when illegally imported goods were offered for sale. In ports such as Curaçao in the Dutch West Indies, American merchants could easily dispose of enumerated goods and purchase foreign items on which duty had not been paid. Consequently, Parliament in 1696 enacted another Navigation Act designed to strengthen enforcement of the first three. This law established in America a number of vice-admiralty courts, which operated without juries. In England such courts dealt only with cases involving piracy, vessels taken as wartime prizes, and the like. But since American juries had already demonstrated a tendency to favor local smugglers over customs officers (a colonial customs service had been started in 1671), Parliament decided to remove Navigation Act cases from the regular colonial courts.

England took another major step in colonial administration in 1696 by creating the Board of Trade and Plantations to replace the loosely structured standing committee of the Privy Council that had handled colonial affairs since 1675. The fifteen-member Board of Trade thereafter served as the chief organ of government concerned with the American colonies. It gathered information, reviewed Crown appointments in America, scrutinized legislation passed by colonial assemblies, supervised trade policies, and advised successive ministries on colonial issues. Still, the Board of Trade did not have any direct powers of enforcement. Furthermore, it shared jurisdiction over American affairs not only with the customs service and the navy but also with the secretary of state for the southern department (the member of the ministry responsible for the colonies). In short, although the Stuart monarchs' reforms considerably improved the quality of colonial administration, supervision of the American provinces remained decentralized and haphazard.

As part of the same campaign to bring more order into the administration of the colonies, successive kings began to chip away at the privileges granted in colonial charters and to reclaim proprietorships for the Crown. New Hampshire (1679), its parent colony Massachusetts (1691), New Jersey (1702), and the Carolinas (1729) all became royal colonies. The charters of Rhode Island, Connecticut, Maryland, and Pennsylvania were temporarily suspended as well, but were ultimately restored to their original status.

The most drastic reordering of colonial administration was attempted in 1686 through 1689, and its chief target was Puritan New England. Reports from America had convinced English officials that New England was a hotbed of smuggling. Moreover, the Puritans refused to allow freedom of religion and insisted on maintaining laws that often ran counter to English practice. New England thus seemed an appropriate place to exert English authority with greater vigor. The charters of all the colonies from New Jersey to Maine (part of Massachusetts) were revoked, and a Dominion of New England established in 1686.

Dominion of New England Sir Edmund Andros, the governor, was given immense power: all the assemblies were dissolved, and he needed only the consent of an appointed council to make laws and levy taxes. New Englanders endured Andros's autocratic rule for more than two years. Then, after hearing that William and Mary had assumed the throne in England, they overthrew Andros and resumed their customary form of government.

In other American colonies too, the Glorious Revolution proved to be a signal for revolt. In Maryland the Protestant Association overturned the government of the Catholic proprietor, and in New York Jacob Leisler, a militia officer of German origin, assumed control of the province. When these three uprisings are seen in conjunction with those of the previous decade—Bacon's Rebellion in Virginia (1676) and Culpeper's Rebellion in North Carolina (1677)—it is clear that the late seventeenth century was a time of turmoil for the American colonies.

What had caused the rash of rebellions? Certainly the Stuart monarchs' attempts to tighten England's control over the colonies were a major contributing factor. The new class of alien officials who arrived in America determined to implement the policies of king and Parliament owed nothing to the colonists. By distributing patronage in the form of offices and land grants, they tried to create "court parties" that would support their claims to expanded power. In the process they won the gratitude of those they favored and the hostility of those they did not. Many members of the developing colonial social and economic elites—whose wealth derived from staple-crop production in the south and commerce in the north—resented their exclusion from political power and opposed the new regimes.

The difficulties resulting from imperial reorganization were compounded by political instability in most of the colonies. Only in New England was a majority of the population native-born in the latter decades of the seventeenth century. Continuing immigration in the South and ethnic diversity in the recently settled middle colonies heightened the disorders that would have existed in any event. Not until the end of the first quarter of the eighteenth century did native-born Americans predominate in all the colonies. It was then that American-born elite families consolidated their hold on economic power and social status. And it is no coincidence that at the same time the colonial political systems outside New England assumed more mature form.

In eighteenth-century American politics, the representative assembly became the chief vehicle through

Important events

1642	English Civil War begins
1649	Charles I executed
1655	Dutch conquer Swedish settlements on Delaware River
1656	Iroquois-Huron Wars end with defeat of Hurons
1658	Oliver Cromwell dies
1660	Stuarts restored to throne; Charles II becomes king First Navigation Act passed
1662	Halfway Covenant drafted Connecticut granted charter
1663	Rhode Island granted charter
1664	English conquer New Netherland; New York founded New Jersey established
1669	Carolina chartered
1670	Charleston founded
1673	Jacques Marquette and Louis Jolliet explore Great Lakes and Mississippi Valley
1674	Netherlands permanently cede New York to England
1675–76	King Philip's (Metacomet's) War (New England)
1676	Bacon's Rebellion (Virginia)
1677	Culpeper's Rebellion (North Carolina)
1679	New Hampshire becomes royal colony
1670s	Imports of African slaves to southern colonies increase dramatically
1680	Pueblo revolt (New Mexico)
1681	Pennsylvania chartered
1682	Sieur de La Salle reaches mouth of Mississippi River
1684	Massachusetts Bay charter revoked
1685	James II becomes king
1686–89	Dominion of New England
1688–89	James II deposed in Glorious Revolution; William and Mary ascend throne
1689	Protestant Association Rebellion (Maryland) Leisler's Rebellion (New York)
1691	Massachusetts Bay and Plymouth colonies combined under one royal charter
1692	Witchcraft outbreak in Salem Village
1696	Board of Trade and Plantations established
1690s	Rice cultivation begins in South Carolina
1702	New Jersey becomes royal colony
1710	Blacks become a majority in South Carolina
1711–13	Tuscarora War (North Carolina)
1715	Yamasee War (South Carolina)
1720s	Native-born Americans become a majority in Chesapeake
1729	North and South Carolina become separate royal colonies
1732	Georgia chartered
1740s	Indigo cultivation begins in South Carolina Black population of Chesapeake begins to grow chiefly through natural increase

which politically talented Americans expressed their

Rise of the
representative
assembly

opinions on colonial policy. Denied access to top appointive posts (which were usually filled with the friends and relatives of English politicians), such men sought to increase their power by expanding the role of the assembly. Colonial assemblies began to claim privileges associated with the House of Commons, such as the right to initiate all tax legislation and to control the militia. The assemblies also developed effective ways of influencing governors, judges, customs officers, and other appointed officials (including threats to withhold their salaries). Colonial assemblies were often wracked by internal disputes among competing factions; though Virginia and South Carolina elite families usually presented a united front to royal officials, New Yorkers fought with each other so long and so bitterly that the provincial government was at times virtually paralyzed. Nevertheless, Americans agreed on one point: members of the assembly represented the people in a way that appointed English officials did not.

By the middle of the eighteenth century, the colonists had developed a standard way of thinking about their political system. They believed that their governments mimicked the balance between king, lords, and commons found in Great Britain—a combination that was thought to produce a stable polity. Although the analogy was not exact, the colonists equated their governors with the monarch, their councils with the aristocracy, and their assemblies with the House of Commons. All three were thought essential to good government, but the colonists did not regard them with the same degrees of approval. They saw the governors and appointed councils as aliens who posed a potential threat to colonial freedoms and customary ways of life. As representatives of England rather than America, the governors and councils were to be feared and guarded against rather than trusted. The colonists saw the assemblies, on the other hand, as the people's protectors. Elected in most colonies by men who met minimal property-holding requirements, the assemblies regarded themselves as representatives of the people. Their constituents shared the same view; in some colonies, notably Massachusetts, towns even began to instruct their representatives how to vote on some controversial issues.

That vision of politics, which emerged slowly over the first half of the eighteenth century, was to be of immense importance in the revolutionary crisis that developed in the years following 1763. The notions of government's proper role expounded then in innumerable pamphlets did not appear out of thin air, but rather rested on generations of political experience. The colonists had become accustomed to a political structure in which the executive was feared and the legislature trusted, in which authority was widely dispersed and decentralized, and in which the supreme power (England, in this case) had little direct effect on most people. What they were familiar with, in other words, was a *limited* government—though limited more by circumstances than by design. When Americans had to create governmental structures for themselves after 1775, they incorporated all those elements of their past experience into a formal political theory.

Suggestions for further reading

General

Charles M. Andrews, *The Colonial Period of American History,* vol. 4 (1938); George Louis Beer, *The Old Colonial System, 1660–1754,* 2 vols. (1912); Carl Bridenbaugh, *Cities in the Wilderness: The First Century of Urban Life in America, 1625–1742* (1938); Stuart Bruchey, *Roots of American Economic Growth, 1607–1861* (1965); Wesley Frank Craven, *The Colonies in Transition, 1660–1713* (1968); George M. Wrong, *The Rise and Fall of New France,* 2 vols. (1928).

Africa and the slave trade

Philip D. Curtin, *The Atlantic Slave Trade: A Census* (1969); Basil Davidson, *The Africans: An Entry to Cultural History* (1969); Basil Davidson, *Black Mother* (1969); David B. Davis, *The Problem of Slavery in Western Culture* (1966); Herbert S. Klein, "Slaves and Shipping in Eighteenth-Century Virginia," *Journal of Interdisciplinary History,* 5 (1974–1975), 383–412.

Blacks in Anglo-America

Richard S. Dunn, *Sugar and Slaves: The Rise of the Planter Class in the English West Indies, 1624–1713* (1972); Lorenzo

Johnson Greene, *The Negro in Colonial New England* (1942); Allan Kulikoff, "A 'Prolifick' People: Black Population Growth in the Chesapeake Colonies, 1700–1790," *Southern Studies,* 16 (1977), 391–428; Edgar J. McManus, *Black Bondage in the North* (1973); Russell Menard, "From Servants to Slaves: The Transformation of the Chesapeake Labor System," *Southern Studies,* 16 (1977), 355–390; Edmund S. Morgan, *American Slavery, American Freedom: The Ordeal of Colonial Virginia* (1975); Peter H. Wood, *Black Majority: Negroes in Colonial South Carolina from 1670 through the Stono Rebellion* (1974).

Indian-white relations

James Axtell, "The White Indians of Colonial America," *William and Mary Quarterly,* 3rd ser., 32 (1975), 55–88; Judith K. Brown, "Economic Organization and the Position of Women among the Iroquois," *Ethnohistory,* 17 (1970), 151–167; David H. Corkran, *The Creek Frontier, 1540–1783* (1967); Verner W. Crane, *The Southern Frontier, 1670–1732* (1929); George T. Hunt, *The Wars of the Iroquois: A Study in Intertribal Relations* (1940); Douglas Leach, *Flintlock and Tomahawk: New England in King Philip's War* (1958); Allen W. Trelease, *Indian Affairs in Colonial New York: The Seventeenth Century* (1960); Alden T. Vaughan and Daniel K. Richter, "Crossing the Cultural Divide: Indians and New Englanders, 1605–1763," *Proceedings of the American Antiquarian Society,* 90, 1 (1980), 23–99; C.A. Weslager, *The Delaware Indians: A History* (1972).

New England

Bernard Bailyn, *The New England Merchants in the Seventeenth Century* (1955); Paul Boyer and Stephen Nissenbaum, *Salem Possessed: The Social Origins of Witchcraft* (1974); Richard Bushman, *From Puritan to Yankee: Character and the Social Order in Connecticut, 1690–1765* (1967); John Demos, "Underlying Themes in the Witchcraft of Seventeenth-Century New England," *American Historical Review,* 75 (1970), 1311–1326; Mary Maples Dunn, "Saints and Sisters: Congregational and Quaker Women in the Early Colonial Period," *American Quarterly,* 30 (1978), 582–601; Kenneth A. Lockridge, "Land, Population, and the Evolution of New England Society, 1630–1790," *Past and Present,* 39 (1968), 62–80; Perry Miller, *The New England Mind: From Colony to Province* (1953); Robert G. Pope, *The Half-Way Covenant: Church Membership in Puritan New England* (1969); Richard Pares, *Yankees and Creoles: The Trade Between North America and the West Indies before the American Revolution* (1956); Laurel Thatcher Ulrich, "Virtuous Women Found: New England Ministerial Literature 1668–1735," *American Quarterly,* 28 (1976), 20–40.

New Netherland and the Restoration colonies

Edwin B. Bronner, *William Penn's "Holy Experiment": The Founding of Pennsylvania 1681–1701* (1962); Thomas J. Condon, *New York Beginnings: The Commercial Origins of New Netherland* (1968); Wesley Frank Craven, *New Jersey and the English Colonization of North America* (1964); Mary Maples Dunn, *William Penn: Politics and Conscience* (1967); Michael Kammen, *Colonial New York: A History* (1975); Lawrence Lee, *The Lower Cape Fear in Colonial Days* (1965); Robert C. Ritchie, *The Duke's Province: A Study of Politics and Society in Colonial New York, 1660–1691* (1977); M. Eugene Sirmans, *Colonial South Carolina: A Political History, 1663–1763* (1966).

Colonial politics

Bernard Bailyn, *The Origins of American Politics* (1968); Bernard Bailyn, "Politics and Social Structure in Virginia," in *Seventeenth-Century America: Essays in Colonial History,* ed. James M. Smith (1959), 90–115; Lois Green Carr and David W. Jordan, *Maryland's Revolution of Government 1689–1692* (1974); Jack P. Greene, *The Quest for Power: The Lower Houses of Assembly in the Southern Royal Colonies, 1689–1776* (1963); Kenneth A. Lockridge and Alan Kreider, "The Evolution of Massachusetts Town Government, 1640–1740," *William and Mary Quarterly,* 3rd ser., 23 (1966), 549–574; David S. Lovejoy, *The Glorious Revolution in America* (1972); Charles S. Sydnor, *"Gentlemen Freeholders": Political Practices in Washington's Virginia* (1952).

Imperial administration

Viola F. Barnes, *The Dominion of New England: A Study in British Colonial Policy* (1923); Thomas C. Barrow, *Trade and Empire: The British Customs Service in Colonial America 1660–1775* (1967); Lawrence A. Harper, *The English Navigation Laws: A Seventeenth-Century Experiment in Social Engineering* (1939); Michael Kammen, *Empire and Interest: The American Colonies and the Politics of Mercantilism* (1970); I.K. Steele, *Politics of Colonial Policy: The Board of Trade in Colonial Administration* (1968); Stephen Saunders Webb, *The Governors-General: The English Army and the Definition of the Empire, 1569–1681* (1979).

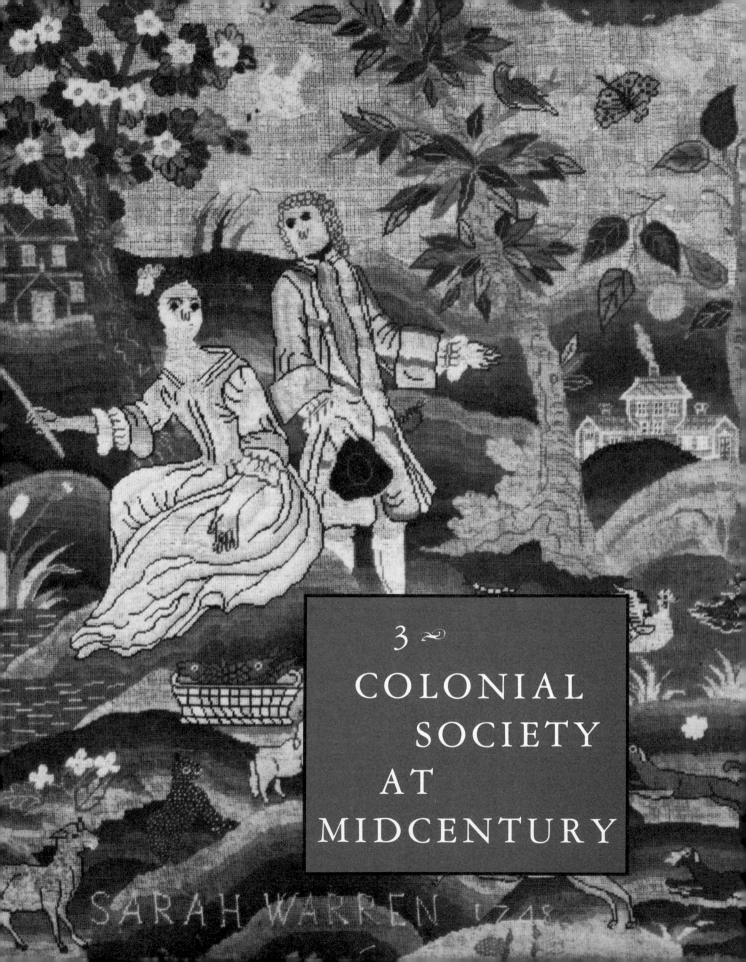

3 ~

COLONIAL
SOCIETY
AT
MIDCENTURY

SARAH WARREN 1748

Around the middle of the eighteenth century, the immigrant Alexander McAllister received a letter from a cousin in Scotland asking whether he too should consider moving to the American colonies. McAllister, who had settled in North Carolina along with many fellow Scotsmen, responded encouragingly. "As for the country it is a very good one a poor man that will incline to work may have the value of his labour for ther is nothing that he puts in the ground but what yealds beyount any Idea that a Strenger can conceive," he told his cousin. Indeed, he continued, "you would do well to advise all poor people whom you wish well to take curradge and com to this Country it will be of Benefite to ther riseing generation."

A few years later Martha McClouting, a Scotch-Irish woman living in Charleston, expressed the same attitude to her mother in Derry: "I am marred Now and fowlos the Stoar Ceping I have got three Cheldren two Sons and wan Dauther. . . . I have got Sex Negros wich keps me Easey From hard Lebar and I wish that meney moor of you had the good fortun to Cum to this Contry with me. . . . Many days have I worked hard in Ireland but many days her I Live at Ease—this Country very few works hard in it."

McAllister and McClouting were two among the hundreds of thousands of European immigrants who flooded into England's mainland colonies during the years from 1715 to 1775. Their attitude was representative. Migrants from overpopulated and distressed areas of Europe, especially Scotland, northern Ireland (Ulster), and Germany, found opportunities in America undreamed of in their homelands. That these opportunities were more restricted than they had been in the previous century meant little to men and women who had owned almost nothing in the Old World and could acquire property in the New. The arrival of these immigrants was one of the most important occurrences in eighteenth-century America.

The life they found in the colonies was less primitive and precarious than it had been during the first century of settlement. The entire coastal plain was free of any threat of Indian attack; representative politics allowed colonists a voice in their own government; and the economy was flourishing, despite occasional wild fluctuations. A majority of colonists, black and white, were now native-born, and the colonies were beginning to develop a distinctive identity of their own. Colleges had been founded, newspapers established, social clubs and literary societies formed, a regular postal service begun, roads built, laws codified, and histories of the colonies written. Life in America, in short, had started to fall into set, predictable, and distinctive patterns. The provinces could no longer be seen as extensions of England. Individually and collectively, they had become quite different.

Population growth

One of the most striking characteristics of the mainland colonies in the eighteenth century was their rapid population growth. Only about 250,000 people (excluding Indians) resided in the colonies in 1700; thirty years later that number had more than doubled, and by 1775 it had become 2.5 million. Although immigration accounted for a considerable share of the growth, most of it resulted from natural increase. By 1750 the sex ratio among both whites and blacks was approximately equal throughout the mainland colonies; thus almost all Americans could marry and have children. Most white women married in their early twenties, most black women in their late teens. Their husbands were usually a few years older. Most women bore between five and eight children, becoming pregnant every two or three years throughout their fertile years, and a large proportion of their children survived to maturity. In 1775 about half the American population, white and black, was under sixteen years of age. (In 1980, by contrast, only about one-third of the American population was under sixteen.)

Such a dramatic phenomenon did not escape the attention of contemporaries. As early as the 1720s, Americans began to point with pride to their fertility, citing population growth as evidence of the advantages of living in the colonies. In 1755 Benjamin Franklin published his *Observations Concerning the Increase of Mankind,* which attributed America's striking population growth to early marriages made possible by the availability of land. (Franklin was partly right, but he did not realize that the greater length of marriages and the high proportion of American women who married and bore children also contributed to the rate of increase.) Franklin estimated that the Ameri-

This portrait of an eighteenth-century family shows the typical colonial childbearing pattern in the large number of "stairstep" children, born at approximately two-year intervals.   Museum of Fine Arts, Boston, Julia Knight Knox Fund.

can population would double every twenty years, and he predicted that in another century "the greatest Number of Englishmen will be on this Side the Water. What an Accession of Power to the British Empire by Sea as well as Land!" he rhapsodized. "What Increase of Trade and Navigation!"

Interestingly enough, Franklin's purpose in writing his *Observations* was to argue that Britain should stop allowing Germans to emigrate to Pennsylvania. Since the English population in America was increasing so rapidly, he asked, "why should the Palatine Boors be suffered to swarm into our Settlements? . . . Why should Pennsylvania, founded by the English, become a Colony of *Aliens,* who will shortly be so numerous as to Germanize us instead of Anglifying them, and will never adopt our Language or Customs?" Franklin was exaggerating the potential effects of German immigration, but his fears were not wholly misplaced. By the late eighteenth century, emigrants from the

Rhineland—known as "Pennsylvania Dutch," a corruption of *Deutsch*—comprised one-third of the colony's residents.

Not all the approximately 100,000 Germans who emigrated to Pennsylvania, mainly between 1730 and 1755, stayed in that colony. Some who landed at Philadelphia moved west and then south along the eastern slope of the Appalachian mountains, eventually finding homes in western Maryland and Virginia. Others sailed first to Charleston or Savannah and settled in the interior of South Carolina or Georgia. The German immigrants belonged to a wide variety of Protestant sects—primarily Lutheran, German Reformed, and Moravian—and therefore added to the already substantial religious diversity of the middle colonies.

German immigration

Many Germans arrived in America as redemptioners. Under that variant form of indentured servitude,

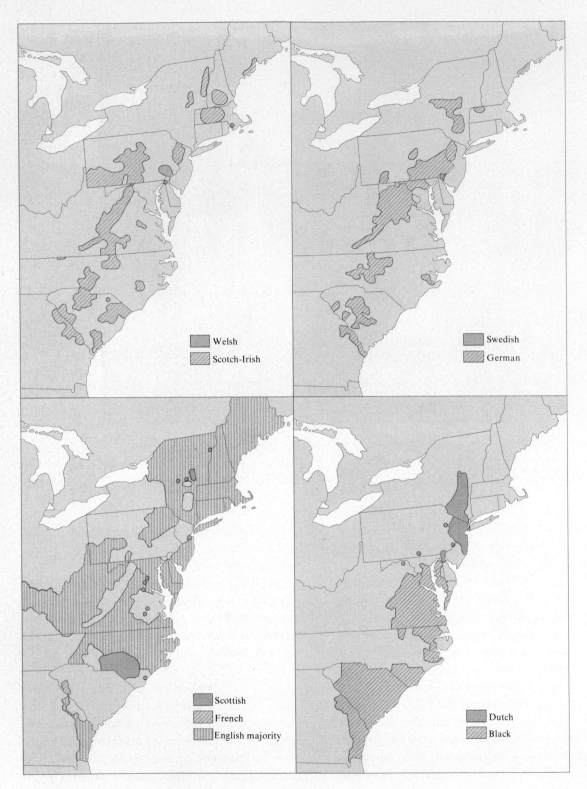

	Welsh
	Scotch-Irish

	Swedish
	German

	Scottish
	French
	English majority

	Dutch
	Black

Non-English white settlements 1775, black population, c. 1775.
Source: Reprinted by permission of Princeton University Press.

Chapter 3: Colonial society at midcentury

immigrants paid as much as possible of the cost of their passage before sailing from Europe. After they landed in the colonies, the rest of the fare had to be "redeemed." If poor immigrants had no friends or relatives in America willing to take on the burden of payment, they were indentured for a term of service proportional to the amount they still owed. That term could be as brief as a year or two, but was more likely to be four. In contrast to the unmarried English indentured servants who had migrated to the Chesapeake in the seventeenth century, German redemptioners often traveled in family groups. In America, the family was sometimes divided among different purchasers and separated for the term of their indentures.

The largest group of white non-English emigrants to America was the Scotch-Irish, chiefly descended from Presbyterian Scots who had settled in Protestant

Scotch-Irish and Scottish immigration

portions of Ireland during the seventeenth century. Perhaps as many as 250,000 Scotch-Irish people moved to the colonies. Fleeing economic distress and religious discrimination—Irish law favored Anglicans over Presbyterians and other dissenters—at home, they were lured as well by hopes of obtaining land in America. Like the Germans, the Scotch-Irish often landed in Philadelphia. They also moved west and south from that city, settling chiefly in the western portions of Pennsylvania, Maryland, Virginia, and the Carolinas. Frequently unable to afford any acreage, they simply squatted where they wished, building crude houses and carving fields out of the wilderness. Such squatters simply ignored the Indian tribes, land speculators, or colonial governments that nominally owned the land.

The more than 25,000 Scots who came directly to America from Scotland should not be confused with the Scotch-Irish. Many Scottish immigrants were Jacobites—supporters of Stuart claimants to the throne of England. After the death of William and Mary's successor Queen Anne in 1714, the British throne had passed to the German house of Hanover, in the person of King George I. In 1715 and again in 1745, Jacobite rebels attempted unsuccessfully to capture the crown for the Stuart pretender, and many were exiled to America as punishment for their treason. (The British also imposed the same punishment on some ordinary criminals.) Most of the Jacobites

A ceramic pie plate manufactured in southeastern Pennsylvania in 1786 shows the continuing use of German by Pennsylvania Dutch immigrants. Philadelphia Museum of Art.

settled in North Carolina. Ironically, they tended to become loyalists during the Revolutionary War because of their strong commitment to monarchy. Another wave of Scottish immigration began in the 1760s and flowed mainly into northern New York; most of these new arrivals settled as tenants on large tracts of land in the Mohawk River valley.

Due to these migration patterns and the concentration of slaveholding in the South, half the colonial population south of New England was of non-English origin by 1775 (see map). Yet, with the exception of certain religious sects like the Mennonites, Amish, and Dunkards (all of whom preserved their traditional lifestyles), most immigrants assimilated fairly readily into Anglo-American culture. In Germantown, Pennsylvania, for example, German continued to be spoken in churches and within families. But English soon became the language of public communication. Although the immigrant generation used both German and English, their children and grandchildren spoke English almost exclusively. Instruction in the town's first school was conducted in English (classes in German were later added). People baptized "Maria Holtz" and "Jacob Zimmermann" changed their names to "Mary Wood" and "James Carpenter." It was chiefly the continuing influx of new settlers from Germany and the retention of German for religious purposes that kept some of the old ways alive in Germantown.

Social stratification

The vast majority of eighteenth-century immigrants entered white society at the bottom of the social scale and on the geographic fringes of settlement. By the time they arrived, American society was dominated by wealthy, native-born elite families. Furthermore, the

| Distribution of wealth |

social and economic structure was more rigid than it had been before 1700. Unlike their seventeenth-century predecessors, the new non-English immigrants had little opportunity to improve their circumstances dramatically. The most they could realistically hope for was to accumulate a modest amount of property over a lifetime of hard work. Even that limited goal appears to have become more difficult to attain as the century progressed, but—considering the poverty they had left behind in Europe—it is unlikely that many regretted their decision to emigrate.

Increasing social stratification—a widening gap between rich and poor—was most noticeable in the cities, which contained less than 10 percent of the population but displayed greater extremes of wealth and poverty than did rural areas outside the plantation South. There were few large cities in mid-eighteenth-century America. The biggest—as it had been since 1630—was Boston, with about 17,000 residents. Next came Philadelphia (approximately 13,000), closely followed by New York (about 11,000). Charleston, South Carolina, the only city of appreciable size in the South, had approximately 7,000 inhabitants, about half of whom were black. Smaller but still important were Newport, New Haven, Salem, and Hartford in the North and Norfolk, Annapolis, and Savannah in the South. In such cities lived the wealthy merchants who dominated the Atlantic trade, and the impoverished sailors employed on their ships; well-paid skilled artisans who made furniture, silver, fancy clothing, and carriages for the rich, and common laborers who had trouble making ends meet; well-to-do appointed officials who supervised colonial governments, and

hundreds, if not thousands, of poor folk who owned little more than the clothes on their backs.

In late seventeenth- and early eighteenth-century America, there was little dire poverty and little ostentatious wealth. Surviving city tax records show that at the turn of the century the bottom half of the population possessed about one-tenth of the property, and the richest 10 percent owned perhaps 40 percent. By contrast to European cities of the same period, this division of wealth was relatively equitable. Sixty to seventy years later, conditions had changed significantly, although American society was still far less stratified than Europe's. The poor relief systems of all the northern cities—especially Boston—were overwhelmed with applicants for assistance. Meanwhile, families with large fortunes were building luxurious mansions and filling them with imported furniture. By 1774, the most prosperous tenth of Philadelphia's population possessed 55 percent of the wealth, while the poorest third owned less than 2 percent.

What had happened? In the cities, obviously, the rich had gotten significantly richer and the poor had gotten poorer. But who were the rich? And who were the poor? The first question is easier to answer than the second. The rich were those American families who had begun the century with sufficient capital to

| Merchants and professionals |

take advantage of changes in the colonial economy. The rapidly increasing population had added both consumers and producers to the economy. Exports of raw materials skyrocketed and so did purchases of imported goods; the colonies developed into a major market for British manufactures. Controlling much of this expanded commerce, and earning sizable profits from it, were the merchants of urban America. (British merchants, their chief competitors, dominated only the tobacco and sugar trades.) In contrast to the late seventeenth century, when most voyages were joint ventures by a large number of small investors, mid-eighteenth-century voyages were funded by fewer merchants with larger amounts of capital. That meant greater individual risk (making marine insurance a thriving field) but also potentially greater individual profits.

In addition to the merchants, the cities contained a growing well-to-do professional class composed of doctors, lawyers, and government officials. Many appointive colonial offices carried substantial salaries;

Work and Leisure
in the Mature Colonies, 1750–1775

Colonial women combined work with leisure by using their sewing skills,
essential for making the family's clothing, to create fancy needlework.
Often they devoted their few leisure hours to the art, stitching samplers
and pictures or embellishing clothing.

These needlework pictures, both
from the mid-eighteenth century,
show two of colonial women's
most time-consuming tasks, spinning and dairying. The spinner is
using a hand-held drop spindle
rather than a wheel, which was
easier to use but more expensive
and cumbersome. The picture of
the milker is probably of
Pennsylvania Dutch Origin.   The
Henry Francis du Pont Winterthur
Museum, Winterthur,
Delaware.

Mercy Otis Warren, who was to become a leading intellectual and author of the Revolutionary era, embroidered the top of this card table sometime before 1770. She and her husband James, like other genteel eighteenth-century Americans, probably spent many leisure hours playing cards. The Pilgrim Society, Plymouth, Massachusetts.

Weddings provided an opportunity for colonists to relax and socialize. The Massachusetts couple whose 1756 wedding is shown in the needlework picture at left was well-to-do, as is indicated by the carriage, the uniformed footmen, and the elaborate clothing of the guests. American Antiquarian Society, Worcester, Mass.

Those colonists who could afford instruments and music lessons could spend their leisure hours like this family, painted late in the century but typical of earlier Americans in their entertainment. The daughter probably learned to play the piano at a school for well-to-do young ladies like herself. The Corcoran Gallery of Art, Washington, D.C.

Africans did not leave their cultural heritage behind when they were forced into slavery. This unique painting, done in 1775 or after, shows slaves passing their few hours of leisure on a Sunday or holiday with a dance. Several identifiably African elements appear in the picture. The drum and banjo-like instrument are both of African origin, as are the scarves and cane used in the tribal dance. The blue-and-white bandannas worn by two of the women are similar to Yoruba cloth (from West Africa).   Abby Aldrich Rockefeller Folk Art Collection, Williamsburg, Virginia.

judges, members of governors' councils, customs officers, and the like were amply rewarded for their labors on behalf of the crown. Prominent families thus often sought political alliances with colonial governors or English administrators, for it was through such connections that coveted positions could be won. As the economy became more complex, the legal system also grew more elaborate. In the seventeenth century, America had had few formally trained lawyers. By the 1750s, lawyers who had studied in London were practicing in all the major cities. They were needed to deal with the intricacies of commerce, property transfers, and all the other legal transactions that undergirded economic development. Successful lawyers could earn sizable incomes, as could the doctors educated in England or Scotland who had begun to practice medicine in Boston, Philadelphia, and smaller colonial cities. (In medicine as in law, the second quarter of the eighteenth century witnessed the shift from amateur to professional practitioner, and men with formal training could command high fees.)

The urban poor are more difficult to identify. Recent immigrants must have been among the poor; whether indentured or not, they often hired themselves out as live-in servants so as at least to have food and lodging, however low their wages. The elderly and disabled—who would have found it hard to obtain work—were another component of the urban poor. Women, mostly widows, also accounted for a large proportion of the urban poor. In the eighteenth century, like today, women were paid less than men for comparable work. (Female servants, for example, earned about half the salary of male servants.) And, though opportunities for employment were better in the city than in the countryside, a woman's chances of finding well-paid work were considerably more limited than a man's. Sewing and nursing commanded far lower fees than did blacksmithing, shipbuilding, and other male occupations.

The effects of increasing poverty can be seen in city records. Philadelphia is a case in point. From the 1730s on, city taxpayers were assessed a three-penny annual fee to supply the needy with food and firewood (distributed to applicants by city officials). A private Hospital for the Sick Poor was founded in 1751 under the leadership of Benjamin Franklin. But in the 1760s, in the aftermath of the French and Indian War and the sub-

| Poor relief |

Mary and Elizabeth Royall, painted by the Boston artist John Singleton Copley in 1758. The thirteen- and eleven-year-old daughters of the wealthy Medford merchant Isaac Royall wear elaborate gowns that display the Royall family's elite status. The sumptuous setting mimics portraits of the English nobility. National Gallery of Art, Gift of Edgar William and Bernice Chrysler Garbisch.

sequent depression (see pages 88–90 and 92–93), such arrangements proved inadequate. The poor tax was raised to five pennies, then to six; a Bettering House—a combined almshouse and workhouse—was founded to shelter the growing number of poor people and to give employment to the able-bodied among them. The problem, however, was insoluble. No matter what method they tried, eighteenth-century Philadelphians were unable to reduce the incidence of poverty in their midst.

Circumstances were still worse in Boston, which suffered serious losses of manpower during the colonial wars (see pages 86–87). The city's economy began to stagnate at midcentury. Boston's merchants had built their fortunes on exporting fish to the West Indies and southern Europe; when England and Spain went to war in 1739, that trade collapsed. (Trading with the enemy was illegal, and the Spanish navy also harassed colonial shipping.) At the same time, a series of poor grain harvests in Europe caused flour prices to rise rapidly. Philadelphia and New York, which could draw on large fertile grain- and livestock-producing areas, thus gained the lead in the foodstuffs trade. Boston never fully recovered, partly because its hinterland was limited in both size and fertility, and partly because of the competition from such nearby ports as Salem, New Haven, and Newport. As one indication of Boston's economic problems, the records of an overseer of the poor in the late 1760s show that about 15 percent of the people in his district were receiving some form of relief—a sizable proportion indeed. In 1790 Boston had only 1,000 more inhabitants than it had had in 1750 (for a total of 18,000), while Philadelphia already boasted over 42,000 residents and New York more than 33,000.

Stratification was increasing in the countryside as well. In the Chesapeake, the fact that the slave population had begun to grow through natural increase spurred the development of very large plantations and helped to create an aristocracy of wealthy planters. Such planters increased their wealth still further by serving as middlemen in the tobacco trade. They loaned less well-to-do planters money, marketed their crops, sold them imported goods, and enriched themselves in the process. In New England, meanwhile, the continuing population growth and the relatively static amount of land under cultivation forced more and more men either to migrate or accept landless status. The same trend appeared even in such fertile areas as Chester County, Pennsylvania, which participated in and contributed to Philadelphia's prosperity. In the late seventeenth century the bottom third of Chester County's residents had owned 17 percent of the wealth, and the top tenth just 24 percent. By 1760 the poorest third possessed only 6 percent of the property, and the top tenth had increased its share to 30 percent.

The trend seems clear, but interpreting it is difficult. Certain families were indeed growing richer, but were other families growing poorer? That is, had individual members of the urban poor (or their parents) once been better off? Or were those increasing numbers of applicants for relief either the victims of unusual circumstances (such as war widows) or recently arrived immigrants who would eventually be self-supporting? It is impossible to tell from the available evidence whether a class of permanently impoverished

people was forming in eighteenth-century America, or whether poverty was a phase many people passed through (usually during youth or old age). But this much can be said: the gap between rich and poor was widening, and it had become more difficult for a person starting out at the bottom of the economic ladder to reach its upper rungs.

The transition to a more rigid social and economic structure did not occur without conflict. People who had trouble earning a living wage occasionally exploded into violence when goaded by particularly blatant examples of profiteering.

| Social conflict |

Such riots were not unique to colonial cities; for centuries, European crowds had taken to the streets to protest unpopular measures. Urban crowds tended to direct their hostility at merchants suspected of monopolizing or hoarding necessary commodities in hopes of driving up prices. In Boston in both 1710 and 1713, for example, rioters prevented a wealthy merchant from exporting large quantities of grain at a time of severe bread shortages. (On the second occasion they cleaned out his warehouse.) Forty years later New York workers took to the streets to protest a devaluation of coinage that, in effect, reduced their meager wages still further. And city dwellers throughout the colonies resisted collectively when the British navy attempted to press them into service. Navy press gangs would roam the streets of colonial cities, gathering up all the able-bodied men they found. The poor had less chance of escaping their clutches than the rich, and frequently had to fight for their freedom.

Rural riots frequently erupted over land titles—a matter of much concern to farmers, regardless of their relative prosperity. In the 1740s, for example, New Jersey farmers holding land under grants from the governor of New York (dating from the brief period when both provinces were owned by the Duke of York) clashed repeatedly with agents of the East Jersey proprietors. The proprietors claimed the land as theirs and demanded annual payments, called quitrents, for the use of the property. Similar violence occurred in the 1760s in the region that later became Vermont. There, farmers (many of them migrants from eastern New England) holding land grants issued by New Hampshire battled with speculators claiming title to the area through grants from New York authorities. In both cases the rioters saw themselves as virtuous yeomen defending their way of life against monied interlopers.

The same theme can be detected in the most serious land riots of the period, which took place along the Hudson River in 1765 and 1766. Late in the seventeenth century, Governor Benjamin Fletcher of New York had granted several huge tracts in the lower Hudson valley to prominent colonial families. The proprietors in turn divided these estates into small farms, which they rented chiefly to poor Dutch and German immigrants, who evidently regarded tenancy as a way station on the road to independent freeholder status. By the 1750s, some proprietors were earning as much as £1,000 to £2,000 annually from quitrents and other fees.

After 1740, though, increasing migration from New England brought conflict to the great New York estates. The mobile New Englanders, who had moved in search of land, did not want to become tenants. Many squatted on vacant portions of the manors and resisted all attempts to evict them. In the mid-1760s, the Philipse family brought suit against the New Englanders, some of whom had lived on Philipse land for twenty or thirty years. New York courts upheld the Philipse claim and ordered the squatters to make way for tenants with valid leases. Instead of complying, the farmers organized a rebellion against the proprietors. For nearly a year the insurgent farmers controlled much of the Hudson valley. They terrorized proprietors and loyal tenants, freed their friends from jail, and on one occasion fought a pitched battle with a county sheriff and his posse. The rebellion was put down only after British troops dispatched from New York City captured its most important leaders.

The land riots in New York, New Jersey, and Vermont revealed the tenacity with which eighteenth-century Americans would defend their cherished positions as independent yeomen farmers. That status played a major part in colonial Americans' perceptions of themselves and their culture.

Colonial culture

From 1754 to 1756, John Dickinson, a Pennsylvanian who would later become a somewhat reluctant revolutionary, studied law at the Middle Temple in London in preparation for a legal career in Philadelphia. Dickinson's letters to his parents provided a running commentary on British politics, the many attractions of the mother country, his studies, and—perhaps most interestingly—his attitudes toward what he was seeing. The young American described England unhesitatingly as a land of "luxury & corruption," observing that "it is grown a vice here to be virtuous."

Dickinson saw his own country as quite different. "Notwithstanding all the diversions of England," he told his parents, "I shall return to America with rapture. . . . Tis rude, but it's innocent. Tis wild, but its private. There life is a stream pure & unruffled, here an ocean briny & tempestuous. There we enjoy life, here we spend it."

John Dickinson was expressing what had become the prevailing view among the colonists: life in America was simpler, purer, and less corrupt than life in England. If America could not boast of a literary culture equal to London's, it could at least point to publications displaying good common sense. If the colonists lacked polish, they nevertheless had unaffected manners. If residence in the colonies meant remoteness from centers of power and influence, it also conveyed immunity to the vice that automatically accompanied the exercise of power. Dickinson and his fellow Americans were, in other words, making a virtue out of a necessity. By no stretch of the imagination could their culture be considered comparable to England's. Instead of trying to compete with their undeniable superior, they changed the terms of the contest: they glorified their lack of the attributes usually considered essential to a proper, civilized existence.

But it was not quite that easy. Fifty years later Americans developed an ideology of republicanism (see Chapter 6) that affirmed and solidified their image of themselves as simple, virtuous yeomen. But while they were still part of the British Empire, they could not reject categorically the standards by which English people were commonly judged. In mid-eighteenth-century America, two opposing tendencies prevailed in the thinking of the colonial cultural, political, and economic elite. One—reflected in John Dickinson's letters—celebrated the simple virtues of life in the colonies and openly criticized England's failings. The other stressed the links between European and American culture. Colonial intellectuals prided themselves on reading the latest English books and corresponding with leading thinkers in the mother country and on the Continent. Wealthy colonists imitated as best they could the manners, dress, and behavior of English aristocrats, and professionals introduced English practices into the conduct of their daily business. (Judges and some lawyers, for example, adopted the English custom of wearing long white wigs and black robes in courtrooms.)

The most important aspect of the transatlantic cultural connection was Americans' participation in the European intellectual movement known as the Enlightenment. Since the sixteenth century, some conti-

| American Enlightenment |

nental thinkers had been analyzing nature in an effort to determine the laws that govern the universe. They employed experimentation and abstract reasoning to discover general principles behind such everyday phenomena as the motions of the planets and stars, the behavior of falling objects, and the characteristics of light and sound. Above all, Enlightenment philosophers emphasized acquiring knowledge through reason, rather than intuition and revelation. Many European Enlightenment thinkers, like John Locke—whose *Essay on Human Understanding* disputed the Calvinist notion that human beings were innately depraved—wrote abstract analytical philosophy. Colonial participants in the Enlightenment, meanwhile, oriented their studies toward the concrete and particular.

For example, Americans were intensely interested in their natural surroundings. The Western Hemisphere housed many plants and animals unknown in the Old World. Naturalists like John Bartram of Pennsylvania and Cadwallader Colden of New York eagerly assisted a trans-Atlantic attempt to identify and classify plant species. Bartram traveled widely through the South, gathering specimens and sending reports of his findings to the Swedish naturalist Linnaeus, whose *Systema Naturae* (1735) had advanced the idea that all plants could be fitted into a universal classification system. American naturalists also sought evidence to disprove the claim that the American environment was unhealthy. Some Enlightenment natural scientists had written that life forms native to the Western Hemisphere were inferior to those found in Europe, and that human beings who emigrated to the Americas would degenerate into savagery and sterility within a few generations.

The American Philosophical Society epitomized the colonists' participation in the Enlightenment. The society was founded in Philadelphia in 1769 as the result of a merger of two rival groups, one of which had focused on natural history and the other on basic science, especially astronomy. Among its first members were political leaders, educators, physicians, and skilled artisans (notably the clockmaker David Rittenhouse, who was constructing an orrery, a mechanical model of the solar system). Benjamin Franklin, the best-known American scientist, was selected as the organization's president even though he was living in London. Over the next few years the society elected new members from other colonies and published a volume of its *Transactions*—a sure sign of scientific prestige and respectability. (Not until after the Revolution did additional volumes appear.)

It was in the realm of medicine that Enlightenment activity had the greatest impact on the lives of ordinary colonists. The key figure in the drama was the Reverend Cotton Mather, the Puritan divine, who was a member of England's Royal Society (the model for the American Philosophical Society). In a Royal Society publication Mather read about the benefits of inoculation (deliberately infecting a person with a

| Smallpox inoculations |

mild case of a disease) as a protection against the dreaded smallpox. In 1720 and 1721, when Boston suffered a major smallpox epidemic, Mather and a doctor ally urged people to be inoculated; there was fervent opposition, including that of Boston's leading physician. When the epidemic had ended, the statistics bore out Mather's opinion: of those inoculated, fewer than 3 percent died; of those who became ill without inoculation, nearly 15 percent perished. Though it was midcentury before inoculation was generally accepted as a preventive procedure, enlightened methods had provided colonial Americans protection from the greatest killer disease of all.

On the whole, though, few Americans were affected by the transatlantic intellectual currents of the day. Only a limited number of well-to-do colonists saw Shakespeare's "Romeo and Juliet," the most popular play in America, or more modern productions such as Richard Cumberland's "The Fashionable Lover." Only a well-educated minority could appreciate the carefully constructed phrases of the great English essayist Joseph Addison or enjoy reading that daring new literary form, the novel. (Samuel Richardson's novels *Pamela, Clarissa,* and *Sir Charles Grandison* were practically required reading for genteel colonial young people.)

Indeed, of all the arts, music alone had a significant effect on the general public. And the roots of American music were less European than local. The music of the common people was vocal and chiefly religious, for communal singing was an important part of both Congregational and Presbyterian church ritual. It was no accident that the first book printed in the colonies was *The Bay Psalm Book* (1640), consisting of Old Testament psalms recast in metrical prose so they could be sung during worship services. The participation of the entire congregation was considered more important than the quality of the music they produced. Such questions as which version of the psalms to use and whether instruments should accompany the singing were resolved by majority vote. Seating in church was assigned by the church leaders: each family had its own pew, whose location at the front, back, or sides depended on the family's relative wealth and social prominence. But communal singing reduced the significance of such hierarchical arrangements, adding an egalitarian element to American religion and bringing a kind of crude democracy into Presbyterian and Congregational churches.

One of the chief reasons why music was the only art that had a broad impact in America was its adaptability for use in a society filled with people who could neither read nor write. Colonial hymns were written in short, rhyming, metrical lines that were easy to learn and remember. Many churches also aided singing by "lining-out"—that is, having a leader read each line aloud before the congregation sang it.

The shortcomings of colonial education ensured that there would be many illiterate Americans who needed such assistance. In New England, which probably had the highest literacy rates in the colonies, 80 to 90 percent of adult men but only about 50 percent of adult women could sign their names at the time of the Revolution. Why did so many people never learn to read and write? Literacy was certainly less essential in eighteenth-century America than it is today. People—especially women—could live their entire lives without ever being called upon to read a book or write a letter. Important information tended to be transmitted orally rather than in writing. Thus education—especially education beyond the rudi-

Dr. William Glysson (1740–1793) treating a smallpox patient. Painted by his brother-in-law Winthrop Chandler in the early 1780s. Campus Martius Museum.

ments of reading, writing, and "figuring"—was usually regarded as a frill for either sex. Massachusetts Bay alone among the colonies attempted (in a law passed in 1647) to require its towns to maintain public schools, but that law was widely ignored.

Whether colonial children learned to read and write thus depended largely on their parents. Most youngsters learned their ABCs at home, often using the Bible or an almanac—the most commonly owned books—as a text. Their first teachers were their parents or older siblings. Later, if their parents were willing and able to pay for further education, they might attend a private "dame school" run by a local widow, where they would learn more of the basics. A few fortunate boys might then go on to a grammar school, to study with a minister and prepare to enter college at age fourteen or fifteen.

| Primary education |

Girls were usually not educated beyond the rudiments. One Harvard graduate declared, for example, that his daughters "knew quite enough if they could make a shirt and a pudding." Only a very few daughters of elite families received any advanced intellectual training. One such girl was Eliza Lucas, whose father,

Benjamin Franklin (1706–1789), painted by the itinerant artist Robert Feke in 1746, when Franklin was forty. The portrait shows Franklin at the height of his business career, a prosperous Philadelphian.   Harvard University Portrait Collection, Bequest, Dr. John C. Warren in 1856.

sachusetts Bay had a higher proportion of learned men in its population than did England.) New England's founders placed heavy emphasis on the need for an institution of higher learning to train young men for the ministry. In 1636 the General Court of Massachusetts voted to set up a college, and two years later instruction began in Newtown, renamed Cambridge. The college itself was named for John Harvard, a minister who died in the fall of 1638, leaving the college his library and half his estate. Throughout the seventeenth and much of the eighteenth century, Harvard College primarily trained clergymen; lawyers and doctors usually received their education through formal or informal apprenticeships. Its curriculum stressed Greek and Hebrew (a thorough knowledge of Latin was required for admission), logic, theology, rhetoric, and metaphysics.

> Founding of
> Harvard

The other early colonial colleges were also designed to educate clerics. The College of William and Mary in Williamsburg, Virginia, chartered in 1693 but not a regularly functioning entity until 1726, prepared Anglican ministers to serve in parishes throughout the Chesapeake region. Yale College was founded in New Haven, Connecticut, in 1701 by a group of ministers who thought Harvard's theological teachings had become too liberal. The College of New Jersey (Princeton, 1747), King's College (Columbia, 1754), the College of Rhode Island (Brown, 1756), and Queen's College (Rutgers, 1766), were begun by Presbyterians, Anglicans, Baptists, and Dutch Reformed clergy, respectively. All wanted to ensure adequate supplies of ministers to fill the pulpits of their churches. Dartmouth College (1769), though not explicitly aimed at educating clerics, also had a religious purpose: Christianizing the Indians. Of all the major colonial colleges, only the College of Philadelphia (later the University of Pennsylvania, 1755), had nonsectarian origins, and it too eventually fell under the domination of the Anglican Church.

The College of Philadelphia was largely the creation of two men: Benjamin Franklin, who first outlined its purposes and curriculum, and William Smith, a Scots emigrant who became its first provost. Franklin, born in Boston in 1706, was the perfect example of a self-made, self-educated man. Indentured at an early age to his older brother James, a Boston printer and newspaper publisher, Franklin ran away to

a West Indian planter, sent her to school in England because he did not want her mind to be "vacant and uninformed." Just before she married Charles Pinckney in 1745, Eliza thanked her father "[for] the pains and mony you laid out in my Education which I esteem a more valuable fortune than any you could now have given me." Eliza Lucas Pinckney was to demonstrate the value of her education by helping to develop a successful means of cultivating indigo (see Chapter 2) and by giving her sons, Thomas and Charles Cotesworth, the rigorous training that enabled them to become national leaders in the 1790s (see Chapter 7).

Ironically, the colonial system of higher education for males was more fully developed than was basic instruction for either sex. In part, the disparity resulted from the large number of university graduates who participated in the Puritan migration; by the mid-1640s, 130 graduates of Oxford and Cambridge had moved to America. (In its early days, therefore, Mas-

Chapter 3: Colonial society at midcentury

Philadelphia in 1723. There he worked as a printer and eventually started his own publishing business, printing the *Pennsylvania Gazette* and *Poor Richard's Almanack* among other books. The business was so successful that Franklin was able to retire from active control in 1748, at forty-two. He thereafter devoted himself to intellectual endeavors and public service (as deputy postmaster general for the colonies, as an agent representing colonial interests in London, and eventually as a diplomat during the Revolution). Franklin's *Experiments and Observations on Electricity* (1751) was the most important scientific work by a colonial American; it established the terminology and basic theory of electricity still in use today.

In 1749 and 1751 Franklin published pamphlets proposing the establishment of a new educational institution in Pennsylvania. The purpose of Franklin's "English School" was not to produce clerics or scholars but to prepare young men "for learning any business, calling or profession, except such wherein languages are required." He wanted to enable them "to pass through and execute the several offices of civil life, with advantage and reputation to themselves and country." The College of Philadelphia, in other words, was intended to graduate youths who would resemble Franklin himself—talented, practical men of affairs competent in a number of different fields.

Benjamin Franklin on education

Franklin and the student he envisioned were perfect representatives of colonial culture. Free of the Old World's traditions and corruptions, the ideal American would achieve distinction through hard work and the application of common-sense principles. He would be unlettered but not unlearned, simple but not ignorant, virtuous but not priggish. The American would be a true child of the Enlightenment, knowledgeable about European culture yet not bound by its fetters, advancing through reason and talent alone. To him all things would be possible, all doors open.

The contrast with the original communal ideals of the early New England settlements could not have been sharper. Franklin's American was an individual, free to make choices about his future, able to contemplate a variety of possible careers. John Winthrop's American, outlined in his "Modell of Christian Charity" (see pages 22–23), had been a component of a greater whole that required his unhesitating, unquestioning submission. But the two visions had one point in common: both described only white males. Neither blacks—nearly one-fifth of the total population—nor females—about half of the population—played any part in them. Yet both groups were of crucial importance in American society.

Life on farms and in towns

The basic unit of colonial society was the household. Headed by a white male (or perhaps his widow), the household was the chief mechanism of production and consumption in the colonial economy. Its members—bound by ties of blood or servitude—worked together to produce goods for consumption or sale. The white male head of the household represented it to the outside world, serving in the militia or political posts, casting the household's sole vote in elections. He managed the finances and held legal authority over the rest of the family—his wife, his children, and his servants or slaves. (Eighteenth-century Americans used the word *family* for people who lived together in one house, whether or not they were blood kin.) Such households were considerably larger than American families today; in 1790, the average home contained seven people, one of whom was black.

The vast majority of eighteenth-century American families—more than 90 percent of them—lived in rural areas. The unique qualities of large southern plantations will be discussed in the next section. But other farm households, whether in the North or the South, had many characteristics in common, as did rural people throughout the colonies. Nearly all adult men were farmers and all adult women farm wives. Though men might work as millers, blacksmiths, or carpenters, and women might sell surplus farm produce to neighbors, they typically did so in addition to their primary agricultural tasks. The tasks different members of the household performed were clearly differentiated by sex. Servants, slaves, and children aided either the master or the mistress of the household, laboring under his or her supervision. Thus the following summary describes the work of all members of a farm family above the age of eight.

At the Loom. One of the earliest known pictures of an American woman at work, this painting shows the mistress of a household making an elaborate coverlet. Note the spinning wheel beside the fireplace.   Downtown Gallery Papers, American Folk Art Gallery. Microfilm roll ND/47, Archives of American Art, Smithsonian Institution.

The mistress of the rural household was responsible for its daily operations. Her task was to ensure that food was properly prepared, clothing was made and cared for, and the house was kept clean and neat. In colonial America, these basic chores were enormously complex and arduous. Preparing food involved planting and cultivating a garden, harvesting and preserving vegetables, salting and smoking meat, drying apples and pressing cider, milking cows and making butter and cheese, not to mention cooking and baking. Making clothing meant processing raw wool and flax fibers (a lengthy process in itself), spinning thread, weaving cloth, dyeing and fulling (softening by repeated beating and washing) the cloth, and finally cutting out and sewing garments by hand. Nor was keeping one's clothes and home clean an easy job, since the soap had to be

Sex roles

made in the household—from ashes, rendered fat, and lye—and water had to be carried by hand from a well or stream. No wonder one harried Long Island housewife filled her diary in 1768 and 1769 with such entries as these: "It has been a tiresome day it is now Bed time and I have not had won minutts rest"; "full of freting discontent dirty and miserabel both yesterday and today."

The head of the household also had a heavy work load. He had to plant and cultivate fields, build fences, chop wood for the fireplaces, harvest and market crops, and butcher cattle and hogs to provide the household with meat. His and his wife's tasks were complementary. A farm needed both a man and a woman to be run properly, since under normal circumstances neither sex would assume the functions of the other. The man's realm was "outdoor affairs"; the

Chapter 3: Colonial society at midcentury

woman's, "indoor" domestic matters. Children and servants or slaves were also needed: given the magnitude of their tasks, both master and mistress had to have help.

Farm households were governed by the seasons and by the hours of daylight. (Candles too had to be manufactured at home; they were too precious to be wasted, so most people rose and went to bed with the sun.) Men and boys had the most leisure in the winter, when there were no crops that needed care.

| Rhythms of rural life | Women and girls were freest in the summer, before embarking on autumn food preservation and winter spinning and weaving. Other activities, including education, had to be subordinated to seasonal work. Thus farm boys attended school in the winter, and their sisters went to classes in the summer. The seasons also affected travel plans. Because the roads were muddy in spring and fall, most visiting took place in summer and especially winter, when sleighs could be used.

Even the conception of children was affected by the seasons. Legitimate conceptions (as indicated by a birth nine months later) peaked in June—after planting but before harvest—and rose to a secondary high point in December, the darkest month of winter. Illegitimate conceptions, by contrast, peaked in late summer. The difference is easily explained: small, crowded colonial houses lacked privacy, and illicit sex was thus possible only outdoors.

Because most farm families were relatively isolated from their neighbors, and because of heavy seasonal work obligations, rural folk took advantage of every possible opportunity for socializing. Men taking grain to be milled would stop at a crossroads tavern for a drink and conversation with friends. Women gathering to assist at childbirth would drink tea and exchange news. The Reverend Charles Woodmason, an Anglican missionary, found to his consternation that residents of the Carolina backcountry regarded his church services as social events. "No making of them sit still during Service—but they will be in and out—forward and backward the whole Time (Women especially) as Bees to and fro to their Hives," he wrote of one congregation in 1768. And work itself provided opportunities for visiting. Harvest frolics, cornhusking bees, barn raisings, quilting parties, spinning bees, and other communal endeavors brought together neighbors from miles around, often for several days of work followed by feasting, dancing, and singing in the evenings.

Even though eighteenth-century cities were nothing but large towns by today's standards, city life differed considerably from rural life in colonial America. A young Massachusetts man who had moved to Providence described one difference to his farmer father: the city, he remarked, was filled with "Noise and Confusion and Disturbance. I must confess, the jolts

| Rhythms of urban life | of Waggons, the Ratlings of Coaches, the crying of Meat for the Market, the Hollowing of Negros and the ten thousand jinggles and Noises, that continually Surround us in every Part almost of the Town, Confuse my thinking." A Philadelphia woman visiting the country had precisely the opposite problem. "I never was disturbed by common noises in the night as many are," she observed in her diary, noting that she missed the chiming of the town clock and the watchman crying the hours. In the country, the clocks so essential to city life were simply irrelevant. City and country people lived on different schedules.

Still, seasonality also touched the lives of city folk. Town women, like their rural counterparts, spent much of the fall preserving food for the winter. And the volume of a merchant's business might depend on the seasons, since weather determined sailing schedules in the Atlantic and the Caribbean. But city dwellers were not tied so inextricably to nature's rhythms. Women could purchase meat, vegetables, butter, and cheese at well-stocked city markets. They could buy cloth at dry goods stores and—if they had the money—even hire seamstresses and milliners to make their family's clothing. Men could purchase wood already chopped, and they had no fields to tend. Nor were visits to friends seasonally determined. The well-to-do in particular had more hours of leisure to read, attend dances, plays, and concerts, take walks around town or rides in the countryside, play cards, or simply relax.

City people had much more contact with the world beyond their own homes than did their rural compatriots. By the middle of the century, every major city had at least one weekly newspaper, and most had two or three. Newspapers printed the latest "advices from London" (usually two to three months old) and news of events in other English colonies, as well as reports on matters of local interest. The local newspaper was available at taverns and inns, so people who could not afford to buy it could nevertheless read it. (Even illiterates could acquaint themselves with the latest news, since the paper was often read aloud by literate customers.) However, contact with the outside world also had drawbacks. Sailors sometimes brought exotic and deadly diseases into port with them. Cities like Boston, New York, and Philadelphia endured terrible epidemics of smallpox and yellow fever, which the countryside largely escaped.

The merchants and professionals at the top of the social and economic scale typically earned more than

| *Urban social structure* | £200 annually. Of similar social but lesser economic standing were teachers and clergymen, whose |

salaries rarely exceeded £100. The yearly incomes of the urban "middling sort," mostly artisans and shopkeepers, ranged from under £50 to over £100. Below them were the unskilled laborers, who earned perhaps £20 a year (bare subsistence for an average family), and then the free servants and apprentices, who were compensated mainly with room and board and no more than £10 a year. At the very bottom of the social ladder were indentured servants and, finally, slaves, who could earn money only with the permission of their masters.

Cities attracted many migrants from rural areas. Young men came to learn a skill through an apprenticeship, ordinary laborers came seeking work, and widows came looking for a means of supporting their families. Without an adult man in the household, a woman had a difficult time running a farm. Consequently, widows tended to congregate in port cities, where they could sell their services as nurses, teachers, seamstresses, servants, or prostitutes, or (if they had some capital) open shops, inns, or boardinghouses. In rural areas, where the economy was based largely on subsistence agriculture and most families produced nearly all their own necessities, there was little demand for the services that landless women and men could perform. In the cities, though, someone always needed another servant, blacksmith, or laundress.

Only widows and the very few never-married women in the colonies could run independent businesses, because of the provisions of English and colonial laws regarding women's status. Under the common law doctrine of coverture, a married woman

| *Status of women* | became one person with her husband. She could not sue or be sued, make contracts, buy or sell |

property, or draft a will. Any property she owned prior to marriage became her husband's after the wedding; any wages she earned were legally his; and all children of the marriage fell under his absolute control. A married woman, in other words, was completely subordinate to her husband by law, and she had little chance to escape a bad marriage. Divorces were practically impossible to obtain. (An unmarried woman, though, had the same legal rights as a man, with the exception of voting.)

A wife's subordination to her husband was more than just legal. Colonial men expected their wives to defer to their judgment, and most wives seem to have accepted secondary status without murmuring. When girls married, they were commonly advised to devote themselves to their husbands' interests. "Let your Dress your Conversation & the whole Business of your life be to please your Husband & to make him happy & you need not fail of being so your self," a New Yorker told his daughter in the 1730s. That women followed such advice is evident in their diaries. A Virginia woman remarked, for example, that "one of my first resolutions I made after marriage, was never to hold disputes with my husband." It was wives' responsibility, she declared, "to give up to their husbands" whenever differences of opinion arose between them. Not until very late in the eighteenth century, during and after the American Revolution, would such women as Abigail Adams begin to question these traditional notions.

The man's authority extended to his children as well. Eighteenth-century Americans regarded child rearing as primarily the father's responsibility. That responsibility did not, however, encompass the day-to-day care of children, which was the mother's task. Instead, the father disciplined the children and determined the general standards by which they were raised. Colonial children tended to be indulged as in-

| *Childrearing* | fants and toddlers, but strictly reared thereafter. Parents usually |

insisted on unquestioning obedience from their offspring, and many fathers freely used physical punishment to break a child's will. The sexual division of tasks within the home brought mothers and daugh-

Chapter 3: Colonial society at midcentury

ters especially close together, for a daughter was her mother's assistant and apprentice in housewifery. Colonial mothers and daughters accordingly often referred to each other as "friend" and "companion." Fathers and sons rarely developed the same sort of egalitarian relationship, possibly because the father's position as head of the household made him unwilling to accept any of his subordinates, even his sons, as equals.

In seventeenth-century New England, as was pointed out in Chapter 1, parents had exercised considerable control over their children's marriages. By the middle of the eighteenth century, though, there is evidence indicating that such traditions were losing their force. Children were marrying out of birth order and choosing spouses from other towns and of lesser economic standing. Most important of all, the premarital pregnancy rate soared. In one Massachusetts town in the latter decades of the century, nearly 40 percent of brides were pregnant at the time of their marriage. In the early seventeenth-century Chesapeake, where similar patterns had prevailed, parents had not been alive to supervise their adult children. A hundred and fifty years later, parents were alive but apparently were losing either the ability or the desire to control their children's lives. The reasons for this shift are not entirely clear. Probably changes in the economy and in parental attitudes toward their offspring both contributed to the striking results, as did the changing mores of the young people themselves.

Life on plantations

A plantation was a rural household writ large. The planter and his wife perceived everyone in the household, white and black alike, as belonging to their family, and, indeed, the plantation was organized along familial lines. The master and mistress of the household were responsible for the same tasks as their counterparts on small farms, but on plantations they supervised black workers instead of doing the jobs themselves. The planter directed the planting, cultivating, and harvesting of crops, while his wife oversaw food processing and preparation, the manufacture of clothing, the operation of the dairy, and so forth.

Both sets of tasks were considerably more complex than on farms, because of the number of people who had to be fed, clothed, housed, and supervised. Children of planter families, like northern youngsters, learned from the parent of the same sex, but the skills they acquired were those involved in supervising slaves rather than mastery of the jobs themselves.

The lives of wealthy white planter families differed markedly from those of their poorer compatriots in both North and South. For one thing, the presence of many slaves altered the relationship between white parents and their children. Since mothers did not have to perform the household chores themselves, they

| White family and social life |

could devote much more time to their offspring. In ordinary homes, children over the age of two (when the mother usually bore another child) had to fend largely for themselves, since their mother was fully occupied with the new infant and the housework. White women on plantations, though, had even more leisure than did well-to-do city women, and they tended to spend that time with their children. Accordingly, wealthy southern youngsters received more attention than did most of their contemporaries. They were also probably the first American children whose parents were not centrally concerned with matters of discipline and control. Their more relaxed upbringing foreshadowed nineteenth-century Americans' greater indulgence of children.

Though life on the larger plantations was comfortable whites still led an isolated existence. Thus like other colonists they took advantage of all opportunities for socializing. In tidewater Virginia and Maryland, attending church was just as much a social occasion as it was in backcountry South Carolina—more formal, to be sure, but nevertheless a time to see friends and exchange news. The Sunday entries in the diary of one Virginia teenager, for instance, barely mentioned the sermon topic but devoted many lines to listing the people she had seen and talked to. Barbecues and week-long house parties were popular, as were horse racing, cock fighting, and gambling. When the House of Burgesses met in Williamsburg, or the Maryland House of Delegates in Annapolis, planters took their families to town for a round of dinners and balls. In South Carolina, planters from the swampy lowcountry traditionally lived in Charleston from May until December to escape the worst

A convivial dinner party in Charleston, around 1760. George Roupell, a customs officer in the city, drew this picture of himself and his friends. One guest inquires drunkenly, "Whose to[a]st is it?" while another shouts, "Success to Caroline!" and a third cautions, "pray less noise gent[lemen]." A slave boy waits by the window. Henry Francis du Pont Winterthur Museum.

heat—and seasonal illnesses like malaria. Consequently Charleston, unlike Williamsburg and Annapolis, developed as wide a variety of diversions as northern cities. Concerts, dances, plays, and similar entertainments enlivened the season wealthy whites spent in the city.

Yet the whites who lived on southern farms and plantations and in the South's few cities made up only slightly more than half the region's population. In South Carolina, a majority of the population was black; in Georgia, about half; and in the Chesapeake, 40 percent. Although the populations of some back-country areas of Virginia, Maryland, and the Carolinas were less than one-fifth black, some parts of the Carolina lowcountry were nearly 90 percent black by 1790. The trend toward consolidation of landholding and slave ownership after 1740 had a pro-

found effect on the lives of Afro-Americans. In the tidewater Chesapeake in the 1780s, nearly three-quarters of all blacks lived on plantations with more than ten slaves, and 43 percent were owned by planters with at least twenty slaves. In the lowcountry, where most of South Carolina's slaves lived in the 1760s, 88 percent were on plantations with ten or more slaves, and 40 percent lived in units of fifty or more. The following discussion will thus focus on the lives of slaves in relatively large households. It must always be remembered, however, that a sizable minority of southern blacks lived on farms with only one or two other slaves; their lives were probably quite different, but historians have not yet investigated them in detail.

The large size of many plantation households allowed for the specialization of labor. Encouraged by

An Overseer Doing His Duty, by Benjamin H. Latrobe. Most slave women were field hands like these, sketched in 1798 near Fredericksburg, Virginia. White women were believed to be unsuited for heavy outdoor labor.   Maryland Historical Society.

planters whose goal was to create as self-sufficient a household as possible, Afro-American men and women became highly skilled at various tasks. Each plantation had its own blacksmiths, carpenters, dairy maids, seamstresses, cooks, valets, shoemakers, gardeners, and at least one midwife, who attended pregnant white and black women alike. These skilled slaves—between 10 and 20 percent of the black population—were as essential to the smooth functioning of the plantation as the ordinary male and female field hands who worked "in the crop." Their presence also meant that the colonial South required the services of fewer white artisans than did the North. Until several decades after the Revolution, much of the skilled labor in the region was performed by blacks.

The typical Chesapeake tobacco plantation or Georgia or Carolina rice-indigo plantation was divided into small "quarters" located at some distance from one another. In the Chesapeake, white overseers supervised work on the distant quarters, while the planter personally took charge of the "home" quarter (which included the planter's house). In the Carolina lowcountry, where the planters were usually absent many months of the year, black drivers often supervised their fellow slaves. The work force on the outlying quarters was typically composed of both Africans and Afro-Americans, whereas Afro-Americans alone lived at the home quarter. Planters usually sent "outlandish" (African-born) slaves to do field labor on outlying quarters in order to accustom them to plantation work routines and to enable them to learn some English. (The proportion of Africans was higher in South Carolina than in the Chesapeake because of the ongoing slave trade to that colony.) Artisans were most often chosen from among the plantation's Afro-

| Operation of the plantation |

Americans. In such families skills like carpentry and midwifery were passed down from father to son and from mother to daughter; such knowledge often constituted a slave family's most valuable possession.

Eighteenth-century planters were considerably less worried that their slaves might run away than were their counterparts fifty years later. Only in special circumstances did they establish regular slave patrols, and blacks could normally pass freely from quarter to quarter. In part their relative freedom of movement resulted from the geographical layout of the plantations. Since slave families were frequently dispersed among widely separated quarters, planters had no means of preventing a good deal of casual visiting, especially on Sundays, the slaves' one day of rest. But the whites' flexibility had another cause as well: since all the colonies legally permitted slavery, blacks had nowhere to go to escape bondage. Sometimes recently arrived Africans tried to steal boats to return home or escaped in groups to the frontier, where they attempted to establish traditional villages. Afro-Americans, on the other hand, clearly recognized that they had few long-term alternatives to remaining on their home plantations.

This is not to say that Afro-American slaves never ran away. They did, in large numbers. But they did so to visit friends or relatives, or simply to escape their normal work routines for a few days or months; they could have had little hope of remaining permanently at large. In a society in which blackness automatically connoted perpetual servitude, no black person anywhere could claim free status without being challenged. And, from the blacks' perspective, violent resistance had even less to recommend it than running away. Whites may have been in the minority in some areas, but they controlled the guns and ammunition. Even if a revolt succeeded for a time, whites could easily muster the armed force necessary to put it down. Only in very unusual circumstances, therefore—as will be seen in the last section of this chapter—did colonial blacks attempt to rebel against their white oppressors.

Eighteenth-century Afro-Americans, then, could do little to free themselves from enslavement. They could nevertheless try to improve the conditions of their bondage and gain some measure of control over their lives. Their chief vehicle for doing so was the family. Planters' records reveal how members of ex-

Black family life

tended kin groups provided support, assistance, and comfort to each other. On the quarters of the Virginia plantation Nomini Hall, for example, Nanny's complaint about the excessive punishment an overseer had inflicted on her sons caused her master Robert Carter to admonish the overseer; Kitty's mother arranged for her to be tended by a particular black doctor; George won his daughter's transfer from one quarter to another so that she could live with her stepmother; and Carter agreed not to part Rebecca from her children. Robert's cousin Landon Carter of Sabine Hall was less responsive to the requests of his slaves. As a result, Sukey retaliated for her granddaughter's mistreatment by turning Landon's cows loose, and Manuel freed his daughter Sarah from the building in which Landon had confined her as punishment for pretending to be ill and then running away. (Manuel's act earned him a whipping.)

Siblings were close, even in adulthood; many blacks named their children after their brothers and sisters, as well as parents, grandparents, and even great-grandparents. The extended-kin ties that developed among Afro-American families who had lived on the same plantation for several generations served as insurance against the uncertainties of existence under slavery. If a nuclear family was broken up by sale, there were always relatives around to help with child rearing and other tasks. Among colonial blacks, in other words, the extended family probably served a more important function than it did among whites.

Blacks were always subject to white intrusions into their lives. Black house servants had to serve the white family rather than their own, and even field hands were constantly at the whites' beck and call. Still, most black families managed to carve out a small measure of autonomy. On many plantations, slaves were allowed to plant their own gardens, hunt, or fish in order to supplement the standard diet of corn and salt pork. Some Chesapeake mistresses permitted their female slaves to raise chickens, which they could then sell or exchange for such items as extra clothing or blankets.

In South Carolina, slaves were often able to accumulate property, because most rice and indigo plantations operated on a task system. Once slaves had

Chapter 3: Colonial society at midcentury

completed their assigned tasks for the day, they were free to work for themselves. (Occasionally they could even cultivate rice or indigo crops of their own.) In Maryland and Virginia, where by the end of the century some whites had begun to hire out their slaves to others, blacks were sometimes allowed to keep a small part of the wages they earned. Such advances were slight, but against the bleak backdrop of slavery they deserve to be highlighted. There were numerous cracks in the slave system, and blacks took advantage of them to increase their limited share of independence.

Relations between blacks and whites varied considerably from household to household. In some, like Landon Carter's, masters and mistresses enforced their will chiefly through physical coercion. Thus one woman's diary noted matter-of-factly: "December 1:

Black-white relations

Lucy whippt for getting key of Celler door & stealing apples. December 2: Plato Anthoney & Abraham Pegg's housband whipt for Hog stealing." On other plantations, like Robert Carter's, masters were more lenient and respectful of slaves' property and their desire to live with other members of their families. (Once, for example, Robert Carter rebuked an overseer who had seized an iron pot belonging to two slave women, ordering it returned to them.) Yet even in households where whites and blacks displayed genuine affection for one another, there were inescapable tensions. Such tensions were caused not only by the whites' uneasiness about the slave system in general but also by the dynamics of day-to-day relationships when a small number of whites wielded absolute legal power over the lives of many blacks.

A confrontation in a Virginia household illustrates some of the complexities of master-slave relationships. Polly Brown decided to whip her slave woman Senah for being "very impudent & disobedient." Senah, however, "rebeled & jerked the switch out of her hand." When Polly's husband Samuel learned of Senah's misbehavior, he began to beat her with his walking stick. But Senah's husband Daniel, in an effort to protect his wife, grabbed an ax from the woodpile. The Browns threatened him with a gun, forced him to lay down the ax, and "tied him, whipt him a little & next morning sent him to jail." After Daniel had been imprisoned for two weeks, Samuel reported

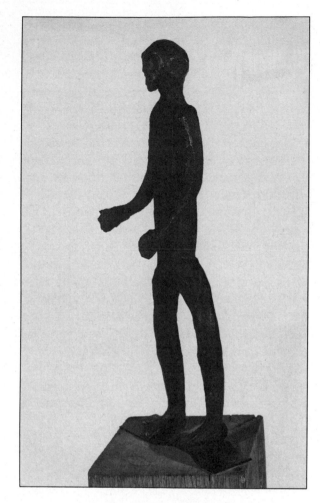

This sculpture, created by an eighteenth-century slave blacksmith, was found in Alexandria, Virginia, on the site of a plantation's slave quarters. It must have been fashioned and kept in secret, for what master would have allowed his slave to use valuable iron—not to mention time—to make such an object? The sculptor must have felt an intense artistic drive to have taken the risk.   Collection of Adele Earnest.

that he was "compleatly cooled, very humble & does very well." As a result, he refused an offer to buy Daniel, explaining, "he is a good coarse shoemaker, & as my family is large, very useful to me." Even though Daniel had tried to attack him, in other words, Samuel Brown found him too valuable to part with; even though the Browns had beaten his wife Senah, Daniel could not continue to resist them for fear of being sold and losing Senah completely. These four people were bound together in ways none of them may have fully understood.

A few thoughtful white Americans were deeply concerned about the implications of the system in which they were enmeshed. But what troubled them was not so much the plight of enslaved blacks as the impact of slavery on whites. Thomas Jefferson summed up the common viewpoint when he observed: "The whole commerce between master and slave is a perpetual exercise of the most boisterous passions, the most unremitting despotism on the one part, and degrading submission on the other. Our children see this, and learn to imitate it. . . . The man must be a prodigy who can retain his manners and morals undepraved by such circumstances." Before the Revolution, only a tiny number of Quakers (most notably John Woolman in his *Some Considerations on the Keeping of Negroes,* published in 1754) took a different approach, criticizing slavery out of sympathy for blacks. The few other white colonists who questioned slavery took Jefferson's approach, stressing the institution's adverse effect on whites.

Underlying anxieties

During the entire colonial period, there were only two (or perhaps three) occasions when blacks sought to win their freedom through rebellion. The first was in New York City in 1712, when about twenty-five slaves set fire to a building, killed nine whites, and wounded others who came to put out the fire. The conspirators were caught and executed, some barbarously (by burning or starvation). In 1741 white residents of New York, fearing another similar plot, embarked on a summer-long reign of terror that resulted in the execution of thirty-one blacks and four whites. In that case, though, it is likely that hysterical whites greatly exaggerated the threat to the city. The so-called conspirators appear to have been a biracial gang of thieves who were also arsonists. The other colonial rebellion, though, posed a real danger to whites.

Early one morning in September 1739, about twenty South Carolina slaves, most of them Ango-

| Stono Rebellion | lans, gathered near the Stono River south of Charleston. After seizing guns and ammunition from a store, they killed the storekeepers and some nearby planter families.

Then, joined by other slaves from the area, they headed south toward Florida in hopes of finding refuge in that Spanish colony. By midday, however, the alarm had been sounded among whites in the district. In the late afternoon a troop of militia caught up with the fugitives, then numbering about a hundred, and attacked them, killing some and dispersing the rest. More than a week later, the whites finally captured most of the remaining conspirators. Those not killed on the spot were later executed, but for more than two years afterward renegades were rumored to be still at large.

The Stono Rebellion shocked white South Carolinians and residents of other colonies as well. Especially when it was coupled with the 1741 New York City scare, the uprising seemed to indicate the precariousness with which whites were clinging to power over their slaves. And there were other signs of conflict within the colonies at midcentury. In the late 1760s, the so-called Regulator movement erupted in the South Carolina backcountry. Angry frontier dwellers, most of them Scotch-Irish, protested that they had little voice in the government of the colony, which was dominated by lowcountry planters. For some months they policed the countryside in vigilante bands, contending that regular law enforcement was too lax. The early 1770s saw the rise of another Regulator movement in North Carolina; there, the western farmers and eastern grandees were unable to resolve their difficulties without bloodshed in a battle at Alamance in 1771. But the most significant evidence of unrest in the colonies was the Great Awakening, the extraordinary religious revival that swept America from the late 1730s to the mid-1760s, reaching its peak in the early 1740s.

The first decades of the eighteenth century had witnessed two unmistakable trends in American religion: a decline in the influence of the clergy (continuing the process of erosion that had begun in the last half of the seventeenth century) and a movement toward rationalism in theology. Protestant clerics never entirely abandoned the Calvinist emphasis on people's powerlessness to affect their own fates. But over time they too—like other well-educated Americans—were affected by the Enlightenment's view of God as a rational creator rather than an irrational (by human standards) and unforgiving judge. Their sermons came to reflect that "enlightened" vision, and to stress the need for preparation for salvation—that is, doing good works and adopting moral lifestyles.

But in the late 1720s new themes began to appear in the preaching of certain clerics—first in Dutch Reformed and Presbyterian churches in the middle colonies, and then in western Massachusetts congregations. The Dutch Reformed clergyman Theodore Frelinghuysen, the Presbyterian Gilbert Tennent, and most notably the Congregationalist Jonathan Edwards all returned to more basic Calvinist principles in their sermons. Individuals, they argued, could attain salvation only through recognition of their own depraved natures and the need to surrender completely to God's will. Such surrender, when it came, brought release from worry and sin. It was above all an irrational emotional experience, distinctly at odds with the prevailing rationalist trend in American theology. People in Edwards's congregation in particular began to experience that surrender as a single identifiable moment of conversion.

The effects of such conversions remained isolated until 1739, when George Whitefield, an English adherent of the Methodist branch of Anglicanism, arrived in America. For fifteen months Whitefield toured the colonies, preaching to large audiences from Georgia to New England and concentrating his efforts in the major cities: Boston, New York, Philadelphia, and Charleston. An effective orator, Whitefield was the chief generating force behind the Great Awakening. Everywhere he traveled, his fame preceded him; thousands turned out to listen—and to experience conversion. At first, regular clerics welcomed Whitefield and the native itinerant evangelist preachers who sprang up to imitate him. Soon, though, many clergymen began to realize that "revived" religion, though it filled their churches, ran counter to their own more rational approach to matters of faith. Furthermore, they disliked the emotional style of the untrained revivalists, whose itinerancy also disrupted normal patterns of church attendance.

Opposition to the Awakening heightened rapidly, and large numbers of churches splintered in its wake. "Old Lights"—traditional clerics and their followers—engaged in bitter disputes with the "New Light" evangelicals. American religion, already characterized by numerous sects, became further divided as the major denominations split into Old Light and New

First Great Awakening

George Whitefield (1714–1770), an English evangelist who made frequent tours of the American colonies. This portrait, painted in England, shows the effects his powerful preaching had on his listeners. National Portrait Gallery, London.

Light factions, and as new evangelical sects—Methodists and Baptists—quickly gained adherents. This rapid rise in the number of distinct denominations contributed to Americans' growing willingness to tolerate religious diversity. No longer could any one sect make unequivocal claims to orthodoxy.

The most important effect of the Awakening, though, was its impact on American modes of thought. Colonial society was deferential; that is, common folk were expected to accept unhesitatingly the authority of their "betters," whether wealthy gentry, government officials, or educated clergymen. The message of the Great Awakening directly challenged that tradition of deference. The revivalists, many of whom were not ordained clergymen (some were even illiterate), claimed they understood the word of God far better than orthodox clerics. The Awakening's emphasis on emotion rather than learning as the road to salvation further undermined the validity of received wisdom. Supported by the belief that God was with them, New Lights began to question not only religious but also social and political orthodoxy.

Nowhere was this trend more evident than in Virginia, where the plantation gentry and their ostentatious lifestyle clearly dominated society. By the 1760s, Baptists had gained a major foothold in Virginia, and their beliefs and behavior were openly at odds with the way most gentry families lived. They rejected as sinful the horse racing, gambling, and dancing that occupied much of the gentry's leisure time. Like the Quakers before them, they dressed plainly and simply, in contrast to the fashionable opulence of the gentry. Most strikingly of all, they addressed each other as "brother" and "sister" and organized their congregations on the basis of equality. And at least some Bap-

tist congregations included blacks as well as whites, which was truly revolutionary.

By midcentury the Great Awakening had injected an egalitarian strain into American life. Although primarily a religious movement, the Awakening also had important social and political consequences, calling into question habitual modes of behavior in the secular as well as the religious realm. By the 1750s, some Americans were challenging previously unassailed colonial authorities; during the next decade, Americans began to challenge English rule as well.

Suggestions for further reading

General

Patricia U. Bonomi, *A Factious People: Politics and Society in Colonial New York* (1971); Alice Hanson Jones, *Wealth of a Nation To Be: The American Colonies on the Eve of the Revolution* (1980); James A. Henretta, *The Evolution of American Society, 1700–1815* (1973); Richard Hofstadter, *America at 1750: A Social Portrait* (1971); Richard B. Morris, *Government and Labor in Early America* (1946); Robert V. Wells, *The Population of the British Colonies in America before 1776: A Survey of Census Data* (1975).

Rural society

Carl Bridenbaugh, *Myths and Realities: Societies of the Colonial South* (1963); Charles S. Grant, *Democracy in the Connecticut Frontier Town of Kent* (1961); Sung Bok Kim, *Landlord and Tenant in Colonial New York: Manorial Society, 1664–1775* (1978); Aubrey C. Land, "Economic Base and Social Structure: The Northern Chesapeake in the Eighteenth Century," *Journal of Economic History,* 25 (1965), 639–654; James T. Lemon, *The Best Poor Man's Country: A Geographical Study of Early Southeastern Pennsylvania* (1972); Michael Zuckerman, *Peaceable Kingdoms: New England Towns in the Eighteenth Century* (1970).

Urban society

Carl Bridenbaugh, *Cities in Revolt: Urban Life in America, 1743–1776* (1955); Gary B. Nash, *The Urban Crucible: Social Change, Political Consciousness, and the Origins of the American Revolution* (1979); Jacob M. Price, "Economic Function and the Growth of American Port Towns in the Eighteenth Century," *Perspectives in American History,* 8 (1974),

123–186; Frederick B. Tolles, *Meeting House and Counting House: The Quaker Merchants of Colonial Philadelphia 1682–1763* (1948); Stephanie Grauman Wolf, *Urban Village: Population, Community, and Family Structure in Germantown, Pennsylvania, 1683–1800* (1976).

Immigration

R.J. Dickson, *Ulster Immigration to Colonial America 1718–1775* (1966); Albert B. Faust, *The German Element in the United States,* 2 vols. (1909); Ian C.C. Graham, *Colonists from Scotland: Emigration to North America 1707–1783* (1956); Marcus L. Hanson, *The Atlantic Migration, 1607–1860: A History of the Continuing Settlement of America* (1940); James G. Leyburn, *The Scotch-Irish: A Social History* (1962).

Blacks

Ira Berlin, "Time, Space, and the Evolution of Afro-American Society in British Mainland America," *American Historical Review,* 85 (1980), 44–78; Allan Kulikoff, "The Origins of Afro-American Society in Tidewater Maryland and Virginia, 1700 to 1790," *William and Mary Quarterly,* 3rd ser., 35 (1978), 228–259; Gary D. Mills, "Coincoin: An Eighteenth-Century 'Liberated' Woman," *Journal of Southern History,* 42 (1976), 205–222; Gerald W. Mullin, *Flight and Rebellion: Slave Resistance in Eighteenth-Century Virginia* (1972).

Women and family

Nancy F. Cott, "Eighteenth-Century Family and Social Life Revealed in Massachusetts Divorce Records," *Journal of Social History,* 10 (1976), 20–43; J. William Frost, *The Quaker Family in Colonial America* (1972); Philip J. Greven, *The Protestant Temperament: Patterns of Child-Rearing, Religious Experience, and the Self in Early America* (1977); Alexander Keyssar, "Widowhood in Eighteenth-Century Massachusetts: A Problem in the History of the Family," *Perspectives in American History,* 8 (1974), 83–119; Mary Beth Norton, *Liberty's Daughters: The Revolutionary Experience of American Women 1750–1800* (1980); Daniel Blake Smith, *Inside the Great House: Planter Family Life in Eighteenth-Century Chesapeake Society* (1980); Daniel Scott Smith, "Parental Power and Marriage Patterns: An Analysis of Historical Trends in Hingham, Massachusetts," *Journal of Marriage and the Family,* 35 (1973), 419–428; Daniel Scott Smith and Michael Hindus, "Premarital Pregnancy in America, 1640–1971: An Overview and Interpretation," *Journal of Interdisciplinary History,* 5 (1975), 655–668.

Colonial culture and the Enlightenment

Daniel J. Boorstin, *The Americans: The Colonial Experience* (1958); Richard Crawford, "A Historian's Introduction to Early American Music," *Proceedings of American Antiquarian Society,* 89, 2 (1979), 261–298; Richard Beale Davis, *Intellectual Life in the Colonial South, 1585–1763,* 2 vols. (1978); Howard Mumford Jones, *O Strange New World. American Culture: The Formative Years* (1964); Michael Kraus, *The Atlantic Civilization–Eighteenth-Century Origins* (1949); Henry F. May, *The Enlightenment in America* (1976); Louis B. Wright, *The Cultural Life of the American Colonies, 1607–1763* (1957).

Education

James Axtell, *The School upon a Hill: Education and Society in Colonial New England* (1974); Bernard Bailyn, *Education in the Forming of American Society* (1960); Lawrence A. Cremin, *American Education: The Colonial Experience 1607–1783* (1970); Jurgen Herbst, "The First Three American Colleges: Schools of the Reformation," *Perspectives in American History,* 8 (1974), 7–52; Kenneth A. Lockridge, *Literacy in Colonial New England: An Inquiry into the Social Context of Literacy in the Early Modern West* (1974).

Science and medicine

Jane Donegan, *Women and Men Midwives: Medicine, Morality, and Misogyny in Early America* (1978); John Duffy, *Epidemics in Colonial America* (1953); Brooke Hindle, *The Pursuit of Science in Revolutionary America* (1956); Raymond P. Stearns, *Science in the British Colonies of America* (1970); Joan Hoff Wilson, "Dancing Dogs of the Colonial Period: Women Scientists," *Early American Literature,* 7 (1973), 225–235.

Religion and The Great Awakening

Carl Bridenbaugh, *Mitre and Sceptre: Transatlantic Faiths, Ideas, Personalities, and Politics, 1689–1775* (1962); J.M. Bumsted and John E. Van de Wetering, *What Must I Do To Be Saved? The Great Awakening in Colonial America* (1976); Edwin S. Gaustad, *The Great Awakening in New England* (1957); Alan E. Heimert, *Religion and the American Mind: From the Great Awakening to the Revolution* (1966); Rhys Isaac, "Evangelical Revolt: The Nature of the Baptists' Challenge to the Traditional Order in Virginia, 1765 to 1775," *William and Mary Quarterly,* 3rd ser., 31 (1974), 345–368; William C. McLoughlin, *New England Dissent, 1630–1833,* 2 vols. (1971); Sidney E. Mead, *The Lively Experiment: The Shaping of Christianity in America* (1963).

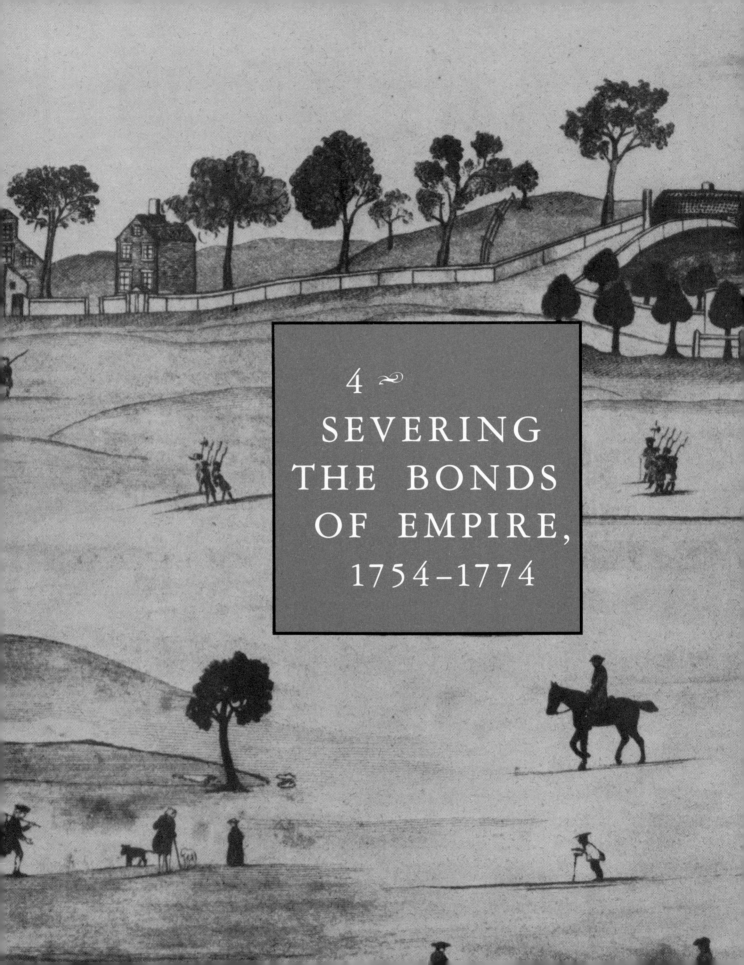

4 ∾

SEVERING
THE BONDS
OF EMPIRE,
1754–1774

"Who shall write the history of the American revolution?" John Adams wrote to Thomas Jefferson in 1815. "Who can write it? Who will ever be able to write it?" Adams and Jefferson were by this time old men, recently reconciled to their former friendship after decades of hostility caused by their political disagreements in the 1790s and early 1800s. The correspondence they had begun in 1812 ranged widely over a variety of topics, but repeatedly returned to the great events in which both had participated, the events that had led to the establishment of American independence. Adams took up the same theme three weeks later, asking Jefferson, "What do We Mean by the Revolution?" His own response to that question, Adams remarked, might be thought "peculiar, perhaps singular." To him, "the Revolution was in the Minds of the people, and this was effected, from 1760 to 1775, in the course of fifteen Years before a drop of blood was drawn at Lexington."

At first glance, Adams's statement does indeed seem peculiar. His view of what constituted the Revolution certainly differs from that held by most Americans today. To us, the Revolution was the war for independence fought from 1775 to 1783—a military, political, and constitutional struggle. To Adams, the Revolution was quite a different thing: it was the American colonists' change of heart about their traditional loyalty to the mother country. Adams's opinion has much to recommend it. In 1750 white colonists gloried in their identity as Britons. Just twenty-five years later, they were engaged in open revolt. What had caused the dramatic shift, a change so startling that it can be termed revolutionary?

The answer lies largely in the events of the two decades preceding the outbreak of war. To be sure, some friction had always marred the relationship between colonies and mother country. Disputes over charters, unpopular royal and proprietary policies, problems with the enforcement of customs regulations, and other such matters had frequently caused difficulties in the imperial relationship. Yet none of these disputes had involved more than one or two colonies, and few had lasted long.

Accordingly, no one on either side of the Atlantic was prepared for the explosive protests against parliamentary acts that began in the mid-1760s. Crisis followed crisis as the British government adopted, then repealed, a stamp tax and new trade duties; as Ameri-

cans clashed with British soldiers in the streets of Boston; as the colonists gradually became convinced that Britain intended to oppress them. Finally a decisive confrontation developed over the seemingly minor issue of a tea tax. To the Americans, that levy on tea had come to symbolize British tyranny. To officials in London, it was a sign of imperial authority. Neither side was willing to compromise, and so the final crisis developed.

Ironically, the event that may be said to have started the movement toward revolution was England's overwhelming victory in the worldwide war that ended in 1763. That victory altered the balance of power in America and fundamentally changed the nature of the British Empire. As a result, Parliament and successive ministries adopted a new approach to Britain's colonial possessions. It was in response to those measures that the North American colonists eventually turned to revolution.

1763: a turning point

Pontiac, the war chief of an Ottawa village near Detroit, was one of the first Americans to understand the changes wrought by the British triumph. A man of vision and commanding bearing, Pontiac had dedicated himself to promoting the welfare of his people. His reaction to Britain's victory was unhesitating. Using all his powers of persuasion, he forged an unprecedented alliance among the Ottawas and their neighbors. Then, in May and June 1763, combined bands of Hurons, Chippewas, Potawatomis, Iroquois, Delawares, and Shawnees launched devastating attacks on settlements and forts on the frontier. But why did the British triumph motivate Pontiac and his allies to take such a drastic step?

For hundreds of years Britain and France had fought each other in Europe. After they established outposts in North America, the continuing warfare enveloped their colonial possessions as well. The two countries were formally at war for nearly half of the three-quarters of a century between 1689 and 1763. Inhabitants of the colonies—white, black, and red alike—thus found themselves in-

Anglo-French warfare in the colonies

volved in armed struggles that had begun in Europe over such issues as France's attempts to expand its territory and the succession to the throne of Austria. These questions mattered little to Americans, but because they did care which nation controlled the chief portion of their continent, they fought willingly on England's side. In the colonies, the War of the League of Augsberg (1689–1697) was called King William's War, the War of the Spanish Succession (1702–1713) was Queen Anne's War, and the War of the Austrian Succession (1740–1748) was King George's War. All three conflicts were inconclusive; neither side was ever able to achieve an unqualified success in America or Europe.

In the colonies, most of the fighting took place along the coast and on the fringes of settlement, where the subjects of the two nations had the easiest access to each other. Since large-scale inland attacks were impractical in a wilderness with few roads, colonial militia and their Indian allies instead conducted swift raids on frontier settlements. In 1689, during King William's War, Iroquois warriors allied with the British destroyed a French village near Montreal. A year later a force of French and Indians retaliated by nearly wiping out the isolated community of Schenectady, New York; and in the winter of 1704, during Queen Anne's War, raiders devastated the Massachusetts town of Deerfield.

The major attacks launched during the three wars were seaborne, since both sides could transport men and weapons more easily on shipboard than by wagon or horseback. Accordingly, the English settlers obtained their most important victories through assaults from the sea. In 1690 they captured Port Royal in Nova Scotia. In 1745 they seized the fortress of Louisbourg on Cape Breton Island, particularly important because of its strategic position at the entrance to the St. Lawrence River, the lifeline of French settlement. (Both prizes were eventually returned to France in treaty negotiations.)

If the European disputes that started the three wars seemed irrelevant to white colonists, they were even less meaningful to American Indians. But the tribes reaped many advantages from the whites' quarrels. Above all, the Indians of the interior wanted to protect their territory from white settlement and to avoid the fate already suffered by their seacoast counterparts. Most of the tribes concluded that their goals could

best be achieved by maintaining outward neutrality and playing off the European powers against one another. Their strategy proved resoundingly successful—as long as the Europeans were evenly matched.

Therefore, after a brief alliance with the British during King William's War, the Iroquois Confederacy signed neutrality treaties with both sides (1701) and persisted in that neutrality for over fifty years. Two Iroquois tribes, though, did take sides: the Mohawks usually supported the British, while the Senecas favored the French. In the South the Creeks adopted a similar policy, maintaining formal nonalignment and placing some of their villages under the protection of the British, others under the Spanish. Since the English were the stronger threat, however, the Creeks commonly aided Britain's Indian enemies, such as the Yamasees, and attacked its Indian allies, especially the Cherokees.

The conditions that allowed the tribes to preserve the balance of power in the American interior ended forever with the close of the conflict known in Europe as the Seven Years' War, in America as the French and Indian War. What distinguished this war from its three predecessors was not only its decisive outcome, but also the fact that it began on the North American continent. For the first time a war spread to Europe from America rather than vice versa. Specifically, the war arose from the clash between England and France over which nation would dominate the land west of the Appalachian Mountains (see map, page 88). Because that land was the home of the interior tribes, they necessarily became involved in the struggle.

In 1753 the French began to push southward from Lake Erie into the Ohio country, building fortified outposts in a region previously inhabited only by Indians and occasional white traders. The French threat stimulated an intercolonial conference in June 1754. Encouraged by authorities in London, delegates from

Albany Congress

seven northern and middle colonies met with representatives of the Iroquois at Albany, New York, in an attempt to persuade the confederated Indian nations to ally themselves with the British. But the Albany Congress failed to convince the Iroquois tribes to abandon their traditional neutrality.

The delegates at Albany also adopted a Plan of Union designed to coordinate the defenses of the colonies. They proposed the establishment of an elected

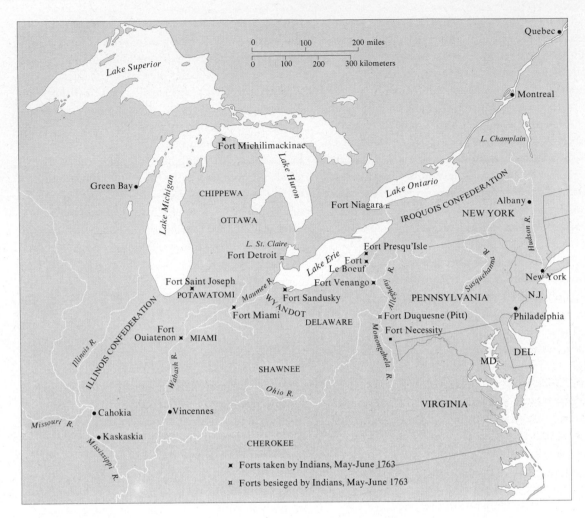

Forts taken by Indians, May-June 1763

Forts besieged by Indians, May-June 1763

The Northwest, 1754–1763

intercolonial legislature with the power to tax, headed by a president-general appointed by the king. But their home governments, fearing the resulting loss of autonomy, uniformly rejected the idea. The Congress thus failed to achieve its major objectives, but it did produce an enduring symbol of union. Benjamin Franklin, the delegate who wrote the first draft of the Plan of Union, published in his *Pennsylvania Gazette* the famous cartoon of a segmented snake captioned "Join, or Die." It was later to be reprinted many times by supporters of unified colonial resistance to Britain.

The delegates to the Congress did not know that, while they deliberated, the war they sought to prepare for was already beginning. Governor Robert Dinwiddie of Virginia had sent a small militia force west-

Beginning of the Seven Years' War

ward to counter the French moves. Virginia claimed ownership of the region that is now western Pennsylvania, and Dinwiddie was eager to prevent the French from establishing a permanent post there. But the Virginia militiamen arrived too late. The French had already taken possession of the strategic point—now Pittsburgh—where the Allegheny and Monongahela rivers meet to form the Ohio, and they were busily engaged in constructing Fort Duquesne. The foolhardy and inexperienced young colonel who commanded the Virginians allowed himself to be trapped by the French in his crudely built Fort Necessity at Great Meadows, Pennsylvania. After a day-long battle in which more than one-third of his men were killed or wounded, the twenty-two-year-old George Washington surrendered. He signed a document of capitulation, and he and his men were allowed to return to Virginia.

Washington had blundered grievously. He had started a war that would eventually encompass nearly the entire world. He had also ensured that the Indians of the Ohio Valley would for the most part support France in the coming conflict. The Indians took Washington's mistakes as an indication of Britain's inability to win the war, and nothing that occurred in the next four years made them change their minds. In 1755 a combined force of French and Indians ambushed General Edward Braddock, two regiments of British regulars, and some colonial troops a few miles south of Fort Duquesne. Braddock was killed and his men demoralized by their complete defeat. For three more years one disaster followed another for Great Britain. Everywhere the two sides clashed, the French were consistently victorious.

Finally, under the leadership of William Pitt, who was named secretary of state in 1757, the British mounted the effort that won them the war in North America. In July 1758 they recaptured the fortress at Louisbourg. In a surprise night attack in September 1759 they broke down the defenses of Quebec, a victory that gained them the Iroquois as allies. A year later the British took Montreal, the last French stronghold. The war in America ended then, though fighting continued for three more years in the Caribbean, India, and Europe. When the Treaty of Paris was finally signed in 1763, France ceded its major North American holdings to Britain. Spain, an ally of France toward the end of the war, gave Florida to the victorious English. And since Britain feared the presence of France in Louisiana, it forced the cession of that region to Spain, a weaker power. No longer would the English seacoast colonies have to worry about the threat to their existence posed by France's extensive North American territories.

In order to achieve this stunning victory, Pitt had had to alter many of the policies his predecessors had pursued in their dealings with the colonies. When the war began, the British intended to rely heavily on American enlistments. But Braddock's fate and later British defeats raised serious questions in the colonists' minds about London's ability to conduct the war. Enlistments lagged, and British officers adopted coercive

Franklin's Join, or Die cartoon, produced at the beginning of the French and Indian War, was used during the Revolution as a symbol of America's need to unite.   The Library Company of Philadelphia.

techniques to fill the ranks. In 1757, American crowds resisted forced recruitment in New York City and

Anglo-American tensions

elsewhere. Other clashes developed over the army's heavy-handed attempts to commandeer wagons and supplies from American farmers and merchants and to house troops in private homes wherever public accommodations were inadequate. Over the objections of local authorities, for example, householders in Albany, New York, were required to take in an average of seven soldiers each during the winter of 1756.

In 1758, Pitt acted to ease the strains that were threatening to disrupt the Anglo-American war effort. He agreed to reimburse the colonies for their military expenditures, and placed the recruitment of American troops in their hands. Each province could control both the number of soldiers to be recruited and the methods used to do so. The result was an immediate increase in the number and enthusiasm of colonial volunteers. The colonial governments, assured of financial aid from the mother country, began to devote more of their resources to the task of winning the war. At the same time, Pitt dispatched a large number of British regulars to the colonies. The well-trained redcoats did most of the actual fighting, with colonial militia relegated to support roles.

Pitt's measures won the war, but they also caused discord within the Anglo-American ranks. British commanders could not understand why the colonies seemed so reluctant to contribute to the war effort; they were especially angry at the merchants who continued to trade with the French West Indies and accused them of prolonging the conflict by supplying the enemy with food. Redcoat officers and enlisted men alike looked down on their American counterparts as undisciplined and ignorant of military procedures. As one arrogant colonel declared, "The Provincials [are] sufficient to work our Boats, drive our Waggons, and fell our Trees, and do the Work that in inhabited Countrys are performed by Peasants." For their part, the Americans resented the Britons' condescension, and soldiers and civilians both chafed at the restrictions imposed on their behavior by military regulations. In sum, even though the combined efforts of colonies and mother country resulted in victory, the first large-scale encounter between British regulars and American colonists was less than satisfactory to both sides.

Over the decade and a half following 1760, as the colonies and Great Britain moved slowly toward a confrontation, each drew on impressions of the other gained during the French and Indian War. The British dismissed any suggestion of American military prowess with a laugh, recalling the colonists' evident lack of fighting ability. The Americans, meanwhile, remembered the threat of arbitrary military power embodied in coercive recruiting, the seizure of supplies, and the quartering of troops in private homes. Nor had they forgotten the British officers' arrogance and their own wounded pride. In both cases the victorious alliance of colonies and mother country had done nothing to dispel—and possibly much to promote—the gathering clouds of disagreement.

It was several years before white colonists felt the full impact of the British victory in the French and Indian War. The Indians, however, felt it almost immediately. After 1760 they could no longer pursue their traditional balancing strategy, for France had been ousted from North America and Spain was too weak to pose a serious threat to British power. The Ottawas and their neighbors, the Chippewas and the Potawatomis, became angry when Britain, lacking competition, raised the price of trade goods and ended the French custom of giving them ammunition for hunting. Even more significantly, the British refused to pay the customary rent for forts established within tribal territory. They also permitted white settlers to move into the Monongahela and Susquehanna valleys, which belonged to the Iroquois and Delawares. Thus the British signalled their disregard for Indian claims to sovereignty over the interior.

Pontiac, the Ottawa chief who realized the meaning of the British victory, had been a loyal ally of the French since the 1740s. When he organized the Indian alliance in the spring of 1763, he was probably in his midforties and at the height of his power and prestige. Pontiac planned to seize the fort at Detroit through a ruse, but failed when an informer betrayed his plot. In early May, he laid siege to the fort while his war parties attacked the other British outposts in the Great Lakes region. Detroit withstood the siege, but by the end of June all the other forts west of Niagara and north of Fort Pitt (old Fort Duquesne) had fallen to the Indian alliance.

Pontiac's uprising

That was the high point of the uprising. The tribes raided the Virginia and Pennsylvania frontiers at will throughout the summer, killing at least two thousand whites. But they could not take the strongholds of Niagara, Fort Pitt, or Detroit. In early August, a combined force of Delawares, Shawnees, Hurons, and Mingoes (Pennsylvania Iroquois) was soundly defeated at Bushy Run, Pennsylvania, by troops sent from the coast. Conflict ceased when Pontiac broke off the siege of Detroit in late October, after most of his warriors had returned to their villages. A formal treaty ending the war was finally negotiated in 1766.

In the aftermath of the bloody summer of 1763, white frontiersmen from Paxton Township, Pennsylvania, sought revenge on the only Indians within reach, a peaceful band of Christian converts living at Conestoga. In December the whites raided the Indian village twice, killing twenty people. Two months later hundreds of frontier dwellers known to history as the Paxton Boys marched on Philadelphia to demand military protection against future Indian attacks. City officials feared violence and mustered the militia to repel the westerners, but the protesters presented their request in an orderly fashion and returned home.

Pontiac's uprising and the march of the Paxton Boys showed that Great Britain would not find it easy to govern the huge territory it had just acquired from

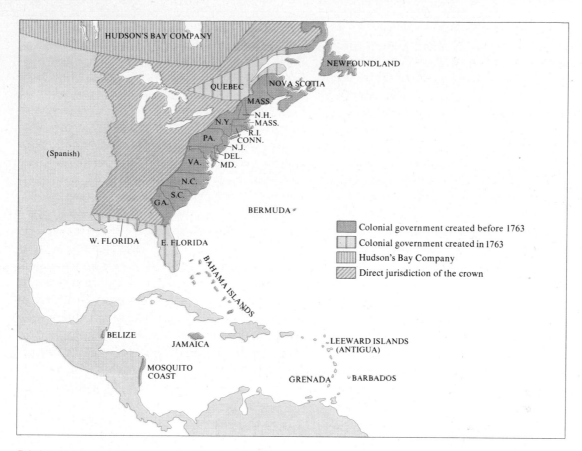

 shows a map with the following labels:

HUDSON'S BAY COMPANY

NEWFOUNDLAND

QUEBEC   NOVA SCOTIA

MASS.

N.H.
N.Y. — MASS.
        R.I.
PA.   CONN.
        N.J.
        DEL.
VA.   MD.

N.C.

S.C.

GA.

(Spanish)

BERMUDA

W. FLORIDA   E. FLORIDA

BAHAMA ISLANDS

BELIZE

JAMAICA

LEEWARD ISLANDS
(ANTIGUA)

MOSQUITO
COAST

GRENADA   BARBADOS

Legend:
- Colonial government created before 1763
- Colonial government created in 1763
- Hudson's Bay Company
- Direct jurisdiction of the crown

Britain's American empire after the Proclamation of 1763

France. The central administration in London had had no prior experience in managing such a vast tract of land, particularly one inhabited by two hostile peoples—the remaining French settlers along the St. Lawrence and the many Indian tribes. In October, in a futile attempt to assert control over the interior, the

Proclamation of 1763

ministry issued the Proclamation of 1763, which declared the headwaters of rivers flowing into the Atlantic from the Appalachian Mountains to be the temporary western boundary for colonial settlement (see map). The proclamation was intended to prevent future clashes between Indians and colonists by forbidding whites to move onto Indian lands until the tribes had given up their land by treaty. But many whites had already established farms west of the proclamation line, and the policy was doomed to failure from its outset.

The beginnings of colonial protest

At the close of the war George Grenville, who had been named prime minister, and George III, who became king in 1760, faced an immediate problem: Britain's immense war debt. The figures were staggering. England's burden of indebtedness had nearly doubled since 1754, from £73 million to £137 million. Annual expenditures before the war had amounted to no more than £8 million; now the yearly interest on the debt alone came to £5 million. Clearly Grenville's ministry had to find new sources of funds, and the English people themselves were already heavily taxed. Since the colonists had been major beneficiaries of the wartime expenditures, Grenville concluded that the Americans should be asked to pay a greater share of the cost of running the empire.

When Grenville decided to tax the colonies, he did not stop to consider whether Parliament had the authority to do so. Like all his countrymen, he believed that the government's legitimacy derived ultimately from the consent of the people, but he defined consent far more loosely than did the colonists. Americans had come to believe that they could be represented only by men for whom they or their property-holding neighbors had actually voted; otherwise they could not count on legislators to be faithful to their interests. To Grenville and his English contemporaries, however, Parliament by definition represented all English subjects, wherever they resided and whether or not they could vote. According to this theory of government, called *virtual representation,* the colonists were said to be virtually, if not actually, represented in Parliament. Thus their consent to acts of Parliament could be presumed.

Theories of representation

With regard to the basis for a government's legitimacy, in other words, the Americans and the English began at the same theoretical starting-point, but arrived at different conclusions in practice. In England, members of Parliament were viewed as representing the entire nation, whatever constituency elected them. (Indeed, some districts had few or no inhabitants; holders of those seats in the House of Commons were hand-picked by the king or local nobles.) In the colonies, by contrast, members of the lower houses of the assemblies were expected to speak for the particular voters who had chosen them. Before Grenville proposed to tax the colonists, the two notions existed side by side without apparent contradiction. But the events of the 1760s pointed up the difference between the English and colonial definitions of representation.

The same events threw into sharp relief Americans' attitudes toward political power. The colonists had become accustomed to a government that wielded only limited authority over them and affected their daily lives very little. In consequence, they believed that a good government was one that largely left them alone, a view in keeping with the theories of a group of British writers known as the Real Whigs. Drawing on a tradition of English dissenting thought that reached back to the days of the Civil War in the mid-seventeenth century, the Real Whigs stressed the dangers inherent in a powerful government, particularly one headed by a monarch. They warned that

the people had to guard constantly against the government's attempts to encroach on their liberties. Political power, wrote John Trenchard and Thomas Gordon in their essay series *Cato's Letters* (originally published in England in 1720–1723 and reprinted many times thereafter in the colonies), was always to be feared. Rulers would try to corrupt and oppress the people. Only the perpetual vigilance of the people and their elected representatives could possibly preserve their fragile yet very precious freedoms.

Britain's attempts to tighten the reins of colonial government in the 1760s and early 1770s convinced many Americans that the Real Whigs' reasoning applied to their circumstances. They began to interpret British measures in light of the Real Whigs' warnings, and to see evil designs behind the actions of Grenville and his successors. Historians disagree over the extent to which those perceptions were correct, but by 1775 a large number of colonists unquestionably believed they were. In the mid-1760s, the colonists did not, however, immediately accuse Grenville of an intent to oppress them. They at first simply questioned the utility of the new laws.

The first such measures, the Sugar and Currency Acts, were passed by Parliament in 1764. The Sugar Act revised the existing system of customs regulations; laid new duties on certain foreign imports into the colonies; established a vice-admiralty court at Halifax, Nova Scotia; and included special provisions aimed at stopping the widespread smuggling of molasses, one of the chief commodities in American trade. The Currency Act in effect outlawed colonial issues of paper money. (For years, the colonies had printed their own money to supplement the private bills of exchange that circulated chiefly among merchants.) Americans could accumulate little hard cash, since they imported more than they exported; thus the act seemed to the colonists to deprive them of the means of doing business.

Sugar and Currency Acts

The Sugar and Currency Acts were visited upon an economy already in the midst of depression. A business boom had accompanied the French and Indian War, but the brief spell of prosperity had ended abruptly in 1760, when the war shifted overseas. Urban merchants could not sell all their imported goods to colonial customers alone, and without the military's demand for foodstuffs, American farmers found

Chapter 4: Severing the bonds of empire, 1754–1774

fewer buyers for their products. The bottom dropped out of the European tobacco market, threatening the livelihood of Chesapeake planters. Sailors were thrown out of work and onto the streets of port cities, and artisans found few employers to hire them. In such circumstances, the prospect of increased customs duties and inadequate supplies of currency naturally aroused merchants' hostility.

It is not surprising that both individual colonists and colonial governments decided to protest the new policies. But, lacking any precedent for a united campaign against acts of Parliament, Americans in 1764 took only hesitant and uncoordinated steps. Eight colonial legislatures sent separate petitions to Parliament requesting repeal of the Sugar Act. They argued that the act placed severe restrictions on their commerce (and would therefore hurt Britain as well), and that they had not consented to its passage. They also instructed their agents in London to lobby against another proposed levy, the stamp tax.

That tax was modeled on a law that had been in effect in England for nearly a century. It would touch nearly every colonist by requiring tax stamps on most printed materials. Anyone who purchased a news-

| Stamp Act | paper or pamphlet, made a will, transferred land, bought dice or

playing cards, needed a liquor license, accepted a government appointment, or borrowed money would have to pay the tax. Never before had a revenue measure of such scope been proposed for the colonies. The act would also require that tax stamps be paid for with hard money and that violators be tried in vice-admiralty courts, without juries. Finally, such a law would break decisively with the colonial tradition of self-imposed taxation.

The most important colonial pamphlet protesting the Sugar Act and the proposed stamp act was *The Rights of the British Colonies Asserted and Proved,* by James Otis, Jr., a brilliant young Massachusetts attorney who later went insane. Otis starkly exposed the ideological dilemma that was to confound the colonists for the next decade. How could they justify their opposition to certain acts of Parliament without questioning Parliament's authority over them? On the one hand, Otis asserted that Americans were "entitled to all the natural, essential, inherent, and inseparable rights" of Britons, including the right not to be taxed without their consent. "No man or body of men, not

Test impressions of one of the tax stamps intended for use in America. Inland Review Library.

excepting the parliament . . . can take [those rights] away," he declared. On the other hand, Otis was forced to admit that, under the British system, "the power of parliament is uncontrollable, but by themselves, and we must obey. . . . Let the parliament lay what burthens they please on us, we must, it is our duty to submit and patiently bear them, till they will be pleased to relieve us."

Otis's first contention, drawing on colonial notions of representation, implied that Parliament could not constitutionally tax the colonies because Americans were not represented in its ranks. Yet his second point both acknowledged political reality and accepted the prevailing theory of British government—that Parliament was the sole, supreme authority in the empire. Even unconstitutional laws enacted by Parliament had to be obeyed until Parliament decided to repeal them. According to orthodox British political theory, there could be no middle ground between absolute submission to Parliament and a frontal challenge to its authority. Otis tried to find such a middle ground by proposing colonial representation in Parliament, but his idea was never taken seriously on either side of the Atlantic. The British believed that the colonists were already virtually represented in Parliament, and the Americans quickly realized that a handful of colonial delegates to London would simply be outvoted.

The Stamp Act crisis

When Americans learned of the passage of the Stamp Act in the spring of 1765, they did not at first know how to proceed. Few colonists publicly favored the law; opposition to it was nearly universal, even among government officials. But the colonists had already failed to prevent its adoption, and further lobbying appeared futile. Perhaps Otis was right, and the only course open to them was to pay the stamp tax, reluctantly but loyally. Acting on that assumption, colonial agents in London sought the appointment of their American friends as stamp distributors, so that the law would at least be enforced equitably.

Not all the colonists were resigned, however, to paying the new tax without a fight. One who was not was a twenty-nine-year-old lawyer serving his first term as a member of the Virginia House of Burgesses. Patrick Henry later recalled that he was at the time "young, inexperienced, unacquainted with the forms *Patrick Henry* of the House and the members that composed it," and appalled by his fellow legislators' unwillingness to oppose the Stamp Act openly. Henry decided to act. "Alone, unadvised, and unassisted, on a blank leaf of an old law book," he wrote the Virginia Stamp Act Resolves.

Little in Henry's earlier life foreshadowed his success in the political arena he entered so dramatically. The son of a prosperous Scottish immigrant to western Virginia, Henry had had little formal education. After marrying at eighteen, he failed at both farming and storekeeping before turning to the law as a means of supporting his wife and their six children. Henry

lacked legal training, but his oratorical skills made him an effective advocate, first for his clients and later for his political beliefs. As a prominent Virginia lawyer wrote in 1774, "He is by far the most powerful speaker I ever heard. Every word he says not only engages, but commands the attention; and your passions are no longer your own when he addresses them."

Patrick Henry introduced his proposals in late May, near the end of the legislative session; many members of the House of Burgesses had already departed for home. Henry's fiery speech in support of his resolutions led the Speaker of the House to accuse him of treason. (Henry quickly denied the charge, contrary to the nineteenth-century myth that had him exclaiming in reply, "If this be treason, make the most of it!") The small number of burgesses remaining in Williamsburg formally adopted five of Henry's resolutions by a bare majority. Though they repealed the most radical resolution the next day, their action had far-reaching effects. Some colonial newspapers printed Henry's seven original resolutions as if they had been uniformly passed by the House, even though one had been rescinded and two others were evidently never debated or voted on at all.

The four propositions adopted by the burgesses resembled the arguments James Otis had advanced the previous year. The colonists had never forfeited the rights of British subjects, they declared, and consent to taxation was one of the most important of those rights. The other three resolutions went much further. The one that was repealed claimed for the burgesses "the only exclusive right" to tax Virginians. The final two asserted that residents of the colony did not have to obey tax laws passed by other legislative bodies (namely Parliament) and termed any opponent of that opinion "an Enemy to this his Majesty's Colony."

The burgesses' decision to accept only the first four of Henry's resolutions was a clear expression of the position most Americans took throughout the following decade. Though willing to contend for their rights, the colonists did not seek independence. They merely wanted some measure of self-government. Accordingly they backed away from the dangerous assertions that they owed Parliament no obedience and that their own assemblies alone could tax them. Indeed, declared the Maryland lawyer Daniel Dulany, whose *Considerations on the Propriety of Imposing Taxes on the British Colonies* was the most widely read pamphlet of 1765, "The colonies are dependent upon Great Britain, and the supreme authority vested in the king, lords, and commons, may justly be exercised to secure, or preserve their dependence." But, warned Dulany, a superior did not have the right "to seize the property of his inferior when he pleases"; there was a crucial distinction between a condition of "dependence and *inferiority*" and one of "absolute *vassalage and slavery.*"

Over the course of the next ten years, Americans searched for a political formula that would enable them to control their internal affairs, especially taxation, but remain within the British Empire. The chief difficulty lay in British officials' inability to compromise on the issue of parliamentary power. The notion that Parliament could exercise absolute authority over all colonial possessions was basic to the orthodox British theory of government. Even the harshest British critics of the ministry's colonial policy questioned only the wisdom of that policy, not the principles on which it was based. In effect, the Americans wanted British leaders to revise their fundamental understanding of the workings of their government. That was simply too much to expect, given the circumstances.

The ultimate effectiveness of Americans' opposition to the Stamp Act did not rest on ideological arguments over parliamentary power. What gave the resistance its primary force were the decisive and inventive actions of the colonists during the late summer and fall of 1765.

In August the Loyal Nine, a Boston social club of printers, distillers, and other artisans, organized a demonstration against the Stamp Act. Hoping to show

| Loyal Nine |

that people of all social and economic ranks opposed the act, they approached the leaders of the city's rival laborers' associations, the North End and South End mobs. The two mobs, composed of unskilled workers and poor tradesmen, often fought pitched battles with each other, but the Loyal Nine convinced them to lay aside their differences and participate in the demonstration. After all, the stamp taxes would have to be paid by all colonists, not just affluent ones.

Early in the morning of August 14, the demonstrators hung an effigy of Andrew Oliver, the province's stamp distributor, from a tree on Boston Common.

That night a large crowd led by a group of about fifty well-dressed tradesmen paraded the effigy around the city. The crowd tore down a small building they thought was intended as the stamp office and built a bonfire with the wood near Oliver's house. They then beheaded the effigy and added it to the flames. Members of the crowd broke most of Oliver's windows—an apparently unplanned gesture—and threw stones at officials who tried to disperse them. In the midst of the melee, the North End and South End leaders drank a toast to their successful union. The Loyal Nine's demonstration achieved its objective when Oliver publicly promised not to fulfill the duties of his office. One Bostonian jubilantly told a relative, "I believe people never was more Universally pleased not so much as one could I hear say he was sorry, but a smile sat on almost every ones countinance."

But another crowd action twelve days later, aimed this time at Oliver's brother-in-law Lieutenant Governor Thomas Hutchinson, drew no praise from the respectable citizens of Boston. On the night of August 26, a mob reportedly led by the South End leader, Ebenezer MacIntosh, attacked the homes of several customs officers. The crowd then completely destroyed Hutchinson's elaborately furnished townhouse in one of Boston's most fashionable districts. The lieutenant governor reported that by the next morning "one of the best finished houses in the Province had nothing remaining but the bare walls and floors." His trees and garden were ruined as well, and the mob had "emptied the house of every thing whatsoever except a part of the kitchen furniture." But Hutchinson took some comfort in the fact that "the encouragers of the first mob never intended matters should go this length and the people in general express the utmost detestation of this unparalleled outrage."

Thoughtful residents of other colonies drew two important conclusions from the Boston mob actions of August 14 and 26. First, they realized that they could prevent enforcement of the Stamp Act simply by imitating the Bostonians and forcing the stamp distributors (one for each colony) to resign. Second, they recognized the danger of inciting mob action to achieve their goals. Although mobs could be useful, they would have to be carefully controlled to avoid the kind of excessive violence that had destroyed Hutchinson's house.

The Stamp Act crisis

This woodcut, produced half a century after the event, shows a crowd parading the effigy of the New Hampshire stamp distributor through the streets of Portsmouth in 1765. The procession is led, as it was in many cities, by men carrying a coffin to symbolize the death and burial of the Stamp Act.   The Metropolitan Museum of Art, Bequest of Charles Allen Munn.

The Stamp Act controversy drew disfranchised Americans into the vortex of imperial politics for the first time. Lower-class whites, blacks, and even women began to participate in public discussions and demonstrations. Such people had long expressed their opinions on local issues, often through crowd action, but never before had they been aroused by broad questions of imperial policy. In 1765, though, as Sally Franklin wrote to her father Benjamin, then serving as a colonial agent in London, "nothing else is talked of, the Dutch [Germans] talk of the stompt act the Negroes of the tamp, in short every body has something to say."

The aims of such newly politicized Americans were often quite different from those of resistance leaders. The Loyal Nine had accomplished their end when Oliver agreed not to distribute stamps, but the Boston crowd had its own goals. Chief among them seems to have been a desire to punish the haughty

Hutchinson for his ostentatious display of wealth, in a city whose average citizen's share of the economic pie had steadily decreased since about 1750. Hutchinson's losses that night amounted to more than £900 sterling; most personal estates in Boston at the time were worth less than £30. Although Hutchinson was erroneously believed to be a supporter of the Stamp Act, his self-advertised wealth probably contributed significantly to motivating the crowd's "hellish Fury."

The Loyal Nine's tactics were immediately imitated elsewhere in the colonies. The organizers of subsequent anti-Stamp Act demonstrations made certain, however, that crowds remained orderly. They were so successful that by November 1, when the law was scheduled to go into effect, not a single stamp distributor was willing to carry out the duties of his office. To coordinate their efforts at directing opposition into acceptable channels, resistance leaders throughout the colonies formed an association known as the Sons of

Liberty. The first such group was created in New York City in early November, and branches spread rapidly through the colonies.

Sons of Liberty

Largely composed of merchants, lawyers, prosperous tradesmen, and the like, the Sons of Liberty linked resistance leaders in cities from Charleston, South Carolina, to Portsmouth, New Hampshire, by early 1766 (see map).

But not even the Sons of Liberty could control all reactions in the new climate of protest. In Charleston in late October 1765 an organized crowd shouting "Liberty Liberty and stamp'd paper" forced the resignation of the South Carolina stamp distributor. The event was celebrated a few days later in the largest demonstration the city had ever known, at which was displayed a British flag with the word LIBERTY written across it. But white resistance leaders were horrified when in January 1766 local slaves paraded through the streets similarly crying "Liberty." The local militia was mustered, messengers were sent to outlying areas with warnings of a possible plot, and one black was banished from the colony.

In Philadelphia, resistance leaders were dismayed when an angry mob threatened to attack Benjamin Franklin's house. The city's laborers believed Franklin to be partly responsible for the Stamp Act, since he had obtained the post of stamp distributor for a close friend. But Philadelphia's artisans—the backbone of the opposition movement there and elsewhere—were fiercely loyal to Franklin, one of their own who had made good. They gathered to protect his home and family from the crowd. The house was saved, but the resulting split between the better-off tradesmen and the common laborers prevented Philadelphians from establishing a successful workingmen's alliance like that of Boston.

During the fall and winter of 1765 and 1766, opposition to the Stamp Act proceeded on three separate fronts. The colonial legislatures petitioned Parliament to repeal the hated law and sent delegates to an intercolonial congress, the first since 1754. In October the Stamp Act Congress met in New York to draft a unified but relatively conservative statement of protest. At the same time, the Sons of Liberty held mass meetings in an effort to win public support for the resistance movement. Finally, American merchants organized nonimportation associations to put economic pressure on British exporters. Recognizing that the

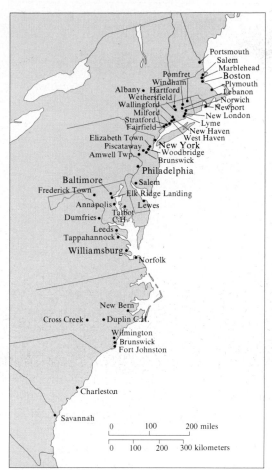

Stamp Act crisis.   Source: Reprinted by permission of Princeton University Press.

The Stamp Act crisis   97

colonial market contributed greatly to the exporters' profits, they reasoned that London merchants whose sales suffered would lobby for repeal. Since times were bad and American merchants were finding few customers for imported goods in any case, a general moratorium on future purchases would also help to reduce their bloated inventories.

In March 1766, Parliament repealed the Stamp Act. The nonimportation agreements had had the antici-

| Repeal of the Stamp Act |

pated effect, creating allies within the powerful circle of wealthy London merchants. But boycotts, formal protests, and crowd actions were less important in winning repeal than was Grenville's replacement as prime minister in summer 1765. Lord Rockingham, the new minister, had opposed the Stamp Act, not because Parliament lacked power to tax the colonies but because he thought the law unwise and divisive. Thus, although Rockingham proposed repeal, he linked it to passage of the Declaratory Act, which asserted Parliament's ability to tax and legislate for Britain's American possessions "in all cases whatsoever."

News of the repeal arrived in Newport, Rhode Island, in May, and the Sons of Liberty quickly transmitted the welcome tidings to all parts of the colonies. They also organized many celebrations commemorating the glorious event, all of which stressed the Americans' unwavering loyalty to Great Britain. Their goal achieved, the Sons of Liberty dissolved. Few colonists recognized the ominous implications of the Declaratory Act.

Resistance to the Townshend Acts

The colonists had accomplished their aim, but they had not developed a consistent ideological defense against parliamentary taxation. Some had raised the basic question of consent, others had objected primarily to the amount of taxation, and still others had criticized the type of tax chosen. Yet Benjamin Franklin confidently assured a parliamentary committee that Americans uniformly acknowledged Parliament's unlimited right to regulate their trade, even while they rejected internal taxes. Charles Townshend, a Grenvil-

lite who became chancellor of the exchequer in the coalition ministry that succeeded Rockingham's in the summer of 1766, decided to use Franklin's erroneous statement as a means of obtaining additional funds from the colonies.

The new taxes Townshend proposed in 1767 were levied on trade goods like paper, glass, and tea, and thus seemed on the surface to be nothing more than

| Townshend Acts |

extensions of the existing Navigation Acts. But the Townshend duties differed from previous customs taxes in two ways. First, they were levied on items imported into the colonies from Britain, not from foreign countries. Thus they were at odds with mercantilist theory. Second, they were designed to raise money, not to regulate the availability and use of certain commodities in America. The receipts, moreover, would pay the salaries of royal officials in the colonies. That posed a direct challenge to the colonial assemblies, which derived considerable power from threatening to withhold officials' salaries. In addition, Townshend's scheme provided for the establishment of an American Board of Customs Commissioners and for the creation of vice-admiralty courts at Boston, Philadelphia, and Charleston. Both moves angered merchants, whose profits would be threatened by more vigorous enforcement of the Navigation Acts. Lastly, Townshend proposed the appointment of a secretary of state for American affairs and the suspension of the New York legislature for refusal to comply with an act requiring colonial governments to supply certain items (like firewood and candles) to British troops stationed permanently in America.

Unlike 1765, when months passed before the colonists began to protest the Stamp Act, the Townshend Acts drew a quick response. One series of essays in particular, *Letters from a Farmer in Pennsylvania* by the prominent lawyer John Dickinson, expressed a consensus that had not existed two years earlier. Eventually all but four colonial newspapers printed Dickinson's essays; in pamphlet form they went through at least seven American editions. Dickinson contended that Parliament could regulate colonial trade, but could not exercise that power for the purpose of raising revenues. He thus avoided the complicated question of colonial consent to parliamentary legislation. But his argument had another flaw: it was clearly unworkable for Americans to assess Parliament's motives

Silver bowl crafted for the Sons of Liberty by Paul Revere in 1768 to commemorate the ninety-two members of the Massachusetts House of Representatives who refused to rescind the circular letter.   Museum of Fine Arts, Boston, Gift by Subscription and Francis Bartlett Fund.

for passing a trade law before deciding whether to obey it.

The Massachusetts assembly responded to the acts by drafting a circular letter to the other colonial legislatures, calling for unity and suggesting a joint petition of protest to the king. It was less the letter itself than the ministry's reaction to it that united the colonies. When Lord Hillsborough, the first secretary of state for America, learned of the circular letter, he ordered Governor Francis Bernard of Massachusetts to insist that the assembly recall it. He also directed other governors to prevent their assemblies from discussing the letter. Hillsborough's order gave the colonial assemblies the incentive they needed to forget their differences and join forces to meet the new threat to their prerogatives. In late 1768 the Massachusetts legislature met, debated, and resoundingly rejected recall by a vote of 92 to 17. Bernard immediately dissolved the assembly, and other governors followed suit when their legislatures debated the circular letter.

> *Massachusetts assembly dissolved*

The figure 45 had become a symbol of resistance to Great Britain when John Wilkes, a radical Englishman sympathetic to the American cause, had been jailed for libel because of his publication of the essay *The North Briton No. 45.* Now 92, the number of votes cast against recalling the circular letter, assumed ritual significance as well. In Charleston, the city's tradesmen decorated a tree with 45 lights and set off 45 rockets. Carrying 45 candles, they adjourned to a tavern whose tables were set with 45 bowls of wine, 45 bowls of punch, and 92 glasses. In Newport, 45 members of the revived Sons of Liberty dined on 45 dishes and drank 92 toasts. And in Boston, the silversmith Paul Revere made a punchbowl weighing 45 ounces, which held 45 gills (half-cups) and was engraved with the names of the 92 legislators; James Otis, John Adams, and others drank 45 toasts from it. (Not surprisingly, newspapers often described these affairs as having been full of "mirth and jollity.")

Pleasant social occasions though they were, such public rituals served an important educational function. Many colonists—especially men in the lower

example, a Maryland nonimportation agreement identified its signers as "Merchants, Traders, Free-holders, Mechanics [artisans], and other Inhabitants" of the colony, all of whom agreed not to import or consume certain British goods. As a result of these tactics, an increasing number of Americans found themselves aligned in a united cause.

Even women, who had previously regarded politics as outside their proper sphere, joined in the formal resistance movement. In towns throughout America, young women calling themselves Daughters of Liberty met to spin in public, in an effort to spur other

A Society of Patriotic Ladies, painted by Philip Dawes(?) in 1775. A disapproving Briton produced this grotesque caricature of female patriots. At left the women empty their tea canisters into a chamber pot. The cartoon bears no resemblance to the actual event, the signing of an anti-British petition by female residents of Edenton, North Carolina.   Library of Congress.

| Daughters of Liberty |

women to make homespun and end the colonies' dependence on English cloth. These symbolic displays of patriotism, often held in the minister's house, served the same purpose as the male rituals involving the numbers 45 and 92. When young ladies from well-to-do families sat publicly at spinning wheels all day, eating only American food and drinking herbal tea, and afterwards listening to patriotic sermons, they were serving as political instructors. Many women took great satisfaction in their new-found role. When a New England satirist hinted that women discussed only "such triffling subjects as Dress, Scandal and Detraction" during their spinning bees, three Boston women replied angrily: "Inferior in abusive sarcasm, in personal invective, in low wit, we glory to be, but inferior in veracity, sincerity, love of virtue, of liberty and of our country, we would not willingly be to any."

Women also took the lead in promoting non-consumption of tea. In Boston more than three hundred matrons publicly promised not to drink tea, "Sickness excepted." The women of Wilmington, North Carolina, burned their tea after walking through town in a solemn procession. Housewives throughout the colonies exchanged recipes for tea substitutes or drank coffee instead. The best known of the protests (because it was satirized by a British cartoonist), the so-called Edenton Ladies Tea Party, actually had little to do with tea; it was a meeting of prominent North Carolina women who pledged formally to work for the public good and to support resistance to British measures.

Not all Americans acquiesced in nonimportation. Many merchants continued to import British goods,

ranks of society and most women—could neither read nor write, and they learned about political issues not by reading closely reasoned pamphlets but by watching and participating in public activities. When Boston's Sons of Liberty invited hundreds of the city's residents to dine with them each August 14 to commemorate the first Stamp Act uprising, and the Charleston Sons of Liberty held their meetings in public, crowds gathered to watch and listen. The participants in such events were openly expressing their commitment to the cause of resistance and encouraging others to join them.

During the two-year campaign against the Townshend duties, the Sons of Liberty and other American leaders made a deliberate effort to broaden the base of the resistance movement. In addition to asking merchants not to import British products, they urged ordinary citizens not to buy them. In June 1769, for

Chapter 4: Severing the bonds of empire, 1754–1774

some as a matter of principle and others for economic reasons. The earlier boycotts of 1765 and 1766 had helped to revive a depressed economy; but in 1768 and 1769 merchants were enjoying boom times and had no financial incentive to support a boycott. In the commercial cities of the North and in Charleston in the South, merchants signed the agreements only reluctantly. Artisans, on the other hand, supported nonimportation enthusiastically, recognizing that the absence of British goods would create a ready market for their own manufactures. Thus tradesmen formed the core of the crowds that coerced both importers and their customers by picketing stores, publicizing offenders' names, and sometimes destroying property.

Such tactics were effective: colonial imports from England dropped dramatically in 1769 (see figure), especially in New York, New England, and Pennsylvania. But they also aroused significant opposition. Some Americans who supported resistance to British measures began to question the use of violence to force others to join the boycott. The wealthier and more conservative colonists were frightened by the threat to private property inherent in the campaign. Moreover, political activism on the part of colonists who had once deferred to the judgment of their superiors posed a threat to the local ruling classes. In 1769 a Charleston essayist warned that "the industrious mechanic [is] a useful and essential part of society . . . in his own sphere," but "when he steps out of it, and sets up for a statesman! believe me he is in a fair way to expose himself to ridicule, and his family to distress, by neglecting his private business." Pretending concern for tradesmen's welfare, the author obviously feared for his own position in society.

All Americans were relieved when the news arrived in April 1770 that a new prime minister, Lord North, had persuaded Parliament to repeal the Townshend duties, except the tea tax, on the grounds that duties on trade within the empire were bad policy. Although the more radical Americans argued that nonimportation should be maintained until even the tea tax was repealed, merchants quickly resumed importing. The rest of the Townshend Acts remained in force, but repeal of the taxes made the other laws appear less objectionable to the colonists.

Repeal of the Townshend duties

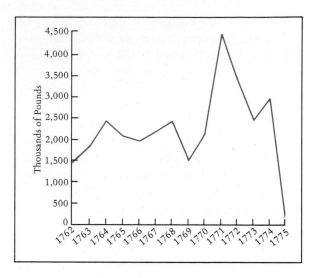

Goods exported to the thirteen colonies, 1762–1775. Source: Adapted from John J. McCusker, "The Current Value of English Exports, 1677 to 1800," *William and Mary Quarterly, 28* (October 1971), Table IIIc, pp. 625–626.

Growing rifts

At first the new ministry did nothing to antagonize the colonists. Yet on the very day Lord North proposed repeal of the Townshend duties, a clash between civilians and soldiers in Boston led to the death of five Americans. The origins of the event patriots called the Boston Massacre lay in repeated clashes between customs officers and the people of Massachusetts. The Townshend Acts' creation of an American Board of Customs Commissioners had been error enough, but basing it in Boston severely compounded the mistake.

From the day of their arrival in November 1767, the customs commissioners were frequent targets of mob action. In June 1768, their seizure of the patriot leader John Hancock's sloop *Liberty* on suspicion of smuggling caused a violent riot in which prominent customs officers' property was destroyed. The riot in turn helped to convince the ministry in London that troops were needed to maintain order in the unruly port. The assignment of two regiments of regulars to their city confirmed Bostonians' worst fears; the redcoats were a constant reminder of the oppressive potential of British power.

Bostonians, accustomed to leading their lives with a minimum of interference from government, now found themselves hemmed in at every turn. Guards on Boston Neck, the entrance to the city, checked all travelers and their goods. Redcoat patrols roamed the city day and night, questioning and sometimes harassing passers-by. Military parades were held on Boston Common, accompanied by loud martial music and often the brutal public whipping of deserters and other violators of army rules. Parents began to fear for the safety of their daughters, who were subjected to the soldiers' coarse sexual insults when they ventured out on the streets. But the greatest potential for violence lay in the uneasy relationship between the soldiers and Boston laborers. Many redcoats sought employment in their off-duty hours, competing for unskilled jobs with the city's ordinary workingmen, and members of the two groups brawled repeatedly in taverns and on the streets.

On March 2, 1770, workers at a ropewalk (a ship-rigging factory) attacked some redcoats seeking jobs; a pitched battle resulted when both groups acquired reinforcements. Three days later, the tension exploded. Early on the evening of March 5, a crowd began throwing hard-packed snowballs at sentries *Boston Massacre* guarding the Customs House. Goaded beyond endurance, the sentries fired on the crowd against express orders to the contrary, killing four and wounding eight, one of whom died a few days later. Among the dead were Samuel Maverick, Ebenezer MacIntosh's brother-in-law, and a mulatto sailor, Crispus Attucks. Resistance leaders idealized the dead rioters as martyrs for the cause of liberty, holding a solemn funeral three days later and commemorating March 5 annually with patriotic orations. The best-known engraving of the massacre, by Paul Revere, was itself a part of the propaganda campaign. It depicts a peaceful crowd, an officer ordering the soldiers to fire, and shots coming from the window of the Customs House.

The leading patriots wanted to make certain the soldiers did not become martyrs as well. Furthermore, despite the political benefits the patriots derived from the massacre, it is unlikely that they approved of the crowd action that provoked it. Ever since August 1765 the men allied with the Sons of Liberty had supported orderly demonstrations and expressed distaste

for uncontrolled riots, of which the Boston Massacre was a prime example. Thus when the soldiers were tried for the killings in November, they were defended by John Adams and Josiah Quincy, Jr., both unwavering patriots. All but two of the accused men were acquitted, and those convicted were released after having been branded on the thumb. Undoubtedly the favorable outcome of the trials prevented London officials from taking further steps against the city.

For more than two years after the Boston Massacre and the repeal of the Townshend duties, a superficial calm descended on the colonies. Local incidents, like the burning of the customs vessel *Gaspée* in 1772 by Rhode Islanders, marred the relationship of individual colonies and the mother country, but nothing caused Americans to join in a unified protest. Even so, the resistance movement continued to gather momentum. The most radical colonial newspapers, such as the *Boston Gazette,* the *Pennsylvania Journal,* and the *South Carolina Gazette,* published essays drawing on Real Whig ideology and accusing Great Britain of a deliberate plan to oppress America. After repeal of the Stamp Act, the patriots had praised Parliament; following repeal of the Townshend duties, they warned of impending tyranny. What had seemed to be an isolated mistake, a single ill-chosen tax, now appeared to be part of a plot against American liberties. Among other things, essayists pointed to Parliament's persecution of the English radical John Wilkes, the stationing of troops in Boston, the growing number of vice-admiralty courts, and a host of other matters (including England's policies toward Ireland and Corsica) as evidence of a plan to enslave the colonists. Indeed, patriot writers played repeatedly on the word *enslavement.* Most white colonists had direct knowledge of slavery (either being slaveholders themselves or having slave-owning neighbors), and the threat of enslavement by Britain must have hit them with peculiar force.

Still, no one yet advocated complete independence from the mother country. Though the patriots were becoming increasingly convinced that they should seek freedom from parliamentary authority, they continued to acknowledge their British identity and to pledge their allegiance to George III. Indeed, they hoped to ally themselves with English radicals in working for imperial reform. They began, therefore, to try to envision a system that would enable them to

Chapter 4: Severing the bonds of empire, 1754–1774

Paul Revere's engraving of the Boston Massacre, a masterful
piece of propaganda. At right the British officer seems to be ordering the soldiers to fire on a peaceful, unresisting crowd. The
Customs House has been labeled Butcher's Hall, and smoke drifts
up from a gun barrel sticking out the window. American Antiquarian Society.

be ruled largely by their own elected legislatures while
remaining loyal to the king. But any such scheme was
totally alien to Britons' conception of the nature of
their government, which was that Parliament held
sole undivided sovereignty over the empire. Conservative colonists recognized the dangers inherent in the
patriots' new mode of thinking. The former stamp
distributor Andrew Oliver, for example, predicted in
1771 that "serious consequences" would follow from
the fact that "the leaders of the people were never [be-
fore] so open in asserting our independence of the
British Legislature," even though "there is an inter-
mission of Acts of violence at present."

Oliver's prediction proved correct when, in the fall
of 1772, the North ministry began to implement the
portion of the Townshend Acts that provided for
governors and judges to be paid from customs revenues. In early November, voters at a Boston town
meeting established a Committee of Correspondence

*Committees of
correspondence*

to publicize the decision by exchanging letters with other Massachusetts towns. Heading the
committee was the man who had proposed its formation, Samuel Adams. As much as a year earlier, Adams
had described in a letter to a Virginia friend the benefits of organizing an official communications network

Samuel Adams (1722-1803), painted by John Singleton Copley. Copley's famous portrait, painted two years before Adams headed the Boston Committee of Correspondence, shows the patriot leader at his most determined. Adams points a finger at the Massachusetts Charter, the symbol of the traditional liberties he sought to protect. Museum of Fine Arts, Boston, Deposited by the city of Boston.

within and among the separate colonies. "If conducted with a proper spirit," Adams had asked, "would it not afford reason for the Enemies of our common Liberty, to tremble?"

Samuel Adams was fifty-one years old in 1772, thirteen years the senior of his distant cousin John and a decade older than most other leaders of American resistance. He had been a Boston tax collector, a member and clerk of the Massachusetts Assembly, and an

ally of the Loyal Nine (though evidently not a member). Unswerving in his devotion to the American cause, Adams drew a sharp contrast between a corrupt Britain and the virtuous colonies. His primary forum was the Boston town meeting. An experienced political organizer, Adams continually stressed the necessity of prudent collective action. His Committee of Correspondence thus undertook to create an informed consensus among all the citizens of Massachusetts, including residents of rural areas. The formal resistance movement had until then been largely confined to cities and towns.

The Boston town meeting directed the Committee of Correspondence "to state the Rights of the Colonists and of this Province in particular," to list "the Infringements and Violations thereof that have been, or from time to time may be made," and to send copies to the other towns in the province. In return, Boston requested "a free communication of their Sentiments on this Subject."

Samuel Adams, James Otis, Jr., and Josiah Quincy, Jr., prepared the statement of the colonists' rights. Declaring that Americans had absolute rights to life, liberty, and property, the committee asserted that the idea that "a British house of commons, should have a right, at pleasure, to give and grant the property of the colonists" was "irreconcileable" with "the first principles of natural law and Justice . . . and of the British Constitution in particular." The list of grievances, drafted by another group of prominent patriots, was similarly sweeping. It complained of taxation without representation, the presence of unnecessary troops and customs officers on American soil, the use of imperial revenues to pay colonial officials, the expanded jurisdiction of vice-admiralty courts, and even the nature of the instructions given to American governors by their superiors in London.

The entire document, which was printed as a pamphlet for distribution to the towns, exhibited none of the hesitation that had characterized colonial claims against Parliament in the 1760s. That body had become nothing more than "a British house of commons." No longer were patriots—at least in Boston—concerned about defining the precise limits of parliamentary authority. No longer did they mention the necessity of obedience to Parliament. Clearly, they were committed to a course that placed American rights first, loyalty to Great Britain a distant second.

The response of the Massachusetts towns to the committee's pamphlet must have caused Samuel Adams to rejoice. Some towns disagreed with Boston's assessment of the state of affairs, but most aligned themselves with the city. From Braintree came the assertion that "all civil officers are or ought to be Servants to the people and dependent upon them for their official Support, and every instance to the Contrary from the Governor downwards tends to crush

and destroy civil liberty." The town of Holden declared that "the People of New England have never given the People of Britain any Right of Jurisdiction over us." The citizens of Petersham commented that resistance to tyranny was "the first and highest social Duty of this people." And Pownallborough warned, "allegiance is a relative Term and like Kingdoms and commonwealths is local and has its bounds." It was beliefs like these that made the next crisis in Anglo-American affairs the final one.

The Boston Tea Party

The only one of the Townshend duties still in effect by 1773 was the tax on tea. In the years since 1770 some Americans had continued to boycott English tea, while others had resumed drinking it either openly or in secret. At one inn, John Adams requested tea "provided it has been honestly smuggled," but found that the landlady had on principle banished all tea from the premises. Less scrupulous colonists purchased smuggled Dutch tea, drank tea from coffeepots, or hid when they consumed it.

Even though the boycott was less than fully effective, tea retained its explosive symbolic character. When in May 1773 Parliament passed an act designed to save the East India Company from bankruptcy, which changed the way British tea was sold in the colonies, resistance leaders were immediately suspicious. Under the Tea Act, certain duties paid on tea were to

| Tea Act |

be returned to the company. Furthermore, tea was to be sold only by designated agents, which would enable the East India Company to control the price and undersell any competitors, even smugglers. The net result would be cheaper tea for American consumers. But many colonists interpreted the new measure as a pernicious device to make them admit Parliament's right to tax them, since the less expensive tea would still be taxed under the Townshend law. Others saw the Tea Act as the first step in the establishment of an East India Company monopoly of all colonial trade. Residents of the four cities singled out to receive the first shipments of tea prepared to respond to what they perceived as a new threat to their freedom.

A 1789 engraving of the Boston Tea Party. A large crowd of bystanders looks on as colonists disguised as Indians break open the tea chests and empty them into the harbor.   Library of Congress.

In New York City, the tea ships failed to arrive on schedule. In Philadelphia, the captain was persuaded to turn around and sail back to England. In Charleston, the tea was unloaded, stored under the direction of local tradesmen, and later destroyed. The only confrontation occurred in Boston, where both sides—the town meeting, joined by participants from nearby towns, and Governor Thomas Hutchinson, two of whose sons were tea agents—rejected compromise.

The first of three tea ships, the *Dartmouth,* entered Boston Harbor on November 28. Under the customs laws, duty had to be paid within twenty days of a ship's arrival or its cargo would be seized by customs officers. After a series of mass meetings, Bostonians voted to prevent the tea from being unloaded and to post guards on the wharf. Hutchinson, for his part, refused to permit the vessels to leave the harbor, since that too would violate the law.

On December 16, 1773, one day before the cargo would have to be confiscated, more than five thousand people (nearly a third of the city's population)

crowded into Old South Church. The meeting, chaired by Samuel Adams, made a final attempt to persuade Hutchinson to send the tea back to England. But Hutchinson remained adamant. At about 6 p.m., Adams reportedly announced "that he could think of nothing further to be done—that they had now done all they could for the Salvation of their Country." As if his statement were a signal, cries rang out from the back of the crowd: "Boston harbor a tea-pot night! The Mohawks are come!" Small groups pushed their

> Boston Tea
> Party

way out of the meeting. Within a few minutes, about sixty men crudely disguised as Indians assembled at the wharf, boarded the three ships, and dumped the cargo into the harbor. By 9 p.m. their work was done: 342 chests of tea worth approximately £10,000 floated in splinters on the ebbing tide.

Among the "Indians" were many representatives of Boston's artisans. Five masons, eleven carpenters and builders, three leatherworkers, a blacksmith, a hatter,

Important events

1689–98	War of League of Augsberg (King William's War)
1701	Iroquois neutrality treaties
1702–13	War of Spanish Succession (Queen Anne's War)
1740–48	War of Austrian Succession (King George's War)
1754	Albany Congress George Washington's defeat
1755	Braddock's defeat
1756	Seven Years' War formally declared
1757	William Pitt becomes secretary of state
1759	Quebec falls to British
1760	Montreal falls to British; American phase of war ends George III becomes king
1763	Treaty of Paris George Grenville becomes prime minister Pontiac's uprising Proclamation of 1763
1764	Sugar Act Currency Act James Otis, Jr., *Rights of the British Colonies Asserted and Proved* March of Paxton Boys
1765	Stamp Act Sons of Liberty formed
1766	Repeal of Stamp Act Hostilities between British and Ottawas end
1767	Townshend Acts John Dickinson, *Letters of a Pennsylvania Farmer*
1768	*Liberty* riot British troops stationed in Boston
1770	Lord North becomes prime minister Repeal of Townshend duties except tea tax Boston Massacre
1772	*Gaspée* incident
1773	Tea Act Boston Tea Party
1774	Coercive Acts First Continental Congress

three coopers, two barbers, a coachmaker, a silver-smith, and twelve apprentices have been identified as participants. Their ranks also included four farmers from outside Boston, ten merchants, two doctors, a teacher, and a bookseller. The next day John Adams exulted in his diary that the Tea Party was "so bold, so daring, so firm, intrepid and inflexible" that "I can't but consider it as an epocha in history."

The North administration reacted with considerably less enthusiasm when it learned of the Tea Party. In March, after failing in an attempt to charge the Boston resistance leaders with high treason, the ministry proposed a bill closing the port of Boston until the tea was paid for, and prohibiting all but

Coercive and Quebec Acts

coastal trade in food and firewood. Colonial sympathizers in Parliament were easily outvoted by those who wished to punish the city that had been the center of opposition to British policies, and American hopes for an alliance with English radicals collapsed. Later in the spring, Parliament passed three further punitive measures. The Massachusetts Government Act altered the province's charter, substituting an appointed council for an elected one, increasing the powers of the governor, and forbidding special town meetings. The Justice Act provided that a person accused of committing murder in the course of suppressing a riot or enforcing the laws could be tried outside the colony where the incident had occurred. Finally, the Quartering Act gave broad authority to military commanders seeking to house their troops in private dwellings.

After passing the last of what became known as the Coercive Acts in early June, Parliament turned its attention to much-needed reforms in the government of Quebec. The Quebec Act, though unrelated to the Coercive Acts, thus became linked with them in the minds of the patriots. Intended to ease the strains that had arisen since the British conquest of the formerly French colony, the Quebec Act granted greater religious freedom to Catholics—alarming the Protestant colonists, who regarded Roman Catholicism as a mainstay of religious and political despotism. It also reinstated French civil law, which had been replaced by British procedures in 1763, and established an appointed council (rather than an elected legislature) as the governing body of the colony. Finally, in an attempt to provide the northern Indian tribes some protection against white settlement, the act annexed to Quebec the area east of the Mississippi River and north of the Ohio River. Thus that region, parts of which were claimed by individual seacoast colonies, was removed from their jurisdiction.

The members of Parliament who had voted for the punitive legislation believed that the acts would be obeyed, that at long last they had solved the problem posed by the troublesome Americans. But the patriots showed little inclination to bow to the wishes of Parliament. In their eyes, the Coercive Acts and the Quebec Act proved what they had feared since 1768: that Great Britain had embarked on a deliberate plan to oppress them. If the port of Boston could be closed, why not those of Philadelphia or New York? If the royal charter of Massachusetts could be changed, why not that of South Carolina? If certain people could be removed from their home colonies for trial, why not all violators of all laws? If troops could be forcibly quartered in private houses, did not that pave the way for the occupation of all of America? If the Roman Catholic Church could receive favored status in Quebec, why not everywhere? It seemed as though the full dimensions of the plot against American rights and liberties had at last been revealed.

The Boston Committee of Correspondence urged all the colonies to join in an immediate boycott of British goods. But the other provinces were not yet ready to take such a drastic step. Instead, they suggested that another intercolonial congress be convened to consider an appropriate response to the Coercive Acts. Few people wanted to take hasty action; even the most ardent patriots still hoped for reconciliation with Great Britain. Despite their objections to British policy, they continued to see themselves as part of the empire. Americans were approaching the brink of confrontation, but they had not committed themselves to an irrevocable break. And so the colonies agreed to send delegates to Philadelphia in September.

Over the preceding decade, momentous changes had occurred in the ways the colonists thought about themselves and their allegiance. Once linked unquestioningly to Great Britain, they had begun to develop a sense of their own identity as Americans. Though they had not yet taken the final step, they had started to sever the bonds of empire. During the next decade, they would forge the bonds of a new American nationality to replace those rejected Anglo-American ties.

Suggestions for further reading

General

Charles M. Andrews, *The Colonial Background of the American Revolution* (1924); Ian R. Christie, *Crisis of Empire: Great Britain and the American Colonies 1754–1783* (1966); Ian R. Christie and Benjamin W. Labaree, *Empire or Independence, 1760–1776: A British-American Dialogue on the Coming of the American Revolution* (1976); Lawrence Henry Gipson, *The Coming of the Revolution 1763–1775* (1954); Merrill Jensen, *The Founding of a Nation: A History of the American Revolution, 1763–1776* (1968); Edmund S. Morgan, *The Birth of the Republic, 1763–1789* (1956).

Colonial warfare and the British Empire

Lawrence Henry Gipson, *The British Empire Before the American Revolution,* 15 vols. (1936–1970); Robert C. Newbold, *The Albany Congress and Plan of Union of 1754* (1955); Richard Pares, *War and Trade in the West Indies, 1739–1763* (1936); Howard H. Peckham, *The Colonial Wars, 1689–1762* (1963); Alan Rogers, *Empire and Liberty: American Resistance to British Authority, 1755–1763* (1974); Neil R.

Stout, *The Royal Navy in America, 1760–1775* (1973); John Shy, *Toward Lexington: The Role of the British Army in the Coming of the American Revolution* (1965).

British politics and policy

George L. Beer, *British Colonial Policy 1754–1765* (1907); John Brewer, *Party Ideology and Popular Politics at the Accession of George III* (1976); John Brooke, *King George III* (1972); Bernard Donoughue, *British Politics and the American Revolution: The Path to War, 1773–1775* (1965); Michael Kammen, *A Rope of Sand: The Colonial Agents, British Politics, and the American Revolution* (1968); Lewis B. Namier, *England in the Age of the American Revolution,* 2nd ed. (1961); Lewis B. Namier, *The Structure of Politics at the Accession of George III,* 2nd ed. (1957); P.D.G. Thomas, *British Politics and the Stamp Act Crisis* (1975); Carl Ubbelohde, *The Vice-Admiralty Courts and the American Revolution* (1960); Franklin B. Wickwire, *British Subministers and Colonial America, 1763–1783* (1966).

Indians and the West

Thomas P. Abernethy, *Western Lands and the American Revolution* (1959); John R. Alden, *John Stuart and the Southern Colonial Frontier: A Study of Indian Relations, War, Trade, and Land Problems in the Southern Wilderness, 1754–1775* (1944); David H. Corkran, *The Cherokee Frontier: Conflict and Survival, 1740–1762* (1962); R.S. Cotterill, *The Southern Indians: The Story of the Civilized Tribes Before Removal* (1954); James T. Flexner, *Mohawk Baronet: Sir William Johnson of New York* (1959); Georgiana C. Nammack, *Fraud, Politics, and the Dispossession of the Indians: The Iroquois Land Frontier in the Colonial Period* (1969); Howard H. Peckham, *Pontiac and the Indian Uprising* (1947); Jack M. Sosin, *Whitehall and the Wilderness: The Middle West in British Colonial Policy, 1760–1775* (1961).

Revolutionary ideology

Bernard Bailyn, *The Ideological Origins of the American Revolution* (1967); Edwin G. Burrows and Michael Wallace, "The American Revolution: The Ideology and Psychology of National Liberation," *Perspectives in American History,* 6

(1972), 167–302; H. Trevor Colbourn, *The Lamp of Experience: Whig History and the Intellectual Origins of the American Revolution* (1965): Isaac Kramnick, *Bolingbroke and His Circle: The Politics of Nostalgia in the Age of Walpole* (1968); J.G.A. Pocock, "Machiavelli, Harrington, and English Political Ideologies in the Eighteenth Century," *William and Mary Quarterly,* 3rd ser., 22 (1965), 547–583; Caroline Robbins, *The Eighteenth-Century Commonwealthman: Studies in the Transmission, Development, and Circumstance of English Liberal Thought from the Restoration of Charles II until the War with the Thirteen Colonies* (1959); Clinton Rossiter, *Seedtime of the Republic: The Origin of the American Tradition of Political Liberty* (1953).

American resistance

David Ammerman, *In the Common Cause: American Response to the Coercive Acts of 1774* (1974); Richard Beeman, *Patrick Henry: A Biography* (1974); Richard D. Brown, *Revolutionary Politics in Massachusetts: The Boston Committee of Correspondence and the Towns, 1772–1774* (1970); Joseph Albert Ernst, *Money and Politics in America, 1755–1775: A Study in the Currency Act of 1764 and the Political Economy of Revolution* (1973): Dirk Hoerder, *Crowd Action in Revolutionary Massachusetts, 1765–1780* (1977); Benjamin W. Labaree, *The Boston Tea Party* (1964); Jesse Lemisch, "Jack Tar in the Streets: Merchant Seamen in the Politics of Revolutionary America," *William and Mary Quarterly,* 3rd ser., 25 (1968), 371–407; Pauline R. Maier, *From Resistance to Revolution: Colonial Radicals and the Development of American Opposition to Britain, 1765–1776* (1972); Pauline R. Maier, *The Old Revolutionaries: Political Lives in the Age of Samuel Adams* (1980); Edmund S. Morgan and Helen M. Morgan, *The Stamp Act Crisis: Prologue to Revolution* (1953); Gary B. Nash, *The Urban Crucible: Social Change, Political Consciousness, and the Origins of the American Revolution* (1979); Richard Ryerson, *The Revolution is Now Begun: The Radical Committees of Philadelphia, 1765–1776* (1978); Arthur M. Schlesinger, *The Colonial Merchants and the American Revolution 1763–1776* (1918); Richard Walsh, *Charleston's Sons of Liberty: A Study of the Artisans, 1763–1789* (1959); John J. Waters, Jr. *The Otis Family in Provincial and Revolutionary Massachusetts* (1968); Alfred H. Young, ed. *The American Revolution: Explorations in the History of American Radicalism* (1976); Hiller B. Zobel, *The Boston Massacre* (1970).

5

A
REVOLUTION,
INDEED,
1775–1783

One April morning in 1775, Hannah Winthrop awoke with a start to drumbeats, bells, and the continuous clang of the Cambridge fire alarm. She and her husband, a professor at Harvard, soon learned that redcoat troops had left Boston late the evening before, bound for Concord. A few hours later they watched British soldiers march through Cambridge to reinforce the first group. The Winthrops quickly decided to leave home and seek shelter elsewhere. Along with seventy or eighty other refugees, mostly wives and children of patriot militiamen, they made their way to an isolated farmhouse near Fresh Pond. But it was no secure haven. They were, Mrs. Winthrop later wrote, "for some time in sight of the Battle, the glistening instruments of death proclaiming by an incessant fire that much blood must be shed, that many widowd and orphand ones be left as monuments of that persecuting Barbarity of British Tyranny."

Afraid to abandon their refuge even after the sounds of battle ceased, the Winthrops and their companions remained in the farmhouse overnight, sleeping in chairs and on the floor. The next morning, warned that Cambridge was still unsafe, the couple headed west toward Andover. The roads were filled with other frightened families, some carrying all their belongings. Their route took them through Menotomy (now Arlington), scene of some of the bloodiest fighting the day before. The battlefield, Mrs. Winthrop recorded, was "strewd with the mangled bodies." Along the way they encountered a farmer gathering the corpses of his neighbors and searching for the body of his son, who had reportedly been killed in battle. As she walked toward Andover, Hannah Winthrop mentally compared herself with Eve expelled from the Garden of Eden; lines from John Milton's *Paradise Lost,* she later told a friend, had echoed repeatedly in her mind. She was convinced that nothing would be the same again.

In that expectation, Hannah Winthrop was wrong. She and her husband soon returned to their Cambridge home and resumed their normal lives. But their experience in 1775 was typical of that of thousands of other Americans over the next eight years. The Revolution, one of only two major conflicts ever fought on American soil—the other was to be the Civil War—was more than just a series of clashes between British and patriot armies. It also uprooted thousands of civilian families, disrupted the economy,

reshaped society by forcing many colonists into permanent exile, and led Americans to develop new conceptions of politics. Indeed, even before the shooting began the patriots had established functioning revolutionary governments throughout the colonies.

In the war itself, the Americans were on the defensive most of the time. British ministers and army officers persisted in comparing the conflict to wars they had fought in Europe, and consequently made numerous errors in strategy and tactics. They also failed to realize that winning a few battles would not achieve their goal of retaining the colonies' allegiance. The patriots, meanwhile, had to worry not only about the redcoat army but also about the blacks, Indians, and loyalists who constituted potentially subversive elements within their own society. That the patriots eventually triumphed over all their foes was more a tribute to their endurance than to their military prowess.

Government by congress and committee

When the fifty-five delegates to the First Continental Congress convened in Philadelphia in September 1774, they knew that any measures they adopted were

| First Continental Congress |

likely to enjoy strong support among their fellow countrymen and women. During the summer of 1774, open meetings held in towns, cities, and counties throughout the colonies had endorsed the idea of another nonimportation pact. Participants in such meetings had promised (in the words of the freeholders of Johnston County, North Carolina) to "strictly adhere to, and abide by, such Regulations and Restrictions as the Members of the said General Congress shall agree to, and judge most convenient." The committees of correspondence that had been established in many communities publicized these popular meetings so effectively that Americans everywhere knew about them. Most of the congressional delegates were selected by extralegal provincial conventions whose members were chosen at such local gatherings, since the royal governors had forbidden the regular assemblies to conduct formal elections. Thus the very act of designating delegates to attend the congress involved Americans in open defiance of British authority.

The colonies' leading political figures—most of them lawyers, merchants, or planters—were sent to the Philadelphia congress. The Massachusetts delegation included both Samuel Adams, the experienced organizer of the Boston resistance, and his younger cousin John, an ambitious lawyer. Among others New York sent John Jay, a talented young attorney. From Pennsylvania came the conservative Joseph Galloway, speaker of the assembly, and his long-time rival John Dickinson. Virginia elected Richard Henry Lee and Patrick Henry, both noted for their patriotic zeal, as well as the stolid and reserved George Washington. Most of these men had never met, but in the weeks, months, and years that followed they were to become the chief architects of the new nation.

The congressmen faced three tasks when they convened at Carpenters Hall on September 5, 1774. The first two were explicit: defining American grievances and developing a plan for resistance. The third was implicit—outlining a theory of their constitutional relationship with England—and proved troublesome. The delegates readily agreed on a list of the laws they wanted repealed (notably the Coercive Acts) and chose as their method of resistance an economic boycott coupled with petitions for relief. But they could not reach a consensus on the constitutional issue. Their discussion of this crucial question was rendered all the more intense by events in Massachusetts.

On the second day of the meeting, word arrived that the British had attacked the Massachusetts countryside and were bombarding Boston from land and sea. This rumor was proven false two days later, but it nevertheless lent a sense of urgency to the congressmen's discussions. That thousands of militiamen had gathered in Cambridge to repel the rumored attack demonstrated how close to the brink of war Great Britain and the colonies had already come. The congressmen accordingly set about their work with particular fervor and commitment.

Since the colonists' resistance was based on the claim that their constitutional rights had been violated, it seemed necessary to define what the colonies' constitutional relationship with England was. But the delegates held widely differing views on that subject.

The most radical congressmen, like Lee of Virginia and Roger Sherman of Connecticut, agreed with the position published a few weeks earlier by Thomas Jefferson—who was not a delegate—in his *Summary View of the Rights of British America*. Jefferson argued that the colonists owed allegiance only to George III, and that Parliament was nothing more than "the legislature of one part of the empire." As such, he declared, it could not exercise legitimate authority over the American provinces, which had historically been governed by their own assemblies.

Meanwhile the conservative Joseph Galloway and his ally James Duane of New York insisted that the congress should acknowledge Parliament's supremacy over the empire and its right to regulate American trade. Galloway embodied these ideas in a formal plan of union, like the one his friend Benjamin Franklin had presented at the Albany Congress in 1754. His plan proposed the establishment of an American legislature, its members chosen by individual colonial assemblies, which would have to consent to laws pertaining to America. The delegates rejected Galloway's proposal, though, eventually accepting instead a position outlined by John Adams.

The clause Adams drafted in the congress's Declaration of Rights and Grievances read in part: "From the necessity of the case, and a regard to the mutual interest of both countries, we cheerfully consent to the operation of such acts of the British parliament, as are bona fide, restrained to the regulation of our external commerce." Note the key phrases. "From the necessity of the case" indicated Americans' abandonment, once and for all, of the unquestioning loyalty to the mother country that had so bedeviled James Otis, Jr., just a decade earlier. The colonists were now declaring that they owed obedience to Parliament only because they had decided it was in the best interest of both countries. "Bona fide, restrained to the regulation of our external commerce" resonated with overtones of the Stamp Act controversy and Dickinson's arguments in his *Farmer's Letters*. The delegates intended to make clear to Lord North that they would continue to resist taxes in disguise, like the Townshend duties. Most striking of all was that such language, which only a few years before would have been regarded as irredeemably radical, could be presented and accepted as a

Declaration of Rights and Grievances

compromise in the fall of 1774. The Americans had come a long way since their first hesitant protests against the Sugar Act.

Once the delegates had resolved the constitutional issue, they discussed the tactics by which to force another British retreat. They quickly agreed on nonimportation of all goods from Great Britain and Ireland, as well as tea and molasses from other British possessions and slaves from any source, effective December 1. An end to the consumption of British products was also readily accepted as part of the agreement that became known as the Continental Association; it would become effective on March 1, 1775. Nonexportation, on the other hand, generated considerable debate. The Virginia delegation adamantly refused to accept a ban on exports to England until after its planters had had a chance to market their 1774 tobacco crop. As a result, the congress provided that nonexportation would not begin until September 10, 1775.

More influential than the details of the Continental Association was the method the congress recommended for its enforcement: the election of committees of observation and inspection in every county, city, and town in America. Such committees were officially charged only with overseeing enforcement of the association, but over the next six months they became de facto governments. Since the congress specified that committee members be chosen by all persons qualified to vote for members of the lower house of the colonial legislatures, the committees were guaranteed a broad popular base. Furthermore, their large size ensured that many new men would be incorporated into the resistance movement. In some places the committeemen were former local officeholders; in other places they were obscure men who had never before held office. Everywhere, however, these committeemen—perhaps seven to eight thousand of them in the colonies as a whole—found themselves increasingly linked to the cause of American resistance.

At first the committees confined themselves to enforcing the nonimportation clause—examining merchants' records and publishing the names of those who continued to import or sell British goods. But the Continental Association also promoted home manufactures and encouraged Americans to adopt simple modes of dress and behavior. Wearing homespun garments became a sign of patriotism, just as it had been in the late 1760s. Since expensive leisure-time activities were symbols of vice and corruption (characteristic of England, not the virtuous colonies), the congress urged Americans to forgo dancing, gambling, horse racing, cock fighting, and other forms of "extravagance and dissipation." In enforcing these injunctions, the committees gradually extended their authority over nearly all aspects of American life.

Committees forbade public and private dancing, extracted apologies from people caught gambling or racing, prohibited the slaughter of lambs (due to the need for wool), and offered prizes for the best locally made cloth. The Baltimore County committee even advised citizens not to attend the upcoming town fair, which they described as nothing more than an occasion for "riots, drunkenness, gaming, and the vilest immoralities."

The committees also attempted to identify opponents of American resistance. Although seeking to protect American rights—which presumably included freedom of speech and thought—the patriots saw no reason to grant those rights to people who disagreed with them. They viewed the resistance movement as a collective endeavor that would succeed only if all colonists supported it. Consequently, the committees developed elaborate spy networks, circulated copies of the association for signatures, and investigated reports of dissident remarks and activities. Suspected dissenters were first urged to convert to the colonial cause; if that failed, the committees had them watched or restricted their movements. Sometimes people engaging in casual political exchanges with friends one day found themselves charged with "treasonable conversation" the next. Committees cooperated with each other, too. In 1775, for example, the Northampton, Massachusetts, committee told its counterpart in nearby Hadley that a townsman had been heard to call the congress "a Pack or Parcell of Fools" that was "as tyrannical as Lord North and ought to be opposed & resisted." The Hadley committee examined the accused man, who admitted his statements and refused to recant. The committee thereafter had him watched.

What is striking about such incidents is not that there were so many but that there were so few. The committees were extralegal bodies, drawing on no source of authority other than popular election. They

Committees of observation

had no connection—except in some cases overlapping membership—with the ordinary organs of government Americans were accustomed to obeying. Furthermore, they assumed unprecedented powers of supervision over the daily lives, actions, and even thoughts of the citizenry. That most colonists apparently submitted to their rule without overt complaint certainly suggests, if it does not altogether prove, broad public support for resistance to Great Britain. As the patriots were to discover, however, this did not necessarily mean that independence would later have the same broad support. Many people who were willing to work for reform within the empire by means of boycotts and petitions were unwilling to seek independence by force of arms.

While the committees were expanding their power during the winter and early spring of 1775, the established governments of the colonies were collapsing. Only in Connecticut, Rhode Island, Delaware, and Pennsylvania did regular assemblies continue to meet without encountering patriot challenges to their authority. In every other colony, popularly elected provincial conventions took over the task of running the

> Provincial conventions

government, sometimes entirely replacing the legislatures and at other times holding concurrent sessions. In late 1774 and early 1775, these conventions approved the Continental Association, elected delegates to the Second Continental Congress (scheduled for May), organized militia units, and gathered arms and ammunition. The British-appointed governors and councils, unable to stem the tide of resistance, watched helplessly as their authority crumbled.

The frustrating experience of Governor Josiah Martin of North Carolina is a case in point. When a provincial convention was called to meet at New Bern on April 4, 1775—the same day the legislature was to convene—Martin proclaimed that "the Assembly of this province duly elected is the only true and lawful representation of the people." He asked all citizens to "renounce disclaim and discourage all such meetings cabals and illegal proceedings . . . which can only tend to introduce disorder and anarchy." Martin's proclamation had no visible effect, and when the convention met at New Bern its membership proved to be virtually identical to that of the colonial legislature. The delegates proceeded to act alternately in both capacities and even passed some joint resolves. Continuing

the farce, the exasperated Martin delivered a speech to the assembly denouncing the election of the convention. On April 7, Martin admitted to Lord Dartmouth, the American Secretary in North's ministry, that his government was "absolutely prostrate, impotent, and that nothing but the shadow of it is left."

Royal officials in the other colonies suffered the same frustrations. Courts were prevented from holding sessions; taxes were paid to agents of the conventions rather than provincial tax collectors; sheriffs' powers were questioned; and militiamen refused to muster except by order of the local committees. In short, during the six months preceding the battles at Lexington and Concord, independence was being won at the local level, but without formal acknowledgment and for the most part without shooting or bloodshed. Not many Americans fully realized what was happening. Most were carried along by events, unaware of the ultimate implications of their acts and arguments. The vast majority of colonists still proclaimed their loyalty to Great Britain and denied that they sought to leave the empire. Among the few Americans who did recognize the trend toward independence were those who opposed it.

Internal enemies

The first protests against British measures, in the mid-1760s, had won the support of most colonists. Only in the late 1760s and early 1770s did a significant number of Americans begin to question both the aims and the tactics of the resistance movement. In 1774 and 1775 such people found themselves in a difficult position. Like their more radical counterparts, most of them objected to parliamentary policies and wanted some kind of constitutional reform. (Joseph Galloway, for instance, was a conservative by American standards, but his plan for restructuring the empire was too novel for Britain to accept.) Nevertheless, if forced to a choice, these colonists sympathized with Great Britain rather than with an independent America. The events of the crucial year between the passage of the Coercive Acts and the outbreak of fighting in Massachusetts had crystallized their thinking. Their doubts about violent protest, their desire to uphold the legally constituted colonial governments, and their fears of anarchy combined to make them especially sensitive to the dangers of resistance.

In 1774 and 1775 some conservatives began to publish essays and pamphlets critical of the congress and its allied committees. In New York City, a group of Anglican clergymen jointly wrote seven pamphlets, as well as numerous shorter essays, arguing the importance of maintaining a cordial connection between England and America. In Pennsylvania, Joseph Galloway published *A Candid Examination of the Mutual Claims of Great Britain and the Colonies,* attacking the Continental Congress for rejecting his plan of union. In Massachusetts, the young attorney Daniel Leonard, writing under the pseudonym Massachusettensis, engaged in a prolonged newspaper debate with Novanglus (John Adams). All the conservative authors stressed the point that Leonard put so well in his sixth essay in January 1775: "There is no possible medium between absolute independence and subjection to the authority of parliament." Leonard and his fellows realized that what had begun as a dispute over the extent of American subordination within the empire had now raised the question of whether the colonies would remain linked to Great Britain at all. "Rouse up at last from your slumber!" the Reverend Thomas Bradbury Chandler of New Jersey cried out to Americans. "There is a set of people among us . . . who have formed a scheme for establishing an independent government or empire in America."

Some colonists heeded the conservative pamphleteers' warnings. About one-fifth of the white American population remained loyal to Great Britain, actively

| *Loyalists, patriots, and neutrals* |

opposing independence. With notable exceptions, most people of the following types became loyalists: British-appointed government officials; merchants whose trade depended on imperial connections; Anglican clergy everywhere and lay Anglicans in the North—where their denomination was in the minority—since the king was the head of their church as well as the state; former officers and enlisted men from the British army, many of whom had settled in America after 1763; non-English ethnic minorities, especially Scots; tenant farmers, particularly those whose landlords sided with the patriots; members of persecuted religious sects; and many of the backcountry southerners who had rebelled against

eastern rule in the 1760s and early 1770s. All these people had one thing in common: the patriot leaders were their long-standing enemies, though for different reasons. Local and provincial disputes thus helped to determine which side a person chose in the imperial conflict.

The active patriots, who accounted for about two-fifths of the population, came chiefly from the groups that had dominated colonial society, either numerically or politically. Among them were yeoman farmers, members of dominant Protestant sects (both Old and New Lights), Chesapeake gentry, merchants dealing mainly in American commodities, city artisans, elected officeholders, and people of English descent. Wives usually but not always adopted their husbands' political beliefs.

There remained in the middle perhaps two-fifths of the white population. Some of those who tried to avoid taking sides were sincere pacifists, such as Pennsylvania Quakers. Others opportunistically shifted their allegiance depending on which side happened to be winning at the time. Still others simply wanted to be left alone to lead their lives; they cared little about politics and normally obeyed whichever side controlled their area. But such colonists also resisted the British and the Americans alike when the demands made on them seemed too heavy—when taxes became too high, for example, or when calls for militia service came too often. Their attitude might best be summed up in the phrase "a plague on both your houses." Such persons made up an especially large proportion of the population in the southern backcountry, where the Scots-Irish settlers had little love for either the patriot gentry or the English authorities.

To American patriots, that sort of apathy or neutrality was a crime as heinous as loyalism. Those who were not for them were against them; in their minds, there could be no conscientious objectors. By the winter of 1775 and 1776, less than a year after Lexington and Concord, the Continental Congress was recommending to the states that all "disaffected" or "inimical" persons be disarmed and arrested. The state legislatures quickly passed laws prescribing severe penalties for suspected loyalists. Many began to require all voters (or, in some cases, all free adult males) to take oaths of allegiance; the punishment for refusal was usually banishment or extra taxes. In 1778 and thereafter, many states formally confiscated the property of

The text within the illustration reads:

A PROSPECTIVE VIEW OF Old NEWGATE Connecticuts STATE PRISON.

The subterranean Vault, over which this place is built was wrought about the middle of the 17ᵗʰ Century for the purpose of obtaining Copper Ore. the opening into those Gloomy Caverns is a Decent of 35 feet, from thence Descending in various Serpentine Directions 75 Yards, opens to the Well 15 in depth 74 feet from the Surface to the Water.

1 The Commandants apartment. 2. the Guard Room. 3. the work shop 4 the store for Nails 5. the Bake house 6 the Cole house 7 the Smiths shop. 8 the Well 9 the gate for Entrance 10 the Pickets & inclosure of the Prison 11 the path leading from the work shop to the Taverns

Connecticut imprisoned many of its loyalists in notorious New-gate prison, a converted copper mine. The offenders were housed in caverns below the large structure left of center. Some prominent loyalists (like Benjamin Franklin's son William, the last royal governor of New Jersey) were held in private homes. The Connecticut Historical Society.

banished loyalists. At the end of the war, perhaps as many as 100,000 white Americans were exiled to England, Canada, or the West Indies because of their loyalism.

The patriots' policies helped to ensure that the weak, scattered, and persecuted loyalists could not band together to threaten the revolutionary cause. But loyalists were not the only internal enemies the resistance leaders had to contend with. As they embarked on war against the crown, they also had to fear potential subversion by blacks and Indians.

In late 1774 and early 1775 news of slave conspiracies surfaced in different parts of the colonies. All shared a common element: a plan to assist the British

Slave conspiracies

in return for freedom. A group of black Bostonians petitioned General Thomas Gage, who had replaced Thomas Hutchinson as governor of Massachusetts, promising to fight for the redcoats if he would liberate them. In Virginia, whites learned that a number of blacks were preparing to join the British. The governor of Maryland authorized the issuance of extra guns to militiamen in four counties where slave uprisings were expected. The most serious incident occurred during the summer of 1775 in Charleston, where Thomas Jeremiah, a free black harbor pilot, was brutally executed after being convicted of attempting to foment a slave revolt.

Internal enemies

> R UN away from *Hampton*, on *Sunday*
> laft, a lufty Mulatto Fellow named ARGYLE, well
> known about the Country, has a Scar on one of his Wrifts, and
> has loft one or more of his fore Teeth; he is a very handy Fel-
> low by Water, or about the Houfe, &c. loves Drink, and is very
> bold in his Cups, but daftardly when fober. Whether he will go
> for a Man of War's Man, or not, I cannot fay; but I will give
> 40s. to have him brought to me. He can read and write.
> NOVEMBER 2, 1775. JACOB WRAY.

An advertisement for a runaway slave suspected of joining Lord Dunmore—a common sight in Virginia and Maryland newspapers during the fall and winter of 1775 to 1776. Virginia State Library.

It was fear of acts such as these that made white residents of the British West Indian colonies far more cautious in their opposition to parliamentary policies than their counterparts on the mainland. On most of the Caribbean islands, blacks outnumbered whites by six or seven to one. The planters simply could not afford to risk opposing Britain, their chief protector, with the ever-present threat of black revolt hanging over their heads. The Jamaica assembly agreed with the mainland colonial legislatures that citizens should not be bound by laws to which they had not consented. Nevertheless its members assured the king in 1774 that "it cannot be supposed, that we now intend, or ever could have intended Resistance to Great Britain." They cited as reasons Jamaica's "weak and feeble" condition, "its very small number of white inhabitants, and . . . the incumbrance of more than Two hundred thousand Slaves."

Racial composition affected politics in the continental colonies as well. In the North, where whites greatly outnumbered blacks, revolutionary fervor was at its height. In Virginia and Maryland, where whites constituted a safe majority of the population, there was occasional alarm over potential slave revolts but no disabling fear. But in South Carolina, which was over 60 percent black, and Georgia, where the racial balance was nearly even, whites were noticeably less enthusiastic about resistance. Georgia, in fact, sent no delegates to the First Continental Congress, and reminded its representatives at the Second Continental Congress to consider its circumstances, "with our

blacks and tories within us," when voting on the question of independence.

The whites' worst fears were realized in November 1775, when Lord Dunmore, the governor of Virginia, offered to free any slaves and indentured servants who would leave their patriot masters to join the British forces. Dunmore hoped to use black manpower in his fight against the revolutionaries, and to disrupt the economy by depriving white Americans of their labor force. But fewer blacks than expected rallied to the British standard in 1775 and 1776 (there were at most two thousand). Many of those who did perished in a smallpox epidemic that raged through the naval vessels housing them in Norfolk harbor.

Though black Americans did not pose a serious threat to the revolutionary cause in its early years, the patriots managed to turn rumors of slave uprisings to their own advantage. In South Carolina in particular, they won adherents by promoting white unity under the revolutionary banner. The Continental Association was needed, they argued, to protect whites from blacks at a time when the royal government was unable to muster adequate defense forces. Undoubtedly many wavering Carolinians were drawn into the revolutionary camp by fear that an overt division among the colony's whites would encourage a slave revolt.

A similar factor—the threat of Indian attacks—helped to persuade some reluctant westerners to support the struggle against Great Britain. In the years since the Proclamation of 1763, British officials had won the trust and respect of the interior tribes by attempting to protect them from land-hungry whites.

| *Indian neutrality* |

The British-appointed superintendents of Indian affairs, John Stuart in the South and Sir William Johnson in the North, lived among and sympathized with the Indians. In 1768, Stuart and Johnson negotiated separate agreements modifying the proclamation line and attempting to draw realistic defensible boundaries between tribal holdings and white settlements. The two treaties—signed respectively at Hard Labor Creek, South Carolina, in October and at Fort Stanwix, New York, in November—supposedly established permanent borders for the colonies. But just a few years later, in the treaties of Lochaber (1770) and Augusta (1773), the British pushed the southern boundary even farther west to accommodate the demands of whites in western Georgia and the "overmountain" region known as Kentucky.

By the time of the Revolution, the Indians were impatient with the Americans' aggressive pressure on their lands. They also recognized the colonists' contempt for the Indians' way of life and resented the whites' unwillingness to prosecute frontiersmen who wantonly killed innocent natives. In combination with the tribes' confidence in Stuart and Johnson, these grievances predisposed most Indians toward an alliance with the British. Only two tribes favored the colonists: the northern Oneidas, who had been converted to Christianity by Boston-based missionaries, and the southern Catawbas, who were heavily dependent on American traders. Even so, the British hesitated to make full and immediate use of their potential Indian allies. The superintendents were well aware that the tribes might prove a liability, since their aims and style of fighting were not necessarily compatible with those of the British. Accordingly, John Stuart and Guy Johnson (who became northern superintendent following his uncle's death) sought nothing more from the tribes than a promise of neutrality. The superintendents even helped to prevent a general Indian uprising in the summer of 1774. Because of the royal officials' clever maneuvering, the Shawnees found no allies when they decided to attack frontier villages in Kentucky. They were defeated by the Virginia militia in Lord Dunmore's War and consequently withdrew north and west of the Ohio, leaving Kentucky open to white settlement.

John Murray, Lord Dunmore (1730–1809), the last royal governor of Virginia. Dunmore tried in vain to raise a black army to combat the Revolution.   Virginia Historical Society.

The patriots, recognizing that their standing with the tribes was poor, also sought the Indians' neutrality. In 1775 the Second Continental Congress sent a general message to the tribes describing the war as "a family quarrel between us and Old England" and requesting that they "not join on either side," since "you Indians are not concerned in it." The Overhill Cherokees, led by Chief Dragging Canoe, nevertheless decided that the whites' "family quarrel" would allow them to settle some old scores. They attacked white settlements along the western borders of the Carolinas and Virginia in the summer of 1776. But a coordinated campaign by Carolina and Virginia militia destroyed many of their towns, along with crops and large quantities of supplies. Dragging Canoe and his diehard followers fled west to the Tennessee River,

Broadside authorizing the purchase of muskets for the Conti-
nental troops beseiging Boston. Published by the New York
Provincial Congress in August 1775.   John Carter Brown
Library.

where they established new outposts, while the rest of
the Cherokees agreed to a treaty that ceded more of
their land to the whites.

The other major southern tribe–the Creeks–failed
to come to the Cherokees' aid in the 1776 war. The
Creeks were preoccupied by a long-standing feud with
the Choctaws, and resentful that both the British and
the Americans had devoted most of their attention
(and gifts) to wooing the Cherokees. This sort of factionalism was the Indians' chief problem during the
Revolutionary War. Had the tribes ever arrived at a
unified position–whether an alliance with the British,
with the Americans, or even a consistently independent role–they could have protected their common interests better. But they had distrusted each other too
long to set aside their differences for the sake of a common goal.

Thus, although the patriots could never completely ignore the threats posed by loyalists, blacks,
neutrals, and Indians, only rarely did fear of these
groups seriously hamper the revolutionary movement. Occasionally frontier militia refused to turn out

for duty on the seaboard because they feared Indians
would attack in their absence. Sometimes southern
troops refused to serve in the North because they (and
their political leaders) were unwilling to leave the
South unprotected against a slave insurrection. But
the practical impossibility of a large-scale slave revolt,
coupled with tribal feuds and the patriots' successful
campaign to disarm and neutralize loyalists, ensured
that the revolutionaries would remain firmly in control as they fought for independence.

War begins

On January 27, 1775, the secretary of state for
America, Lord Dartmouth, addressed a fateful letter
to General Thomas Gage, the British commander-in-
chief at Boston. Expressing his belief that American
resistance was nothing more than the response of a
"rude rabble without plan," Dartmouth ordered
Gage to arrest "the principal actors and abettors in the
provincial congress." If such a step were taken swiftly
and silently, Dartmouth observed, no bloodshed need
occur. Opposition could not be "very formidable,"
Dartmouth wrote, and even if it were, "it will surely
be better that the Conflict should be brought on,
upon such ground, than in a riper state of Rebellion."

Because of poor sailing weather, Dartmouth's letter did not reach Gage until April 14. The major patriot leaders had by then already left Boston, and in
any event Gage did not believe that arresting them
would serve a useful purpose. The order nevertheless
spurred him to action: he decided to send an expedition to confiscate provincial military supplies stock-
piled at Concord. Bostonians dispatched two messengers, William Dawes and Paul Revere (later joined by
a third, Dr. Samuel Prescott), to rouse the countryside. Thus when the British vanguard approached
Lexington at dawn on April 19, they found a strag-
gling group of 70 militiamen–approximately half the adult male
population of the town–drawn
up before them on the town com-
mon. The Americans' commander, Captain John
Parker, ordered his men to withdraw, realizing that
they were too few to halt the redcoat advance. But as

| Battles of
Lexington and
Concord |

Chapter 5: A revolution, indeed, 1775–1783

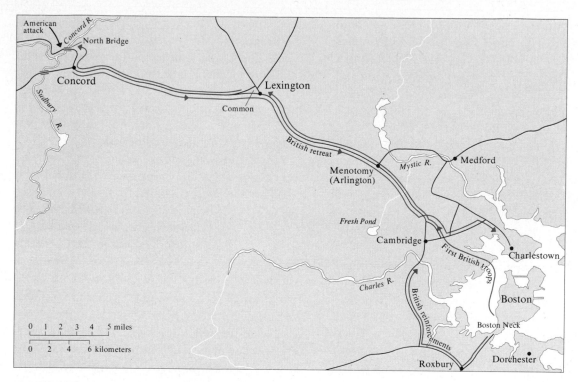

Lexington and Concord, April 19, 1775

they began to disperse, a shot rang out; the British soldiers then fired several volleys. When they stopped, 8 Americans lay dead and another 10 had been wounded. The British moved on to Concord, five miles away (see map).

There the contingents of militia were larger; the men of Concord had been joined by groups from Lincoln, Acton, and other nearby towns. The Americans allowed the British to enter Concord unopposed, but later in the morning they attacked the British infantry companies guarding the North Bridge. The brief exchange of gunfire there spilled the first British blood of the Revolution: 3 men were killed and 9 (including 4 officers) wounded. On their march back to Boston, the British were attacked by thousands of militiamen, firing from behind trees, bushes, and houses along the road. By the end of the day, the redcoats had suffered 272 casualties, 70 of whom were dead. Only the arrival of reinforcements from the city and the militia's lack of coordination prevented much heavier British losses. The patriots suffered just 93 casualties.

By the evening of April 20, perhaps as many as twenty thousand American militiamen had gathered around Boston, summoned by local committees that spread the alarm across the New England countryside. Many did not stay long, since they were needed at home for spring planting, but those who remained dug in along siege lines encircling the city. For nearly a year the two armies sat and stared at each other across those lines. During that period the redcoats attacked their besiegers only once, on June 17, when they drove the Americans from trenches atop Breed's Hill in Charlestown. In that misnamed Battle of Bunker Hill, the British incurred their greatest losses of the entire war: over 800 wounded and 228 killed. The Americans, though forced to abandon their position, lost fewer than half that number. During the same eleven-month period, the patriots captured Fort Ticonderoga, a British post on Lake Champlain, acquiring much-needed cannon. In the hope of bringing Canada into the war on the American side, they also mounted an uncoordinated northern campaign that ended in disaster at Quebec in early 1776. But the chief significance of the first year of the war lay in the long lull in fighting between the main armies at Boston. The delay gave both sides a chance to regroup, organize, and plan their strategies.

War begins

Lord North and his new American secretary, Lord George Germain, made three major assumptions about the war they faced. First, they concluded that

British strategy

patriot forces could not withstand the assaults of trained British regulars. They and their generals were convinced that the campaign of 1776 would be the first and last of the war. Accordingly, they dispatched to America the largest single force Great Britain had ever assembled anywhere: 370 transport ships carrying 32,000 troops (including thousands of German mercenaries) and tons of supplies, accompanied by 73 naval vessels and 13,000 sailors. Such an extraordinary effort would, they thought, ensure a quick victory.

Second, British officials and army officers persisted in comparing this war to wars they had fought successfully in Europe. Thus they adopted a conventional strategy of capturing major American cities and defeating the rebel army decisively without suffering serious casualties themselves. Third, they assumed that a clear-cut military victory would automatically bring about their goal of retaining the colonies' allegiance.

All these assumptions proved false. North and Germain, like Lord Dartmouth before them, vastly underestimated the Americans' commitment to armed resistance. Defeats on the battlefield did not lead the patriots to abandon their political aims and sue for peace. The ministers also failed to recognize the significance of the American population's dispersal over an area 1,500 miles long and more than 100 miles wide. Although at one time or another during the war the British would control each of the most important American ports, less than 5 percent of the population lived in those cities. And the coast offered so many excellent harbors that essential commerce was easily rerouted. In other words, the loss of the cities did little to damage the American cause, while the desire for such ports repeatedly led redcoat generals astray.

Most of all, the British did not at first understand that a military victory would not necessarily bring about a political victory. Securing the colonies permanently would require hundreds of thousands of Americans to return to their original allegiance. The conquest of America was thus a far more complicated task than the defeat of France twelve years earlier. The British needed not only to overpower the patriots, but

also to convert them. After 1778, they adopted a strategy designed to achieve that goal through the expanded use of loyalist forces and the restoration of civilian authority in occupied areas. But the new policy came too late. The British never fully realized that they were not fighting a conventional European war at all, but rather an entirely new kind of conflict: the first modern war of national liberation.

Yet the British at least had a bureaucracy ready to supervise the war effort. The Americans had only the Second Continental Congress, originally intended

Second Continental Congress

merely as a brief gathering of colonial representatives to consider the British response to the Continental Association. Instead, the delegates who convened in Philadelphia on May 10, 1775, found that they had to assume the mantle of intercolonial government. "Such a vast Multitude of objects, civil, political, commercial and military, press and crowd upon us so fast, that we know not what to do first," John Adams wrote a close friend early in the session. Yet as the summer passed the congress slowly organized the colonies for war. It authorized the printing of money with which to purchase necessary goods, modified the Continental Association to allow trade in needed military supplies with friendly European nations, and took steps to strengthen the militia. Most important of all, the congress created the Continental Army and appointed its generals.

Until the congress met, the Massachusetts provincial congress had taken responsibility for organizing the massive army of militia encamped at Boston. But that army, composed of men from all the New England states, was proving to be a heavy drain on limited local resources. Consequently, on May 16 Massachusetts asked the Continental Congress to assume the task of directing the army. One of the first decisions the congress had to make was to choose a commander-in-chief. Since the war had thus far been a wholly northern affair, many delegates recognized the importance of naming a non-New Englander to command the army in order to ensure colonial unity in the struggle. There seemed only one obvious candidate. The delegates unanimously selected their fellow delegate, the Virginian George Washington.

Washington was no fiery radical, nor was he a reflective political thinker. He had not played a promi-

George Washington (1732–1799), painted in his uniform as commander in chief. His stalwart bearing, so vividly conveyed in this portrait, was one of his prime assets as a leader. Washington and Lee University, Washington-Custis-Lee Collection.

nent role in the prerevolutionary agitation, but his

George Washington: his traits

devotion to the American cause was unquestioned. He was dignified, conservative, respectable, and a man of unimpeachable integrity. The younger son of a Virginia planter, Washington had not expected to inherit substantial property and had planned to make his living as a surveyor. But the early death of his older brother and his marriage to the wealthy widow Martha Custis had made him a rich man. Though unmistakably an aristocrat, Washington was unswervingly committed to representative government. And he had other desirable traits as well.

His stamina was remarkable: in more than eight years of war Washington never had a serious illness and took only one brief leave of absence. Moreover, he both looked and acted like a leader. Six feet tall in an era when most men were five inches shorter, his presence was stately and commanding. Other patriots praised his judgment, steadiness, and discretion, and even a loyalist admitted that Washington could "atone for many demerits by the extraordinary coolness and caution which distinguish his character."

Washington needed all the coolness and caution he could muster when he took command of the army outside Boston in July 1775. It took him months to impose hierarchy and discipline on the unruly troops and to bring order to the supply system. But by March 1776, when the arrival of cannon from Ticonderoga enabled him at last to put direct pressure on the redcoats in the city, the army was prepared to act. As it happened, an assault on Boston proved unnecessary. Sir William Howe, who had replaced Gage as the British commander-in-chief, had been considering an evacuation for some time; he wanted to move his troops to a more central location, New York City. The patriots' bombardment of Boston early in the month decided the matter. On March 17, the British and more than a thousand of their loyalist allies abandoned Boston forever.

That spring of 1776, as the British fleet left Boston for the temporary haven of Halifax, Nova Scotia, the colonies were moving inexorably toward the act the Massachusetts loyalists on board the ships feared most: a declaration of independence. Even months after fighting had begun, American leaders still denied they sought a break with the empire. Then in January 1776 there appeared a pamphlet by a man who not only thought the unthinkable but advocated it.

Thomas Paine's *Common Sense* exploded on the American scene like a bombshell. Within three

| Thomas Paine's Common Sense |

months of publication, it sold 120,000 copies. The author, a radical English printer who had lived in America only since 1774, called stridently and stirringly for independence. More than that: Paine challenged many common American assumptions about government and the colonies' relationship to England. Rejecting the notion that a balance of monarchy, aristocracy, and democracy was necessary to preserve freedom, he advocated the establishment of a republic. Instead of acknowledging the benefits of a connection with the mother country, Paine insisted that Britain had exploited the colonies unmercifully. In place of the frequent assertion that an independent America would be weak and divided, he substituted an unlimited confidence in America's strength when freed from European control. These striking statements were clothed in equally striking prose. Scorning the polite, rational style of his classically educated predecessors, Paine adopted a furious, raging tone. His work was couched in the language of the common people and relied heavily on the Bible—the only book familiar to

most Americans—as his primary source of authority. No wonder the pamphlet had a wider distribution than any other political publication of its day.

There is no way of knowing how many people were converted to the cause of independence by reading *Common Sense*. But by late spring 1776 independence had clearly become inevitable. On May 10, the Second Continental Congress formally recommended that individual colonies "adopt such governments as shall, in the opinion of the representatives of the people, best conduce to the happiness and safety of their constituents in particular, and America in general." From that source flowed the first state constitutions. Perceiving the trend of events, the few loyalists still connected with the congress severed their ties to that body.

Then on June 7 came the confirmation of the movement toward independence. Richard Henry Lee of Virginia, seconded by John Adams of Massachusetts, introduced the crucial resolution: "that these United Colonies are, and of right ought to be, free and independent States, that they are absolved of all allegiance to the British Crown, and that all political connection between them and the State of Great Britain is, and ought to be, totally dissolved." The congress debated but did not immediately adopt Lee's resolution. Instead, consideration was postponed until early July, to allow time for consultation and public reaction. In the meantime, a committee composed of Thomas Jefferson, John Adams, Benjamin Franklin,

| Declaration of Independence |

Robert R. Livingston of New York, and Roger Sherman of Connecticut was directed to draft a declaration of independence.

The committee in turn assigned primary responsibility for writing the declaration to Jefferson, who was well known for his apt and eloquent style. Years later John Adams recalled that Jefferson had modestly protested his selection, suggesting that Adams prepare the initial draft. The Massachusetts revolutionary recorded his frank response: "You can write ten times better than I can."

Thomas Jefferson was at the time thirty-four years old, a Virginia lawyer educated at the College of William and Mary and in the law offices of the prominent attorney George Wythe. He had also read widely in history and political theory, especially after his election to the House of Burgesses. His broad knowledge

Edward Savage never completed this engraving of the July 2 vote in the Second Continental Congress, but the likenesses of the members of the committee that drafted the Declaration of Independence dominate the center. Thomas Jefferson places a draft of the document on the table. Grouped around Jefferson are the other members of the drafting committee: John Adams, Roger Sherman, Robert R. Livingston, and Benjamin Franklin (seated). American Antiquarian Society.

was evident not only in the declaration but also in his draft of the Virginia state constitution, completed just a few days before his appointment to the committee. Jefferson, an intensely private man, loved his home and family deeply. This early stage of his political career was marked by his beloved wife Martha's repeated difficulties in childbearing. While he wrote and debated in Philadelphia during the summer of 1776, she suffered a miscarriage at their home, Monticello. Only after her death in 1782, from complications following the birth of their sixth (but only third surviving) child in ten years of marriage, did Jefferson fully commit himself to a career of public service.

The draft of the declaration was laid before congress on June 28. The delegates officially voted for independence four days later, then debated the wording of the declaration for two more days, adopting it with some changes on July 4. Since Americans had long since ceased to see themselves as legitimate subjects of Parliament, the Declaration of Independence concentrated on George III. It accused the king of attempting to destroy representative government in the colonies and of oppressing Americans through the unjustified use of excessive force. But the declaration's chief importance did not lie in its lengthy catalogue of grievances against the king (including, in a section omitted by congress, Jefferson's charge that George III had introduced slavery into America). It lay instead in the ringing statements of principle that have served ever since as the ideal to which Americans adhere, nominally at least. "We hold these truths to be self evident, that all men are created equal; that they are endowed by their creator with certain inalienable rights; that among these are life, liberty and the pursuit of happiness; that, to secure these rights, governments are instituted among men, deriving their just powers from the consent of the governed, that whenever any form of government becomes destructive of these ends, it is the right of the people to alter or abolish it, and to institute new government." These phrases have echoed down through American history like no others.

The delegates in Philadelphia who voted to accept the Declaration of Independence did not have the advantage of our two hundred years of hindsight. When they adopted the declaration, they risked their necks; they were unequivocally committing treason against the crown. Thus when they concluded the declaration with the assertion that they "mutually pledge[d] to each other our lives, our fortunes, and our sacred honor," they spoke no less than the truth. The real struggle still lay before them, and few of them had Thomas Paine's boundless confidence in success.

The long struggle in the North

In late June 1776, the first of the ships carrying Sir William Howe's troops from Halifax appeared off the coast of New York. On July 2, the day the congress voted for independence, the redcoats landed on Staten Island. But Howe waited until mid-August, after the

| Battle for New York City |

arrival of troop transports from England, to begin his attack on the city. The delay gave Washington sufficient time to march his army south to meet the threat. To defend New York, Washington had approximately 17,000 soldiers: 10,000 Continentals who had promised to serve until the end of the year, and 7,000 militiamen who had enlisted for shorter terms. Neither he nor most of his men had ever fought a major battle against the British, and their

lack of experience led to disastrous mistakes. The difficulty of defending New York City only compounded the errors.

Washington's problem was as simple as the geography of the region was complex. To protect the city adequately, he would have to divide his forces among Long Island, Manhattan Island, and the mainland. But the British fleet under Admiral Lord Richard Howe, Sir William's brother, controlled the harbors and rivers that separated the American forces. The patriots thus constantly courted catastrophe, for swift action by the British navy could cut off the possibility of retreat and perhaps even communication. But despite these dangers, Washington could not afford to surrender New York to the Howes without a fight. Not only did the city occupy a strategic location, but the region that surrounded it was known to contain many loyalist sympathizers. A show of force was essential if the revolutionaries were to retain any hope of persuading waverers to join them.

Washington fortified strong entrenchments atop Brooklyn Heights, overlooking lower Manhattan, and awaited the British attack. It came on August 27. Sir William Howe brilliantly outflanked the untried American troops posted in poorly designed forward positions, forcing them back into the Brooklyn trenches with heavy losses. But instead of pressing his advantage by making a frontal assault on the Americans, Howe delayed. Perhaps the memory of Bunker Hill casualties was still fresh in his mind. Nor did he order his brother's ships to sail into the East River to prevent the Americans from retreating. As a result, the patriots escaped. On the night of August 29, a troop of Marblehead, Massachusetts, fishermen ferried the entire Brooklyn contingent of 9,000 men to Manhattan in less than nine hours.

But Washington was not safe. Indeed, he still faced possible defeat, for the British could easily trap him and his men on the southern tip of Manhattan by means of combined sea and land movements. The Howe brothers again let their quarry escape, maneuvering their huge force so slowly that Washington was able to retreat northward onto the mainland. Once more the American commander-in-chief erred, leaving nearly 3,000 men in the supposedly impregnable Fort Washington on the west shore of Manhattan. When Sir William Howe finally decided to stop chasing Washington through Westchester County

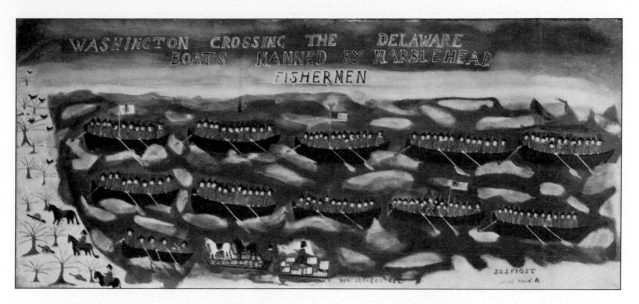

Years after Marblehead fishermen ferried Washington's troops across the Delaware to attack the Hessians at Trenton, J.O.J. Frost, an untrained artist, celebrated his townsmen's heroism. Private Collection.

and turned his attention back to the fort, its defenses quickly collapsed. The large garrison surrendered in early November. Only when Charleston fell to the British in May 1780 did the Americans lose more men on a single occasion.

George Washington had defended New York, but he had done a bad job of it. He had repeatedly broken a primary rule of military strategy: never divide your force in the face of a superior enemy. In the end, though, the Howe brothers' failure to move quickly prevented a decisive defeat of the Americans. Although Washington's army had been seriously reduced by battlefield casualties, the surrender of Fort Washington, and the loss of most of the militiamen (who had headed home for the harvest), its core remained. Through November and December, Washington led his men in a retreat across New Jersey. Howe followed at a leisurely pace, setting up a string of outposts manned mostly by Hessian mercenaries. After Washington crossed the Delaware River into Pennsylvania, the British commander turned back and settled into comfortable winter quarters in New York City.

The British now controlled most of New Jersey. Hundreds of Americans accepted the pardons offered by the Howes. Among them were Joseph Galloway, the one-time delegate to the First Continental Congress, and Richard Stockton, a signer of the Declaration of Independence. The occupying troops met with little opposition, and the revolutionary cause appeared to be in disarray. "These are the times that try men's souls," wrote Thomas Paine in his pamphlet *The Crisis.* "The summer soldier and the sunshine patriot will, in this crisis, shrink from the service of his country; . . . yet we have this consolation with us, that the harder the conflict, the more glorious the triumph."

In the aftermath of battle, as at its height, the British generals let their advantage slip away. The redcoats stationed in New Jersey went on a rampage of rape and plunder. Because loyalists and patriots were indistinguishable to the British and Hessian troops, families on both sides suffered equally. Livestock, crops, and firewood were seized for use by the army. Houses were looted and burned, churches and public buildings desecrated. But nothing was better calculated to rally doubtful Americans to the cause of independence than the wanton murder of innocent civilians and the epidemic of rape inflicted on the women of New Jersey. Sixteen girls from Hopewell were held captive for days in the British camp and repeatedly molested; a thirteen-year-old was raped by six soldiers;

Jean Baptiste Antoine de Verger, a sublieutenant in the French army in America, painted this watercolor of revolutionary soldiers in his journal. They are, from left to right, a black light infantryman, a musketman, a rifleman, and an artilleryman. The Anne S. K. Brown Military Collection.

another thirteen-year-old, two of her friends, and her aunt were similarly attacked. A resident of Princeton, in his eyewitness account of the occupation of the state, lamented that "against both justice and reason we despise these poor innocent sufferers." Consequently, he observed, "many honest virtuous women have suffered in this manner and kept it secret for fear of making their lives misserable."

The soldiers' marauding alienated potentially loyal New Jerseyites and Pennsylvanians whose allegiance the British could ill afford to lose. It also spurred Washington's determination to strike back. The enlistments of most of the Continental troops were to expire on December 31, and Washington also wanted to take advantage of short-term Pennsylvania militia who had recently joined him. Thus he had to move quickly. And he did, attacking the Hessian encamp-

| Battle of Trenton |

ment at Trenton early in the morning of December 26, while the redcoats were still reeling from their Christmas celebration. The patriots captured more than 900 Hessians and killed another 30; only 3 Americans were wounded. A few days later, after persuading many of his men to stay on beyond the term of their enlistments, Washington attacked again at Princeton. Having gained command of the field and buoyed American spirits with the two swift victories, Washington set up winter quarters at Morristown, New Jersey.

The campaign of 1776 established patterns that were to persist throughout much of the war, despite changes in British leadership and strategy. British forces were usually more numerous and often better led than the Americans. But their ponderous style of

Chapter 5: A revolution, indeed, 1775–1783

maneuvering, lack of familiarity with the terrain, and inability to live off the land without antagonizing the populace helped to offset those advantages. Furthermore, although Washington always seemed to lack regular troops—the Continental Army never numbered more than 18,500 men—he could usually count on the militia to join him at crucial points. American militiamen did not like to sign up for long terms of service or to fight far from home, but when their homes were threatened they would rally to the cause. Washington and his officers frequently complained about the militia's habit of disappearing during planting or harvesting. But time and again their presence, however brief, enabled the Americans to launch an attack or counter an important British thrust.

As the war dragged on, the Continental Army and the militia took on decidedly different characters. State governments, responsible for filling military quotas, discovered that most men willing to enlist for long periods in the regular army were young, single, and footloose. Farmers with families tended to prefer short-term militia duty. As the supply of whites willing to sign up for the Continentals diminished, recruiters in the northern states turned increasingly to blacks, both slave and free. (White southerners continued to resist this approach.) Perhaps as many as 5,000 blacks eventually served in the Revolutionary army, and most of them won their freedom as a result. Also attached to the American forces were a number of women, mostly wives and widows of poor soldiers. Such camp followers worked as cooks, nurses, and launderers, performing vital services for the army in return for rations and extremely low wages. The presence of the women, as well as the militiamen who floated in and out of the American camp at irregular intervals, made for an unwieldy army its officers found difficult to manage. Yet the army's shapelessness also reflected its greatest strength: an almost unlimited reservoir of man and woman power.

In 1777, the chief British effort was planned by the flashy "Gentleman Johnny" Burgoyne, a playboy general as much at home at the gaming tables of London as on the battlefield. Burgoyne, a subordinate of Howe, had spent the winter of 1776 and 1777 in London, where he gained the ear of Lord George Germain. Burgoyne convinced Germain that he could lead an invading force of redcoats and Indians down the Hudson River from Canada, cutting off New

Deborah Sampson (1760–1827), a patriot who disguised herself as a man and enlisted in the Continental Army under the name Robert Shurtleff. She served from May 1782 to October 1783, when her sex was discovered and she was discharged. In later years she made a living by giving public lectures describing her wartime experiences. After her death her husband became the only man to receive a pension as the "widow" of a revolutionary soldier. Rhode Island Historical Society.

England from the rest of the states. He proposed to rendezvous near Albany with a similar force that would move east from Niagara along the Mohawk River valley. The combined force would then presumably link up with that of Sir William Howe in New York City.

That Burgoyne's scheme would give "Gentleman Johnny" all the glory and relegate Howe to a supporting role did not escape Howe's notice. In fact, while Burgoyne was plotting in London, Howe was laying his own plans in New York City. Joseph Galloway and other Pennsylvania loyalists persuaded Howe that Philadelphia could be taken easily and that his troops would be welcomed by many residents of the region.

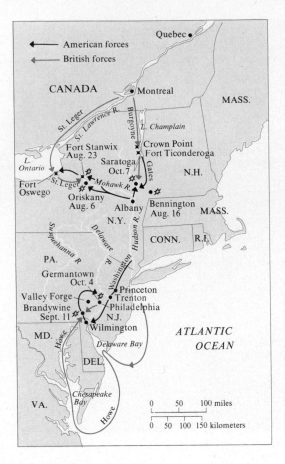

American forces
British forces

CANADA

Quebec
Montreal

MASS.

St. Leger
St. Lawrence R.
Burgoyne
L. Champlain

Fort Stanwix
Aug. 23

Crown Point
Fort Ticonderoga

L.
Ontario

Saratoga
Oct. 7

Gates

N.H.

Fort
Oswego

St. Leger
Mohawk R.

Oriskany
Aug. 6

Albany

Bennington
Aug. 16

MASS.

N.Y.

Hudson R.

CONN.

R.I.

Susquehanna R.
Delaware R.
Washington

PA.

Germantown
Oct. 4

Valley Forge
Brandywine
Sept. 11

Princeton
Trenton
Philadelphia
N.J.

Wilmington

ATLANTIC
OCEAN

MD.
Howe
Delaware Bay

DEL.

VA.
Chesapeake
Bay

Howe

0   50   100 miles

0   50 100 150 kilometers

Campaign of 1777

Just as Burgoyne left Howe out of his plans, Howe left Burgoyne out of his. Thus the two major British armies in America would operate independently in 1777, and the result would be a disaster (see map).

Howe accomplished his objective: he captured Philadelphia. But he did so in an inexplicable fashion, delaying for months before beginning the campaign,

Howe takes Philadelphia

then taking six weeks to transport his troops by sea to the head of Chesapeake Bay instead of marching them overland. That maneuver cost him at least a month, debilitated his men, and depleted his supplies. Incredibly, due to contrary winds and a change of destination, he was only forty miles closer to Philadelphia at the end of the lengthy voyage than when he had begun. Two years later, when Parliament formally inquired into the conduct of the war, Howe's critics charged that his errors were so extraordinary he must have deliberately committed treason. Even today, his-

torians have not been able to explain his motives adequately. In any event, by the time Howe was ready to move on Philadelphia, Washington had had time to prepare its defenses. Twice, at Brandywine Creek and again at Germantown, the two armies clashed near the rebel capital. Though the British won both engagements, the Americans handled themselves well. The redcoats took control of Philadelphia in late September, but to little effect. The campaign season was nearly over; the Revolutionary army had gained confidence in itself and its leaders; few welcoming loyalists had materialized; and, far to the north, Burgoyne was going down to defeat.

Burgoyne and his men had set out from Montreal in mid-June, floating down Lake Champlain into New York in canoes and flat-bottomed boats. In early

Burgoyne's campaign in New York

June they had easily taken Fort Ticonderoga from its outnumbered and outgunned defenders. But trouble began as Burgoyne started his overland march. His clumsy artillery carriages and baggage wagons foundered in the heavy forests and ravines. Progress was further slowed by patriot militia, who felled giant trees across the army's path. As a result, Burgoyne's troops took 24 days to travel the 23 miles to Fort Edward, on the Hudson River. Short of supplies, the general dispatched 800 German mercenaries into Vermont to forage the countryside. On August 16 American militia companies nearly wiped out the Germans at Bennington, a severe blow to the redcoats. Yet Burgoyne failed to recognize the seriousness of his predicament and continued to dawdle, giving the Americans more than enough time to prepare for his coming. By the time he finally crossed the Hudson in mid-September, bound for Albany, Burgoyne's fate was sealed. After several bloody clashes with the American force commanded by Horatio Gates, Burgoyne was surrounded near Saratoga, New York. On October 17, 1777, he surrendered his entire force of more than 6,000 men.

Long before, the 1,400 redcoats and Indians marching along the Mohawk River toward Albany had also been turned back. Under the command of Colonel Barry St. Leger, they had advanced easily until they reached the isolated American outpost at Fort Stanwix in early August. After they had laid siege to the well-fortified structure, they learned that a patriot relief column was en route to the fort. Leaving only a

Chapter 5: A revolution, indeed, 1775–1783

The Mohawk chief Joseph Brant (1742–1807), painted in London in 1786 by Gilbert Stuart. New York State Historical Association, Cooperstown.

small detachment at Fort Stanwix, the British ambushed the Americans at Oriskany on August 6. The British claimed victory in the ensuing battle, one of the bloodiest of the war, but they and their Indian allies lost their taste for further fighting. The Americans tricked them into believing that another large patriot force was on the way, and in late August the British abandoned the siege and returned to Niagara.

The battle of Oriskany marked the division of the Iroquois Confederacy. In 1776 the Six Nations had

> Crumbling of
> the Iroquois
> Confederacy

formally pledged to remain neutral in the Anglo-American struggle. But two influential Mohawk leaders, Joseph and Mary Brant, worked tirelessly to persuade their fellow Iroquois to join the British. Mary Brant, a powerful

tribal matron in her own right, was also the widow (in fact if not in law) of the respected Indian superintendent Sir William Johnson. Her younger brother Joseph, a renowned warrior who visited London early in the war, was convinced that the Six Nations should ally themselves with the British in order to prevent American encroachment on their lands. As an observer said of Mary, "one word from her goes farther with them [the Iroquois] than a thousand from any white man without exception." The Brants won over to the British the Senecas, Cayugas, and Mohawks, all of whom contributed warriors to St. Leger's expedition. But the Oneidas persisted in their traditional preference for the Americans, bringing the Tuscaroras with them. (The remaining Iroquois tribe, the Onondagas, split into three factions, one on each side and

The long struggle in the North

one supporting neutrality.) At Oriskany, the Oneidas and the Tuscaroras joined the patriot militia to fight their Iroquois brethren; thus a league of friendship that had survived for more than three hundred years was torn apart by the whites' family quarrel.

For the Indians, Oriskany was the most significant battle of the northern campaign; for the whites, it was Saratoga. The news of Burgoyne's surrender brought joy to patriots, discouragement to loyalists and Britons. In exile in London, Thomas Hutchinson wrote of the "universal dejection" among loyalists there. "Everybody in a gloom," he commented; "most of us expect to lay our bones here." The disaster prompted Lord North to authorize a peace commission to offer the Americans everything they had requested in 1774—in effect, a return to the imperial system of 1763. It was, of course, far too late for that: the patriots rejected the overture and the peace commission sailed back to England empty-handed in mid-1778.

Most important of all, the American victory at Saratoga drew France into the war. Ever since 1763, the French had been seeking ways to avenge their defeat in the Seven Years' War, and the American Revolution was the perfect opportunity to do so. King Louis XVI and his ministers had covertly aided the revolutionaries with money and supplies since 1776, and American emissaries in France (notably the clever Benjamin Franklin) had worked tirelessly to strengthen those ties. Not until Saratoga, though, did France agree to a formal alliance with the patriots. After 1778, the British could no longer focus their attention on the American mainland alone, for they had to fight the French in the West Indies and elsewhere. Spain's entry into the war in 1779 as an ally of France (but not the United States) further magnified Britain's problems. In the last years of the war, French assistance was to prove vital to the Americans.

| French entry into the war |

The long struggle in the South

In the aftermath of the Saratoga disaster, Lord George Germain and the military officials in London reassessed their strategy. Maneuvering in the North had done them little good; perhaps shifting the field of battle southward would bring success. The many loyalist exiles in England encouraged this line of thinking. They argued that loyal southerners would welcome the redcoat army as liberators, and that once the region had been pacified and returned to civilian control it could serve as a base for attacking the North.

By early 1778 Sir William Howe had resigned and been replaced by Sir Henry Clinton, a former subordinate who had sharply criticized Howe in 1776 for failure to act decisively. But as commander-in-chief Clinton too was afflicted with sluggishness and lack of resolution. Clinton oversaw the regrouping of British forces in America, ordering the evacuation of Philadelphia in June 1778 and dispatching a small expedition to Georgia at the end of the year. When Savannah and then Augusta fell easily into British hands, Clinton became convinced that a southern strategy would work. In late 1779 he sailed down the coast with an invasion force of 8,500 troops to attack Charleston, the most important American city in the South.

Although the Americans worked hard to bolster Charleston's defenses, the city fell to the British on May 12, 1780. General Benjamin Lincoln surrendered the entire southern army—5,500 men—to the invaders. In the weeks that followed, the redcoats spread throughout South Carolina, establishing garrisons at key points in the interior. As in New Jersey in 1776, hundreds of South Carolinians renounced allegiance to the United States and proclaimed their loyalty to the crown. Clinton organized loyalist regiments and the process of pacification began.

| Fall of Charleston |

Yet the British triumph was less complete and secure than it appeared. The success of the southern campaign depended on British control of the seas, for only by sea could the widely dispersed British armies remain in communication with one another. For the moment the Royal Navy safely dominated the American coastline, but French naval power posed a threat to the entire southern enterprise. Moreover, the redcoats never managed to establish full control of the areas they seized. As a result, patriot bands operated freely throughout the state, and loyalists could not be guaranteed protection against their enemies. Last but not least, the fall of Charleston did not dishearten the patriots; instead, it spurred them to greater exertions.

As one Marylander declared confidently, "The Fate of America is not to be decided by the Loss of a Town or Two." Patriot women in four states formed the Ladies Association, which collected money to purchase shirts for needy soldiers. Recruiting efforts were stepped up.

Throughout most of 1780, though, the war in South Carolina went badly for the patriots. In August, a reorganized southern army under the command of Horatio Gates was crushingly defeated at Camden by the forces of Lord Cornwallis, who had been placed in charge of the southern campaign. The British army was joined wherever it went by hundreds, even thousands, of blacks seeking freedom with the redcoats on the basis of Lord Dunmore's proclamation. Slaves ran away from their patriot masters individually and as families, in such numbers that they seriously disrupted planting and harvesting in 1780 and 1781. More than 55,000 blacks were lost to their owners as a result of the war. Not all of them joined the British or won their freedom if they did, but their flight had just the effect Dunmore wanted. And a good many served the British as scouts, guides, and laborers.

After the defeat at Camden, Washington (who had to remain in the North to oppose the British army occupying New York) gave command of the southern campaign to General Nathanael Greene of Rhode Island. Greene was appalled by what he found in South Carolina. As he wrote to a friend, "the word difficulty when applied to the state of things here . . . is almost without meaning, it falls so far short" of reality. His troops needed clothing, blankets, and food, but "a great part of this country is already laid waste and in the utmost danger of becoming a desert." The constant guerrilla warfare had, he commented, "so corrupted the principles of the people that they think of nothing but plundering one another." Under such circumstances, Greene had to move cautiously. He adopted a conciliatory policy toward loyalists and

| *Greene rallies South Carolina* |

neutrals, persuading the governor of South Carolina to offer complete pardons to those who had fought for the British if they would join the patriot militia. He also ordered his troops not to loot loyalist property and to treat captives fairly. Greene recognized that the patriots could win only by convincing the people that they could bring stability to the region. He thus helped the shattered provincial con-

Esther DeBerdt Reed (1746–1780), founder of the Ladies Association of 1780. Reed coordinated fund raising for the war effort until her untimely death from dysentery in the fall of 1780. Reed Collection.

gresses of Georgia and South Carolina to begin reestablishing civilian authority in the interior—a goal the British were never able to accomplish, even along the coast.

Greene also took a conciliatory approach to the southern Indians, in contrast to the policy adopted in the North. After Iroquois bands allied with the British made bloody raids on the New York frontier settlements of Wyoming and Cherry Valley in 1778, the whites had retaliated by burning Iroquois crops and villages in 1779. The following years were filled with even more bloodshed as both sides sought revenge for past wrongs. But Greene, with his desperate need for soldiers, could not afford to have frontier militia companies occupied in defending their homes against Indian attacks. Since he had so few regulars (only 1,600 when he took command), Greene had to rely on western volunteers. Thus he negotiated with the Indians.

His policy eventually met with success, although at first royal officials cooperating with the British invasion forces won allies among the Creeks, Choctaws,

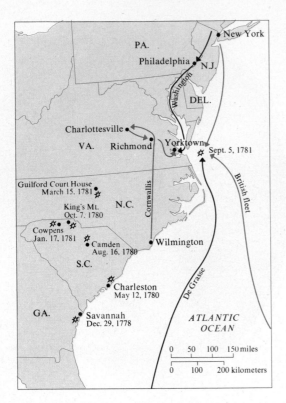

The war in the South

coats and loyalists. Then in January 1781 Greene's trusted aide, Brigadier General Daniel Morgan, brilliantly defeated the crack British regiment Tarleton's Legion at Cowpens, near the border between North and South Carolina. Greene himself confronted the main body of British troops under Lord Cornwallis at Guilford Court House, North Carolina, in March. Cornwallis controlled the field at the end of the day, but his army had been largely destroyed. He had to retreat to Wilmington, on the coast, to receive supplies and fresh troops from New York by sea. In the meantime Greene returned to South Carolina, where, in a series of swift strikes, he forced the redcoats to abandon their posts in the interior and retire to Charleston.

Cornwallis had already ignored explicit orders not to leave South Carolina unless the state was safely in British hands. Evidently bent on his own destruction, he now headed north into Virginia, where he joined forces with a detachment of redcoats commanded by the American traitor Benedict Arnold. (Arnold had fought heroically with the patriots early in the war, but defected to the British in 1780 in the belief that the Americans did not fully appreciate him.) Instead of acting decisively with his new army of 7,200 men, Cornwallis withdrew to the tip of the peninsula between the York and James rivers, where he fortified Yorktown and in effect waited for the end. Seizing the opportunity, Washington quickly moved over 7,000 troops south from New York City. When a French fleet under the Comte de Grasse arrived from the West Indies to cut the Britons' vital sea supply line, Cornwallis was trapped (see map). On October 19, 1781, four years and two days after Burgoyne's defeat at Saratoga, Cornwallis surrendered to the combined

Surrender at Yorktown

American and French forces while his military band played "The World Turned Upside Down."

When news of the surrender reached England, Lord North's ministry fell. Parliament voted to cease offensive operations in America and authorized peace negotiations. But guerrilla warfare between patriots and loyalists continued to ravage the Carolinas and Georgia for more than a year, and in the North vicious retaliatory raids by Indians and whites kept the frontier aflame. Indeed, the single most brutal massacre of the war occurred in March 1782, at Gnadenhuetten, Pennsylvania. There a group of white militia-

Chickasaws, and especially Dragging Canoe's Cherokees. But these southern tribes, recalling the disastrous defeat the Cherokees had suffered in 1776, never committed themselves wholeheartedly to the British. In 1781 the Cherokees began negotiations with the patriots, and the next year the other tribes too sued for peace. By the end of the war only the Creeks remained allied to the redcoats. A group of Chickasaw chiefs explained their reasoning to American agents in July 1782, after Greene's battlefield successes had forced the British to withdraw into Savannah and Charleston: "The English put the Bloody Tomahawk into our hands, telling us that we should have no Goods if we did not Exert ourselves to the greatest point of Resentment against you, but now we find our mistake and Distresses. The English have done their utmost and left us in our adversity. We find them full of Deceit and Dissimulation."

Even before Greene took command of the southern army in December 1780, the tide had begun to turn. At King's Mountain in October, a force of "overmountain men" from the settlements west of the Appalachians had defeated a large party of red-

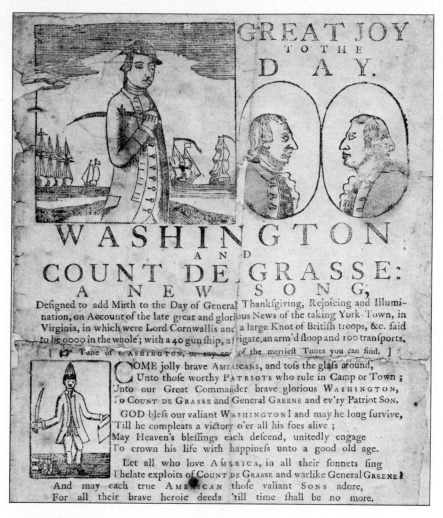

GREAT JOY TO THE DAY.

WASHINGTON AND COUNT DE GRASSE: A NEW SONG,

Designed to add Mirth to the Day of General Thanksgiving, Rejoicing and Illumination, on Account of the late great and glorious News of the taking York-Town, in Virginia, in which were Lord Cornwallis and a large Knot of British troops, &c. said to be 0000 in the whole; with a 40 gun ship, a frigate, an arm'd sloop and 100 transports.

[☞ Tune of WASHINGTON, or any one of the merriest Tunes you can find.]

COME jolly brave AMERICANS, and toss the glass around,
Unto those worthy PATRIOTS who rule in Camp or Town;
Unto our Great Commander brave glorious WASHINGTON,
To Count DE GRASSE and General GREENE and ev'ry Patriot Son.

GOD bless our valiant WASHINGTON! and may he long survive,
Till he compleats a victory o'er all his foes alive;
May Heaven's blessings each descend, unitedly engage
To crown his life with happiness unto a good old age.

Let all who love AMERICA, in all their sonnets sing
The late exploits of Count DE GRASSE and warlike General GREENE!
And may each true AMERICAN those valiant SONS adore,
For all their brave heroic deeds 'till time shall be no more.

Part of a broadside ballad celebrating the American victory at Yorktown. Published in Boston, probably in early 1782. The Henry Francis du Pont Winterthur Museum.

men, seeking the Indians who had killed a frontier family, encountered a peaceful band of Delawares. The Indians, who had been converted to both Christianity and pacifism by Moravian missionaries, were slaughtered unmercifully. Ninety-six men, women, and children died that day, some burned at the stake, others tomahawked. Two months later, hostile members of the Delaware tribe captured three white militiamen and subjected them to gruesome tortures in reprisal. The persistence of this sort of warfare after Yorktown, all too often overlooked in accounts of the Revolution, should serve to underline that the British and American armies were not the only combatants in the conflict.

The fighting finally ended when Americans and Britons learned of the signing of a preliminary peace treaty at Paris in November 1782. The American negotiators—Benjamin Franklin, John Jay, and John Adams—ignored their instructions to be guided by France and instead struck a separate agreement with Great Britain. Their instincts were sound: the French government was more an enemy to Britain than a friend to the United States. In fact, French ministers worked secretly behind the scenes to try to prevent the establishment of a strong, unified, independent republic in America. The new British ministry, headed by Lord Shelburne (formerly a persistent critic of Lord

Treaty of Paris

Important events

1768	Treaty of Hard Labor
	Treaty of Fort Stanwix
1770	Treaty of Lochaber
1773	Treaty of Augusta
1774	Lord Dunmore's War
	First Continental Congress
	Continental Association; committees of observation formed
1775	Battles of Lexington and Concord
	Battle of Bunker Hill
	Lord Dunmore's Proclamation
	Second Continental Congress
	American invasion of Canada
1776	Thomas Paine, *Common Sense*
	British evacuate Boston
	Declaration of Independence
	New York campaign
	Battle of Trenton
	Cherokee War
1777	Battle of Princeton
	British take Philadelphia
	Battle of Oriskany
	Burgoyne surrenders at Saratoga
1778	British Peace Commission
	French alliance
	British evacuate Philadelphia
	British take Savannah
1779	Sullivan expedition against Iroquois villages
1780	British take Charleston
	Battle of Camden
	Battle of King's Mountain
1781	Battle of Guilford Court House
	Cornwallis surrenders at Yorktown
1782	North's ministry falls
	Gnadenhuetten massacre
	British evacuate Savannah
	Preliminary peace treaty
	British evacuate Charleston
1783	Treaty of Paris
	British evacuate New York City

North's harsh American policies), was weary of war and made numerous concessions—so many, in fact, that Parliament ousted the ministry shortly after the peace terms were approved.

Under the treaty, finalized on September 3, 1783, the Americans were granted unconditional independence and unlimited fishing rights off Newfoundland. The boundaries of the new nation were generous: to the north, approximately the current boundary with Canada; to the south, the thirty-first parallel; to the west, the Mississippi River. The British conveniently overlooked the fact that their Indian allies, particularly the Iroquois and the Creeks, had joined them precisely because of their promise to protect Indian lands from white encroachment. Thus the tribes found themselves and their interests sacrificed to European power politics. Loyalists were also poorly served by the British negotiators. In effect the treaty legalized the wartime confiscation of loyalist property and forced people like Joseph Galloway into permanent exile.

The long war finally over, the victorious Americans could look back on their achievement with satisfaction and awe. In 1775, with an inexperienced ragtag army, they had taken on the greatest military power in the world—and eight years later they had won. They had accomplished their goal more through persistence and commitment than through brilliance on the battlefield. Actual victories had been few, but their army had always survived defeat and stand-offs to fight again. Ultimately, the Americans had simply worn their enemy down.

Suggestions for further reading

Essay collections

Larry Gerlach, ed., *Legacies of the American Revolution* (1978); *Journal of Interdisciplinary History,* 6, No. 4 (spring 1976), *Interdisciplinary Studies of the American Revolution;* Stephen G. Kurtz and James H. Hutson, eds., *Essays on the American Revolution* (1973); Library of Congress, *Symposia on the American Revolution,* 5 vols. (1972–1976); Edmund S. Morgan, *The Challenge of the American Revolution* (1976); *William and Mary Quarterly,* 3rd ser., 33, No. 3 (July 1976), *The American Revolution;* Alfred Young, ed., *The American Revolution: Explorations in the History of American Radicalism* (1976).

Military

John Richard Alden, *The American Revolution 1775–1783* (1964); Ira Gruber, *The Howe Brothers and the American Revolution* (1972); Don Higginbotham, *The War of American Independence: Military Attitudes, Policies, and Practice, 1763–1789* (1971); Piers Mackesy, *The War for America, 1775–1783* (1964); Charles Royster, *A Revolutionary People at War: The Continental Army and American Character, 1775–1783* (1980); John Shy, *A People Numerous & Armed: Reflections on the Military Struggle for American Independence* (1976); Marshall Smelser, *The Winning of Independence* (1972); Herbert T. Wade and Robert A. Lively, *This Glorious Cause: The Adventures of Two Company Officers in Washington's Army* (1958); Willard M. Wallace, *Appeal to Arms: A Military History of the American Revolution* (1950); William Willcox, *Portrait of a General: Sir Henry Clinton in the War of Independence* (1964).

Local and regional

Jeffrey Crow and Larry Tise, eds., *The Southern Experience in the American Revolution* (1978); Robert A. Gross, *The Minutemen and Their World* (1976); Ronald Hoffman, *A Spirit of Dissension: Economics, Politics, and the Revolution in Maryland* (1973); Robert J. Taylor, *Western Massachusetts in the Revolution* (1954).

Indians and blacks

Barbara Graymont, *The Iroquois in the American Revolution* (1972); Winthrop Jordan, *White Over Black: American Attitudes toward the Negro 1550–1812* (1968); Duncan J. MacLeod, *Slavery, Race, and the American Revolution* (1974); James H. O'Donnell, III, *Southern Indians in the American Revolution* (1973); Benjamin Quarles, *The Negro in the American Revolution* (1961); Anthony F.C. Wallace, *The Death and Rebirth of the Seneca* (1969).

Loyalists

Bernard Bailyn, *The Ordeal of Thomas Hutchinson* (1974); Robert McCluer Calhoon, *The Loyalists in Revolutionary America 1760–1781* (1973); William H. Nelson, *The American Tory* (1961); Mary Beth Norton, *The British-Americans: The Loyalist Exiles in England, 1774–1789* (1972); Mary Beth Norton, "Eighteenth-Century American Women in Peace and War: The Case of the Loyalists," *William and Mary Quarterly,* 3rd ser., 33 (1976), 486–409; Paul H. Smith, *Loyalists and Redcoats: A Study in British Revolutionary Policy* (1964); James W. St. G. Walker, *The Black Loyalists: The Search for a Promised Land in Nova Scotia and Sierra Leone 1783–1870* (1976).

Women

Linda Grant DePauw, *Founding Mothers: Women of America in the Revolutionary Era* (1975); Linda Grant DePauw and Conover Hunt, *"Remember the Ladies": Women in America 1750–1815* (1976); Linda K. Kerber, *Women of the Republic: Intellect & Ideology in Revolutionary America* (1980); Mary Beth Norton, *Liberty's Daughters: The Revolutionary Experience of American Women, 1750–1800* (1980).

Diplomacy

Samuel F. Bemis, *The Diplomacy of the American Revolution* (1935); Richard B. Morris, *The Peacemakers: The Great Powers and American Independence* (1965); Gerald Stourzh, *Benjamin Franklin and American Foreign Policy,* 2nd ed. (1969); Richard W. Van Alstyne, *Empire and Independence: The International History of the American Revolution* (1965).

Patriot leaders

Fawn M. Brodie, *Thomas Jefferson: An Intimate History* (1974); Verner W. Crane, *Benjamin Franklin and a Rising People* (1954); Marcus Cunliffe, *George Washington: Man and Monument* (1958); James T. Flexner, *George Washington,* 4 vols. (1965–1972); Eric Foner, *Tom Paine and Revolutionary America* (1976); Claude A. Lopez and Eugenia Herbert, *The Private Franklin: The Man and His Family* (1975); Dumas Malone, *Jefferson and His Time,* 5 vols. (1948–1974); Peter Shaw, *The Character of John Adams* (1976).

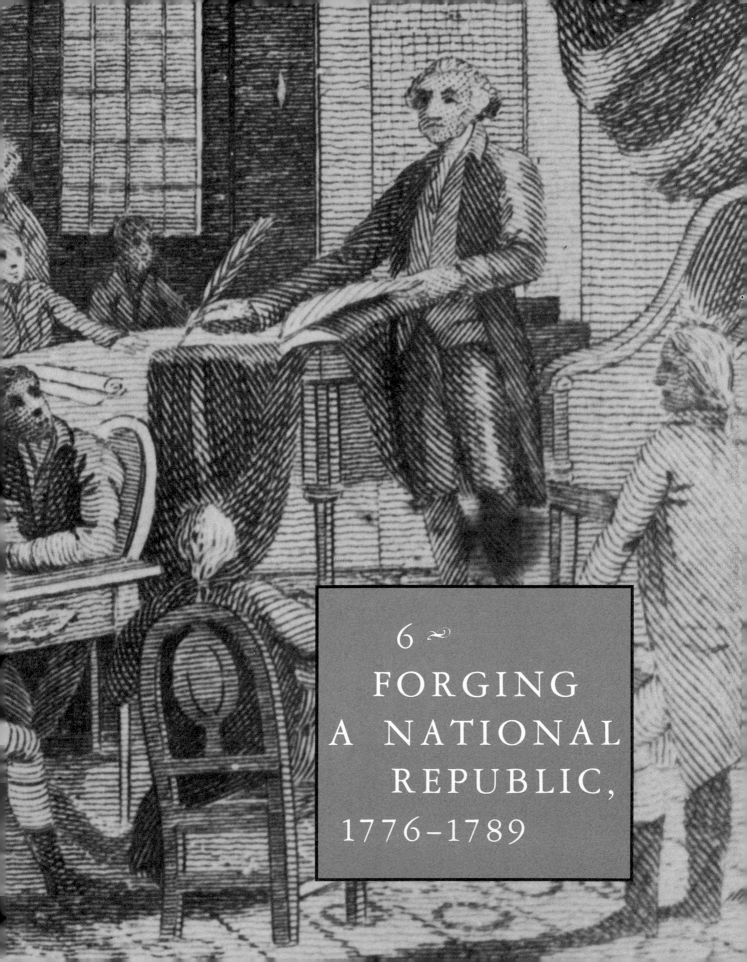

6

FORGING
A NATIONAL
REPUBLIC,
1776–1789

"In the new Code of Laws which I suppose it will be necessary for you to make I desire you would Remember the Ladies," Abigail Adams wrote her congressman husband John on March 31, 1776. "Remember all Men would be tyrants if they could," she continued. "If perticuliar care and attention is not paid to the Laidies we are determined to foment a Rebelion, and will not hold ourselves bound by any Laws in which we have no voice, or Representation."

With these words, Abigail Adams took a step that was soon to be duplicated by other disfranchised Americans. She was deliberately employing the ideology that had been developed to combat Great Britain's claims to political supremacy, but applying it to the legal status of women. Since men were "Naturally Tyrannical," she argued, America's new legal code should "put it out of the power of the vicious and the Lawless to use us with cruelty and indignity."

John Adams failed to take his wife's suggestion seriously. Two weeks later he replied, "As to your extraordinary Code of Laws, I cannot but Laugh. We have been told that our Struggle has loosened the bands of Government every where"—that children, apprentices, slaves, Indians, and college students had all become "disobedient" and "insolent." Her letter was the first indication that "another Tribe more numerous and powerfull than all the rest were grown discontented." But women, he insisted, had little reason for complaint. "In Practice you know We are subjects. We have only the Name of Masters, and rather than give up this, which would compleatly subject Us to the Despotism of the Peticoat, I hope General Washington and all our brave Heroes would fight."

Abigail Adams's famous words have often been cited as the first stirrings of feminism in America. Whether or not such an interpretation is accurate, her comments were, as John Adams recognized, a sign of the impact the Revolution and its ideology had had on American society. The colonists had ventured into revolution to protect their rights as English people, especially their right of consent to taxation. Gradually they had developed broader definitions of those rights and rejected monarchy once and for all. The accompanying abandonment of some political commonplaces, like the notion of absolute parliamentary supremacy, had called others into question. For example, the Americans' prolonged effort to define the relationship between the British government and their own local political institutions led them to question the traditional notion that sovereignty—the ultimate authority in any political unit—was indivisible. As a result, they created a federal system, in which the states and the central government shared political authority.

The experience of revolution prompted Americans to rethink their assumptions on nonpolitical matters as well. In the years before the Revolution, members of dissenting religious sects had protested their unequal status in colonies with a state-supported, or established, church. In those colonies (all but Rhode Island, Pennsylvania, New Jersey, and Delaware, which guaranteed complete religious freedom), dissenters could be taxed to support the established church. They also had to have the permission of the legislature to hold their own worship services. Revolutionary ideology helped dissenters combat such policies. Isaac Backus, a New England Baptist, observed forcefully that "many, who are filling the nation with the cry of LIBERTY and against *oppressors* are at the same time themselves violating that dearest of all rights, LIBERTY of CONSCIENCE." Legislators could not resist the logic of these arguments. Many states dissolved their ties to churches during the war; others vastly reduced state support for established denominations.

It was not just in the realms of religion and women's rights that revolutionary ideology had unexpected consequences. Propertyless men, who had always been denied the vote, began to claim that they too should have access to the ballot box. Other men argued that representation in state and national governments should be proportional to population, rather than allotted equally to governmental units (towns, counties, and states) of varying sizes. Some questioned the institution of slavery. Still others asked why one American citizen should be expected to defer automatically to the judgment of another, no matter how wealthy or well educated. Veterans returned home with a new sense of national pride, and with political loyalties that transcended state boundaries. They accordingly viewed politics differently than they had before the war. The cultural climate had changed: an independent America would be something more than a collection of former colonies.

In redefining their politics and society between 1775, when the war began, and 1787, when the new

Constitution was drafted, Americans drew their ideas from the ideology of resistance and from their own experiences. They designed state and national governments incorporating the features they had decided would best protect their rights: weak executives and powerful legislatures, separation of powers among branches of government, and division of sovereignty between national and state governments. Over time they modified their ideas somewhat, but these basic elements remained intact. The Articles of Confederation and the Constitution, which historians have often seen as reflecting opposing political philosophies (the "democratic" Articles versus the "aristocratic" Constitution), should instead be viewed as separate and successive attempts to solve the same problems. Both represented Americans' efforts to apply the lessons of the Revolution to their form of government.

Learning the lessons of the Revolution

Abigail Adams seems an unlikely revolutionary. In 1776 she was thirty-one years old, daughter of a minister, wife of a lawyer, and mother of four growing children. Throughout her life she emphasized the "Relative Duties" of her roles as wife, mother, and mistress of a household. She believed that women were more tender and delicate than men, that each sex had its distinct role to fulfill, and that ladies like herself should avoid the rough-and-tumble world of politics and public affairs. She had little formal education (as is apparent in her spelling and punctuation), but she read widely and thoughtfully. More important still, she had the intelligence to perceive the incongruities in her society and the initiative to point them out.

> *Abigail Adams*

Yet not until the American Revolution began did Abigail Adams think to question the assumptions that had previously defined her world. Her husband, like many other leaders of the Revolution, was away from home for long periods of time. John Adams served first in congress and then in the fledgling diplomatic corps; other male patriots enlisted in the Continental Army or the militia. In their absence their wives, who had previously handled only the "indoor affairs"

of the household, had to shoulder the responsibility for "outdoor affairs" as well. As the wife of a Connecticut militiaman later recalled, her husband "was out more or less during the remainder of the war [after 1777], so much so as to be unable to do anything on our farm. What was done, was done by myself."

In the Adams household and many others, the necessary shift of responsibilities that occurred during the war taught men and women that their traditional notions of proper sex roles had to be rethought. Both Adamses took great pride in Abigail's developing skills as a "farmeress," and John praised her courage repeatedly. "You are really brave, my dear, you are an Heroine," he told her in 1775. Abigail Adams, like her female contemporaries, stopped calling the farm "yours" in letters to her husband, and began referring to it as "ours." (This simple change of pronoun spoke volumes.) Both men and women realized that female patriots had made a vital contribution to winning the war through their work at home. Thus, in the years after the Revolution, Americans began to develop new ideas about the role women should play in a republican society.

Only a very few thought that role should include the right to vote. Abigail Adams called women's patriotism "the most disinterested of all virtues" because women were "excluded from honours and from offices" and "deprived of a voice in Legislation, obliged to submit to those Laws which are imposed upon us." Nevertheless, she did not press for female suffrage, believing that women's influence was best exerted in private. But some women thought differently, as events in New Jersey proved. The men who drafted the state constitution in 1776 had defined voters loosely as "all free inhabitants" who met certain property qualifications. They thereby unintentionally gave the vote to property-holding white spinsters and widows, as well as free black men. In the 1780s and 1790s women successfully claimed the right to vote in New Jersey's local and congressional elections. They continued to exercise that right until 1807, when women and blacks were disfranchised by the state legislature on the grounds that their votes could be easily manipulated. Yet the fact that they had voted at all was evidence of their altered perception of their place in political life.

Such dramatic episodes were unusual. On the whole the re-evaluation of women's position had its

In the mid-1780s Abigail Adams (1744–1818) and her husband John (1735–1826) sat for these portraits in London, where they had been reunited after a five-year wartime separation. John Adams was then American ambassador to Great Britain. Left, Boston Athenaeum. Right, New York State Historical Association, Cooperstown.

greatest impact on private life. For instance, the traditional colonial view of marriage had stressed the subordination of wife to husband. But in 1790 a female "Matrimonial Republican" asserted that "marriage

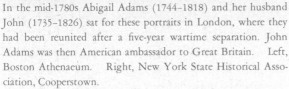
Revolutionary ideal of womanhood

ought never to be considered as a contract between a superior and an inferior, but a reciprocal union of interest. . . . The obedience between man and wife is, or ought to be mutual." This new understanding of the marital relationship seems to have contributed to a rising divorce rate after the war. Dissatisfied wives proved less willing to remain in unhappy marriages than they had been previously. At the same time, state judges became more sympathetic to women's desires to be freed from abusive or unfaithful husbands.

Furthermore, though the father had previously been seen as the most influential parent, the republican decades witnessed an ever-increasing emphasis on

the importance of mothers. A list of "Maxims for Republics" first published in 1779 and reprinted in 1788 declared that "it is of the utmost importance, that the women should be well instructed in the principles of liberty in a republic. Some of the first patriots of antient times, were formed by their mothers." In 1790 one woman even argued publicly for female superiority, resting her claim on woman's maternal role. Men, she said, had assumed primacy in the past "on the vain presumption of their being assigned the most important duties of life." But God had clearly intended otherwise, since to women He had "assigned the care of making the first impressions on the infant minds of the whole human race, a trust of more importance than the government of provinces, and the marshalling of armies."

Other Americans did not go that far. To be sure, they were more willing than before to expand the meaning of the phrase "all men are created equal" to

Chapter 6: Forging a national republic, 1776–1789

apply to women, but they still viewed woman's role in traditional terms. Like Abigail Adams, eighteenth-century Americans assumed that women's place was in the home, and that their primary function was to be good wives and mothers. They accepted the notion of equality, but within the context of men's and women's separate spheres. Whereas their forebears had seen women as inferior and subordinate to men, members of the revolutionary generation regarded the sexes and their roles as more nearly equal in importance. However, equality did not mean sameness. Despite the shift in opinion, it would be more than half a century before some Americans began to argue formally for women's rights.

To white men, too, the Revolution brought change. It is estimated that 40 percent of adult white male patriots served six months or more in the Revolutionary armies. (The total number of deaths in battle and from disease, approximately 25,000, seems small until one realizes that the proportional equivalent today would be two million.) In the ranks, American men learned four new political lessons. The first was nationalism. According to David Ramsay, a

Beginnings of nationalism

South Carolina physician and Continental Army veteran who was an early historian of the Revolution, the war "set them on thinking, speaking and acting in a line far beyond that to which they had been accustomed." The army and the congress, by "freely mixing together" men from all the states, "assimilated [them] into one mass." Thus, concluded Ramsay, "a foundation was laid for the establishment of a nation out of discordant materials."

Ramsay's statement was too sweeping, but he had correctly recognized that the experience of fighting, sacrificing, and working together for a common goal had given men from different regions a new notion of where their loyalties lay. At the First Continental Congress in 1774, John Adams made no secret of his preference for New England and its inhabitants, openly criticizing the beliefs and behavior of fellow congressmen from the southern and middle states. Yet within only a few years Adams had reordered his loyalties, putting primary emphasis not on his birthplace but on the nation as a whole.

Soldiers' letters confirm that Adams's change of heart was typical. In March 1776 a Massachusetts shoemaker in the Continental Army told his wife that "I am willing to serve my contery in the Best way & manner that I am Capeble of." Reporting to her the likelihood that his regiment would be moved south to New York City, he commented, "I would not Be understood that I should Chuse to March But as I am ingaged in this glories Cause I am will[ing] to go whare I am Called." Similarly, a surgeon assigned to Valley Forge during the difficult winter of 1777 and 1778 observed that "nothing tends to the establishment of the firmest Friendship like Mutual Sufferings." When such men returned to their homes after the war, they retained their patriotism and pride in their accomplishments. They had also acquired a knowledge of other parts of the country that few earlier Americans had possessed.

The second and third lessons concerned the theory and practice of republicanism. As John Dickinson later recalled, "there was no question concerning forms of Government, no enquiry whether a Republic or a limited Monarchy was best. . . . We knew that the people of this country must unite themselves under some form of Government and that this could be no other than the Republican form." To Dickinson and other Americans, a republican government had to rest directly and solely on the consent of the people. By definition it did not contain the balance of monarchical and aristocratic elements Europeans believed necessary for political stability. Members of the revolutionary generation therefore devoted much time and attention to molding state governments into proper republican shapes. They also attempted to order their lives in accordance with republican principles.

Nowhere was this more true than in the ranks of the Revolutionary army and navy, where enlisted men repeatedly revealed their commitment to the concept of government by mutual consent. Captured Ameri-

Republican soldiers

can sailors on British prison hulks lived by mutually agreed-upon rules formalized in written "constitutions." One such group of more than 100 seamen imprisoned in Plymouth, England, declared that "we are determined to stand, and so remain as long as we live, true and loyal to our Congress, our country, our wives, children and friends." When a thousand Pennsylvania soldiers mutinied at the American army's main winter encampment at Morristown, New Jersey, on January 2, 1781, their chief complaint was not poor food and clothing but that their rights had been violated. They had enlisted for three years, they argued, and their term of service was up; Pennsylvania contended that they had signed on for the duration of the war. The disgruntled soldiers chose a proper republican solution to their problem, leaving camp peacefully en masse to lay their case before Pennsylvania's civilian leaders. The military authorities agreed to a compromise that discharged most of the men.

Another republican lesson soldiers learned had to do with status and its prerequisites. Before the war, only men of distinguished social and economic standing had held political or military office in the colonies. But the unwieldy Revolutionary army required numerous officers (perhaps 15,000 to 20,000 in all). Consequently, men with no pretenses to gentlemanly status achieved posts of prestige and responsibility. At the same time, close contact with genteel officers gave many common soldiers a more realistic view of their betters. Privates who saw inexperienced officers make mistakes that cost both battles and men—there were many such mistakes during the long years of war—became less inclined to defer automatically to the gentry's judgment. Furthermore, military service at any rank brought honor to veterans in their home towns. After the war, former soldiers and sailors commanded the sort of respect from their fellow townsmen previously accorded only to clergymen and some secular leaders. Veterans accounted for a very high proportion of postwar officeholders, both elected and appointed. And since many states paid their soldiers in land grants rather than cash, propertyless young men could become independent yeoman farmers after they were mustered out of the service.

The fourth lesson of the Revolution was less heartening. In the heady days of 1775 and early 1776, before the British victories around New York City, the patriots had been convinced of their invincibility and of the willingness of the people to make necessary wartime sacrifices. But as the war dragged on and patriotic fervor subsided, the men serving their country grew bitter. The Valley Forge surgeon complained that those who sat comfortably at home around a warm fire "enjoying their wives & families" wanted the soldiers to "suffer everything for their Benefit & advantage, and yet are the first to Condemn us for not

doing more!" Soldiers were often underfed and underclothed, short of guns and ammunition, and unpaid—all because state legislatures failed to support the war with adequate appropriations and because war profiteers sold the army shoddy merchandise and spoiled food. For many soldiers, military salaries were the sole source of income. When skyrocketing inflation destroyed the value of the currency in 1779 and 1780, they had nothing to show for their years of service. Thus once-optimistic patriots learned that many Americans were unwilling to sacrifice personal gain for public good, and that it would be unwise to put too much confidence in their new governments.

Ironies of the Revolution

For white Americans, male and female, the war did more than change the way they thought about themselves. It also exposed them to one of the primary contradictions in their society. Just as Abigail Adams pointed out to her husband his failure to apply revolutionary doctrines to the status of women, both blacks and whites recognized the irony of slaveholding Americans claiming they wanted to prevent Britain from enslaving them.

As early as 1764, James Otis, Jr., had identified the basic problem in his pamphlet *The Rights of the British Colonies Asserted and Proved* (see pages 93–94). If according to natural law all people were born free and equal, that meant *all* humankind, black and white. "Does it follow that 'tis right to enslave a man because he is black?" Otis asked. "Can any logical inference in favor of slavery be drawn from a flat nose, a long or short face?" The same theme was later voiced by other revolutionary leaders. In 1773 the Philadelphia doctor Benjamin Rush called slavery "a vice which degrades human nature," warning ominously that "the plant of liberty is of so tender a nature that it cannot thrive long in the neighborhood of slavery." Common folk too saw the contradiction. When Josiah Atkins, a Connecticut soldier marching south, saw George Washington's plantation, he observed in his journal: "Alas! That persons who pretend to stand for the *rights of mankind* for the *liberties of society,* can delight in oppression, & that even of the worst kind!"

Elizabeth Freeman, known as Mumbet, whose suit for freedom in the mid-1780s prompted Massachusetts courts to outlaw slavery. The portrait was painted by Susan Sedgwick, daughter of Theodore Sedgwick, the Federalist lawyer who presented Mumbet's case in court. Mumbet later worked for Sedgwick as a paid servant. Massachusetts Historical Society.

Blacks themselves were quick to recognize the implications of revolutionary ideology. In 1779 a group of slaves from Portsmouth, New Hampshire, asked the state legislature "from what authority [our masters] assume to dispose of our lives, freedom and property," and pleaded "that the name of slave may not more be heard in a land gloriously contending for the sweets of freedom." That same year several black residents of Fairfield, Connecticut, petitioned the legislature for their freedom, characterizing slavery as a "dreadful Evil" and "flagrant Injustice." Surely, they declared pointedly, "your Honours who are nobly contending in the Cause of Liberty, whose Conduct excited the Admiration, and Reverence, of all the great Empires of the World; will not resent, our thus freely animadverting, on this detestable Practice."

Both legislatures responded negatively. But the postwar years did witness the gradual abolition of slavery in the North. Massachusetts courts decided in the 1780s that the clause in the state constitution declaring that "all men are born free and equal, and have certain natural, essential, and unalienable rights" had abolished slavery in the state. Pennsylvania passed an abolition law in 1780; four years later Rhode Island and Connecticut provided for gradual emancipation, followed by New York (1799) and New Jersey (1804). Although New Hampshire did

Gradual emancipation

The Reverend Richard Allen (1760–1831) of Philadelphia, founder of the African Methodist Episcopal Church. Allen was attracted to Methodism because "the Methodists were the first people that brought glad tidings to the colored people." Later elected bishop of the AME Church, he was the first black bishop in the United States.   Historical Society of Pennsylvania.

not formally abolish slavery, only eight slaves were reported on the 1800 state census and none remained a decade later.

In the South the pattern differed. Antislavery impulses prompted the state legislatures of Virginia (1782), Delaware (1787), and Maryland (1790 and 1796) to pass laws allowing masters to free their slaves without legal restrictions. But South Carolina and Georgia never considered adopting such acts, and North Carolina decided to insist that all manumissions—emancipations of individual slaves—be approved by county courts. None of the southern states came close to adopting general emancipation laws.

Thus revolutionary ideology had limited impact on the well-entrenched economic interests of large slaveholders. Only in the North, where there were few slaves and where little money was invested in human capital, could state legislatures vote to abolish slavery

with relative ease. Even there, legislators' concern for property rights—the Revolution was, after all, fought for property as well as life and liberty—led them to favor gradual emancipation over immediate abolition. Most states provided only for the freeing of children born after passage of the law, not for the emancipation of adults. And even those children were to remain slaves until age twenty-one or twenty-eight. As a result, some northern states still had a few legally held slaves at the time of the Civil War.

Despite the slow progress of abolition, the free black population of the United States grew dramatically in the first years after the Revolution. Before the war there had been few free blacks in America. (According to a 1755 Maryland census, for example, only 4 percent of the blacks in the colony were free.) Most prewar free blacks were mulattoes, born of unions between white masters and enslaved black women. But wartime disruptions radically changed the size and composition of the free black population. Slaves who had escaped from plantations during the war, others who had served in the American army, and still others who had been emancipated by their owners or by state laws were now free. Because most of them were not mulattoes, dark skin was no longer an automatic sign of slave status. By 1790 there were nearly 60,000 free people of color in the United States; ten years later they numbered more than 108,000 and represented nearly 11 percent of the total black population. The effects of postwar manumissions were felt most sharply in the upper South, where they were fostered by such economic changes as declining soil fertility and a shift from tobacco to grain production. The free Negro population of Virginia more than doubled between 1790 and 1810, and by the latter year nearly a quarter of Maryland's black population was no longer in legal bondage.

Growth of the free black population

But the trend toward abolition of slavery was not a trend toward racial equality. Even whites who recognized blacks' right to freedom were unwilling to accept them as equals. Laws discriminated against emancipated blacks as they had against slaves—South Carolina, for example, did not permit free blacks to testify against whites in court. Public schools often refused to educate the children of free black parents. Freedmen found it difficult to purchase property and find good jobs. And though in many areas blacks were accepted as members—even ministers—of evangelical churches, whites rarely allowed them an equal voice in church affairs.

Gradually free blacks developed their own separate institutions, sometimes by choice, sometimes because whites imposed segregation on them. In Charleston,

mulattoes formed the Brown Fellowship Society, which provided insurance coverage for its members, financed a school for free children, and helped to support black orphans. In 1787 blacks in Philadelphia and Baltimore founded churches that eventually became the African Methodist Episcopal (AME) denomination. AME churches later sponsored schools in a number of cities and often became cultural centers of the free black community.

For freed blacks, then, the lesson of the Revolution was that freedom from bondage did not necessarily mean freedom from discrimination. If they were to survive and prosper, they would have to rely on their own efforts rather than the benevolence or goodwill of their white compatriots.

American Indians had long since learned the same lesson. Even so, the Revolution meant the end of an independent tribal existence for most of those who lived east of the Mississippi River. They tried to resist the whites' westward thrust, but to no avail. Though tribal claims were not discussed by British and American diplomats at the end of the war, the United States assumed that the Treaty of Paris (1783) cleared its title to all land east of the Mississippi except the areas still held by Spain. But recognizing that some sort of land cession should be obtained from the major tribes, Congress initiated negotiations with both northern and southern Indians. At Fort Stanwix, New York, in 1784, and at Hopewell, South Carolina, in late 1785 and early 1786, American representatives signed treaties of questionable legality with the Iroquois and with Choctaw, Chickasaw, and Cherokee chiefs respectively (see map). The United States took the treaties as final confirmation of its sovereignty over the Indian territories, and authorized white settlers to move onto the land. Whites soon poured over

the southern Appalachians, provoking the Creeks—who were receiving supplies from the Spanish and who had not agreed to the Hopewell treaties—to defend their territory by declar-

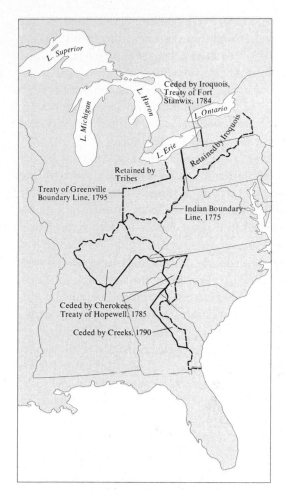

Cession of Indian lands to U.S., 1775–1790.   Source: Reprinted by permission of Princeton University Press.

ing war. Only in 1790, when the Creek chief Alexander McGillivray traveled to New York to negotiate a treaty, did the Creeks finally come to terms with the United States.

In the North, meanwhile, the Iroquois Confederacy was in disarray. The retaliatory raids Americans launched against their villages in 1779 had forced many tribesmen to flee to Canada. Most of them, including the Mohawk leaders Joseph and Mary Brant, never returned to live within the borders of the United States. Instead they established villages on lands set aside for them by the British north of the St. Lawrence River. The Iroquois who did remain soon found that they had little bargaining power. In 1786 they formally repudiated the Fort Stanwix treaty and warned of new attacks on frontier settlements, but both whites and Indians knew the threat was an empty one. The flawed treaty was permitted to stand by default. At intervals during the remainder of the decade the state of New York purchased large amounts of land from individual Iroquois tribes. By 1790 the once-proud Iroquois Confederacy was confined to a few scattered reservations.

It is one of the crueler ironies of American history that a revolution fought in the name of personal liberty and property rights failed to deliver those benefits to large segments of the population. The loyalists were exiled from their homes and deprived of their property for exercising what could have been seen as their right to dissent. Indians and blacks suffered even more grievously. Because of the Revolution the eastern Indian tribes lost much of their traditional homeland. Most blacks remained slaves. And the sizable number of blacks who did acquire freedom discovered that emancipation from slavery did not bring equality of treatment. However, the war had caused white men and women to look at their political and social roles in a new light. That development was to influence Americans' efforts to establish new state and national governments during and after the war.

Designing republican governments

About two months after his wife urged him to "Remember the Ladies," John Adams received a letter from a friend requesting advice on drafting the suffrage provisions of a new Massachusetts constitution and proposing that propertyless men be given the vote. It is clear from Adams's reply that he had begun to think seriously about the issues raised by his wife and by the changing circumstances in America. Government must be founded on the consent of the people, Adams observed, but what precisely did that mean? "How then does the right arise in the majority to govern the minority against their will? Whence arises the right of the men to govern the women without their consent? whence the right of the old to bind the young without theirs?"

In response to his own questions, Adams drew a parallel between disfranchised groups. "Very few men

who have no property, have any judgment of their own," he asserted. Therefore, if the franchise was to be broadened to include men without property, "the same reasoning . . . will prove that you ought to admit women and children: for, generally speaking, women and children have as good judgment, and as independent minds, as those who are wholly destitute of property." Thus Adams used the specter of women and children at the polls to argue for maintaining traditional property requirements for voting. "Depend upon it, sir," he declared, "it is dangerous to open so fruitful a source of controversy and altercation, as would be opened by attempting to alter the qualifications of voters. There will be no end of it. . . . It tends to confound and destroy all distinctions, and prostrate all ranks to one common level."

Clearly, although Adams was a revolutionary and a republican, he was not a democrat by today's standards. Neither he nor the other leaders of the Revolution wanted to establish a democracy in the twentieth-century meaning of the term. They believed that government had to be based on the consent of the people, and that republics, with elected rather than hereditary rulers, were preferable to monarchies and aristocracies. But they still wanted to define the electorate—those who had a direct voice in the government—as white male property-holders.

Politically aware Americans believed that republics were especially fragile forms of government that risked chronic instability. A study of the histories of popular governments in such places as Greece and Rome convinced Americans that republics could succeed only if they were small in size and homogeneous in population. Furthermore, unless the citizens of a republic were especially virtuous, willing to sacrifice their own private interests for the good of the whole, the government would inevitably collapse. In return for sacrifices, though, a republic offered its citizens equality of opportunity. Under such a government, rank would be based on merit rather than inherited wealth and status. Society would be ruled by members of a "natural aristocracy," men of talent who had risen from what might have been humble beginnings to positions of power and privilege. As John Adams had indicated, rank would not be abolished but instead placed on a different footing.

Designing governments that put such precepts into effect proved difficult. On May 10, 1776, even before passage of the Declaration of Independence, the Continental Congress directed the states to devise new republican governments to replace the provincial congresses and committees that had met since 1774. Thus

| *Drafting of state constitutions* |

Americans initially concentrated on drafting state constitutions and devoted little attention to their national government—an oversight they were later forced to remedy. At the state level, they immediately faced the problem of defining just what a constitution was. The British constitution could not serve as a model because it was an unwritten mixture of law and custom; Americans wanted tangible documents specifying the fundamental structures of government. Several years passed before the states agreed that their constitutions could not be drafted by regular legislative bodies, like ordinary laws. Following the lead established by Massachusetts in 1780, they began to call conventions for the sole purpose of drafting constitutions. Thus the states sought direct authorization from the people—the theoretical sovereigns in a republic—before establishing new governments. After the new constitutions had been drawn up, delegates submitted them to the people for ratification.

Those who wrote the state constitutions concerned themselves primarily with outlining the distribution of and limitations on governmental power. Both questions were crucial to the survival of republics. If authority was improperly distributed among the branches of government or not confined within reasonable limits, the states might become tyrannical, as Britain had. Indeed, Americans' experience with British rule affected every provision of their new constitutions.

Under their colonial charters, Americans had learned to fear the power of the governor—in most cases the appointed agent of the king or the proprietor—and to look on the legislature as their defender. Accordingly, the first state constitutions typically provided for the governor to be elected annually (usually by the legislature), limited the number of terms any one governor could serve, and gave him little independent authority. At the same time the constitutions expanded the powers of the legislature. They redrew the lines of electoral districts to reflect population patterns more accurately and increased the number of members in both the upper and lower houses. Finally,

despite John Adams's dire predictions, most states lowered property qualifications for voting. As a result the legislatures came to include some men who before the war would not even have been eligible to vote. Thus the revolutionary era witnessed the first deliberate attempt to broaden the base of American government, a process that has continued into our own day.

But the authors of the state constitutions knew that governments designed to be responsive to the people would not necessarily provide sufficient protection should tyrants be elected to office. Consequently, they included limitations on governmental authority in the documents they composed. Seven of the constitutions contained formal bills of rights, and the others had similar clauses. Most of them guaranteed citizens freedom of the press and of religion, the right to a fair trial, the right of consent to taxation, and protection against general search warrants. An independent judiciary was charged with upholding such rights.

In sum, the constitution-makers put far greater emphasis on preventing state governments from becoming tyrannical than on making them effective wielders of political authority. Their approach to the process of shaping governments was understandable, given the American experience with Great Britain. But establishing such weak political units, especially in wartime, practically ensured that the constitutions would soon need revision. As early as the 1780s some states began to rewrite the constitutions they had drafted in 1776 and 1777. Invariably, the revised versions increased the powers of the governor and reduced the scope of the legislature's authority. Only then, a decade after the Declaration, did Americans start to develop a formal theory of checks and balances as the primary means of controlling governmental power. Once they realized that legislative supremacy did not in itself guarantee good government, Americans attempted to achieve their goal by balancing the powers of the legislative, executive, and judicial branches against one another. The national constitution they drafted in 1787 would embody that principle.

The constitutional theories that Americans applied at the state level did not at first influence their conception of the nature of a national government. The powers and structure of the Continental Congress evolved by default early in the war, since Americans had little time to devote to legitimizing their de facto government while organizing the military struggle against Britain. Not until late 1777, after Burgoyne's defeat at Saratoga, did Congress send the Articles of Confederation to the states for ratification.

The articles by and large wrote into law the arrangements that had developed, unplanned and largely unheeded, in the Continental Congress. The chief organ of national government was a unicameral

| Articles of Confederation |

legislature in which each state had one vote. Its powers included the conduct of foreign relations, the settlement of disputes between states, control over maritime affairs, the regulation of Indian trade, and the valuation of state and national money. The articles did not give the national government the ability to tax effectively or to enforce a uniform commercial policy. The United States of America was described as "a firm league of friendship" in which each state "retains its sovereignty, freedom and independence, and every Power, Jurisdiction and right, which is not by this confederation expressly delegated to the United States, in Congress assembled."

The articles required the unanimous consent of the state legislatures for ratification or amendment, and a clause concerning western lands turned out to be troublesome. The draft accepted by Congress allowed the states to retain all land claims derived from their original colonial charters. But states with definite western boundaries in their charters (like Maryland, Delaware, and New Jersey) wanted the other states to cede the lands west of the Appalachian Mountains to the national government. Otherwise, they feared, states with large claims could expand and overpower their smaller neighbors. Maryland absolutely refused to accept the articles until 1781, when Virginia finally promised to surrender its western holdings to national jurisdiction (see map).

The fact that a single state could delay ratification for three years was a portent of the fate of American government under the Articles of Confederation. The unicameral legislature, whether it was called the Second Continental Congress (until 1781) or the Confederation Congress (thereafter), was too inefficient and unwieldy to govern effectively. The authors of the articles had not given adequate thought to the distribution of power within the national government or to the relationship between the Confederation and the states. The congress they created was simultaneously

a legislative body and a collective executive, but it had no independent income and no authority to compel the states to accept its rulings. What is surprising, in other words, is not how poorly the Confederation functioned in following years, but rather how much the government was able to accomplish.

Trials of the confederation

During and after the war the most persistent problem faced by the American governments, state and national, was finance. Because legislators at all levels were understandably reluctant to levy taxes on their fellow countrymen, both Congress and the states tried to finance the war by simply printing currency. Even though the money was backed by nothing but good faith, it circulated freely and without excessive depreciation during 1775 and most of 1776. Demand for military supplies and civilian goods was high, stimulating trade (especially with France) and local production. Indeed, the amount of money issued in those years was probably no more than what a healthy economy required as a medium of exchange.

But in late 1776, as the American army suffered major battlefield reverses in New York and New Jersey, prices began to rise and inflation set in. The value of

| Monetary problems |

the currency rested on Americans' faith in their government, a faith that was sorely tested in the years that followed, especially during the dark days of the early British triumphs in the South (1779 and 1780). Some state governments fought inflation by controlling wages and prices, requiring acceptance of paper currency on an equal footing with hard money, borrowing, and even levying taxes. Their efforts were futile. So too was Congress's attempt to stop printing currency altogether and to rely solely on state contributions. By early 1780 it took forty paper dollars to purchase one in silver. A year later Continental currency was worthless.

The severe wartime inflation seriously affected people on fixed incomes—including many soldiers and civilian leaders of the Revolution. Abigail Adams managed to keep her family solvent during the war primarily by selling small luxury items her husband

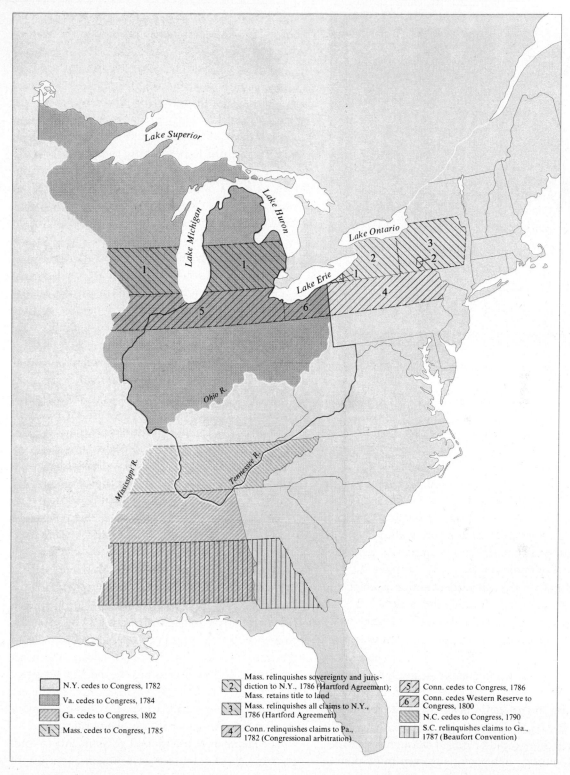

Legend:

- N.Y. cedes to Congress, 1782
- Va. cedes to Congress, 1784
- Ga. cedes to Congress, 1802
- 1 Mass. cedes to Congress, 1785
- 2 Mass. relinquishes sovereignty and jurisdiction to N.Y., 1786 (Hartford Agreement); Mass. retains title to land
- 3 Mass. relinquishes all claims to N.Y., 1786 (Hartford Agreement)
- 4 Conn. relinquishes claims to Pa., 1782 (Congressional arbitration)
- 5 Conn. cedes to Congress, 1786
- 6 Conn. cedes Western Reserve to Congress, 1800
- N.C. cedes to Congress, 1790
- S.C. relinquishes claims to Ga., 1787 (Beaufort Convention)

Western land claims and cessions, 1782–1802

Trials of the confederation

Privateers—privately owned warships licensed by Congress or the states—recruited sailors with promises of quick wealth. Captured enemy ships were sold and the proceeds divided among the crew and owners.   American Antiquarian Society.

urging him to take advantage of the new opportunities, "it was Never better times here for Seamen then it is Now."

But accumulations of private wealth did not help Congress with its financial problems. In 1781, faced with the total collapse of the monetary system, the delegates undertook major reforms. After establishing a department of finance under the wealthy Philadelphia merchant Robert Morris, they asked the states to amend the Articles of Confederation to allow Congress to levy a duty on imported goods. Morris put national finances on a solid footing, but the customs duty was never adopted. First Rhode Island, then New York refused to agree to the tax. The states' resistance reflected genuine fear of a too-powerful central government. As one worried citizen wrote in 1783, "If permanent Funds are given to Congress, the aristocratical Influence, which predominates in more than a major part of the United States, will fully establish an arbitrary Government."

Congress also faced major diplomatic problems at the close of the war. Chief among them were issues involving the peace treaty itself. Article 4, which promised the repayment of prewar debts (most of them owed by Americans to British merchants), and Article 5, which suggested that loyalists might recover their confiscated property, aroused considerable opposition. States passed laws denying British subjects the right to sue for recovery of debts or property in American courts, and town meetings decried the loyalists' return. As residents of Norwalk, Connecticut, put it, few Americans wanted to permit the "Tory Villains" to return "while filial Tears are fresh upon our Cheeks and our Murdered Brethren scarcely cold in their Graves." The state governments also had reason to oppose enforcement of the treaty. Sales of loyalists' land, houses, and other possessions had helped to finance the later stages of the war; since most of the purchasers were prominent patriots, the states had no desire to raise questions about the legitimacy of their property titles.

The failure of state and local governments to comply with Articles 4 and 5 gave Britain an excuse to maintain posts on the Great Lakes long after its troops were supposed to be withdrawn. Furthermore, Congress's inability to convince the states to implement the treaty pointed up its lack of power, even in an

Failure to enforce the Treaty of Paris

John sent at her request from his diplomatic posts in Europe. The prices of such goods as fine handkerchiefs, gloves, fans, and ribbons climbed so precipitously that she was able to keep pace with rising food costs. Most people in similar circumstances were less fortunate. Common laborers, small farmers, clergymen, and poor folk in general could do nothing to stop the declining value of their incomes.

Yet there were people who benefited from such economic conditions. Military contractors could make sizable profits. Large-scale farmers who produced surpluses of meat, milk, and grains could sell their goods at high prices to the army or to civilian merchants. People with money could invest in lucrative trading voyages. If Abigail Adams could profit by occasional sales, much more could be gained through systematic effort. More risky, but potentially even more profitable, was privateering against enemy shipping—an enterprise that attracted venturesome sailors and wealthy merchants alike. Indeed, as a Nantucket, Massachusetts, mother wrote her son in early 1778,

area—foreign affairs—in which it had been granted specific authority by the Articles of Confederation. Concerned nationalists argued publicly that enforcement of the treaty, however unpopular, was a crucial test for the republic. "Will foreign nations be willing to undertake anything with us or for us," asked Alexander Hamilton, "when they find that the nature of our governments will allow no dependence to be placed on our engagements?"

Congress's weakness was especially evident in the realm of trade, because the Articles of Confederation specifically denied it the power to establish a national commercial policy. Immediately following the war, both Britain and France restricted American trade with their colonies. Americans, who had hoped independence would bring about free trade with all nations, were outraged but could do little to change matters. Members of Congress watched helplessly as British and French manufactured goods flooded the United States while American produce could no longer be sold in the British West Indies, once its prime market, or even the French islands. The South Carolina indigo industry, deprived of the British bounty that had supported it, suffered a setback after the war. Though Americans opened a profitable trade with China in 1784, it was no substitute for access to closer and larger markets.

Congress also had difficulty dealing with the threat posed by Spain's presence on the southern and western borders of the United States. Determined to prevent the new nation's expansion, Spain in 1784 closed the Mississippi River to American navigation. It thus deprived the growing settlements west of the Appalachians of their major access route to the rest of the nation and the world. If Spain's policy were not reversed, westerners might have to accept Spanish sovereignty as the necessary price for survival. Congress opened negotiations with Spain in 1785, but even John Jay, one of the nation's most experienced diplomats, could not win the necessary concessions on navigation. The talks collapsed the following year after Congress divided sharply on the question of whether agreement should be sought on other issues. Southerners, voting as a bloc, insisted on navigation rights on the Mississippi, while northerners were willing to abandon that claim in order to win commercial concessions. The impasse raised questions about the possibility of a national consensus on foreign affairs.

Diplomatic problems of another sort confronted the congressmen when they considered the status of the territory north of the Ohio River. The United States had nominally acquired that land from Great Britain by the Treaty of Paris, and state land cessions had then placed the domain directly under congressional jurisdiction. But in actuality the land was still occupied by Indians—and by tribes, moreover, that had not participated in the negotiations at Fort Stanwix in 1784. The Shawnee, Chippewa, Ottawa, Potawatomi, and other western tribes had once allowed the Iroquois to speak for them. In the aftermath of the Revolution, though, they formed their own confederacy and demanded direct negotiations with the United States. Their aim was to present a united front, so as to avoid the piecemeal surrender of land by individual tribes.

At first the national government ignored the western Indian confederacy. Shortly after the state land cessions were completed, Congress began to organize the Northwest Territory, bounded by the Mississippi River, the Great Lakes, and the Ohio River. Ordinances passed in 1784, 1785, and 1787 outlined the

Northwest Ordinances

process through which the land could be sold to settlers and formal governments organized. To ensure orderly development, Congress directed that the land be surveyed into townships six miles square, each divided into thirty-six sections of 640 acres (one square mile). Revenue from the sale of the sixteenth section of each township was to be reserved for the support of public schools—the first instance of federal aid to education in American history. The minimum price per acre was set at one dollar, and the minimum sale was to be 640 acres. Congress was clearly not especially concerned about helping the small farmer: the minimum outlay of $640 was beyond the reach of most Americans (except, of course, veterans who had received part of their army pay in land warrants). The proceeds from the land sales were the first independent revenues available to the national government.

The most important ordinance was the third, passed in 1787. The Northwest Ordinance contained a bill of rights guaranteeing settlers in the territory freedom of religion and the right to a jury trial, prohibiting cruel and unusual punishments, and abolishing slavery. It also specified the process by which residents of the territory could eventually organize state

The town of Marietta being laid out by the Ohio Company in the midst of earthworks left by the Mound Builders. Ohio Historical Society.

governments and seek admission to the union "on an equal footing with the original States." Early in the nation's history, therefore, Congress laid down a policy of admitting new states on the same basis as the old and assuring residents of the territories the same rights as citizens of the original states. Both provisions stemmed from the congressmen's experience as colonists resentful of their inferior status. Having suffered under the rule of a colonial power, they understood the importance of preparing the United States' first "colony" for eventual self-government. Nineteenth- and twentieth-century Americans were to be less generous in their attitudes toward residents of later territories, many of whom were nonwhite or non-Protestant. But the nation never fully lost sight of the egalitarian principles of the Northwest Ordinance.

In a sense, though, the ordinance was purely theo-

retical at the time it was passed. The Indians in the region refused to acknowledge American sovereignty and insisted on their right to the land. They opposed white settlement violently, attacking unwary pioneers who ventured too far north of the Ohio River. In 1788 the Ohio Company, to which Congress had sold a large tract of land at reduced rates, established the town of Marietta at the juncture of the Ohio and Muskingum rivers. But the Indians prevented the company from extending settlement very far into the interior. It was soon apparent that the United States would have to negotiate with the western confederacy.

In January 1789 General Arthur St. Clair, the first governor of the Northwest Territory, asked the tribes to come to a council at Fort Harmar, on the Muskingum. Only a few Indians attended, none of them ma-

Chapter 6: Forging a national republic, 1776–1789

General Anthony Wayne accepting the surrender of the Indian leader Little Turtle after the United States Army's victory in the Battle of Fallen Timbers, August 1794. Chicago Historical Society.

jor chiefs. According to one of the Americans present, the negotiations were conducted in French, which St. Clair did not speak, through a Canadian interpreter who had to "guess at" St. Clair's meaning "for he can neither write nor speak the [English] language so as to make himself understood in any matter of importance." The treaty signed by St. Clair and the Indians was utterly meaningless.

After that fiasco, war was inevitable. General Josiah Harmar (1790) and then St. Clair himself (1791) were defeated in major battles near the present border

War in the Northwest

between Indiana and Ohio. More than six hundred of St. Clair's men were killed and scores more wounded; it was the whites' worst defeat in the entire history of the American frontier. In 1793 the tribal confederacy declared that peace could be achieved

only if the United States recognized the Ohio River as the boundary between white and Indian lands. But the national government refused to relinquish its claim to the Northwest Territory. A new army under the command of General Anthony Wayne, a Revolutionary War hero, attacked and defeated the tribesmen in August 1794, at the Battle of Fallen Timbers (near Toledo, Ohio). This victory made it possible for serious negotiations to begin.

By the summer of 1795, Wayne had reached agreement with delegates from the western tribes. The Treaty of Greenville gave each side a portion of what it wanted. The United States gained the right to settle much of what was to become the state of Ohio, the tribes retaining only the northwest corner of the region. The Indians received the acknowledgment they had long sought: American recognition of their rights to the soil. At Greenville, the United States formally accepted the principle of Indian sovereignty, by virtue of residence, over all lands the tribes had not yet ceded. Never again would the United States government claim that it had acquired Indian territory solely through negotiation with a European or American country.

The problems the United States encountered in ensuring safe settlement of the Northwest Territory pointed up, once again, the basic weakness of the Confederation government. Not until after the Articles of Confederation were replaced with a new Constitution could the United States muster sufficient force to implement all the provisions of the Northwest Ordinance. Thus, although the ordinance is often viewed as one of the few major accomplishments of the Confederation Congress, it must be seen within a context of political impotence.

From crisis to a constitution

The Americans most deeply concerned about the inadequacies of the Articles of Confederation were those involved in overseas trade and foreign affairs. It was in those areas that the articles were most obviously deficient: Congress could not impose its will on the states to establish a uniform commercial policy or to ensure the enforcement of treaties. The problems involving trade were particularly serious. Less than a year after the end of the war, the American economy slid into a depression; both exporters of staple crops and importers of manufactured goods were adversely affected by the postwar restrictions on American commerce imposed by European powers. Although recovery had begun by 1786, the war's effects proved impossible to erase entirely.

Indeed, the economy was significantly changed by the Revolution. Whereas the thirteen colonies had sold their goods primarily to foreign markets, the domestic market began to assume greater overall importance in the independent United States. As the nation was winning political independence, in other words, it was also beginning to gain economic independence. Americans lost access to their traditional markets, but steady population growth and the spread of settle-

ment helped to create new internal ones. In addition, freed from the mercantilist restrictions of the British Empire and drawing on European technological innovations, Americans began to establish manufacturing enterprises. The first American textile mill opened in Pawtucket, Rhode Island in 1793; later, in the early nineteenth century, textile manufacturing would come to play a major role in the American economy.

Recognizing the Confederation Congress's inability to deal with the nation's trade problems, Virginia invited the other states to a conference at Annapolis, Maryland, to discuss commercial policy. Although eight states named representatives to the meeting in September 1786, only five delegations attended. Those present realized that they were too few in number to have any real impact on the political system. They issued a call for another convention, to be held in Philadelphia in nine months, "to devise such further provisions as shall . . . appear necessary to render the constitution of the federal government adequate to the exigencies of the Union."

That fall an incident occurred in western Massachusetts that helped to convince other Americans that broad changes were necessary in their national government. Crowds of farmers angered by high taxes

> Shays' Rebellion

and the low supply of money halted court proceedings in which the state was trying to seize property for nonpayment of taxes. The insurgents were led by Daniel Shays, a farmer who had risen to the rank of captain in the American army; many of them were respected war veterans, described as gentlemen in contemporary accounts of the riots. Clearly the incident could not be dismissed as the work of an unruly rabble. What did the uprising mean for the future of the republic? Was it a sign of impending anarchy? Those were the questions that worried the nation's political leaders.

The protesters explained their position in an address to the governor and council of Massachusetts. They "were not induced to rise from a disaffection to the Commonwealth, or instigated by British Emissaries but from those sufferings which dissenabled them to provide for their Wives and Children or to Discharge their honest debts though in possession of the lands of their Country." Referring to their experience as revolutionary soldiers, they asserted that they "es-

A woodcut of Daniel Shays and one of his chief officers, Job Shattuck, in 1787. National Portrait Gallery, Smithsonian Institution, Washington, D.C.

teem[ed] one moment of Liberty to be worth an eternity of Bondage."

To residents of eastern Massachusetts and other citizens of the United States, the most frightening aspect of the uprising was the rebels' attempt to forge direct links between themselves and the earlier struggle for independence. The state legislature issued an address to the people, asking and replying to a rhetorical question: "Because they could not have everything as they wished, could they be justified in resorting to force? . . . In a republican government the majority must govern. If the minor part governs it becomes aristocracy, if every one opposed at his pleasure, it is no government, it is anarchy and confusion." Thus Massachusetts officials asserted that the formation of the republic had narrowed the range of acceptable political alternatives. The crowd actions that had once been a justifiable response to British tyranny were no longer legitimate. In a republic, reform had to come about through the ballot box rather than by force. If the nation's citizens refused to submit to legitimate authority, the result would be chaos and collapse of the government.

It was this issue that made Shays' Rebellion seem to challenge the existence of the entire United States, though it never seriously threatened even the state of Massachusetts. The rebels were easily dispersed by militia early in 1787. Shays and some of his followers fled to Vermont; many others were quickly caught and jailed. The reality of the threat the insurgents posed was never at issue: the importance of the uprising lay in its symbolic meaning. Of the major American political thinkers, only Thomas Jefferson could view the Massachusetts incidents without alarm. "What country can preserve its liberties, if its rulers are not warned from time to time that their people preserve the spirit of resistance?" Jefferson wrote from Paris, where he was serving as American ambassador. "What signify a few lives lost in a century or two? The tree of liberty must be refreshed from time to time, with the blood of patriots and tyrants. It is its natural manure."

But Jefferson was clearly exceptional. Shays' Rebellion unquestionably accelerated the movement toward comprehensive revision of the Articles of Confederation. In February 1787, after most of the states had already appointed delegates, the Confederation Congress belatedly en-

Calling of the Constitutional Convention

James Madison (1751–1836), the youthful scholar and skilled politician who earned the title Father of the Constitution.   Mr. Albert Errol Leeds, Philadelphia.

dorsed the convention. In mid-May, fifty-five men, representing all the states but Rhode Island, assembled in Philadelphia to begin their deliberations.

The vast majority of the delegates were men of property and substance. Among their number were merchants, planters, physicians, generals, governors, and especially lawyers—twenty-three had studied the law. Most had been born in America, and many came from families that had immigrated in the seventeenth century. In an era when only a tiny proportion of the population had any advanced education, more than half had attended college. A few had been educated in Britain, but most were graduates of American institutions: Princeton (ten), William and Mary (four), Yale (three), Harvard and Columbia (two each). The youngest delegate was twenty-six, the oldest—Benjamin Franklin—eighty-one. Like George Washington, whom they elected chairman, most were in their vigorous middle years. A dozen men did the bulk of the convention's work: Oliver Ellsworth and Roger Sherman of Connecticut; Elbridge Gerry and Rufus King of Massachusetts; William Paterson of New Jersey; Gouverneur Morris of New York; James Wilson of Pennsylvania; John Rutledge and Charles Pinckney of South Carolina; and Edmund Randolph, George Mason, and James Madison of Virginia. Of those leaders, Madison was by far the most important; he truly deserves the title Father of the Constitution.

The frail, shy, slightly built James Madison was thirty-six years old in 1787. Raised in the Piedmont country of Virginia, he had attended Princeton, served

| *James Madison: his early life* |

on the local committee of safety, and been elected successively to the Virginia provincial convention, the state's lower and upper houses, and finally the Continental Congress (1780–1783). Although Madison returned to Virginia to serve in the state legislature in 1784, he remained in touch with national politics, partly through his continuing correspondence with his close friend Thomas Jefferson. A promotor of the Annapolis convention, he strongly supported its call for further reform.

Madison was unique among the delegates in his systematic preparation for the Philadelphia meeting. Through Jefferson in Paris he bought more than two hundred books on history and government, and carefully analyzed their accounts of past confederacies and republics. In April 1787, a month before the convention began, he summed up the results of his research in a lengthy paper entitled "Vices of the Political System of the United States." After listing the eleven major flaws he perceived in the current structure of the government (among them "encroachments by the states on the federal authority" and "want of concert in matters where common interest requires it"), Madison revealed the conclusion that would guide his actions over the next few months. "The great desideratum [desire] in Government is such a modification of the sovereignty as will render it sufficiently neutral between the different interests and factions, to controul one part of the society from invading the rights of another, and at the same time sufficiently controuled itself, from setting up an interest adverse to that of the whole Society."

Thus Madison set forth the principle of checks and balances. The government, he believed, had to be constructed in such a way that it could not become tyrannical or fall wholly under the influence of a particular interest group. He regarded the large size of a potential national republic as an advantage in that respect. Rejecting the common assertion that republics had to be small to survive, Madison argued that a large, diverse republic was in fact to be preferred. Because the nation would include many different interest groups, no one of them would be able to control the government. Political stability, he declared, would result from compromises among the contending parties.

Madison's conception of national government was embodied in the so-called Virginia plan, introduced on May 29 by his colleague Edmund Randolph. The

Virginia and New Jersey plans

plan provided for a two-house legislature with proportional representation in both houses, an executive and a judiciary (both of which the Confederation government lacked), and congressional veto over state laws. It gave Congress the broad power to legislate "in all cases to which the separate states are incompetent." Had the Virginia plan been adopted intact, it would have created a government in which national authority reigned unchallenged and state power was greatly diminished.

But the convention included many delegates who, while recognizing the need for change, believed that the Virginians had gone too far in the direction of national consolidation. After Randolph's proposal had been debated for several weeks, the disaffected delegates united under the leadership of William Paterson. On June 15 Paterson presented an alternative scheme, the New Jersey plan, calling for modifications in the Articles of Confederation rather than a complete overhaul of the government. Even before introducing his proposals, Paterson had made his position clear in debate. On June 9 he had asserted that the articles were "the proper basis of all the proceedings of the convention," and warned that if the delegates did not confine themselves to amending the articles they would be charged with "usurpation" by their constituents. All that was needed, Paterson contended, was "to mark the orbits of the states with due precision and provide for the use of coercion" by the national government. Although the delegates rejected Paterson's narrow interpretation of their task, he and his allies won a number of major victories in the months that followed.

Debate quickly focused on three key questions involving representation. Should there be proportional representation in both houses of the national legislature? (Paterson's group readily agreed to replace Congress with a bicameral body.) What should the representation in either or both houses be proportional to—people, property, or a combination of the two? And, finally, how should the representatives to the two houses be elected? The three questions were intertwined, since a decision on one could determine the answers to the others; yet each had to be considered on its own merits. Matters were further complicated by the existence of more than two opinions on each issue.

The easiest question to resolve was the mode of electing representatives. The Virginia plan suggested that the lower house be elected at large by the people, and that the upper house be elected by the lower. The latter proposal was quickly discarded, and a compromise was reached as early as June 21. John Dickinson best expressed the somewhat reluctant consensus. It was, he declared, "essential that one branch of the legislature should be drawn immediately from the people and expedient that the other should be chosen by the legislatures of the states." The delegates, in other words, agreed that the people should have a direct say in the choice of some national legislators (thus the House of Representatives). They also knew that the state governments, which had named delegates to the Confederation Congress, would insist on a similar privilege in the new government. In providing for senators to be selected by state legislatures, they thus adhered to republican principles but recognized political reality.

The most difficult problem was the issue of proportional representation in the Senate. On June 11 the convention accepted the principle of proportional rep-

Debate over representation

resentation in the lower house, reaffirming its vote on June 29. The Senate was quite another matter. Speaking for the states with large populations, the democratically minded James Wilson inquired, "Can we forget for whom we are forming a government? Is it for *men,* or for the imaginary beings called *states?*" But Luther Martin of Maryland, the major spokesman for the smaller states, argued that "an equal vote in each state was essential to the federal idea and was founded in justice and freedom, not merely in policy; . . . the states, like individuals, were in a state of nature equally sovereign and free."

For weeks both sides remained adamant. An impasse was reached on July 2 when a motion to give each state one vote in the Senate failed on a tie vote of five states in favor, five against. (Three states were absent at the time.) In desperation, the convention appointed a committee to work out a compromise. Three days later the committee recommended equal representation for states in the Senate, coupled with a proviso that all appropriation bills must originate in the lower house. The large states were still dissatisfied, but fears that the meeting would collapse led delegates to urge reconciliation. On July 16, by a vote of 5 to 4 with one state (Massachusetts) divided, the convention at last agreed to the small states' demand for equal representation in the Senate. But not until a week later, when the convention adopted Roger Sherman's suggestion that the two senators from each state vote as individuals rather than as a bloc, was a breakdown averted.

One potentially divisive question remained unresolved: how was representation in the lower house to be apportioned among the states? Aside from the few who wanted representation distributed according to wealth, most delegates fell into one of three groups: those who wanted representation proportional to total population; those who wanted to count only the free population; and those who proposed counting three-fifths of the slaves as well. (The three-fifths formula for counting slaves was not

| Three-fifths compromise |

original to the convention; it had been developed by the Confederation Congress in 1783 as a means of allocating taxation.) Delegates from Georgia and South Carolina wanted to count the entire population, slave and free alike, because doing so would increase their total number of representatives. New Englanders wanted to count only free people, fearing that their representatives would be outvoted in the lower house by southern slaveholders. Delegates from the middle states and the upper South insisted on compromise. After the three-fifths formula was linked to a clause allowing Congress to stop the slave trade after twenty years (thus preventing the slave population from increasing indefinitely), it was unanimously accepted. Only two delegates, Gouverneur Morris and George Mason, spoke out strongly against the institution of slavery.

Once agreement was reached on the knotty problem of representation, the delegates had little diffi-

culty achieving consensus on the other major issues confronting them. Instead of giving Congress the nearly unlimited scope proposed in the Virginia plan, the delegates enumerated congressional powers and then provided for flexibility by granting all authority "necessary and proper" to carry out those powers. Discarding the legislative veto contained in the Virginia plan, the convention implied a judicial veto instead. The Constitution plus national laws and treaties would constitute "the supreme law of the land; and the judges in every state shall be bound thereby." The convention placed primary responsibility for the conduct of foreign affairs in the hands of the president, who was also designated commander-in-chief of the armed forces. The delegates established an elaborate independent mechanism, the electoral college, to select the president, and agreed that the chief executive should serve a short term but be eligible for re-election.

The final document still showed signs of its origins in the Virginia plan, but compromises had created a system of government less powerful at the national level than Madison and Randolph had envisioned. The key to the Constitution was the distribution of political authority—separation of powers among the

| Separation of powers |

executive, legislative, and judicial branches of the national government, and division of powers between states and nation. The branches were balanced against one another, their powers deliberately entwined to prevent them from acting independently. The president was given a veto over congressional legislation, but his treaties and major appointments required the consent of the Senate. Congress could impeach the president and the federal judges, but the courts appeared to have the final say on interpretation of the Constitution. The system of checks and balances would make it difficult for the government to become tyrannical, as Madison had intended. At the same time, though, the elaborate system would sometimes prevent the government from acting quickly and decisively. Finally, the line between state and national powers was so ambiguously and vaguely drawn that the United States was to fight a civil war in the next century before the issue was fully resolved.

The convention held its last session on September 17, 1787. Of the forty-two delegates present, only three refused to sign the Constitution. (Two of the three, George Mason and Elbridge Gerry, declined because of the lack of a bill of rights.) Benjamin Franklin had written a speech calling for unity; because his voice was too weak to be heard, James Wilson read it for him. "I confess that there are several parts of this constitution which I do not at present approve," Franklin admitted. Yet he urged its acceptance "because I expect no better, and because I am not sure, that it is not the best." Only then was the Constitution made public. The convention's proceedings had been entirely secret—and remained so until the delegates' private notes were published in the nineteenth century.

Opposition and ratification

Later that same month the Confederation Congress submitted the Constitution to the states but did not formally recommend approval. The ratification clause of the Constitution provided for the new system to take effect once it was approved by special conventions in at least nine states. The delegates to each state convention were to be elected by the people. Thus the national constitution, unlike the Articles of Confederation, would rest directly on popular authority (and the presumably hostile state legislatures would be circumvented).

As the states began to elect delegates to the special conventions, debate over the proposed government grew more heated. It quickly became apparent that the disputes within the Constitutional Convention had been minor compared to the divisions of opinion within the country as a whole. After all, the delegates at Philadelphia had agreed on the need for basic reforms in the American political system. Many citizens, though, not only rejected that conclusion but believed that the proposed government, despite its built-in safeguards, held the potential for tyranny.

Critics of the Constitution, who became known as Antifederalists, fell into two main groups: those who emphasized the threat to the states embodied in the

| Antifederalists |

new national government, and those who stressed the dangers to individuals posed by the lack of a bill of rights. Ultimately, though, the two positions were one. The Antifederalists saw the states as the chief protectors of in-

dividual rights, and their weakening as the onset of arbitrary power.

Fundamentally the Antifederalists were traditionalists, steeped in the notion that a republican form of government could succeed only in a small geographical area. James Madison had concluded from his study of ancient republics that increasing the size of the political unit might help to reduce destructive factionalism. But the Antifederalists regarded Madison's argument as heretical nonsense. "It is the opinion of the most celebrated writers on government, and confirmed by uniform experience," the Antifederalist delegates to the Pennsylvania convention pointed out, "that a very extensive territory cannot be governed on the principles of freedom, otherwise than by confederation of republics." The same men went on to charge that "the powers vested on Congress by this constitution, must necessarily annihilate and absorb the legislative, executive, and judicial powers of the several States." The result, they predicted, would be "*an iron handed despotism,* as nothing short of the supremacy of despotic sway could connect and govern these United States under one government."

As the months passed and public debate continued, the Antifederalists focused more sharply on the Constitution's lack of a bill of rights. Even if the states were weakened by the new system, they believed, the people could still be protected from tyranny if their rights were specifically guaranteed. The Constitution did contain some prohibitions on congressional power—for example, the writ of habeas corpus, which prevented arbitrary imprisonment, could not be suspended except in dire emergencies—but the Antifederalists found these provisions inadequate. Nor were they reassured by the Federalists' assertion that, since the new government was one of limited powers, it had no authority to violate the people's rights. *Letters of a Federal Farmer,* perhaps the most widely read Antifederalist pamphlet, listed the rights that should be protected: freedom of the press and of religion, the right to trial by jury, and guarantees against unreasonable search warrants.

From Paris, Thomas Jefferson added his voice to the chorus. Replying to Madison's letter conveying a copy of the Constitution, Jefferson wrote: "I like much the general idea of framing a government which should go on of itself peaceably, without needing continual recurrence to the state legislatures." He

Important events

1776	Second Continental Congress directs states to draft constitutions
1777	Articles of Confederation sent to states for ratification
1780	Pennsylvania becomes first state to abolish slavery
	Massachusetts becomes first state to call constitutional convention
1781	Articles of Confederation ratified
1782	Virginia becomes first southern state to allow individual manumissions without legal restrictions
1784	Treaty of Fort Stanwix
	Spain closes Mississippi River to American navigation
1785–86	Treaty of Hopewell
1786	Iroquois repudiate Treaty of Fort Stanwix
	Annapolis Convention
1786–87	Shays' Rebellion (Mass.)
1787	Northwest Ordinance
	Constitutional Convention
1788	Hamilton, Jay, and Madison, *The Federalist*
	Constitution ratified
1789	Treaty of Fort Hamar
1791	St. Clair's defeat
1794	Battle of Fallen Timbers
1795	Treaty of Greenville

also approved of the separation of powers among the three branches of government and declared himself "captivated" by the compromise between the large and small states. Nevertheless, he added, he did not like "the omission of a bill of rights. . . . A bill of rights is what the people are entitled to against every government on earth, general or particular, and what no just government should refuse, or rest on inference."

As the state conventions met to consider ratification, the lack of a bill of rights loomed larger and larger as a flaw in the new form of government. Four of the first five states to ratify did so unanimously, but serious disagreements then began to surface. Massachusetts ratified by a majority of only 19 votes out of 355 cast; in New Hampshire the Federalists won by a majority of 57 to 47. When New Hampshire ratified, in June 1788, the requirement of nine states had been satisfied. But New York and Virginia had not yet voted, and everyone realized the new constitution could not succeed unless those key states accepted it. In Virginia, despite a valiant effort by the Antifederalist Patrick Henry, the pro-Constitution forces won 89 to 79. In New York James Madison, John Jay, and Alexander Hamilton campaigned for ratification by publishing *The Federalist,* one of the most important political tracts in American history. Their reasoned arguments, coupled with the promise that a bill of rights would be added to the Constitution, helped carry the day. On July 26, 1788, New York ratified the Constitution by the slim margin of 3 votes. The new government was a reality, even though the last state (Rhode Island, which had not participated in the convention) did not formally join the union until 1790.

Ratification of the Constitution

In the years since 1776, Americans had altered their political ideas and their social practices. Once wedded to a conception of politics and government drawn almost entirely from traditional definitions of republicanism, they had gradually forged their national government out of a combination of direct experience and political theory. They had begun to think more deeply than ever before about themselves and their society, raising questions about the institution of slavery, the position of women, and the role of the citizen in a republic. Still the question remained: could they successfully implement the new system?

Suggestions for further reading

General

Stuart Bruchey, *The Roots of American Economic Growth, 1607-1861* (1965); Staughton Lynd, *Class Conflict, Slavery, & the United States Constitution: Ten Essays* (1967); Forrest McDonald, *E Pluribus Unum: The Formation of the American Republic 1776-1790* (1965); Jackson Turner Main, *The Social Structure of Revolutionary America* (1965); Curtis P. Nettels, *The Emergence of a National Economy, 1775-1815* (1962); Robert R. Palmer, *The Age of the Democratic Revolution: A Political History of Europe and America 1760-1800*, 2 vols. (1959, 1964); Morton White, *The Philosophy of the American Revolution* (1978); Chilton Williamson, *American Suffrage from Property to Democracy 1760-1860* (1960); Garry Wills, *Inventing America: Jefferson's Declaration of Independence* (1978); Benjamin F. Wright, Jr., *Consensus and Continuity, 1776-1787* (1958); Gordon S. Wood, *The Creation of the American Republic, 1776-1787* (1969).

Continental Congress and Articles of Confederation

Jack Eblen, *The First and Second United States Empires: Governors and Territorial Government, 1784-1912* (1968); E. James Ferguson, *The Power of the Purse: A History of American Public Finance, 1776-1790* (1961); H. James Henderson, *Party Politics in the Continental Congress* (1974); Merrill Jensen, *The Articles of Confederation: An Interpretation of the Social-Constitutional History of the American Revolution, 1774-1781*, 2nd ed. (1959); Merrill Jensen, *The New Nation: A History of the United States during the Confederation, 1781-1789* (1950); Jack N. Rakove, *The Beginnings of National Politics: An Interpretive History of the Continental Congress* (1979); Clarence L. VerSteeg, *Robert Morris, Revolutionary Financier* (1954).

State politics

Willi Paul Adams, *The First American Constitutions: Republican Ideology and the Making of the State Constitutions in the Revolutionary Era* (1980); Elisha P. Douglass, *Rebels & Democrats: The Struggle for Equal Political Rights & Majority Rule During the American Revolution* (1955); Richard T. McCormick, *Experiment in Independence: New Jersey in the Critical Period 1781-1789* (1950); Jackson Turner Main, "Government by the People: The American Revolution and the Democratization of the Legislatures," *William and Mary Quarterly*, 3rd ser., 23 (1966), 391-407; Jackson Turner Main, *Political Parties Before the Constitution* (1973); Jackson Turner Main, *The Sovereign States, 1775-1783* (1973); Jackson Turner Main, *The Upper House in Revolutionary America, 1763-1788* (1967); Allan Nevins, *The American States during and after the Revolution, 1775-1789* (1924); Stephen E. Patterson, *Political Parties in Revolutionary Massachusetts* (1973); J.R. Pole, *Political Representation in England and the Origins of the American Republic* (1966); Irwin H. Polishook, *Rhode Island and the Union, 1774-1795* (1969); Marion L. Starkey, *A Little Rebellion* (1955); Robert J. Taylor, *Western Massachusetts in the Revolution* (1954).

The Constitution

Douglass Adair, *Fame and the Founding Fathers* (1974); Charles A. Beard, *An Economic Interpretation of the Constitution of the United States* (1913); Irving Brant, *James Madison*, 6 vols. (1941-1961); Linda Grant DePauw, *The Eleventh Pillar: New York State and the Federal Constitution* (1966); Max Farrand, *The Framing of the Constitution of the United States* (1913); Forrest McDonald, *We the People: The Economic Origins of the Constitution* (1958); Jackson Turner Main, *The Anti-Federalists: Critics of the Constitution, 1781-1788* (1961); Frederick W. Marks, III, *Independence on Trial: Foreign Affairs and the Making of the Constitution* (1973); Clinton Rossiter, *1787: The Grand Convention* (1973); Robert A. Rutland, *The Ordeal of the Constitution* (1966); Gerald Stourzh, *Alexander Hamilton and the Ideal of Republican Government* (1970); Carl Van Doren, *The Great Rehearsal: The Story of the Making and Ratifying of the Constitution of the United States* (1948).

Women

Charles Akers, *Abigail Adams: An American Woman* (1980); Ruth Bloch, "American Feminine Ideals in Transition: The Rise of the Moral Mother, 1785-1815," *Feminist Studies*, 4, No. 2 (June 1978), 100-126; Nancy F. Cott, "Divorce and the Changing Status of Women in Massachusetts," *William and Mary Quarterly*, 3rd ser., 33 (1976), 586-614; Linda K. Kerber, *Women of the Republic: Intellect & Ideology in Revolutionary America* (1980); Mary Beth Norton, *Liberty's Daughters: The Revolutionary Experience of American Women, 1750-1800* (1980).

Blacks and Indians

Ira Berlin, *Slaves without Masters: The Free Negro in the Antebellum South* (1974); David Brion Davis, *The Problem of Slavery in the Age of Revolution, 1770-1823* (1975); Winthrop D. Jordan, *White Over Black: American Attitudes Toward the Negro, 1550-1812* (1968); Duncan J. MacLeod, *Slavery, Race, and the American Revolution* (1974); Bernard Sheehan, *Seeds of Extinction: Jeffersonian Philanthropy and the American Indian* (1973); Anthony F.C. Wallace, *The Death and Rebirth of the Seneca* (1969); Arthur Zilversmit, *The First Emancipation: The Abolition of Slavery in the North* (1967).

7 ~

POLITICS
AND
SOCIETY
IN THE
EARLY
REPUBLIC,
1790–1800

Charles Thomson, secretary to Congress, arrived at Mount Vernon, Virginia, around noon on April 14, 1789. He brought momentous news: the first electoral college convened under the new Constitution had unanimously elected George Washington president of the United States, and Congress had confirmed the choice.

Washington had been expecting the summons to New York City, the nation's capital. Two days later he and Thomson began the journey north. The new president hoped in vain for an uneventful trip. After being honored at formal dinners in Alexandria, Baltimore, and Wilmington, he arrived on April 20 at a bridge across the Schuylkill River. Charles Willson Peale, a Philadelphia painter and naturalist, had turned the crude bridge into a triumphal avenue, beginning and ending with laurel-bedecked arches twenty feet high and flanked on both sides by flags. As Washington rode a white horse beneath the first arch, Peale's daughter Angelica operated a machine that placed a laurel wreath on his head. In Philadelphia, on the other side of the river, more than 20,000 people lined the streets for a glimpse of the first president of the new republic.

Entering Trenton the next day, Washington rode under another triumphal arch, this one emblazoned with the words, "The Defender of the Mothers will be the Protector of the Daughters." The women of New Jersey had not forgotten that Washington's victories at Princeton and Trenton had put an end to the epidemic of rape they endured when the British occupied the state. A group of girls dressed in white threw flowers in his path while singing an ode composed for the occasion.

Each New Jersey town Washington passed through greeted him with speeches, music, pealing bells, and military salutes. Finally, at Elizabeth on April 23, he was met by a congressional committee sent to escort him to Manhattan. The official party traveled up the Hudson on a specially constructed fifty-foot barge draped in red. When the barge arrived at the foot of Wall Street, church bells rang and thirteen guns fired a salute. On the night of Washington's inauguration one week later, New York City was illuminated by lanterns and the festivities ended with a spectacular two-hour fireworks display.

The United States formally honored its first president with an outpouring of affection and respect that

has rarely been equalled since. Washington's inauguration allowed the people to express their pride in the Revolution, the new Constitution, and most of all in the nation itself. The struggle against Britain had nurtured in Americans an intense nationalism that quickly manifested itself in attempts to create a distinctive cultural style. They reformed their educational system in accordance with republican principles, and pursued artistic and literary independence along with political autonomy. Their goal was to establish a nation of virtuous, self-sacrificing yeomen dedicated to the public good rather than private gain.

Yet Americans were ultimately unsuccessful in their quest for unity and unqualified independence. Nowhere was their failure more evident than in the realm of national politics. The fierce battle over the Constitution foreshadowed an even wider division over the major political issues the republic had to confront. To make matters worse, Americans' belief in the tenets of republicanism prevented them from fully anticipating the political disagreements that characterized the 1790s. They believed that the Constitution would resolve the problems that had arisen during the Confederation period, and they expected the new government to rule largely by consensus. Accordingly, they found it difficult to understand and deal with partisan tensions that developed out of disputes over such fundamental questions as the extent to which authority, especially fiscal authority, should be centralized in the national government; the formulation of foreign policy in an era of continual warfare in Europe; and the limits of dissent within the republic. By the close of the decade they still had not come to terms with the implications of partisan politics.

Creating a virtuous republic

"Virtue, Virtue alone . . . is the basis of a republic," declared Dr. Benjamin Rush, a leading Philadelphia physician and ardent patriot, in 1778. His fellow Americans fully concurred. Every aspect of their culture should, they believed, reflect and foster the virtue so necessary to a republic. Accordingly, in the 1780s and 1790s those who sought to define American identity looked to painting, literature, and architecture, as well as politics and society, to express republican virtue. In 1786 the editors of the *Columbian Magazine* asserted confidently that their publication would document "the progress of literature and the arts among [American] citizens." Since literature was "the natural concomitant of FREEDOM," and the United States was the freest country in the world, it followed that the new nation would soon produce literary works that rivaled Europe's.

The Americans took their artistic standards less from contemporary England and Europe than from ancient Greece and Rome—the source of their political heroes as well. The style they used is called *neoclassical,* for it was an explicit adaptation of classical forms to contemporary circumstances. Paradoxically, educated Americans wanted to create a culture embodying the highest artistic and literary ideals outlined by European Enlightenment thinkers, but free of the corrupting influence of vice-ridden Europe. When the *Columbian Magazine* began a monthly book review section devoted exclusively to American publications in 1790, the editors proudly proclaimed, "We are no longer the servile copyists of foreign manners, fashions, and vices. We begin to think and act in a manner better adapted to the genius of our government."

The first American literary productions were highly moralistic. William Hill Brown's *The Power of Sympathy* (1789), the first novel written in the United States, was a lurid tale of seduction intended as a warning to young women, who made up a large proportion of America's fiction readers. In Royall Tyler's *The Contrast* (1787), the first successful American play, the virtuous conduct of Colonel Manly was contrasted (hence the title) to the reprehensible behavior of the fop Billy Dimple. Jonathan, Colonel Manly's brashly independent Yankee servant, was an American original, the prototype of a long line of untutored and aggressively democratic men who filled the pages of American fiction and biography. The most popular book of the era, Mason Locke Weems' *Life of Washington,* published in 1800 shortly after its subject's death, was, the author declared, designed to "hold up his great Virtues . . . to the imitation of Our Youth." Weems could hardly have been accused of being subtle. The famous tale he invented—six-year-old George bravely admitting cutting down his father's favorite cherry tree—ended with George's father ex-

claiming, *"Run to my arms, you dearest boy. . . . Such an act of heroism in my son, is worth more than a thousand trees, though blossomed with silver, and their fruits of purest gold."*

Painting, too, was expected to embody high moral standards. The major artists of the republican period—Gilbert Stuart, John Trumbull, and Ralph Earl—studied in London under Benjamin West and John Singleton Copley, the first great American-born painters, both of whom had emigrated to England before the Revolution. Stuart and Earl painted innumerable portraits of upstanding republican citizens—the political, economic, and social leaders of the day. Trumbull's vast canvases depicted such milestones of American history as the Battle of Bunker Hill, Burgoyne's surrender at Saratoga, and Cornwallis's capitulation at Yorktown. Both portraits and historical scenes were intended to arouse patriotic virtues in their viewers.

Architects likewise hoped to convey in their buildings a sense of the young republic's ideals, and most of them consciously rejected British models. When the Virginia government asked Thomas Jefferson, then ambassador to France, for advice on the design of a state capitol in Richmond, Jefferson unhesitatingly recommended copying a Roman building, the Maison Carrée at Nîmes. "It is very simple," he explained, "but it is noble beyond expression." Jefferson set forth ideals that would guide American neoclassical architecture for a generation to come: simplicity of line, harmonious proportions, a feeling of grandeur. Nowhere were these rational goals of republican art manifested more clearly than in Benjamin H. Latrobe's plans for the majestic domed United States Capitol in Washington, built shortly after the turn of the century.

But republican theorists did not always influence artistic trends so directly. In the realm of music, for example, the 1780s and 1790s marked the consolidation of certain anticommunal and antiegalitarian tendencies that had first appeared in the 1760s. Group singing had always been an important part of worship services in colonial Protestant churches. Such total participation by the congregation promoted precisely the sort of cooperation and equality that was the hallmark of republican ideology. After about 1770, however, congregations relied increasingly on professional musicians and trained choirs (usually composed of local young people). William Billings, the first major

The title page of William Billings's *Psalm-Singers' Amusement* (1781) illustrates the new musical trends opposed by traditionalists. In the upper left and lower right corners choirs of women and men practice fuguing pieces and anthems. In the other corners musicians play stringed instruments, and above the title a soloist plays an oboe.

American composer, published such works as *The New-England Psalm-Singer* (1770) and *The Psalm-Singers' Amusement* (1781) for use in the special singing schools that instructed choir members. Traditionalists resisted the trend, partly because it required altering the standard hierarchical seating patterns in the church, but also because it excluded most of the congregation from music-making.

Music was not the only realm in which disturbing tendencies occurred. By the mid-1780s, some Americans were beginning to detect signs of luxury and corruption all around them. The end of the war and resumption of European trade brought a return to fashionable clothing styles for both men and women, and abandonment of the simpler homespun garments patriots had once worn with such pride. Balls and concerts resumed in the cities and were attended by well-dressed elite families. Parties no longer seemed complete without gambling and card-playing. Social clubs for young people multiplied; Samuel Adams worried in print about the possibilities for corruption lurking behind innocent plans for tea drinking and genteel conversation among Boston youths. Especially alarming to fervent republicans was the establishment of the Society of the Cincinnati, a hereditary organization of Revolutionary War officers and their descendants. Many feared that the group would become the nucleus of a native-born aristocracy. All these developments directly challenged the United States's image as a virtuous, self-sacrificing republic.

Their deep-seated concern for the future of the infant republic focused Americans' attention on their children, the "rising generation." Education acquired new significance in the context of the republic. Since

Educational reform

the early days of the colonies, education had been seen chiefly as a private means to personal advancement, and thus a matter of concern only to individual families. Now, though, it would serve a public purpose. If young people were to resist the tempta-

Chapter 7: Politics and society in the early republic, 1790–1800

tion of vice, they would have to learn the lessons of virtue at home and at school. In fact, the very survival of the nation depended on it. The early republican period was thus a time of major educational reform.

The 1780s and 1790s brought three significant changes in American educational practice. First, the states began to be willing to use tax money to support public elementary schools. Until that time nearly all education in the colonies had been privately financed. Parents who wanted their children taught any subject, from the rudiments of reading and writing to advanced Latin and Greek, had to pay individually for the privilege. But the provision in the Northwest Ordinance of 1787 setting aside land to support public education reflected Americans' new attitude toward schooling. In the republic, schools had a claim on tax dollars. Consequently, the Massachusetts legislature in 1789 adopted a law requiring towns to supply their citizens with free public elementary education.

Second, the college curriculum was reformed. Since their founding, American colleges—with the notable exception of Franklin's College of Philadelphia, later the University of Pennsylvania—had offered students a classical education aimed primarily at producing well-trained clerics. But the end of the eighteenth century brought major changes in the traditional course of study. Although colleges like Harvard, Yale, and William and Mary continued to instruct their students in classical languages and theology, they added classes in history, geography, modern languages, and "natural philosophy" (science). At its highest level, then, American education broadened its scope and focused on producing well-informed republican citizens rather than future clergymen.

Third, schooling for girls was vastly improved. Because the colonists placed little emphasis on formal education for girls, at least half the American female population was illiterate at the time of the Revolution. But Americans' new recognition of the importance of the rising generation led to the realization that mothers would have to be properly educated if their children were to be educated. Therefore Massachusetts insisted in its 1789 law that town elementary schools be open to girls as well as boys. Throughout the United States, private academies were founded to give teenage girls from well-to-do families an opportunity for advanced schooling. No one yet proposed opening colleges to women, but a few fortu-

Judith Sargent Murray (1751–1820), painted by John Singleton Copley about the time of her marriage to the sea captain John Stevens. Although her steady gaze suggests clear-headed intelligence, there is little in the stylized portrait—typical of Copley's work at the time—to suggest her later emergence as the first notable American feminist theorist. Frick Art Reference Library.

nate girls could now study history, geography, rhetoric, and mathematics. The academies also trained female students in fancy needlework—the only artistic endeavor open to women.

The chief theorist of women's education in the early republic was Judith Sargent Murray, of Gloucester, Massachusetts. Born in 1751, Murray married a sea captain at age eighteen. Widowed in 1786, she took as her second husband John Murray, the founder of the Universalist sect.

| Judith Sargent Murray on education |

Though she began to think and write about woman's status during the American Revolution, her first published essay did not appear until 1784. Murray argued that women and men had equal intellectual capacities, though women's inadequate education might make them seem to be less intelligent. "We can only reason from what we know," she declared, "and if an opportunity of acquiring knowledge hath been denied us, the inferiority of our sex cannot fairly be deduced from thence." Therefore, concluded Murray, boys and girls should be offered equivalent scholastic training. She further contended that girls should be taught to support themselves by their own efforts: "Independence should be placed within their grasp." Because she rejected the prevailing notion that a young woman's chief goal in life should be finding a husband, Judith Sargent Murray deserves the title of the first American feminist. (That distinction is usually accorded to better-known nineteenth-century women like Margaret Fuller or Sarah Grimké.)

By 1800, therefore, the struggle for political independence had prompted Americans to think about their society and culture in new ways. The process of breaking away from their colonial origins had already had a profound influence on the arts. Americans were also attempting to ensure their nation's future by instructing their children—and themselves—in the principles of virtue and morality. All their efforts would prove useless, though, if the new federal government was not placed on a sound footing.

Building a workable government

In 1788 Americans celebrated the ratification of the Constitution with a series of parades, held in many cities on the Fourth of July. The processions were carefully planned to symbolize the unity of the new nation and to recall its history to the minds of the watching throngs. The Philadelphia parade, planned largely by Charles Willson Peale, was more or less typical.

About 5,000 people participated in the procession, which stretched for a mile and a half and lasted three hours. Twelve costumed "axe-men" representing the first pioneers were followed by a mounted military troop and a group of men with flags symbolizing independence, the peace treaty, the French alliance, and other revolutionary events. A band played a "Federal March" composed for the occasion. There followed a Constitution float, displaying a large framed copy of the Constitution and a thirteen-foot-high eagle. A

number of local dignitaries marched in front of the next float, "The Grand Federal Edifice," a domed structure supported by thirteen columns (three of which were left unfinished to signify the states that had not yet ratified).

The remainder of the parade consisted of groups of artisans and professionals marching together and dramatizing their work. One of the farmers scattered seed in the streets; on the manufacturers' float, cloth was being made; the printers operated a press, distributing copies of a poem written to honor the Constitution. More than forty other groups of tradesmen, such as barbers, hatters, and clockmakers, sponsored similar floats. The artisans were followed by lawyers, doctors, clergymen of all denominations, and congressmen. Bringing up the rear was a symbol of the nation's future, a contingent of students from the University of Pennsylvania and other city schools. Marching with their teachers, they carried a flag labelled "The Rising Generation."

The nationalistic spirit expressed in the ratification processions carried over into the first session of Congress. In the congressional elections, held late in 1788, only a few Antifederalists had run or been elected to office. Thus the First Congress was composed chiefly of men who were considerably more inclined toward a strong national government than had been the delegates to the Constitutional Convention. Since the Constitution had deliberately left many key issues undecided, the nationalists' domination of Congress meant that their views on those points quickly prevailed.

First Congress

Congress faced four immediate problems when it convened in April 1789: raising revenue to support the new government, responding to the state ratification conventions' calls for amendments to the Constitution, establishing executive departments, and organizing the federal judiciary. The latter task was especially important. The Constitution declared only that there should be a Supreme Court and other lower federal courts, leaving it to Congress to work out not just the details of the national judiciary but also its basic structure.

The Virginian James Madison, who had been elected to the House of Representatives, soon became as influential in Congress as he had been at the Philadelphia convention. Only a few months into the session, he persuaded Congress to impose a tariff on certain imported goods. Consequently, the First Congress quickly achieved what the Confederation Congress never had: an effective national tax law. The new government was to have its problems, but lack of sufficient revenue was not one of them.

Madison also took the lead on the issue of constitutional amendments. At the convention and thereafter, he had consistently opposed additional limitations on the national government on the grounds that it was unnecessary to guarantee the people's rights when the government was one of limited, delegated powers. But Madison recognized that public opinion, as expressed by the state ratifying conventions, was against him, and accordingly placed nineteen proposed amendments before the House. Congress eventually sent twelve amendments to the states for ratification. Two, having to do with the number of congressmen and their salaries, were not accepted by a sufficient number of states. The other ten amendments officially became part of

| Bill of Rights |

the Constitution on December 15, 1791. Not for many years, though, did they become known collectively as the Bill of Rights.

The first amendment specifically prohibited Congress from passing any law restricting the people's right to freedom of religion, speech, press, peaceable assembly, or petition. The next two arose directly from the former colonists' fear of standing armies as a threat to freedom. The second guaranteed the people's right "to keep and bear arms" because of the need for a "well regulated Militia"; the third defined the circumstances in which troops could be quartered in private homes. The next five amendments pertained to judicial procedures. The fourth amendment prohibited "unreasonable searches and seizures"; the fifth and sixth established the rights of accused persons; the seventh specified the conditions for jury trials in civil, as opposed to criminal, cases; and the eighth forbade "cruel and unusual punishments." Finally, the ninth and tenth amendments reserved to the people and the states other unspecified rights and powers. In short, the authors of the amendments made clear that in listing some rights explicitly they did not mean to preclude the exercise of others.

While debating the proposed amendments, Congress also concerned itself with the organization of the executive branch. It was readily agreed to continue the three administrative departments established un-

der the Articles of Confederation: War, Foreign Affairs (renamed State), and Treasury. Congress also instituted two lesser posts: the attorney general – the nation's official lawyer – and the postmaster general, who would oversee the Post Office. The only serious controversy was whether the president alone could dismiss officials whom he had originally appointed with the consent of the Senate. After some debate, the House and Senate agreed that he had such authority. Thus was established the important principle that the heads of the executive departments are responsible solely to the president. Though it could not have been foreseen at the time, this precedent paved the way for the development of the president's cabinet.

Aside from the constitutional amendments, the most far-reaching piece of legislation enacted by the First Congress was the Judiciary Act of 1789. That act

| Judiciary Act of 1789 |

was largely the work of Senator Oliver Ellsworth of Connecticut, a veteran of the Constitutional Convention who in 1796 would become the third chief justice of the United States. The Judiciary Act provided for the Supreme Court to have six members: a chief justice and five associate justices. It also defined the jurisdiction of the federal judiciary and established thirteen district courts and three circuit courts of appeal.

The act's most important provision may have been its section 25, which allowed appeals from state courts to the federal court system when certain types of constitutional issues were raised. This section was intended to implement Article VI of the Constitution, which stated that federal laws and treaties were to be considered "the supreme Law of the Land." If Article VI was to be enforced uniformly, the national judiciary clearly had to be able to overturn state court decisions in cases involving the Constitution, federal laws, or treaties. Yet nowhere did the Constitution explicitly permit such action by federal courts. The nationalistic First Congress accepted Ellsworth's argument that the right of appeal from state to federal courts was implied in the wording of Article VI. Eventually, however, judges and legislators committed to the ideal of states' rights were to challenge that interpretation.

During the first decade of its existence, the Supreme Court handled few cases of any importance. Indeed, for its first three years it heard no cases at all.

The first political buttons in the United States were just that—buttons sewn on clothing. These proclaimed the wearer's support of George Washington during his first term in office. Edmund B. Sullivan Collection, University of Hartford.

John Jay, the first chief justice, served only until 1795, and only one of the first five associate justices remained on the bench in 1799. But in a significant 1796 decision, *Ware* v. *Hylton,* the Court—acting on the basis of section 25 of the Judiciary Act of 1789—for the first time declared a state law unconstitutional. That same year it also reviewed the constitutionality of an act of Congress, upholding its validity in the case of *Hylton* v. *US.* The most important case of the decade, *Chisholm* v. *Georgia* (1793), established that states could be freely sued in federal courts by citizens of other states; this decision, unpopular with the states, was overruled five years later by the eleventh amendment to the Constitution.

Domestic policy under Washington and Hamilton

George Washington did not seek the presidency. When he returned to Mount Vernon in 1783, he was eager for the peaceful life of a Virginia planter. He rebuilt his house, redesigned his gardens, experimented with new agricultural techniques, improved the breeding of his livestock, and speculated in western lands. Yet his fellow countrymen never regarded Washington as just another private citizen. Although he took little part in the political maneuverings that preceded the Constitutional Convention, he was unanimously elected its presiding officer. As a result, he did not participate in debates, but he consistently voted for nationalistic positions. Once the proposed structure of the government was presented to the public, Americans concurred that only George Washington had sufficient prestige to serve as the republic's first president. The vote of the electoral college was just a formality.

Election of the first president

Washington was reluctant to return to public life, but knew he could not resist his country's call. Awaiting the summons to New York, he wrote to an old friend, "My movements to the chair of Government will be accompanied by feelings not unlike those of a culprit who is going to the place of his execution. . . . I am sensible, that I am embarking the voice of my Countrymen and a good name of my own, on this voyage, but what returns will be made for them, Heaven alone can foretell."

During his first months in office Washington acted cautiously, knowing that whatever he did would set precedents for the future. He held weekly receptions at which callers could pay their respects, and toured different areas of the country in turn. When the title by which he should be addressed aroused a good deal of controversy (John Adams favored "His Highness, the President of the United States of America, and Protector of their Liberties"), Washington said nothing; the accepted title soon became a plain "Mr. President." Washington also concluded that he should exercise his veto power over congressional legislation very sparingly—only, indeed, if he was convinced a bill was unconstitutional.

Washington's first major task as president was to choose the men who would head the executive departments. For the War Department he selected an old comrade-in-arms, Henry Knox, who had been his reliable general of artillery during much of the Revolution. His choice for the State Department was his fellow Virginian Thomas Jefferson, who had just returned to the United States from his post as ambassador to France. Finally, for the crucial position of secretary of the treasury, the president chose the brilliant, intensely ambitious Alexander Hamilton.

The illegitimate son of a Scottish aristocrat and a woman divorced by her husband for adultery and desertion, Hamilton was born on the British West

| *Alexander Hamilton: his early life* | Indian island of Nevis in 1757. His early years were spent in poverty; after his mother's death when he was eleven, he worked as a clerk |

for a mercantile firm. In 1773 Hamilton enrolled in King's College (later Columbia University) in New York City; only eighteen months later the precocious seventeen-year-old contributed a major pamphlet to the prerevolutionary publication wars of late 1774. Devoted to the patriot cause, Hamilton volunteered for service in the American army, where he came to the attention of George Washington. In 1777 Washington appointed the young man as one of his aides-de-camp, and the two developed great affection for one another. Indeed, in some respects Hamilton became the son Washington never had.

The general's patronage enabled the poor youth of dubious background to marry well. At twenty-three he took as his wife Elizabeth Schuyler, the daughter of a wealthy New York family. After the war, Hamilton practiced law in New York City and served as a delegate first to the Annapolis Convention in 1786 and the following year to the Constitutional Convention.

Though he exerted little influence at either convention, his contributions to *The Federalist* in 1788 revealed him to be one of the chief political thinkers in the republic.

In his dual role as secretary of the treasury and one of Washington's major advisors, two traits distinguished Hamilton from most of his contemporaries. First, he displayed an undivided, unquestioning loyalty to the nation as a whole. As a West Indian who had lived on the mainland only briefly before the war, Hamilton had no ties to an individual state. He showed little sympathy for, or understanding of, demands for local autonomy. Thus his fiscal policies aimed always at consolidation of power at the national level. Furthermore, he never feared the exercise of centralized executive authority, as did his older counterparts who had clashed repeatedly with colonial governors.

Second, he regarded his fellow human beings with unvarnished cynicism. Perhaps because of his difficult early life and his own overriding ambition, Hamilton believed people to be motivated primarily, if not entirely, by self-interest—particularly economic self-interest. He placed absolutely no reliance on people's capacity for virtuous and self-sacrificing behavior. That outlook immediately set him apart from other republicans who foresaw a rosy future in which public-spirited citizens would pursue the common good rather than their own private advantage. More important, his beliefs significantly influenced the way in which he tackled the monumental task before him: straightening out the new nation's tangled finances.

In 1789 Congress ordered the new secretary of the treasury to study the state of the public debt and to submit recommendations for supporting the government's credit. Hamilton discovered that the country's remaining war debts fell into three categories: those owed by the United States to foreign governments and investors, mostly to France (about $11 million); those owed by the national government to merchants, former soldiers, holders of revolutionary bonds, and the like (about $27 million); and, finally, similar debts owed by state governments (roughly estimated at $25 million). With respect to the national debt, there was little disagreement: Americans uniformly recognized that if their new government was to succeed it would have to pay the obligations the nation incurred while winning independence.

Alexander Hamilton (1737–1804), painted by John Trumbull in 1792. Hamilton was then at the height of his influence as secretary of the treasury, and his haughty, serene expression reveals his supreme self-confidence. Trumbull, an American student of the English artist Benjamin West, painted the portrait at the request of John Jay.   National Gallery of Art, Gift of the Avalon Foundation.

The state debts were quite another matter. Some states—notably Virginia, Maryland, North Carolina, and Georgia—had already paid off most of their war debts. They would oppose the national government's assumption of responsibility for other states' debts, since their citizens would be taxed to pay such obligations in addition to their own. Massachusetts, Connecticut, and South Carolina, on the other hand, still had sizable unpaid debts, and would welcome a system of national assumption. The possible assumption of state debts also had political implications. Consolidation of the debt in the hands of the national government would unquestionably help to concentrate both economic and political power at the national level. A contrary policy would reserve greater independence of action for the states.

Hamilton's "Report on Public Credit," sent to Congress in January 1790, reflected both his national loyalty and his cynicism. It proposed that Congress assume outstanding state debts, combine them with national obligations, and issue new securities covering both principal and accumulated unpaid interest. Current holders of state or national debt certificates would have the option of taking a portion of their payment in western lands.

Hamilton's "Report on Public Credit"

Chapter 7: Politics and society in the early republic, 1790–1800

Hamilton's aims were clear: he wanted to expand the financial reach of the United States government and reduce the economic power of the states. He also wanted to ensure that the holders of public securities—many of them wealthy merchants and speculators—would have a significant financial stake in the survival of the national government.

Hamilton's plan stimulated lively debate in Congress. The opposition coalesced around his former ally James Madison. Madison opposed the assumption of state debts, since his own state of Virginia had already paid off most of its obligations. As a congressman tied to agrarian rather than moneyed interests, he opposed the notion that only current holders of public securities should receive payments. Believing with some reason that speculators had purchased large quantities of debt certificates at a small fraction of their face value, Madison proposed that the original holders of the debt also be compensated by the government. But Madison's plan, though probably more just than Hamilton's—in that it would have directly rewarded those people who had actually supplied the revolutionary governments with goods or services—was exceedingly complex and perhaps impossible to administer. The House of Representatives accordingly rejected it.

At first, however, the House also rejected the assumption of state debts. Since the Senate, by contrast, adopted Hamilton's plan largely intact, a series of compromises followed. Hamilton agreed to changes in the assumption plan that would benefit Virginia in particular. The assumption bill also became linked in a complex way to the other major controversial issue of that congressional session: the location of the permanent national capital. Northerners and southerners both wanted the capital in their region. The traditional story that Hamilton and Madison agreed over Jefferson's dinner table to exchange assumption of state debts for a southern site is distorted and simplistic, but in the end the Potomac River was designated as the site for the capital. Simultaneously, the four congressmen from Maryland and Virginia whose districts contained the most likely locations for the new city switched from opposition to support for assumption. As a result, the first part of Hamilton's financial program became law in August 1790.

Four months later Hamilton submitted to Congress a second report on public credit, recommending the chartering of a national bank. Like his proposal for assumption of the debt, this recommendation too aroused considerable opposition. Unlike the earlier debate, which involved matters of policy, this one focused on constitutional issues. It also arose primarily after Congress had already passed the law.

Hamilton modeled his proposed bank on the Bank of England. The Bank of the United States was to be capitalized at $10 million, with only $2 million coming from public funds. The rest would be supplied by private investors. Its charter was to run for twenty years, and one-fifth of its directors were to be named by the government. Its bank notes would circulate as the nation's currency; it would also act as the collecting and disbursing agent for the treasury, and lend money to the government. Most people recognized that such an institution would benefit the country, especially because it would solve the problem of America's perpetual shortage of an acceptable medium of exchange. But there was another issue: did the Constitution give Congress the power to establish such a bank?

First Bank of the United States

James Madison, for one, answered that question with a resounding no. He pointed out that the delegates at the Philadelphia convention had specifically rejected a clause authorizing Congress to issue corporate charters. Consequently, he argued, that power could not be inferred from other parts of the Constitution.

Washington was sufficiently disturbed by Madison's contention that he decided to request other opinions before signing the bill. Edmund Randolph, the attorney general, and Thomas Jefferson, the secretary of state, agreed with Madison that the bank was unconstitutional. Jefferson referred to Article I, section 8 of the Constitution, which gave Congress the power "to make all Laws which shall be necessary and proper for carrying into Execution the foregoing Powers." *Necessary* was the key word, Jefferson argued: Congress could do what was needed but it could not do what was merely desirable without specific constitutional authorization.

Washington asked Hamilton to reply to these negative assessments of his proposal. Hamilton's "Defense of the Constitutionality of the Bank," presented to Washington in February 1791, was a brilliant exposition of what has become known as the broad-con-

Washington's strong response to the Whiskey Rebellion inspired artists to commemorate the event in pictures. Here a soldier says good-bye to his girlfriend before leaving to help put down the rebellion.   Historical Society of Pennsylvania.

structionist view of the Constitution. Hamilton argued forcefully that Congress could choose any means not specifically prohibited by the Constitution to achieve a constitutional end. In short, he said, if the end was constitutional and the means was not *un*constitutional, then the means was also constitutional.

Washington was convinced. The bill became law; the bank proved successful. So did the scheme for funding and assumption: the new nation's securities became desirable investments for its own citizens and for wealthy foreigners. But two other aspects of Alexander Hamilton's wide-ranging financial scheme did not fare so well.

In December, Hamilton presented to Congress his "Report on Manufactures," the third and last of his prescriptions for the American economy. In it he outlined an ambitious plan for encouraging and protecting the United States's infant industries, like shoemaking and textile manufacturing. Hamilton argued that the nation could never be truly independent as long as it had to rely heavily on Europe for its manufactured goods. He thus urged Congress to promote the immigration of technicians and laborers, enact protective tariffs, and support industrial development. Although many of Hamilton's ideas were implemented in later decades, few congressmen in 1791 could see much merit in his proposal. They firmly believed that America's future was agrarian. The mainstay of the republic was, after all, the virtuous yeoman farmer. Therefore, Congress rejected the report.

That same year Congress did accept the other part of Hamilton's financial program, an excise tax on whiskey, because of the need for additional government revenues. The tax fell most heavily on New England, where most of the nation's large distilleries were located, and on western farmers. Because transportation over the mountains was difficult and expensive, the frontier-dwellers' most salable "crop" was whiskey made from the corn they raised. Jugs of spirits were, after all, much more easily handled than wagonloads of bulky corn. Whiskey was also much in demand; the citizens of the new nation were already notorious for their heavy consumption of alcohol.

News of the excise law set off immediate protests in frontier areas of Pennsylvania and the Carolinas. But matters did not come to a head until the summer of 1794, when western Pennsylvania farmers tried to stop a federal marshal from arresting some men charged with violating the law. The only person killed in the disturbances was a leader of the rioters, but President Washington was determined to prevent a recurrence of Shays' Rebellion. On August 7, he issued a proclamation calling on the insurgents to disperse by September 1, and he summoned more than 12,000 militia from Pennsylvania and neighboring states. By the time the federal forces marched westward in October and November (headed some of the time by Washington himself), the riots had long since ended. The troops, who met with no resistance, arrested a number of suspects. Only two were ever convicted of treason, and Washington pardoned both. The rebellion, such as it was, ended almost without bloodshed.

The chief importance of the Whiskey Rebellion was not military victory over the rebels—for there was none—but rather the message it forcefully conveyed to the American public. The national government, Washington had demonstrated, would not allow violent organized resistance to its laws. In the new republic, change would be effected peacefully, by legal means. Those who were dissatisfied with the law should try to amend or repeal it, not take extralegal action.

Whiskey Rebellion

By 1794, a group of Americans had already begun to seek change systematically within the confines of electoral politics, even though traditional political theory regarded organized opposition—especially in a republic—as illegitimate. The leaders of the opposition were Thomas Jefferson and James Madison, who became convinced as early as 1792 that Hamilton and his supporters intended to impose a corrupt, aristocratic government on the United States. Jefferson and Madison justified their opposition to Hamilton and his policies by contending that they were the true heirs of the revolution, whereas Hamilton was actually plotting to subvert republican principles. To emphasize their point, they and their followers in Congress began calling themselves *Republicans.* Hamilton in turn accused Jefferson and Madison of the same crime: attempting to destroy the republic. To legitimize their claim to being the rightful interpreters of the Constitution, Hamilton and his supporters called themselves *Federalists.* In short, each group accused the other of being an illicit faction. (A faction was, in the traditional sense of the term, by definition opposed to the public good.)

At first, President Washington tried to remain aloof from the political dispute that divided his chief advisors, Hamilton and Jefferson. Even so, the controversy helped to persuade him to seek a second term of office in 1792 in hopes of promoting political unity. But in 1793 and thereafter, a series of developments in foreign affairs magnified the disagreements.

The beginnings of partisan politics

The first years under the Constitution were blessed by international peace. Eventually, however, the French Revolution, which began in 1789, brought about the resumption of hostilities between France, America's wartime ally, and Great Britain, America's most important trading partner.

At first, Americans welcomed the news that France was turning toward republicanism. The French people's success in limiting, then overthrowing, the monarchy seemed to vindicate the United States revolution. Now more than ever, Americans could see themselves as being in the vanguard of an inevitable historical trend that would reshape the world for the better. But by the early 1790s the reports from France were disquieting. Outbreaks of violence continued, ministries succeeded each other with bewildering rapidity, and executions were commonplace. The king himself was beheaded in early 1793. Although many Americans, including Jefferson and Madison, retained their sympathy for the French revolutionaries, others began to view France as a prime example of the perversion of republicanism. As might be expected, Alexander Hamilton fell into the latter group.

At that juncture, France declared war on Britain, Spain, and Holland. The Americans thus faced a dilemma. The 1778 treaty with France bound them to that nation "forever," and a mutual commitment to republicanism created ideological bonds. Yet the United States was connected to Great Britain as well. Aside from sharing a common history and language, America and England were economic partners. Americans still purchased most of their manufactured goods from Great Britain and sold their own produce chiefly in British and British colonial markets. Indeed, since the Hamiltonian financial system depended heavily on import tariffs as a source of revenue, and America's imports came primarily from Britain, the nation's economic health in effect required uninterrupted trade with the former mother country.

The political and diplomatic climate was further complicated in April 1793, when Citizen Edmond Genet, a representative of the French government,

| Citizen Genet |

landed in Charleston. As Genet made his leisurely way northward toward New York City, he was wildly cheered and lavishly entertained at every stop. En route, he recruited Americans for expeditions against British and Spanish possessions in the Western Hemisphere and distributed privateering commissions with a generous hand. Genet's arrival raised a series of key questions for President Washington. Should he receive Genet, thus officially recognizing the French revolutionary government? Should he acknowledge the United States obligation to aid France under the terms of the 1778 treaty? Or should he proclaim American neutrality in the conflict?

For once, Hamilton and Jefferson saw eye to eye. Both told Washington that the United States could not afford to ally itself firmly with either side. Washington agreed; thus he received Genet officially, but

also issued a proclamation informing the world that the United States would adopt "a conduct friendly and impartial toward the belligerent powers." In deference to Jefferson's continued support for France, the word *neutrality* did not appear in the declaration—but its meaning was nevertheless clear.

Genet himself was removed as a factor in Franco-American relations at the end of the summer. His faction, the Girondists, fell from power in Paris, and instead of returning home to face almost-certain execution he sought political asylum in the United States. But his disappearance from the diplomatic scene did not lessen the continuing impact of the French Revolution in America. The domestic divisions Genet helped to widen were perpetuated by clubs called Democratic-Republican societies, formed by Americans sympathetic to the French Revolution and worried about trends in the Washington administration. The societies thus expressed grass-roots concern about the same developments that troubled Jefferson and Madison.

| Democratic-Republican societies |

More than forty Democratic-Republican societies were organized between 1793 and 1800, in both rural and urban areas. Their members saw themselves as heirs of the Sons of Liberty, seeking the same goal as their predecessors: protection of the people's liberties against encroachments by corrupt and evil rulers. To that end, they publicly protested government policies and published "addresses to the people" warning of impending tyranny. The societies repeatedly proclaimed their belief in "the equal rights of man," stressing in particular the rights to free speech, free press, and assembly. Like the Sons of Liberty, the Democratic-Republican societies were composed chiefly of artisans and craftsmen of various kinds, although professionals, farmers, and merchants also joined.

The rapid growth of such groups, outspoken in their criticism of the Washington administration for its failure to come to the aid of France and for its domestic economic policies, deeply disturbed Hamilton and eventually Washington himself. Newspapers sympathetic to the Federalists charged that the societies were subversive agents of a foreign power. Their "real design," one asserted, was "to involve the country in war, to assume the reins of government and tyrannize over the people." The climax of the attack came in the fall of 1794, when Washington accused the societies of having fomented the Whiskey Rebellion.

In retrospect, Washington's and Hamilton's reaction to the Democratic-Republican societies seems hysterical, overwrought, and entirely out of proportion to whatever challenge they may have posed to the administration. But it must be kept in mind that "faction" was believed to be dangerous to the survival of a republic. In a monarchy, opposition groups were to be expected, even encouraged. In a government of the people, though, serious and sustained disagreement was taken as a sign of corruption and subversion. The Democratic-Republican societies were the first formally organized political dissenters in the United States. As such, they aroused the fear and suspicion of elected officials who had not yet accepted the idea that one component of a free government was an organized loyal opposition.

That same year George Washington decided to send Chief Justice John Jay to England to try to reach agreement on four major unresolved questions affecting Anglo-American affairs. Jay's diplomatic mission had important domestic consequences. The first point at issue was recent British seizures of American merchant ships trading in the French West Indies. The United States wanted to establish the principle of freedom of the seas and to assert its right, as a neutral nation, to trade freely with both sides. Second, Great Britain had not yet carried out its promise in the Treaty of Paris (1783) to evacuate its posts in the American Northwest. Western settlers believed that the British were responsible for the renewed Indian warfare in the region (see pages 154–156), and they wanted that threat removed. Third and fourth, the Americans hoped for a commercial treaty and sought compensation for the slaves who had left with the British army at the end of the war.

The negotiations in London proved difficult, since Jay had little to offer Britain in exchange for the concessions he wanted. In the end, Britain did agree to

| Jay Treaty |

evacuate the western forts and ease the restrictions on American trade to England and the West Indies. (Some limitations were retained, however, violating the Americans' stated commitment to open commerce.) No compensation for lost slaves was agreed to, but Jay accepted a provision establishing an arbitration commis-

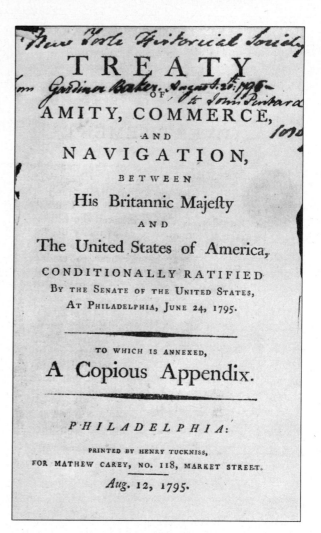

TREATY

OF

AMITY, COMMERCE,

AND

NAVIGATION,

BETWEEN

His Britannic Majesty

AND

The United States of America,

CONDITIONALLY RATIFIED

BY THE SENATE OF THE UNITED STATES,
AT PHILADELPHIA, JUNE 24, 1795.

TO WHICH IS ANNEXED,

A Copious Appendix.

PHILADELPHIA:

PRINTED BY HENRY TUCKNISS,
FOR MATHEW CAREY, NO. 118, MARKET STREET.

Aug. 12, 1795.

Title page of the Jay Treaty. Publication of the document after its secret ratification by the Senate aroused widespread protest against its terms. The House of Representatives tried but failed to halt its implementation. The New-York Historical Society.

sion to deal with the matter of prewar debts owed to British creditors. A similar commission was to handle the question of compensation for the seizures of American merchant ships. Under the circumstances, Jay had done remarkably well: the treaty averted war with England at a time when the United States, which lacked an effective navy, could not have hoped to win a conflict with its former mother country. Nevertheless, most Americans, including the president, were dissatisfied with at least some parts of the treaty.

At first, however, potential opposition was blunted, because the Senate debated and ratified the treaty in secret. Not until after it was formally approved on June 24, 1795, was the public informed of its provisions. The Democratic-Republican societies led protests against the treaty, which were especially intense in the South. Planters criticized Jay's failure to obtain compensation for runaway slaves as well as the commitment to repay prewar debts. Once President Washington had reluctantly signed the treaty, though, there seemed to be little the Republicans could do to prevent it from taking effect. Just one opportunity remained: Congress had to appropriate funds to carry out the treaty provisions, and according to the Constitution money bills had to originate in the House of Representatives.

When the House took up the issue in March 1796, opponents of the treaty tried to prevent approval of the appropriations. To that end, they called on Washington to submit to the House all documents pertinent to the negotiations. In successfully resisting the House's request, Washington developed the doctrine of executive privilege—that is, the power of the president to withhold information from Congress if he believes circumstances warrant doing so. Although the treaty's opponents initially appeared to be in the majority, pressure for approval built as time passed. Frontier residents were eager for evacuation of the British posts, fearing a new outbreak of Indian war despite the signing of the Treaty of Greenville the previous year (see page 155). Merchants wanted to reap the benefits of widened trade with the British Empire. Furthermore, Thomas Pinckney of South Carolina had negotiated a popular treaty with Spain giving the United States navigation privileges on the Mississippi, which would be an economic boost to the West and South. Federalist senators threatened not to ratify Pinckney's Treaty if the Jay Treaty appropriations were defeated. For all these reasons the House on April 30, 1795, voted the necessary funds by the narrow margin of 51 to 48.

Analysis of the vote reveals both the regional nature of the division and the growing cohesion of the Republican and Federalist factions in Congress. Voting in favor of the appropriations were 44 Federalists and 7 Republicans; voting against were 45 Republicans and 3 Federalists. The final tally was also split by region. The vast majority of votes against the bill

Republicans and Federalists

were cast by southerners (including the three Federalists, who were Virginians). The bill's supporters were largely from New England and the middle states, with the exception of two South Carolina Federalists. The seven Republicans who broke ranks with their faction to vote for the appropriations were from commercial areas in New York, Pennsylvania, and Maryland.

The small number of defectors revealed a new force at work in American politics: partisanship. Voting statistics from the first four congresses show the ever-increasing tendency of members of the House of Representatives to vote as coherent groups, rather than as individuals. If factional loyalty is defined as voting together at least two-thirds of the time on national issues, the percentage of nonaligned congressmen dropped from 42 percent in 1790 to just 7 percent in 1796. Also, the majority slowly shifted from Federalist to Republican. Federalists controlled the first three congresses, through spring 1795; Republicans gained the ascendancy in the Fourth Congress; Federalists returned to power with slight majorities in the Fifth and Sixth Congresses; and the Republicans took over in the Seventh Congress in 1801.

To describe these shifts is easier than to explain them. The growing division cannot be accurately explained in the terms used by Jefferson and Madison (aristocrats versus the people) or by Hamilton and Washington (true patriots versus subversive rabble). Simple economic differences between agrarian and commercial interests do not provide the answer either, since more than 90 percent of Americans in the 1790s lived in rural areas. Yet certain distinctions can be made. Republicans tended to be self-assured, confident, and optimistic about both politics and the economy. They did not fear instability, at least among the white population, and they sought to widen the people's participation in government. They foresaw a prosperous future, and looked first to the United States's own resources, second to her position in the world. Republicans also remained sympathetic to France in international affairs.

Federalists, on the other hand, were insecure, uncertain of the future. They stressed the need for order, authority, and regularity in the political world. Unlike Republicans, they had no grass-roots political organization and put little emphasis on involving ordinary people in government. The nation was, in their eyes, perpetually threatened by potential enemies, both internal and external, and best protected by a continuing alliance with Great Britain. Their vision of international affairs may have been more accurate, given the warfare in Europe, but it was also narrow and unattractive. Since it held out little hope of a better future to the voters of any region, it is not surprising that the Republicans eventually became dominant.

If the factions' respective attitudes are translated into economic and regional affiliations, the pattern is clear. Northern merchants and commercially oriented farmers, well aware of the uncertainties of international trade, tended to be Federalists. Since New England's soil was poor and agricultural production could not be expanded, northern subsistence farmers also gravitated toward the more conservative party, which wanted to preserve the present (and past) rather than look to the future.

Republican southern planters, on the other hand, firmly in control of their region and of a class of enslaved laborers, could anticipate unlimited westward expansion. Many Tidewater planters successfully shifted from cultivating soil-draining tobacco to grains and other foodstuffs. The invention of the cotton gin in 1793 allowed them to plant many more acres of cotton (see Chapter 10). For their part, small farmers in the South found the Republicans' democratic rhetoric (despite aristocratic leadership) more congenial than the approach of the Federalists, who said and did little to attract the allegiance of such folk.

Finally, the two sides drew supporters from different ethnic groups. Americans of English stock tended to be Federalists, while those of Celtic origin (Welsh, Irish, Scots) were more likely to be Republicans. The third largest group, the Germans, were split fairly evenly at first but eventually moved into the Republican camp. To what degree traditional antagonisms between English and Celts in particular contributed to the growing political split is impossible to say. But since patterns of migration to and within America (see pages 61–64) rendered regional and ethnic lines largely parallel, it is conceivable that ethnicity was as important as other factors in determining eventual political alignments.

The presence of the two organized groups, not yet parties in the modern sense but nonetheless active contenders for office, made the presidential election of

1796 the first that was seriously contested. George Washington, tired of the criticism to which he had been subjected, decided to retire from office. (Presidents had not yet been limited to two terms by constitutional amendment.) In September Washington published his famous "Farewell Address," most of which was written by Hamilton. Washington outlined two principles that guided American foreign policy at least until the late 1940s: maintain commercial but not political ties to other nations and enter no permanent alliances. He also drew a sharp distinction between the United States and Europe, stressing America's uniqueness and the need for independent action.

Domestically, Washington lamented the existence of factional divisions among his fellow countrymen. His call for an end to partisan strife has often been interpreted by historians as the statement of a man who could see beyond political affiliations to the good of the whole. But it is more accurately read in the context of its day as an attack on the legitimacy of the Republican opposition. What Washington wanted was unity behind the Federalist banner, which he saw as the only proper political stance. The Federalists (like the Republicans) continued to see themselves as the sole guardians of the truth, the only true heirs of the Revolution, and they perceived their opponents as misguided, unpatriotic troublemakers.

To succeed Washington, the Federalists put forward the candidacy of Vice President John Adams, with the diplomat Thomas Pinckney of South Caro-

| Election of 1796 |

lina as his vice-presidential running mate. The Republicans in Congress chose Thomas Jefferson as their candidate; the lawyer, revolutionary war veteran, and active Republican politician Aaron Burr of New York agreed to run for vice president.

That the election was contested did not mean that its outcome was decided by the people. Voters could cast their ballots only for electors, not for the candidates themselves. Many voters did not even have that opportunity, since more than 40 percent of the members of the electoral college that year were chosen by state legislatures, some even before the candidates had been selected. Furthermore, the method of voting prescribed for the electoral college by the Constitution tended to work against the new factions,

John Adams and political dissent

THE PROVIDENTIAL DETECTION

This Federalist political cartoon was probably drawn shortly after the presidential election of 1796. Jefferson kneels in front of the altar of French despotism, kindling a fire from the controversial writings of radicals. He is stopped from adding the Constitution to the flames by an American eagle—meant to symbolize John Adams, whose election has saved the nation from disorder.   The Library Company of Philadelphia.

which was not surprising, since the authors of the Constitution had not foreseen the development of opposing national political organizations. Members of the electoral college were required to vote for two persons, without specifying the office. The man with the highest total became president; the second highest became vice president. In other words, there was no way an elector could explicitly support one person for president and another for vice president.

This procedure proved to be the Federalists' undoing. Adams won the presidency with 71 votes, but a number of Federalist electors (especially those from New England) failed to cast ballots for Pinckney. Thomas Jefferson won 68 votes, 9 more than Pinckney, and became vice president. The incoming administration was thus politically divided. The next four years were to see the new president and vice president, once allies and close friends, become bitter enemies.

John Adams took over the presidency peculiarly blind to the partisan developments of the past four years. As president he never abandoned the outdated notion George Washington had discarded as early as 1794: that the president should be above politics, an independent and dignified figure who did not seek petty factional advantage. Thus Adams kept Washington's cabinet intact, despite its key members' allegiance to his chief rival, Alexander Hamilton. He often adopted a passive posture, letting others (usually Hamilton) take the lead, when he should have acted decisively. As a result his administration gained a reputation for inconsistency. When Adams's term ended, the Federalists were severely divided and the Republicans had won the presidency. But at the same time Adams's detachment from Hamilton's maneuverings enabled him to weather the greatest international crisis the republic had yet faced: the so-called Quasi-War with France.

The Jay Treaty improved America's relationship with England, but it provoked retaliation from France. Angry that the United States had, in effect, abandoned the 1778 French-American treaty, the Directory (the coalition then in power in Paris) ordered French vessels to seize American ships carrying British goods. In response, Adams appointed three special commissioners to try to reach a settlement with France: Elbridge Gerry, an old friend from Massachusetts; John Marshall, a Virginia Federalist; and Charles Cotesworth Pinckney of South Carolina, Thomas's older brother. At the same time Congress increased military spending, authorizing the building of ships and the stockpiling of weapons and ammunition.

For months, the American commissioners futilely sought to open negotiations with Talleyrand, the French foreign minister. But Talleyrand's agents demanded a bribe of $250,000 before talks could begin.

| XYZ Affair | The Americans retorted, "No, no; not a sixpence," and reported the incident in dispatches that President Adams received in early March 1798. Adams informed Congress of the impasse and recommended increased appropriations for defense.

Convinced that Adams had deliberately sabotaged the negotiations, congressional Republicans insisted that the dispatches be turned over to Congress. Aware that releasing the reports would work to his advantage, Adams complied. He withheld only the names of the French agents, referring to them as X, Y, and Z. The revelation that the Americans had been treated with utter contempt by the Directory stimulated a wave of anti-French sentiment in the United States. A journalist's version of the commissioners' reply, "Millions for defense, but not a cent for tribute," became the national slogan. Cries for war filled the air. Congress formally abrogated the 1778 treaty and authorized American ships to seize French vessels.

The Republicans, who opposed war and continued to sympathize with France, could do little to stem the tide. Since Agent Y had boasted of the existence of a "French party in America," Federalists flatly accused the Republicans of traitorous designs. A New York newspaper declared that anyone who remained "lukewarm" after reading the XYZ dispatches was a "criminal—and the man who does not warmly reprobate the conduct of the French must have a soul black enough to be *fit* for *treason Strategems* and *spoils."* John Adams wavered between calling the Republicans traitors and acknowledging their right to oppose administration measures. His wife was less tolerant: "Those whom the French boast of as their Partizans," Abigail Adams told her older sister, deserved to be "adjudged traitors to their country." If Jefferson had been president, she observed, "we should all have been sold to the French."

The Federalists saw this climate of opinion as an opportunity to deal a death blow to their Republican opponents. Now that the country seemed to see the truth of what they had been saying ever since the Whiskey Rebellion in 1794—that the Republicans were subversive foreign agents—the Federalists sought to codify that belief into law. In the spring and summer of 1798, the Federalist-controlled Congress adopted a set of four laws known as the Alien and Sedition Acts, intended to suppress dissent and prevent further growth of the Republican party.

Three of the acts were aimed at immigrants, whom the Federalists quite correctly suspected of being Republican in their sympathies. The Naturalization Act lengthened the residency period required for citizenship from five to fourteen years and ordered all resident aliens to register with the federal government. The Alien Enemics Act provided for the detention of

Alien and Sedition Acts

enemy aliens in time of war. The Alien Friends Act, which was to be in effect for only two years, gave the president almost unlimited authority to deport any alien he deemed dangerous to the nation's security. (Adams never used that authority. The Alien Enemies Act was not implemented either, since war was never formally declared.)

The fourth law, the Sedition Act, sought to control both citizens and aliens. It outlawed conspiracies to prevent the enforcement of federal laws and set the maximum punishment for such offenses at five years in prison and a $5,000 fine. The act also tried to control speech. Writing, printing, or uttering "false, scandalous and malicious" statements "against the government of the United States, or the President of the United States, with intent to defame . . . or to bring them or either of them, into contempt or disrepute" became a crime punishable by as much as two years imprisonment and a fine of $2,000. Today the Supreme Court would declare unconstitutional any such law punishing speech alone. But in the eighteenth century, when organized political opposition was regarded with suspicion, the Sedition Act was legally acceptable.

In all, there were fifteen indictments and ten convictions under the Sedition Act. Most of the accused were outspoken Republican newspaper editors who failed to mute their criticism of the administration in response to the law. But the first victim—whose story may serve as an example of the rest—was a Republican congressman from Vermont, Matthew Lyon. The Irish-born Lyon, a former indentured servant who had purchased his freedom and fought in the Revolution, was indicted for declaring in print that John Adams had displayed "a continual grasp for power" and "an unbounded thirst for ridiculous pomp, foolish adulation, and selfish avarice." Though convicted, fined $1,000, and sent to prison for four months, Lyon was not silenced. He conducted his re-election campaign from jail, winning an overwhelming majority. The fine, which he could not afford, was ceremoniously paid by contributions from leading Republicans around the country.

Faced with the prosecutions of their major supporters, Jefferson and Madison sought an effective means of combating the Alien and Sedition Acts. Petitioning the Federalist-controlled Congress to repeal the laws

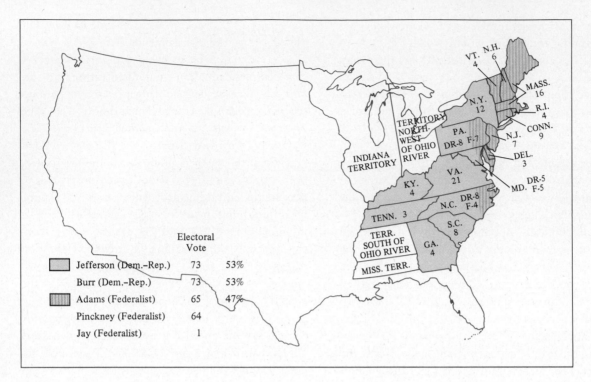

	Electoral Vote	
Jefferson (Dem.–Rep.)	73	53%
Burr (Dem.–Rep.)	73	53%
Adams (Federalist)	65	47%
Pinckney (Federalist)	64	
Jay (Federalist)	1	

Presidential election, 1800

would clearly do no good. Furthermore, Federalist judges refused to allow accused persons to question the Sedition Act's constitutionality. Accordingly, the Republican leaders turned to the only other possible mechanism for protest: the state legislatures. Carefully concealing their own role (it would hardly have been desirable for the vice president to be indicted for sedition), Jefferson and Madison each drafted a set of resolutions. Introduced into the Kentucky and Virginia legislatures respectively in the fall of 1798, the resolutions differed somewhat but their import was the same. Since the Constitution was created by a compact among the states, they contended, the people speaking through their states had a legitimate right to judge the constitutionality of actions by the federal government. Both sets of resolutions pronounced the Alien and Sedition Acts unconstitutional and asked other states to join in the protest.

Although no other state replied positively to the Virginia and Kentucky resolutions, they nevertheless had major significance. In the first place, they were superb political propaganda, rallying Republican opinion throughout the country. They placed the opposition party squarely in the revolutionary tradition of

resistance to tyrannical authority. Second, the theory of union they proposed was expanded on by southern states'-rights advocates in the 1830s and thereafter. Jefferson and Madison had identified a key constitutional issue: how far could the states go in opposing the national government? How could a conflict between the two be resolved? These questions were not to be finally answered until 1865.

Ironically, just as the Sedition Act was being implemented and northern state legislatures were rejecting the Virginia and Kentucky resolutions, Federalists split badly over the course of action the United States should take toward France. Hamilton and his supporters still called for a declaration legitimizing the undeclared naval war the two nations had been waging for months. But Adams had received a number of private signals that the Directory now regretted its treatment of the three American commissioners. Acting on these assurances, he dispatched the envoy William Vans Murray to Paris. In September 1800 Murray reached agreement with Napoleon Bonaparte, who had seized power in France, thus ending the threat of war. The results of the negotiations were not known in the United States until after the presidential election of

Although the camp meeting shown here occurred in the later years of the Second Great Awakening, the scene was typical of the period. Note the preponderance of women in the crowd. The New-York Historical Society.

1800. Even so, Adams's decision to seek a peaceful settlement probably cost him re-election because of the divisions it caused in Federalist ranks.

In sharp contrast, the Republicans entered the 1800 presidential race firmly united behind the Jefferson-Burr ticket. Though they won the election, their lack of foresight almost cost them dearly. The problem was caused by the system of voting in the electoral college, which the Federalists understood more clearly than the Republicans. The Federalists arranged in advance for one of their electors to fail to vote for Charles Cotesworth Pinckney, their vice-presidential candidate. John Adams thus received the highest number of Federalist votes (65 to Pinckney's 64). The Republicans failed to make the same distinction between their candidates, and all 73 cast ballots for both Jefferson and Burr (see map). Because neither Republican had a plurality, the Constitution required that the contest be decided in the House of Representatives, with each state's congressmen voting as a unit. Since the new House, dominated by Republicans,

| Election of 1800 |

would not take office for some months, Federalist congressmen decided the election. It took them thirty-five ballots to decide that Jefferson would be a lesser evil than Burr. As a result of the tangle, the twelfth amendment to the Constitution (1804) changed the method of voting in the electoral college to allow for a party ticket.

Religious dissent and racial ferment

Ever since the fervor of the Great Awakening (see pages 80–82) had burned itself out in the 1760s, America's churches had been largely quiescent. Clergymen, like their congregations, had become preoccupied with secular issues—the Revolution, the Constitution, foreign threats. But in the late 1790s a few revivals began to occur in New England, and in 1800 a full-fledged Second Awakening broke

| Second Great Awakening |

Mourning scenes like this one were common in women's art during the late eighteenth and early nineteenth centuries. The concern for grieving widows and orphans revealed in such works also found expression in church-sponsored female charitable associations.   Museum of Fine Arts, Boston, M. and M. Karolik Collection.

out in Kentucky and Tennessee. Itinerant Presbyterian and Methodist ministers spread over the countryside, carrying the word of salvation to all who would listen.

Frontier folk, for the most part poor, uneducated, and rootless, were particularly receptive to the enthusiastic preachers. At camp meetings, sometimes attended by thousands of people and usually lasting from three days to a week, clergymen exhorted their audiences to repent their sins and become genuine Christians. They stressed that salvation was open to all, downplaying the doctrine of predestination that had characterized orthodox colonial Protestantism. The emotional nature of the conversion experience was emphasized far more than the need for careful study and preparation. Such preachers thus brought the message of religion to the people in more ways than one. They were in effect "democratizing" American religion, making it available to all rather than to a preselected and educated elite.

The most famous camp meeting took place at Cane Ridge, Kentucky, in 1801. At a time when the largest settlement in the state had no more than 2,000 inhabitants, attendance at Cane Ridge was estimated at from 10,000 to 25,000. One witness, a Presbyterian cleric, marvelled that "no sex nor color, class nor description, were exempted from the pervading influence of the spirit; even from the age of eight months to sixty years, there were evident subjects of this marvellous operation." He went on to recount how people responded to the preaching with "loud ejaculations of prayer, . . . some struck with terror, . . . others, trembling, weeping and crying out . . . fainting and swooning away, . . . others surrounding them with melodious songs, or fervent prayers for their happy resurrection, in the love of Christ." Such scenes

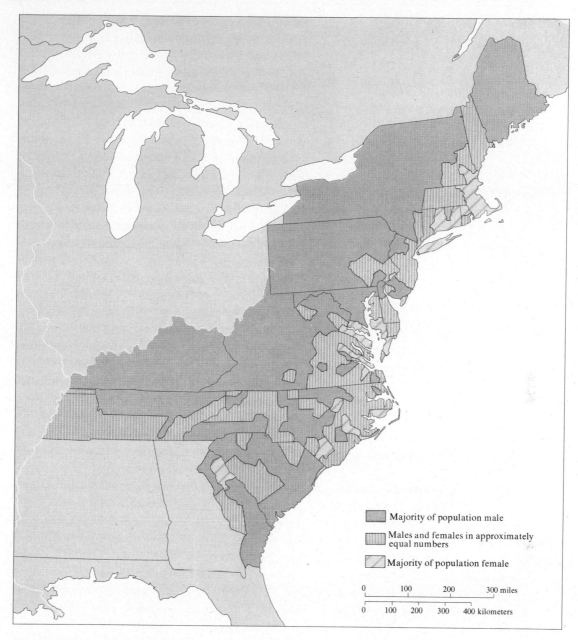

Sex ratio of white population, 1790

<table>
<tr><td>■</td><td>Majority of population male</td></tr>
<tr><td>▥</td><td>Males and females in approximately equal numbers</td></tr>
<tr><td>▨</td><td>Majority of population female</td></tr>
</table>

were to be repeated many times in the decades that followed. Revivals swept across different regions of the country until nearly the middle of the century, leaving an indelible legacy of evangelism to American Protestant churches.

The revivals also led to increasingly female church congregations. Unlike the First Great Awakening, when converts were evenly divided by sex, more women than men—particularly young women—an-swered the call of Christianity during the Second Awakening. The increase in female converts seems to have been directly related to major changes in women's circumstances at the end of the eighteenth century. In some areas of the country, especially New England (where the revival movement flourished), women outnumbered men after 1790, since many men had migrated westward in search of land (see map). Thus girls could no longer count on finding

Religious dissent and racial ferment

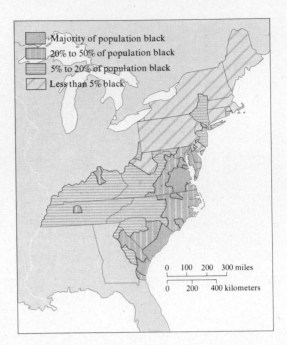

1790 black population: proportion of total population.   Source: Reprinted by permission of Princeton University Press.

Majority of population black
20% to 50% of population black
5% to 20% of population black
Less than 5% black

marital partners. The uncertainty of their social and familial position may well have led them to seek spiritual certainty in the church.

Young women's domestic roles changed dramatically at the same time, as cloth production began to move from the household to the factory (see Chapter 9). Deprived of their chief household role, New England daughters found in the church a realm where they could continue to make useful contributions to society. Church missionary societies and charitable associations provided an acceptable outlet for their talents. One of the most striking developments of the early nineteenth century was the creation of thousands of female associations to aid widows and orphans, collect money for foreign missions, or improve the quality of maternal care.

The religious ferment among both blacks and whites in frontier regions of the upper South contributed to racial ferment as well. People of both races attended the camp meetings, and sometimes black preachers exhorted whites in addition to members of their own race. When revivals spread eastward into more heavily slaveholding areas, white planters became fearful of the egalitarianism implied in the evan-gelical message of universal salvation and harmony. At the same time, revivals created a group of respected black leaders—preachers—and provided them with a ready audience for a potentially revolutionary doctrine.

Recent events in the West Indies gave whites ample reason for apprehension. In the 1790s, over the course of several years, mulattoes and blacks in the French colony of Saint Domingue (Haiti) overthrew European rule under the leadership of a mulatto, Toussaint L'Ouverture. The revolt was bloody, vicious, prolonged, and characterized by numerous atrocities committed by both sides. In an attempt to prevent the spread of such unrest to their own slaves, southern state legislators passed laws forbidding white Haitian refugees from bringing their slaves with them. But North American blacks learned about the revolt anyway. Furthermore, the preconditions for racial upheaval did not have to be imported into the South from the West Indies: they already existed on the spot.

The Revolution had caused immense destruction in the South, especially in the states south of Virginia. The heavy losses of slaves and constant guerrilla warfare, not to mention the changes in American trading patterns brought about by withdrawal from the British Empire, wreaked havoc on the southern economy. Also, the vast postwar increase in the number of free blacks severely strained the system of race relations that had evolved during the eighteenth century. Color, caste, and slave status no longer coincided, as they had when the few free blacks were all mulattoes (see map). Furthermore, like their white compatriots, blacks (both slave and free) had become familiar with notions of liberty and equality. They had also witnessed the benefits of fighting collectively for freedom, rather than resisting individually or running away. The circumstances were ripe for an explosion, and the Second Awakening was the match that lit the fuse in both Virginia and North Carolina.

The Virginia revolt was planned by Gabriel Prosser, a blacksmith who argued that blacks should fight to obtain the same rights as whites, and who ex-

Gabriel's Rebellion

plicitly placed himself in the tradition of the French and Haitian revolutions. At revival meetings led by his brother, Martin, a preacher, Gabriel recruited other blacks like himself—artisans who moved

Chapter 7: Politics and society in the early republic, 1790–1800

easily in both black and white circles and who lived in semifreedom under minimal white supervision. The artisan leaders then enlisted rural blacks in the cause. The conspirators planned to attack Richmond on the night of August 30, 1800, setting fire to the city, seizing the state capital, and capturing the governor. Their plan showed considerable political sophistication, but heavy rain made it impossible to execute the plot as scheduled. Several whites then learned of the plan from their slaves and spread the alarm. Gabriel avoided capture for some weeks, but most of the other leaders of the rebellion were quickly arrested and interrogated. The major conspirators, including Prosser himself, were hanged, but in the months that followed other insurrectionary scares continued to frighten Virginia slaveowners.

Two years later a similar wave of fear swept North Carolina and the bordering counties of Virginia. A slave conspiracy to attack planters' homes, kill all whites except small children, and seize the land was uncovered in Bertie County. Similar plots were rumored elsewhere. Again, slave artisans and preachers played prominent roles in the planned uprisings. Nearly fifty blacks were executed as a result of the whites' investigations of the rumors. Some were certainly innocent victims of the planters' hysteria, but there can be no doubt about the existence of most of the plots.

As the eighteenth century ended, then, white and black inhabitants of the United States were moving toward an accommodation to their new circumstances. The United States was starting to take shape as an independent nation no longer dependent on England. In domestic politics, the Jeffersonian interpretation of republicanism had prevailed over the Hamiltonian approach. The country would be characterized by a decentralized economy, minimal government (especially at the national level), and maximum freedom of action and mobility for individual white males.

But that freedom would be purchased at the expense of white females and black men, women, and children. In the decades to come, both groups would be subject to further control. To prevent a recurrence of outbreaks of violence like those of 1800 through 1802, slaveholders increased the severity of the slave codes, further restricting their human property. Before long, all talk of emancipation (gradual or other-

Important events

1789	George Washington inaugurated
	Judiciary Act of 1789
	French Revolution
1790	Alexander Hamilton's first "Report on Public Credit"
1791	First National Bank chartered
	Hamilton's "Report on Manufactures"
	First ten amendments (Bill of Rights) ratified
	Haitian revolt begins
1793	France declares war on Britain, Spain, and Holland
	Neutrality Proclamation
	Democratic-Republican societies founded
	Invention of cotton gin
	Chisholm v. *Georgia*
1794	Whiskey Rebellion (Pennsylvania)
1795	Jay Treaty
1796	First contested presidential election: John Adams elected president, Thomas Jefferson vice president
	Ware v. *Hylton*
1798	XYZ affair
	Alien and Sedition Acts
	Virginia and Kentucky resolutions
	Eleventh amendment
1798–99	"Quasi-War" with France
1800	United States and France reach peace agreement
	Jefferson elected president, Aaron Burr vice president
	Second Great Awakening begins
	Gabriel's Rebellion (Virginia)
	Mason Locke Weems, *Life of Washington*
1804	Twelfth amendment
	Haiti becomes independent republic

Religious dissent and racial ferment

wise) ceased, and slavery became even more firmly entrenched as an economic institution and way of life. Likewise, the Revolution's implicit promise for women was never fully realized. Woman's place was still in the home; in the first half of the nineteenth century an unprecedented outpouring of books and magazine articles asserted that conclusion with ever greater force and fervor. Jeffersonian Republicans, like almost all Americans before them, failed to extend to women the freedom and individuality they recognized as essential for men.

Among Indians as well, the end of the eighteenth century marked an important turning point. The United States had unquestionably established its independence; henceforth, the influence of European powers in the American interior would be negligible. The tribes accordingly had no alternative but to confront directly the problems posed by land-hungry white Americans. West of the Appalachians, the Indians had yet to feel the full force of the whites' westward thrust. East of the mountains, though, the Iroquois—who well knew the difficulty of trying to stop the white flood—were experiencing their own religious awakening on their small, scattered reservations. Led by their prophet, Handsome Lake, they embraced the traditional values of their culture and renounced such destructive white customs as drinking alcohol and playing cards. At the same time, though, they began abandoning their ancient way of life. The traditional economic system based on male hunters and female cultivators gave way to one, like that of the whites, founded on male farming and female housekeeping. The Indians too had come to the end of one path and the beginning of another that would affect their lives, individually and collectively.

Suggestions for further reading

National government and administration

Ralph Adams Brown, *The Presidency of John Adams* (1975); John R. Howe, *The Changing Political Thought of John Adams* (1966); Richard H. Kohn, *Eagle and Sword: The Federalists and the Creation of the Military Establishment in America, 1783-1802* (1975); Stephen G. Kurtz, *The Presidency of*

John Adams: The Collapse of Federalism, 1795-1800 (1957); Forrest McDonald, *Alexander Hamilton: A Biography* (1979); Forrest McDonald, *The Presidency of George Washington* (1974); John C. Miller, *Alexander Hamilton, Portrait in Paradox* (1959); John C. Miller, *The Federalist Era, 1789-1801* (1960); Merrill D. Peterson, *Thomas Jefferson & The New Nation: A Biography* (1970); Carl E. Prince, *The Federalists and the Origins of the U.S. Civil Service* (1978); Leonard D. White, *The Federalists: A Study in Administrative History* (1948).

Partisan politics

Leland D. Baldwin, *The Whiskey Rebels* (1939); Lance Banning, *The Jeffersonian Persuasion: Evolution of a Party Ideology* (1978); Richard Beeman, *The Old Dominion and the New Nation, 1788-1801* (1972); Richard W. Buel, Jr., *Securing the Revolution: Ideology in American Politics, 1789-1815* (1972); William Nisbet Chambers, *Political Parties in a New Nation: The American Experience, 1776-1809* (1963); Joseph Charles, *The Origins of the American Party System* (1956); Noble E. Cunningham, *The Jeffersonian Republicans: The Formation of Party Organization, 1789-1801* (1957); Manning J. Dauer, *The Adams Federalists* (1953); Paul Goodman, *The Democratic Republicans of Massachusetts* (1964); Richard Hofstadter, *The Idea of a Party System: The Rise of Legitimate Opposition in the United States, 1780-1840* (1970); Adrienne Koch, *Jefferson and Madison: The Great Collaboration* (1950); Eugene P. Link, *Democratic-Republican Societies, 1790-1800* (1942); Norman K. Risjord, *Chesapeake Politics, 1781-1800* (1978); Patricia Watlington, *The Partisan Spirit: Kentucky Politics, 1779-1792* (1972); Alfred F. Young, *The Democratic-Republicans of New York: The Origins, 1763-1797* (1967); John Zvesper, *Political Philosophy and Rhetoric: A Study of the Origins of American Party Politics* (1977).

Diplomacy

Harry Ammon, *The Genet Mission* (1973); Samuel F. Bemis, *Jay's Treaty,* 2nd ed. (1962); Samuel F. Bemis, *Pinckney's Treaty,* 2nd ed. (1960); Jerald A. Combs, *The Jay Treaty* (1970); Alexander DeConde, *Entangling Alliance: Politics and Diplomacy under George Washington* (1958); Alexander DeConde, *The Quasi-War: Politics and Diplomacy of the Undeclared War with France, 1797-1801* (1966); Felix Gilbert, *To the Farewell Address: Ideas of Early American Foreign Policy* (1961); Bradford Perkins, *The First Rapprochement: England and the United States, 1795-1805* (1967); Charles Ritcheson, *Aftermath of Revolution: British Policy Toward the United States, 1783-1795* (1969); Paul A. Varg, *Foreign Policies of the Founding Fathers* (1963).

Chapter 7: Politics and society in the early republic, 1790-1800

Civil liberties

Leonard W. Levy, *Legacy of Suppression: Freedom of Speech and Press in Early American History* (1960); Leonard W. Levy, *Origins of the Fifth Amendment* (1968); Robert A. Rutland, *The Birth of the Bill of Rights, 1776–1791* (1955); James Morton Smith, *Freedom's Fetters: The Alien and Sedition Laws and American Civil Liberties* (1956).

Education and culture

Lawrence A. Cremin, *American Education: The National Experience, 1783–1876* (1981); Joseph J. Ellis, *After the Revolution: Profiles of Early American Culture* (1979); Carl F. Kaestle, *The Evolution of an Urban School System: New York City, 1750–1850* (1973); David P. McKay and Richard Crawford, *William Billings of Boston: Eighteenth-Century Composer* (1975); Russel B. Nye, *The Cultural Life of the New Nation: 1776–1803* (1960); Kenneth Silverman, *A Cultural History of the American Revolution* (1976).

Women and blacks

Nancy F. Cott, *The Bonds of Womanhood: "Woman's Sphere" in New England, 1780–1835* (1977); Nancy F. Cott, "Young Women in the Second Great Awakening in New England," *Feminist Studies*, 3, No. 1/2 (1975), 15–29; Jeffrey J. Crow, "Slave Rebelliousness and Social Conflict in North Carolina, 1775 to 1802," *William and Mary Quarterly*, 3rd ser., 37 (1980), 79–102; Gerald W. Mullin, *Flight and Rebellion: Slave Resistance in Eighteenth-Century Virginia* (1972).

8 ∾
THE
REPUBLIC
ENDURES,
1801–1824

In November 1800, Abigail Adams took up residence in the "wilderness," the new federal capital of Washington. The president's "great castle," she wrote her sister, was still uncompleted. Because the yard was unfenced, the First Lady was forced to dry the family's wash in the "great unfinished audience-room" (the East Room). She shopped for provisions in nearby Georgetown, but found it "the very dirtyest Hole," its streets "a quagmire after every rain." Indeed, mud became the enemy of public affairs whenever it rained. Diplomats, cabinet officers, and congressmen driving to the White House in full dress inevitably had to leave their carriages and drag them from the mud on Pennsylvania Avenue. Even in the Senate chamber, mud was a hazard. Signs warned balcony visitors "not to place their feet on the board in front of the gallery, *as the dirt from them falls upon Senators' heads."*

The politicians and diplomats who had to live in Washington tended to feel cut off from the mainstream of American life. When the government moved to Washington from Philadelphia, its unfinished federal buildings appeared more like ruins than the headquarters of a vibrant new nation. Augustus John Foster, a British diplomat, lamented the move. The diplomatic corps, he reported, found it "difficult to digest" moving from "agreeable," urban Philadelphia "to what was then scarce any better than a mere swamp." On the other hand, Washington offered amusements unlike any other Atlantic capital. "Excellent snipe shooting and even partridge shooting was to be had on each side of the main [Pennsylvania] avenue and even close under the wall of the Capitol," Foster recalled.

Matters did not improve for the next few decades. Washington failed to develop as a city, lacking public accommodations of any kind. The nearest public houses and commercial shops were three miles from the Capitol; six years passed before the first church was built. Government clerks, laborers, and impoverished job seekers were the city's only permanent residents; representatives, bored with the endless political discussions, fled the city as often as possible. A large minority of congressmen pressed for a return to Philadelphia, but the majority feared reopening a question that could fan sectional conflict.

Even so, the creation of this new capital, a planned city, was among the boldest steps of the new nation. Located near the nation's center of population in east-

ern Maryland, Washington was beholden neither to the colonial past nor to any single state. Its design, too, reflected the political philosophy of the new nation. Just as the Constitution divided the government into three branches, so the city had three distinct areas—one centered around Congress, another around the president, and the third around the Supreme Court. At the highest elevation stood the Capitol, a single building that emphasized Congress's role as a collective body. A mile and a half away lay the president's mansion, surrounded by the various buildings of the government departments. Broad boulevards connected the mansion with the Capitol and the surrounding countryside, but the Court stood apart from both Congress and the mansion, without direct access to either.

Few buildings were needed to house the government. In 1802 the federal government had only 2,875 civilian employees, including congressmen; most were postmasters or collectors of revenue. Washington itself housed only 291 federal officials, elected and appointed. Essentially the government collected tariffs, delivered mail, and defended its borders.

A small government suited the republic. Americans tended to distrust the federal government. The adoption of the Constitution and the power of the Federalists in the 1790s had been more a result of their dissatisfaction with the Articles of Confederation than a sign of their confidence in central government. In 1800 they elected the Republican Thomas Jefferson to the presidency; thus began the Virginia dynasty and a swing back to state authority. In an age when it took some congressmen more than a week to reach the capital, most Americans favored government closer to home.

With Jefferson's inauguration in 1801, the nation established a tradition of peaceful transition of power from one political party to another. Competition for voters' allegiance invigorated both parties, as a faction called the Younger Federalists copied the popular electioneering techniques of the Republicans. But though Federalists remained strong in many states, they could not compete on an equal footing at the national level; the party lacked vigorous, popular leaders comparable to Jefferson, Madison, and Monroe. Nonetheless, Federalist ideology came to dominate the Supreme Court during the thirty-four-year tenure of Chief Justice John Marshall. Under Marshall the

Court became an equal branch of government and the voice of a nationalist point of view.

Conflict at home thus proved benign, but problems abroad led to war. Caught between the warring French and British, the young nation found its neutral rights threatened on the high seas. British impressment of American seamen and the disabling of the U.S.S. *Chesapeake* in 1807 left Americans humiliated and angry. Jefferson sought to avoid war by holding American ships in port, but his policy failed. Land-hungry westerners called War Hawks finally prevailed over antiwar easterners, and the nation took up arms.

The War of 1812 was a foolish step from a military point of view. The United States was simply unprepared for combat. Indeed, it was changed conditions in Europe—the end of the Napoleonic wars—that finally made peace possible, not American victories. The peace treaty that ended the two-and-one-half-year conflict merely restored the status quo; it ignored the issues that had led to war. But the war and the treaty nevertheless reaffirmed American independence and determination to steer clear of European conflicts.

The War of 1812 unleashed a wave of nationalism. The growing, expanding nation became more assertive both at home and throughout the hemisphere. In the new atmosphere, Republicans became the unlikely champions of a national bank, protective tariffs, and internal improvements. But this so-called Era of Good Feelings was short-lived. The Panic of 1819 brought hard times and voices of discontent became commonplace as sectional self-interest divided the nation. Southerners opposed the tariff; northern manufacturers lobbied for higher duties. Westerners blamed the tight money policies of the Bank of the United States for their troubles. And the admission of Missouri as a state in 1821 created a new rift, as debate over slavery resounded for the first time in the halls of Congress. Yet through both war and political division, the new nation endured.

Jefferson assumes power

Nearly overnight the formality of the Washington and Adams presidencies disappeared as Thomas Jefferson set the tone for Republican Washington. Gone were the aristocratic wigs, ruffles, and breeches (short trousers) the first two presidents had favored; Jefferson wore plain garb. On March 4, 1801, the president-elect left his New Jersey Street boarding house alone and walked to the Capitol to be sworn in. Ordinary folk who had come to celebrate his inaugural overran Washington and Georgetown, causing Federalists to cluck their tongues at the seeming collapse of authority and order.

Yet for all their suspicion, the Federalists gave up the reins of government peaceably. "I have this morning witnessed one of the most interesting scenes a free people can ever witness," Margaret B. Smith, a Philadelphian, wrote on March 4, 1801, to her sister-in-law. "The changes of administration, which in every government and in every age have most generally been epochs of confusion, villainy and bloodshed, in this our happy country take place without any species of distraction, or disorder." The precedent of an orderly and peaceful change of government had been established.

Jefferson delivered his inaugural address in the Senate chamber, the only part of the Capitol that had been completed. Nearly a thousand people strained to hear his barely audible voice. "We are all republicans, we are all Federalists," he told the assembly in an appeal for national unity. Confidently addressing those with little faith in the people's ability to govern themselves, he called America's republican government "the world's best hope." If "man cannot be trusted with the government of himself," Jefferson argued, "can he, then, be trusted with the government of others? Or have we found angels in the forms of kings to govern him? Let history answer this question."

Jefferson's inaugural address

The new president went on to outline his own and his party's goals:

a wise and frugal government, which shall restrain men from injuring one another, which shall leave them otherwise free to regulate their own pursuits.

. . .

equal and exact justice to all men, of whatever state or persuasion, religious or political. . . .

the support of the state governments in all their rights, as the most competent administrators for our domestic concerns and the surest bulwarks against antirepublican tendencies.

An 1801 Republican victory flag. Above a cameo portrait of Jefferson the eagle holds a banner reading "Jefferson President of the United States of America." He tramples disdainfully on a second banner, "John Adams no more." Smithsonian Institution.

At the same time, he assured Federalists that he shared some of their concerns as well:

the preservation of the general government in its whole constitutional vigor. . . .

the honest payment of our debts and sacred preservation of the public faith. . . .

encouragement of agriculture and of commerce as its handmaid.

But more than lofty principles was at stake in the rivalry between the two groups. On assuming the presidency, Jefferson found that virtually all appointed officials were loyal Federalists: of the 600-odd appointed under Washington and Adams, only 6 were known Republicans. To counteract this Federalist power, Jefferson first refused to recognize Adams's last-minute "midnight appointments" to local offices in the District of Columbia. Next he dis-

missed Federalist customs collectors from New England ports. Vacant treasury and judicial offices were awarded to Republicans, until by July 1803 only 130 of 316 presidentially controlled offices were held by Federalists. Jefferson saw these actions not as distributing the spoils of victory, but as equalizing the power of the parties. Nonetheless, he had used patronage both to reward his friends and to build a party organization.

Meanwhile, the Republican Congress proceeded to affirm its Republicanism. Guided by Secretary of the Treasury Albert Gallatin and John Randolph of Virginia, Jefferson's ally in the House, the federal government went on a diet. Congress repealed all internal taxes, even the whiskey tax. Gallatin cut the army budget in half, to just under $2 million, and reduced the navy budget from $3.5 to $1 million in 1802. Moreover, Gallatin laid plans to reduce the national

Chapter 8: The republic endures, 1801–1824

debt—Hamilton's engine of economic growth—from $83 to $57 million, as part of a plan to retire it altogether by 1817. Jefferson even closed two of the nation's five diplomatic missions abroad—the Hague and Berlin—to save money.

More than frugality, however, separated Republicans from Federalists. Opposition to the Alien and Sedition laws of 1798 had helped to unite Republicans before Jefferson's election (see pages 183–184). Now as president, Jefferson forswore using the acts against his opponents, as President Adams had, and Congress let them expire in 1801 and 1802. Congress also repealed the Naturalization Act of 1798, which had required fourteen years of residency for citizenship. The act that replaced it required only five years of residency, acceptance of the Constitution, and the forsaking of foreign allegiance and titles (1802). The new act would remain the basis of naturalized American citizenship into the twentieth century.

The Republicans turned next to the judiciary, the last stronghold of unchecked Federalist power. During the 1790s not a single Republican had been appointed to the federal bench. Moreover, the Judiciary Act of 1801, passed in the last days of the Adams administration, had created fifteen new judgeships (which Adams filled in his midnight appointments) and reduced by attrition the number of justices on the Supreme Court from six to five. Since that reduction would have deprived Jefferson of the chance to appoint a new justice when the next vacancy occurred, one of the first acts of the new Republican-dominated Congress was to repeal the Judiciary Act of 1801.

Attacks on the judiciary

But Republican grievances against the Court ran deeper than that. Federalist judges had refused to review the Sedition Act, and Federalists had prosecuted critics of the judiciary under the act. At Jefferson's suggestion, the House impeached (indicted) and in 1804 the Senate removed from office Federal District Judge John Pickering of New Hampshire. Although he was an alcoholic and emotionally disturbed, Pickering had not committed any crime.

The same day Pickering was convicted, the House impeached Supreme Court Justice Samuel Chase for judicial misconduct. Chase, an arch-Federalist and leader in pressing convictions under the Sedition Act, had repeatedly denounced Jefferson's administration

from the bench. The Republicans, however, failed to muster the two-thirds majority necessary to convict him; they had gone too far. Their failure to remove Chase preserved the Court's independence and established a precedent for narrow interpretation of the grounds for impeachment (criminal rather than political grounds). Time soon cured Republican grievances; by the year Jefferson left office, he had appointed three new Supreme Court justices.

Far more momentous than frugality in government or the politics of federal appointments was the Louisiana Purchase (1803). The territory of Louisiana was vital to the American West. By 1800 nearly a million Americans living west of the Appalachians were dependent on the Ohio and Mississippi rivers. Farmers shipped their produce down the two rivers to New Orleans for sale and shipment both to American ports and overseas. As long as a weak Spain had held Louisiana, Americans had expected to acquire the land eventually through settlement. But in 1802, Napoleonic France acquired the vast territory. Americans feared Napoleon would try to rebuild the French Empire in the New World and embroil North America in his European wars. At about the same time, the Spanish intendant of Louisiana withdrew from Americans the privilege of duty-free shipping through the port of New Orleans. Most Americans suspected a Napoleonic plot behind the change of policy. Eastern merchants and western farmers, both hurt by the decline in trade, clamored for war.

Louisiana Purchase

To relieve the pressure for war and to prevent westerners from joining Federalists in opposition to his administration, Jefferson simultaneously prepared for war and explored the possibility of purchasing Louisiana. In January 1803 he sent James Monroe to France to help the American minister Robert Livingston in negotiating to buy New Orleans and Florida for $10 million. Meanwhile, Congress authorized a call-up of 80,000 militia if it proved necessary. Arriving in Paris on April 12, Monroe was astonished to learn that on the previous day France had offered to sell all of Louisiana—more than 825,000 square miles—to the United States for $15 million. On April 30 Monroe and Livingston signed a treaty to purchase the territory, whose borders were left undefined.

The Louisiana Purchase doubled the size of the nation, opened the way for westward expansion across the continent, and prevented the United States from being drawn into European politics. The acquisition was the boldest of federal actions and the single most popular achievement of Jefferson's presidency. Yet for Jefferson, the purchase presented a dilemma. It offered fulfillment of the dream of an empire of liberty reaching to the Pacific Coast, "with room enough for our descendants to the hundredth and thousandth generation," as he put it in his second inaugural address. But its legality was questionable. The Constitution gave him no clear authority to acquire new territory and incorporate it into the nation. Jefferson considered requesting a constitutional amendment to allow the purchase, but in the end he justified it on the grounds that it was part of the president's implied powers to protect the nation. The people, he knew, would accept or reject the purchase on election day.

In 1804 the voters expressed their overwhelming approval of Jefferson's action; he and his running mate, George Clinton, rode the wave of popularity to a second term. Charles C. Pinckney and Rufus King, their Federalist opponents, carried only Connecticut and Delaware.

Republicans versus Federalists

Jefferson's re-election was both a personal and a party triumph. The political dissenters of the 1790s had turned their Democratic-Republican societies into a political party—an organization for the purpose of winning elections. More than anything else, opposition to the Federalists had molded and unified them. Indeed, it was where the Federalists were strongest—in New York and Pennsylvania in the 1790s and in New England in the 1800s—that the Republicans had organized most effectively.

Until the Republican successes in 1800 and 1804, Federalists had disdained widespread electioneering. They believed in government by the "best" people—those whose education, wealth, and experience marked them as leaders. For candidates to debate their qualifications before their inferiors—the voters—was unnecessary and undignified. The direct appeals of the Republicans therefore struck them as a subversion of the natural political order.

But after their resounding defeat in 1800, a younger generation of Federalists began to imitate the Republicans. They organized statewide, and led by

Younger Federalists

men like Josiah Quincy, a young congressman from Massachusetts, they began to campaign for popular support. Quincy cleverly identified the Federalists as the people's party, attacking Republicans as autocratic planters. "Jeffersonian Democracy," Quincy satirized in 1804, was "an indian word, signifying '*a great tobacco planter who had herds of black slaves.*'" The self-styled Younger Federalists also exploited westerners' concern about Indians, New Englanders' concern about commerce, and everyone's concern about national strength.

In the states where both parties organized and ran candidates, participation in elections increased markedly. In some states more than 90 percent of the eligible voters—nearly all of whom were white males—cast ballots between 1804 and 1816. People became more interested in politics generally, especially at the local level; and as participation in elections increased, the states expanded suffrage.

In response to the new competition, the Republicans introduced the political barbecue, which became the symbol of grassroots campaigning. In New York they roasted oxen; on the New England coast they fried fish and baked clams; in Maryland they served turtles and oysters. The guests washed down their meals with beer and punch and sometimes competed in corn shuckings or horse pulls. Throughout the barbecue, candidates and party leaders spoke from the stump. Oratory was a popular form of entertainment, and the speakers delivered lengthy and uninhibited speeches. They often made wild accusations, which—given the slow speed of communications—might not be answered until after the election. In 1808, for example, a New England Republican accused the Federalists of causing the Boston Massacre.

Soon both parties were using barbecues to appeal directly to voters. Holidays became occasions for partying and electioneering, a practice that helped to make the Fourth of July a day of national celebration and local oratory. But although the Younger Federalists adopted the political barbecue, the Federalist party never fully mastered the art of wooing voters. Older Federalists still opposed such blatant campaigns. And although they were strong in a few states

Chapter 8: The republic endures, 1801–1824

Citizens gather at the State House in Philadelphia to whip up support for their candidates and parties. This picture, drawn on Election Day in 1816, suggests the overwhelmingly white, exclusively male composition of the electorate.   Historical Society of Pennsylvania.

like Connecticut and Delaware, the Federalists never offered the Republicans sustained competition. Divisions between Older and Younger Federalists often hindered them, and the extremism of some Older Federalists tended to discredit the party. A case in point was Timothy Pickering, a Massachusetts congressman and former secretary of state who opposed the Louisiana Purchase, feared Jefferson's re-election, and urged the secession of New England in 1803 and 1804. Pickering won some support among the few Federalists in Congress, but others opposed his plan for a northern confederacy. When Vice President Burr lost his bid to become governor of New York in 1804, the plan collapsed. (Burr, more an opportunist than a loyal Republican, was to have led New York into secession, with the other states to follow.)

Both political parties suffered from factionalism. In 1804, for instance, the Federalist Alexander Hamilton backed a rival Republican faction against Burr in his race for the governorship of New York; Hamilton

| Hamilton-Burr duel |

had caught wind of the Pickering-Burr conspiracy. Burr, his political career in ruins, turned his resentment on Hamilton and challenged him to a duel. The specific insult was Hamilton's description of Burr as dangerous and unfit to hold office. Three years before, Hamilton's son Philip had been killed in a duel when he refused to fire at his opponent. Now, with his own honor at stake, Hamilton accepted Burr's challenge, although he found duelling repugnant. He faced Aaron Burr on July 11, 1804, at Weehawken, New Jersey, and followed his son's lead: he did not fire. Hamilton paid for that decision with his life.

The Burr-Hamilton duel reflected the intensity of party factionalism, which combined with the personal nature of political conflict to keep both Republicans and Federalists from becoming full-blown parties in the modern sense. Where Federalists were too weak to

John Marshall (1755–1835), chief justice of the Supreme Court from 1801 to 1835. This portrait shows the strength of personality that enabled Marshall to make the Court into a Federalist stronghold. Note the head of Solon, an Athenian lawgiver of the sixth century B.C., at the top of the portrait. Supreme Court of the United States.

level. Indeed, after the death of Alexander Hamilton, only one Federalist played a strong and sustained role in national politics: Chief Justice John Marshall.

Marshall was an astute lawyer who was always to be found on the winning side. A Virginia Federalist who had served under George Washington in the Revolutionary War, he had been minister to France and then secretary of state under President Adams before being named chief justice in the midnight appointments. An autocrat by nature, Marshall nevertheless possessed a grace and openness of manner well suited to the new Republican political style. Under Marshall's domination from 1801 until 1835, the Supreme Court remained a Federalist stronghold even after Republican justices achieved a majority in 1811. Throughout his tenure the Court upheld federal supremacy over the states and protected the interests of commerce and capital.

John Marshall

More important, Marshall made the Court the equal of the other branches of government in practice as well as theory. First, he made a place on the Court a coveted honor. Prior to Marshall it had been difficult to keep the Court filled. Fifteen justices had served on the six-member Court during its first twelve years; after Marshall's appointment it would take 40 years for fifteen new members to be appointed. Marshall's presence had made the Court worthy of ambitious and talented men. Second, he built a unified Court, influencing the justices to issue a single majority opinion rather than individual concurring judgments. Marshall himself became the voice of the majority. From 1801 through 1805 he wrote 24 of the Court's 26 decisions; through 1810 he wrote 85 percent of the 171 opinions, including every important decision.

Finally, Marshall increased the Court's power. Ironically *Marbury* v. *Madison* (1803), the landmark case that enabled Marshall to strengthen the Courts, involved another of Adams's midnight appointees. William Marbury, whom Adams had designated a justice of the peace in the District of Columbia, sued the new secretary of state, James Madison, for canceling Marbury's appointment so Jefferson could appoint a Republican. In his suit Marbury requested a writ of mandamus, or a court order compelling Madison to appoint him.

Marbury v. Madison

At first glance, the case presented a political dilemma. It was highly possible that even if the Su-

be a threat, Republicans succumbed to the temptation to fight among themselves. Even Jefferson's congressional leader, John Randolph, abandoned the president in 1806 to start a third party.

Parties also had shallow roots; they tended to organize from the top down, with control resting in a legislative caucus. In Virginia, the Carolinas, and Georgia, there were no statewide elections and hence no statewide parties. Governors were chosen by the legislature, and members of the electoral college and congressmen were elected in districts. Candidates in these states nominated themselves, since party committees and caucuses did not exist. Congressional representatives joined party caucuses in Washington but had no party ties at home.

Thus, although this period is commonly called the era of the first party system, parties as such never fully developed. Competition encouraged party organization, but personal ambition, personality clashes, and local, state, and regional loyalties worked against it. And as the election of 1804 revealed, the Federalists could offer only weak competition at the national

preme Court ruled in favor of Marbury and issued a writ of mandamus, the president would not comply. After all, why should the president, sworn to uphold the Constitution, allow the Court to decide for him what was constitutional? But if, on the other hand, the Court refused to issue the writ, it would be handing the Republicans a victory. Marshall avoided both alternatives and turned what seemed like a no-win situation into a Federalist triumph. Speaking for the Court, he ruled that Marbury had a right to his commission but that the Court could not compel Madison to honor it, because the Constitution did not grant the Court power to issue a writ of mandamus. Thus Marshall declared unconstitutional section 13 of the Judiciary Act of 1789, which authorized the Court to issue such writs. Marbury lost his job and the justices denied themselves the power to issue writs of mandamus, but the Supreme Court claimed its great power of judicial review.

In succeeding years Marshall fashioned the theory of judicial review. Since the Constitution was the supreme law, he reasoned, any act of Congress contrary to the Constitution must be null and void. And since the Supreme Court was responsible for upholding the law, it had a duty to decide whether a conflict existed between a legislative act and the Constitution. If such a conflict did indeed exist, the Court would declare the congressional act unconstitutional.

Marshall's decision rebuffed Republican attacks on the Court's independence. He avoided a confrontation with the Republican-dominated Congress by not ruling on their repeal of the Judiciary Act of 1801, which had created positions for the midnight appointees. And he enhanced the Court's independence.

Under Marshall, the Supreme Court also became the bulwark of a nationalist point of view. In *McCulloch* v. *Maryland* (1819), the Court struck down a

McCulloch *v.* Maryland

Maryland law taxing the federally chartered Second Bank of the United States. Maryland had adopted the tax in an effort to destroy the bank's Baltimore branch. The issue was thus one of state versus federal power. Speaking for a unanimous Court, Marshall asserted the supremacy of the federal government over the states. "The Constitution and the laws thereof are supreme," he declared; "they control the constitution and laws of the respective states and cannot be controlled by them."

Having established federal supremacy, the Court went on to consider whether Congress could issue a bank charter. No such power was specified in the Constitution. But Marshall noted that Congress had the authority to pass "all laws which shall be necessary and proper for carrying into execution" the enumerated powers of the government (Article I, Section 8). Therefore Congress could legally exercise "those great powers on which the welfare of the nation essentially depends." If the ends were legitimate and the means were not prohibited, Marshall ruled, a law was constitutional. The Constitution was in Marshall's words, "intended to endure for ages to come, and consequently, to be adapted to the various causes of human affairs." The bank charter was declared legal.

In *McCulloch* v. *Maryland* Marshall combined Federalist nationalism with Federalist economic views. By asserting federal supremacy he was protecting the commercial and industrial interests that favored a national bank. This was Federalism in the tradition of Alexander Hamilton. The decision was only one in a series. In *Fletcher* v. *Peck* (1810) the Court voided a Georgia law that violated individuals' right of contract. Similarly, in the famous *Dartmouth College* v. *Woodward* (1819), the Court nullified a New Hampshire act altering the charter of Dartmouth College, which Marshall ruled constituted a contract. In protecting such contracts, Marshall thwarted state interference in commerce and business.

The struggle for power between Marshall's Federalist court and Republican legislatures, though fierce, proved benign. A certain amount of sparring was to be expected in the process of hammering out governmental relationships in a new republic. If the nation were to be threatened in these times, it would be not from within, but from without.

Preserving American neutrality

"Peace, commerce, and honest friendship with all nations, entangling alliance with none," President Jefferson had sensibly proclaimed in his first inaugural address. And Jefferson's efforts to stand clear of European conflict worked until 1805. Thereafter he found peace and undisturbed commerce an elusive goal, though pursuit of it occupied nearly his entire second administration.

After the Senate ratified Jay's Treaty in 1795 (see pages 179–180), the United States and Great Britain had appeared to reconcile their differences. Britain withdrew from its western forts and interfered less in American trade with France. More importantly, trade between the United States and Britain increased: the republic became Britain's best customer, and the British Empire in turn bought the bulk of American exports.

But renewal of the Napoleonic wars in May 1803 — two weeks after Napoleon sold Louisiana to the United States—again trapped the nation between the two unfriendly superpowers. For two years American commerce actually benefited from the conflict. As the world's largest neutral carrier, the United States became the chief supplier of food to Europe. American merchants also gained control of most of the West Indian trade, which was often transshipped through American ports to Europe.

Meanwhile, the United States victory over Tripolitan pirates on the north coast of Africa provided Jefferson with his one clear success in protecting American trading rights. In 1801 Jefferson had refused the demands of the Sultan of Tripoli for payment of tribute. Instead he sent a naval squadron to the Mediterranean to protect American merchant ships from Barbary Coast pirates. In 1803 and 1804, under Lieutenant Stephen Decatur, the navy blockaded Tripoli Harbor while seven marines marched overland from Egypt to seize the port of Derna. The United States signed a peace treaty with Tripoli in 1805, but continued to pay tribute to other Barbary states.

That same year American merchants became victims of Anglo-French enmity. First Britain tightened its control over the high seas with its victory over the French and Spanish fleets at the Battle of Trafalgar in October 1805. Two months later Napoleon defeated the Russian and Austrian armies at Austerlitz. Stalemated, the two powers waged commercial war, blockading and counterblockading each other's trade. As a trading partner of both countries, the United States paid a high price.

At the same time the British navy stepped up impressments of American sailors. Britain, whose navy was the world's largest, was suffering a severe shortage

Impressment of American sailors

of sailors. Few enlisted, and those already in service frequently deserted, discouraged by poor food and living conditions and brutal discipline. The Royal Navy resorted to stopping American ships and forcibly removing British deserters, British-born naturalized American seamen, and other unlucky sailors mistakenly suspected of being British. About six to eight thousand Americans were drafted in this manner between 1803 and 1812.

Americans saw impressment as a direct assault on their new republic. It violated America's rights as a neutral nation, and the British principle of "once a British subject, always a British subject" ignored American citizenship and sovereignty. Moreover, the practice exposed the weakness of the new nation; the United States was in effect unable to protect its citizens from impressment.

In February 1806 the Senate denounced British impressment as aggression and a violation of neutral rights. To protest the insult Congress passed the Non-Importation Act, prohibiting importation from Great Britain of a long list of cloth and metal articles. In November Jefferson suspended the act temporarily while William Pinckney joined James Monroe in London in an attempt to negotiate a settlement. But the treaty Monroe and Pinckney carried home violated their instructions—it did not mention impressment—and Jefferson never submitted it to the Senate for ratification.

Less than a year later the *Chesapeake* Affair exposed American military weakness and revealed the emotional impact of impressment on the public. In June 1807 the forty-gun frigate U.S.S. *Chesapeake* left Norfolk, Virginia, on a mission to protect American ships trading in the Mediterranean. About ten miles out, still inside American territorial waters, it met the fifty-gun British frigate *Leopard*. When the *Chesapeake* refused to be searched for deserters, the *Leopard* repeatedly emptied its guns broadside into the American ship. Three Americans were killed and eighteen wounded, including the ship's captain, Commodore James Barron. Four sailors were impressed—three of them American citizens, all of them deserters from the Royal Navy. Wounded and humiliated, the *Chesapeake* crept back into port.

Chesapeake Affair

THE MPRESSMENT OF AN

American Sailor Boy,

SUNG ON BOARD THE BRITISH PRISON SHIP CROWN PRINCE, THE FOURTH OF JULY, 1814
BY A NUMBER OF THE AMERICAN PRISONERS.

THE youthful sailor mounts the bark,
　　And bids each weeping friend adieu :
Fair blows the gale, the canvass swells :
　　Slow sinks the uplands from his view.

Three mornings, from his ocean bed,
　　Resplendent beams the God of day :
The fourth, high looming in the mist,
　　A war-ship's floating banners play.

Her yawl is launch'd ; light o'er the deep,
　　Too kind, she wafts a ruffian band :
Her blue track lengthens to the bark,
　　And soon on deck the miscreants stand.

Around they throw the baleful glance :
　　Suspense holds mute the anxious crew—
Who is their prey ? poor sailor boy !
　　The baleful glance is fix'd on you.

Nay, why that useless scrip unfold ?
　　They damn'd the " lying yankee scrawl,"
Torn from thine hand, it strews the wave—
　　They force thee trembling to the yawl.

Sick was thine heart as from the deck,
　　The hand of friendship wav'd farewell ;
Mad was thy brain, as far behind,
　　In the grey mist thy vessel fell.

One hope, yet, to thy bosom clung,
　　The captain mercy might impart ;

Vain was that hope, which bade thee look,
　　For mercy in a Pirate's heart.

What woes can man on man inflict,
　　When malice joins with uncheck'd power ;
Such woes, unpitied and unknown,
　　For many a month the sailor bore !

Oft gem'd his eye the bursting tear,
　　As mem'ry linger'd on past joy ;
As oft they flung the cruel jeer,
　　And damn'd the " chicken liver'd boy."

When sick at heart, with " hope deferr'd,"
　　Kind sleep his wasting form embrac'd,
Some ready minion ply'd the lash,
　　And the lov'd dream of freedom chas'd.

Fast to an end his miseries drew :
　　The deadly hectic flush'd his cheek :
On his pale brow the cold dew hung,
　　He sigh'd, and sunk upon the deck !

The sailor's woes drew forth no sigh ;
No hand would close the sailor's eye :
Remorseless, his pale corse they gave,
Unshrouded to the friendly wave.

And as he sunk beneath the tide,
　　A hellish shout arose ;
Exultingly the demons cried,
　　" So f re all Albion's Rebel Foes !"

Ballad of an American sailor impressed by the British during the
War of 1812. References to the British captain as a "Pirate" and
the British crew as "demons" reveal the intense indignation felt
by the American public.　The New-York Historical Society.

Preserving American neutrality

Had the United States been better prepared for war, the howl of public indignation that resulted might have brought about a declaration of war. But the United States was ill equipped to defend its neutral rights with force; it was no match for the British navy. Fortunately, Congress was not in session at the time of the *Chesapeake* Affair, and Jefferson was able to avoid hostilities. The president responded instead by strengthening the military and putting economic pressure on Great Britain: in July Jefferson closed American waters to British warships to prevent similar incidents and soon thereafter he increased military and naval expenditures. On December 14, 1807, Jefferson again invoked the Non-Importation Act, followed eight days later by a new measure, the Embargo Act.

Intended as a short-term measure, the Embargo Act forbade virtually all exports from the United

> **Embargo Act**

States to any country. Imports came to a halt as well, since foreign ships delivering goods would have to leave American ports with empty holds. Smuggling blossomed overnight.

Few American policies have been as unsuccessful as Jefferson's embargo. The lucrative American merchant trade collapsed; exports fell 80 percent from 1807 to 1808. New England, the heart of Federalist opposition to the Virginia dynasty, felt the brunt of the depression. Ships rotted in harbors and grass grew on wharves; unemployment soared. In the winter of 1808 and 1809, talk of secession spread through New England port cities. Great Britain, in contrast, was only mildly affected by the embargo. Those English citizens who were hurt most—West Indians and English factory workers—had no voice in policy. English merchants actually gained, since they took over the Atlantic carrying trade from the stalled American merchant marine. Moreover, because the British blockade of Europe had already ended most trade with France, the embargo had little practical effect on the French. Indeed, it gave France an excuse to privateer against American ships that had managed to escape the embargo by avoiding American ports. The French argued that such ships must be British ships in disguise, since the embargo barred American ships from the seas.

In the election of 1808, the Republicans faced the Federalists, the embargo, and factional dissent in their own party. Jefferson followed Washington's example, renouncing a third term and supporting James Madison, his secretary of state, as the Republican standard-bearer. Madison won the endorsement of the congressional caucus, but Virginia Republicans put forth James Monroe (who later withdrew), and some eastern Republicans supported Vice President George Clinton. This was the first time the Republican nomination had been contested.

Charles C. Pinckney and Rufus King again headed the Federalist ticket, but with new vigor. The Younger Federalists pounded away at the widespread disaffection with Republican policy, especially the embargo. Although Pinckney received only 47 electoral votes to Madison's 122, the Federalists did manage to make the election a race. Pinckney carried all of New England except Vermont, and won Delaware and some electoral votes in two other states as well. Federalists also gained seats in Congress and captured the New York state legislature. For the Younger Federalists, the future looked bright.

As for the embargo, it eventually collapsed under the weight of domestic opposition. Jefferson withdrew it in his last days in office, replacing it with the Non-Intercourse Act of 1809. The act reopened trade

> **Non-Intercourse Act**

with all nations except Britain and France, and authorized the president to resume trade with either country if it ceased to violate neutral rights. But the new act solved only the problems that had been created by the embargo; it did not convince Britain and France to change their policies. For one brief moment it appeared to work: President Madison reopened trade with England in June 1809 after the British minister to the United States assured him that Britain would offer the concessions he sought. His Majesty's government in London, however, repudiated the minister's assurances, and Madison renewed nonintercourse.

When the Non-Intercourse Act expired in spring 1810, the United States tried to sell old wine in a new bottle, relabeled Macon's Bill Number 2. A congressional invention, the bill reopened trade with both Great Britain and France, but provided that if either nation ceased to violate American rights, the president could shut down American commerce with the other. Madison, eager to use the bill rather than go to war, was tricked at his own game. When Napoleon declared that French edicts against United States shipping would be lifted, Madison declared nonintercourse against Great Britain in March 1811. But Napoleon did not keep his word. The French continued to seize American ships, and nonintercourse failed a second time.

Because the British navy controlled the Atlantic, Britain was the main target of American hostility, not France. New York harbor was virtually blockaded by the Royal Navy, so reopening trade with any nation had little practical effect. Angry American leaders tended to blame even Indian resistance in the West on British agitation, ignoring the Indians' legitimate protests against white encroachment and treaty violations. Frustrated and having exhausted all efforts to alter British policy, the United States in 1811 and 1812 drifted into war with Great Britain.

Meanwhile, unknown to the president and Congress, Great Britain was changing its policy. The Anglo-French conflict had ended much of British commerce with the European continent, and exports to the United States had fallen 80 percent. Depression had hit the British Isles. On June 16, 1812, Britain opened the seas to American shipping. But two days later, before word had crossed the Atlantic, Congress declared war.

The War of 1812 was the logical outcome of United States policy since the renewal of war in Europe in 1803. The grievances enumerated in President Madison's message to Congress on June 1, 1812, were old ones: impressment, interference with neutral commerce, and the stirring-up of western Indians. Unmentioned was the resolve to defend American independence and honor—and the thirst of expansionists for British Canada. Yet Congress and the country were divided. Much of the sentiment for war came from the War Hawks, land-hungry southerners and westerners led by Henry Clay of Kentucky and John C. Calhoun of South Carolina. Most representatives from the coastal states opposed war, since armed conflict with the great naval power threatened to close down all American shipping. The vote for war—79 to 49 in the House, 19 to 13 in the Senate—was close and reflected these sharp regional differences. The split would also be reflected in the way Americans fought the war.

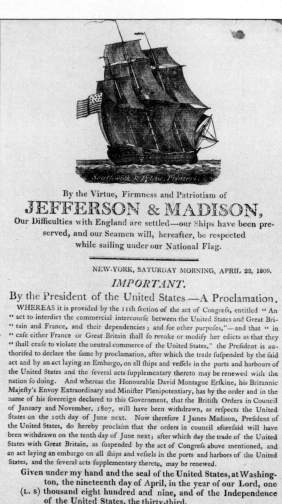

A broadside celebrating the brief reopening of trade with Britain in 1809. This Republican propaganda made the most of a small victory resulting from the generally unsuccessful and highly unpopular policy of nonintercourse. *The New-York Historical Society.*

The War of 1812

Militarily, war was a foolish adventure for the United States in 1812; despite six months of preparation, American forces were still ill equipped. Because the army had neither an able staff nor an adequate force of enlisted men, the burden of fighting fell on the state militia—and not all the states cooperated. The navy did have a corps of well-trained, experienced

Major campaigns of the War of 1812

officers who had proven their mettle in protecting American merchantmen from Mediterranean pirates. But next to the Royal Navy, the ruler of the seas, the U.S. Navy was minuscule. Jefferson's warning that "our constitution is a peace establishment—it is not calculated for war" proved a wise one.

For the United States, the only readily available battlefront on which to confront Great Britain was Canada. The mighty Royal Navy was useless on the waters separating the United States and Canada, since no river afforded it access from the sea. In-

Invasion of
Canada

vasion of Canada, thousands of miles from British supply sources, therefore would give the United States an edge. And England, preoccupied with fighting Napoleon on the European continent, was unlikely to reduce its continental forces to defend Canada.

Begun with high hopes, the invasion of Canada proved disastrous. The American strategy was to concentrate on the West, splitting Canadian forces and isolating the Indians who supported the British. General William Hull marched his troops into lower Canada, near Detroit. But the British anticipated the invasion, moved troops into the area, and demanded

Cameo portraits of the naval heroes of the War of 1812 surround a lithograph of the Battle of Put-in-Bay (1813), in which the United States gained control of Lake Erie. Clockwise from top center: Oliver H. Perry, Stephen Decatur, Johnston Blakeley, William Bainbridge, David Porter, and James Lawrence. Drawn and published by Currier in 1846. The New-York Historical Society.

Hull's surrender. When pro-British Indians captured Fort Dearborn, near Detroit, Hull capitulated (see map). Farther to the west, other American forts surrendered. By the winter of 1812 and 1813, the British controlled about half the Old Northwest (Ohio, Indiana, Illinois, Michigan, and Wisconsin).

The United States had no greater success on the Niagara front, where New York borders Canada. At the Battle of Queenstown, north of Niagara, the United States regular army met defeat because the New York state militia refused to leave the state. This scene was repeated near Lake Champlain, where American plans to attack Montreal were foiled when the militia declined to cross the border.

The navy provided the only bright note in the first year of the war: the U.S.S. *Constitution,* the U.S.S. *Wasp,* and the U.S.S. *United States* all bested British warships on the Atlantic. But their victories gave the United States only a brief advantage. In defeat the British lost just 1 percent of their strength; in victory the Americans lost 20 percent. The British admiralty simply shifted its fleet away from the American ships, and by 1813 the Royal Navy again dominated the seas.

In 1813 the two sides also vied over control of the Great Lakes, the key to the war in the Northwest. The contest was largely a ship-building race. Under Master Commandant Oliver Hazard Perry and shipbuilder Noah Brown, the United States outbuilt the British on Lake Erie and defeated them at the bloody Battle of Put-in-Bay on September 10. The ships fought fiercely and at close range; of 103 men on duty on the U.S.S. *Lawrence,* 21 were killed and 63 wounded. With this costly victory, the Americans gained control of Lake Erie.

> Great Lakes campaign

Silk bandanna glorifying Andrew Jackson (1767–1845), hero of the Battle of New Orleans. Edmund B. Sullivan Collection, University of Hartford.

clined nearly 90 percent since 1811, and the decline in revenues from customs duties threatened to bankrupt the federal government.

Following their overthrow of Napoleon in April 1814, the British stepped up the land campaign against the United States, concentrating their efforts in the Chesapeake. In retaliation for the burning of York—and to divert American troops from Lake Champlain, where the British planned a new offensive—royal troops occupied Washington and set it to the torch. The attack on the capital was, however, only a raid. The major battle occurred at Baltimore, where the Americans held firm. Although the British inflicted heavy damages both materially and psychologically, they achieved no more than a stalemate.

The last campaign of the war was waged in the South, along the Gulf of Mexico. It began when Tennessee militia general Andrew Jackson defeated the Creeks and Cherokees at the Battle of Horseshoe Bend in March 1814. The battle ended the year-long Creek War, which had begun after a series of skirmishes between Indians and settlers. As a result, the Creeks ceded two-thirds of their land and withdrew to southern and western Alabama. Jackson became a major general in the regular army and continued south toward the Gulf. To forestall a British invasion at Pensacola Bay, which provided an overland route to New Orleans, Jackson seized Pensacola—in Spanish Florida—on November 7, 1814. After securing Mobile, he marched on to New Orleans and prepared for a British attempt to capture the city.

The Battle of New Orleans was the final engagement of the war. Early in December the British fleet had landed east of New Orleans, 1,500 strong, hoping to gain control of the Mississippi River. They faced an American force of regular army troops, plus a larger contingent of Tennessee and Kentucky frontiersmen and two companies of free black volunteers from New Orleans. For three weeks the British under Sir Edward Pakenham and the Americans under Jackson played cat-and-mouse, each trying to gain a major strategic position. Finally, on January 8, 1815, the two forces met head on. Jackson and his mostly untrained army held their ground against two frontal assaults. It was a massacre. More than 2,000 British soldiers lay dead or wounded at the day's end; the Americans suffered only 21 casualties. Andrew Jackson was a na-

Battle of New Orleans

General William Henry Harrison then began the campaign that would prove to be the United States' brightest moment in the war. Harrison's 4,500-man force, mostly Kentucky volunteers, crossed Lake Erie and pursued the British and their Indian allies into Canada, defeating them at the Battle of the Thames on October 5. The great Shawnee Chief Tecumseh died in that battle, and with him, the Indian confederacy he had formed to resist American expansion (see Chapter 11). Once again the United States controlled the Old Northwest.

The American success on Lake Erie could not be repeated on Lake Ontario. After the Battle of the Thames, both sides seemed to favor petty victories over strategic goals in the Northwest. The Americans raided York (now Toronto), the Canadian capital, and looted and burned the Parliament before withdrawing, too few in number to hold the city.

Outside the Old Northwest the British dominated the war. In December 1812 the Royal Navy blockaded the Chesapeake and Delaware bays. By May 1813 the blockade had closed nearly all southern and Gulf of Mexico ports, and by November it had reached north to Long Island Sound. By 1814 all New England ports were closed. American trade had de-

British naval blockade

tional hero. Ironically, the Battle of New Orleans was fought two weeks after the end of the war; unknown to Jackson, a treaty had been signed in Ghent, Belgium, on December 24, 1814.

The United States government had gone to war only reluctantly, and during the conflict had continued to probe for a diplomatic end to hostilities. In 1813, for instance, President Madison had eagerly accepted a Russian offer to mediate, but Great Britain had refused to participate. Then in November, three months after the Russian offer failed, British Foreign Minister Lord Castlereagh had suggested opening peace talks. It took over ten months to arrange for meetings, but in August 1814 a team of American negotiators, including John Quincy Adams and Henry Clay, began talks with the British in Ghent.

The Ghent treaty made no mention of the issues that had led to war. The United States received no satisfaction on impressment, blockades, or other maritime rights. Likewise, British demands for a neutral Indian buffer state in the Northwest and territorial cessions from Maine to Minnesota went unmet. Essentially, the Treaty of Ghent restored the prewar status quo. It provided for an end to hostilities, release of prisoners, restoration of conquered territory, and arbitration of boundary disputes. Other questions—notably compensation for losses and fishing rights—would be negotiated by joint commissions.

Treaty of Ghent

Why did the negotiators settle for so little? Events in Europe had made peace and the status quo acceptable at the end of 1814, as they had not been in 1812. Napoleon's fall from power allowed the United States to abandon its demands, since peace in Europe made impressment and interference with American commerce moot questions. Similarly, war-weary Britain, its treasury nearly depleted, gave up pressing for a military victory.

The war did reinforce the independence of the young American republic. Although conflict with Great Britain continued, it never again led to war. The experience strengthened America's resolve to steer clear of European politics, for it had been the British-French conflict that had drawn the United States into war. For the rest of the century the nation would shun involvement with Europe.

Domestically, the war prompted recognition of the need for better transportation and an efficient army.

American generals had found American roads inadequate to move an army and its supplies among widely scattered fronts. In the Northwest, General Harrison's troops had depended on homemade cartridges and gifts of clothing from Ohio residents. In Maine, troops had melted down spoons to make bullets. Clearly, improved transportation and a well-equipped army were major priorities. In 1815 President Madison made a beginning by centralizing control of the army. And Congress voted a standing army of 10,000 men, one-third of the army's wartime strength but three times its size during Jefferson's administration.

The war also sealed the fate of the Federalist party. Realizing that their chances of winning a presidential election in wartime were slight, the Federalists had joined dissatisfied Republicans in supporting De Witt Clinton of New York in 1812. This was the high point of Federalist organization at the state level, and the Younger Federalists campaigned hard. Clinton nevertheless lost to President Madison by 128 to 89 electoral votes; areas that favored the war (the South and West) voted solidly Republican. The Federalists did, however, gain some congressional seats, and they carried many local elections.

But once again extremism was the Federalists' undoing. During the war Older Federalists had revived talk of secession, and from December 15, 1814, to January 5, 1815, Federalist delegates from New England met in Hartford, Connecticut, to take action. With the war in a stalemate and trade in ruins, they planned to revise the national compact or pull out of the republic. Moderates prevented a resolution of secession, but convention members continued to call for radical changes in the Constitution. In particular, they wanted constitutional amendments restricting the presidency to one term and requiring a two-thirds congressional vote to admit new states. They also hoped to abolish the three-fifths compromise, whereby slaves were counted in the apportionment of congressional representatives, and to forbid naturalized citizens from holding office. These proposals were aimed at the growing West and South—the heart of Republican electoral strength—and at Irish immigrants.

Hartford Convention

If nothing else, the timing of the Hartford Convention proved fatal. The victory at New Orleans and news of the peace treaty made the Hartford Convention, with its talk of secession and proposed constitutional amendments, look ridiculous. Rather than harassing a beleaguered wartime administration, the Federalists now retreated before a rising tide of nationalism. Though it remained strong in a handful of states until the 1820s, the Federalist party began to dissolve. The war, at first a source of revival as opponents of war flocked to the Federalist banner, had killed the party.

Possibly most important of all, the war stimulated economic change. The embargo, the Non-Importation and Non-Intercourse acts, and the war itself had spurred the production of manufactured goods—cloth and metal—to replace banned imports. And in the absence of commercial opportunities abroad, New England capitalists had begun to invest in manufactures. The effects of these changes were to be far reaching (see Chapter 9).

Postwar nationalism

With peace came a new sense of American nationalism. Five new states joined the union: Indiana (1816), Mississippi (1817), Illinois (1818), and Alabama (1819). (Louisiana had been admitted in 1812.) Self-confidently, the nation asserted itself at home and abroad as Republicans aped Federalists in encouraging economic development and commerce. In his last message to Congress in December 1815, President Madison embraced Federalist doctrine by recommending military expansion and a program to stimulate development and growth. Wartime experiences had, he said, demonstrated the need for a national bank (the first bank had expired) and for better transportation. To raise government revenues and perpetuate the wartime growth in manufacturing, Madison called for a protective tariff—a tax on imported goods. Yet in straying from Jeffersonian Republicanism, Madison did so within limits. Only a constitutional amendment, he argued, could give the federal government authority to build roads and canals that were less than national in scope.

The congressional leadership pushed Madison's nationalist program energetically. Representative John C. Calhoun and Speaker of the House Henry Clay, who named the program the American System, believed it would unify the country. They looked to the tariff on imported goods to stimulate industry. New mills would purchase raw materials; new millworkers would buy food from the agricultural South and West. New roads would make possible the flow of produce and goods, and tariff revenues would provide the money to build them. Finally, the national bank would facilitate all these transactions.

American System

Indeed, Hamilton's original plan for a Bank of the United States became fundamental to the new Republican policy. Fearing the concentration of economic power in a central bank, the Republicans had allowed the charter of the first Bank of the United States to expire in 1811. State banks, however, proved inadequate to the nation's needs. Their resources had been insufficient to assist the government in financing the War of 1812. Moreover, people distrusted currency issued by banks in distant localities. Because many banks issued notes without gold to back them up, and counterfeit notes were common, merchants hesitated to accept strange currency. Republicans therefore came to favor a national bank. In 1816 Congress chartered for twenty years the Second Bank of the United States, to be headquartered in Philadelphia. The government provided $7 million of the $35 million capital and appointed one-fifth of the directors, and the bank opened its doors on January 1, 1817.

Congress did not share Madison's reservations about the constitutionality of using federal funds to build local roads. "Let us, then, bind the republic together," Calhoun declared, "with a perfect system of roads and canals." But Madison vetoed Calhoun's internal improvements bill, which provided for the construction of roads of mostly local benefit, adamantly insisting that it was unconstitutional. Internal improvements were the province of the states and of private enterprise. (Madison did, however, approve funds for the continuation of the National Road, on the grounds that it was a military necessity.)

Protective tariffs completed Madison's nationalist program. Though the embargo and the war had stimulated domestic industry, especially cloth and iron manufacturing, resumption of trade after the war brought competition from abroad. Americans

This watercolor by George Tattersall shows the primitive state of American roads in the early nineteenth century.   Museum of Fine Arts, Boston, M. and M. Karolik Collection.

charged that British firms were dumping their goods on the American market at below cost to stifle American manufacturing. To aid the new industries, Madison recommended and Congress passed the Tariff of 1816, the first protective tariff in American history. The act levied taxes on imported woolens and cottons, especially inexpensive ones, and on iron, leather, hats, paper, and sugar. In effect it raised the cost of these imported goods. Some New England representatives viewed the tariff as interference in free trade, and southern representatives (except Calhoun and a few others) opposed it because it raised the cost of imported goods to southern farmers with no interest in industry. But the western and Middle Atlantic states backed it, and the tariff passed.

James Monroe, Madison's successor as president, retained Madison's domestic program, supporting the bank and tariffs and vetoing internal improvements on constitutional grounds. Monroe, Madison's secretary of state, was nominated by the Republican congressional caucus in 1816. Later that year he easily defeated Rufus King, the last Federalist nominee, sweeping all the states except the Federalist strongholds of Massachusetts, Connecticut, and Delaware. Monroe optimistically declared that "discord does not belong to our system." The American people were, he said, "one great family with a common interest." And for his first term that was true.

Monroe's secretary of state, John Quincy Adams, managed the nation's foreign policy brilliantly from 1817 to 1825. An experienced diplomat who had served in the Netherlands, Prussia, Russia, and Great Britain and negotiated the Treaty of Ghent, Adams stubbornly pushed for expansion, political distance from

John Quincy Adams as secretary of state

John Quincy Adams (1767–1848), secretary of state from 1817 to 1825, in an early daguerreotype taken by Southworth and Hawes shortly before his death. This famous photograph suggests Adams's bulldog tenacity. The Metropolitan Museum of Art, Gift of I. N. Phelps Stokes, Edward S. Hawes, Alice Mary Hawes, Marion Augusta Hawes, 1937.

the Old World, and peace. Party politics, he firmly believed, had no place in foreign relations; the national interest, not loyalty or good intentions, should guide American policy. A small, austere man who described himself as a bulldog, Adams was a giant as a diplomat.

Adams's first step was to strengthen the peace with Great Britain. In April 1817 the two nations agreed to the Rush-Bagot Treaty, which grew out of negotiations Adams had begun the previous year in his capacity as diplomatic minister in London. Britain and the United States agreed in this pact to limit their Great Lakes naval forces to one ship each on Lake Ontario and Lake Champlain and two vessels each on the other lakes. This first disarmament treaty of modern times began the process that led to demilitarization of the United States–Canadian border.

Adams then pushed for the Convention of 1818—also a sequel to the Treaty of Ghent—which fixed the United States–Canadian border from Lake of the Woods west to the Rockies. When agreement could

Chapter 8: The republic endures, 1801–1824

not be reached on the territory west of the mountains, the two nations settled on joint occupation of Oregon for ten years. Adams, who wanted to fix the border at the 49th parallel, hoped for a better negotiating position at the end of that period.

Adams moved next to settle long-term disputes with Spain. During the War of 1812, the United States had seized Mobile and West Florida. Afterward it took advantage of Spain's preoccupation with domestic and colonial troubles to negotiate for the purchase of Florida. Talks took place in 1818, while General Andrew Jackson's troops occupied much of Florida on the pretext of suppressing Seminole raids against American settlements across the border. The following year, under dictated terms, Spain agreed to cede Florida to the United States without payment. In this Transcontinental, or Adams-Onís Treaty, the United States also defined the southern boundary of the Louisiana Purchase from the Gulf of Mexico to the Pacific Ocean. In return, the United States government assumed $5 million worth of claims by American citizens against Spain and gave up its dubious claim to Texas. Expansion had thus been achieved at little cost and without bloodshed, and American claims now stretched from the Atlantic to the Pacific.

The Panic of 1819 and renewed sectionalism

Monroe's domestic achievements could not match his diplomatic successes. The period of harmony that began his presidency—dubbed the Era of Good Feelings by a Boston newspaper—was short-lived. By 1819 postwar nationalism and confidence had eroded, and financial panic darkened the land. (Neither panic nor the resurgence of sectionalism hurt Monroe politically; without a rival political party to rally opposition, he won a second term unopposed.)

But hard times spread. The postwar expansion had been built on loose money and widespread speculation. When it slowed, the manufacturing depression that had begun in 1818 deepened, and prices spiraled downward. Distressed urban workers lobbied for relief and began to take a more active role in politics.

Manufacturers demanded greater tariff protection—and eventually got it in the Tariff of 1824. Farmers, on the other hand, wanted lower tariffs. Hurt by a sharp decline in the price of cotton, southern planters railed at the protective Tariff of 1816, which had raised prices at the same time their incomes were falling sharply. The Virginia Agricultural Society of Fredericksburg, for example, argued that the tariff violated the very principles on which the nation had been founded. In a protest to Congress in January 1820, the society called the tariff an unequal tax that awarded exclusive privileges to "oppressive monopolies, which are ultimately to grind both us and our children after us 'into dust and ashes.'"

Western farmers suffered too. Those who had purchased public land on credit could not repay their loans. To avoid mass bankruptcy, Congress delayed payment of the money, and western state legislatures passed "stay laws" restricting mortgage foreclosures. Many westerners blamed the panic on the Second Bank of the United States, which in self-protection had cut off loans it had issued in the previous three years. Having fueled the boom with credit, the bank now sped the contraction by tightening the money supply. Many state banks, in debt to the national bank, folded, and westerners bitterly accused the bank of saving itself while the nation went to ruin. Although the economy recovered in the mid-1820s, the seeds of the Jacksonian movement (see Chapter 12) had been sown.

Even more divisive was the question of slavery. Ever since the drafting of the Constitution, political leaders had avoided the issue. In February 1819, however, slavery finally crept into the political agenda when Missouri residents petitioned Congress for admission to the Union as a slave state. For the next two-and-one-half years the issue dominated all congressional action. "This momentous question," Thomas Jefferson wrote, fearful for the life of the Union, "like a fire bell in the night, awakened and filled me with terror."

The debate transcended slavery in Missouri. At stake was the undoing of the compromises that had kept the issue quarantined since the Constitutional Convention. Missouri was on the same latitude as free Illinois, Indiana, and Ohio, and its admission as a slave state would thus thrust slavery further northward. It would also tilt the political balance toward the states

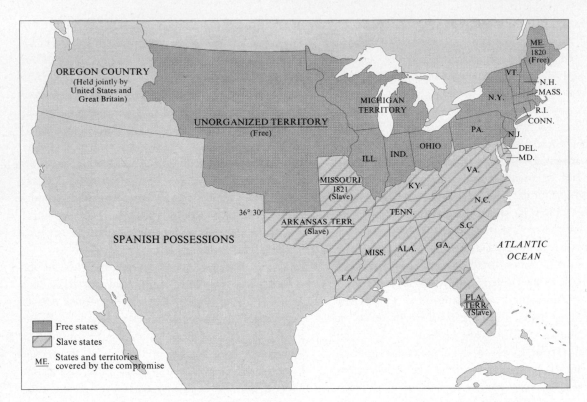

The Missouri Compromise of 1820

committed to slavery. In 1819 the Union consisted of an uneasy balance of eleven slave and eleven free states. (Of the five new states admitted since 1812, three—Louisiana, Mississippi, and Alabama—were slave states.) If Missouri entered as a slave state, the slave states would have a two-vote edge in the Senate.

But what made the issue so divisive was not the politics of admission to statehood, but people's emotional attitudes toward slavery. The settlers of Missouri were mostly Kentuckians and Tennesseeans who had grown up with slavery. But in the North, slavery was slowly dying out, and many northerners had come to the conclusion that it was evil. Thus when Representative James Tallmadge, Jr., of New York introduced an amendment providing for gradual emancipation in Missouri, it led to passionate and sometimes violent debate on moral grounds. The House, which had a northern majority, passed the Tallmadge amendment, but the Senate rejected it. The two sides were deadlocked.

A compromise emerged in 1820 under pressure from House Speaker Henry Clay: the admission of

free Maine, carved out of Massachusetts, was linked with that of slave Missouri. In the rest of the Louisiana Territory north of 36°30' (Missouri's southern boundary), slavery was prohibited forever (see map). The compromise carried, but the agreement almost came apart in November when Missouri submitted a constitution barring free blacks from settling in the state. Opponents contended that the proposed state constitution violated the federal Constitution's provision that "the Citizens of each state shall be entitled to all privileges and immunities of Citizens in the several States." Advocates argued that restrictions on free blacks were common in state law both North and South. In 1821 Clay produced a second compromise: Missouri guaranteed that none of its laws would discriminate against citizens of other states. (Once admitted to the Union, however, Missouri twice adopted laws banning free blacks from entering the state.)

Although political leaders had successfully removed slavery from the congressional agenda, the is-

Missouri Compromise

sue ultimately destroyed Republican unity and ended the reign of the Virginia dynasty. The Republican party would come apart in 1824 as presidential candidates from different sections of the country scrambled for caucus support (see Chapter 12).

In foreign policy, one thorny issue remained to be resolved: recognition of revolutionary forces in Latin America. The United Provinces of the Rio de la Plata (Argentina), Chile, Peru, Colombia, and Mexico had broken free of Spain between 1808 and 1822, and Americans clamored to recognize them officially. But Monroe and Adams moved slowly in acknowledging Latin American independence. They sought to avoid conflict with European powers and to assure themselves of the stability of the revolutionary regimes. Shortly after the Adams-Onís Treaty with Spain was safely signed and ratified, in 1823, however, the United States became the first nation outside Latin America to recognize the new states.

Later the same year, events in Europe again threatened the stability of the New World. Spain experienced a domestic revolt, and France occupied Spain in an attempt to bolster the weak monarchy against the rebels. The United States feared that France and its allies might also seek to overturn the new Latin American states and restore them to Spanish rule. Great Britain, which shared this concern, proposed joint United States–British protection of South America. But Adams rejected the British overture, fearing any European intervention in the New World. He insisted that the United States act independently and on its own initiative; action in concert with Britain would violate the long-standing principle of avoiding foreign entanglements.

To thwart an alliance with Great Britain, the bulldog Adams tenaciously outargued other Cabinet members. Those who favored joint action believed that Britain alone had the power to prevent French or Russian intervention. They were supported by former President Jefferson, then in retirement at Monticello. Adams, however, won out. "It would be more candid, as well as more dignified," he argued, "to avow our principles explicitly to Russia and France, than to come in as a cock-boat in the wake of the British man-of-war."

The result was the Monroe Doctrine, a unilateral declaration against European interference in the New

We Owe Allegiance to No Crown, painted by John A. Woodside, shows the self-confident nationalism that prevailed at the time of the Monroe Doctrine. Liberty crowns an American sailor with a laurel wreath as he tramples on the symbols of British tyranny. Collection of Davenport West, Jr.

World. The president enunciated the famous doctrine in his last message to Congress on December 2, 1823. Monroe called for, first, *noncolonization* of the Western

| Monroe Doctrine |

Hemisphere by European nations, a principle that expressed American anxiety not only about Latin America but also about Russian expansion in Alaska. Second, he demanded *nonintervention* by Europe in the affairs of independent New World nations. Finally, Monroe pledged *noninterference* by the United States in European affairs, including those of Europe's existing New World colonies.

The Monroe Doctrine proved popular at home as an anti-British, anti-European assertion of American nationalism, and it eventually became the foundation of American policy in the Western Hemisphere. Monroe's words, however, had no force behind them. Indeed, the policy could not have succeeded without the support of the British, who were already committed to keeping other European nations out of the New

Important events

1801	John Marshall becomes Chief Justice Jefferson inaugurated
1801–05	Tripoli War
1803	*Marbury* v. *Madison* Louisiana Purchase
1803–12	British impressment of American seamen
1804	Jefferson re-elected
1806	Non-Importation Act
1807	*Chesapeake* Affair Embargo Act
1808	James Madison elected president
1809–10	Non-Intercourse Acts
1810	Macon's Bill No. 2
1812–15	War of 1812
1814	Treaty of Ghent
1814–15	Hartford Convention
1815	Battle of New Orleans
1816	James Monroe elected; last Federalist presidential candidate
1817	Second Bank of the United States Rush-Bagot Treaty
1819	*McCulloch* v. *Maryland* Adams-Onís Treaty
1819–23	Financial panic; depression
1820	Missouri Compromise
1821	Missouri admitted as state
1823	Monroe Doctrine

The mother country often treated its former colony as if it had not won its independence. A second war—the War of 1812—had to be fought to reiterate American independence; thereafter the nation was able to settle most disputes at the bargaining table. And like Third World nations today, the young United States steered clear of alliances with superpowers, preferring neutrality and unilateralism.

At home the United States worked to establish an enduring central government. As a union of states whose boundaries were an inheritance from the colonial past, the republic was no more than a shaky federation. And although Federalist talk of secession never led to action, sectional differences ran deep. Some issues, like slavery, seemed beyond resolution, though compromise did succeed in delaying the judgment day. Political division in itself proved benign, and the young country established a tradition of peaceful transition of power through presidential elections. It was the Supreme Court that made the first advances toward national unity, establishing federal power over the states and encouraging commerce. After the war all branches of the government, responding to the popular mood, pursued a more vigorous national policy. Their efforts would help to transform the nation and its economy.

Suggestions for further reading

General

Henry Adams, *History of the United States of America During the Administration of Thomas Jefferson and of James Madison,* 9 vols. (1889–1891); Marcus Cunliffe, *The Nation Takes Shape, 1789–1837* (1959); Marshall Smelser, *The Democratic Republic, 1801–1815* (1968); Charles M. Wiltse, *The New Nation, 1800–1845* (1961).

Party politics

James M. Banner, *To The Hartford Convention: The Federalists and the Origins of Party Politics in the Early Republic, 1789–1815* (1967); Noble E. Cunningham, Jr., *The Jeffersonian Republicans in Power: Party Operations, 1801–1809* (1963); David Hackett Fischer, *The Revolution of American Conservatism: The Federalist Party in the Era of Jeffersonian De-*

World. Europeans ignored the doctrine; it was the Royal Navy they respected, not American policy.

The foreign-policy problems confronting the infant republic from the turn of the century through the mid-1820s strikingly resembled those faced today by the newly established nations of the Third World.

mocracy (1965); Richard Hofstadter, *The Idea of a Party System* (1969); Linda K. Kerber, *Federalists in Dissent* (1970); James S. Young, *The Washington Community, 1800–1828* (1966).

The Virginia presidents

Harry Ammon, *James Monroe: The Quest for National Identity* (1971); Irving Brant, *The Fourth President: A Life of James Madison* (1970); Irving Brant, *James Madison*, 6 vols. (1941–1961); Noble E. Cunningham, Jr., *The Process of Government Under Jefferson* (1978); Alexander De Conde, *The Affair of Louisiana* (1976); James Ketcham, *James Madison* (1970); Forrest McDonald, *The Presidency of Thomas Jefferson* (1976); Dumas Malone, *Jefferson and His Time*, 5 vols. (1948–1974); Merrill D. Peterson, *The Jefferson Image in the American Mind* (1960); Merrill D. Peterson, *Thomas Jefferson and the New Nation* (1970).

The Supreme Court and the law

Leonard Baker, *John Marshall: A Life in Law* (1974); Albert Beveridge, *The Life of John Marshall*, 4 vols. (1916–1919); Richard E. Ellis, *The Jeffersonian Crisis: Courts and Politics in the Young Republic* (1971); Charles G. Haines, *The Role of the Supreme Court in American Government and Politics, 1789–1835* (1944); Morton J. Horowitz, *The Transformation of American Law, 1780–1860* (1977); R. Kent Newmyer, *The Supreme Court under Marshall and Taney* (1968).

The War of 1812

Roger H. Brown, *The Republic in Peril: 1812* (1964); A. L. Burt, *The United States, Great Britain, and British North America* (1940); Harry L. Coles, *The War of 1812* (1965); Reginald Horsman, *The Causes of the War of 1812* (1962); Reginald Horsman, *The War of 1812* (1969); Bradford Perkins, *Prologue to War: England and the United States, 1805–1812* (1961); Julius W. Pratt, *Expansionists of 1812* (1925).

Nationalism and sectionalism

George Dangerfield, *The Awakening of American Nationalism, 1815–1828* (1965); George Dangerfield, *The Era of Good Feelings* (1952); Shaw Livermore, *Twilight of Federalism: The Disintegration of the Federalist Party, 1815–1830* (1962); Glover Moore, *The Missouri Compromise 1819–1821* (1953); Murray N. Rothbard, *The Panic of 1819* (1962).

The Monroe Doctrine

Samuel F. Bemis, *John Quincy Adams and the Foundations of American Foreign Policy* (1949); Walter LaFeber, ed., *John Quincy Adams and American Continental Empire* (1965): Ernest R. May, *The Making of the Monroe Doctrine* (1976); Dexter Perkins, *Hands Off: A History of the Monroe Doctrine* (1941); Dexter Perkins, *The Monroe Doctrine 1823–1826* (1927).

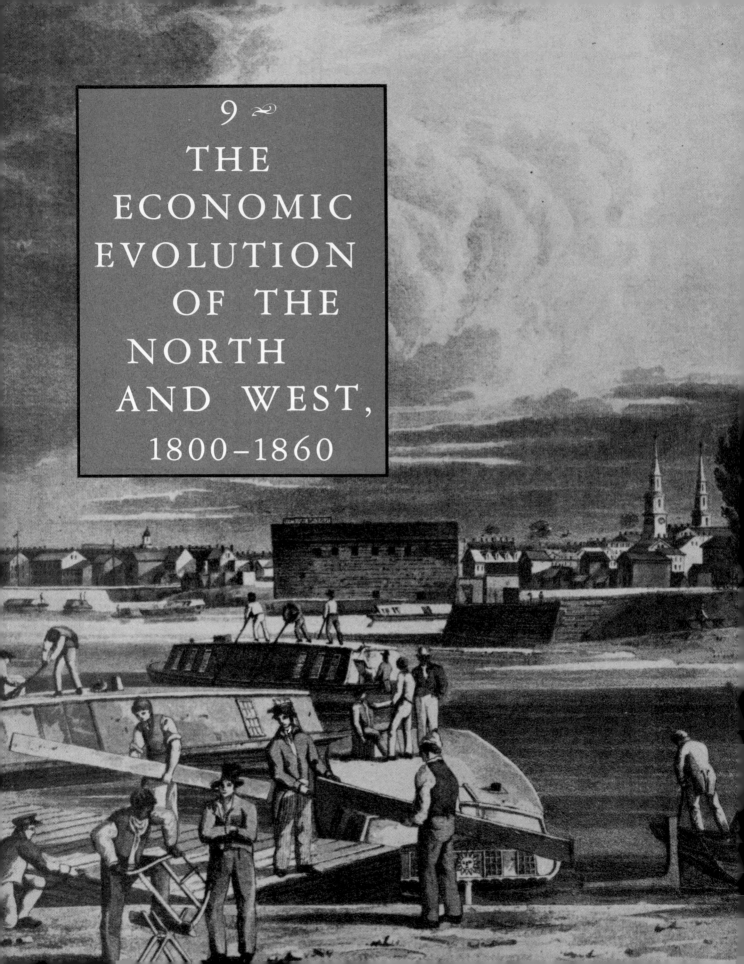

9 ~
THE ECONOMIC EVOLUTION OF THE NORTH AND WEST, 1800–1860

John Jervis suffered from canal fever and railroad fever nearly all his life. He first contracted the obsession in 1817, when at age twenty-two he left his father's upstate New York farm to clear a cedar swamp for the Erie Canal. Like the other laborers, as well as the men directing the project, Jervis had had no experience in canal construction. Indeed, he had never built anything according to a plan or diagram.

Together the directors and workers learned enough on the job to construct 363 well-engineered miles of canal. Jervis's education began his first day. Though he was an expert axeman, he had never had to down a line of trees along a precise path. With "a little trouble" he learned to hew with precision. Jervis learned new skills each year, advancing from axeman to surveyor to engineer to superintendent of a division.

When the Erie Canal was completed in 1825, Jervis moved on to become second-in-command of the Delaware and Hudson Canal project. To reduce costs, he substituted a railroad line for the last seventeen miles of the canal. Since there was not a single locomotive in the United States in 1828, Jervis had one sent from England. The engine that was delivered, however, was heavier than the one he had ordered, and on both tests it crushed the hemlock rails.

Undaunted, the self-trained engineer left the Delaware canal company to supervise construction of another early rail experiment, the Mohawk and Hudson Railroad from Albany to Schenectady. In building the railroad Jervis redesigned the locomotive's wheel assembly, and his design became standard throughout America.

Jervis spent the next two decades building the 98-mile Chenango Canal and the fresh-water supply—Croton Reservoir, 33-mile aqueduct, and pumping system—for New York City. Later he built other railroads, including the Michigan Southern, the Rock Island, and the Nickel Platte. In 1864, at age sixty-nine, Jervis returned home to Rome, New York, and organized an iron mill. He had spent his life constructing the mechanisms—canals and railroads—that would change America.

John Jervis's life bridged the old and the new. His roots lay in the rural farm country that was typical of the United States at the beginning of the nineteenth century. He had learned to read and write during occasional attendance at common school, and to farm and handle an axe from his father. But in 1817 he left behind much of that tradition and became involved in undertakings that would lead to a new, far different nation. He had to acquire skills not used on the farm: the ability to follow and create construction plans, to calculate weight stresses, and to work precisely in tandem with others.

The canals and railroads John Jervis helped build were the most visible signs of the evolution of the American economy from 1800 through 1860. The canal boat, the steamboat, the locomotive, and the telegraph were all agents of change and economic growth. They helped to open up the frontier and brought mostly self-sufficient farmers into the market economy. They made it profitable to manufacture cloth in New England and ship the finished goods to retail outlets in New Orleans or St. Louis or even, by the 1850s, San Francisco. They forged the beginnings of a national, capitalist economy.

Public and private investment and a growing population stimulated economic growth during these years. Government, especially state government, promoted an environment in which farming and industry could blossom, however unevenly and unsteadily. Banks, insurance companies, and corporations amassed the capital for large-scale enterprises like factories and railroads. Meanwhile, farming and manufacturing methods became more complex. Factories and precision-made machinery began to replace home workshops and hand-made goods, and mechanized reapers and sowers revolutionized the farming industry.

But for Americans living in this era of rapid economic growth, the rewards of economic improvement were accompanied by problems and tensions. Not everyone profited, as John Jervis did, in wealth and opportunity. The journeyman cobbler who had to abandon his tools for a machine had a far different experience from the master shoemaker who became a factory owner. As traditional ways began to give way to the demands of a market economy, survival required that most free Americans sell their labor for wages. By the second half of the nineteenth century, the engine of economic change and growth roared ahead full-steam; economic growth would not be derailed.

The transition to a market economy

The base of the old economy had been staple exports—grain, tobacco, and other crops grown by free farmers and slaves for overseas markets. Farmers who did not cultivate for export tended to be self-sufficient, producing nearly everything they needed—clothing, candles, soap, and the like—and bartering for the few items they could not produce, such as cooking pots and horseshoes. By the Civil War, however, the United States had an industrializing economy in which an increasing number of men and women worked in factories or offices for a wage, and in which most citizens—farmers and workers—had become dependent on store-bought necessities. The export of agricultural products was still important to the economy, but the revenues it brought in were increasingly used to finance industrial growth.

In the new economy crops were grown and goods were produced for sale in the marketplace, at home or abroad. The money received in market transactions,

| Definition of a market economy |

whether from the sale of goods or of a person's labor, was used to purchase items produced by other people—such as the candles and soap no longer made at home. Such a system encouraged specialization. Formerly self-sufficient farmers, for example, began to grow just one or two crops, or to concentrate on raising only cows, pigs, or sheep for market. Farm women gave up spinning and weaving at home and purchased fabric produced by wage-earning farm girls in Massachusetts textile mills.

Sustained growth was the result of this economic evolution. Improvements in transportation and technology, the division of labor, and new methods of financing all fueled expansion of the economy—that is, the multiplication of goods and services. In turn, this growth prompted new improvements. The effect was cumulative; by the 1840s the economy was growing more rapidly than in the previous four decades. Per-capita income doubled between 1800 and 1860.

The Ohio dairy industry illustrated this process. In the first decades of the century, Ohio farmers made whatever cheese they needed for their own tables. Some made cheese to sell elsewhere, but only because they had a surplus of milk. However, the development of canals and railroads in the 1830s and 1840s changed Ohio farming. Farmers began to specialize, finding it more profitable to invest in better tools and spend all their time on one product. Some chose to grow wheat or tobacco for market, and to purchase whatever dairy products they needed. Other Ohioans, especially in the Western Reserve, decided to devote full time to dairy farming. Beginning in 1847, entrepreneurs built cheese factories in rural towns and contracted to buy curd from these local dairy farmers. In 1851 one such factory in Gustavus, Ohio, produced a daily average of 5,000 pounds of cheese from the milk of 2,500 cows. The cheese was shipped by canal and railroad to cities and eastern ports. In Boston and New York, some merchants turned to handling cheese and other dairy products exclusively, selling to consumers as far away as California, England, and China. By 1860 Ohio dairymen were producing 21.6 million pounds of cheese a year for market—a huge leap in production over the early 1800s.

Though such economic growth was sustained, it was not even. Prosperity reigned during two long periods, from 1823 to 1835 and from 1843 to 1857. But there were long stretches of economic contraction as well. During the time from Jefferson's 1807 embargo

| Boom-and-bust cycles |

through 1815, in fact, upheaval was so great that the growth rate was actually negative—that is, fewer goods and services were produced. Contraction and deflation occurred again during the depressions of 1819 through 1823, 1839 through 1843, and 1857. These periods were characterized by the collapse of banks, business bankruptcies, and a decline in wages and prices. Workers faced increasing insecurity as a result of these cycles; on the down side, they suffered not only lower incomes but also unemployment.

Working people, a Baltimore physician noted during the depression of 1819, felt hard times "a thousand fold more than the merchants." Yet even during good times wage earners could not build up sufficient financial reserves to get them through the next depression; often they could not make it through the winter without drawing on charity for food, clothing, and firewood. In the 1820s and 1830s, free laborers in Baltimore found steady work from March through October and unemployment and hunger from November through February.

If good times were hard on workers and their families, depressions devastated them. In 1839 in Baltimore, all small manufacturers for the local market closed their doors; tailors, shoemakers, milliners, and shipyard and construction workers lost their jobs. Ninety miles to the north, Philadelphia took on an eerie aura. "The streets seemed deserted," Sidney George Fisher observed in 1842; "the largest [merchant] houses are shut up and to rent, there is no business . . . no money, no confidence." Only auctions boomed, as the sheriff sold off seized property at a quarter of predepression prices. Elsewhere in the city, soup societies fed the hungry. In New York, breadlines and beggars crowded the sidewalks. In smaller cities like Lynn, Massachusetts, those who did not leave became scavengers, digging for clams and harvesting dandelions.

In 1857 hard times struck again. The Mercantile Agency recorded 5,123 bankruptcies in 1857—nearly double the number in the previous year. The bankrupt firms had a total debt of $300 million, only half of which would be paid off. Contemporary reports estimated 20,000 to 30,000 unemployed in Philadelphia, and 30,000 to 40,000 in New York City. Benevolent societies expanded their soup kitchens and distributed free firewood to the needy. In Chicago, charities reorganized to meet the needs of the poor; in New York, the city hired the unemployed to fix streets and develop Central Park. And in Fall River, Massachusetts, a citizens' committee disbursed public funds on a weekly basis to nine hundred families. The soup kitchen, the breadline, and public aid had become permanent fixtures in urban America.

What caused the cycles of boom and bust that brought about such suffering? In general, they were a direct result of the new market economy. Prosperity inevitably stimulated greater demand for staples and finished goods. Increased demand led in turn to higher prices and still higher production, to speculation in land, and to the flow of foreign currency into the country. Eventually production surpassed demand, leading to lower prices and wages; and speculation outstripped the true value of land and stocks. The inflow of foreign money led first to easy credit and then to collapse when unhappy investors withdrew their funds.

Cause of boom-and-bust cycles

Some economists considered this process healthy—a self-adjusting cycle in which unprofitable economic ventures were eliminated. In theory, people concentrated on the activities they did best, and the economy as a whole became more efficient. Advocates of the system argued also that it furthered individual freedom, since ideally each seller, whether of goods or labor, was free to determine the conditions of the sale. But in fact the system put workers on a perpetual rollercoaster; they had become dependent on wages—and the availability of jobs—for their very existence.

Many also felt a distinct loss of status. For Joseph T. Buckingham, foreman of the Boston printing shop of West & Richardson, wage labor represented failure. Buckingham had been a master printer, running the shop of Thomas & Andrews on commission and doing some publishing of his own. In 1814 he purchased the shop, but did not get enough work to pay his debts. Without the capital to sustain his losses or to compete with larger shops, Buckingham had to sell his presses at auction. He became a wage earner, albeit a foreman. Though his wages were about the equal of an ordinary printer's income, Buckingham was unhappy. In his own words, he was "nothing more than a journeyman, except in responsibility."

Government promotion of the economy

To stimulate economic growth, the federal and state governments intervened actively during these years in the economy. Beginning with the purchase of Louisiana in 1803, the nation embarked on a deliberate program of westward expansion, western settlement, and promotion of agriculture. In 1803 President Jefferson dispatched Meriwether Lewis and William Clark to explore the new territory and report on its flora, fauna, minerals, and metals. The Lewis and Clark expedition was the beginning of a continuing federal interest in geographic and geologic surveying, which were the first steps in opening western land to exploitation and settlement.

Survey and sale of land

New steps followed quickly. In 1817 and 1818 Henry Rowe Schoolcraft explored the Missouri and Arkansas region, reporting on its geologic features and mineral resources. In 1819 and 1820 Major Stephen Long explored the Great Plains, mapping the area between the Platte and Canadian rivers. Between 1827 and 1840 the government surveyed about fifty railroad routes. The final door to western settlement was opened in 1843 and 1844 by John C. Frémont's expedition, which followed the Oregon Trail to the Pacific, then traveled south to California and returned east by way of the Great Salt Lake. An officer in the U.S. Topological Corps, Frémont published a report of his journey dispelling a long-standing myth that the center of the continent was a desert.

To encourage western agriculture, the federal government offered public lands for sale at reasonable prices (see page 153) and evicted Indian tribes from their traditional lands. And because transportation was crucial to development of the frontier, the government financed roads and subsidized railroad construction through land grants. Even the State Department aided agriculture: its consular offices overseas collected horticultural information, seeds, and cuttings and published technical reports in an effort to improve American farming.

The federal government also played a key role in technological and industrial growth. Federal arsenals pioneered new manufacturing techniques and helped to develop the machine-tool industry. The United States Military Academy at West Point, founded in 1802, emphasized technical and scientific subjects in its curriculum. And the U.S. Post Office stimulated interregional trade and played a brief but crucial role in the development of the telegraph: the first telegraph line, from Washington to Baltimore, was constructed under a government grant, and during 1845 the Post Office ran it, employing inventor Samuel F. B. Morse as superintendent. Finally, to create an atmosphere conducive to economic growth, the government protected inventions and domestic industries. Patent laws gave inventors a seventeen-year monopoly on their inventions, and tariffs protected American industry from foreign competition.

The federal judiciary also promoted business enterprise. In *Gibbons* v. *Ogden* (1824), the Supreme Court

| Legal foundations of commerce |

overturned a New York state law that had given Robert Fulton and Robert Livingston a monopoly on the New York–New Jersey steamboat trade. Ogden, their successor, lost his monopoly when Chief Justice Marshall ruled that the trade fell under the sway of the commerce clause of the Constitution. Thus Congress, not New York, had the controlling power. Since the federal government issued such licenses on a nonexclusive basis, the decision ended monopolies on waterways throughout the nation. Within a year, 43 steamboats were plying Ogden's route.

In defining interstate commerce broadly, the Marshall Court expanded federal powers over the economy while limiting the ability of states to control economic activity within their borders. Its action was consistent with its earlier decision in *Dartmouth College* v. *Woodward* (1819), which protected the sanctity of contracts against interference by the states (see page 201). "If business is to prosper," Marshall wrote, "men must have assurance that contracts will be enforced."

Federal and state courts, in conjunction with state legislatures, also encouraged the proliferation of corporations—groups of investors that could hold property and transact business as one person. In 1800 the United States had about 300 incorporated firms; in 1817 about 2,000. By 1830 the New England states alone had issued 1,900 charters, one-third to manufacturing and mining firms. At first each firm needed a special legislative act to incorporate, but after the 1830s applications became so numerous that incorporation was authorized by general state laws. Though legislative action created corporations, the courts played a crucial role in defining their status, extending their powers, and protecting them.

State governments far surpassed the federal government in promoting economic growth. From 1815

| State promotion of the economy |

through 1860, for example, 73 percent of the $135 million invested in canals was government money, mostly from the states. In the 1830s the states shifted their investments to rail construction. Even though the federal government played a larger role in building railroads than canals, state and local governments provided more than half of southern rail capital. Overall, railroads received 131 million acres in land subsidies, 48 million of which was provided by the states. State governments also invested in corporation and bank stocks, providing those institutions with much-needed capital. Pennsylvania, probably the most active of the states in promoting its economy, invested a total of $100 million in canals, railroads, banks, and manufacturing firms; its appointees sat on more than 150 corporate boards of directors.

States actually equaled or surpassed private enterprise in their investments. But they did more than invest in industry. By establishing bounties for agricultural prizes, they stimulated commercial agriculture, especially sheep raising and wool manufacture (see page 232). Through special acts and general incorporation laws, states regulated the nature and activities of both corporations and banks. They also used their licensing capacity to regulate industry; in Georgia, for example, grading and marketing of tobacco was state-regulated.

From the end of the War of 1812 until 1860 the United States experienced uneven but sustained economic growth largely as a result of these government efforts. Though political controversy raged over questions of state versus federal activity—especially with regard to internal improvements and banking—all parties agreed on the general goal of economic expansion (see Chapters 8 and 12). Indeed, the major restraint on government action during these years was not philosophical but financial: both the government and the public purse were small.

Transportation and regionalization

From 1800 through 1860 the North, South, and West followed distinctly different paths economically. Everywhere agriculture remained the foundation of the American economy. Nevertheless, factories and merchant houses came to characterize the North, plantations the South, and frontier farms the West. Paradoxically, this tendency toward regional specialization made the sections at once more different and more dependent on each other.

The revolution in transportation and communications was probably the single most important cause of these changes. It was the North's heavy investment in canals and railroads that made it the center of American commerce; its growing seaboard cities distributed western produce and New England textiles. New York financial and commercial houses linked even the southern cotton-exporting economy to the North. The South, with most of its capital invested in slave labor, built fewer canals, railroads, and factories and remained largely rural and undeveloped (see Chapter 10).

Before the canal fever of the 1820s and 1830s and the railroad fever of the 1830s and after became epidemic, it was by no means self-evident that New England and the Middle Atlantic states would dominate American economic life. In fact, the natural orientation of the 1800 frontier—Tennessee, Kentucky, and Ohio—was to the South. The southward-flowing Ohio and Mississippi rivers were the lifelines of early western settlement. Flatboats transported western grain and hogs southward for consumption or transfer to oceangoing vessels at New Orleans. Southern products—first tobacco, then lumber and cotton—flowed directly to Europe. Settlement of southern Illinois and Indiana and the appearance of steamboats on western rivers only intensified this pattern.

Change in trade routes

But the pattern changed in the 1820s and 1830s. New roads and turnpikes opened up east-west travel. The National Road, a stone-based, gravel-topped highway beginning in Cumberland, Maryland, reached Wheeling (then in Virginia) in 1818 and Columbus, Ohio, in 1833. More important, the Erie Canal, completed in 1825, forged an east-west axis from the Hudson River to Lake Erie, linking the Great Lakes with New York City and the Atlantic Ocean. The canal carried easterners and then immigrants to settle the Old Northwest and the frontier beyond; in the opposite direction, it bore western grain to the large and growing eastern markets. Railroads and later the telegraph would solidify these east-west links. By contrast, only at one place—Bowling Green, Kentucky—did a northern railroad actually connect with a southern one. Although trade still continued southward along the Ohio and Mississippi rivers, the bulk of western trade flowed eastward by 1850. Thus, by the eve of the Civil War, the northern and Middle Atlantic states were closely tied to the former frontier of the Old Northwest.

Construction of the 363-mile-long Erie Canal was a visionary enterprise. When the state of New York authorized it in 1817, the longest existing American canal was only 28 miles long. Vigorously promoted by Governor De Witt Clinton, the Erie cost $7 million, much of it

Canals

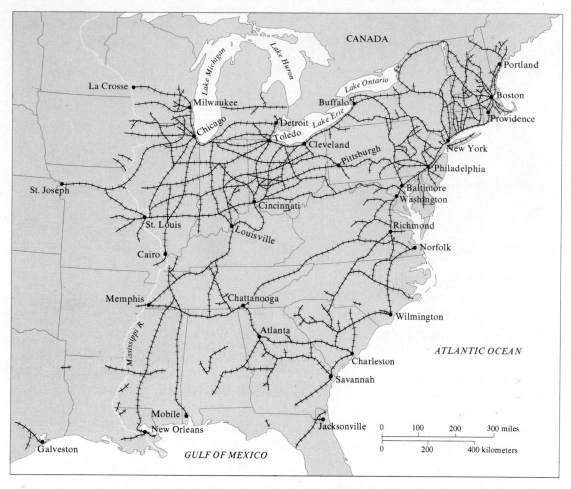

Major railroads in 1860

raised by loans from British investors. The canal shortened the journey between Buffalo and New York City from twenty to six days and reduced freight charges from $100 to $5 a ton. By 1835 traffic was so heavy that the Erie had to be widened from forty to seventy feet and deepened from four to seven feet. The skeptics who had called the canal "Clinton's big ditch" had long since been silenced.

The Erie triggered an explosion of canal building. Other states and cities, fearing the advantage New York had gained, rushed to follow suit. By 1840 canals crisscrossed the Northeast and Midwest, and canal mileage in the United States had reached 3,300 — an increase of more than 2,000 miles in a single decade. Unfortunately for investors, none of these canals enjoyed the financial success achieved by the Erie. The high cost of construction, lack of federal financing,

and economic contraction after 1837 all lowered profitability. As a result, investment in canals began to slump in the 1830s. By 1850 more miles were being abandoned than built, and the canal era had ended.

Meanwhile, railroad construction was on the upswing. The railroad era began in 1830 when Peter

| Railroads |

Cooper's locomotive *Tom Thumb* first steamed along 13 miles of track constructed by the Baltimore and Ohio Railroad. In 1833 a second railroad ran 136 miles from Charleston to Hamburg, South Carolina. By 1850 the United States had nearly 9,000 miles of railroad; by 1860, roughly 31,000 (see map). Canal fever stimulated this early railroad construction. Promoters of the Baltimore and Ohio had turned to the railroad in an effort to compete with the Canal. Similarly, the line between Boston and Worcester, Massachusetts, was

intended as the first link in a line to Albany, at the eastern end of the Erie Canal.

The earliest railroads connected two cities or one city and its surrounding area. Not until the 1850s would railroads offer long-distance service at reasonable rates. And the early lines also had technical problems to contend with. As John Jervis had discovered, locomotives heavy enough to climb steep grades and pull long trains required strong rails and resilient roadbeds. Engineers met those needs by replacing wooden track with iron rails and by supporting the rails with ties embedded in gravel. John Jervis's wheel alignment—called the swivel truck—removed another major obstacle by enabling engines to hold the track on sharp curves. Other problems persisted, though:

notably the continued use of hand brakes, which severely restricted speed, and the lack of a standard gauge for track. The Pennsylvania and Ohio railroads, for instance, had no fewer than seven different track widths. Thus a journey from Philadelphia to Charleston involved eight changes in gauge.

In the 1850s technological improvements, competition, and economic recovery prompted the development of regional and later national rail networks. The West experienced a railroad boom. By 1853 rail lines linked New York to Chicago, and a year later track had reached the Mississippi River. By 1860 rails stretched as far west as St. Joseph, Missouri—the edge of the frontier. In that year the railroad network east of the Mississippi approximated its physical pattern for the next century, but the process of corporate integration had only begun. In 1853 seven short lines combined to form the New York Central system, and the Pennsylvania Railroad was unified from Philadelphia to Pittsburgh. Most lines, however, were still independently run, separated by gauge, scheduling, differences in car design, and a commitment to serve their home towns first and foremost.

Railroads did not completely replace water transportation. Steamboats, first introduced in 1807 when Robert Fulton's *Clermont* paddled up the Hudson

| Steamboats |

from New York City, still plied the rivers. They had proven their value on western rivers in 1815 when the *Enterprise* first carried cargo upstream on the Mississippi and Ohio rivers. Until the 1850s, when western rail development blossomed, steamboats outdid railroads in carrying freight. Great Lakes steamers managed to hold their own even into the fifties, for the sea-like lakes permitted the construction of giant ships and the widespread adoption of propellers in place of paddle wheels. These unique ships, lying as whales in the water, were especially well suited to carrying heavy bulk cargoes like lumber, grain, and ore.

Gradually steamboats began to replace sailing vessels on the high seas. In days gone by, sailing ships—whalers, sleek clippers, and square-rigged packets—had been the pride of American commerce. But sailing ships were dependent on prevailing winds and weather, and thus could not schedule regular crossings. In 1818 packets began making four round trips a year between New York and Liverpool, sailing on schedule rather than waiting for a full cargo as had ships before then. The breakthrough came in 1848, though, when steamship owner Samuel Cunard began the Atlantic Shuttle, which reduced travel time between Liverpool and New York from 25 days eastbound and 49 days westbound to 10–14 days each way. Sailing ships quickly lost their first-class passengers and light cargo to these swift new ocean steamships. For the next decade they continued to carry immigrants and bulk cargo, but by 1860 only the freight trade remained to them.

By far the fastest spreading technological advance of the era was the magnetic telegraph. Samuel F. B.

| Telegraph |

Morse's invention freed messages from the restraint of traveling no faster than the messenger; instantaneous communication became possible even over long distances. By 1853, only nine years after construction of the first experimental line, 23,000 miles of telegraph wire spread across the United States; by 1860, 50,000. The first transatlantic cable was laid in 1858, and by 1861 the telegraph bridged the continent, connecting the east and west coasts. The new invention revolutionized news gathering, provided advance information for railroads and steamships, and altered patterns of business and finance. Rarely has innovation had so great an impact so quickly.

The changes in transportation and communications from 1800 to 1860 were revolutionary. Railroads reduced the number of loadings and unloadings, were cheap to build over difficult terrain, and remained in use all year. But time was the key. In 1800 it took four days to travel from New York City to Baltimore, and nearly four weeks to reach Detroit. By 1830 Baltimore was only a day-and-a-half away and Detroit only a two-week journey. By 1857 Detroit was but an overnight trip; in a week one could reach Texas, Kansas, or Nebraska. This reduced travel time saved money and facilitated commerce. During the first two decades of the century, wagon transportation cost 30 to 70 cents per ton per mile. By 1860, railroads in New York state carried freight at an average charge of 2.2 cents per ton per mile; wheat moved from Chicago to New York for 1.2 cents a ton-mile. In sum, the transportation revolution had transformed the economy—and with it the relationships of the North, West, and South.

The North: merchants and farmers

The development of the North as the nation's clearing-house was hastened by its rapid population growth. Between 1800 and 1860, the number of Americans increased sixfold to 31.4 million. As the population grew, the frontier receded, and rural settlements became towns and cities (see figure). In 1800 the nation had only 33 towns with 2,500 or more people and only 3 with more than 25,000. By 1860, 392 towns exceeded 2,500 in population and 35 had more than 25,000.

In the Northeast, the percentage of people living in

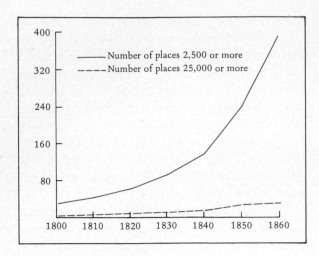

```
400

320

240

160

80

      ——— Number of places 2,500 or more
      ----- Number of places 25,000 or more

   1800  1810  1820  1830  1840  1850  1860
```

Number of urban areas, 1800–1860

urban areas grew from 9.3 to 35.7 from 1800 to 1860. Significantly, most of this growth occurred in northern and western communities located along the new

| Growth of cities |

transportation routes, where increased commerce created new jobs and opportunities. Kingston, New York, 90 miles north of New York City on the Hudson River, was one example. The Delaware and Hudson Canal, which extended from the Hudson Valley to the coalfields of Pennsylvania, rapidly transformed Kingston from a sleepy farm village of 1,000 in the 1820s to an urban community of more than 10,000 in 1850.

The hundreds of small new cities like Kingston were surpassed by stars of even greater magnitude: the great metropolitan cities. In 1860 21 cities exceeded 40,000 in population and 9 exceeded 100,000 (see maps). By 1810 New York City had overtaken Philadelphia as the nation's most populous city; its population soared thereafter, reaching 1,174,779 in 1860. Baltimore and New Orleans dominated the South, and San Francisco became the leading West Coast city. In the Midwest the new lake cities (Chicago, Detroit, Milwaukee, and Cleveland) began to surpass the frontier river cities (Cincinnati, Louisville, and Pittsburgh) founded a generation earlier. These cities formed a nationwide urban network whose center was the great metropolises of the North.

Rapid urban growth in turn brought about a radical change in American commerce and trade. In 1800 most merchants performed the functions of retailer, wholesaler, importer and exporter, shipper, banker, and insurer. Some even engaged in manufacturing, as master craftsmen. But in New York and Philadelphia in the 1790s, and increasingly in all large cities after the War of 1812, the general merchant gave way to the specialist. As a result, the distribution of goods

| Specialization of commerce |

became more systematic. By the 1830s and 1840s, urban centers had been transformed into a pattern we would recognize today: retail shops featured such specialized lines as shoes, wines and spirits, dry goods, groceries, and hardware. Within the downtown area importers and exporters, wholesalers, jobbers, bankers, and insurance brokers clustered on particular streets, near transportation and the merchant exchanges that made it convenient to carry on their businesses more efficiently.

Thus Kingston in the 1850s differed from Kingston in the 1820s not just in size and population density but also in the complexity of its institutions. In the small rural village of the 1820s, homes and workplaces were often combined; thirty years later Kingston had separate commercial and residential districts. By 1858 Kingston's downtown boasted six china and glassware shops, ten clothing stores, two fancy-goods outlets, and ten dry-goods stores, as well as other retail shops, doctors' and lawyers' offices, and financial firms. Beyond the commercial center, two small industrial zones housed nearly all of the city's manufacturing.

On a personal level the specialization of commerce was illustrated by the cotton trader. Cotton had become a staple export following the invention of the cotton gin in 1793; exports rose from half a million pounds in that year to 83 million pounds in 1815. At first northern cotton traders sold the crop abroad or in New England; in turn they bought household goods, supplies, and equipment for southern plantations, extending credit to the purchasers. Gradually some agents came to specialize in finance alone: cotton brokers appeared, men who brought together buyers and sellers for a commission. Similarly, wheat and hog brokers sprang up in the West—in Cincinnati, Louisville, and St. Louis. The supply of finished goods also became more specialized. Wholesalers bought large quantities of a particular item from manufacturers, and jobbers broke down the wholesale lots for retail stores and county merchants.

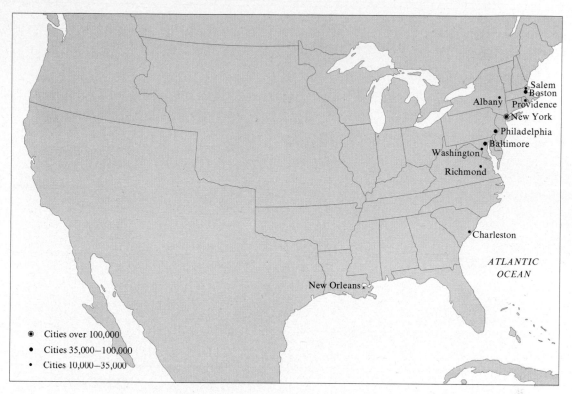

Major American cities, 1820

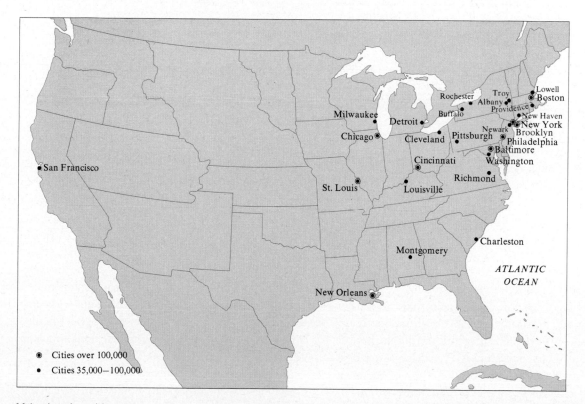

Major American cities, 1860

The North: merchants and farmers

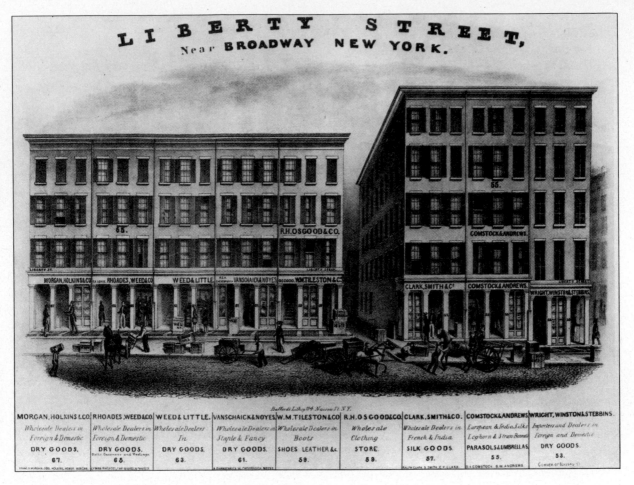

LIBERTY STREET, Near BROADWAY NEW YORK.

MORGAN, HOLKINS & CO.	RHOADES, WEED & CO.	WEED & LITTLE.	VANSCHAICK & NOYES	W. M. TILESTON & CO.	R. H. OSGOOD & CO.	CLARK, SMITH & CO.	COMSTOCK & ANDREWS	WRIGHT, WINSTON & STEBBINS
Wholesale Dealers in Foreign & Domestic	*Wholesale Dealers in Foreign & Domestic*	*Wholesale Dealers In*	*Wholesale Dealers in Staple & Fancy*	*Wholesale Dealers in*	*Wholesale Clothing*	*Wholesale Dealers in French & India*	*European & India Silks Leghorn & Straw Bonnets*	*Importers and Dealers in Foreign and Domestic*
DRY GOODS.	DRY GOODS.	DRY GOODS.	DRY GOODS.	BOOTS SHOES LEATHER &c.	STORE.	SILK GOODS.	PARASOLS & UMBRELLAS	DRY GOODS.
67.	65.	63.	61.	59.	59.	57.	55.	53.

A dry goods center on Liberty Street in New York City. The key below the picture identifies most of the proprietors as wholesale dealers.   Museum of the City of New York.

In small towns the general merchant persisted for a longer time. Such merchants continued to sell some goods through barter–exchanging, for example, flour or pots and pans for eggs or other local produce. They left the sale of finished goods, such as shoes and clothing, to local craftsmen. In rural areas and on the frontier, peddlers acted as general merchants. But as transportation improved and towns grew, even small-town merchants began to specialize.

Commercial specialization made some traders in the big cities, especially New York, virtual merchant princes. New York had emerged as the dominant port in the late 1790s, outstripping Philadelphia and Boston. When the Erie Canal opened, the city became a standard stop on every major trade route–from Europe, the ports of the South, and the West. New

York traders were the middlemen in southern cotton and western grain trading; in fact, New York was the nation's major cotton-exporting city. Merchants in other cities played a similar role within their own regions.

These newly rich traders invested their profits in processing and then manufacturing, further stimulating the growth of northern cities. Some cities became leaders in specific industries: Rochester became a milling center and Cincinnati–"Porkopolis"–the first meat-packing center. Boston merchants even founded a new city, Lowell, to house the first textile mills in Massachusetts.

To support their complex commercial transactions, many merchants required large office staffs. In an age before typewriters and carbon paper, much of the office staff—all male—worked on high stools laboriously copying business forms and correspondence. The scratch of their pens was the early nineteenth-century equivalent of the typewriter's clatter. At the bottom of the office hierarchy were messenger boys, often pre-teenagers, who delivered documents. Above them were the ordinary copyists, who hand-copied documents in ink as many times as needed. Clerks handled such assignments as customs-house clearances and duties, shipping papers, and translations. Above them were the bookkeeper and the confidential chief clerk. Those seeking employment in such an office, called a counting house, could take a course from a writing master to acquire a "good hand." All hoped to rise to the status of partner.

Because the entire trading system was built on credit, it was extremely susceptible to the boom-and-bust cycles that characterized the era. In boom times credit was easy to come by and merchants flourished. During slumps and depressions—1819 through 1823, 1837 through 1843, and 1857—bank credit and investment loans contracted sharply and many merchant houses collapsed. Merchants learned to evaluate their customers carefully before shipping them goods on credit. One response to the need to minimize risk was Lewis Tappan's mercantile agency, founded in 1841. The forerunner of Dun and Bradstreet, Tappan furnished his subscribers with confidential credit reports on country merchants. One such report read:

James Samson is a peddler, aged 30; he comes to Albany to buy his goods, and then peddles them out along the canal from Albany to Buffalo. He is worth $2,000; owns a wooden house at Lockport . . . has a wife and three children . . . drinks two glasses cider brandy, plain, morning and evening—never more; drinks water after each; chews fine cut; never smokes; good teeth generally; has lost a large double tooth on lower jaw, back, second from throat on left . . . purchases principally jewelry and fancy articles.

Beyond the town and city limits, agriculture remained the backbone of the New England economy. For although urban areas were growing quickly, America was still overwhelmingly rural; even in 1860 rural residents far outnumbered urban dwellers (see

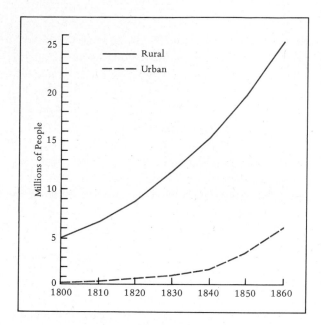

Urban-rural population, 1800–1860

figure). Indeed, it was rural population growth that transformed so many farm villages into bustling small cities. And it was the ability of northeastern farmers to feed the growing town and village populations that made possible the concentration of population and the resulting development of commerce and industry.

In the early part of the century New England and Middle Atlantic farmers supplied their own needs and produced a surplus of crops for sale to the growing towns. Farmers achieved their surpluses by using homemade goods and implements—wooden plows, rakes, shovels, and yokes—as their fathers had done. For iron parts, they turned to the local blacksmith.

But then canals and railroads began transporting grains, especially wheat, eastward from the fertile Old Northwest. And at the same time, northeastern agriculture developed some serious problems. North-

Northeastern
agriculture

eastern farmers had already cultivated all the land they could; expansion was impossible. Moreover, these small New England farms with their uneven terrain did not lend themselves to the new labor-saving farm implements introduced in the 1830s—mechanical sowers, reapers, threshers, and balers. Many northeastern farms also suffered from soil exhaustion: the worn-out land produced lower yields while requiring a greater investment in seed.

The North: merchants and farmers

In response to all these problems, and to competition from the West, many northern farmers either went west or gave up farming for jobs in the merchant houses and factories. For eastern farm sons and daughters, western New York was the first frontier. After the Erie Canal was completed, these Yankees and Yorkers settled on more fertile, cheaper land in Ohio and Illinois, and then in Michigan, Indiana, and Wisconsin. Farm daughters who did not go west flocked to the early textile mills and became the first large-scale American industrial work force. Still other New Englanders—urban, better educated, and often experienced in trade—entered the counting houses of New York and other cities.

Neither the counting house nor the factory, however, depleted New England agriculture. The farmers who remained proved as adaptable at farming as their children did at copy desks and water-powered looms. By the 1850s New England and Middle Atlantic farmers were successfully adjusting to competition from western agricultural products. They abandoned commercial production of wheat and corn and stopped tilling poor land. Instead they improved their livestock, especially cattle, and specialized in vegetable and fruit production and dairy farming. They financed these changes through land sales or borrowing. In fact, their greatest profit was made from increasing land values, not from farming itself.

State governments promoted commercial agriculture in order to spur economic growth and sustain the values of an agrarian-based republic. Massachusetts in 1817 and New York in 1819 subsidized agricultural prizes and county fairs. New York required contestants to submit written descriptions of how they grew their prize crops; the state then published the best essays to encourage the use of new methods and to promote specialization. Farm journals also helped to familiarize farmers with developments in agriculture. By 1860 there were nearly sixty journals with a combined circulation of from 250,000 to 300,000.

Even so, the Old Northwest gradually and inevitably replaced the northeastern states as the center of American agriculture. Farms in the Old Northwest were much larger than northeastern ones, and better suited to the new mechanized farming implements.

| Mechanization of agriculture |

The farmers of the region bought machines such as the McCormick reaper on credit and paid for them with the profits from their high yields. By 1847 Cyrus McCormick was selling a thousand reapers a year. Using interchangeable parts, he expanded production to five thousand a year, but still demand outstripped supply. Similarly, John Deere's steel plow, invented in 1837, replaced the inadequate iron plow; steel blades kept the soil from sticking and were tough enough to break the roots of prairie grass. By 1856, Deere's sixty-five employees were making 13,500 plows a year.

These machines eased the problem of scarce farm labor and permitted a 70-percent surge in wheat production in the 1850s alone. By that time the area that had been the western wilderness in 1800 had become one of the world's leading agricultural regions. Midwestern farmers fed an entire nation and a generation of immigrants, and had food left over to export.

The western frontier

Between 1800 and 1860 the frontier moved westward at an incredible pace (see map). In 1800 the edge of settlement formed an arc from western New York through the new states of Kentucky and Tennessee,

| Movement of the frontier |

south to Georgia. Twenty years later it had shifted to Ohio, Indiana, and Illinois in the North and Louisiana, Alabama, and Mississippi in the South. By 1860 settlement had reached the West Coast; the 1800 frontier was long-settled, and once-unexplored regions were dotted with farms and mines, towns and villages. Unsettled land remained—mostly between the Mississippi River and the Sierra Nevadas—but essentially the frontier and its native inhabitants, the Indians, had given way to white settlement (see Chapter 11). All that remained for whites was to people the plains and mountain territories.

The legal boundaries of the country also changed rapidly during this period. Between 1803 and 1857 the United States pushed its original boundaries to their present continental limits (except for Alaska). The Louisiana Purchase roughly doubled the nation's size, and the War of 1812 and acquisition of Florida from Spain in 1819 secured the Southeast. In the 1840s the United States annexed the Republic of Texas, defined its northern border with Canada, and purchased Cali-

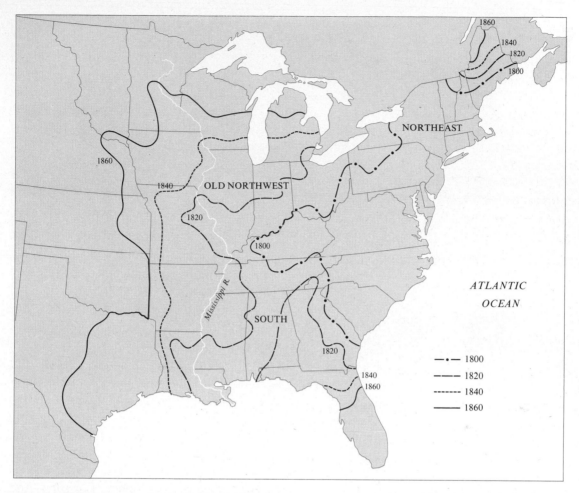

The moving frontier: the edge of settlement, 1800–1860.
Source: From Ross M. Robertson, *History of the American Economy,* 2nd edition. N.Y.: Harcourt Brace & World, 1964.

fornia, Nevada, Utah, and most of Arizona from Mexico (see Chapter 12). In the 1850s the Gadsden Purchase added southern Arizona and New Mexico (see Chapter 13).

The lore of the vanishing frontier forms part of the mythology of America: fur trappers, explorers, and pioneers braving an unknown environment and hostile Indians; settlers crossing the arid plains and snow-covered Rockies by Conestoga wagon to bring civilization to the wilderness; Mormons finding Zion in the Great American Desert; forty-niners sailing on clipper ships to California in search of gold.

Americans have only recently come to recognize that there are other sides to these familiar stories. Women as well as men were pioneers. The fur trappers, explorers, and pioneers did not discover North America by themselves, nor did the wagon trains fight their way across the plains—Indians guided them along traditional paths and led them to food and water. And rather than civilizing the frontier, settlers at first brought a rather primitive economy and society, which did not compare favorably with the well-ordered Indian civilizations. In the South, frontier settlement carried with it slavery. The Mormons who sought a new Jerusalem by Salt Lake were fleeing the gehenna (hell) imposed on them by intolerant, violent frontier folk farther east (see Chapter 12). And all those who sought furs, gold, and lumber spoiled the virgin landscape in the name of progress and development.

This was the ironic contrast between the ideal and the reality of the frontier. If pioneers were attracted by

The western frontier

Spring rendezvous at Green River, Wyoming, painted by W. H. Jackson. Western History Department, Denver Public Library.

the beauty and bounty of the American wilderness, if they were lured by the opportunity to live a simple, rewarding life close to the soil, they were also destroying the natural landscape in the process. It was almost as if the vast forests, prairies, and lakes were enemies to be conquered and bent to their will. Millions of trees were felled to make way for farms. Michigan lumbermen denuded the land. And farther west, miners in search of gold leveled the hills.

No figure has come to symbolize the frontier more aptly than the footloose, rugged fur trapper, who roamed thousands of unmapped miles in search of pelts. Fur trading, especially for beaver, had been economically important since the early colonial period.

| Fur trade | Traders were the last link in an elaborate network that reached from beyond the settled frontier to sophisticated European shops. But after 1800 American investors organized to compete with foreign trading companies such as Hudson's Bay. The German immigrant John Jacob Astor, for instance, became a millionaire

through his American Fur Trading Company. And Americans also changed the method by which furs were acquired. In the 1820s the St. Louis merchant William Henry Ashley pioneered the rendezvous system. Instead of buying beaver furs from Indians, Ashley sent out trappers to roam the Rockies and farther west; at a meeting on the Green River at season's end, the trappers exchanged their pelts for goods Ashley had brought in from St. Louis. This annual spring rendezvous was the hallmark of the American fur-trading system through the 1840s, when silk hats replaced beaver hats and trapping declined. In many areas the beaver had been virtually trapped out of existence.

The history of trapping was in essence the history of the opening up of the frontier. Early fur traders exploited friendly Indian tribes; then pioneers—mountain trappers—monopolized the trade through the systematic organization and financial backing of trading companies. Soon settlements and towns sprang up along the trappers' routes. By the 1840s, with demand at a low ebb and the beaver nearing extinction, fur

Chapter 9: The economic evolution of the North and West, 1800–1860

Ships lie rotting in San Francisco Harbor as their crews seek gold in the California hills. Photographed in the winter of 1852 to 1853 by William Shaw.   Smithsonian Institution.

trading declined. The mining and cattle frontiers were to continue for another half-century, following the development of the fur-trading frontier.

But not all regions followed this pattern. By contrast, California and the Pacific Slope were settled almost overnight. In January 1848 James Marshall, a carpenter, spotted a few gold-like particles in the | *California gold rush* | millrace at Sutter's Mill (now Coloma, California). When the owner confirmed that the granules were indeed gold, Marshall rode back at night through driving rain in search of more. Word of the discovery spread, and other Californians rushed in search of instant fortunes. When John C. Frémont reached San Francisco in June, 1848, he found that "all, or nearly all, its male inhabitants had gone to the mines." The town, "which a few months before was so busy and thriving, was then almost deserted."

By 1849 the news had spread eastward; hundreds of thousands of fortune-seekers flooded in. Most forty-niners never found enough gold to pay their expenses.

"The stories you hear frequently in the States," one gold-seeker wrote home, "are the most extravagant lies imaginable—the mines are a humbug. . . . the almost universal feeling is to get home." But many stayed, unable to afford the passage back home, or tempted by the growing labor shortage in California's cities and agricultural districts. San Francisco, the gateway from the coast to the interior, became an instant city, ballooning from 1,000 people in 1848 to 35,000 just two years later.

Although those who came produced almost nothing, they had to be fed. Thus began the great California agricultural boom, centered along the natural waterways in the fertile interior of the state. Wheat was the great staple; it required minimal investment, was easily planted, and offered a quick return at the end of a relatively short growing season. California farmers became eager importers of machinery, since wages were high in the labor-scarce district and the extensive flat, treeless plains were well suited to horse-drawn machines. By the mid-1850s, California was exporting wheat. In its growing cities, merchant princes arose to supply, feed, and clothe the new settlers. One such merchant was Levi Strauss, whose tough mining pants eventually became synonymous with American jeans.

Gold altered the pattern of settlement along the entire Pacific Coast. Before 1848 most overland traffic flowed north over the Oregon Trail; few pioneers turned south to California. But by 1849 a pioneer observed that the Oregon Trail "bore no evidence of having been much traveled this year." Traffic was instead flowing south, and California was becoming the new population center of the Pacific Slope. One measure of the shift was the overland mail routes. In the 1840s the Oregon Trail had been the major communications link between the Pacific and the Midwest. But the Post Office officials who organized mail routes in the 1850s terminated them in California; there was no route farther north than Sacramento.

By 1860 California, like the Great Plains and prairies farther east, had become a farmers' and merchants' frontier. Though the story of these settlers is less dramatic than that of the trappers and forty-niners, it is nevertheless the story of the overwhelming majority of westerners before 1860. The farming frontier started first on the western fringes of

| *Farming frontier* |

the eastern seaboard states and in the Old Northwest, then moved to the edge of the Great Plains and California. Pioneer families cleared the land of trees or prairie grass, hoed in corn and wheat, fenced in animals, and constructed cabins of logs or sod. If they were successful—and many were not—they slowly cleared more land. As settled areas expanded, farmers built roads to carry their stock and produce to market and bring back supplies they could not produce themselves. Growth brought specialization; as western farmers shifted from self-sufficiency to commercial farming, they too tended to concentrate on one crop. By this time the area was no longer a frontier, and families seeking new land had to go farther west. In John Jervis's time a farmer from Rome, New York, might have gone to Michigan via the Erie Canal and Lake Erie. A later generation would go farther west to Iowa, Nebraska, or even California.

What made farm settlement possible was the availability of land and credit. Some public lands were granted as a reward for military service: veterans of the

| *Land grants and sales* |

War of 1812 received 160 acres; veterans of the Mexican War (see Chapter 12) could purchase land at reduced prices. And until 1820, civilians could buy government land at $2 an acre (a relatively high price) on a liberal four-year payment plan. More important, from 1804 to 1817 the government successively reduced the minimum purchase from 320 to 80 acres. However, when the availability of land prompted a flurry of land speculation that ended in the Panic of 1819, the government discontinued credit sales. Instead it reduced the price further, to $1.25 an acre.

Some eager pioneers settled land before it had been surveyed and put up for sale. Such illegal settlers, or squatters, then had to buy the land they lived on at auction, and faced the risk of being unable to purchase it. In 1841, to facilitate settlement, simplify land sales, and end property disputes, Congress passed the Preemption Act, which legalized settlement prior to surveying.

Since most settlers, squatters or not, needed to borrow money, private credit systems arose. Banks, private investors, country storekeepers, and speculators all extended credit to farmers. Railroads also sold land on credit—land they had received from the government as construction subsidies. (The Illinois Central, for example, received 2.6 million acres in 1850.) Indeed, nearly all economic activity in the West involved credit, from land sales to the shipping of produce to railroad construction. And again in 1836, 1855, and 1856 the credit system helped to fuel land prices. Much land fell into the hands of speculators, and as a result tenancy became more common in the West than it had been in New England.

Towns and cities were the lifelines of the agricultural West. Cities along the Ohio and Mississippi rivers—Pittsburgh, Louisville, Cincinnati, and St. Louis—

| *Frontier cities* |

preceded most of the settlement of the early frontier. A generation later the lake cities of Cleveland, Detroit, and Chicago spearheaded settlement farther west. Steamboats connected farms with these river and lake cities, carrying grain east to market and bringing back finished goods in return. As in the Northeast, these western cities eventually developed into manufacturing centers when merchants shifted their investments from commerce to industry. Chicago became a center for the

CINCINNATI-1800.

Cincinnati in 1800 (above) and 1848 (below). These two pictures show the rapid growth of the city from a frontier hamlet to a major urban center. The steamboats lined up along the riverfront in the bottom picture helped to link the frontier to southern and eastern cities. Above: The Cincinnati Historical Society; below: Rare Book Room, Cincinnati Public Library.

The western frontier

manufacture of farm implements, Louisville of textiles, and Cleveland of iron. Smaller cities specialized in flour mills, and all produced consumer goods for the hinterlands.

Urban growth in the West was so spectacular that by 1860 Cincinnati, St. Louis, and Chicago had populations exceeding 100,000, and Buffalo, Louisville, San Francisco, Pittsburgh, Detroit, Milwaukee, and Cleveland had surpassed 40,000. Thus commerce, urbanization, and industrialization eventually overtook the farmers' frontier, wedding the Old Northwest and areas beyond to the Northeast.

The rise of manufacturing

The McCormick reaper, ridiculed the London *Times,* looked like "a cross between a flying-machine, a wheelbarrow, and an Astley chariot." Put to a competitive test through rain-soaked wheat, however, the Chicago-made reaper alone passed, to the spontaneous cheers of the skeptical English spectators. The reaper and hundreds of other American products made their international debut at the 1851 London Crystal Palace Exhibition, the first modern world's fair. There the design and quality of American machines and wares—from familiar farm tools to such exotic devices as an ice-cream freezer and the reaper—astonished observers. American manufacturers returned home with dozens of medals, including all three prizes for piano making. But more impressive to the Europeans were three simple machines: Alfred C. Hobb's unpickable padlocks, Samuel Colt's revolvers, and Robbins and Lawrence's six rifles with completely interchangeable parts. All were machine-made rather than hand-tooled, products of what the British called the American system of manufacturing.

So impressed were the British—the leading industrial nation of the time—that in 1853 they sent a parliamentary commission to study the American system. A year later a second committee returned to examine the firearms industry in detail. In their report to the British government, the committee described an astonishing experiment performed at the federal armory in Springfield, Massachusetts. To test the interchangeability of machine-made muskets, they selected

rifles made in each of the previous ten years. While the committee watched, the guns were dismantled "and the parts placed in a row of boxes, mixed up together." The Englishmen "then requested the workman, whose duty it is to 'assemble' the arms, to put them together, which he did—the Committee handing him the parts, taken at hazard—with the use of a turnscrew only, and as quickly as though they had been English muskets, whose parts had carefully been kept separate." Britain's Enfield arsenal subsequently converted to American equipment. Within the next few years other nations followed Great Britain's lead, sending delegations across the Atlantic to bring back American machines.

The American system of manufacturing used precision machinery to produce interchangeable parts that needed no filing or fitting. In 1798 Eli Whitney had used a primitive system of interchangeable parts when he contracted with the federal government to make ten thousand rifles in twenty-eight months. By the 1820s the Connecticut manufacturer Simeon North, the Springfield, Massachusetts, Arsenal, and the Harpers Ferry, Virginia, Armory were all producing machine-made interchangeable parts for firearms. From the arsenals the American system spread, giving birth to the machine-tool industry—the mass manufacture of specialized machines for other industries. One by-product was an explosion in consumer goods: since the time and skill involved in manufacturing had been greatly reduced, the new system permitted mass production at low cost. Waltham watches, Yale locks, Singer sewing machines, and Colt revolvers became household items, inexpensive yet of uniformly high quality.

Interchangeable parts and the machine-tool industry were uniquely American contributions to the industrial revolution. Both paved the way for America's swift industrialization following the Civil War. The process of industrialization began, however, in a simple and traditional way, not unlike that of other nations. In 1800 manufacturing was relatively unimportant to the American economy. What manufacturing there was took place mostly in small workshops and homes, where journeymen and apprentices worked with and under master craftsmen. These tailors, shoemakers, and blacksmiths made articles by hand for a specific customer.

American system of manufacturing

It was the rise of merchant-investors, wholesalers, and retailers, in combination with the transportation revolution, that transformed this system. First the "putting-out" system of home manufacture estab-

| Putting-out system |

lished the merchant as a middle-man between the worker and the customer. In the shoe industry, for instance, shoemakers worked in their homes from 1800 until about 1840, receiving the materials—leather, thread, and so on—from a merchant or master cordwainer and delivering the finished product to him. Then in the 1820s, entrepreneurs set up central shops where leather was cut into soles and uppers before being put out. The upper parts were then sent to one group of workers and the soles and finished uppers to another group. This system introduced a division of labor, in which workers performed specialized tasks—cutting leather, shaping and sewing uppers, or finishing the shoe. By the 1840s, machinery had begun to replace the traditional tools, and by the 1850s steam-powered factory production had become widespread. In the process the master craftsman had disappeared, the journeyman had become a factory worker, and shoes were produced impersonally for distant markets.

Even more dramatic and influential was the development of the New England textile industry. The first American textile mill, built in Pawtucket, Rhode Island, in 1790, used water-powered spinning machines constructed by the English immigrant Samuel Slater. By 1800 the mill employed one hundred people, and its cloth was sold from Maine to Maryland. Soon other mills sprang up, stimulated by the embargo on English imports from 1807 through 1815.

These early mills also used the putting-out system. Traditionally women had spun their own yarn and woven it into cloth for their own families; now many women received yarn from the mills and returned finished cloth. The change was subtle but significant: although the work itself was familiar, women now operated their looms for piece-rate wages and produced cloth for the market, not for their own use.

Textile manufacturing was radically transformed in 1813 by the construction of the first American power loom and the chartering of the Boston Manufacturing Company. The corporation was capitalized at $400,000—ten times the amount behind the Rhode Is-

land mills—by Francis Cabot Lowell and other Boston merchants. Its goal was to eliminate problems of timing, shipping, coordination, and quality control inherent in the putting-out system. The owners erected their factories in Waltham, Massachusetts, combining

| Waltham (Lowell) system |

all the manufacturing processes at a single location. They also employed a resident manager to run the mill, thus separating ownership from management. The company produced cheap, coarse cloth suitable for the mass market.

In the rural setting of Waltham not enough hands could be found to staff the mill, so the managers recruited New England farm daughters, accepting responsibility for their living conditions and their virtue. To persuade young women to come, they offered high wages, company-run boarding houses, and such cultural events as evening lectures—none of which were available on the farm. This paternalistic approach, called the Waltham or Lowell system, was adopted in other mills erected alongside New England rivers. The Hamilton Corporation (1825), the Appleton and Lowell corporations (1828), and the Suffolk, Tremont, and Lawrence firms (1831) all followed suit. By the 1850s, though, another work force had entered the mills—Irish immigrants. With a surplus of cheap labor available, Lowell and other mill towns abandoned their model systems. By 1860 a cotton mill had become a modern factory, and work relationships in American society had been radically altered.

Textile manufacturing changed New England. Lowell, the famous "city of spindles" that came to symbolize early American industrialization, grew from 2,500 people in 1826 to 33,000 in 1850. The industry became the most important in the nation before the Civil War, employing 115,000 workers in 1860, more than half of whom were women. The key to its success was that the machines, not the women, spun the cloth. The workers watched the machines and intervened to maintain smooth operation. When a thread broke, for instance, the machine stopped automatically; the worker would find the break, piece the ends together, and restart the machine. The mills used increasingly specialized machines, relying heavily on advances in the machine-tool industry. Here was the American system of manufacturing applied.

Though shoe factories and textile mills were in the

CLOTH MADE AND PRINTED BY THE
MERRIMACK MANUFACTURING CO
LOWELL, MASS.
INCORPORATED 1822.
Warranted Fast Colors.

A Merrimack Manufacturing Company label shows the mill
girls who came from rural areas to work at the looms in Lowell,
Massachusetts.   Merrimack Valley Textile Museum.

vanguard of industrialization, the United States experienced broad-based growth in many kinds of manufacturing. Woolen textiles, farm implements, machine tools, iron, glass, and finished consumer goods
all became major industries. "White coal"—water
power—was widely used to run the machines. Yet by
1860, the United States was still predominantly an agricultural nation; just over one-half of the work force
was engaged in agriculture. Manufacturing accounted
for only a third of total production, even though that
percentage had doubled in twenty years.

To a great extent, industrialization in this period
must be seen as the result of other changes in American life rather than the agent of change. Ever since
Alexander Hamilton's report on manufactures, national self-consciousness and pride had led to emphasis on the development of home industry. Contrary to
Hamilton's hopes, however, more money flowed into
the merchant marine than into industry between 1789

and 1808. In the early republic, greater profits could
be made by transporting British products to the
United States than by producing the same items at
home. But the embargo and the War of 1812 reversed
the situation, and merchants began to shift their capital from shipping to manufacturing (see pages
210–211). It was in this new economic environment
that the Waltham system took root.

Other factors also helped to stimulate industry.
Population growth, especially in urban areas and the
Old Northwest, created a large domestic market for
finished goods (see maps). The rise of commercial agriculture further increased demand by replacing self-
sufficient farming. Specialty merchants and new
modes of transportation speeded up the development
of these new markets. And the relative scarcity of
skilled craftsmen encouraged mechanization—as more
workers moved westward than entered the factories,
merchants had to find some way to produce more

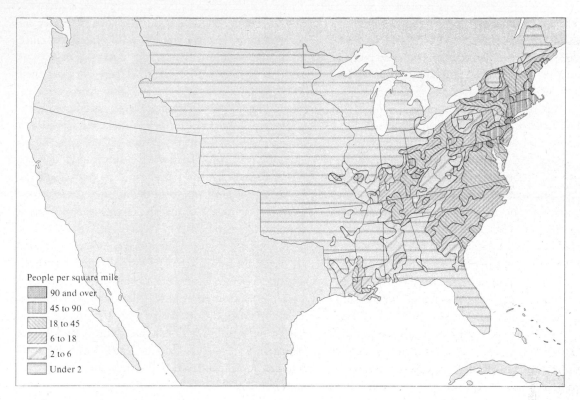

People per square mile

90 and over
45 to 90
18 to 45
6 to 18
2 to 6
Under 2

United States population, 1820

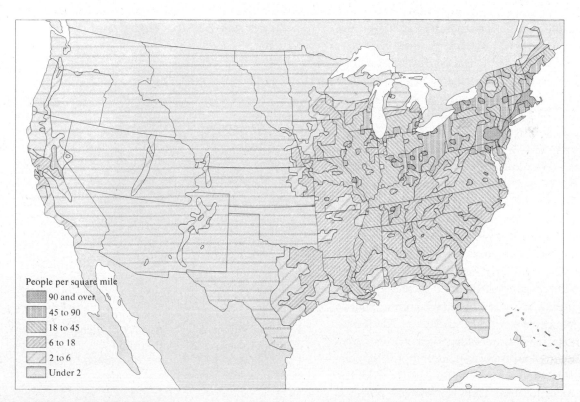

People per square mile

90 and over
45 to 90
18 to 45
6 to 18
2 to 6
Under 2

United States population, 1860

The rise of manufacturing

goods with less labor. Finally, beginning with the Tariff of 1816 and culminating in the Tariff of Abominations of 1828, Congress passed tariffs more to protect the market for domestic manufacturers than to increase the treasury.

Equally important to the rise of manufacturing was the development of financial institutions (banks, insurance companies, and corporations) linking savers—

| Banking and credit systems |

those who put money in the bank—with producers or speculators—those who wished to borrow money for equipment. The expiration of the Bank of the United States in 1811 after Congress refused to renew its charter, acted as a stimulus to state-chartered banks, and in the next five years the number of banks more than doubled. Nonetheless, state banks proved inadequate to spur national growth, and in 1816 Congress chartered the Second Bank of the United States (see page 210). From then until 1832, however, many farmers, local bankers, and politicians denounced the bank as a monster, and finally succeeded in killing it (see Chapter 12).

The closing of the Second Bank in 1836 caused a nationwide credit shortage that, along with the Panic of 1837, stimulated some major reforms in banking. Michigan and New York introduced charter laws promoting what was called *free banking*. Previously every new bank had required a special legislative charter, which made each bank incorporation a political decision. Under the new laws, any proposed bank that met certain minimum conditions—amount of money, notes issued, and types of loans to be made—would automatically receive a state charter. Although banks were thus freer to incorporate, more restrictions were placed on their practices, slightly reducing the risk of bank failure. Other states soon followed suit.

Free banking proved a significant stimulus to the economy in the late 1840s and 1850s. New banks sprang up everywhere, providing merchants and manufacturers the credit they needed. The free banking laws also served as a precedent for general incorporation statutes, which allowed manufacturing firms to receive state charters without special acts. Investors in corporations, called shareholders, were granted *limited liability,* or freedom from responsibility for the company's debts. An attractive feature to potential investors, limited liability thus encouraged people to back new business ventures.

Changes in insurance companies also promoted industrialization. In the course of business, insurance companies accumulated large amounts of money as reserves against future claims. Then as now, their greatest profits came from investing those reserves. Beginning in the 1840s and 1850s, insurance companies lent money for longer periods than banks, and they bought shares in corporations. They were able to do so by persuading customers to buy whole-life policies rather than annual term insurance. They also took advantage of improvements in communications to establish networks of local agencies, thus expanding the number of customers they served.

In the 1850s, with credit and capital both more easily obtainable, the pace of industrialization increased. In the North, industry began to rival agriculture and commerce in dollar volume. Meanwhile commercial farming, financed by the credit boom, integrated the early frontier into the northern economy. By 1860 six northern states—Massachusetts, New York, Pennsylvania, Connecticut, Rhode Island, and Ohio—were highly industrialized. The clothing, textile, and shoe industries employed more than 100,000 workers each, lumber 75,000, iron 65,000, and woolens and leather 50,000. Although agriculture still predominated even in these states, industrial employment would soon surpass it.

Mill girls and mechanics

Oh, sing me the song of the Factory Girl!
So merry and glad and free!
The bloom in her cheeks, of health how it speaks,
Oh! a happy creature is she!
She tends the loom, she watches the spindle,
And cheerfully toileth away,
Amid the din of wheels, how her bright eyes kindle,
And her bosom is ever gay.

Oh, sing me the song of the Factory Girl!
Whose fabric doth clothe the world.
From the king and his peers to the jolly tars
With our flag o'er all seas unfurled.
From the California's seas, to the tainted breeze
Which sweeps the smokened rooms,
Where "God save the Queen" to cry are seen
The slaves of the British looms.

This idyllic portrait of factory work was an anachronism when it appeared in the Chicopee, Massachusetts, *Telegraph* in 1850. But it was a fitting song for the first women who entered the New England textile mills: young women, mostly single and between fifteen and thirty years old, who left the villages and farms of New England to work in the mills. They went on their own, lured by the chance to be independent and self-supporting, to get away from home, to save for a trousseau, and to enjoy city life. The mill owners, believing that the degradation of English factory workers arose from their living conditions and not from the work itself, designed a model community offering airy courtyards and river views, secure dormitories, prepared meals, and cultural activities. Housekeepers enforced strict curfews, banned alcohol, and reported to the corporations on workers' behavior and church attendance.

Some workers saw factory life as an escape from the drudgery of farming and home manufacture. At home, farm daughters spent their extra time spinning wool by hand and weaving it into cloth. One sixteen-year-old, after weaving steadily for three months and producing 176 yards of cloth, recorded in her diary: "Welcome Sweet Liberty, once more to me. How I have longed to meet again with thee." Her freedom would soon be lost when the annual cycle of spinning and weaving resumed. Factory workers were guaranteed leisure time—not much, but enough to tempt a farm girl. Eventually the New England textile mills replaced home manufacture of cloth altogether.

By the 1840s the songs of the factory girls had become rebellious. "The Factory Girl's Come-All-Ye" (about 1850) expressed the workers' desire to leave the oppressive mill:

No more I'll take my bobbins out,
No more I'll put them in,
No more the overseer will say
"You're weaving your cloth too thin!"

No more will I eat cold pudding,
No more will I eat hard bread,
No more will I eat those half-baked beans,
For I vow! They're killing me dead!

I'm going back to Boston town
And live on Tremont Street;
And I want all you fact'ry girls
To come to my house and eat!

What had happened to dash the hopes of these young women? The corporation's goal of building an industrial empire had taken precedence over its concern for workers' living conditions. In the race for profits, owners had lengthened hours, cut wages, and tightened discipline. Eliza R. Hemingway, a six-year veteran of the Massachusetts mills, told a state House of Representatives committee that the worker's hours were too long, "her time for meals too limited. In the summer season, the work is commenced at 5 o'clock, A.M., and continued 'til 7 o'clock, P.M., with half an hour for breakfast and three quarters of an hour for dinner." When Hemingway worked evenings—which was compulsory—293 small lamps and 61 large ones lit the room. There was no bloom of health in her cheeks.

New England mill workers responded to their deteriorating working conditions by organizing and

| Mill girl protests |

striking. In 1834, in reaction to a 25-percent wage cut, they unsuccessfully "turned out" (struck) against the Lowell mills. Two years later, when boarding-house rates were raised, they turned out again. Following the period from 1837 to 1842, when most mills ran only part-time because of a decline in demand for cloth, managers applied still greater pressures on workers. The speedup, the stretch-out, and the premium system became common methods of increasing production. The speedup increased the speed of the machines; the stretch-out increased the number of machines each worker had to operate. Premiums were paid to overseers whose departments produced the most cloth. The result was that in Lowell between 1836 and 1850, the number of spindles and looms increased 150 and 140 percent respectively, while the number of workers increased by only 50 percent. Mill workers began to think of themselves as slaves.

As conditions worsened, workers changed their methods of resistance. By the 1850s strikes had given way to a concerted effort to shorten the workday. Massachusetts mill women joined forces with other workers to press for legislation mandating a ten-hour day. They aired their complaints in worker-run newspapers—the *Factory Girl* appeared in New Hampshire and the *Wampanoag and Operatives' Journal* in Massachusetts, both in 1842. Two years later the *Factory Girl's Garland* and the *Voice of Industry,* nicknamed "the factory girl's voice," were founded. Even the

TIME TABLE OF THE LOWELL MILLS,

Arranged to make the working time throughout the year average 11 hours per day.

TO TAKE EFFECT SEPTEMBER 21st., 1853,

The Standard time being that of the meridian of Lowell, as shown by the Regulator Clock of AMOS SANBORN, Post Office Corner, Central Street.

From March 20th to September 19th, inclusive.

COMMENCE WORK, at 6.30 A. M. LEAVE OFF WORK, at 6.30 P. M., except on Saturday Evenings.
BREAKFAST at 6 A. M. DINNER, at 12 M. Commence Work, after dinner, 12.45 P. M.

From September 20th to March 19th, inclusive.

COMMENCE WORK at 7.00 A. M. LEAVE OFF WORK, at 7.00 P. M., except on Saturday Evenings.
BREAKFAST at 6.30 A. M. DINNER, at 12.30 P. M. Commence Work, after dinner, 1.15 P. M.

BELLS.

From March 20th to September 19th, inclusive.

Morning Bells.	*Dinner Bells.*	*Evening Bells.*
First bell,...........4.30 A. M.	Ring out,.............12.00 M.	Ring out,...........6.30 P. M.
Second, 5.30 A. M.; Third, 6.20.	Ring in,..........12.35 P. M.	Except on Saturday Evenings.

From September 20th to March 19th, inclusive.

Morning Bells.	*Dinner Bells.*	*Evening Bells.*
First bell,...........5.00 A. M.	Ring out,..........12.30 P. M.	Ring out at..........7.00 P. M.
Second, 6.00 A. M.; Third, 6.50.	Ring in,.............1.05 P. M.	Except on Saturday Evenings.

SATURDAY EVENING BELLS.

During APRIL, MAY, JUNE, JULY, and AUGUST, Ring Out, at 6.00 P. M.
The remaining Saturday Evenings in the year, ring out as follows :

SEPTEMBER.

First Saturday, ring out 6.00 P. M.
Second   "   "   5.45   "
Third   "   "   5.30   "
Fourth   "   "   5.20   "

OCTOBER.

First Saturday, ring out 5.05 P. M.
Second   "   "   4.55   "
Third   "   "   4.45   "
Fourth   "   "   4.35   "
Fifth   "   "   4.25   "

NOVEMBER.

First Saturday, ring out 4.15 P. M.
Second   ".   "   4.05   "

NOVEMBER.

Third Saturday ring out 4.00 P. M.
Fourth   "   "   3.55   "

DECEMBER.

First Saturday, ring out 3.50 P. M.
Second   "   "   3.55   "
Third   "   "   3.55   "
Fourth   "   "   4.00   "
Fifth   "   "   4.00   "

JANUARY.

First Saturday, ring out 4.10 P. M.
Second   "   "   4.15   "

JANUARY.

Third Saturday, ring out 4.25 P. M.
Fourth   "   "   4.35   "

FEBRUARY.

First Saturday, ring out 4.45 P. M.
Second   "   "   4.55   "
Third   "   "   5.00   "
Fourth   "   "   5.10   "

MARCH.

First Saturday, ring out 5.25 P. M.
Second   "   "   5.30   "
Third   "   "   5.35   "
Fourth   "   "   5.45   "

YARD GATES will be opened at the first stroke of the bells for entering or leaving the Mills.

•.• *SPEED GATES commence hoisting three minutes before commencing work.*

This 1853 timetable from the Lowell Mills illustrates the regimentation workers had to submit to in the new environment of the factory. Note that workers frequently began before daylight, finished after sunset, and were given only half an hour for meals. Merrimack Valley Textile Museum.

Lowell Offering, the owner-sponsored paper that was the pride of mill workers and managers alike, became embroiled in controversy when some workers charged that articles critical of working conditions had been suppressed.

But not all the militant native-born mill workers stayed on to fight the managers and owners, and gradually fewer New England daughters entered the mills. The immigrant women, mostly Irish, who constituted a majority of mill workers by the end of the 1850s were driven to the mills by the need to support their families. Most could not afford to complain about their working conditions.

What happened in the New England mills occurred in less dramatic fashion throughout the nation. Workers experienced undesirable changes in their tasks and in their relationships with their employers. In the old journeyman-apprentice system that skilled workers had known for centuries, the master had worked alongside his employees, often living in the same household. Work relationships were intensely personal, and there was little social distance between master and journeyman—after all, the journeymen and apprentices expected to become masters themselves someday. All had an interest in the standards of their craft, and they made their finished goods to order and with pride.

| Changes in the workplace |

But textile mills, shoe factories, insurance companies, wholesale stores, canals and railroads were the antithesis of the old master-journeyman tradition. Supervisors separated the workers from the owners. The division of labor and the use of machines reduced the skills required of workers. And the coming and going of the large work forces was governed by the bell, the steam whistle, or the clock. In 1844 the *Factory Girl's Garland* published a poem describing how the ringing of the factory bell controlled when the workers awoke, ate, began and ended work, and went to sleep. The central problem, of course, was the quickening of the work between the bells. Since owners and managers no longer shared the workers' tasks, it was easy for them to expect faster and faster performance.

Like the mill women, most workers at first welcomed the new manufacturing methods; new jobs and higher wages seemed adequate compensation. But later wage reductions, speed-ups, and stretch-outs changed their minds. Other adjustments were difficult too. Young women in the mills had to become used to the roar of the looms, and all workers on power machines risked accidents that could kill or maim. Most demoralizing of all, they had to accept that their future was relatively fixed. Opportunities to become an owner or manager in the new system were virtually nil.

The growing division between worker and owner was mirrored in commercial agriculture by the gap between hired hands or tenants and farm owners. Though the United States was still primarily an agricultural nation—and many saw the frontier farm as the antidote to commerce and industrialization—not all farmers were yeomen. Farm laborers, once scarce in the United States, had become commonplace. In the North in 1860 there was one hired hand for every 2.3 farms. Given the high cost of land and of farming by that time, hired hands had little opportunity to acquire farms of their own. By the 1850s it took from ten to twenty years for a rural laborer to save enough money to farm for himself. For the same reason, the number of tenant farmers increased.

One response to increasing economic insecurity and social rigidity was the active participation of workers in reform politics. In the 1820s labor parties arose in Pennsylvania, New York, and Massachusetts; they eventually spread to a dozen states. These parties advocated free public education, abolition of imprisonment for debt, revision of the militia system (in which workers bore the greatest burden) and opposed banks and monopolies. Workers' reform often crossed paths with middle-class benevolent movements, since the two groups shared a concern not only for public education but also for public morals: temperance, observance of the Sabbath, and suppression of vice (see Chapter 12). Ironically, however, reform politics tended to divide workers. Many of the reforms—moral education, temperance, Sabbath closings—served merchants and industrialists seeking a more disciplined work force. Others broadened the divisions between native-born and immigrant workers. Anti-immigrant and anti-Catholic movements spread.

| Emergence of a labor movement |

Due both to these divisions and to economic upheaval, organized labor was not a strong force during this period. Labor unions tended to be local in nature; the strongest resembled medieval guilds. The first

Women shoe workers strike for higher wages at Lynn,
Massachusetts, in 1860.   Culver.

unions arose among urban journeymen in printing,
woodworking, shoemaking, and tailoring. These
craftsmen sought to protect themselves against the
competition of inferior workmen by regulating apprenticeship and establishing minimum wages. In the
1820s and 1830s craft unions—unions organized by
occupation—forged larger umbrella organizations in
the cities, including the National Trades Union
(1834). But in the depression of 1839 through 1843,
the movement fell apart amidst wage reductions and
unemployment. In the 1850s the deterioration of
working conditions strengthened the labor movement again. Workers won a reduction in hours, and
the ten-hour day became standard. Though the Panic
of 1857 wiped out the umbrella organizations, some
of the new national unions for specific trade groups—

notably printers, hat finishers, and stonecutters—survived. By 1860 five more national unions had been organized by the painters, cordwainers, cotton spinners,
iron molders, and machinists.

Organized labor's greatest achievement during this
period was in gaining recognition of its right to exist.
When journeymen shoemakers organized in the first
decade of the century, employers turned to the courts,
charging criminal conspiracy. The cordwainers' conspiracy cases, which involved six trials from 1806
through 1815, left labor organizations in a tenuous
position. Although the journeymen's right to organize was recognized, the courts ruled unlawful any
coercive action that harmed other businesses or the
public. In effect, therefore, strikes were unlawful.
Eventually a Massachusetts case, *Commonwealth* v.

Hunt (1842), effectively reversed the decision when

| Right to strike |

Chief Justice Lemuel Shaw ruled that Boston journeymen boot-makers had a right to combine and strike "in such manner as best to subserve their own interests."

The impact of economic and technological change, however, fell more heavily on individual workers than on their organizations. As a group, the workers' share of the national wealth declined after the 1830s. Individual producers—craftsmen, factory workers, and farmers—had less economic power than they had had a generation or two before. And workers were increasingly losing control over their own work.

For the nation as a whole, the period from 1800 through 1860 was one of sustained growth. The population grew from 5.3 to 31.5 million. Settlement, once restricted to the Atlantic seaboard and the eastern rivers, extended more than a thousand miles inland by 1860 and was spreading east from the Pacific Ocean as well. Whereas agriculture had completely dominated the nation at the turn of the century—in 1800 nearly every American not engaged in farming either processed food or provided services for farmers—by mid-century farming was being challenged by a booming manufacturing sector. And agriculture itself was becoming mechanized.

Still, traditional work persisted. Every town had its blacksmith and tailor, stablehands and day laborers, seamstresses and domestic servants. And in the South, although some black slaves worked in the new factories and mills, the overwhelming majority of slaves still performed traditional agricultural work.

Suggestions for further reading

General

W. Elliot Brownlee, *Dynamics of Ascent: A History of the American Economy* (1979); Stuart Bruchey, *The Roots of American Economic Growth, 1607–1861: An Essay in Social Causation* (1965); North Douglass, *Economic Growth of the United States, 1790–1860* (1961); David Klingaman and Richard Vedder, eds., *Essays in 19th Century History* (1975); Susan Previant Lee and Peter Passell, *A New Economic View of American History* (1979); Nathan Rosenberg, *Technology and American Economic Growth* (1972).

Important events

1803–06	Lewis and Clark expedition
1807	Fulton's steamboat, *Clermont*
1810	New York becomes the most populous city
1813	Boston Manufacturing Company founded
1817–30	Canal era
1818	National Road reaches Wheeling, Virginia
1819	*Dartmouth College* v. *Woodward*
1819–23	Depression
1820s	New England textile mills expand
1824	*Gibbons* v. *Ogden*
1825	Erie Canal completed
1830	Baltimore and Ohio Railroad begins operation *Tom Thumb*
1830–86	Railroad era
1831	McCormick invents the reaper
1834	Mill women strike at Lowell
1837	Financial panic
1839–43	Depression
1841	Tappan's mercantile agency
1844	Baltimore-Washington telegraph line
1848	Cunard's Atlantic shuttle
1849	Gold rush
1853	British study of American system of manufacturing
1854	Railroad reaches the Mississippi
1857	Depression
1858	Transatlantic cable

Transportation

Robert G. Albion, *The Rise of New York Port, 1815–1860* (1939); Albert Fishlow, *American Railroads and the Transformation of the Ante-Bellum Economy* (1965); Carter Goodrich, *Government Promotion of American Canals and Railroads, 1800–1890* (1960); Erik E. Haites, *et al., Western River Transportation: The Era of Internal Development, 1810–1860* (1975); Louis C. Hunter, *Steamboats on the Western Rivers* (1949); Samuel E. Morison, *Maritime History of Massachusetts, 1789–1860* (1921); Harry N. Scheiber, *Ohio Canal Era: A Case Study of Government and the Economy, 1820–1861* (1969); Ronald E. Shaw, *Erie Water West: Erie Canal, 1797–1854* (1966); George R. Taylor, *The Transportation Revolution, 1815–1860* (1951).

Commerce and manufacturing

Alfred D. Chandler, Jr., *The Visible Hand: Managerial Revolution in American Business* (1977); Victor Clark, *History of Manufactures in the United States,* 3 vols. (1929); Arthur H. Cole, *The American Wool Manufacture,* 2 vols. (1926); H. J. Habakkuk, *American and British Technology in the Nineteenth Century* (1962); Diane Lindstrom, *Economic Development in the Philadelphia Region, 1810–1850* (1978); Louis Hartz, *Economic Policy and Democratic Thought: Pennsylvania, 1776–1860* (1954); James D. Norris, *R. G. Dun & Co. 1841–1900* (1978); Merritt Roe Smith, *Harpers Ferry Armory and the New Technology* (1977); Peter Temin, *Iron and Steel in Nineteenth-Century America* (1964); Joseph E. Walker, *Hopewell Village: A Social and Economic History of an Ironmaking Community* (1966); Caroline F. Ware, *Early New England Cotton Manufacturing* (1931).

Agriculture

Percy Bidwell and John Falconer, *History of Agriculture in the Northern United States 1620–1860* (1925): Allan G. Bogue, *From Prairie to Corn Belt: Farming on the Illinois and Iowa Prairies in the Nineteenth Century* (1963); Clarence Danhof, *Change in Agriculture: The Northern United States, 1820–1870* (1969); Paul W. Gates, *The Farmer's Age: Agriculture, 1815–1860* (1962); Paul W. Gates, *The Illinois Central and Its Colonization Work* (1934); Benjamin H. Hibbard, *A History of Public Land Policies* (1939); Julie Roy Jeffrey, *Frontier Women: The Trans-Mississippi West 1840–1880* (1979); Edward C. Kendall, *John Deere's Steel Plow* (1959); William T. Hutchinson, *Cyrus Hall McCormick,* 2 vols. (1930–1935).

The western frontier

Ray A. Billington, *The Far Western Frontier, 1830–1860* (1956); Ray A. Billington, *Westward Expansion* (1974); Hiram M. Chittenden, *The American Fur Trade of the Far West,* 3 vols. (1935); Gloria G. Cline, *Exploring the Great Basin* (1963); John Mack Faragher, *Women and Men on the Overland Trail* (1979); William H. Goetzmann, *Exploration and Empire: The Explorer and the Scientist in the Winning of the American West* (1966); John A. Hawgood, *America's Western Frontier: The Exploration and Settlement of the Trans-Mississippi West* (1967); Rodman W. Paul, *California Gold: The Beginning of Mining in the Far West* (1974); John D. Unruh, Jr., *The Overland Emigrants and the Trans-Mississippi West, 1840–1860* (1979); David J. Wishart, *The Fur Trade of the American West, 1807–1840* (1979).

Workers

Alan Dawley, *Class and Community: The Industrial Revolution in Lynn* (1977); Thomas Dublin, *Women at Work: The Transformation of Work and Community in Lowell, Massachusetts, 1826–1860* (1979); Philip S. Foner, ed., *The Factory Girls* (1977); Susan E. Hirsch, *Roots of the American Working Class: The Industrialization of Crafts in Newark, 1800–1860* (1978); Hannah Josephson, *The Gold Threads: New England's Mill Girls and Magnates* (1949); Bruce Laurie, *Working People of Philadelphia, 1800–1850* (1980); Norman Ware, *The Industrial Worker, 1840–1860* (1924).

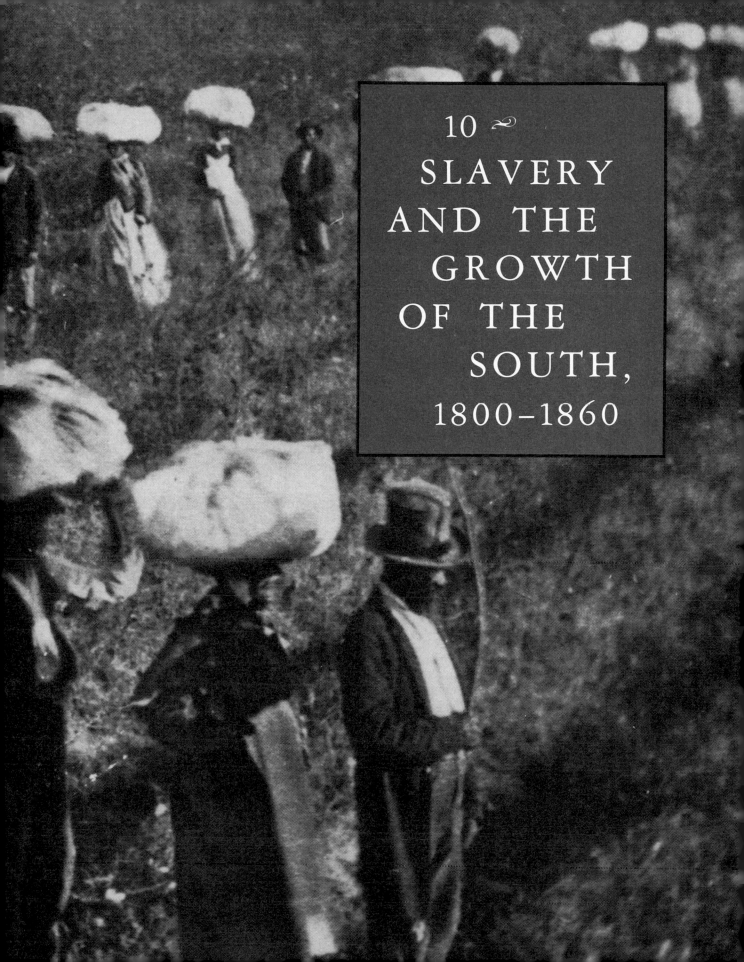

10 ∽

SLAVERY
AND THE
GROWTH
OF THE
SOUTH,
1800–1860

He was weeping, sobbing. In a humble voice he had begged his master not to give him to Mr. King, who was going away to Alabama, but it had done no good. Now his voice rose and he uttered "an absolute cry of despair." Raving and "almost in a state of frenzy," he declared that he would never leave the Georgia plantation that was home to his father, mother, wife, and children. He twisted his hat between clenched fists and flung it to the ground; he would kill himself, he said, before he lost his family and all that made life worth living.

To Fanny Kemble, watching from the doorway, it was a horrifying and disorienting scene. One of the most famous British actresses ever to tour America, Fanny had grown up breathing England's antislavery tradition as naturally as the air. In New England she had become friends with such enlightened antislavery thinkers as William Ellery Channing, the liberal Boston minister who founded Unitarianism; Catharine Maria Sedgwick, America's foremost woman novelist; and Elizabeth Dwight Sedgwick, an educator and Catharine's sister-in-law. Amid such company, Fanny understandably assumed that attitudes in America were advanced and civilized. Then the man she married took her away from New England to a Georgia rice plantation, where hundreds of dark-skinned slaves produced the white grain that was his source of wealth.

Pierce Butler, Fanny's husband, was all that a cultured Philadelphia gentleman should be. He had lived all his life in the North, though part of his family's fortune had always sprung from southern slavery. When Fanny chose him from dozens of suitors, he had seemed an attractive exemplar of American culture. Yet now he shattered his slave's hopes without hesitation. Quietly "leaning against a table with his arms folded," Butler advised the distraught black man not to "make a fuss about what there was no help for."

Fanny wondered what America was really like. In the South, the northerner she thought she knew seemed a different man. Only with tears and vehement pleas was she able to convince Butler to keep the slave family together. He finally agreed as a favor to her, not as an act of principle.

This incident, which occurred in 1839, illustrates both the similarities between South and North and the differences that were beginning to emerge. Though racism existed in the North, its influence was far more visible on southern society. And though some northerners, like Pierce Butler, were undisturbed by the idea of human bondage, a growing number considered it shocking and backward. In the years after the Revolution, these northerners, possessing few slaves and influenced by the revolutionary ideal of natural rights, had adopted gradual emancipation laws (see Chapter 11). At the same time they had embarked on an industrial revolution that transformed their economy, gradually mechanizing their farms and rendering forced labor obsolete.

In the South too, the years from 1800 to 1860 were a time of growth and prosperity; new lands were settled and new states peopled. But as the North grew and changed, economically the South merely grew; change there only reinforced existing economic patterns. Steadily the South emerged as the world's most extensive and vigorous slave economy. Its people were slaves, slaveholders, and nonslaveholders rather than farmers, merchants, mechanics, and manufacturers. Its well-being depended on agriculture alone, rather than agriculture plus commerce and manufacturing. Its population was almost wholly rural rather than rural and urban.

These facts meant that the social lives of southerners were unavoidably distinct from those of northerners. Nonslaveholders operated their family farms in a society dominated by slaveholding planters. A handful of planters developed an aristocratic lifestyle, while slaves—one-third of the South's people—lived without freedom, struggling to develop a culture that sustained hope. The influence of slavery spread throughout the social system, affecting not just southern economics but southern values, customs, and laws. It created a society that was noticeably different.

The South remains rural

The South in the early 1800s was the product of precisely the kind of resource-exploiting commercial agriculture that most of the early colonies had aspired to develop. Only there, nonmechanized agriculture remained highly profitable, as it did not in the Northeast. Southern planters were not sentimentalists who held onto their slaves for noneconomic reasons even in the face of the industrial revolution. Like other Americans, they were profit-oriented. Circumstances dictated that the most profitable investment lay in the continuation of a plantation economy.

At the time of the Revolution, slave-based agriculture was not exceedingly lucrative. Debt hung heavily over most of Virginia's extravagant and aristocratic tobacco growers, prodding them to consider the disadvantages of slavery. Cotton was a lucrative export crop only for sea-island planters, who grew the luxurious long-staple variety. The short-staple cotton that grew readily in the interior was unmarketable because its sticky seeds lay tangled in the fibers. But in spite of the limited usefulness of slavery, social inertia and fear of slave revolts prevented its abolition.

Then England's burgeoning textile industry changed the southern economy. English mills needed more and more cotton. Sea-island cotton was so profitable between 1785 and 1795 that thousands of farmers in the interior experimented with the short-staple variety; by the early 1790s southern farmers were planting 2 to 3 million pounds of it each year. Some of this cotton was meant for domestic use, but most was grown in the hope that some innovation would make the crop salable to the English. In such circumstances the invention of a cotton gin was almost inevitable, and Eli Whitney responded in 1793 with a simple machine that removed the seeds from the fibers. By 1800 cotton was spreading rapidly westward from the seaboard states.

So the antebellum South, or Old South, became primarily a cotton South. Tobacco continued to be grown in Virginia and North Carolina, and rice and

| Rise of the Cotton South | sugar were still very important in certain coastal areas, especially in South Carolina, Georgia, and |

Louisiana. But cotton was the largest crop, the most widespread, and the force behind the South's hunger for new territory. Ambitious cotton growers poured into the West, pushing the Indians off their fabulously fertile Gulf lands and across the Appalachians (see Chapter 11). The boom in the cotton economy came in the 1830s in Alabama and Mississippi. But not until the 1850s did the wave of cotton expansion cross Louisiana and pour into Texas (see maps page 254). Migration into Texas was still strong in 1860.

Thus the Old South was not old at all; in 1860 it was still growing. For although prices plunged sharply at least once a decade after 1820, overall demand for cotton soared. Since English mills would buy virtually all the cotton a planter could grow, eager southerners bought more slaves and more land. Soon they were exporting more than three-quarters of their crop and supplying almost the same proportion of England's purchases. In just a few decades some of these planters amassed great personal fortunes and rose to an aristocratic position in society. Though some old Virginia and South Carolina families were represented among the proud new "cotton snobs," most of the wealthy were newly rich.

To the hard-working and lucky, riches came quickly. A good example is the family of Jefferson Davis. Like Abraham Lincoln, Davis was born in humble circumstances. His father was one of the

| Jefferson Davis: his early life | thousands of American farmers on the frontier who moved frequently, unwisely buying land |

when prices were high and selling when they were low, never making his fortune. Luckily for Davis, his older brother migrated to Mississippi and became successful. Settling on rich bottomlands next to the Mississippi River, Joseph Davis made profits, expanded his holdings of land and slaves, and made more profits. Soon he was an established figure in society, and he used his position to arrange an education at West Point for his younger brother. A large plantation awaited Jefferson's retirement from the army. Thus the Davis family became aristocrats in one generation.

A less fortunate consequence of the cotton boom was the relative indifference of farmers to the long-term fertility of the soil. In an expanding economy, with cheap and superior land available farther west, most people preferred to exhaust the land and move on rather than invest heavily in preserving it. Only in the older states of the upper South, where the major landholders stayed behind, and where the cotton boom had less impact, did serious interest in diversified farming develop.

An even more important consequence of the boom was thin population distribution. Producers spread

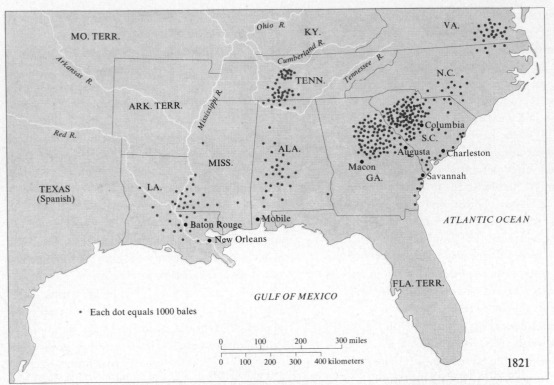

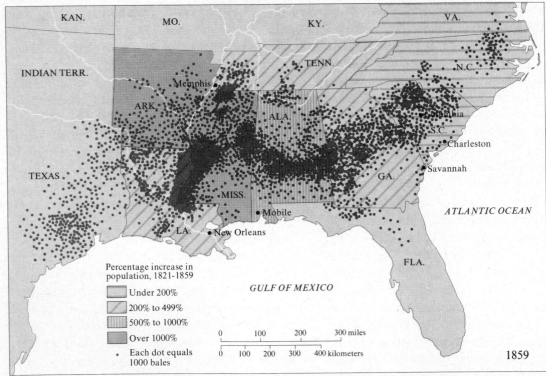

Cotton production in the South

Chapter 10: Slavery and the growth of the South, 1800–1860

Charleston, one of the South's larger cities, remained small compared to many urban centers in the industrializing North. Painted in 1831 by S. Barnard. The Yale University Art Gallery, Mabel Brady Garvan Collection.

out over as large an area as possible in order to maximize production and income. Because farms were far apart, southern society remained predominantly rural. Population density, low even in the older plantation states, was especially so in the frontier areas being brought under cultivation. In 1860 there were only 2.3 people per square mile in Texas, 15.6 in Louisiana, and 18.0 in Georgia. By contrast, population density in the nonslaveholding states east of the Mississippi River was almost three times higher. The northeast had an average of 65.4 persons per square mile, and in some places the density was much higher. Massachusetts had 153.1 people per square mile, and New York City, where overcrowding reached epic proportions, compressed 86,400 people into each square mile.

Even in the 1850s, much of the South seemed al-

Population distribution

most uninhabited, a virtual wilderness. Frederick Law Olmsted, a northerner who later became famous as a landscape architect, made several trips through the South in the 1850s as a reporter. He found that the few trains and stagecoaches available to travelers offered only rough accommodations and kept their schedules poorly. Indeed, he had to do most of his traveling on horseback along primitive trails. Passing from Columbus, Georgia, to Montgomery, Alabama, Olmsted observed "a hilly wilderness, with a few dreary villages, and many isolated cotton farms." Alabama was, of course, on the frontier in 1800, but Olmsted encountered the same conditions in parts of eastern Virginia: "For hours and hours one has to ride through the unlimited, continual, all-shadowing, all-embracing forest, following roads in the making of which no more labor has been given than was necessary to remove the timber which would obstruct the

The South remains rural

passage of wagons; and even for days and days he may sometimes travel and see never two dwellings of mankind within sight of each other."

Society in such rural areas was characterized by relatively weak institutions, for it takes people to create and support organized activity. Where the concentration of people was low, it was difficult to finance and operate schools, churches, libraries, or even hotels, restaurants, and other urban amenities. Southerners were strongly committed to their churches, and some believed in the importance of universities, but all such institutions were far less developed than those in the North.

The few southern cities were likewise smaller and less developed than those in the North. As exporters, southerners did not need large cities; a small group of merchants working in connection with northern brokers sufficed to ship their cotton overseas and to import necessary supplies and luxuries. As planters,

| Economic development |

southerners invested most of their capital in slaves; they had little money left to build factories—another source of urban growth. A few southerners did invest in iron or textiles on a small scale. But the largest southern industrial plants were cigar factories, where slaves finished tobacco products. As a result, in 1860 only 49,000 out of 704,000 South Carolinians lived in towns with 2,500 or more residents. Less than 3 percent of Mississippi's population lived in places of comparable size. In 1860 the population of Charleston was only 41,000, Richmond 38,000, and Mobile 29,000. New Orleans, by far the largest southern city, had only 169,000 residents.

Thus, although it was economically attuned to an international market, the South was only semi-developed in comparison with other sections of the country. Its people prospered, but neither as rapidly nor as independently as residents of the North. There commerce and industry brought unprecedented advances in productivity, widening the range of affordable goods and services and raising the average person's standard of living. In the South, change was quantitative rather than qualitative; farming techniques remained essentially the same. To prosper, southerners increased their acreage and hoped for continued high demand from foreign customers—decisions that worked to the ultimate disadvantage of the region.

The society that developed in this largely agrarian economy was a society of extremes. The social distance between a wealthy planter and a small slaveholder was as great as the distance between a slaveholder and a nonslaveholder (to say nothing of the distance between whites and slaves). And, contrary to popular belief, planters were neither the most numerous nor the most typical group. The typical white southerner was a yeoman farmer.

Yeoman farmers

More than two-thirds of white southern families owned no slaves. Some of them lived in towns and ran stores or businesses, but most were farmers who owned their own land and grew their own food. Independent and self-respecting, with a hearty share of frontier individualism, they settled the southern wilderness, first by herding livestock and then by planting crops.

Successive waves of these herdsmen and farmers moved down the southern Appalachians into the new regions of the Southwest following the War of 1812. The herdsmen grazed their cattle and pigs on the abundant natural vegetation in the woods. Before long, however, the next wave of settlers arrived and broke ground for crops. These yeomen farmers forced the herdsmen farther and farther west, and eventually across the Mississippi. Some yeomen acquired large tracts of level land and became wealthy planters. Others clung to the beautiful mountainous areas they loved, or pressed farther into the wilds because they "couldn't stand the sound of another man's axe." As they moved, they tended to stick to the climate and soils they knew best. Yeomen could not afford the richest bottomlands, which were swampy and required expensive draining, but they owned land almost everywhere else.

Observers sometimes concluded that these people were poor and idle, especially the herdsmen who sat on their cabin porches while their stock foraged in the woods. It would be more accurate to say that they were frontiersmen and farmers who did not manage to become rich. They worked hard, as farmers do everywhere, and enjoyed a folk culture based on fam-

Chapter 10: Slavery and the growth of the South, 1800–1860

Many southern yeomen led an almost frontier style of life, farming and raising livestock in sparsely populated areas.   Culver.

ily, church, and community. They spoke with a drawl and their inflections were reminiscent of their Scottish and Irish backgrounds. Once a year they flocked to religious revivals called protracted meetings or camp meetings, and in between they enjoyed house raisings, log rollings, corn shuckings, and the ancient Scottish habit of burning the woods (to remove underbrush or clear land). The men did most of the farming; though the women occasionally helped in the fields, they commonly spent their time preserving and preparing food, making clothes, blankets, and candles, and tending to household matters.

> *Folk culture of the yeoman*

Beyond these basic facts, historians know little about the yeomen. Because their means were modest, they did not generate the voluminous legal papers, such as contracts, wills, and inventories of estates, that document the activities of the rich. Only a few letters have found their way into libraries and archives. It is reasonable to suppose, though, that yeomen held a variety of opinions and pursued individual goals. Some envied the planters and strove to be rich; others were content with their independence, recreation, family life, and religion.

At the first extreme was a North Carolinian named John F. Flintoff, whose rare diary records the ambitions of a nonslaveholder who hungered to be rich. Flintoff was born in 1823 and at age eighteen went to Mississippi to seek his fortune. Like other aspiring yeomen, he worked as an overseer, but often found it impossible to please his employers. At one time he gave up and returned to North Carolina, where he married and lived in his parents' house. But Flintoff was "impatient to get along in the world," so he tried Louisiana next and then Mississippi again.

For Flintoff, the fertile Gulf region had its disadvantages. "My health has been very bad here," he noted; "chills and fever occasionally has hold of me."

Yeoman farmers

"First rate employment" alternated with "very low wages." Moreover, as a young man working on isolated plantations, Flintoff often felt "all alone." Even a revival meeting in 1844 proved "an extremely cold time" with "but little warm feeling." His uncle and other employers found fault with his work, and in 1846 Flintoff concluded in despair that "managing negroes and large farms is soul destroying."

Still, a desire to succeed kept him going. At twenty-six, before he owned a foot of land, Flintoff bought his first slave, "a negro boy 7 years old." Soon he had purchased two more children, the cheapest slaves available. Conscious of his status as a slaveowner, Flintoff resented the low wages he was paid and complained that his uncle offered him "*hand pay*," the wages of a day laborer rather than a slaveowner and manager. In 1853, with nine young slaves and a growing family, Flintoff faced "the most unhappy time of my life." He was fired by his uncle, "treated shamefully." Finally he said, "I will have to sell some of my negroes to buy land. This I must have. I want *a home*."

Returning to North Carolina, Flintoff purchased 124 acres with help from his in-laws. He grew corn, wheat, and tobacco and earned extra cash hauling wood in his wagon. By 1860 he owned 3 horses, 26 hogs, 10 cattle, and several slaves, and was paying off his debts. Eventually Flintoff owned 217 acres and became a fairly prosperous tobacco and grain farmer. He was able to send his sons to college, and prided himself that his wife "has lived a *Lady*." But the struggle upward had not been easy, and Flintoff never became the cotton planter he had aspired to be.

Probably more typical of the southern yeoman was Ferdinand L. Steel. As a young man Steel moved from North Carolina to Tennessee to work as a hatter and river boatman, but he eventually settled down to farming in Mississippi. He rose every day at five and worked until sundown. With the help of his family he raised corn, wheat, pork, and vegetables for the family table. Cotton was his cash crop: like other yeomen he sold five or six bales a year to obtain money for sugar, coffee, salt, calico, gunpowder, and a few other store-bought goods.

Steel picked his cotton himself (never exceeding 120 pounds per day—less than many slaves averaged) and regretted that cotton cultivation was so arduous and time-consuming. He was not tempted to grow more of it. The market fluctuated, and if cotton prices fell, a small grower like himself could be driven into debt and lose his farm. Steel, in fact, wanted to grow less cotton. "We are too weak handed" to manage it, he noted in his diary. "We had better raise small grain and corn and let cotton alone, raise corn and keep out of debt and we will have no necessity of raising cotton."

Steel's life in Mississippi in the 1840s retained much of the flavor of the frontier. He made all the family's shoes; his wife and sister sewed dresses, shirts, and "pantiloons." The Steels also rendered their own soap, spun and wove cotton into cloth, and hunted for game. House raisings and corn shuckings provided entertainment, and Steel doctored his illnesses with boneset tea and other herbs.

The focus of Steel's life was his family and his religion. The family prayed together every morning and night, and he prayed and studied Scripture for an hour after lunch. Steel joined a temperance society and looked forward to church and camp meetings. "My Faith increases, & I enjoy much of that peace which the world cannot give," he wrote in 1841. Seeking to improve himself and be "ready" for judgment, Steel borrowed histories, Latin and Greek grammars, and religious books from his church. Eventually he became a traveling Methodist minister. "My life is one of toil," he reflected, "but blessed be God that it is as well with me as it is."

Toil was also the lot of another group of free southerners: free blacks. In 1860 nearly a quarter million of them faced conditions that were worse than

| Free blacks |

the yeoman's, and often little better than the slave's. The free blacks of the upper South were descendants of men and women emancipated by their owners in the 1780s and 1790s, a period of post-Revolutionary idealism that coincided with a decline in tobacco prices. They had few material advantages; most did not own land and had to labor in someone else's field, frequently beside slaves. By law they could not own a gun or liquor, violate curfew, assemble except in church, testify in court, or (everywhere after 1835) vote. Despite these obstacles, a minority bought land, and others found jobs as artisans, draymen, boatmen, and fishermen. A few owned slaves, who were almost always their wives and children, purchased from bondage.

Chapter 10: Slavery and the growth of the South, 1800–1860

Farther south, in the cotton and Gulf regions, a large proportion of free blacks were mulattoes, the privileged offspring of wealthy planters. Some received good educations and financial backing from their fathers, who recognized a moral obligation to them. In a few cities such as New Orleans and Mobile, extensive interracial sex had produced a mulatto population that was recognized as a distinct class. Mulattoes formed a society of their own and sought a status above slaves and other freedmen, if not equal to planters. But outside New Orleans and Mobile such groups were rare, and most mulattoes encountered disadvantages more frequently than they enjoyed benefits from their light skin tone. (For a more detailed discussion of free blacks, see Chapter 11.)

Slaveholding planters

At the opposite end of the spectrum from free blacks were the slaveholders. As a group slaveowners lived well, on incomes that enabled them to enjoy superior housing, food, clothing, and luxuries. But most did not live on the opulent scale that legend suggests. A few statistics tell the story: 88 percent of southern slaveholders had fewer than twenty slaves; 72 percent had fewer than ten; 50 percent had fewer than five. Thus the average slaveholder was not a man of great wealth but an aspiring farmer. Nor was he a polished aristocrat, but more usually a person of humble origins, with little formal education and many rough edges to his manner. In fact, he probably had little beyond a degree of wealth and a growing ambition to distinguish him from a nonslaveholder.

Even wealthy slaveowners often lacked the refined manner of aristocrats. A Louisiana planter named Bennet Barrow, for example, was neither especially polished nor unusually coarse. Barrow's plantation lay in a wealthy parish in Louisiana, but his wealth was new and Barrow was preoccupied with money-making. He worried constantly over his cotton crop, filling his diary with tedious weather reports and gloomy predictions of his yields. Yet Barrow also strove to appear above such worries, and in boom times he grandly endorsed notes for men who left him saddled with debt.

Barrow hunted frequently, and he had a passion for racing horses and raising hounds. Each year he set aside several weeks to attend the races in New Orleans, where he entered stallions brought from as far away as Tennessee. Barrow could report the loss of a slave without feeling, but emotion shattered his laconic manner when misfortune struck his sporting animals. "Never was a person more unlucky than I am," he complained; "My favorite pup never lives." His strongest feelings surfaced when his horse Jos Bell—equal to "the best Horse in the South"—"broke down in running a mile . . . ruined for Ever." That same day the distraught Barrow gave his field hands a "general Whipping." Barrow was rich, but his wealth had not softened his rough, direct style of life.

The wealth of the greatest planters gave ambitious men like Barrow something to aspire to. If most planters lived in spacious, comfortable farmhouses, some did live in mansions. If most slaveowners sat down at mealtimes to an abundance of tempting country foods—pork and ham, beef and game, fresh vegetables and fruits, tasty breads and biscuits, cakes and jams—the sophisticated elite consumed such delights as "gumbo, ducks and olives, *supreme de volaille,* chickens in jelly, oysters, lettuce salad, chocolate cream, jelly cake, claret cup, etc." On formal and business occasions such as county court days, a traveler in Mississippi would see gentlemen decked out in "black cloth coats, black cravats and satin or embroidered silk waistcoats; all, too, sleek as if just from a barber's hands, and redolent of perfumes." The ladies wore the latest fashions to parties and balls.

Among the wealthiest and oldest families, a paternalistic ideology prevailed. Instead of stressing the acquisitive aspects of commercial agriculture, these people focused on *noblesse oblige.* They saw themselves as custodians of the welfare of society as a whole and of the black families who depended on them. The paternalistic planter saw himself not as an oppressor but as the benevolent guardian of an inferior race. He developed affectionate feelings toward his slaves (as long as they kept in their place) and was genuinely shocked at outside criticism of his behavior.

A few words from the letters of Paul Carrington Cameron, North Carolina's largest slaveholder, illustrate this mentality. After a period of sickness among

Southern paternalism

The North Carolina planter Duncan Cameron (1776–1853) built this spacious and comfortable farmhouse for his bride, Rebecca Bennehan, in 1804. The house, called Fairntosh, is more typical of the average planter's home than the elaborate Greek-revival-style mansions of popular legend. Courtesy of the North Carolina Division of Archives and History, Raleigh.

his approximately one thousand North Carolina slaves (he owned hundreds more in Alabama and Mississippi), Cameron wrote, "I fear the Negroes have suffered much from the want of proper attention and kindness under this late distemper . . . no love of lucre shall ever induce me to be cruel, or even to make or permit to be made any great exposure of their persons at inclement seasons." On another occasion he described to his sister the sense of responsibility he felt: "I cannot better follow the example of our venerated Mother than in doing my duty to her faithful old slaves and their desendants. Do you remember a cold & frosty morning, during her illness, when she said to me 'Paul my son the people ought to be shod' this is ever in my ears, whenever I see any ones shoes in bad order; and in my ears it will be, so long as I am master."

There is no doubt that the richest southern planters saw themselves in this way. It was comforting to do so, and slaves, accommodating themselves to the realities of power, encouraged their masters to think their benevolence was appreciated. Paternalism also provided a welcome defense against abolitionist criticism. Still, for most planters, paternalism affected the manner and not the substance of their behavior. It was a matter of style. Its softness and warmth covered harsher assumptions: Negroes were inferior; planters should make money.

Southern women and their servants, photographed in 1860. The Western Reserve Historical Society.

Even Paul Cameron's concern vanished with changed circumstances. Following the Civil War he bristled at their efforts to be free and made sweeping economic decisions without regard to their welfare. Writing on Christmas Day 1865, Cameron showed little Christian charity (but a healthy profit motive) when he expressed his desire to get "free . . . of the negro. I am convinced that the people who gets rid of the free negro first will be the first to advance in improved agriculture. Have made no effort to retain any of mine [and] will not attempt a crop beyond the capacity of 30 hands." With that he turned out nearly a thousand black agriculturalists, rented his lands to several white farmers, and invested in industry.

Relations between men and women in the planter class were similarly paternalistic. The southern woman was raised and educated to be a companion and helpmate to men. At an age when her brothers were studying science, law, or medicine, the wealthy young woman was expected to devote herself to drawing, music, literature, and social life. Her proper responsibility was home management. She was not to venture into politics and other worldly affairs. If she did, she met universal condemnation. Within the domestic circle, furthermore, the husband reigned supreme. "He is master of the house," wrote South Carolina diarist Mary Boykin Chesnut. "To hear is to obey . . . all the

Woman's role

comfort of my life depends upon his being in a good humor." In a darker mood Chesnut once observed that "there is no slave . . . like a wife." Unquestionably there were some, possibly many, close and satisfying relationships between men and women in the planter class. But it is clear that many women were oppressed.

Childbearing brought grief and sickness as well as joy to southern women. In 1840 the birthrate for southern women in their fertile years was almost 20 percent higher than the national average. At the beginning of the nineteenth century, the average southern woman could expect to bear eight children; by 1860 the figure had decreased only to six, and a miscarriage was likely among so many pregnancies. The high birthrate took a toll on women's health, for complications of childbirth were a major cause of death. Moreover, a mother had to endure the loss of many of the infants she bore. Infant mortality in the first year of life exceeded 10 percent. In the South in 1860 almost five out of ten children died before age five, and among all South Carolinians younger than twenty, fewer than four in ten survived to reach the 20-to-60-year-old category. For those women who wanted to plan their families, methods of contraception were not always reliable. And doctors had few remedies for infection or irritation of the reproductive tract.

Slavery was another source of trouble, a nasty sore that women sometimes had to bandage but were not supposed to notice. "Violations of the moral law . . . made mulattoes as common as blackberries," protested a woman in Georgia, but wives had to play "the ostrich game." "A magnate who runs a hideous black harem," wrote Mrs. Chesnut, "under the same roof with his lovely white wife, and his beautiful accomplished daughters . . . poses as the model of all human virtues to these poor women whom God and the laws have given him. From the height of his awful majesty, he scolds and thunders at them, as if he never did wrong in his life."

In the early 1800s, some southern women, especially Quakers, had spoken out against slavery. But in the 1840s and 1850s, as national and international criticism of slavery increased, southern men published a barrage of articles stressing that women should restrict their concerns to the home. A writer in the *Southern Literary Messenger* bemoaned "these days of Women's Rights." Perhaps in fear of women's politi-

cal opinions, the *Southern Quarterly Review* declared, "The proper place for a woman is at home. One of her highest privileges, to be politically merged in the existence of her husband." Thomas Dew, one of the nineteenth century's first proslavery theorists, advised that "women are precisely what the men make them," and another writer promoted "affection, reverence, and duty" as a woman's proper attitudes.

But southern women were beginning to chafe at their customary exclusion from financial matters. Education was another sore spot. Some of the most privileged women were acquiring a taste for knowledge, and schools for women were multiplying. These academies emphasized domestic skills, but their students nevertheless picked up some knowledge of the world's affairs that they were not, after graduation, permitted to use.

For another large category of southern men and women, education in any form was not allowed. Male or female, slaves were expected to accept ignorance as part of their condition.

Slaves and the conditions of their servitude

For Afro-Americans, slavery was a curse that brought no blessings other than the strengths they developed to survive it. Slaves knew a life of poverty, coercion, toil, heartbreak, and resentment. They had few hopes that were not denied; often they had to bear separation from their loved ones; and they were despised as an inferior race. That they endured and found loyalty and strength among themselves is a tribute to their courage, but it could not make up for a life without freedom or opportunity.

Southern slaves enjoyed few material comforts beyond the bare necessities. Their diet was plain and limited, though generally they had enough to eat. The basic ration was cornmeal, fat pork, molasses, and occasionally coffee. Many masters allowed slaves to tend gardens, which provided the variety and extra nutrition of greens and sweet potatoes. Fishing and hunting benefited some

Slave diet, clothing, and housing

Most slave families lived in crude and crowded quarters, but the five generations pictured here drew strength from their close family ties. Photographed in Beaufort, South Carolina, in 1862.   Library of Congress.

slaves. "It warn't nothin' fine," recalled one woman, "but it was good plain eatin' what filled you up." Most slaveowners were innocent of the charge that they starved their slaves, but there is considerable evidence that slaves often suffered the effects of beriberi, pellagra, and other dietary-deficiency diseases.

Clothing too was plain, coarse, and inexpensive. Children of both sexes ran naked in hot weather and wore long cotton shirts in cool. When they were big enough to go to the fields, the boys received a work shirt and a pair of britches and the girls a simple dress. On many plantations slave women made their own

clothing of cheap osnaburg, or "nigger cloth." Probably few received more than one or two changes of clothing for hot and cold seasons and one blanket each winter. Those who could earn a little money by doing extra work often bought additional clothing. Many slaves had to go without shoes until December, even as far north as Virginia. The shoes they received were frequent objects of complaint—uncomfortable brass-toed brogans or stiff wraparounds made from leather tanned on the plantation.

Summer and winter, slaves lived in small one-room cabins with a door and possibly a window opening, but no glass. Logs chinked with mud formed the walls, dirt was the only floor, and a wattle or stone chimney vented the fireplace that provided heat and light. Bedding consisted of straw, straw mattresses, or wooden bedframes lashed to the walls with rope. A few crude pieces of furniture and cooking utensils completed the furnishings of most cabins. More substantial houses survive today from some of the richer plantations, but the average slave lived in crude accommodations. The gravest drawback of slave cabins was not their appearance and lack of comfort but their unhealthfulness. In each small cabin lived one or two whole families. Crowding and lack of sanitation fostered the spread of infection and contagious diseases. Many slaves (and whites) carried worms and intestinal parasites picked up from fecal matter or the soil. Lice were widespread among both races, and flies and other insects spread such virulent diseases as typhoid fever, malaria, and dysentery.

Hard work was the central fact of the slaves' existence. Overseers rang the morning bell before dawn, so early that some slaves remembered being in the fields

| Slave work routines |

"before it was light enough to see clearly . . . holding their hoes and other implements—afraid to start work for fear that they would cover the cotton plants with dirt because they couldn't see clearly." And, as one woman testified, when interviewed by workers in the Federal Writers' Project of the 1930s, "it was way after sundown 'fore dey could stop dat field wuk. Den dey had to hustle to finish deir night wuk in time for supper, or go to bed widout it." Except on some rice plantations, where slaves were assigned daily tasks to complete at their own pace, working from "sun to sun" became universal in the South. These long hours and hard work were at the heart of the advantage of slave labor. As one planter put it, slaves were the best labor because "you could command them and *make* them do what was right." White workers, by contrast, were few and couldn't be *driven;* "they wouldn't stand it."

Planters aimed to keep all their laborers busy all the time. Slave women did heavy field work, often as much as the men and even during pregnancy. Old people—of whom there were few—were kept busy caring for young children, doing light chores, or carding, ginning, or spinning cotton. Children had to gather

kindling for the fire, carry water to the fields, or sweep the yard. But slaves had a variety of ways to keep from being worked to death. It was impossible for the master to supervise every slave every minute, and slaves slacked off when they were not being watched. Thus travelers frequently described lackadaisical slaves who seemed "to go through the motions of labor without putting strength into them," and owners complained that slaves "never would lay out their strength freely . . . it was impossible to make them do it." Stubborn misunderstanding and literal-mindedness was another defense. One exasperated Virginia planter exclaimed, "You can make a nigger work, *but you cannot make him think.*"

Of course the slave could not cheat too much, because the owner enjoyed a monopoly on force and violence. Whites throughout the South believed that

| Physical and mental abuse of slaves |

Negroes "can't be governed except with the whip." One South Carolinian frankly explained to a northern journalist that he had whipped his slaves occasionally, "say once a fortnight; . . . the Negroes knew they would be whipped if they didn't behave themselves, and the fear of the lash kept them in good order." Evidence suggests that whippings were less frequent on small farms than on large plantations, but the reports of former slaves show that a large majority even of small farmers plied the lash. These beatings symbolized authority to the master and tyranny to the slaves, who made them a benchmark for evaluating a master. In the words of former slaves, a good owner was one who did not "whip too much," whereas a bad owner "whipped till he'd bloodied you and blistered you."

As this testimony suggests, terrible abuses could and did occur. The master wielded virtually absolute authority on his plantation; courts did not recognize the word of chattel, and southern society was slow to put pressure on all but the most debased and vicious slaveowners. One slave told of a sadistic owner who several times opened a jug of whiskey, tied up some slaves, and staged a "whippin' frolic" that lasted for hours. Other owners refined the cruelty of whipping by cutting open the blisters on a slave's back and dripping sealing wax into them, or throwing salt or pepper water onto the sores. Sometimes, pregnant women received terrible lashings after their master

Chapter 10: Slavery and the growth of the South, 1800–1860

In some parts of the South slaves and even free blacks had to wear demeaning identification tags like these, issued in Charleston. The Charleston Museum.

had dug a hole in the ground in which to lay their bellies. There were burnings, mutilations, tortures, and murders.

Slavery in the United States was physically cruel, but less so than elsewhere in the New World. In some parts of the Western Hemisphere in the 1800s, slaves were regarded as an expendable resource and scheduled for replacement after seven years. Treatment was so poor and families so uncommon that death rates were high and the heavily male slave population did not replace itself, and rapidly shrank in size. In the United States, by contrast, the slave population showed a steady natural increase, births exceeded deaths, and each generation grew larger.

The worst evil of American slavery was not its physical cruelty but the fact of slavery itself: coercion, loss of freedom, belonging to another person. Recalling their days in bondage, some former slaves emphasized the physical abuse—those were "bullwhip days"

to one woman; another said, "W'at I t'ink 'bout slabery? Huh—nigger get back cut in slabery time, enty [didn't he]?" But their comments focused on the tyranny of whipping as much as the pain. A woman named Delia Garlic cut to the core when she said, "It's bad to belong to folks dat own you soul an' body. I could tell you 'bout it all day, but even den you couldn't guess de awfulness of it." And a man named Thomas Lewis put it this way: "There was no such thing as being good to slaves. Many people were better than others, but a slave belonged to his master and there was no way to get out of it."

As these comments show, American slaves retained their mental independence and self-respect despite their bondage. They hated their oppression, and contrary to some whites' perceptions, they were not grateful to their oppressors. Although they had to be subservient and speak honeyed words in the presence of their masters, they talked quite differently later on among themselves. The evidence of their resistant attitudes comes from their actions and from their own life stories.

Former slaves reported some kind feelings between masters and slaves, but the overwhelming picture was one of antagonism and resistance. Slaves mistrusted kindness from whites and suspected self-interest in their owners. A woman whose mistress "was good to us Niggers" said her owner was kind " 'cause she was raisin' us to wuk for her." A man recalled that his owners "allus thunk lots of their niggers and Grandma Maria say, 'Why shouldn't they—it was their money.' " Christmas presents of clothing from the master did not mean anything, observed another, " 'cause he goin' to [buy] that anyhow."

| Slaves' attitudes toward whites |

Slaves also saw their owners as people who used human beings as beasts of burden. "Massa was purty good," said one man. "He treated us jus' 'bout like you would a good mule." Another said that his master "fed us reg'lar on good, 'stantial food, jus' like you'd tend to you hoss, if you had a real good one." A third recalled his master saying, " 'A well-fed, healthy nigger, next to a mule, is de bes' propersition a man kin' ves' his money in.' "

Slaves were sensitive to the thousand daily signs of their degraded status. One man recalled the general rule that slaves ate cornbread and owners ate biscuits. If blacks did get biscuits, "de flour dat we made de biscuits out of wus de third-grade shorts." A woman reported that on her plantation "Ol' Marster hunted a heap, but us never did get none of what he brought in." "Us cotch lots of 'possums, but mighty few of 'em us Niggers ever got a chance to eat or rabbits neither," said another. "Dey made Niggers go out and hunt 'em and de white folks et 'em." If the owner took slaves' garden produce to town and sold it for them, the slaves suspected him of pocketing part of the profits.

Suspicion and resentment often grew into hatred. According to a former slave from Virginia, "the white folks treated the nigger so mean that all the slaves prayed God to punish their cruel masters." When a yellow fever epidemic struck in 1852, many slaves saw it as God's retribution. As late as the 1930s an elderly woman named Minnie Fulkes cherished the conviction that God was going to punish white people for their cruelty to blacks. She described the whippings that her mother had had to endure and then exclaimed, "Lord, Lord, I hate white people and de flood waters gwine drown some mo." A young slave girl who had suffered abuse as a house servant admitted that she took cruel advantage of her mistress when the woman had a stroke. Instead of fanning the mistress to keep flies away, the young slave struck her in the face with the fan whenever they were alone. "I done that woman bad," the slave confessed, but "she was so mean to me."

The bitterness between blacks and whites was vividly expressed by a former slave named Savilla Burrell, who visited her former master on his deathbed long after the Civil War. Sitting beside him, she reflected on the lines that "sorrow had plowed on dat old face and I 'membered he'd been a captain on hoss back in dat war. It come into my 'membrance de song of Moses: 'de Lord had triumphed glorily and de hoss and his rider have been throwed into de sea.' " She felt sympathy for a dying man, but she also felt satisfaction at God's revenge.

On the plantation, of course, slaves had to keep such thoughts to themselves. Often they expressed one feeling to whites, another to their own race. When one mistress died, "all the slaves come in the house just a hollering and crying and holding their hands over their eyes, just hollering for all they could. Soon as they got outside of the house they would say, 'Old Goddamn son-of-a-bitch, she gone on down to hell.' " A young girl who appeared overcome with tears of emotion when her newly married young mistress chose her as a servant was in reality only glad her new owner "didn't beat." And filing solemnly by the coffin of her cruel and much-hated master, one girl recounted, "I jist happened to look up and caught my sister's eye and we both jist natchelly laughed—Why shouldn't we? We was glad he was dead."

Slave culture and everyday life

The force that helped slaves to maintain such defiance was their culture. They had their own view of the world, a body of beliefs and values born of both their past and their present, as well as the fellowship

The Old Plantation. Slaves do the Juba, a dance of Yoruba origin, to the music of a stringed *molo* and a *gudugudu* (drum). The women's colorful headscarves recall African styles and customs, as does the man's use of a cane in his dance. Drawn in the late eighteenth century on a plantation between Charleston and Orangeburg.   The Abby Aldridge Rockefeller Folk Art Center, Williamsburg, Virginia.

and support of their own community. With power overwhelmingly in the hands of whites, it was not possible for slaves to change their world. But drawing strength from their culture, they could refuse to accept their condition or to give up the struggle against it.

Slave culture changed significantly after the turn of the century. Between 1790 and 1808, when Congress banned further importation of slaves, there was a rush to import Africans. After that the proportion of native-born blacks rose steadily, reaching 96 percent in 1840 and almost 100 percent in 1860. (For this reason blacks can trace their American ancestry back further than many white Americans.) Meanwhile, more and more slaves adopted Christianity. With time the old African culture faded further into memory, though it

did not disappear. Differences among slaves from various tribes became less noticeable. An Afro-American culture was emerging.

In many ways African influences remained primary. For African practices and beliefs reminded the slaves that they were and ought to be different from their oppressors, and thus encouraged them to resist. The most visible aspects of African culture were the slaves' dress and recreation. Some slave men plaited their hair into rows and fancy designs; slave women often wore their hair "in string"—tied in small bunches with a string or piece of cloth. A few men and many women wrapped their heads in kerchiefs following the styles and colors of West Africa.

Remnants of African culture

For entertainment slaves made musical instruments with carved motifs that resembled some African stringed instruments. Their drumming and dancing clearly followed African patterns; whites marveled at them. One visitor to Georgia in the 1860s described a ritual dance of African origin: "A ring of singers is formed . . . and they . . . walk slowly around and around in a circle. . . . They then utter a kind of melodious chant, which gradually increases in strength, and in noise, until it fairly shakes the house, and it can be heard for a long distance. This chant is responded to at intervals. . . . The dancers usually bend their bodies into an angle of about forty-five degrees, and thus bent, march around, accompanying their steps, every second or so, with a quick, jerking motion, or jump, which I can compare to nothing else than the brisk jumping of a frog. . . . The songs are . . . handed down by tradition from their ancestors."

Many slaves continued to see and believe in spirits. Some whites believed in ghosts, but the belief was more widespread among slaves. It closely resembled the African concept of the living dead—the idea that deceased relatives visited the earth for many years until the process of dying was complete. Slaves also practiced conjuration, voodoo, and quasi-magical root medicine. By 1860 the most notable conjurers and root doctors were reputed to live in South Carolina, Georgia, Louisiana, and other isolated coastal areas of heavy slave importation.

These cultural survivals provided slaves with a sense of their separate past. Black achievement in music and dance was so exceptional that whites felt entirely cut off from it; in this one area some whites became aware that they stood completely outside the slave community. Conjuration and folklore also directly fed resistance; slaves could cast a spell or direct the power of a hand (a bag of articles belonging to the person to be conjured) against the master. Not all masters felt confident enough to dismiss such a a threat.

In adopting Christianity, slaves fashioned it too into an instrument of support and resistance. Theirs was a religion of justice quite unlike that of the propa-

Slave religion | ganda their masters pushed at them. Former slaves scorned the preaching arranged by their masters. "You ought to heared that preachin'," said one man. " 'Obey your massa and missy, don't steal chickens and eggs and meat,' but nary a word 'bout havin' a soul to save." To the slaves, Jesus cared about their souls and their present plight. They rejected the idea that in heaven whites would have "de colored folks . . . dar to wait on em." Instead, when God's justice came, the slaveholders would be "brillin' in hell fur dey sin." "God is punishin' some of dem ol' suckers an' their chillun right now fer de way dey use to treat us poor colored folks," said one woman.

For slaves Christianity was a religion of personal and group salvation. Devout men and women worshipped and prayed every day, "in de field or by de side of de road," or in special "prayer grounds" such as a "twisted thick-rooted muscadine bush" that afforded privacy. Beyond seeking personal guidance, these worshippers prayed "for deliverance of de slaves." Some waited "until the overseer got behind a hill" and then laid down their hoes and called on God to free them. Others held fervent secret prayer meetings that lasted far into the night. From such activities many slaves gained the unshakeable belief that God would end their bondage. As one man asserted, "hit was de plans of God to free us niggers." This faith and the joy and emotional release that accompanied their worship sustained blacks.

Slaves also developed a sense of racial identity. The whole experience of southern blacks taught them that whites despised their race. White people, as one exslave put it, "have been and are now and always will be against the Negro." Even "the best white woman that ever broke bread wasn't much," said another, " 'cause they all hated the po' nigger." Blacks naturally drew together, helping each other in danger, need, and resistance. "We never tole on each other," one woman declared. Former slaves were virtually unanimous in denouncing those who betrayed the group or sought personal advantage through allegiance to whites.

Of course, different jobs and circumstances created natural variations in attitude among slaves. But for most slaves, there was no overriding class system within the black community. Only one-quarter of all slaves lived on plantations of fifty blacks or more, so few knew a wide chasm between exalted house servants and lowly field hands. In fact, many slaves did both housework and field work, depending on their age and the season. Their primary loyalty was to each other.

Arise! Arise! and weep no more dry up your tears, we shall part no more. Come rose we go to Tennessee, that happy shore To old virginia never — never — return.

Hundreds of thousands of slaves were forced to move west as the South expanded. Almost always they traveled on foot, either with their masters or as shown here, under the supervision of slave traders.   The Virginia State Library, Richmond.

The main source of support was the family. Slave families faced severe dangers. At any moment the master could sell a husband or wife, give a slave child away as a wedding present, or die in debt, forcing a division of his property. Many families were broken in such ways. Others were uprooted in the trans-Appalachian expansion of the South, which caused a large interregional movement of the black population. Between 1810 and 1820 alone, 137,000 slaves were forced to move from North Carolina and the Chesapeake states to Alabama, Mississippi, and other western regions. An estimated 2 million persons were sold between 1820 and 1860. When the Union Army registered thousands of black marriages in Mississippi and Louisiana in 1864 and 1865, 25 percent of the men over forty reported that they had been forcibly separated from a previous wife. A similar proportion of former slaves later recalled that slavery had de-

Slave family life

stroyed one of their marriages. Probably a substantial minority of slave families suffered disruption of one kind or another.

But this did not mean that slave families could not exist. American slaves clung tenaciously to the personal relationships that gave meaning to life. For although American law did not protect slave families, masters permitted them. In fact, slave owners expected slaves to form families and have children. As a result, even along the rapidly expanding edge of the cotton kingdom, where the effects of the slave trade would have been most visible, there remained a normal ratio of men to women, young to old.

Following African kinship taboos, Afro-Americans avoided marriage among cousins (a frequent occurrence among aristocratic slaveowners). Adapting to the circumstances of their captivity, they did not condemn unwed mothers, although they did expect a young girl to form a stable marriage after one preg-

Chapter 10: Slavery and the growth of the South, 1800–1860

These examples of slave craftsmanship show some African influences, as well as the painstaking skill invested in the manufacture of even the most common objects. Left to right: a diamond-pattern quilt; a hand-carved cane with African motifs; and hand-made egg and vegetable baskets. Cane from the National Gallery of Art, Washington, D.C., Index of American Design. Quilt and baskets from the Old Slave Mart.

Slave culture and everyday life

nancy, if not before. By naming their children after relatives of past generations, Afro-Americans emphasized their family histories. If they chose to bear the surname of a white slaveowner, it was often not their current master's but that of the owner under whom their family had begun.

Slaves abhorred interference in their family lives. Some of their strongest protests sought to prevent the break-up of a family. Indeed, some individuals refused to accept such separations and struggled for years to maintain or re-establish contact. Rape was a horror for both men and women. Some husbands faced death rather than permit their wives to be sexually abused; and women sometimes fought back. In other cases slaves seethed with anger at the injustice but could do nothing except to soothe each other with human sympathy and understanding. Significantly, blacks condemned the guilty party, not the victim.

Because of the pressures of bondage, black couples had more equal relationships than their white owners. Each member of the immediate family, as well as grandparents, uncles, and aunts, had to take on extra duties as the need arose; thus there was no opportunity to restrict women to narrow responsibilities. Women often worked in the fields with men, but they still cooked the meals and performed traditional household chores. The men cared for the livestock in the evening or fished and hunted on the weekends. Female house servants attained a high level of skill in sewing, weaving, embroidery, and cooking, but only on the largest plantations did male slaves have the chance to develop skill in a craft. Even so, the slave husband and father held a respected place in his home. And though the marriage ceremony consisted only of jumping over a broomstick, partners "stuck lots closer den," in one woman's words. "[When] they married they stayed married," said another. When husbands and wives lived on neighboring plantations, visits on Wednesday and Saturday nights included big dinners of welcome and celebration. Christmas was a similarly joyous time " 'cause husbands is comin' home an' families is gittin' 'nited again."

Slaves brought to their efforts at resistance the same common sense, determination, and practicality that characterized their family lives. American slavery produced some fearless and implacable revolutionaries. Gabriel's conspiracy apparently was known to more

than a thousand slaves when it was discovered in 1800, just before it was put into motion (see Chapter 7). A similar conspiracy in Charleston in 1822, headed by a free black named Denmark Vesey, involved many of the most trusted slaves of leading families. But the most famous rebel of all, Nat Turner, rose in violence in Southampton County, Virginia, in 1831.

The son of an African woman who passionately hated her enslavement, Nat was a precocious child who learned to read very young. Encouraged by his first owner to study the Bible, he enjoyed some special privileges but also knew changes of masters and hard work. His father, who successfully ran away to freedom, stood always before him as an example of defiance. In time young Nat became a preacher, an impressive orator with a reputation among whites as well as blacks. He also developed a tendency toward mysticism, and he became increasingly withdrawn. After nurturing his plan for several years, Turner led a band of rebels from house to house in the predawn darkness of August 22, 1831. The group severed limbs and crushed skulls with axes or killed their victims with guns. Before they were stopped, Nat Turner and his followers had slaughtered sixty whites of both sexes and all ages. Nat and as many as two hundred blacks lost their lives as a result of the rebellion.

But most slave resistance was not violent, for the odds against revolution were especially poor in North America. The South had the highest ratio of whites to blacks in the hemisphere; at the same time plantations were relatively small, which meant that whites had ample opportunity to supervise the slaves' activities. There was thus literal truth to one slave's remark that "the white man was the slave's jail." Moreover, the South lacked vital geographic and demographic features that had aided revolution elsewhere. The land offered relatively few jungles and mountain fastnesses to which rebels could flee. And compared to South America, southern slave importations were neither large nor prolonged. The South therefore lacked a preponderance of young male slaves. Nor were its military forces weak and overtaxed, like those of many South American colonies.

Thus the scales weighed heavily against revolution, and the slaves knew it. Consequently they directed

Chapter 10: Slavery and the growth of the South, 1800–1860

The most famous of all slave rebels, Nat Turner, led an uprising that took the lives of sixty whites and spread fear throughout the South.   Library of Congress.

their energies toward improving their lot as slaves. A desperate slave could run away for good, but as often or probably more often slaves simply ran off temporarily to hide in the woods. There they were close to friends and allies who could help them escape capture in an area they knew well. Every day that a slave "lay out" in this way the master lost a day's labor. Most owners chose not to mount an exhaustive search and sent word instead that the slave's grievances would be redressed. The runaway would then return to bargain with the master. Most owners would let the matter pass, for, like the owner of a valuable cook, they were "glad to get her back."

Other modes of resistance had the same object: to better the conditions of slavery. Appropriating food (stealing, in the master's eyes) was so common that even whites sang humorous songs about it. Blacks were also alert to the attitudes of individual whites, and learned to ingratiate themselves or play off one white person against another. Field hands frequently tested a new overseer to intimidate him or win more favorable working conditions. Other blacks fought with patrollers. Some slaves engaged in verbal arguments and even physical violence to deter or resist beatings. The harshest masters were the most strongly resisted. "Good masters had good slaves 'cause they treated 'em good," but "whar the ole master was mean an' ornery," his slaves were ornery too.

Harmony and tension in a slave society

Not only for blacks but for whites too, slave labor stood at the heart of the South's social system. A host of consequences flowed from its existence, from the organization of society to an individual's personal values.

For blacks, the nineteenth century brought a strengthening and expansion of the legal restrictions of slavery. In all things, from their workaday movements to Sunday worship, slaves fell under the supervision of whites. Courts held that a slave "has no civil right" and could not even hold property "except at the will and pleasure of his master." When slaves revolted, legislators tightened the legal straitjacket: after the Nat Turner insurrection in 1832, for example, they prohibited owners from teaching their slaves to read.

The weight of this legal and social framework fell on nonblacks as well. All white male citizens bore an obligation to ride in patrols to discourage slave movements at night. Whites in strategic positions, such as ship captains and harbor masters, were required to scrutinize the papers of blacks who might be attempting to escape bondage. White southerners who criticized the slave system out of moral conviction or class resentment were intimidated, attacked, or legally prosecuted. (Some, like James Birney, went north to join the antislavery movement.) Urban residents who did not supervise their domestic slaves as closely as planters found themselves subject to criticism. And the South's few manufacturers felt pressure to use slave rather than free labor.

Small wonder, for slavery was the main determinant of wealth in the South. Ownership of slaves guaranteed the labor to produce cotton and other crops on a large scale—labor otherwise unavailable in a rural society. Slaves were therefore vital to the acquisition of a fortune. Beyond that, slaves were a commodity and an investment, much like gold; people bought them on speculation, hoping for a steady rise in their value. In fact, for southern society as a whole, slaves equaled wealth almost completely. Important economic enterprises not based on slavery were so rare that the correspondence between geographic variations in wealth and variations in slaveholding was nearly one-to-one.

Slavery as the basis of wealth and social standing

It was therefore natural that slaveholding should be the main determinant of a person's social position. Wealth in slaves was the foundation on which the ambitious built their reputations. Ownership of slaves also brought political power: a solid majority of political officeholders were slaveholders, and the most powerful of them were generally large slaveholders. Though lawyers and newspaper editors were sometimes influential, they did not hold independent positions in the economy or society. Dependent on the planters for business and support, they served planters' interests and reflected their outlook.

As slavery became entrenched, its influence spread throughout the social system until even the values and mores of nonslaveholders bore its imprint. For one thing, the availability of slave labor tended to devalue free labor. Where strenuous work under another was reserved for an enslaved race, few free people relished working "like a nigger." Nonslaveholders therefore preferred to work for themselves rather than to hire out. This kind of thinking engendered an aristocratic value system ill-suited to a newly established democracy.

In modified form, the attitudes characteristic of the planter elite gained a considerable foothold among the masses. The ideal of the aristocrat emphasized lineage, privilege, power, pride, and refinement of person and manner. Some of those qualities were necessarily in short supply in an expanding economy, however; they mingled with and were modified by the tradition of the frontier. In particular, masculinity and defense of one's honor were highly valued by planter and frontier farmer alike.

Aristocratic values and frontier individualism

Fights and even duels over personal slights were not uncommon in southern communities. This custom sprang from both frontier lawlessness and aristocratic tradition. Throughout the sparsely settled regions of America in the early nineteenth century, pugnacious people took the law into their own hands. Thus it was not unusual for a southern slaveowner who had warned patrollers to stay off his property to shoot at the next group of trespassers. But instead of gradually disappearing, as it did in the North, the

Chapter 10: Slavery and the growth of the South, 1800–1860

code duello, which required men to defend their honor through the rituals of a duel, hung on in the South and gained an acceptance that spread throughout the society.

An incident that occurred in North Carolina in 1851 will illustrate. There a wealthy planter named Samuel Fleming responded to a series of disputes with the rising lawyer William Waightstill Avery by cowhiding him on a public street. According to the code, Avery had two choices: to redeem his honor through violence or to brand himself a coward through inaction. Three weeks later Avery shot Fleming dead at point-blank range during a session of Burke County Superior Court, with Judge William Battle and numerous spectators looking on. A jury took just ten minutes to find Avery not guilty, and the spectators gave him a standing ovation. Some people, including Judge Battle, were troubled by the victory of the unwritten code over the law, but most white males seemed satisfied.

Other aristocratic values that marked the planters as a class were less acceptable to the average citizen. Simply put, planters believed they were better than other people. In their pride, they expected not only to wield power but to receive special treatment. By the 1850s, some planters openly rejected the democratic creed, vilifying Jefferson for his statement that all men were equal.

These ideas, which shaped the outlook of the southern elite for generations, were inappropriate to a democratic political system. Throughout America democratic ideals were gaining strength; even in the South the majority of voters rejected the principle of the superiority of a few. Thus there were frequent conflicts between aristocratic pretensions and democratic zeal. As Mary Boykin Chesnut pointed out, a wealthy planter who sought public office could not announce his status too haughtily. She described the plight of Colonel John S. Preston, a South Carolinian with great ambitions. Preston, a perfect aristocrat, carried his high-flown manners too far; he refused to make the necessary gestures of respect toward the average voter—mingling with the crowd, exchanging jokes and compliments. Thus his highest aspiration, political leadership, could never be fulfilled. The voters would not accept him.

Such tensions found significant expression in the western parts of the seaboard states during the 1820s and 1830s. There yeomen farmers and citizens resented their underrepresentation in state legislatures,

| Democratic reform movements |

corruption in government, and undemocratic control over local government. After vigorous debate, the reformers won most of their battles. Five states—Alabama, Mississippi, Tennessee, Arkansas, and Texas—adopted what was for that time a thoroughly democratic system: popular election of governors; white manhood suffrage; legislative apportionment based on the white population; and locally chosen county government. Georgia, Florida, and Louisiana were not far behind, and reformers won significant concessions in North Carolina and Maryland. Kentucky was democratically governed except in its counties. Only South Carolina and Virginia effectively defended property qualifications for office, legislative malapportionment, appointment of county officials, and selection of the governor by the lawmakers. Democracy had expanded with the cotton kingdom.

Even in Virginia, nonslaveholding westerners raised a basic challenge to the slave system. Following the Nat Turner rebellion, advocates of gradual abolition forced a two-week legislative debate on slavery, arguing that it was injurious to the state and inherently dangerous. When the House of Delegates finally voted, the motion favoring abolition lost by just 73 to 58. This was the last major debate on slavery in the antebellum South.

With such tensions in evidence, it was perhaps remarkable that slaveholders and nonslaveholders did not experience frequent and serious conflict. Why were class confrontations among whites so infrequent? Historians who have considered this question have given many answers. In a rural society, family bonds and kinship ties are valued, and some of the poor nonslaveholding whites were related to the rich new planters. The experience of frontier living must also have created a relatively informal, egalitarian atmosphere. And there is no doubt that the South's racial ideology, which stressed whites' superiority to blacks and race, not class, as the social dividing line, tended to reduce conflict among whites.

Finally, it is important to remember that the South was a new and mobile society. Many people had risen in status, and far more were moving away geographically. Yeomen often moved several times during a lifetime of farming, and many slaveowners did too. Even in cotton-rich Alabama in the 1850s, fewer than half the richest families in a county belonged to its elite category ten years later. Most had not died or lost their wealth; they had merely moved on to some new state. This constant mobility meant that southern society had not settled into a rigid, unchanging pattern.

But two other factors, social and economic, were probably more important. First, the South was rural and uncrowded. Travel was difficult, and people stayed much to themselves. Consequently slaveowners and nonslaveowners rarely collided. Where there is little contact, there can be little conflict. Second, the two groups were economically independent. The yeomen farmed for themselves; planters farmed for themselves and for the market. The complementary growing patterns of corn and cotton allowed planters to raise food for their animals and laborers without lowering cotton production: from spring through December, cotton and corn needed attention alternately, but never at the same time. Thus the planter did not need to depend on the nonslaveholder, and yeomen needed nothing from the planters.

There were signs, however, that the relative lack of conflict between slaveholders and nonslaveholders was coming to an end. As the region grew older, nonslaveholders saw their opportunities beginning to narrow; meanwhile wealthy planters enjoyed an expanding horizon. In effect, the risk involved in substantial cotton production was becoming too great for most nonslaveholders. Thus from 1830 to 1860 the percentage of white southern families holding slaves declined steadily from 36 percent to 25 percent. At the same time, the monetary gap between the classes was widening. Though nonslaveholders were becoming more prosperous, slaveowners' wealth was increasing much faster. And though slaveowners made up a smaller portion of the population in 1860, their share of the South's agricultural wealth remained between 90 and 95 percent. In fact, the average slaveholder was almost 14 times as rich as the average nonslaveholder.

Pre-Civil War politics reflected these realities. Facing the prospect of a war to defend slavery, slave-

Hardening of class lines

owners expressed growing fear for the loyalty of nonslaveholders and discussed schemes to widen slave ownership. In North Carolina, a prolonged and increasingly bitter controversy over the combination of high taxes on land and low taxes on slaves erupted under the influence of a class-conscious nonslaveholder named Hinton R. Helper. Convinced that slavery had impoverished many whites and retarded the whole region, Helper attacked the institution in his book *The Impending Crisis,* published in New York in 1857. Discerning planters knew that such fiery controversies lay close at hand in every southern state.

But for the moment slaveowners stood secure. They held from 50 to 85 percent of the seats in state legislatures and a similarly high percentage of the South's congressional seats. In addition to their near-monopoly on political office, they had established their point of view in all the other major social institutions. Professors who criticized slavery had been dismissed from colleges and universities; schoolbooks that contained "unsound" ideas had been replaced. And almost all the Methodist and Baptist clergy, some of whom had criticized slavery in the 1790s, had given up preaching against the institution. In fact, except for a few obscure persons of conscience, southern clergy had become the most vocal defenders of the institution. Society as southerners knew it seemed stable, if not unthreatened.

Elsewhere in the nation, however, society was anything but stable. Social diversity was becoming one of the major characteristics of northern society, and social conflict an increasingly common phenomenon.

Suggestions for further reading

Southern society

W. J. Cash, *The Mind of the South* (1941); Avery O. Craven, *The Growth of Southern Nationalism, 1848–1861* (1953); Clement Eaton, *Freedom of Thought in the Old South* (1940); Clement Eaton, *The Growth of Southern Civilization, 1790–1860* (1961); William W. Freehling, *Prelude to Civil War* (1965); W. Conard Gass, " 'The Misfortune of a High Minded and Honorable Gentleman': W. W. Avery and the Southern Code of Honor," *North Carolina Historical Review,* LVI (Summer 1979), 278–297; Eugene D. Genovese, *The*

World the Slaveholders Made (1964); Eugene D. Genovese, "Yeoman Farmers in a Slaveholders' Democracy," *Agricultural History,* 49 (April 1975), 331–342; William Sumner Jenkins, *Pro-Slavery Thought in the Old South* (1935); Robert McColley, *Slavery and Jeffersonian Virginia* (1964); Frederick Law Olmsted, *The Slave States,* ed. Harvey Wish (1959); Edward Phifer, "Slavery in Microcosm: Burke County, North Carolina," *The Journal of Southern History,* XXVIII (May 1962), 137–165; Charles S. Sydnor, *The Development of Southern Sectionalism, 1819–1848* (1948); Ralph A. Wooster, *The People in Power* (1969); Ralph A. Wooster, *Politicians, Planters, and Plain Folk* (1975); Gavin Wright, *The Political Economy of the Cotton South* (1978).

Slaveholders and nonslaveholders

Bennet H. Barrow, *Plantation Life in the Florida Parishes of Louisiana, as Reflected in the Diary of Bennet H. Barrow,* ed. Edwin Adams Davis (1943); Ira Berlin, *Slaves Without Masters* (1974); Mary Boykin Chesnut, *A Diary from Dixie,* ed. Ben Ames Williams (1949); William J. Cooper, *The South and the Politics of Slavery, 1828–1856* (1978); Everett Dick, *The Dixie Frontier* (1948); Clement Eaton, *The Mind of the Old South* (1967); Drew Faust, *A Sacred Circle: The Dilemma of the Intellectual in the Old South* (1977); John Hope Franklin, *The Militant South, 1800–1861* (1956); John Hope Franklin, *The Free Negro in North Carolina, 1790–1860* (1943); Luther P. Jackson, *Free Negro Labor and Property Holding in Virginia, 1830–1860* (1942); Frances Anne Kemble, *Journal of a Residence on a Georgian Plantation in 1838–1839* (1863); Donald G. Mathews, *Religion in the Old South* (1977); Robert Manson Myers, ed., *The Children of Pride* (1972); Frank L. Owsley, *Plain Folk of the Old South* (1949); Mary D. Robertson, ed., *Lucy Breckinridge of Grove*

Hill (1979); Anne Firor Scott, *The Southern Lady* (1970); J. Mills Thornton, III, *Politics and Power in a Slave Society* (1978).

Conditions of slavery

Kenneth F. Kiple and Virginia H. Kiple, "Black Tongue and Black Men," *The Journal of Southern History,* XLIII (August 1977), 411–428; Ronald L. Lewis, *Coal, Iron, and Slaves* (1979); Richard G. Lowe and Randolph B. Campbell, "The Slave Breeding Hypothesis," *The Journal of Southern History,* XLII (August 1976), 400–412; Leslie Howard Owens, *This Species of Property* (1976); Willie Lee Rose, ed., *A Documentary History of Slavery in North America* (1976); Todd L. Savitt, *Medicine and Slavery* (1978); Kenneth M. Stampp, *The Peculiar Institution* (1956); Robert S. Starobin, *Industrial Slavery in the Old South* (1970).

Slave culture and resistance

Herbert Aptheker, *American Negro Slave Revolts* (1943); John W. Blassingame, *The Slave Community* (1972); Judith Wragg Chase, *Afro-American Art and Craft* (1971); Jeffrey J. Crow, *The Black Experience in Revolutionary North Carolina* (1977); Dena J. Epstein, *Sinful Tunes and Spirituals* (1977); Paul D. Escott, *Slavery Remembered* (1979); Eric Foner, ed. *Nat Turner* (1971); Eugene D. Genovese, *From Rebellion to Revolution* (1979); Eugene D. Genovese, *Roll, Jordan, Roll* (1974); Herbert G. Gutman, *The Black Family in Slavery and Freedom, 1750–1925* (1976); Lawrence W. Levine, *Black Culture and Black Consciousness* (1977); Gerald W. Mullin, *Flight and Rebellion* (1972); Stephen B. Oates, *The Fires of Jubilee* (1975); Albert J. Raboteau, *Slave Religion* (1978); Robert S. Starobin, *Denmark Vesey* (1970); Peter H. Wood, *Black Majority* (1974).

11 ～
THE
AMERICAN
SCENE,
1800–1860

For twenty years Edwin Forrest and his English rival William Charles Macready had vied for the favor of American audiences. Literary and intellectual circles lionized Macready; artisans and mechanics preferred Forrest, an American who stressed his love of flag, country, and democracy. When the two actors appeared simultaneously in New York City in May 1849, posters went up challenging Macready:

WORKING MEN,
shall
AMERICANS OR ENGLISH RULE
in this city?

Macready's opening night was ruined by noise and a barrage of objects, including four chairs, thrown from the gallery. Later in his run a crowd gathered outside the theater, protesting Macready's appearance as a symbol of "English ARISTOCRATS!! and Foreign Rule!" Adding to the fray were Anglophobic Irish immigrants, recently escaped from the bootheel of English rule. As Macready left the theater under police protection, the mob surged. The militia, on guard to maintain order, fired above the heads of the crowd, missing the rioters but felling dozens of bystanders. Twenty-two people were killed, thirty-six injured.

This incident was an extreme version of the chaos typical of theaters. The Englishwoman Frances Trollope, in her *Domestic Manners of the Americans* (1832), described the audience at a Cincinnati theater: "The spitting was incessant," accompanied by "the mixed smell of onions and whiskey. . . . The noises, too, were perpetual, and of the most unpleasant kind." An 1830 theater poster forbade "personal altercations in any part of the house," "the uncourteous habit of throwing nut shells, apples, etc., into the Pit," and "clambering over the balustrade into the Boxes, either during or at the end of the Performance." Indeed, theater regularly evoked the strongest of passions among Americans. "When a patriotic fit seized them, and 'Yankee Doodle' was called for," Trollope observed, "every man seemed to think his reputation as a citizen depended on the noise he made."

That the theater could elicit such emotions, and that class, ethnic, and patriotic conflicts spilled into its arena, reflected its pre-eminent role in American life. Theater was an early development in the rise of mass popular culture in the United States. It was also a mirror of American social life. Like society itself, theater audiences were divided by occupation, wealth, status, sex, and race. On the floor of the theater were the benches of the pit, where the mass of mechanics and artisans sat. In the tiers of boxes beyond the pit were the most expensive seats, where merchants, professionals, and ladies gathered. The third tier of boxes was generally reserved for less respectable women—boarding-house keepers and other gainfully employed women. Above these boxes, farthest from the stage, was the gallery (balcony). If the theater permitted blacks, they sat in the gallery, along with prostitutes and those of the working class unable to afford a seat in the pit.

As the American scene changed, so did the theater. As cities and towns grew larger, they boasted more than one or two theaters, and different houses began to cater to different classes. In New York, the Park Theater enjoyed the patronage of the carriage trade, the Bowery drew the middle class, and the Chatham attacted workers. The opera house generally became the upper-class playhouse. Again, the theater mirrored society, for with the increasing pace of urbanization and industrialization, the gap between the classes yawned wider. It was economic hardship as much as patriotism that sent Edwin Forrest's admirers into the streets of New York in 1849. The theater was the stage for their much larger drama.

Indeed, as the United States grew, its society became at once more diverse and more turbulent. More and more people lived in cities, where poverty, overcrowding, and crime set them against each other. Opulent mansions existed within sight of notorious slums, and both wealth and poverty reached extremes unknown in traditional agrarian America.

Immigration further increased social diversity. Within large cities and in the countryside, whole districts became European enclaves. The immigrants helped to build transportation and industry, in the process reshaping American culture.

The position of free blacks and Indians within this society was uncertain. Their very presence disturbed many Americans. Free people of color were second-class citizens at best, struggling to better their lot against overwhelming legal and racial barriers. Eastern Indians, forced to abandon their lands for resettlement beyond the Mississippi River, fared no better.

Private life changed too during these years. With increasing industrialization, the home began to lose its

A performance of an English farce at the fashionable Park Street Theatre in 1822. Faces in the audience are portraits of upper-class New Yorkers known to the artist, John Searle. The New-York Historical Society.

function as a workplace. Especially among the middle and upper classes, it became woman's domain, a refuge from the jungle of a man's world. At the same time birth control was more widely practiced and families became smaller.

To a great degree, many Americans were uncomfortable with the new direction of American life. Antipathy toward immigrants was common among native-born Americans, who feared competition for jobs. Blacks fought unceasingly for equality, and Indians tried unsuccessfully to resist forced removal. And some women began to raise their voices against the restrictions they faced. In a diverse and complex society, conflict became common.

Country life, city life

Surprisingly, it was the isolated pioneer—the frontier hunter, the fur trapper, the lonesome farm family—who came to symbolize the United States in the decades before the Civil War. These were the legendary Americans, as Frances Trollope observed, who were as independent as Robinson Crusoe. In the late 1820s Mrs. Trollope visited a self-sufficient farm family living near Cincinnati. The family grew or produced all their necessities except for coffee, tea, and whiskey, which they got by sending butter or chickens to market. But until other settlers came to live near them, they lacked the human contact that a community offered. For their inexpensive land and self-sufficiency they paid the price of isolation and loneliness. " 'Tis strange to us to see company," lamented the mother. "I expect the sun may rise and set a hundred times before I shall see another *human* that does not belong to the family."

It was, however, the farm community rather than the isolated family that dominated rural America. The farm village was the center of rural life—the farmers'

| Farm communities |

link with religion, politics, and the outside world. But rural social life was not limited to trips to the village; families gathered on each other's farms to do as a community what they could not do individually. Barn-raising was among the activities that regularly brought people together. In preparation for the event, the farmer and an itinerant carpenter built a platform and cut beams, posts, and joists. When the neighbors arrived by buggy and wagon, they put together the sides and raised them into position. After the roof was up, everyone celebrated with a communal meal, and perhaps with singing and dancing. Similar gatherings took place at harvest time and on other special occasions.

Rural women met more formally than did men. Farm men had frequent opportunities to gather informally at general stores, markets, and taverns. Women, though, had to prearrange their regular work and social gatherings: weekly after-church dinners; sewing, quilting, and husking bees; and preparations for marriages and baptisms. These were times to exchange experiences and thoughts, offer each other support, and swap letters, books, and news.

Irene Hardy, who spent her childhood in rural southwestern Ohio in the 1840s, left a record of the gatherings she attended as a girl. Most vivid in her memory fifty years later were the apple bees. Since canning was unknown at the time, neighbors gathered to make apple butter, preserves, or dried apples. "Usually invitations were sent about by word of mouth," she recalled. " 'Married folks' came and worked all day or afternoon, peeling by hand and with peelers, coring and quartering, and spreading out . . . in the sun to dry." A dinner feast followed, for which the visiting women made biscuits, vegetables, and coffee. After cleaning up, "the old folks went home to send their young ones for their share of work and fun." The elders had gossiped to pass the time; the youngsters played tricks, joked, and teased each other in a comic-serious precourting ritual. "Then came supper, apple and pumpkin pies, cider, doughnuts, cakes, cold chicken and turkey," Hardy wrote, "after which games, 'Forfeits,' 'Building a Bridge,' 'Snatchability,' even 'Blind Man's Buff' and 'Pussy Wants a Corner.' "

Traditional country bees had their town counterparts. Fredrika Bremer, a Swedish visitor to the United States, described a sewing bee in 1849 in Cambridge, Massachusetts, at which neighborhood women made clothes for "a family who had lost all their clothing by fire." Yet these town bees were not the all-day family affairs typical of the countryside, and when the Hardy family moved to the town of Eaton in 1851, young Irene missed the country gatherings. The families of Eaton seldom held bees; they purchased their goods at the store.

City people had more formal amusements. As work and family life grew apart, there were fewer opportunities to turn work into festivals or family gatherings.

| City life |

Entertainment became a separate activity for which one purchased a ticket—to the theater, the circus, or P. T. Barnum's American Museum; or in the 1840s, to the race track; or a decade later, to the baseball park. The concentration of population in cities supported this diversity of activities, a luxury unknown in the countryside.

Though population density and cultural diversity animated city life, they also became problems in themselves. Sporting events became so crowded that one New Yorker doubted whether it was worth battling the mobs of people to attend the racetrack. The

Country people looked forward to combining work and play in communal bees. Here Pennsylvanians scutch flax, beating the stalks to separate the linen fibers from the woody ones. National Gallery of Art, Gift of Edgar William and Bernice Chrysler Garbisch.

"crowd and the dust and the danger and the difficulty of getting on and off the course with a carriage," Philip Hone wrote in 1842, "are scarcely compensated by any pleasure to be derived from the amusement." Everywhere there seemed to be mobs of people. When P. T. Barnum brought Jenny Lind, the famous Swedish soprano, to New York in September 1850, twenty thousand people mobbed the hotel entrance for a glimpse of her.

As cities grew in size, public transportation made it easier to get around. Horse-drawn omnibuses appeared in New York in 1827, and horse-drawn streetcars soon followed. The Harlem Railroad, completed in 1832, ran the length of Manhattan. By the 1850s all big cities had streetcars. And they needed them. Cities grew so fast, they seemed to leap overnight into the countryside. George Templeton Strong, a New York lawyer and devoted diarist, recorded in 1856 that

he had attended a party at a Judge Hoffman's "in thirty-seventh!!!—it seems but the other day that thirty-seventh Street was an imaginary line running through a rural district and grazed over by cows."

Strong and other upper-class New Yorkers found the density and diversity of the city repugnant. His diary is filled with his distaste for mixing with the masses. He especially disliked riding the city railroad or the omnibus. One day in 1852, suffering from a "splitting headache," Strong vented his rage at the immigrant population that crowded the city's public transportation. In "the choky, hot railroad car," he gagged on the "stale, sickly odors from sweaty Irishmen in their shirt sleeves." The other people repelled him as well: "German Jew shop-boys in white coats, pink faces, and waistcoats that looked like virulent prickly heat; fat old women, with dirty-nosed babies; one sporting man with black whiskers, miraculously crisp and curly, and a shirt collar insulting stiff, who contributed a reminiscence of tobacco smoke—the spiritual body of ten thousand bad cigars." Even tragedy provoked Strong's distaste: passing by a fire on Elizabeth Street in 1854, he observed "two or three wooden shanties blazing and disgorging an incredible number of cubic feet of Irish humanity and filthy feather beds."

Leaving aside Strong's ugly prejudices, his picture of city life was an accurate one. By twentieth-century standards, early nineteenth-century cities were disorderly, unsafe, and unhealthy. Expansion occurred so suddenly and swiftly that few cities could handle the problems it brought. For example, migrants from rural areas were used to relieving themselves and throwing refuse in any vacant area. But in the city waste spread disease, polluted wells, and gave off obnoxious smells. New York City solved part of the problem in the 1840s by abandoning wells in favor of reservoir water piped into buildings and outdoor fountains. In some districts scavengers and refuse collectors carted away garbage and human waste, but in much of the city it just rotted.

Crime was another problem. To keep order and provide for public safety, Boston supplemented (1837) and New York replaced (1845) its colonial watchmen and constables with paid policemen. Nonetheless, middle-class men and women did not venture out alone at night, and during the day stayed clear of many city districts. And the influx of immigrants to the cities compounded social tensions by pitting people of different backgrounds against each other in the contest for jobs and housing. Ironically, in the midst of the dirt, the noise, the crime, and the conflict, as if to tempt those who struggled to survive, rose the opulent residences of the very rich.

Extremes of wealth

Some observers, notably the young French visitor Alexis de Tocqueville, saw the United States before the Civil War as a place of equality and opportunity. Over a nine-month period in 1831 and 1832, Tocqueville and his companion Gustave de Beaumont traveled four thousand miles and visited all twenty-four states. He later introduced *Democracy in America,* his classic analysis of the American people and nation, with the statement: "No novelty in the United States struck me more vividly during my stay there than the equality of conditions."

Tocqueville saw American equality—the relative fluidity of the United States' social order—as the result of its citizens' geographic mobility. Migration offered people opportunities to start anew regardless of where they came from or who they were. Prior wealth or family or education mattered little; a person could be known by deeds alone. And indeed, ambition for security and success drove Americans on; sometimes they seemed unable to stop. "An American will build a house in which to pass his old age," Tocqueville wrote, "and sell it before the roof is on; he will plant a garden and rent it just as the trees are coming into bearing; he will clear a field and leave others to reap the harvest; he will take up a profession and leave it, settle in one place and soon go off elsewhere with his changing desires."

Talent and hard work, many Americans and Europeans believed, found their just reward in such an atmosphere. It was common advice that anyone could advance by working hard and saving money. A local legend from Newburyport, Massachusetts, sounded this popular theme. Tristram Dalton, a Federalist lawyer, wanted his carriage repaired. Moses Brown, an energetic mechanic, refused to wait for Dalton's servants to tow the carriage to his shop; he sought out the vehicle and fixed it on the spot. After Dalton's death his heirs squandered the family fortune, but Brown's industriousness paid off. Through hard work the humble carriage craftsman became one of Massachusetts' richest men. Eventually he bought the Dalton homestead and lived out his life there. The message was clear: "Men succeed or fail . . . not from accident or external surroundings," as the Newburyport *Herald* put it in 1856, but from "possessing or wanting the elements of success in themselves."

But other observers recorded the rise of a new aristocracy based on wealth and power, and a growing gap between the upper and working classes. Among those who disagreed with the egalitarian view of

| Distribution of wealth |

American life was *New York Sun* publisher Moses Yale Beach, author of twelve editions of *Wealth and Biography of the Wealthy Citizens of New York City.* In 1845 Beach listed a thousand New Yorkers with assets of $100,000 or more. (John Jacob Astor led with a $25 million fortune.) Combining gossip-column tidbits with often erroneous guesses at people's wealth, Beach's book nevertheless provided some idea of the enormous wealth of New York's upper class. Tocqueville himself, ever sensitive to the conflicting trends in American life, had described the growth of an American aristocracy based on industrial wealth. The rich and well educated "come forward to exploit industries," Tocqueville wrote, and become "more and more like the administrator of a huge empire. . . . What is this if not an aristocracy?"

Throughout the United States, wealth was becoming concentrated in the hands of a relatively small number of people. In Brooklyn in 1810 two-thirds of the families owned only 10 percent of the wealth; by 1841 their share had decreased to almost nothing. In New York City between 1828 and 1845, the wealthiest 4 percent of the city's population increased its holdings from an estimated 63 percent to 80 percent of all individual wealth. That slaves accounted for 15 percent of the population in 1840, and that relatively large-scale immigration began in the 1840s, contributed further to the growing disparity. By 1860 the top 5 percent of families owned more than half the nation's wealth; the top tenth owned over 70 percent.

Inequality of wealth prevailed in rural areas as well. The combined income of just 1,000 southern planters nearly equaled that of the remaining 660,000 white families. In southern cotton counties, 10 percent of the landholders owned 40 percent of the taxable assets; wealth was even more concentrated in the sugar-producing parishes of Louisiana. In the Old Northwest—the frontier of the first four decades of the nineteenth century—the richest 10 percent owned nearly 40 percent of taxable wealth. Farther west there was great disparity between the owners of large tracts of unmortgaged land and the easterners and immigrants who bought parcels of it on credit. During economic downturns large numbers of these small farmers abandoned their land or lost it to foreclosures; the number of hired hands, both men and women, grew.

Another manifestation of the growing inequality and insecurity in American society was the frequency of rioting and sporadic incidents of violence. In the 1830s riots became commonplace as skilled workers

| Urban riots | vented their rage against new migrants to the city and other sym-

bols of the new industrial order. In Philadelphia, for instance, native-born workers fought Irish weavers in 1828; whites and blacks rioted on the docks in 1834 and 1835. In 1835 and 1838 antiabolitionist riots broke out. And in North Philadelphia from 1840 to 1842, residents took to the streets continuously until the construction of a railroad through their neighborhood was abandoned. These disturbances climaxed in the great riots of 1844, in which mostly Protestant skilled workers fought Irish Catholics. Nationwide between 1828 and 1833 there were twenty major riots; in the year 1834 alone there were sixteen; in 1835, thirty-seven. By 1840 more than 125 people had died in urban riots, and by 1860 more than a thousand.

A cloud of uncertainty hung over working men and women. Many were afraid that in periods of economic depression they would become part of the urban flotsam and jetsam of able-bodied men and women, white and black, who could not find steady work. They feared the competition of immigrant and slave labor. They feared the insecurities and indignities of poverty, chronic illness, disability, old age, widowhood, and desertion. And they had good reason.

Indeed, poverty and squalor stalked the urban working class. Cities were notorious for the dilapidated districts where newly arrived immigrants, indigent blacks, working poor and thieves, beggars, and prostitutes lived. Five Points in New York City's Sixth Ward was probably the worst slum in pre-Civil War America. Dominated by the Old Brewery, which in 1837 had been privately converted to housing for hundreds of adults and children, the neighborhood was equally divided between Irish and blacks. Ill-suited to human habitation and lacking such amenities as running water and sewers, it exemplified all that was worst in American society.

| Urban slums |

In New York and other large cities lived street rats, children and young men who earned their living off the streets—by boot blacking or petty thievery—and slept on boats, in hay lofts, or in warehouses. Charles Loring Brace, a founder of the Children's Aid Society (1853), described the street rats in his *Dangerous Classes of New York* (1872): "Like the rats, they were too quick and cunning to be often caught in their petty plunderings, so they gnawed away at the foundations of society undisturbed." To Brace and others,

The infamous Five Points section of New York City's Sixth Ward, probably the worst slum in pre–Civil War America. Immodestly dressed prostitutes cruise the streets or gaze from windows, while a pig roots for garbage in their midst. Brown Brothers.

the street rats threatened American society. "They will vote—they will have the same rights as we ourselves," warned the first report of the Children's Aid Society in 1854, "though they have grown up ignorant of moral principle, as any savage or Indian." Moreover, "they will perhaps be embittered at the wealth and luxuries they never share. Then let society beware, when the vicious, reckless multitude of New York boys, swarming now in every foul alley and low street, come to know their power and *use it!*"

A world apart from Five Points and street rats was the upper-class elite society of Philip Hone, one-time mayor of New York. Hone's diary, meticulously kept from 1826 until his death in 1851, records the activities of an American aristocrat. On February 28, 1840, for instance, Hone attended a masked ball at the Fifth Avenue mansion of Henry Breevoort, Jr., and Laura

Carson Breevoort. The ball began at the fashionable hour of 10 P.M., and the five hundred ladies and gentlemen who filled the five rooms of the mansion's first floor wore costumes adorned with ermine, gold, and silver. For more than a week, Hone believed, the affair "occupied the minds of the people of all stations, ranks, and employments. . . . " Few balls attained such grandeur, but at one time or another similar parties were held in Boston, Philadelphia, Baltimore, Charleston, and New Orleans.

At a less rarefied level, Hone's social calendar was filled with elegant dinner parties featuring fine cuisine and imported wines. The New York elite who filled the pages of Hone's diary—the 1 percent of the population who owned 50 percent of the city's wealth—lived in large townhouses and mansions, with corps of servants to tend to their elaborate furniture and fine

Immigration to the United States, 1821–1860

COUNTRY OF ORIGIN	1821–1830	1831–1840	1841–1850	1851–1860
Ireland	51,000	207,000	781,000	914,000
German states	6,800	152,000	435,000	952,000
Great Britain (excluding Ireland)	25,000	76,000	267,000	424,000
British North America	2,300	14,000	42,000	59,000
China	2	8	35	41,000

wine cellars. In the summer, country estates, ocean resorts, mineral spas, and grand tours of Europe afforded them relief from the winter and spring social seasons.

By and large the elite were not idle, although their fortunes were often built on inherited wealth. Nearly all received sizable inheritances, and their inbred marriage patterns enhanced their inherited possessions. Yet as a group they devoted at least some of their energies to increasing their fortunes and their power. Philip Hone, like other urban capitalists and southern planters, was actively engaged in transportation and manufacturing ventures. Wealth begat wealth.

New lives in America

Though they did not bring much wealth with them, immigrants contributed in other ways to the changing American scene. In numbers alone they drastically altered the United States. The 5 million immigrants who settled in the states between 1820 and 1860 outnumbered the entire population of the country at the first census in 1790. They came from all over the world—from North America, the Caribbean, Latin America, Asia, and Africa, though Europeans made up the vast majority (see table). The peak period of pre–Civil War immigration was from 1847 through 1857; in that eleven-year period, 3.3 million immigrants entered the United States, 1.3 million from Ireland and 1.1 million from the German states. By 1860, 15 percent of the white population was foreign-born.

This massive migration had been set in motion decades earlier. In Europe around the turn of the nineteenth century, the Napoleonic wars had begun one of the greatest population shifts in history, which was to last more than a century. One part of the movement, increasingly significant as time went on, was emigration of Europeans to the United States. War and revolution, crop failure and famine, industrialization and economic displacement, political and religious persecution dogged weary Europeans. Meanwhile, the United States beckoned. Millions of unplowed acres awaited Europeans, offering them not only economic opportunity but also the chance to

Background of immigration

found new communities. Large construction projects needed strong young laborers, as did the expanding mills and mines. Europeans' awareness of the United States heightened as employers, states, and shipping companies advertised the opportunities to be found across the Atlantic. Often the message was stark: work and prosper in America or starve in Europe. With regularly scheduled sailing ships commuting across the ocean, the cost of transatlantic travel was within easy reach of millions of Europeans.

So they came, enduring the hardships of travel and of settling in a strange land. The journey was difficult. The average crossing took six weeks; in bad weather it could take three months. Disease spread unchecked among people huddled together like cattle in steerage. More than 17,000 immigrants, mostly Irish, died from "ship fever" in 1847. On disembarking, immigrants became fair game for the con artists and swindlers who worked the docks. Runners and agents greeted them and tried to lure them from their chosen destinations. In 1855, in response to the immigrants' plight, New York state's commissioners of emigration established Castle Garden as an immigrant center. There, at the tip of Manhattan Island, the major port of entry, immigrants were sheltered from fraud. Authorized transportation companies maintained offices in the large rotunda and assisted immigrants with their travel plans.

Most immigrants gravitated toward the cities, since only a minority had farming experience or the means to purchase land and equipment. Many stayed in New York. By 1845, 35 percent of the city's 371,000 people were of foreign birth. Ten years later 52 percent of its 623,000 inhabitants were immigrants, 28 percent from Ireland and 16 percent from Germany. In the Sixth Ward, home of Five Points, no fewer than 70 percent of the residents were immigrants. Boston, an important entry point for the Irish, took on a European tone. Throughout the 1850s the city was about 35 percent foreign-born, of whom more than two-thirds were Irish. In the South, too, major cities had large immigrant populations. In 1860 New Orleans was 44 percent foreign-born, Savannah 33 percent, Charleston 26 percent, and the border city of St. Louis, 61 percent. On the West Coast, San Francisco had a foreign-born majority.

Some immigrants, however, did settle in rural areas. In particular, German, Dutch, and Scandina-vian farmers gravitated toward the Midwest. Greater percentages of Scandinavians and Netherlanders became farmers than other nationalities; both groups came mostly as religious dissenters and migrated in family units. The Dutch who founded the American Holland in Michigan and Wisconsin, for instance, had seceded from the official Reformed Church of the Netherlands. Under such leaders as Albertus C. Van Raalte, they fled persecution in their native land to establish new and more pious communities—Holland, New Groningen, and Zeeland, Michigan, among them.

Success in America bred further emigration. "I wish, and do often say that we wish you were all in this happy land," wrote shoemaker John West of Germantown, Pennsylvania, to his kin in Corsley, England, in 1831. "A man nor woman need not stay out of employment one hour here," he advised. "No war nor insurrection here. *But all is plenty and peace.*" John Down, a weaver from Frome, England, settled in New York City without his family. Writing to his wife in August, 1830, he described the bountiful meal he had shared with a farmer's family: "They had on the table puddings, pyes, and fruit of all kind that was in season, and preserves, pickles, vegetables, meats, and everything that a person would wish, and the servants [farm hands] set down at the same table with their masters." Though Down missed his family dearly, he wrote, "I do not repent of coming, for you know that there was nothing but poverty before me, and to see you and the dear children want was what I could not bear. *I would rather cross the Atlantic ten times than hear my children cry for victuals once.*" To those skeptics who claimed the United States was filling up, he advised, "There is plenty of room yet, and will be for a thousand years to come." These letters and others were widely circulated in England to advertise the success of pauper immigrants in America.

American institutions, both public and private, actively recruited European immigrants. Western states lured potential settlers in the interest of promoting their economies. In the 1850s, for instance, Wisconsin appointed a commissioner of emigration, who advertised the state's advantages in American and European newspapers. Wisconsin also opened a New York office and hired European agents to compete with other

Promotion of immigration

states and with firms like the Illinois Central Railroad for immigrants' attention.

Before the potato blight hit Ireland, tens of thousands of Irish were lured to America by recruiters. They came to swing picks and shovels on American canals and railroads, to dig the foundations of mills and factories. The popular folksong known variously as "Poor Paddy Works on the Erie" and "Working on the Railroad" records their story:

Oh in eighteen hundred and forty-three
I sailed away across the sea,
I sailed away across the sea,
To work upon the railway, the railway.
I'm weary of the railway;
Oh poor Paddy works on the railway!

. . .

Oh in eighteen hundred and forty-five
When Daniel O'Connell he was alive,
When Daniel O'Connell he was alive,
To work upon the railway, the railway . . .

Oh in eighteen hundred and forty-six
I changed my trade to carrying bricks,
I changed my trade to carrying bricks,
From working on the railway, the railway . . .

Oh in eighteen hundred and forty-seven
Poor Paddy was thinking of going to Heaven,
Poor Paddy was thinking of going to Heaven,
After working on the railway, the railway,
He was weary of the railway;
Oh poor Paddy worked on the railway![1]

But as other verses reveal, not all the Irish immigrants were successful; tens of thousands of them returned to their homeland. Among them was Michael

| Immigrant disenchantment |

Gaugin, who had the misfortune of arriving in New York City during the financial panic of 1837. Gaugin, an assistant engineer in the construction of the Ballinasloe Canal in Dublin, had been attracted to the states by the promise that "he should soon become a wealthy man." The Dublin agent for a New York firm had convinced Gaugin to quit his job, which he had held for thirteen years and which included a house and an acre of ground, in order to im-

migrate to the United States. Within two months of arriving in the United States, Gaugin had become a pauper. In August 1837 he declared he was "now without means for the support of himself and his family, and has no employment, and has already suffered great deprivation since he arrived in this country; and is now soliciting means to enable him to return with his family home to Ireland." Many of those who had come with the Gaugins had already returned home.

Such experiences did not deter Irish men and women from coming to the United States. Ireland was the most densely populated European country, and among the most impoverished. From 1815 on, small harvests prompted a steady stream of Irish to immigrate to America. Then in 1845 and 1846 po-

| Irish immigration |

tatoes—the basic Irish food—rotted in the fields. From 1845 to 1849, death in the form of starvation, malnutrition, and typhus stalked the island. In all, 1 million died and about 1.5 million fled, two-thirds of them to the United States. People became Ireland's major export.

In the 1840s and 1850s a total of 1.7 million Irish men and women entered the United States. At the peak of Irish immigration, from 1847 to 1854, 1.2 million came. By the end of the century there would be more Irish in the United States than in Ireland. The immigrants clustered in poverty in the cities, where they met growing anti-immigrant, anti-Catholic sentiment. Everywhere "No Irish Need Apply" signs appeared.

Anti-Catholicism had erupted in the American revolutionary movement when Quebec spurned the Continental Congress's invitation to join the Revolution. Later, though, French support of the colonists and the staunch patriotism of American Catholics had soothed such feelings. As the states freed themselves from established churches and abolished religious tests for office following the Revolution, anti-Catholicism receded. But in the 1830s the trend reversed, and anti-Catholicism appeared wherever the Irish did. At-

| Anti-Catholicism |

tacks on the papacy and the church circulated widely in the form of libelous texts like *The Awful Disclosures of Maria Monk* (1836), which alleged sexual orgies among priests and nuns. Nowhere was anti-Catholicism more open and nasty than in Boston, though such sentiments were widespread.

[1]Quoted in Carl Sandburg, *The American Songbag* (New York: Harcourt Brace Jovanovich, 1927), p. 357. Reprinted with permission.

Anti-Catholic riots were almost commonplace. In Charlestown, Massachusetts, a mob burned a convent (1834); a Philadelphia crowd attacked priests and nuns and vandalized churches (1844); and in Lawrence, Massachusetts, a mob leveled the Irish neighborhood (1854).

The native-born who embraced anti-Catholicism were motivated largely by anxiety. They feared that a militant Roman church would subvert American society, that unskilled Irish workers would displace American craftsmen, and that the slums inhabited in part by the Irish were undermining the nation's values. Every American problem from immorality and the evils of alcohol to poverty and economic upheaval was blamed on immigrant Irish Catholics. Impoverished workers complained to the Massachusetts legislature that the Irish displaced "the honest and respectable laborers of the State . . . and from their manner of living . . . work for much less per day . . . being satisfied with food to support the animal existence alone." American workers, on the other hand, "not only labor for the body but for the mind, the soul, and the State." Friction increased as Irish-Americans fought back against anti-Irish and anti-Catholic prejudice; in the 1850s they began to vote and to become active in politics.

Though potato blight also sent many Germans to the United States in the 1840s, other hardships contributed to the steady stream of German immigrants. Many came from areas where small landholdings | *German immigration* | made it hard to eke out a living and to pass on land to their sons. Others were craftsmen displaced by the industrial revolution. These refugees were joined by middle-class Germans who had sought to unify the three dozen or so German states in a liberal republic. Frustration with abortive revolutions like one that occurred in 1848 led them to immigrate to the United States. For some, the only other choice was jail.

Unlike the Irish, who tended to congregate in towns and cities, Germans settled everywhere. Many came on German cotton boats, disembarked at New Orleans, and traveled up the Mississippi. In the South they became peddlers, traders, and merchants; in the North they worked as farmers, urban laborers, and businessmen. Also unlike the Irish, they tended to mi-grate in families. A strong desire to maintain the German language and culture prompted them to colonize areas as a group.

German immigrants transplanted their Old World institutions in the New World, creating New Germanies in rural areas and transforming the tone and culture of established cities like Cincinnati and Milwaukee. *Turnvereine*—German physical-culture clubs—sprouted in villages and cities; by 1853 sixty such societies were hosting exercise groups and German-language lectures.

In adhering to German traditions, German-Americans also met with antiforeign attitudes. More than half the German immigrants were Catholic, and their Sabbath practices were different from the Protestants'. On Sundays German families typically gathered at beer gardens to eat and drink beer, to dance, sing, and listen to band music, and sometimes to play cards. Protestants were outraged by such violations of the Lord's day. In Chicago riots broke out when Protestants enforced the Sunday prohibition laws.

In rural areas Germans were resented for their success as farmers. Familiar with scientific agriculture, German-Americans dominated farming in Ohio, Wisconsin, and Missouri. Their persistence in using the German language and their different religious beliefs also set them apart. Besides the Catholic majority, a significant number of German immigrants were Jewish. And even the Protestants—mostly Lutherans—founded their own churches and often educated their children in German-language schools. Not all Germans, however, were religious. The failure of the revolution of 1848 had sent to the United States a whole generation of liberals and free thinkers, some of whom were socialists, communists, and anarchists. The free thinkers entered politics with a loud voice, embracing abolitionism and the Republican party.

The conflict between the immigrants and the society they joined was paralleled by the inner tensions most immigrants experienced. On the one hand they felt impelled to commit themselves wholeheartedly to their new country, to learn the language and adapt themselves to American ways. On the other hand they were rooted in their own cultural traditions—the comfortable, tried, and tested customs of the country of their birth, the familiar ways and words that came intuitively and required no education.

The German Turnvereine, or physical-culture club, of Cincinnati, 1850. The Cincinnati Historical Society.

Nearly all found themselves altered in significant ways, even as they successfully resisted other changes. In the process American customs and society changed as well.

Free people of color

No black person was safe, wrote the abolitionist and former slave Frederick Douglass following the Philadelphia riot of 1849. "His life—his property—and all that he holds dear are in the hands of a mob, which may come upon him at any moment—at midnight or mid-day, and deprive him of his all." Between 1832 and 1849 five major antiblack riots occurred in Philadelphia. Mobs stormed black dwellings and churches, set them to the torch, and killed the people inside. For free people of color, mobs could take many forms. They could come in the shape of slave hunters, seeking fugitive slaves but as likely to kidnap a free black as a slave. Or they could take the form of civil authority, as in Cincinnati in 1829, when city officials, frightened by the growing black population, drove one-to-two thousand blacks from the city by enforcing a law requiring cash bonds for good behavior. In whatever form, free blacks faced insecurity daily.

Under federal law, blacks held an uncertain position. The Bill of Rights seemed to apply to free blacks; the Fifth Amendment specified that "no person shall . . . be deprived of life, liberty, or property, without due process of law." Nevertheless, early federal legislation discriminated against free people of color. In 1790 naturalization was limited to white aliens; in 1792 the militia was limited to white male citizens; and in 1810 blacks were barred from carrying the mails. Moreover, Congress approved the admission to the Union of states whose constitutions restricted the rights of blacks. Following the admission of Missouri in 1821, every new state admitted until the Civil War banned blacks from voting. And when the Oregon and New Mexico territories were organized, public land grants were limited to whites.

Dred Scott v. *Sanford* (1857) made the de facto position of free blacks official. Scott, a Missouri slave, had

Dred Scott *v.* Sanford

accompanied his master to the free state of Illinois and the free territory of Wisconsin. Once back in Missouri, he sued for his freedom on the grounds that his presence in areas where there was no slavery had made him free. After a ten-year battle, the Supreme Court ruled against Scott. Speaking for the majority, Chief Justice Roger Taney ruled that blacks "were not intended to be included, under the word 'citizens' in the Constitution, and can therefore claim none of the rights and privileges which that instrument provides for and secures to citizens of the United States." As George Fitzhugh, a defender of slavery, exclaimed in 1854, "A free Negro! Why, the very term seems an absurdity."

The Dred Scott decision affirmed what had already become practice: each state decided the legal condition of blacks within its borders. In the North blacks faced legal restrictions nearly everywhere; Massachusetts was the major exception. Many states barred entry to free blacks or required bonds of $500 to $1,000 to guarantee their good behavior, as in Ohio (1804), Illinois (1819), Michigan (1827), Indiana (1831), Iowa (1839), and Oregon (1849). Although seldom enforced, these laws clearly indicated the less-than-free status of blacks. Only in Massachusetts, New Hampshire, Vermont, and Maine could blacks vote on an equal basis with whites throughout the pre–Civil War period. Blacks gained the right to vote in Rhode Island in 1842, but they had lost it earlier in Pennsylvania and Connecticut. No state but Massachusetts permitted blacks to serve on juries; four midwestern states and California did not allow blacks to testify against whites. In Oregon blacks could not own real estate, make contracts, or sue in court.

Legal status was important, but practice and custom were crucial. Although Ohio repealed its law barring black testimony against whites in 1849, the exclusion persisted as custom in southern Ohio counties. Throughout the North free people of color were either excluded from or segregated in public

Exclusion and segregation of blacks

places. Abolitionist Frederick Douglass was repeatedly turned away from public facilities during a speaking tour of the North in 1844. A doorkeeper refused him admission to a circus in Boston, saying "We don't allow niggers in here." He met the same reply when he tried to attend a revival meeting in New Bedford. At a restaurant in Boston and on an omnibus in Weymouth, Massachusetts, he heard the familiar words. Hotels and restaurants were closed to blacks, as were most theaters and churches. But probably no practice inflicted greater injury than the general discrimination in hiring. Factory and skilled work were virtually closed to northern blacks.

Free people of color faced still severer legal and social barriers in the southern slave states, where their presence was often viewed as an incentive to insurrection. Indeed, southern states responded to fear of mass rebellion by tightening the restrictions on free blacks and forcing them to leave small towns and interior counties. After a successful slave rebellion in Haiti in the 1790s, southern states barred the entry of free blacks for two decades. And in 1806 Virginia required newly freed blacks to leave the state. Following Nat Turner's slave uprising in Southampton County in 1831, the position of free blacks weakened further. Within five years nearly all the southern states prohibited the freeing of any slaves without legislative or court approval, and by the 1850s Texas, Mississippi, and Georgia had banned manumission altogether.

To restrict free blacks and encourage them to migrate north, southern states adopted elaborate "black codes." Blacks were required to have licenses for cer-

Black codes

tain occupations and were barred from others (for example, Virginia and Georgia banned black river captains and pilots). Some states forbade blacks to assemble without a license; some prohibited blacks from being taught to read and write. All the slave states except Delaware barred blacks from testifying against whites. In the late 1830s, when these black codes were enforced with vigor for the first time, free blacks increasingly moved northward, even though northern states discouraged the migration.

Chapter 11: The American scene, 1800–1860

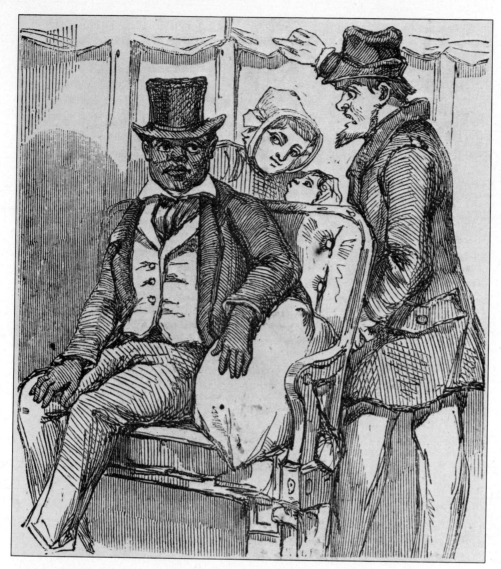

A free black man being expelled from a whites-only railway car in Philadelphia. Prior to the Civil War blacks were commonly segregated or excluded from public places in the North. Library of Congress.

In spite of these obstacles, the free black population rose dramatically in the first part of the nineteenth century, from 108,000 in 1800 to almost 500,000 in 1860 (see table, page 294). Nearly half lived in the North, occasionally in rural settlements like Hammond County, Indiana, but more often in cities like Philadelphia, New York, or Cincinnati. Baltimore had the largest free black community; sizable free black populations also existed in New Orleans, Charleston, and Mobile (see Chapter 10).

The ranks of free blacks were constantly increased by ex-slaves. Some, like Frederick Douglass and Harriet Tubman, were fugitives. Douglass had hired himself out as a ship caulker in Baltimore, paying $3 monthly to his owner. Living among free workers made him yearn to escape slavery. By masquerading as a free black with the help of borrowed seaman's papers, he bluffed his way to Philadelphia and freedom. Tubman, a slave on the eastern shore of Maryland, escaped

Fugitive slaves

Free people of color

Black Population of the United States, 1800–1860

	TOTAL BLACK POPULATION	PERCENTAGE OF TOTAL U.S. POPULATION	FREE PEOPLE OF COLOR	FREE BLACKS AS A PERCENTAGE OF BLACK POPULATION
1800	1,002,000	18.9	108,000	10.8
1810	1,378,000	19.0	186,000	13.5
1820	1,772,000	18.4	234,000	13.2
1830	2,329,000	18.1	320,000	13.7
1840	2,874,000	16.8	386,000	13.4
1850	3,639,000	15.7	435,000	11.9
1860	4,442,000	14.1	488,000	11.0

to Philadelphia in 1849 when her master's death led to rumors that she would be sold out of the state. Within the next two years she returned twice to free her two children, her sister, her mother, and her brother and his family. Other slaves were voluntarily freed by their owners. Some, like a Virginia planter named Sanders who settled his slaves as freedmen in Michigan, sought to cleanse their souls by freeing their slaves in their wills. Others freed elderly slaves after a lifetime of service rather than support them in old age. The parents of the slave Isabella (Sojourner Truth) were freed when whites who inherited the family would not support the father, who was too old to work.

Sojourner Truth's experience reveals that the gradual emancipation laws of northern states had little effect as long as slavery existed elsewhere. In 1817 New York state adopted an emancipation plan whereby all slaves over forty years old were freed, and young slaves would serve ten more years. But owners tried to thwart the law by selling their slaves into other states. In 1826, fearing sale to the South, Sojourner Truth found refuge with a nearby abolitionist couple. With their help she sued successfully for the freedom of her son Peter, who had been sold unlawfully to an Alabaman. One can only guess how many blacks did not receive such help and were permanently deprived of their freedom.

In response to their oppression, free blacks founded strong, independent self-help societies to meet their

Founding of black institutions

unique needs and fight their less-than-equal status. In every black community there appeared black churches, fraternal and benevolent associations, literary societies, and schools. The black Masons (affiliated with London because American Masons refused to accept blacks) grew from a single Boston lodge in 1784 to more than fifty lodges in seventeen states by 1860. Many black leaders believed that these mutual aid societies would encourage thrift,

Sojourner Truth (about 1797–1883), the spellbinding preacher, abolitionist, and crusader for women's rights.   Sophia Smith Collection, Smith College.

industry, and morality, thus equipping their members to improve their lot. But no amount of effort could counteract white prejudice. Blacks remained second-class in status.

The black convention movement, which originated in the 1830s, also promoted education and industriousness. But under the leadership of the small black middle class, which included the Philadelphia sail manufacturer James Forten and the orator Reverend Henry Highland Garnet, the convention movement quickly turned into a protest movement. Increasingly the conventions served as a forum to attack

slavery and agitate for equal rights (see Chapter 12). The struggle was also joined by militant new black publications. *Freedom's Journal,* the first black weekly, appeared in March 1827; in 1837 the *Weekly Advocate* began publication in New York City. Both papers circulated throughout the North, spreading black thought and activism.

Although abolitionism and civil rights remained at the top of the blacks' agenda, the mood of free blacks began to shift in the late 1840s and 1850s. Many were frustrated by the failure of the abolitionist movement and by the passage of the Fugitive Slave Law of 1850 (see Chapter 13). Some black leaders became more militant, and a few joined John Brown in his plans for rebellion. But many more were swept up in the tide of black nationalism, which stressed racial solidarity and

| Black nationalism | unity, self-help, and a growing interest in Africa. Before this time, efforts to send Afro-Americans |

unity, self-help, and a growing interest in Africa. Before this time, efforts to send Afro-Americans "back to Africa" had originated with whites seeking to solve racial problems by ridding the United States of blacks. But in the 1850s blacks held emigrationist conventions of their own under the leadership of Henry Bibb and Martin Delany. In 1859 Delany led a Niger Valley exploration party as the emissary of a black convention. He signed a treaty with Yoruba rulers allowing him to settle American blacks in that African kingdom (the plan was never carried out). With the coming of the Civil War and emancipation, however, the status of free blacks would move back onto the national political agenda, and Afro-Americans would focus with renewed intensity on their position at home.

The Trail of Tears

Indians faced problems similar to blacks'. They too faced massive hostility. Midwesterners and southerners sought their land, and soldiers marched them off it. Missionaries tried to Christianize them. And like blacks, their troubles involved the law, for Indians too were directly dependent on government policy—or the lack of it.

Under the Constitution, Indians had a more clearly defined status than blacks. For all practical purposes they were not part of the American nation. They were not taxed, not counted in apportioning state representation, not citizens. Congress was given the power "to regulate Commerce with foreign Nations, and among the several States, and with the Indian Tribes." In exercising this mandate and its treaty-making and war powers, the federal government had come to treat Indian tribes as separate nations.

The basis of Indian-white relations was the treaty. For its own convenience, the United States government demanded that one person or group have the power to obligate a tribe to a treaty's provisions. But like European nations in colonial times, government officials had difficulty applying this principle. Many tribes' traditions simply did not permit it. The Cherokees, for instance, were a common lingual group rather than a confederation of independent villages. No majority or unanimous leadership could sell the birthrights of all tribal members. Some frustrated United States officials simply designated a tribal leader. During the negotiations leading to the Treaty of Butte des Morts in 1827, for example, Governor Lewis Cass of the Michigan Territory named one Indian leader principal chief of the Menomonies. (The Menomonies, Cass confessed, "appear to us like a flock of geese without a leader.") Chiefs who worked closely with the government were well rewarded with gifts and honors.

Other circumstances made the treaty process less than the bargaining of two equal nations. Treaties were often made between victors and vanquished. In a context of coercion, old treaties often gave way to new ones in which the Indians ceded their traditional holdings in return for different lands in the West. Beginning with President Jefferson, the government withheld payments due to tribes for previous land cessions to pressure them to sign new treaties.

The Shawnee Chief Tecumseh led by far the most significant campaign of resistance to these federal tactics. Convinced that only a federation of nations and tribes could stop the advance of white society, Tecumseh sought in the first decade of the century to unify northern and southern Indians. His brother Laulewasika (the Prophet), like Tecumseh a powerful orator, spread the word of unity as well. Laulewasika, who had undergone a mystical conversion in overcoming alcoholism, contrasted the dignity and salvation of Indian ways with the corrupting influence of white culture.

Under Tecumseh, the Indians refused to cede more land to the whites. In repudiating an Indian land sale, Tecumseh told Indiana's Governor William Henry Harrison at Vincennes in 1810 that "the only way to check and stop this evil is, for all the red men to unite in claiming a common and equal right in the land, as it was at first, and should be yet; for it never was divided, but belongs to all, for the use of each. . . . No part has a right to sell, even to each other, much less to strangers." Tecumseh then warned that the Indians would resist white occupation of the 2.5 million acres on the Wabash they had ceded to the United States in the Treaty of Fort Wayne the year before.

A year later, using a Potawatomi raid on an Illinois settlement as an excuse, Harrison attacked Prophet's Town, Tecumseh's headquarters on Tippecanoe Creek. Losses on both sides were heavy. Indian warriors throughout the Midwest came to Tecumseh's side; Harrison appealed for help to President Madison. When the War of 1812 started, Tecumseh joined the British in return for a promise of an Indian country in the Great Lakes region. But he was killed in the Battle of the Thames in October 1813, and with him died the dream of Indian unity.

By 1820 Indians in Ohio, southern Indiana and Illinois, southwestern Michigan, most of Missouri, central Alabama, and southern Mississippi had been forced to cede their lands. They had given up nearly 200 million acres for pennies an acre. But white settlers' appetites were insatiable; the demand for tribal lands east of the Great Plains continued until nearly all the Indians had been forced out. For this land Indians were paid rations, supplies, and annuities. Because forced migration had destroyed their economic base, the tribes became dependent on these government payments—a dependence that only made them more susceptible to government pressure.

In the 1820s the Cherokees, Creeks, Choctaws, Chickasaws, and Seminoles attempted to resist the whites' tactics and defend their ancestral lands. In 1825 President Monroe proposed that these tribes, the last of the large Indian nations east of the Mississippi, sign new treaties and resettle between the Missouri and Red rivers. The conflict had focused on northwestern Georgia, where lay the Cherokee lands and a small portion of the Creek lands. Georgia had accused the federal government of not fulfilling its 1802 promise to remove the Indians in return for the state's renunciation of its claim to western lands. Although in 1826 the Creeks, under federal pressure, ceded all but a small strip of their Georgia lands, Governor George M. Troup was not satisfied. Troup sent surveyors to the one remaining strip; President John Quincy Adams then threatened to send the army to protect the Indians' claims, and Troup countered with his own threats. Only the eventual removal of the Georgia Creeks to the West in 1826 prevented a clash between the state and the federal government.

In 1827 the Cherokees attempted to resist forced removal by adopting a written constitution and organizing themselves officially as an independent nation. But in 1828 the Georgia legislature annulled the constitution, extended state sovereignty over the Cherokees, and ordered the seizure of tribal lands. Under the new law a Cherokee named Corn Tassel was tried and convicted of murder in a state court. Though the Supreme Court issued a writ of error on appeal, Georgia refused to recognize it and executed Corn Tassel. He was only the first of thousands of victims in the conflict between Georgia and the Cherokees.

In 1829 the Cherokees, with the support of sympathetic whites but without the support of the new president, Andrew Jackson, turned to the federal courts to defend their treaty with the United States and prevent Georgia's seizure of their land. In *Cherokee Nation* v. *Georgia* (1831), Chief Justice John Marshall ruled that under the federal Constitution an Indian tribe was neither a foreign nation nor a state, and therefore had no standing in federal courts. Marshall referred to the Indians as "domestic dependent nations . . . their relation to the United States resembles that of a ward to his guardian." Nonetheless, said Marshall, the Indians had an unquestioned right to their lands; they could lose title only by voluntarily giving it up. A year later, in *Worcester* v. *Georgia,* Marshall defined the Cherokees' position more clearly. The Indian nation was, he declared, a distinct political community in which "the laws of Georgia can have no force," and into which Georgians could not enter without permission or treaty privilege.

"John Marshall has made his decision," President Jackson is reported to have said; "now let him enforce it." Jackson, who as a general had led the expedition against the Seminoles in Spanish Florida in 1818, had little sympathy for the Indians. Concerned with opening up new lands for settlement, he was determined to remove the Cherokees at all costs. (His failure to carry out the Supreme Court decision served his states' rights position as well—see Chapter 12). In the Removal Act of 1830 Congress provided Jackson the funds he needed to negotiate new treaties and resettle the resistant tribes west of the Mississippi. The Choctaw were the first to go; in the winter of 1831 and 1832, they made the forced journey from Mississippi

The *Cherokee Phoenix,* a bilingual newspaper published by the Cherokee nation (top) and the title page of the Cherokee constitution (bottom). This issue of the newspaper details the provisions of a recent treaty with the Creeks.   Rare Book Division, The New York Public Library, Astor, Lenox and Tilden Foundations.

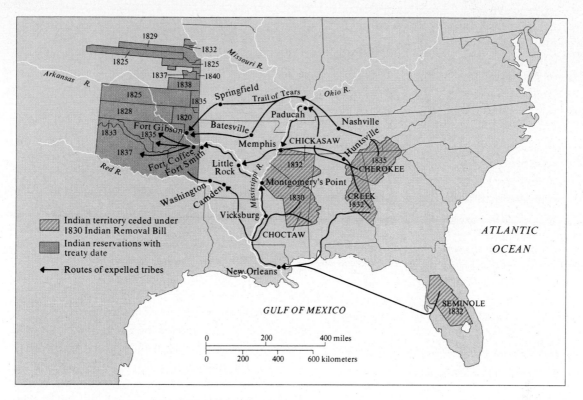

Removal of the Indians from the South, 1820–1840. Source: Redrawn by permission of Macmillan Publishing Company, Inc. From *American History Atlas* by Martin Gilbert, cartography by Peter Kingsland. Copyright © 1968 by Martin Gilbert.

| Trail of Tears | and Alabama to the West (see map). Alexis de Tocqueville was visiting Memphis when they arrived there, "the wounded, the sick, newborn babies, and the old men on the point of death. . . . I saw them embark to cross the great river," he wrote, "and the sight will never fade from my memory. Neither sob nor complaint rose from that silent assembly. Their afflictions were of long standing, and they felt them to be irremediable."

Soon other tribes were forced west. The Creeks in Alabama delayed removal until 1836, when the army pushed them westward. A year later the Chickasaws followed. The Cherokees, having fought to stay through the courts, found themselves divided. Some recognized the hopelessness of further resistance and accepted removal as the only chance to preserve their civilization. The leaders of this minority signed a treaty in 1835 in which they agreed to exchange their southern home for western land. But when the time for evacuation came in 1838, most Cherokees refused to move. President Martin Van Buren then sent federal troops to round up the Indians. About twenty thousand Cherokees were evicted, held in detention camps, and marched to Oklahoma under military escort. Nearly one-quarter died of disease and exhaustion on the famous Trail of Tears. When it was all over, the Indians had traded about 100 million acres of land east of the Mississippi for 32 million acres west of the river plus $68 million. Only a few scattered remnants of the tribes, among them the Seminoles, remained in the East and South.

A small band of Seminoles successfully resisted removal and remained in Florida. In the 1832 Treaty of Payne's Landing, tribal chiefs agreed to relocate to the

| Seminole War | West within three years. Under Osceola, however, a minority refused to vacate their homes, and from 1835 on they

---

waged a fierce guerrilla war against the United States. The army in turn attempted, ruthlessly but unsuccessfully, to exterminate the Seminoles. In 1842 the United States finally abandoned the Seminole War; it had cost 1,500 soldiers' lives and $20 million. Osceola's followers remained in Florida.

Later that decade, when the United States frontier expanded to the Southwest, Indians again fought valiantly to protect their homelands. The annexation of Texas in 1846 and the United States victory in the Mexican War in 1848 led to new Indian-white confrontations (see Chapter 12). Other conflicts developed over the food supply: when white hunters decimated the great herds of buffalo that were the primary source of meat for many Plains tribes, Indians encroached on each other's lands in search of food. The Sioux violated the territory of the Crows and Pawnees, the Crows and Assiniboins that of the Blackfeet, and so forth.

To open up the West to white settlement and end the intertribal warfare, Commissioner of Indian Affairs William Medill in 1848 proposed gathering the western Indians into two great reservations, one northern and one southern. Between the two, in the Kansas and Platte valleys, would be a wide corridor for white settlers to cross on their way westward. In 1853, however, the government took back most of the northern lands in a new round of treaties, and Kansas and Nebraska were opened to white settlement.

Among whites, the forced Indian removals were motivated by a complex set of attitudes. Most whites merely wanted Indian lands; they had little or no respect for the rights or culture of the Indians. Others were aware of the injustice, but believed the Indians must inevitably give way to white settlement. Some, like John Quincy Adams, believed the only way to preserve Indian civilization was to remove the tribes and establish a buffer zone between Indians and whites. Others, including Thomas Jefferson, doubted that white civilization and Indian "savagery" could coexist. Supported by missionaries and educators, they hoped to "civilize" the Indians and assimilate them slowly into American culture. But however the motivation of whites might have varied, the result was the same: the destruction of an American people and their culture.

Woman's sphere

American democracy, Alexis de Tocqueville believed, was built on the foundation of family stability. "In Europe almost all the disorders of society are born around the domestic hearth," he wrote in *Democracy in America*, "and not far from the nuptial bed." By contrast, "when the American returns from the turmoil of politics to the bosom of the family, he immediately finds a perfect picture of order and peace." This regularity of family life was reflected in public affairs, Tocqueville wrote. Religion, too, influenced the family, "and by regulating domestic life it helps to regulate the state."

Whether or not the differences between the United States and Europe can be explained in terms of family stability and contentedness, Tocqueville's distinction between public and private life was an important one in the America of the first half of the nineteenth century. For the middle class and the elite, the public sphere was associated with men and the private, or domestic, sphere with women. The public sphere was the world of business and politics, of conflict and selfishness—a jungle where men fought for economic survival. The private sphere, the home, was a refuge from that jungle. Governed by women, it was the fount of spirituality and purity, a religious and moral institution where selflessness and cooperation ruled.

Changing role of women

The development of separate spheres for men and women reflected, in part, the changing economic and social roles of the family. Once a cradle of production and economic activity, the family was now losing that function to shops and factories outside the home. It became instead a service unit for the domestic needs of its members. Education, religion, morality, domestic arts, and culture were its new concerns.

The development of public and private spheres also reflected the growing class distinctions in American society. Those who could concentrate on developing the home as a spiritual and cultural sanctuary were elite and middle-class women who led lives of material ease and comfort. They employed other women's daughters to free themselves from menial tasks. Yet, paradoxically, the new ideal of womanhood gave

A watercolor and ink portrait of a scrubwoman, made in 1807. Domestic work was still the most common job held by women working outside the home in the early nineteenth century. The New-York Historical Society.

middle-class and elite women less status rather than more; it represented an extremely narrow definition of a woman's proper sphere. Though they were dominant within the home, women were expected to be passive and submissive to men in public. Many women fought and shed this role as active leaders in reform movements (see Chapter 12), but the overall effect was a constriction of women's options and independence.

The range of paying jobs a woman could hold was narrow; most of the crafts and professions were closed to females. Moreover, work outside the home was viewed with disapproval. After all, it conflicted with the ideal of female domesticity. But whether or not society approved of work outside the home, unmarried daughters of laborers and immigrants, mothers without husbands, widows, black women both slave and free, and rural pioneers had no choice: economic necessity required them to work. Gradually work outside the home became associated with the lower classes, and the work women performed—mill work, domestic service—fell in esteem. Lowell and other New England mill towns experienced this transformation. Originally the mills had attracted genteel farm daughters who worked a relatively short time before returning home to be married. But by the 1840s

Pen-and-watercolor drawing of a middle-class family in 1832. The picture suggests the growing emphasis on the home as a spiritual refuge rather than a center of production.   Museum of Fine Arts, Boston.

Irish immigrant women had replaced most of the native-born workers, and wage levels and working conditions had deteriorated. Employment in the mills had been devalued and was shunned by respectable women.

Only two occupations were open to genteel women: nursing and teaching. Both were consistent with the new notion of womanhood, since they represented professional extensions of woman's domestic sphere. And since both nursing and teaching required education and training, they were closed to the daughters of workers and immigrants.

While woman's sphere was narrowing, family size was shrinking. In 1800 an American woman bore, on

| Decline in the birth rate |

the average, six children; in 1860 she would bear five, and by 1900 four. This decline occurred even while many immigrants with large-family traditions were settling in the United States; thus the birth rate for native-born women declined more sharply than

the average. Although rural families were larger than urban ones, birth rates in both areas declined to the same degree.

A number of factors lowered the birth rate. For many people, family life became less important as migration loosened family bonds. In cities, where there was less social pressure to marry than in rural areas, more people remained single. And increasingly, small families were viewed as desirable. Fewer children, it was believed, would enjoy greater opportunities. Parents could pay more attention to them, and would be better able to educate them and help them financially. Finally, contemporary marriage manuals stressed the harmful effects of too many births on a woman's health; too many children weakened women physically and overworked them as mothers.

All this evidence suggests that the decline in family size was the result of deliberate decisions. In rural areas with little cheap land, families were smaller than in other agricultural districts. It appears that parents

Chapter 11: The American scene, 1800–1860

who foresaw difficulty setting up their children as independent farmers chose to have fewer children. Similarly, in urban areas children were more and more an economic burden than an asset. As the family lost its role as a producer of goods, the length of time during which children were only consumers grew, as did the economic costs to parents.

How did men and women limit their families in the early nineteenth century? Many married later, thus shortening the period of childbearing. More important, however, was the widespread use of birth control. The first American book on birth control, *Moral Physiology; or, A Brief and Plain Treatise on the Population Question* (1831), as well as the popular marriage guide by the physician Charles Knowlton, *Fruits of Philosophy; or, the Private Companion of Young Married People* (1832), provide us with a glimpse of contemporary birth control methods. Probably the most widespread practice was *coitus interruptus,* or withdrawal of the male before completion of the sexual act. But mechanical devices were beginning to compete with this ancient folk practice. Although animal-skin condoms imported from France were too expensive for popular use, cheap rubber condoms were widely adopted when they became available in the 1850s. Dr. Knowlton advocated the dubious practice of douching with a chemical solution immediately after intercourse. And some couples used the rhythm method—attempting to confine intercourse to a woman's infertile periods. Knowledge of the "safe period" was so uncertain even among physicians, however, that the directions for avoiding conception were similar to today's advice to couples who want children! Another method was abstinence, or less frequent sexual intercourse. Frequently women abstained and men visited prostitutes.

If all else failed, abortion was widely available, especially after 1830. Ineffective folk remedies for self-induced abortion had been around for centuries, but in the 1830s surgical abortions became common. Abortionists advertised their services in large cities, and middle-class and elite women boldly asked their doctors to perform abortions. One sign of the upswing in abortions was the increase in legislation against it. Between 1821 and 1841, ten states and one territory prohibited abortions; by 1860, twenty states had outlawed it. Only three of those twenty punished the mother, however, and the laws were rarely enforced.

Significantly, the birth control methods women themselves controlled—douching, the rhythm method, abstinence, and abortion—were the ones that were increasing in popularity. For the new emphasis on women's domesticity encouraged women's autonomy in the home and gave them greater control over their own bodies. According to the cult of true womanhood, the refinement and purity of women ruled the family, including the nuptial bed; as one woman put it, "woman's duty was to subdue male passions, not to kindle them."

In turn, smaller families and fewer births changed the position and living conditions of women. At one time birth and infant care had occupied the entire span of women's adult lives, and few mothers had lived to see their youngest child reach maturity. But after the 1830s many women had time for other activities. Smaller families also allowed women to devote more time to their older children, and slowly childhood came to be perceived as a distinct part of the life span. The beginnings of public education in the 1830s (see Chapter 12) and the policy of grouping school children by age tended to reinforce this trend.

Marriage patterns changed as well. Only among elite families did the pattern of marrying kin persist. And among all but the highest classes, young people married spouses of their own choosing, not their parents'. In the new social climate marriages were made between individuals, not families, and romantic love was the yardstick by which proposals were measured.

The experiences of Mollie Dorsey Sandford, a young schoolteacher who came of age in Indiana and Nebraska in the 1850s and kept a careful diary of her adventures, illustrated the new marriage patterns. To Mollie marriage was an uncertainty. "If I live to be an *old maid,*" Mollie wrote, "I will be one of the good kind that is a friend to everybody and that everyone loves. If I *do* ever marry," she promised herself, "it will be someone I love *very, very, very,* much." When finally, after courting, Byron Sandford proposed to marry her, she wrote in her diary that night: "He loves me tenderly, truly, and . . . I know now that I can place my hand in his and go with him this life, be path smooth or stormy." Mollie's aunt Eliza had tried to encourage her "to captivate Mr. Rucker, as he is rich . . . [and] *owns a farm.*" Byron, on the other hand, owned only a few lots. Eliza herself, however, "likes money, but *she* married for love" when she wed a poor itinerant minister.

Not all women accepted or could fulfill the domestic ideal. Mollie Dorsey Sandford was prepared if necessary for the life of a single schoolteacher, boarding out without a home of her own. And mill girls, especially by the 1840s when they organized and resisted wage reductions, were forging new roles for women in the public sphere. So too were the women who assembled at Seneca Falls, New York, in 1848. Modeling their protest on the Declaration of Independence, they called for political, social, and economic equality for women (see Chapter 12).

The United States in 1860 was a far more diverse and divided society than it had been in 1800. Industrialization, urbanization, and immigration had altered the ways people lived and worked. Communities had become larger and more varied, and differences in wealth, ethnicity, religion, race, and sex separated individuals and groups.

As American society changed during these years, conflict became commonplace. Riots, crime, and anti-Catholicism were just a few of the many manifestations of social division in America. But conflict took other forms as well. In reform movements and religious revivals, Americans attempted to deal constructively with social change. In future years the 1820s, 1830s, and 1840s would be known as an age of reform.

Suggestions for further reading

Communities

Stuart M. Blumin, *The Urban Threshold: Growth and Change in a Nineteenth-Century American Community* (1976); Robert Doherty, *Society and Power: Five New England Towns, 1800–1860* (1977); Don H. Doyle, *The Social Order of a Frontier Community: Jacksonville, Illinois, 1825–1870* (1978); Peter R. Knights, *The Plain People of Boston, 1830–1860* (1971); Roger W. Lotchin, *San Francisco, 1846–1856: From Hamlet to City* (1974); Raymond A. Mohl, *Poverty in New York, 1783–1825* (1971); Edward Pessen, *Riches, Class and Power Before the Civil War* (1973); Stephan Thernstrom, *Poverty and Progress: Social Mobility in a Nineteenth Century City* (1964); Alexis de Tocqueville, *Democracy in America*, 2 vols. (1835–1840); Richard C. Wade, *The Urban Frontier: 1790–1830* (1957); Anthony F. C. Wallace, *Rockdale: The Growth of an American Village in the Early Industrial Revolution* (1978).

Immigrants

Rowland Berthoff, *British Immigrants in Industrial America* (1953); Theodore C. Blegen, *Norwegian Migration to America, 1825–1860* (1931); Kathleen Neils Conzen, *Immigrant Milwaukee: 1836–1860* (1976); Jay P. Dolan, *The Immigrant Church: New York's Irish and German Catholics, 1815–1865* (1975); Charlotte Erickson, *Invisible Immigrants* (1972); Robert Ernst, *Immigrant Life in New York City, 1825–1863* (1949); Oscar Handlin, *Boston's Immigrants: A Study in Acculturation,* rev. ed. (1959); Marcus L. Hansen, *The Atlantic Migration, 1607–1860* (1940); Stuart Creighton Miller, *The Unwelcome Immigrant: The American Image of the Chinese 1785–1882* (1969); Harold Runblom and Hans Norman, *From Sweden to America* (1976); Philip Taylor, *The Distant Magnet: European Emigration to the United States of America* (1971); Carl Wittke, *The Irish in America* (1956).

Free people of color

Ira Berlin, *Slaves Without Masters: The Free Negro in the Antebellum South* (1974); Letitia Woods Brown, *Free Negroes in the District of Columbia, 1790–1846* (1972); James Horton and Lois Horton, *Black Bostonians: Family Life and Community Struggle in the Antebellum North* (1979); Luther Porter Jackson, *Free Negro Labor and Property Holding in Virginia, 1830–1860* (1942); David M. Katzman, *Before the Ghetto: Black Detroit in the Nineteenth Century* (1973); Rudolph M. Lapp, *Blacks in Gold Rush California* (1977); Leon Litwack, *North of Slavery: The Negro in the Free States, 1790–1860* (1961); Floyd J. Miller, *The Search for a Black Nationality: Black Colonization and Emigration 1787–1863* (1975); Emma Lou Thornbrough, *The Negro in Indiana* (1957); Arthur Zilversmit, *The First Emancipation: The Abolition of Slavery in the North* (1967).

Native Americans

Robert F. Berkhofer, Jr., *The White Man's Indian* (1978); Arthur De Rosier, *Removal of the Choctaw Indians* (1970); Grant Foreman, *Indian Removal: The Emigration of the Five Civilized Tribes of Indians,* rev. ed. (1953); Charles Hudson, *The Southeastern Indians* (1976); Alvin M. Josephy, Jr., *The Patriot Chiefs: a Chronicle of American Indian Resistance*

Work and Leisure
in the Early Nineteenth Century, 1800–1860

Nineteenth-century American farmers made annual fairs an occasion for demonstrating their agricultural skills. The competition to select the finest cattle, sheep, horses, or pigs not only gave farmers a reason for pride in their work, but provided an opportunity for socializing. As in the colonial period, rural Americans continued to combine work with leisure. Collection of H. T. Peters, Jr.

Some traditional leisure activities took on new, more organized forms in the mid-nineteenth century. Colonial Americans had enjoyed skating on crude, home-made skates and had attended horse races on one another's farms. By mid-century, machine-made ice skates were readily available, and the New Yorkers shown at top right went skating in the newly completed Central Park. At the same time, formally designed race courses like the one in Louisville (bottom right) attracted spectators from miles around to carefully planned and publicized contests. Thus Americans engaged in both participatory and spectator sports early in the nation's history.   Top: The St. Louis Art Museum, Eliza McMillan Fund; bottom: Collection of the J. B. Speed Art Museum, Louisville, Kentucky.

Like livestock competitions, quilting bees allowed Americans to socialize while working. The women at this bee have just completed a quilt, and one of them is removing it from its frame. As another clears leftover scraps from the floor, a black fiddler strikes up a dance tune. The Henry Francis du Pont Winterthur Museum, Winterthur, Delaware.

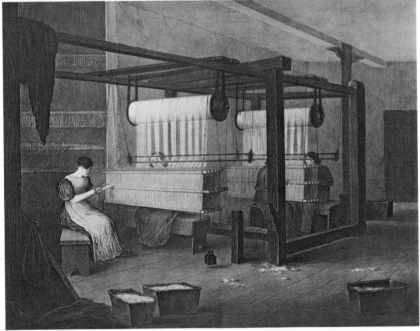

Until the 1850s, northern farm daughters like the girl at left made up most of the work force in the cotton mills: they were the nation's first factory workers. But although they were operating machines and working outside their homes, the mill girls still performed the same tasks their mothers had—spinning and weaving. Though women's work had in one sense changed dramatically, then, in another sense it had remained much the same. Slater Mill Historic Site, Pawtucket, Rhode Island.

Despite the introduction of factories and
farm machinery in the North and West,
the use of manual labor persisted in the
South. This mid-nineteenth-century painting shows the old-fashioned sugar-
harvesting methods used by slaves in
Texas and Louisiana cane fields. Perhaps
because planters gained little by creating
extra leisure time for their enslaved work
force, old ways died slowly.   The
Glenbow-Alberta Institute, Canada.

(1961); John K. Mahon, *History of the Second Seminole War, 1835–1842* (1967); Francis P. Prucha, *American Indian Policy in the Formative Years* (1962); Ronald N. Satz, *American Indian Policy in the Jacksonian Era* (1975); Glen Tucker, *Tecumseh: Vision of Glory* (1956); Wilcomb E. Washburn, *The Indian in America* (1975); Thurman Wilkin, *Cherokee Tragedy* (1970).

Women and the family

Nancy F. Cott, *The Bonds of Womanhood: "Woman's Sphere" in New England, 1780–1835* (1977); Carl N. Degler, *At Odds: Women and the Family in America from the Revolution to the Present* (1980); Linda Gordon, *Woman's Body, Woman's Rights: A Social History of Birth Control in America* (1976); Gerda Lerner, "The Lady and the Mill Girl," *Mid-Continent American Studies Journal,* 10 (Spring 1969), 5–15; James C. Mohr, *Abortion in America: The Origins and Evolution of National Policy, 1800–1900* (1978); James Reed, *From Private Vice to Public Virtue: The Birth Control Movement and American Society Since 1830* (1978); Kathryn Kish Sklar, *Catherine Beecher: A Study in American Domesticity* (1973); Barbara Welter, "The Cult of True Womanhood, 1820–1860," *American Quarterly,* 18 (Summer 1966), 151–174.

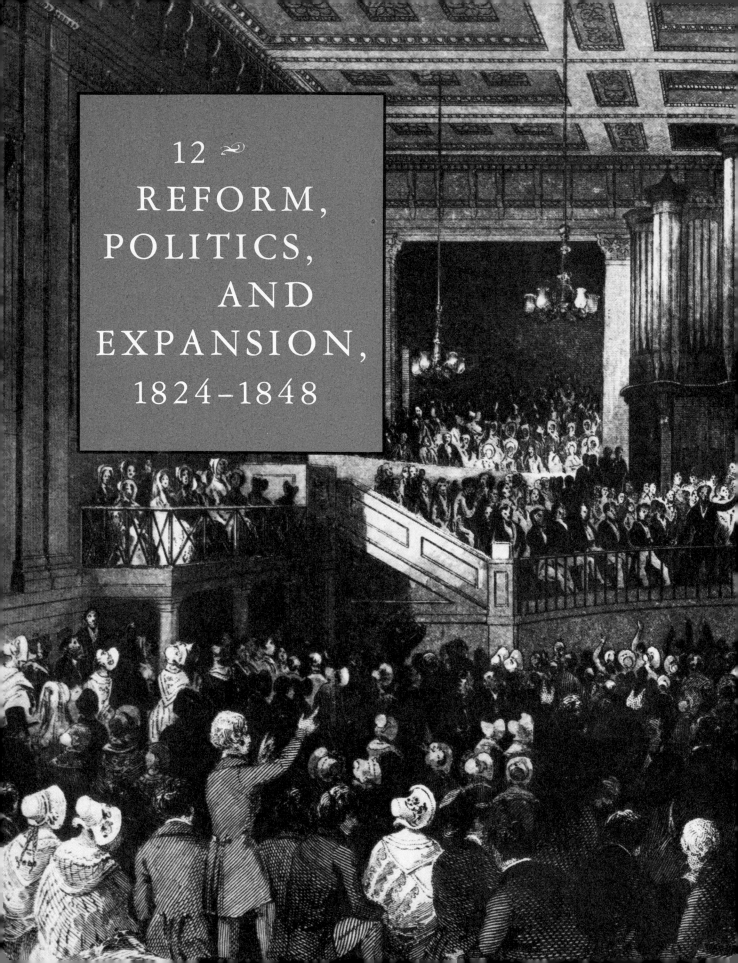

12 ~

REFORM,
POLITICS,
AND
EXPANSION,
1824–1848

Like a biblical prophet, the gaunt, bearded New Englander Henry David Thoreau periodically withdrew from the world to meditate and listen to an inner voice. Then he would emerge, pen in hand, in defense of nature against exploitation, of simplicity against industrialism, of citizen against the state. From July 4, 1845, to September 6, 1847, Thoreau retreated to the wilderness shores of Walden Pond in Concord, Massachusetts. His sojourn there resulted in the classic *Walden, or Life in the Woods* (1854), a romantic account of his thoughts and experiences that exalted nature and individualism.

Thoreau was skeptical of the value of the artifacts of a changing economy and society: railroads, steamboats, the telegraph, factories, and cities. "There is an illusion about" such improvements, he wrote in *Walden.* "There is not always a positive advance. The Devil goes on exacting compound interest to the last for his early share and numerous succeeding investments in them. . . . Men think that it is essential that the *Nation* have commerce, and export ice, and talk through a telegraph, and ride thirty miles an hour . . . but whether we should live like baboons or like men, is a little uncertain."

Thoreau the prophet claimed that it was possible to escape the marketplace, to forgo the world of cities and factories, to live simply in the landscape that existed before the plow and the engine. There was an eternal cycle of seasons, he wrote, and a place for humans within that cycle. By living off the land, one could achieve a good, moral life, in relation both to oneself and to nature.

Yet for all his idealization of the simple life, Thoreau did not withdraw from the world, much less from Concord. While at Walden he visited his mother daily, dined with townsfolk, joined the men congregating around the grocery-store stove, and hosted picnics and blueberrying parties at his cabin. In reality his everyday life was infused with all those modern improvements he seemed to detest so much. Indeed, Thoreau's years as a hermit depended, as James Russell Lowell wrote in a famous attack on *Walden,* on the fruits of organized society. "He squatted on another man's land; he borrows an ax; his boards, his nails, his bricks, his mortar, his books, his lamp, his fishhooks, his plough, his hoe, all turn state's evidence against him as an accomplice in the sin

of that artificial civilization." Thoreau even raised a cash crop—beans—and sold it to support himself at Walden.

Was Thoreau a fraud? No, he was caught up in a basic ambivalence toward industrialization and urbanization. *Walden* was a romantic, idealistic response to the changes that were sweeping America—in essence, a nostalgic return to the world of his youth. Although Thoreau's answer was highly individualistic, he shared his search—and his ambivalence—with millions of other Americans. They were lured on the one hand by the simplicity and beauty of pastoral days gone by, pulled on the other by their belief in progress and the promise of machine-generated prosperity and happiness.

Indeed, in the early nineteenth century artists, writers, and reformers of all kinds sought to find or impose harmony on a society in which discord had reached a crescendo. The Hudson River school of painters sought on canvas to reconcile the pastoral ideal with urban and industrial reality. Reformers, prompted by the evangelical ardor of the Second Great Awakening and convinced of the perfectibility of the human race, crusaded for individual improvement. Some, like the Shakers and the New Englanders of Brook Farm, withdrew from the everyday competitive world to seek perfection in utopian communities. Others sought to improve themselves by renouncing intoxicating spirits. Inevitably the personal impulse to reform oneself led to the creation and reshaping of institutions. Public education, religious orders, hospitals, asylums, and penitentiaries all underwent scrutiny and reform. Women were prominent in the reform movement, and the role of women in public life became an issue in itself.

But eventually one issue overrode all others: antislavery. No single issue evoked the depth of passion that slavery did. On a personal level it pitted neighbor against neighbor, settler against settler, section against section. National expansion in the 1840s and 1850s would make it politically explosive as well.

To a great extent, those favoring and those opposing reform fought their battles in the political arena. Once reformers had formed a cohesive group, they naturally turned to the state as an effective instrument of social and economic change. Opponents of reform were no less concerned with social problems. What

The Lackawanna Valley, by the painter George Inness, a member of the Hudson Valley school. National Gallery of Art, Washington, Gift of Mrs. Huttleston Rogers.

set them apart from reformers was their skepticism about human perfectibility and their distrust of institutions and power, both public and private. To them, coercion was the greater evil. Rather than shaping change, they sought to reverse it.

In the late 1820s the opponents of reform found a champion in Andrew Jackson and a home in the Democratic party. Jackson reversed the activist role previous presidents had played, believing that a strong federal government restricted individual freedom by favoring one group over another. The federally chartered Second Bank of the United States became the target of his opposition to special interests. In response, reformers rallied around the Whig party, which became the vehicle for humanitarian reform. The two parties competed energetically in the second party system, developing strong organizations and intensely loyal followings. Religious and ethnic differences divided the two parties; immigrant Catholics tended to become Democrats, and native-born evangelical Protestants became Whigs.

Following the hard times of 1839 to 1843, the United States renewed its territorial expansion. Manifest Destiny became the byword of those who hoped to extend the United States across the continent. During the 1840s the territory of the United States increased by two-thirds. The Republic of Texas was annexed in 1845, and the next year the United States acquired undisputed control of the Oregon Territory south of the forty-ninth parallel. In 1848 the Treaty of Guadalupe Hidalgo, which ended the Mexican War, gave the United States the Mexican territories encompassing present-day California, Nevada, Arizona, New Mexico, and Utah. The territorial destiny of the United States had indeed become manifest during this period.

Romanticism and reform

The undisputed symbol of change in America was the machine—that fine-tooled, power-driven substitute for men and women's own hands, stamping out interchangeable parts for other machines. Of course it was not machines alone that altered the direction of the nation and its people. Population growth, immigration, the receding frontier, and loosening family and community ties all contributed to the remaking of the United States. But it was the machine that seemed to change the American landscape the most. It threatened to turn America into a giant factory, in which everything was viewed as a commodity to be sold at the marketplace.

What seemed to be most at risk was Thoreau's vision of a life directed by inner impulses, by a deep connection with nature and humanity. Ralph Waldo Emerson, Thoreau's closest friend, saw machines as competing with people for control. He described machines ("things") as the victor:

Things are in the saddle,
And ride mankind.

There are two laws discrete,
Not reconciled,—
Law for man, and law for thing;
The last builds town and fleet,
But it runs wild,
And doth the man unking.

Others disagreed. The locomotive, a business magazine predicted in 1840, "is to be one of the most valuable agents of the present age, because it is swifter than the greyhound, and powerful as a thousand horses; because it is guided by its directors; because it runs and never tires." The advocates of industrial change claimed, in other words, that the machine was an improvement on nature.

The first distinctively American group of artists, the Hudson River school, seemed to look askance at

Hudson River school

urbanization and industrialization. Led by Thomas Cole, who abandoned portrait painting in the 1820s to concentrate on nature, these artists—Asher Brown Durand, William Trost Richards, George Inness, and others—ignored cities and factories to paint romantic scenes of majestic mountains and river valleys. Their northeastern panoramas were not, however, untouched by civilization's advances. Thomas Cole's *The Oxbow* (1836), for instance, portrayed the works of both God and human beings; the focal point of the painting was cleared farm land. Similarly, William Trost Richards's *View in the Adirondacks* (about 1859) focused on an inhabited environment of tool-made houses and plowed fields.

These American landscapists seemed to be saying that the land itself would restrain industrialism; American mill villages would not become slums like Manchester, England. George Inness solved the conflict visually in his painting *The Lackawanna Valley* (1855). Hired by the Lackawanna Railroad to depict a railroad scene, he blended landscape and machine into an organic whole. The railroad and industrial buildings seemed to belong to the landscape without overpowering or obliterating it.

The changing environment was treated more directly in the work of the firm of Currier and Ives,

Currier and Ives

whose prints depicted not grand panoramas but the events of everyday life. Currier and Ives illustrated actual elections, disasters, steamboat races, and sporting events in their popular prints, mass-produced for ordinary homes. Using techniques developed in other retail industries, the two turned art into a large-scale commercial venture.

The artist's search for harmony between the vast physical changes America was experiencing and the simple landscape of the past was paralleled by various reform movements that emerged during the 1820s. Basically, reformers sought to restore order to a society made disorderly by economic and social change. Disturbed by change, convinced that the world could be improved, and confident that they could do something about it, reformers were so active from 1820 through the 1850s that the period became known as an age of reform.

Why were people upset by change? What was it about the growth of cities and industry that disturbed them? For one thing, many people felt they were no

Background of reform

longer masters of their own fate. Change was occurring so rapidly that people had difficulty keeping up with it. An apprentice shoemaker could find his trade obsolete by the time he became a journeyman; a student could find himself lacking sufficient arithmetic or geography to enter a counting house when he graduated. Other aspects of change were simply unpleasant or culturally alien. Respectable citizens found their safety threatened by urban mobs and paupers, and the Protestant majority feared the growing Catholic minority, with their strange customs and beliefs. To many these changes seemed to undermine the values of the American Revolution and the Declaration of Independence. Americans had fought the Revolution to make themselves independent; poverty and obsolescent trades and education made them dependent. And they had waged war to preserve their rights as Englishmen, not to protect alien cultures and religions. By the mid-1830s nearly all the revolutionary leaders and founders of the republic had died. People asked themselves: would the mission of American society follow them to the grave?

Reform was at its core an attempt to impose moral direction on these social, cultural, and economic changes. The movement encompassed both individual improvement (religion, temperance, health) and institutional reform (antislavery, women's rights, and education). A minority of reformers were reactionaries motivated more by fear than by hope—anti-Masonic, nativist, and anti-Catholic. Not all the problems that reformers addressed were new to the nineteenth century; some were generations old. Slavery had existed in the United States for two centuries, and alcohol had been a colonial problem; yet neither became a national issue until the 1820s and after, when the reformist ferment prompted action.

Though reform movements played an important role in all sections of the country, they centered in the North and most reformers were northern. For one thing, slavery and the complex issues surrounding that institution tended to suppress the southern reform impulse. Fear of educating blacks, for instance, led even antislavery southerners to ignore the movement for educational reform.

The prime motivating force behind reform was probably religion. Starting in the late 1790s, a tremendous religious revival, the Second Great Awakening, galvanized Protestants (see Chapter 7). The awakening began in small villages in the East, intensified in the 1820s in western New York, and continued through the late 1840s. Under its influence, Christians in all parts of the country tried to right the wrongs of the world.

Religious revival and utopianism

Evangelical Christianity was a religion of the heart, not the head. In 1821 Charles G. Finney, "the father of modern revivalism," experienced a soul-shaking conversion, which, he said, brought him "a retainer from the Lord Jesus Christ to plead his cause." Finney, a former teacher and lawyer, immediately began his career as a converter of souls, preaching that salvation could be achieved through spontaneous conversion or spiritual rebirth like his own. In everyday language, he told his audiences that "God has made man a moral free agent." In other words, sin was a voluntary, avoidable act; Christians were not doomed by original sin. Hence anyone could achieve salvation through righteous behavior. Finney's brand of revivalism transcended sects, wealth, and race. Presbyterians, Baptists, and Congregationalists became evangelists, as did some Methodists.

The Second Great Awakening raised people's hopes for the Second Coming of | Second Great Awakening | the Christian messiah and the establishment of the Kingdom of God on earth. A millennium—a thousand years—of peace, harmony, and Christian morality was supposed to precede the Day of Judgment. Thus revivalists set out to speed the Second Coming by creating a heaven on earth. They joined the forces of good and light—reform—to combat those of evil and darkness. Some revivalists even believed that the United States had a special mission in God's design, and therefore a special role in eliminating evil.

In this way the Great Awakening bred reform, and evangelical Protestants became missionaries for both religious and secular salvation. Wherever they preached, voluntary societies arose. Evangelists organized an association for each issue—temperance, education, Sabbath observance, antidueling, and later antislavery; collectively these groups formed an empire of benevolent and moral reform societies.

In western New York and Ohio, the reform movement was the direct result of Charles G. Finney's preaching. Western New York experienced such continuous and heated waves of revivalism that it became known as the "burned-over" district. In other areas, revivalist institutions—Ohio's Lane Seminary and Oberlin College were the most famous—sent com-

Men sowing seed at the Bishop Hill Colony (1846–1862), a utopian farm community founded in Illinois by Swedish religious dissenters. At its peak in 1855 the colony had five hundred members. Bishop Hill State Historical Site.

mitted graduates out into the world to spread the gospel of reform. Evangelists also organized grassroots political movements. In the late 1830s and 1840s they rallied around the Whig party in an attempt to use government as an instrument of reform. Their efforts galvanized nonevangelical Protestants, Catholics, and Jews as well as evangelical Christians.

Other people, especially middle-class businessmen and their families, were drawn to revivalism for its efforts to restore traditional communal and familial values. Change had eroded the old ways of neighborliness and kinship. The new market economy tended to separate people from each other by emphasizing self above communal interest. Revivalism brought people back together and promised to restore the old order of things. It was an anchor in a sea of change.

Some of these seekers of a sense of community turned away from the larger society to establish utopian towns and farms. Such settlements offered an antidote to the untamed growth of large urban commu-

nities. Whatever their particular philosophy, utopians attempted to establish order and regularity in their daily lives and to build a cooperative rather than competitive environment. Some experimented with communal living and nontraditional work, family, and sex roles.

America's earliest utopian experiments were organized by the Shakers, who derived their name from the

| Shakers |

way they danced and swayed at worship services. An offshoot of the Quakers, their sect was established in America in 1774 by the English Shaker Ann Lee. Shakers believed that the end of the world was near, and that sin entered the world through sexual intercourse. They regarded existing churches as too worldly, and considered the Shaker family the instrument of salvation.

After the death of Mother Ann Lee in 1784, the Shakers turned to communal living to fulfill their mission. In 1787 they "gathered in" at New Lebanon, New York, to live, worship, and work communally.

Other colonies soon followed. At its peak, between 1820 and 1860, the sect had about six thousand members in twenty settlements in eight states. Shaker communities emphasized agriculture and crafts; most managed to become self-sufficient, profitable enterprises. Shaker furniture became famous for its excellent construction, utility, and beauty of design.

Though economically conservative, the Shakers were social radicals. They abolished individual families, practiced celibacy, and made no distinction between the sexes in their government, economy, or society. Each colony was one large family, with religious authority vested in elders and eldresses and economic leadership in deacons and deaconesses. The Shaker ministry was headed by a woman, Lucy Wright, during its period of greatest growth.

The Shaker experiment in communal living proved both economically rewarding and emotionally satisfying to its members. It was the communities' celibacy that proved to be their eventual downfall. Unable to reproduce naturally, the colonies succumbed to death by attrition in the twentieth century.

Not all utopian communities were founded by religious groups. Robert Owen's New Harmony was a short-lived attempt to found a socialist utopia in Indiana. A wealthy Scottish industrialist, Owen established the cooperative community in 1825. According to his plan, its nine hundred members were to exchange their labor for goods at a communal store. Handicrafts (hat and boot making) flourished at New Harmony. But the economic base of the community, its textile mill, failed after Owen gave it to the community to run. Turnover in membership was too great for the community to develop any cohesion, and by 1827 the experiment had ended.

More successful were the New England transcendentalists who lived and worked at the Brook Farm

| Brook Farm | cooperative in West Roxbury, Massachusetts. Inspired by the

philosophy that the spiritual transcends the worldly, members rejected materialism and sought satisfaction in a communal life combining spirituality, work, and play. Founded in 1841 by the Unitarian minister George Ripley, Brook Farm attracted not only farmers and skilled craftsmen but teachers and writers, among them Nathaniel Hawthorne. Indeed, the fame of Brook Farm rested on the intellectual achievements of its members. Its school attracted students from outside the community, and its residents contributed heavily to the *Dial,* the leading transcendentalist journal. In 1845 Brook Farm's hundred members organized themselves into model phalanxes (work-living units) in keeping with the philosophy of the French utopian Charles Fourier. Rigid regimentation replaced individualism, and membership dropped. Following a disastrous fire in 1846, the experiment collapsed.

Though short-lived, Brook Farm played a significant part in the Romantic movement. During these years Hawthorne, Emerson, and the *Dial*'s editor Margaret Fuller joined Thoreau, James Fenimore Cooper, Herman Melville, and others in creating what is known today as the American Renaissance—the flowering of a national literature. In poetry and prose these Romanticists praised individualism and intuition, rejecting or modifying the ordered world of the Enlightenment in favor of the mysteries of nature. Rebelling against convention, both social and literary, they probed and celebrated the American character and the American experience. Cooper, for instance, wrote of the frontier in the Leatherstocking Tales, and Melville wrote of great spiritual quests in the guise of seafaring adventures.

Far and away the most successful communitarians were the Mormons, who originated in the burned-over district of western New York. Fleeing persecution in Illinois because of their newly adopted practice of polygamy, the Mormons trekked across

| Mormon community of Saints | the continent in 1846 and 1847 to found a New Zion in the Great Salt Lake Valley. There, under

Brigham Young, head of the Twelve Apostles, they established a cohesive community of Saints—a heaven on earth. The Mormons created agricultural settlements and distributed land according to family size. An extensive irrigation system, constructed by men who contributed their labor according to the quantity of land they received and the amount of water they expected to use, transformed the arid valley into a rich oasis. As the colony developed, its cooperative principles gradually gave way to benevolent corporate authority, and the church elders came to control water, trade, industry, and even the territorial government of Utah.

Revivalism encompassed the absurd as well as the sublime. Some naive revivalists, like the followers of Baptist minister William Miller, believed in the literal return of Jesus. Awaiting His appearance in 1843, the "year of the time," the Millerites prepared by holding camp meetings in locations as widely separated as Massachusetts, Iowa, and Kentucky and giving away all their earthly goods. But they did so in vain. Quick recalculations postponed the coming to October 1844. When the End of Days again failed to occur, the Second Coming was indefinitely postponed and most of the faithful abandoned the vigil. Presumably they turned to more earthly concerns, like the evils of alcohol.

Temperance, public education, and feminism

As a group, American men liked to drink alcoholic spirits—whiskey, rum, and hard cider. They gathered in public houses, saloons, taverns, and rural inns to socialize, gossip, discuss politics, play cards, and drink. Men drank on all occasions, social and business: contracts were sealed with a drink; celebrations were toasted with spirits; barn raisings and harvests ended with liquor. And though respectable women did not drink in public, many regularly tippled alcohol-based elixirs, patent medicines promoted as cure-alls.

There were economic and environmental reasons for the popularity of liquor. Spirits were more easily transported than grain; as a result, by 1810 they were surpassed only by cloth and tanned hides in total value of output. And in areas where clean water was either expensive or unobtainable, whiskey was not only cheaper but safer than water. Not until the Croton Reservoir brought clean water to New York City in 1842 did New Yorkers switch from spirits to water.

Why then was temperance such a vital issue? And why were women specially active in the movement? As with all reform, temperance had a strong religious base. "The Holy Spirit," a temperance pamphlet proclaimed, "will not visit, much less dwell with him who is under the polluting, debasing effects of intoxicating drink." To evangelicals, the selling of whiskey was a chronic symbol of Sabbath violation, for workers commonly labored six days a week, then

spent Sunday at the public house drinking and socializing. Alcohol was seen as a destroyer of families as well, since men who drank heavily either neglected their families or could not adequately support them. Indeed, though craftsmen who worked for themselves could mix drink with work, the habit of drinking was not tolerated in the new world of the factory. Timothy Arthur Shay dramatized all these evils in *Ten Nights in a Barroom* (1853), a classic American melodrama.

Demon rum thus became the target of the most widespread and successful of the antebellum reform movements. As the reformers gained momentum, they shifted their emphasis from temperate use of spirits to voluntary abstinence and finally to a crusade to prohibit the manufacture and sale of spirits. The American Society for the Promotion of Temperance, organized in 1826 to urge drinkers to sign a pledge of abstinence, shortly thereafter became a pressure group for state prohibition legislation. By the mid-1830s there were some five thousand state and local temperance societies, and more than a million people had taken the pledge. By the 1840s the movement's success was reflected in a sharp decline in alcohol consumption in the United States. Between 1800 and 1830, annual per capita consumption of alcohol had risen from three to more than five gallons; by the mid-1840s, however, it had dropped below two gallons. Success bred more victories. In 1851 Maine prohibited the manufacture and sale of alcohol except for medicinal purposes, and by 1855 similar laws had been enacted throughout New England and in New York, Delaware, Indiana, Iowa, Michigan, Ohio, and Pennsylvania.

Even though consumption of alcohol was declining, opposition to it did not weaken. Many reformers believed that alcohol was an evil introduced and perpetuated by Catholic immigrants. From the 1820s on, antiliquor reformers based much of their argument on this false prejudice. The Irish and Germans, the *American Protestant Magazine* complained in 1849, "bring the grog shops like the frogs of Egypt upon us." Rum and immigrants defiled the Sabbath; rum and immigrants brought poverty and pauperism; rum and immigrants supported the feared papacy. Some Catholics did join with nonevangelical Protestant sects like the Lutherans to oppose temperance legislation. But

Temperance societies

"The Drunkard's Family," a Currier and Ives print that dramatized the evils of alcohol. With their pockets empty, their children shoeless and exposed to the elements, the drunkard and his
long-suffering wife wander an unmarked trail. Edmund B.
Sullivan Collection, Hartford University.

other Catholics took the pledge of abstinence and
formed their own temperance organizations, such as
the St. Mary's Mutual Benevolent Total Abstinence
Society in Boston. Even nondrinking Catholics
tended to oppose state regulation of drinking, however; temperance seemed to them a question of individual choice, not state coercion.

Another important part of the reform impulse was
the development of new institutions to meet the social needs of citizens. The list of organizations
founded during this era is a long one—Protestant
denominations, Catholic orders, reform Judaism;
schools and colleges, hospitals, asylums, orphanages,
and penitentiaries; new political parties; and myriad
reform societies. Many of these institutions experimented with new techniques for handling old problems. New York state's penitentiary at Auburn, for
example, placed prisoners in rehabilitative cooperative
labor programs during the day, confining them only
at night. Other states soon followed New York's lead.

Public education was one of the more lasting results of the age of institution building. In 1800 there
were no public schools outside New England; by
1860 every state had some public education, although
southern states lagged far behind the North and
West. Massachusetts took the lead, especially under
Horace Mann, secretary of the state board of education from 1837 to 1848. Under
Mann, Massachusetts established a
minimum school year of six
months, increased the number of high schools, formalized the training of teachers, and emphasized secular subjects and applied skills rather than religion.

Horace Mann was an evangelist of public education and school reform; his preaching on behalf of
free state education changed schooling not only in
Massachusetts but also throughout the nation. "If we
do not prepare children to become good citizens,"
Mann prophesied, "if we do not develop their capacities, . . . imbue their hearts with the love of truth and

> Horace Mann
> on education

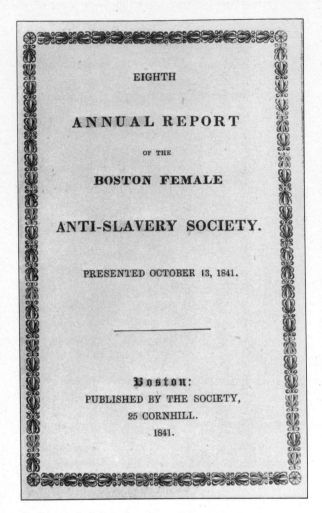

EIGHTH

ANNUAL REPORT

OF THE

BOSTON FEMALE

ANTI-SLAVERY SOCIETY.

PRESENTED OCTOBER 13, 1841.

Boston:
PUBLISHED BY THE SOCIETY,
25 CORNHILL.
1841.

Women organized in Boston in 1833 to fight the evils of slavery. This annual report of their society was published in 1841.   Sophia Smith Collection, Smith College.

American history, arithmetic, and science replaced many of the classics; teachers were trained in the new subjects at normal schools. Moral education was retained, but direct religious indoctrination was dropped.

Many traditionalists, including New England Congregationalists, fought to maintain the old ties between education and religion. Some feared secular public education was a sign of the decline of American morality and virtue. But others, including many deeply religious people reborn in the Second Great Awakening, believed that public education would strengthen religious values. Mann's ideals and motives—the general betterment of society—were similar to theirs, and they saw merit in a democratic school system available to all, rich and poor. They noted, furthermore, that the Bible remained the centerpiece of elementary school education. And free public education would enable Sunday schools to devote full time to their students' religious needs without having to teach reading and writing as well. Thus Sunday-school teachers became Mann's allies.

A more controversial reform movement was the rise of American feminism in the 1840s. Ironically, it was women's traditional image as pious and spiritual that brought them into the public sphere. The Second Great Awakening, with its emphasis on conversion through the heart, had served to elevate women; women were thought to be more emotional than men, and emotion was the most important element in being reborn. In the 1820s and 1830s, using their churches as a base, women began to play a prominent activist role in temperance, antislavery, and other reform movements. Organized into women's groups like the Boston Female Anti-Slavery Society, they slowly entered the public arena.

Reaction to the growing involvement of women in reform movements led many women to re-examine their position in society. In 1837 two antislavery lecturers, Angelina and Sarah Grimké, became objects of

Angelina and Sarah Grimké

controversy when they were attacked for speaking before mixed groups of men and women. Some New England Congregationalists and even abolitionists joined in the criticism; as one pastoral letter put it, women should obey, not lecture, men. This hostile reception turned the Grimkés' attention from slavery to women's condition. The two attacked the concept of

duty, and a reverence for all things sacred and holy, then our republic must go down to destruction." The abolition of ignorance, Mann claimed, would end misery, crime, and suffering. "The only sphere . . . left open for our patriotism," he wrote, "is the improvement of our chidren,—not the few, but the many; not a part of them but all."

In laying the basis of free public schools, Mann also broadened the scope of education. Previously, education had had little practical benefit, other than the discipline fostered by rote reading of the Bible; thus most parents were indifferent to whether or not their children attended school. Under Mann's leadership, the school curriculum became more appropriate for future clerks, farmers, and workers. Geography,

"subordination to man," insisting that both men and women had the "same rights and same duties." Sarah Grimké's *Letters on the Condition of Women and the Equality of the Sexes* (1838) and her sister's *Letters to Catherine E. Beecher*, published the same year, were the opening volleys in the war against the legal and social inequality of women.

In arguing against slavery, some women noticed the similarities between their own position and that of slaves. They saw parallels in their legal disabilities—inability to vote or control their property, except in widowhood—and their social restrictions—exclusion from advanced schooling and from most occupations. "The investigation of the rights of the slave," Angelina Grimké confessed, "has led me to a better understanding of my own." The women who worked in the Lowell mills came to the same conclusion in the 1840s.

Unlike other reform movements, which succeeded in building a broad base of individual and organizational support, the movement for women's rights was confined mostly to women. Some men joined the ranks, notably abolitionist William Lloyd Garrison and ex-slave Frederick Douglass, but most actively opposed the movement. In the 1840s the question of women's rights split the antislavery movement, the majority declaring themselves opposed. Though the Seneca Falls Convention, led by Elizabeth Cady Stanton and Lucretia Mott, issued a much-published indictment of women's disabilities in 1848, it had little effect. By the 1850s feminists were focusing more and more on the single issue of suffrage. If women had the vote, these reformers argued, they would be able both to protect themselves and to realize their potential as moral and spiritual leaders. Their argument fell on deaf ears. Another cause would eclipse their movement, at least for a time.

The antislavery movement

Antislavery began as one among many reform movements. But, sparked by territorial expansion, the issue of slavery eventually became so overpowering that it consumed all other reforms. Passions would become so heated that they would threaten the nation itself. Above all else, those opposed to slavery saw it as a moral issue, evidence of the sinfulness of the American nation. When territorial questions in the 1850s forced the issue of slavery to center stage, the antislavery forces were well prepared (see Chapter 13).

Prior to the 1820s antislavery had played on the conscience of the individual slaveholder. Quakers had led the first antislavery movement in the eighteenth century, freeing their slaves and preaching that it was a sin for Christians to hold people in bondage. But in the North, where most states had abolished slavery by 1800, whites took little interest in an issue that did not concern them directly. It was in the upper South that antislavery sentiment was strongest, at least until the 1820s. But the movement there seemed to be as much concerned with preparing society for the natural death of slavery as with the plight of the slaves themselves. The American Colonization Society, founded in 1816 and supported by slaveholders and white abolitionists alike, worked to rid the nation of blacks by gradually settling them in Africa.

Through the 1820s only free people of color demanded an immediate end to slavery. By 1830 there were at least fifty black antislavery societies in major black communities. These societies assisted fugitive slaves, attacked slavery at every turn, and reminded the nation that its mission as defined in the Declaration of Independence remained unfulfilled. A free black press helped to spread their word. When the climate of opinion changed and whites became more committed to antislavery, black abolitionists like Frederick Douglass, Sojourner Truth, and Harriet Tubman worked with white reformers in the American Anti-Slavery Society. These crusaders also stirred European support for their militant and unrelenting campaign. "Brethren, arise, arise, arise!" Henry Highland Garnet commanded the 1843 national colored convention. "Strike for your lives and liberties. Now is the day and hour. Let every slave in the land do this and the days of slavery are numbered. Rather die freemen than live to be slaves."

Black antislavery movement

In the 1830s a full-fledged abolitionist crusade was ushered in by a small minority of white reformers who made antislavery their primary commitment. The most prominent and uncompromising abolitionist, though clearly not the most representative, was William Lloyd Garrison, who demanded "immediate and

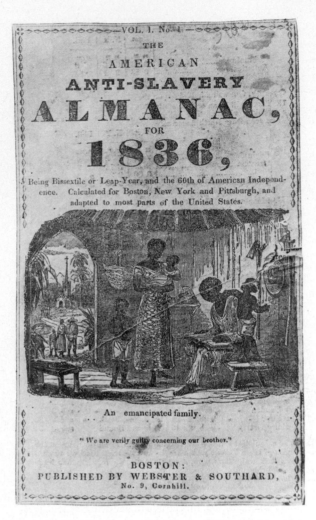

The Anti-Slavery Almanac, propaganda of the American Anti-Slavery Society. Beneath the picture of an emancipated family is the motto "We are verily guilty concerning our brother." Sophia Smith Collection, Smith College.

weapon against slavery for thirty-five years. "I am in earnest—I will not equivocate—I will not excuse—I will not retreat a single inch—and *I will be heard,*" he wrote in the first issue.

Garrison's refusal to work with anyone who even indirectly delayed emancipation left him isolated. He even forswore political action, on the grounds that it was governments that permitted slavery. (On July 4, 1854, Garrison burned a copy of the Constitution, proclaiming, "So perish all compromises with tyranny.") Though not a great organizer, Garrison helped to make antislavery the prevailing issue through sheer force of rhetoric. His "immediatism" is probably best defined as tolerating no delay in ending slavery; he had no specific plan for abolishing it. In essence, Garrison called for an antislavery revival—all those who held slaves or cooperated with institutions supporting slavery should cast off their sins, repent, and join the battle against evil.

Garrison alone could not have made antislavery a central issue. By the 1830s many northern reformers were recognizing the evils of slavery and preparing to act. Moral and religious ferment in the burned-over district and the Old Northwest had primed evangelists to enter the fray. And the reform activities of the 1820s, including antislavery, had built a network of interrelated organizations. A state society in Michigan, for example, met one day as a temperance convention and reconvened the next day as an antislavery society.

Ironically, it was in defense of the constitutional rights of abolitionists, not slaves, that many whites entered the struggle. Wherever they went, abolitionists found their civil rights in danger, especially their right of free speech. Using the new steam press, the American Anti-Slavery Society had increased its distribution of antislavery propaganda tenfold between 1834 and 1835, sending out 1.1 million pieces in 1835. But southern mobs seized and destroyed much of the mail, and South Carolina intercepted and burned abolitionist literature that entered the state (with the approval of the postmaster general). President Andrew Jackson even proposed a law prohibiting the mailing of antislavery tracts.

Another civil rights confrontation developed in Congress. Exercising their constitutional right to petition Congress, abolitionists had mounted a campaign

William Lloyd Garrison

complete emancipation." Garrison had begun his career in the late 1820s editing the *National Philanthropist,* a weekly paper devoted to general reform, but especially to prohibition. It was in 1828, when Benjamin Lundy recruited him to *The Genius of Universal Emancipation,* that Garrison entered the ranks of the abolitionists. But Lundy favored colonization and sought to end slavery through persuasion, a position Garrison rejected. In January 1831 Garrison broke with gradualists like Lundy and published the first issue of the *Liberator,* which was to be his major

Chapter 12: Reform, politics, and expansion, 1824–1848

to abolish slavery and the slave trade in the District of Columbia. (Since the district was under federal rule, states' rights arguments against interfering with slavery did not apply there.) But Congress responded in 1836 by adopting the so-called gag rule, which

| Gag rule |

automatically tabled abolitionist petitions, effectively preventing debate on them. In a dramatic defense of the right of petition, ex-president John Quincy Adams, then a Massachusetts representative, took to the floor repeatedly to defy the gag rule and eventually succeeded in getting it repealed (1844).

Antislavery speakers often faced hostile crowds, and their presses were under constant threat of attack. The martyrdom of Elijah P. Lovejoy at the hands of a mob in Alton, Illinois, in 1837, drew attention to proslavery violence. Lovejoy, who had been driven out of slaveholding Missouri, had re-established his printing plant just across the river in Illinois. He was killed by a mob that had come to sack his office, with the cooperation of local authorities. Public outrage at Lovejoy's murder, as with the gag rule and censorship of the mails, only served to broaden the base of antislavery support in the North.

Frustration with the federal government also fed northern support for antislavery. By and large, politicians and government officials sought to avoid the question of slavery. The Missouri Compromise of 1820 had been an effort to quarantine the issue by adopting a simple formula—banning slavery north of 36°30′, Missouri's southern boundary—that would make debate on the slave or free status of new states unnecessary. Censorship of the mails and the gag rule were similar attempts to keep the issue out of the political arena. Yet the more national leaders, especially Democrats, sought to avoid the matter, the more they hardened the resolve of the antislavery forces.

The effect of the unlawful, violent, and obstructionist tactics used by proslavery advocates cannot be overestimated. Antislavery was not at the outset a unified movement. It was splintered and factionalized, and its adherents fought each other as often as they fought the defenders of slavery. They were divided over Garrison's emphasis on "moral suasion" versus the more practical political approach of James G. Birney, the Liberty party's candidate for president in 1840 (see page 332). They were split over support of other reforms, especially the rights of women. And they disagreed over the place of black people in American society. Even so, abolitionists would eventually manage to unify and make antislavery a major issue in the politics of the 1850s.

Jacksonianism and the beginnings of modern party politics

Reformers were not the only Americans working to create or restore order in the 1820s and 1830s. Though their means differed, political leaders were also seeking to deal with the problems created by an expanding, urbanizing, market-oriented nation. John Quincy Adams advocated a nationalist program and an activist federal government; Andrew Jackson and his followers adhered to the Jeffersonian ideal of a limited federal government, with the primary power vested in the states.

The election of 1824, in which Adams and Jackson faced each other for the first time, signaled the beginning of a new, more open political system. From 1800

| End of the caucus system |

through 1820 a congressional caucus had chosen the Republican presidential nominees: Jefferson, Madison, and Monroe. Jefferson and Madison had both indicated to the caucus that their secretaries of state should succeed them, and the system had worked efficiently. Of course, such a system restricted voter involvement—but this was not a real drawback at first, since in 1800 only five of sixteen states selected presidential electors by popular vote. (In ten states, legislators designated the electors.) In 1816, however, ten out of nineteen states chose electors by popular vote, and in 1824, eighteen out of twenty-four did so.

Moreover, President Monroe never designated an heir apparent. Without direction from the president, therefore, the caucus in 1824 chose William H. Crawford, secretary of the treasury. But others, encouraged by the opportunity to appeal directly to the voters in most states, challenged Crawford. Secretary of State John Quincy Adams drew support from New England, and westerners backed Speaker of the House

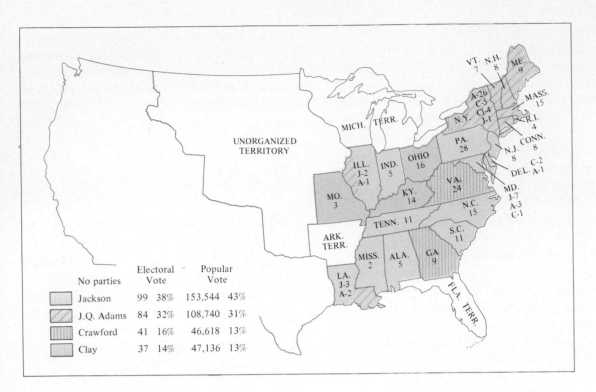

No parties		Electoral Vote		Popular Vote	
Jackson	99	38%	153,544	43%
J.Q. Adams	84	32%	108,740	31%
Crawford	41	16%	46,618	13%
Clay	37	14%	47,136	13%

Presidential election, 1824

Henry Clay of Kentucky. Secretary of War John C. Calhoun looked to the South for support, and hoped to win Pennsylvania as well. Andrew Jackson, a popular military hero whose political views were unknown, was nominated by resolution of the Tennessee legislature and won support everywhere. But Crawford, who had declined to oppose Monroe in 1816 and 1820, had the most widespread support in Washington. Since his choice by the caucus was a foregone conclusion, the other four candidates joined in attacking the caucus system as undemocratic. When their supporters boycotted the deliberations, Crawford's victory became a hollow one, based on a minority vote. The role of the congressional caucus in nominating presidents was over.

Though Andrew Jackson led in both popular and electoral votes in the four-way presidential election of 1824, no one received a majority. Adams finished second, and Clay and Crawford trailed far behind. (Calhoun dropped out of the race before the election.) Under the Constitution, the selection of a president in such circumstances fell to the House of Representatives, which would vote by state delegation, one vote

to a state. Crawford, a stroke victim, never received serious consideration; Clay, who had received the fewest votes, was dropped. But Clay, as Speaker of the House and leader of the Ohio Valley states, was in a position to influence the House vote for either Adams or Jackson. He backed Adams, who received the votes of thirteen out of twenty-four state delegations (see map). Clay was rewarded with the position of secretary of state in the Adams administration—the traditional stepping-stone to the presidency. Angry Jacksonians denounced the arrangement as a "corrupt bargain" that had stolen the office from the clear frontrunner.

As president, John Quincy Adams took a strong nationalist position emphasizing Henry Clay's American System of protective tariffs, a national bank, and internal improvements (see page 210). Adams believed the federal government should take an activist role not only in the economy but in education, science, and the arts; accordingly, he proposed a national university in Washington, D.C.

Tragically, Adams was as inept a president as he was brilliant as a diplomat and secretary of state. He un-

Chapter 12: Reform, politics, and expansion, 1824–1848

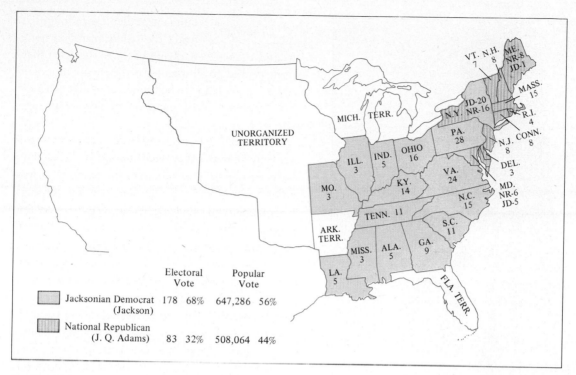

	Electoral Vote		Popular Vote	
▨ Jacksonian Democrat (Jackson)	178	68%	647,286	56%
▨ National Republican (J. Q. Adams)	83	32%	508,064	44%

Presidential election, 1828

derestimated the lingering effects of the Panic of 1819 and the resulting bitter opposition to a national bank and protective tariffs. Distrustful of party organization, Adams failed to build a coalition to support his programs. Meanwhile, supporters of Andrew Jackson sabotaged Adams's administration at every opportunity. They even turned Adams's one success to their advantage: by supporting the extremely high Tariff of Abominations (1828), the Jacksonians won the support of eastern protectionists. "The bill referred to manufactures of no sort or kind," John Randolph observed in noting its effect on Jackson's candidacy, "but the manufacture of a President of the United States."

The 1828 campaign between Adams and Jackson was an intensely personal conflict. Whatever principles the two men stood for were obscured by the mudslinging both sides indulged in. Though Adams won the same states as in 1824, his opposition rallied around one candidate—Jackson—and swamped him. Jackson polled 56 percent of the popular vote and won in the electoral college, 178 to 83 (see map). For him and his supporters, the election of 1828 was the culmination of a long-fought, well-organized cam-

paign based on party organization. Through a lavishly financed coalition of state parties, political leaders, and newspaper editors, a popular movement had elected a president.

Andrew Jackson was nicknamed "Old Hickory," after the toughest American hardwood. A rough-and-tumble, ambitious man, he rose from humble birth to become a wealthy planter and slaveholder. Jackson was the first American president not born into comfortable circumstances, a self-made man at ease among both frontiersmen and southern planters.

Andrew Jackson

Few Americans have been celebrated in myth and legend as has Andrew Jackson. As a general in the Tennessee militia, Jackson had led the battle against the Creeks on the Alabama frontier, forcing them from 22 million acres of land in Georgia and Alabama. He burst onto the national scene as the great hero of the War of 1812, and in 1818 enhanced his glory in an expedition against the Seminoles in Spanish Florida. Jackson also served as a congressional representative and senator from Tennessee, as a judge in his home state, and as the first territorial governor of

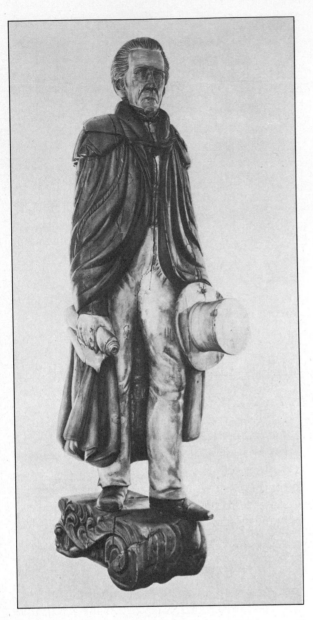

Wooden figurehead of "Old Hickory," Andrew Jackson, carved for the prow of the U.S.S. *Constitution* in 1834. Shortly after it was mounted, an enemy of Jackson sawed the head off.   Museum of the City of New York.

Florida (1821) before being nominated for the presidency in 1824. He was an active presidential aspirant until he won the office in 1828.

Jackson and his supporters offered a distinct alternative to the activist federal government Adams had advocated. They and their party, the Democratic-Republicans (shortened to Democrats), represented a wide range of beliefs but shared some common ideals.

Democrats Fundamentally, they sought to foster the Jeffersonian concept of an agrarian society, harkening back to the belief that a strong central government was the enemy of individual liberty, a tyranny to be feared. Thus, like Jefferson, they favored limited government and emphasized state sovereignty.

Jacksonians were as fearful of the concentration of economic power as they were of political power. They saw government intervention in the economy as benefiting special-interest groups and creating corporate monopolies, and thus rejected an activist economic program as favoring the rich. Jacksonians sought to restore the independence of the individual—the artisan and the yeoman farmer—by ending federal support of banks and corporations and restricting the use of paper currency. Their concept of the proper role of government tended to be negative, and Jackson's political power was largely expressed in negative acts; he used the veto more than all previous presidents combined.

Finally, Jackson and his supporters were hostile to reform as a movement and an ideology. Reformers were increasingly calling for an activist and interventionist government as they organized to turn their programs into legislation. But Democrats tended to oppose programs like educational reform and the establishment of public education. They believed, for instance, that public schools restricted individual liberty by interfering with parental responsibility, and undermined freedom of religion by replacing church schools. Nor did Jackson share reformers' humanitarian concerns. He showed little sympathy for the Indians, ordering their removal from the Southeast to make way for white agricultural settlement (see page 297).

Like Jefferson, Jackson strengthened the executive branch of government at the same time he weakened the federal role. Given his popularity and the strength of his personality, this concentration of power in the presidency was perhaps inevitable; but his deliberate policy of combining the roles of party leader and chief of state did centralize even greater power in the White House. Invoking the principle that rotating officeholders would make government more responsive to the public will, Jackson used the spoils system to reward loyal Democrats with appointments to office. Though he removed fewer than one-quarter of federal officeholders in his two terms, his use of patronage nevertheless strengthened party organization and loyalty.

In office Jackson invigorated the philosophy of limited government. In 1830 he vetoed the Maysville Road bill, which would have provided a federal subsidy to construct a sixty-mile turnpike from Maysville to Lexington, Kentucky. Jackson insisted that an internal improvement confined to one state was unconstitutional, and that such projects were properly a state responsibility. The veto undermined Henry Clay's American System and personally embarrassed Clay, since the project was in his home district.

The nullification and bank controversies

Jackson had to face more directly the question of the proper division of sovereignty between state and federal government. The growing reform crusades, especially antislavery, had made the southern states fearful of federal power—and none more so than South Carolina, where the planter class was strongest and slavery most concentrated. Having watched the growth of abolitionist sentiment in Great Britain, which resulted in 1833 in emancipation in the West Indies, South Carolinians feared the same thing would happen at home. Hard hit by the Panic of 1819, from which they never fully recovered, they also resented the high prices of imported goods created by protectionist tariffs.

To protect their interests, South Carolinian political leaders developed the doctrine of *nullification*, according to which a state had the right to overrule, or nullify, federal legislation that conflicted with its own. The act that directly inspired this doctrine was the passage in 1828 of the Tariff of Abominations. In his unsigned *Exposition and Protest*, John C. Calhoun argued that in any disagreement between the federal government and a state, a special state convention—like those called to ratify the Constitution—would decide the conflict by either nullifying or accepting the federal law. Only the power of nullification could protect the minority against the tyranny of the majority, Calhoun asserted.

South Carolina first invoked its theory of nullification against the tariff of 1832. Though this tariff had the effect of reducing some duties, it retained high taxes on imported iron, cottons, and woolens. A majority of southern representatives supported the new tariff, but South Carolinians refused to go along. In their view, their constitutional right to control their own destiny had been sacrificed to the demands of northern industrialists. They feared the consequences of accepting such an act; it could set a precedent for congressional legislation on slavery. In November 1832 a South Carolina state convention nullified the tariff, making it unlawful for officials to collect duties in the state after February 1, 1833. Immediately recruiters began to organize a volunteer army to ensure nonenforcement of the tariff.

Nullification crisis

President Jackson responded with the toughness that had earned him the nickname "Old Hickory." Privately, he threatened to invade South Carolina and hang Calhoun; publicly, he sought to avoid the use of force. On December 10, 1832, Jackson issued his own proclamation nullifying nullification. He moved troops to federal forts in South Carolina and prepared United States marshals to collect the required duties. At Jackson's request, Congress passed the Force Act, which supposedly renewed Jackson's authority to call up troops; it was actually a scheme to avoid the use of force by collecting duties before ships reached South Carolina. At the same time, Jackson extended the olive branch by recommending tariff reductions. Calhoun, disturbed by South Carolina's drift toward separatism, worked with Henry Clay to draw up the compromise tariff of 1833. Quickly passed by Congress and signed by the president, the revision lengthened the list of duty-free items and reduced duties over the next nine years. Satisfied, South Carolina's convention repealed its nullification law, and in a final salvo nullified Jackson's Force Act. Jackson ignored the gesture.

Although fought over the practical issue of tariffs (and the unspoken issue of slavery), the nullification controversy did represent a genuine debate on the true nature and principles of the republic. Each side believed it was upholding the Constitution. Both felt they were fighting special privilege and subversion of republican values. South Carolina was fighting the tyranny of the federal government and the manufacturers who sought tariff protection; Jackson was

When New York state banks stopped redeeming bank notes for gold or silver during the Panic of 1837, Whigs blamed the crisis on Jackson's opposition to the Second Bank of the United States. This satirical six-cent note drawn on the Humbug Glory Bank ridicules Jackson and Van Buren. Notice the Democratic donkey and the hickory leaf on the face of the paper. The New-York Historical Society.

fighting the tyranny of South Carolina, whose refusal to bow to federal authority threatened to split the republic. Neither side won a clear victory. Another issue, that of a central bank, would define the powers of the federal government more clearly.

At stake was the rechartering of the Second Bank of the United States, whose twenty-year charter expired in 1836. Like its predecessor, the bank served as a

| Second Bank of the United States |

depository for federal funds, on which it paid no interest; and it served the republic in many other ways. Its bank notes circulated as currency throughout the country; they could be readily exchanged for gold, and the federal government accepted them as payment in all transactions. Through its twenty-five branch offices, the bank acted as a clearing-house for state banks, keeping them honest by refusing to accept their notes if they had insufficient gold in reserve.

But the bank had enemies. Many state banks resented the central bank's police role; by presenting state bank notes for redemption all at once, the Second Bank could easily ruin a state bank. Moreover,

state banks, with less money in reserve, found themselves unable to compete on an equal footing with the Second Bank. And many state governments regarded the national bank, with its headquarters in Philadelphia, as unresponsive to local needs. Finally, westerners and urban workers remembered with bitterness the bank's conservative credit policies during the Panic of 1819. And there was some truth to their complaints. Though the Second Bank served some of the functions of a central bank, it was still a private profit-making institution, and its policies reflected the self-interest of its owners. Its president, Nicholas Biddle, controlled the bank completely. Conservative and anti-Jacksonian, Biddle symbolized all that westerners found wrong with the bank.

Although the bank's charter would not expire until 1836, Biddle, aware of Jackson's hostility, sought to make it an issue in the presidential campaign of 1832. His strategy backfired. In July 1832 Jackson vetoed the rechartering bill, and the Senate failed to override the veto. Jackson's veto message was an emotional attack on the undemocratic nature of the bank. "It is to be regretted," he said, "that the rich and pow-

Chapter 12: Reform, politics, and expansion, 1824–1848

erful too often bend the acts of government to their selfish purposes." Rechartering would grant "exclusive privileges, to make the rich richer and the potent more powerful."

The bank became the major symbol and issue in the presidential campaign of 1832. Jackson did not debate its constitutionality or its functions; instead he denounced special privilege and economic power. The Jacksonians had organized a highly effective party, and they used it in the election. Operating in a system in which all the states but South Carolina now chose electors by popular vote, the Jacksonians mobilized voters by advertising the presidential election as the focal point of the political system.

But the most dramatic institutional change that accompanied the rise of parties—the convention system of nominating presidential candidates—did not originate with the Jacksonians. It was the Anti-Masonic party that in 1831 met in a national convention, named William Wirt their standard-bearer for 1832, and adopted a party platform, the first in the nation's history. The Democrats and the major opposition party, the National Republicans, quickly followed suit. Jackson and Martin Van Buren were nominated at the Democratic convention, Clay and John Sergeant at the National Republican. John Floyd ran as South Carolina's candidate. Jackson was re-elected easily in a Democratic party triumph.

After his victory and second inauguration in 1833, Jackson moved not only to dismantle the Second Bank of the United States but to ensure that it would not be resurrected. He deposited federal funds in favored state-chartered ("pet") banks; without federal money, the bank shriveled. When its federal charter expired in 1836, it became just another Pennsylvania-chartered private bank. In 1841 it went bankrupt.

The Whig challenge and the second party system

Once historians described the period from 1834 through the 1840s as the Age of Jackson, and the personalities of the leading political figures dominated history books. Increasingly, however, historians have viewed these years as an age dominated by popularly based political parties and reformers. For it was only when the passionate concerns of evangelicals and reformers spilled into politics that party differences became important and party loyalties solidified. For the first time grassroots political groups organized from the bottom up set the tone of political life.

In the 1830s the Democrats' opponents found shelter under a common umbrella, the Whig party. Resentful of Jackson's domination of Congress, the Whigs borrowed their name from the British party that had opposed the tyranny of the Stuart kings and George III in the previous century. From the congressional elections of 1834 through the 1840s, they and the Democrats competed nearly equally; only a few percentage points separated the two parties in national elections. They fought at every level—city, county, and state—and achieved a stability previously unknown in American politics. Both parties built strong organizations, commanded the loyalty of legislators, and attracted mass popular followings.

The two parties emphasized responsiveness to their supporters, a priority that reflected significant changes in the electoral process. At the local level, direct voting had replaced nomination and election by legislator's and electors. And though many states still permitted only taxpayers to vote in local elections, by the 1830s only a handful significantly restricted adult white male suffrage in nonlocal elections. Some even allowed immigrants who had taken out their first citizenship papers to vote. The effect of these changes was a sharp increase in the number of votes cast in presidential elections. Between 1824 and 1828 the number of votes cast for president increased threefold, from 360,000 to over 1.1 million. In 1840, 2.4 million men cast votes. The proportion of eligible voters who cast ballots also increased. In 1824 an estimated 27 percent of those eligible voted; from 1828 through 1836, about 55 percent; in 1840, more than 80 percent.

On the political agenda during these years were numerous fundamental issues. At the national level, officials struggled with the question of the proper constitutional roles of the federal and state governments, national expansion, and Indian policy. Also during this period, many state conventions were drafting new constitutions and deliberating over such basic issues as the rights of individuals and corporations; the rights of labor and capital; government aid to business; currency and sources of revenue; and public education, temperance, and antislavery.

Increasingly the two parties differed in their approaches to these issues. Though both favored economic expansion, the Whigs sought it through an activist government, the Democrats through limited

| Whigs |

government. Thus the Whigs supported corporate charters, a national bank, and paper currency; the Democrats were opposed. The Whigs also favored more humanitarian reforms than did the Democrats—public schools, abolition of capital punishment, temperance, and prison and asylum reform.

In general, Whigs were simply more optimistic than Democrats, and more enterprising. They did not hesitate to help one group if doing so would promote the general welfare. The chartering of corporations, they argued, expanded economic opportunity for everyone, providing work for laborers and increasing demand for food from farmers. Meanwhile the Democrats, distrustful of the concentration of economic power and of moral and economic coercion, held fast to their Jeffersonian principle of limited government.

For all the rank economic inequality that characterized the era, it was not the major issue that divided the parties. Nor were the conflicts over the bank and government, the issuing of corporate charters battles between the haves and have-nots. Although the Whigs attracted more of the upper and middle classes, both sides drew support from manufacturers, merchants, laborers, and farmers. Instead, it was religion and ethnicity that determined party membership. In the North, the Whigs' concern for energetic government and humanitarian and moral reform won the favor of native-born and British-American evangelical Protestants, especially those involved in religious revival. These Presbyterians, Baptists, and Congregationalists were overwhelmingly Whigs, as were the relatively small number of free black voters. Democrats, on the other hand, tended to be foreign-born Catholics and nonevangelical Protestants, both groups that preferred to keep religious and secular affairs separate.

The Whig party thus became the vehicle of evangelical Christianity. In many locales, the membership of benevolent societies overlapped that of the party.

| Whigs and reformers |

Indeed, Whigs practiced a kind of political revivalism. Their rallies resembled camp meetings; their rhetoric echoed evangelical rhetoric; their programs embodied the perfectionist beliefs of reformers. This potent blend of religion and politics—which, as Tocqueville noted, were "intimately united" in America—greatly intensified political loyalties.

In unifying evangelicals, the Whigs alienated members of other faiths. The evangelicals' ideal Christian state had no room for Catholics, Mormons, Unitarians, Universalists, or religious freethinkers. Sabbath laws, temperance legislation, and Protestant-inspired public education threatened the religious freedom and individual liberty of these groups, which generally opposed state interference in moral and religious questions. As a result, more than 95 percent of Irish Catholics, 90 percent of the Reformed Dutch, and 80 percent of German Catholics voted Democratic.

Vice President Martin Van Buren headed the Democratic ticket in the presidential election of 1836. Hand-picked by Jackson, Van Buren was a shrewd politician who had built the Democratic party in New York. The Whigs, who had not yet coalesced into a national party, entered three sectional candidates: Daniel Webster of New England, Hugh White of the South, and William Henry Harrison of the West. By splintering the vote, they hoped to throw the election into the House, but Van Buren squeaked through with a 25,000-vote edge out of a total of 1.5 million. No vice-presidential candidate received a majority of electoral votes, though, and for the only time in American history the Senate chose a vice president: the Democratic candidate, Richard M. Johnson.

Van Buren took office just weeks before the American credit system collapsed. The economic boom of the 1830s was over. In May 1837 New York banks

| Martin Van Buren and hard times |

stopped redeeming paper currency in gold, and soon all banks suspended payments in hard coin. As confidence faded, banks curtailed loans. The credit contraction only made things worse; after a brief recovery, full-scale depression set in, and persisted from 1839 to 1843.

Not surprisingly, economic issues were paramount during these years. Unfortunately, Van Buren followed Jackson's hard-money policies. He curtailed federal spending, thus adding to the deflation, and opposed the Whigs' advocacy of a national bank, which would have improved matters by expanding credit.

Even worse, Van Buren proposed a new treasury system under which the government would keep all its funds in regional treasury offices rather than banks. The treasury branches would accept and pay out only gold and silver coin; they would not accept paper currency or checks drawn on state banks. Van Buren's independent treasury bill was passed in 1840. By creating a constant demand for hard coin, it deprived banks of gold and added to the general deflation.

Undaunted, the Whigs fought the Democrats at the state level over currency, banks, and corporate charters. No issues were more controversial, since great economic advantages were at stake. The Whigs favored new banks, more paper currency, and more corporations. As the party of hard money, the Democrats favored eliminating paper currency altogether and using only gold or silver coin. Increasingly the Democrats became distrustful even of state banks, and by the mid-1840s a majority favored eliminating all bank corporations. The Whigs, riding the wave of economic distress into office, made banking and corporate charters more readily available.

With the nation in a depression, the Whigs confidently prepared for the election of 1840. Their strategy was simple: keep their loyal supporters and win over independents distressed by hard times. The Democrats renominated President Van Buren in a somber convention. The Whigs rallied behind the military hero General William Henry Harrison, conqueror of Prophet Town on Tippecanoe Creek in 1811. Harrison and his running mate, John Tyler of Virginia, ran a "log cabin and hard cider" campaign—a people's crusade against the aristocratic president in the Palace, as the Whigs called the White House. Using many of the techniques of twentieth-century politics—huge rallies, parades, floats, songs, posters, campaign hats and emblems—the Whigs wooed supporters and independents alike. Harrison stayed carefully above the issues, earning the nickname General Mum, but party hacks bluntly blamed the depression on the Democrats. In the huge turnout that resulted—80 percent of eligible voters cast ballots—Harrison won the popular vote by a narrow margin but swept the electoral college 234 to 60.

Immediately after taking office in 1841, President Harrison called a special session of Congress to enact the Whig economic program: repeal of the independ-

Election of 1840

Using many of the techniques of twentieth-century politics, General William Henry Harrison ran a "log cabin and hard cider" campaign—a popular crusade—against the aristocratic Martin Van Buren. This notice of a preconvention planning meeting pictures Harrison as a simple down-home farmer ("the farmer of North Bend"). Library of Congress.

ent treasury system; a new national bank; and a higher protective tariff. Unfortunately for the Whigs, Harrison died within a month of his inauguration. His successor, John Tyler, a former Democrat who had left the party in opposition to Jackson's Nullification Proclamation, turned out to be more of a Democrat than a Whig. Tyler consistently opposed the Whig congressional program. He repeatedly vetoed Henry Clay's protective tariffs, bills promoting internal improvements, and bills aimed at reviving the Bank of the United States. The only important measures that became law under his administration were the repeal of the independent treasury and a higher tariff. Two days after Tyler's second veto of a bank bill, the entire

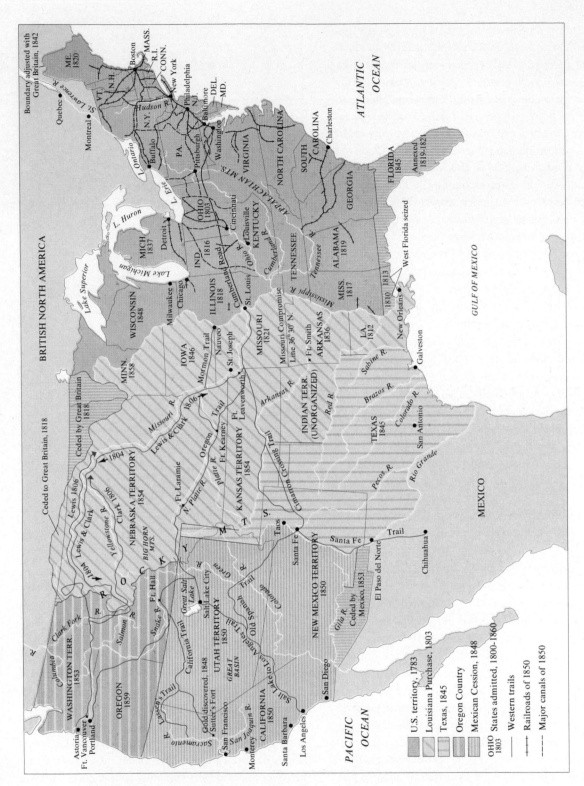

Westward expansion, 1800–1860

BRITISH NORTH AMERICA

Boundary adjusted with Great Britain, 1842

St. Lawrence R.

Quebec

Montreal

L. Ontario

L. Erie

Hudson R.

ATLANTIC OCEAN

ME. 1820

VT.

N.H.

MASS.

R.I.

CONN.

N.Y.

N.J.

PA.

DEL.

MD.

Boston

New York

Philadelphia

Baltimore

Washington

Pittsburgh

Buffalo

APPALACHIAN MTS.

VIRGINIA

NORTH CAROLINA

SOUTH CAROLINA

GEORGIA

Charleston

FLORIDA 1845

Annexed 1819–1821

West Florida seized

1810 1813

GULF OF MEXICO

OHIO 1803

Cincinnati

Louisville

KENTUCKY

TENNESSEE

ALABAMA 1819

MISS. 1817

IND. 1816

Detroit

MICH. 1837

Lake Michigan

Lake Superior

L. Huron

WISCONSIN 1848

Milwaukee

Chicago

ILLINOIS 1818

Cumberland Road

St. Louis

Ohio R.

Cumberland R.

Tennessee R.

Mississippi R.

LA. 1812

New Orleans

Galveston

MINN. 1858

IOWA 1846

Nauvoo

St. Joseph

Mormon Trail

Missouri R.

Oregon Trail

Ft. Kearney

Ft. Leavenworth

MISSOURI 1821

Missouri Compromise Line 36° 30' N.

ARKANSAS 1836

Ft. Smith

INDIAN TERR. (UNORGANIZED)

Arkansas R.

Red R.

Sabine R.

Brazos R.

Colorado R.

TEXAS 1845

San Antonio

Rio Grande

Pecos R.

MEXICO

Ceded by Great Britain, 1818

Ceded to Great Britain, 1818

Lewis 1806

Yellowstone R.

Clark 1806

1804

Lewis & Clark

Platte R.

N. Platte R.

Ft. Laramie

NEBRASKA TERRITORY 1854

BIG HORN MTS.

KANSAS TERRITORY 1854

R O C K Y M T S.

Cimarron Crossing Trail

Taos

Santa Fe

Santa Fe Trail

Trail

Chihuahua

El Paso del Norte

NEW MEXICO TERRITORY 1850

Gila R.

Ceded by Mexico, 1853

Columbia R.

Clark Fork

Lewis & Clark

1806

Salmon R.

Snake R.

Ft. Hall

WASHINGTON TERR. 1853

Astoria

Ft. Vancouver

Portland

OREGON 1859

Lassen's Trail

California Trail

Great Salt Lake

Salt Lake City

UTAH TERRITORY 1850

GREAT BASIN

Green R.

Colorado R.

Old Spanish Trail

Salt Lake to Los Angeles Trail

Sutter's Fort

Gold discovered, 1848

San Francisco

Sacramento

San Joaquin R.

Monterey

Santa Barbara

Los Angeles

CALIFORNIA 1850

San Diego

PACIFIC OCEAN

U.S. territory, 1783

Louisiana Purchase, 1803

Texas, 1845

Oregon Country

Mexican Cession, 1848

OHIO 1803 States admitted, 1800–1860

Western trails

Railroads of 1850

Major canals of 1850

cabinet except Secretary of State Daniel Webster resigned. Webster, involved in negotiating a new treaty with Great Britain, left shortly thereafter. Tyler became a president without a party, and the Whigs lost the presidency without an election.

Virtually expelled from the Whig party and at war with them over domestic policy, Tyler turned his attention to territorial questions. During the late 1830s, Anglo-American relations, which had been friendly since the War of 1812, had again become tense. Southern alarm over West Indian emancipation; northern commercial rivalry with Britain; the default of state governments and corporations on British-held debts during the Panic of 1837; rebellion in Canada; boundary disputes; and American expansionism all fueled Anglo-American tensions.

| Anglo-American tensions |

Among the most troublesome of these disputes was the quarrel resulting from the *Caroline* affair, in which a United States citizen, Amos Durfee, had been killed when Canadian militia set the privately owned steamer *Caroline* afire in the Niagara River. (The *Caroline* had supported an unsuccessful uprising against Great Britain in Upper Canada in 1837.) Britain refused to apologize for its revenge, and patriotic Americans seethed with rage. Fearing that popular support for the Canadian rebels would ignite war, President Van Buren posted troops at the border to discourage border raids. Tensions subsided in November 1840 when Alexander McLeod, a Canadian deputy sheriff, was arrested in New York for the murder of Durfee. Fortunately McLeod was eventually acquitted; had he been found guilty and executed, Lord Palmerston, the British foreign minister, would surely have sought vengeance in war.

At about the same time another quarrel threatened Anglo-American relations. The peace of Ghent that ended the War of 1812 had not solved the boundary dispute between Maine and New Brunswick. Moreover, although Great Britain had accepted an 1831 arbitration decision fixing a new boundary, the United States Senate had rejected it in 1832. Thus when Canadians began to log the disputed region in the winter of 1838 and 1839, Maine attempted to expel them. Soon the lumbermen had captured the Maine land agent and posse; both sides had mobilized their militia; and Congress had authorized a call-up of fifty thousand

men. No blood was spilled, though. General Winfield Scott, who had patrolled the border during the *Caroline* affair, was dispatched to Aroostook, Maine. Scott arranged a truce between the warring state and province, and the two sides compromised on their conflicting claims in the Webster-Ashburton Treaty (1842).

These border disputes with Great Britain prefigured an issue that became prominent in national politics in the mid- to late 1840s: the westward expansion of the United States. Tyler's succession to power in 1841 and a Democratic victory in the presidential election of 1844 ended activist, energetic government on the federal level for the rest of the decade. Meanwhile economic issues were eclipsed by debate over the nation's destiny to stretch from coast to coast. Reform, however, was not dead. Its passions would resurface in the 1850s in the debate over slavery in the territories.

Manifest destiny

The belief that American expansion westward was inevitable, divinely ordained, and just was first called *manifest destiny* by a Democrat, the newspaperman John L. O'Sullivan. The annexation of Texas, O'Sullivan wrote in 1845, was "the fulfillment of our manifest destiny to overspread the continent allotted by Providence for the free development of our yearly multiplying millions." Americans used the concept loosely during the 1840s to justify war and threats of war, and at the end of the century they would use it to justify imperialistic adventures beyond the nation's continental limits.

Americans had been hungry for western land ever since the colonists first turned their eyes westward. There lay virgin soil, valuable mineral resources, and the chance for a better life or a new beginning. Agrarian Democrats saw the West as an antidote to urbanization and industrialization. Enterprising Whigs looked to the new commercial opportunities the West offered. No wonder that between 1833 and 1860 the proportion of Americans living west of the Appalachians grew from one-quarter to one-half (see map).

German settlers in Texas. This watercolor must have been done in 1845 or after, since the title refers to Texas as a state. San Antonio Museum Association.

Equally important in the quest for western land was a fierce national pride. Dampened during times of depression, it reasserted itself during recoveries and booms, as in the 1840s. North or South, Whig or Democrat, Americans were convinced that theirs was the greatest country on earth, with a special role to play in the world. What better evidence of such a role could there be than expansion from coast to coast?

Americans also idealistically believed that westward expansion would extend American freedom and democracy. The acquisition of new territory would, they reasoned, bring the benefits of America's republican system of government to less fortunate people. Of course such idealism was self-serving, and contained an undercurrent of racism as well. Indians were perceived as savages best removed from their homes east of the Mississippi and confined to small areas in the West. Mexicans and Central and South Americans were also seen as inferior peoples, fit to be controlled or conquered. Thus the same racism that justified slavery in the South and discrimination in the North prompted expansion in the West.

Finally, the expansionist fever of the 1840s was fed by the desire to secure the nation from external enemies. The internal enemies of the 1830s—a monster bank, corporations, paper currency, alcohol, Sabbath violation—seemed to pale before the threats Americans found on their borders in the 1840s. Expansion, some believed, was necessary to preserve American independence.

Among the long-standing objectives of expansionists was the Republic of Texas, which included parts of present-day Oklahoma, Kansas, Colorado, and New Mexico as well as all of Texas. This entire territory was originally a part of Mexico. After

Republic of Texas

Chapter 12: Reform, politics, and expansion, 1824–1848

winning its independence from Spain in 1821, Mexico encouraged the development of these rich but remote northern provinces, offering large tracts of land to settlers who agreed to bring two hundred or more families into the area. Americans like Moses and Stephen Austin, who had helped to formulate the policy, responded eagerly, for Mexico was offering rich land virtually free in return for settlers' promises to become Mexican citizens and adopt the Catholic religion.

By 1835, 35,000 Americans, including many slaveholders, lived in Texas. These new settlers ignored local laws and oppressed native Mexicans, and when the Mexican government attempted to tighten its control over the region, it stimulated a rebellion instead. At the Alamo in San Antonio in 1836, 200 Americans made a heroic stand against 3,000 Mexicans under General Santa Anna. All the defenders, including Davy Crockett and Colonel James Bowie, died in the battle, and "Remember the Alamo" became the Texans' rallying cry. By the end of the year the Texans had won their independence, to the delight of most Americans, some of whom saw the victory as a triumph of white Protestantism over Catholic Mexico.

Although they established an independent republic, Texans still sought annexation to the United States. Immediately after independence was declared, President Sam Houston opened negotiations. But the issue was politically explosive. Southerners favored annexing the proslavery territory; antislavery forces, Northerners, and most Whigs opposed it. Abolitionists saw the proposal as a southern plot to enlarge the area of slavery. In view of the political dangers, President Jackson delayed recognition of Texas until after the election of 1836, and President Van Buren ignored annexation altogether.

Rebuffed by the United States, Texans talked about developing close ties with the British and extending their republic all the way to the Pacific Coast. Faced with the specter of a rival republic to the south, and with British colonies already entrenched to the north, Americans feared encirclement. If Texas reached the ocean and became an English ally, would not American independence be threatened?

Now President Tyler—committed to expansion, fearful of the British presence, and hoping to build political support in the South—pushed for annexa-

tion. But in April 1844 the Senate rejected a treaty of annexation. A letter from Secretary of State Calhoun to the British minister justifying annexation as a step in protecting slavery so outraged senators that the treaty was defeated 16 to 35. Seven northern Democrats joined the Whigs in opposition to it.

Just as southerners sought expansion to the Southwest, northerners looked to the Northwest. In 1841 "Oregon fever" struck thousands. Lured by the glowing reports of missionaries, who

| Oregon fever |

showed as much interest in the Northwest's richness and beauty as in the conversion of the Indians, emigrants organized hundreds of wagon trains and embarked on the Oregon Trail. The two-thousand-mile journey took six months or more, but within a few years five thousand settlers had arrived in the fertile Willamette Valley south of the Columbia River. However, the organization of a provisional government in 1843 placed the United States and Britain on a collision course.

Since the Anglo-American convention of 1818, Britain and the United States had jointly occupied the disputed Oregon territory (see page 213). Beginning with the administration of President John Quincy Adams, the United States had tried to fix the boundary at the 49th parallel, but Britain had refused, anxious to maintain access to the Puget Sound and the Columbia River. Time only increased the American appetite. In 1843 a Cincinnati convention called to consider the question demanded that the United States obtain the entire Oregon territory, up to its northernmost border of 54°40'. Soon "Fifty-four Forty or Fight" had become the rallying cry of American expansionists.

The presidential campaign of 1844 was the first to be dominated by foreign-policy issues. At the Democratic convention, southerners blocked Van Buren's

| Election of 1844 |

nomination because of his opposition to the annexation of Texas. (Van Buren feared annexation would lead to war with Mexico.) Instead the party chose House Speaker James K. Polk, a hard-money Jacksonian and avid expansionist. The Whig leader Henry Clay, who opposed annexation, won his party's unanimous nomination. The main plank of the Democratic platform called for occupation of the entire Oregon territory and annexation of Texas. The

Travelers on the Oregon Trail encamped at Independence Rock in Wyoming. Denver Public Library, Western History Department.

Whigs, though they favored expansion, argued that the Democrats' belligerent nationalism would lead the nation to war with Great Britain or Mexico or both. Clay favored expansion through negotiation, not force.

But few militant expansionists supported Clay, and Polk and the Democrats captured the White House by 170 electoral votes to 105 (they won the popular vote by just 38,000 out of 2.7 million). Polk carried New York's 36 electoral votes by just 6,000 votes; abolitionist James G. Birney, the Liberty party candidate, drew almost 16,000 votes away from Clay, handing the state and the election to Polk. Thus abolitionist forces had influenced the choice of a president.

Interpreting Polk's victory as a mandate for annexation, President Tyler proposed in his last days in office that Texas be admitted by joint resolution of Congress. (The usual method of admission, by treaty negotiation, required a two-thirds vote in the Senate—

which expansionists clearly did not have. Joint resolution required only a simple majority in both houses.) Proslavery and antislavery congressmen debated the extension of slavery into the territory, and the resolution passed the House 120 to 98 and the Senate 27 to 25. Three days before leaving office, Tyler signed the measure. Mexico immediately broke relations with the United States.

Faced with the prospect of war in the Southwest, President Polk sought to avoid conflict with Great Britain in the Northwest. Thus he dropped the demand for a 54°40′ boundary in favor of the 49th parallel. But the United States was still demanding the lion's share of Oregon, and Britain rejected the offer. In April 1846 the United States therefore gave the required one-year notice for ending the 1818 joint-occupation agreement. Faced with what amounted to a threat of war, the British accepted the 49th parallel in the Oregon Treaty of 1846 (see map). The United

States gained all of present-day Oregon, Washington, and Idaho and parts of Wyoming and Montana.

Meanwhile, the crisis over Texas was worsening as a direct result of the president's expansionist aims. Polk was determined to have California and New Mexico as well as all of Texas; he intended to fulfill the nation's destiny and expand to the Pacific. After an attempt to buy the tremendous expanse of land failed, Polk resolved to ask Congress for a declaration of war, and set to work compiling a list of grievances. This task became unnecessary when word arrived that Mexican forces had engaged a body of American troops whom Polk had sent to guard the Texas border. American blood had been shed. Polk eagerly declared that "war exists by the act of Mexico itself" and summoned the nation to arms.

Although Congress voted overwhelmingly in May 1846 to recognize a state of war between Mexico and the United States, public opinion was sharply divided. Southwesterners anticipated war with enthusiasm; New Englanders strenuously opposed it. Antislavery Whigs charged that Polk had manipulated the United States into war; abolitionists regarded the war as no less than a plot to extend slavery and proslavery influence. But Whig congressmen remembered the fate of the Federalists, who had been driven into oblivion because of their opposition to the War of 1812. When the test came, they voted for war.

As in previous wars, the United States depended on volunteers raised by the states to augment its small standing army. Nationalist and expansionist fervor generated adequate forces, however, and American troops quickly established their superiority over the Mexicans. General Zachary Taylor attacked and occupied Monterrey, securing northeastern Mexico (see map). Polk then ordered Colonel Stephen Kearney and a small detachment of troops to invade the remote and relatively unpopulated provinces of New Mexico and California. Taking Santa Fe without opposition, Kearney pushed into California, where he joined forces with rebellious American settlers, commanded by Captain John C. Frémont, and a couple of United States naval units. Together they wrested control of California from Mexico with ease.

Meanwhile, General Winfield Scott led an army of fourteen thousand men from Vera Cruz, on the Gulf

| Mexican War |

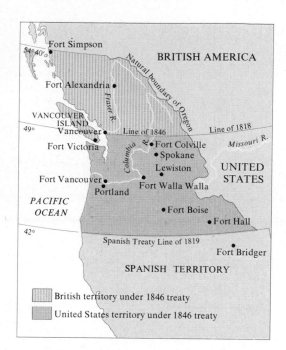

American expansion in Oregon

of Mexico, into Mexico City itself. The daring invasion brought the war to an end, and on February 2, 1848, representatives signed the Treaty of Guadalupe Hidalgo. The United States gained California and New Mexico (including present-day Nevada, Utah, and Arizona) and recognition of the Rio Grande as the southern boundary of Texas. In return, the American government agreed to settle the claims of its citizens against Mexico and to pay Mexico a mere $15 million for the new territory. The nation's manifest destiny had been achieved: the American flag waved on Atlantic and Pacific shores. The cost was thirteen thousand Americans and fifty thousand Mexicans dead, and Mexican-American enmity lasting into the twentieth century.

Ironically enough, instead of unifying the nation, the territorial expansion of the 1840s sparked sectional conflict. The debate over whether Oregon would be slave or free (Polk had recommended excluding slavery) revived old southern fears of congressional power. Northern expansionists, meanwhile, felt abandoned on the Oregon question by a South that

| Sectional conflict over slavery in the territories |

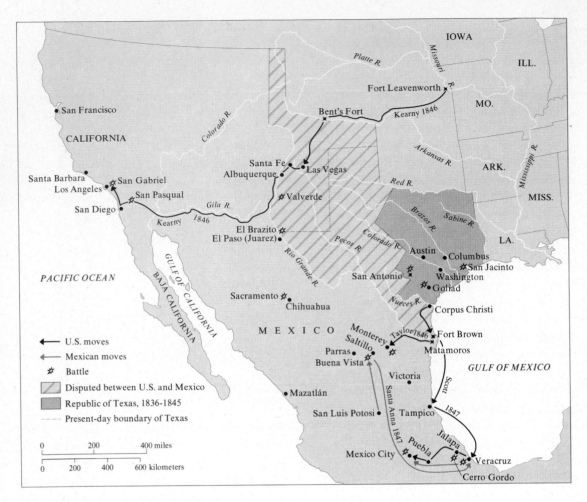

Texas independence and the Mexican War

had already won its plum—Texas. Reformers, charging that expansion was a Slave Power conspiracy, began to find a receptive audience in the North. Under the pressure of these sectional issues, the party unity of both Democrats and Whigs began to loosen. A Democratic faction in New York, for instance, opposed both the annexation of Texas and the war with Mexico.

Early in his administration Polk had renounced a second term, hoping to stem growing factionalism among Democrats. As president, Polk had offered regular Democrats nearly all they could ask—territorial expansion combined with traditional Jacksonian economic policy. He persuaded Congress to reinstitute the independent treasury system and remove protectionist features from the tariff, and he vetoed inter-

nal improvements. But one issue was beyond solution by him or anyone else: slavery in the territories. No position could have avoided splintering the Democratic party.

In the presidental election of 1848, the political agenda changed radically. Prohibition of slavery in the

> Election of
> 1848

territories was the one overriding issue; it dominated the conventions, the campaign, and the election. The Democrats tried to avoid sectional conflict by nominating General Lewis Cass of Michigan for president and General William O. Butler of Kentucky for vice president. Cass personally favored "squatter sovereignty"—letting the inhabitants of a territory decide the question of slavery themselves. The party platform in turn declared that Congress did

A sailor serving under Commodore Robert F. Stockton sketched this picture of Mexican and American troops clashing in southern California. The battle, a United States victory, brought California under American control. Franklin D. Roosevelt Library.

not have the power to interfere with slavery, and criticized those who pressed the question. Some Democrats broke with the party and nominated former President Van Buren. Also backed by members of the Liberty party and abolitionist Whigs, Van Buren became the Free-Soil candidate. The party slogan was "Free soil, free speech, free labor, and free men."

The regular Whigs nominated General Zachary Taylor, the military hero of the Mexican War and a slaveholding southerner, along with Millard Fillmore for vice president. Though the Whig convention refused to assert congressional power over slavery in the territories, its attempt to avoid the issue proved futile. Van Buren divided the Democratic vote, allowing Taylor to carry states he might not otherwise have

won. The former president even outpolled Cass in his home state of Michigan. Again New York, Van Buren's home state, provided the crucial marginal votes—enough to put Taylor in the White House. Antislavery crusaders had influenced the outcome of the election.

The election of 1848 and the conflict over slavery in the territories shaped politics in the 1850s. At the national level, all issues would be seen through the prism of sectional conflict over slavery in the territories. The nation's uncertain attempts to deal with economic and social change would give way to more pressing questions about the nature of the Union itself. And the second party system developed in the 1830s and 1840s would itself succumb to crisis.

Important events

1790s–1840s	Second Great Awakening
1820s	Hudson River School
1824	House of Representatives elects John Quincy Adams president
1825–27	New Harmony, Indiana, experiment
1826	American Society for the Promotion of Temperance founded
1828	Tariff of Abominations Andrew Jackson elected president
1830s–40s	Second party system
1830	Maysville Road bill veto
1831	*Liberator* begins publication
1832	Veto of Second Bank of the United States recharter Jackson re-elected
1832–33	Nullification crisis
1836	Republic of Texas established Martin Van Buren elected president
1837	Financial panic
1837–39	U.S.–Canada border tensions
1837–48	Horace Mann heads Massachusetts Board of Education
1838	Sarah Grimké, *Letters on the Condition of Women and the Equality of the Sexes*
1839–43	Depression
1840	Whigs under William Henry Harrison win presidency
1841–47	Brook Farm
1841	John Tyler assumes the presidency
1844	James K. Polk elected president
1845	Texas admitted to the Union
1846–47	Mormon trek to the Great Salt Lake Valley
1846–48	Mexican War
1846	Oregon Treaty
1848	Treaty of Guadalupe Hidalgo Seneca Falls Convention General Zachary Taylor elected president
1851	Maine Temperance law

Suggestions for further reading

General

Marvin Myers, *The Jacksonian Persuasion: Politics and Belief* (1960); Russel B. Nye, *Society and Culture in America, 1830-1860* (1974); Edward Pessen, *Jacksonian America: Society, Personality, and Politics,* rev. ed. (1979); Arthur M. Schlesinger, Jr., *The Age of Jackson* (1945); John William Ward, *Andrew Jackson: Symbol for an Age* (1955).

Religion and revivalism

Whitney R. Cross, *The Burned-Over District* (1950); Leon A. Jick, *The Americanization of the Synagogue, 1820-1870* (1976); Charles A. Johnson, *The Frontier Camp Meeting* (1955); Paul E. Johnson, *A Shopkeeper's Millennium: Society and Revivals in Rochester, New York, 1815–1837* (1978); William G. McLoughlin, *Revivals, Awakenings, and Reform: An Essay on Religion and Social Change in America, 1607–1977* (1978); Perry Miller, *The Life of the Mind in America: From the Revolution to the Civil War* (1966); Timothy L. Smith, *Revivalism and Social Reform in Mid-Nineteenth Century America* (1957); William W. Sweet, *Revivalism in America* (1949).

Reform

Ray Allen Billington, *The Protestant Crusade, 1800-1860: A Study of the Origins of American Nativism* (1938); Henri Desroche, *The American Shakers from Neo-Christianity to Pre-Socialism* (1971); Clifford S. Griffin, *The Ferment of Reform,*

Chapter 12: Reform, politics, and expansion, 1824–1848

1830–1860 (1967); Clifford S. Griffin, *Their Brother's Keepers: Moral Stewardship in the United States, 1800–1865* (1960); Gerald N. Grob, *Mental Institutions in America: Social Policy to 1875* (1973); Raymond Muncy, *Sex and Marriage in Utopian Communities: 19th Century America* (1973); David J. Rothman, *The Discovery of the Asylum: Social Order and Disorder in the New Republic* (1971); Wallace Stegner, *The Gathering of Zion: The Story of the Mormon Trail* (1964); Alice Felt Tyler, *Freedom's Ferment* (1944); Ronald G. Walter, *American Reformers, 1815–1860* (1978).

Temperance, education, and feminism

Barbara J. Berg, *The Remembered Gate: Origins of American Feminism. The Woman and the City, 1800–1860* (1977); Lawrence A. Cremin, *American Education: The National Experience, 1783–1876* (1980); Ellen C. Du Bois, *Feminism and Suffrage: The Emergence of an Independent Woman's Movement in America 1848–1869* (1978); Michael Katz, *The Irony of Early School Reform* (1968); Jonathan Messerli, *Horace Mann* (1972); W. J. Rorabaugh, *The Alcoholic Republic: An American Tradition* (1979); Stanley K. Schultz, *The Culture Factory: Boston Public Schools, 1789–1860* (1973); Ian R. Tyrrell, *Sobering Up: From Temperance to Prohibition in Antebellum America, 1800–1860* (1979).

Antislavery and abolitionism

Frederick Douglass, *Life and Times of Frederick Douglass* (1881); Martin Duberman, ed., *The Anti-Slavery Vanguard: New Essays on the Abolitionists* (1965); Aileen S. Kraditor, *Means and Ends in American Abolitionism: Garrison and His Critics on Strategy and Tactics* (1967); Gerda Lerner, *The Grimké Sisters of South Carolina: Rebels Against Slavery* (1967); William H. Pease and Jane H. Pease, *They Would Be Free: Blacks' Search for Freedom, 1830–1861* (1974); Lewis Perry and Michael Fellman, eds., *Antislavery Reconsidered: New Perspectives on the Abolitionists* (1979); Benjamin Quarles, *Black Abolitionists* (1969); Leonard L. Richards,

"Gentlemen of Property and Standing": Anti-Abolition Mobs in Jacksonian America (1970); John L. Thomas, *The Liberator: William Lloyd Garrison* (1963); Ronald G. Walter, *The Antislavery Appeal: American Abolitionism After 1830* (1976); Bertram Wyatt-Brown, *Lewis Tappan and the Evangelical War Against Slavery* (1969).

Democrats and Whigs

Lee Benson, *The Concept of Jacksonian Democracy: New York as a Test Case* (1964); William R. Brock, *Parties and Political Conscience: American Dilemmas, 1840–1850* (1979); James C. Curtis, *The Fox at Bay: Martin Van Buren and the Presidency, 1837–1841* (1970); Ronald P. Formisano, *The Birth of Mass Political Parties: Michigan, 1827–1861* (1971); William W. Freehling, *Prelude to Civil War: The Nullification Controversy in South Carolina* (1966); Daniel Walker Howe, *The Political Culture of the American Whigs* (1979); Richard B. Latner, *The Presidency of Andrew Jackson: White House Politics, 1829–1837* (1979); Richard P. McCormick, *The Second American Party System: Party Formation in the Jacksonian Era* (1966); Robert V. Remini, *Andrew Jackson* (1966); Robert V. Remini, *Andrew Jackson and the Bank War* (1967); William G. Shade, *Banks or No Banks: The Money Issue in Western Politics, 1832–1865* (1972).

Manifest destiny

K. Jack Bauer, *The Mexican-American War, 1846–1848* (1974); Bernard De Voto, *The Year of Decision, 1846* (1943); Frederick Merk, *Manifest Destiny and Mission in American History: A Reinterpretation* (1963); David M. Pletcher, *The Diplomacy of Annexation: Texas, Oregon, and the Mexican War* (1973); John H. Schroeder, *Mr. Polk's War: American Opposition and Dissent, 1846–1848* (1973); Charles G. Sellers, Jr., *James K. Polk: Continentalist, 1843–1846* (1966); Otis A. Singletary, *The Mexican War* (1960); Albert K. Weinberg, *Manifest Destiny* (1935).

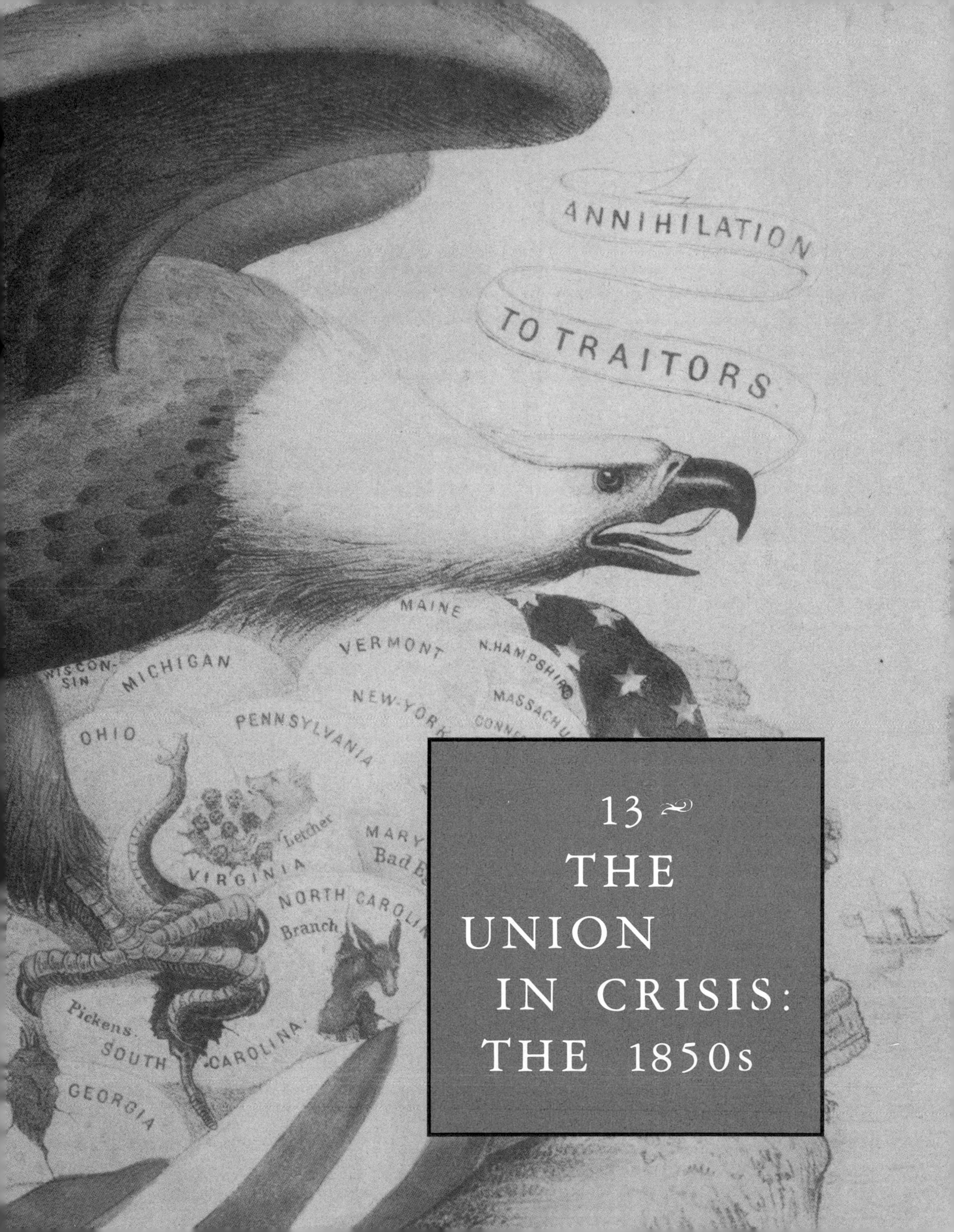

ANNIHILATION

TO TRAITORS.

MAINE

VERMONT   N. HAMPSHIRE

WISCON-SIN   MICHIGAN   NEW-YORK   MASSACHU

OHIO   PENNSYLVANIA   CONNE

Letcher   MARY

Bad B

VIRGINIA   NORTH CAROLI

Branch

Pickens.

SOUTH   CAROLINA.

GEORGIA

13 ~

THE
UNION
IN CRISIS:
THE 1850s

"This great country will continue united," declared the senator from Mississippi. "Trifling politicians in the South, or in the North, or in the West, may continue to talk otherwise, but it will be of no avail. They are like the mosquitoes around the ox; they annoy, but they cannot wound, and never kill." So spoke Jefferson Davis, the future president of the Confederacy, while traveling through New England in the summer of 1858. Like millions of his fellow citizens, North and South, Davis was intensely proud of America and passionate in his nationalism. The United States "is my country," he said, "and to the innermost fibers of my heart I love it all, and every part." Davis was determined, he said, not to "dwarf myself to mere sectionality."

A more pessimistic statement came from Abraham Lincoln in the winter of 1860. An old friend, Alexander Stephens of Georgia, had written to the president-elect. Fearful that the growing momentum of sectional conflict would soon shatter the Union, Stephens appealed to Lincoln to make some gesture to reassure the South. But Lincoln refused to budge from his party's platform; he was unalterably opposed to the extension of slavery to the territories, though he readily acknowledged its right to exist in the southern states. Replying to Stephens, Lincoln wrote, "You think slavery is *right* and ought to be extended; while we think it is *wrong* and ought to be restricted. That I suppose is the rub." To Lincoln the conflict was fundamental.

Was compromise possible? Throughout the 1850s many Americans, North and South, worked for that end. One school of historians has blamed the outbreak of the Civil War on the failure of a blundering generation of politicians who let the possibilities for peace slip through their fingers. Others, like Lincoln, have argued that the split over slavery was deep-seated and unavoidable. In the words of Republican William H. Seward, it was an "irrepressible conflict" that had to lead to war.

There is evidence to support both interpretations. The politicians made mistakes. They passed laws that sparked unexpected controversy, and they seriously misunderstood each other. Their most critical decisions were often based on miscalculations. But there were also fundamental sectional issues that cropped up repeatedly. Some opinions could not have been compromised by even the wisest of leaders.

Circumstances worked against the peacemakers. Though northerners and southerners strove to avoid conflict over slavery, westward expansion continually injected their disagreement into politics by raising the question of whether slavery would be allowed in the territories. This recurring crisis eventually convinced each side that its very way of life was jeopardized. Northerners envisioned a Slave Power intent on trampling basic liberties; southerners imagined that northerners would not stop until they had abolished slavery everywhere. Finally, changes in the political party system magnified sectional divisions. These forces jointly caused far more damage to the Union than they could have separately.

In the 1850s sectional pressures built until they eventually overwhelmed the capacity of the changing political system to deal with them. The result was a tragedy—civil war—that most American voters in 1860 clearly did not want.

The sources of conflict

The bitter debate over the morality of slavery was one cause of sectional strife. Profound questions of morality, social responsibility, and national purpose were at issue. At times the debate was explosive.

In the 1830s and 1840s, a growing body of northern abolitionists—male and female, black and white—had preached against slavery, condemning it as a sin. "There is but one remedy for sin," the mathematician and reformer Elizur Wright, Jr., had warned slaveholders, "and that is available only by a repentance, evidenced by reformation." These missionaries spoke in thousands of churches and public halls, slowly winning converts, indicting slavery as a moral wrong that brutalized all who came in contact with it.

Debate over the morality of slavery

Stung by such criticism, southern slaveowners denied any wrongdoing, asserting that their slaves were well cared-for and protected. Some even argued that slavery was a social good. One of South Carolina's governors declared servitude to be an "essential constituent" of "all political communities." Senator John C. Calhoun agreed, calling slavery "a universal condition," and jurist William Harper wrote in 1837 that

Chapter 13: The Union in crisis: the 1850s

"the exclusive owners of property . . . ought to be the virtual rulers of mankind." Added Harper, "It is as much the order of nature that men should enslave each other as that animals should prey upon each other." Even more extreme were the pronouncements of a Virginian named George Fitzhugh, who analyzed relations between management and labor in both the North and the South and concluded that wage labor in industry was more inhumane than slavery. Fitzhugh went so far as to claim that slavery ought to be practiced in all societies, whatever their racial composition.

These arguments generated strong emotions, but they were not central to the conflict that eventually divided the Union. The abolitionists were significant because they were a growing minority opposed in principle to the status quo. Proslavery advocates also wanted change: greater security and acceptance of their institution. Both constituted a threat to political stability. But their argument was only one cause of sectional strife, and a small one at that. Most northerners were racists, not abolitionists, and most southerners paid scant attention to proslavery theories. The issue that ultimately led to disunion was more obscure and complicated than the morality of slavery. That issue was slavery in the territories.

Throughout the 1850s quarrels over the territories cropped up repeatedly. Abolitionists and proslavery advocates were too weak to impose their views on

Debate over slavery in the territories

each other in the states, but the territories provided them a ready battleground. Americans kept moving west, prompting Congress to create new territories. Thus westward expansion guaranteed that controversy would arise over and over again. The prizes in these contests were both tangible and intangible. On achieving statehood, each territory elected two senators who would support either slavery or freedom in Washington. This gain directly affected sectional power. Indirectly, there was the prestige of victory, of extending influence. Some slaveowners dreamed of a West built on slave-based agriculture and mining; northerners envisioned a frontier of free-labor farms.

Ironically, the territorial question had only limited practical significance. Few slaves entered any territory during the 1850s, and many areas had few white settlers. Thus the territorial issue in itself was probably

manageable. Its explosive power lay in its capacity to stir up other issues and arouse other fears.

The prospect of slaves in the territories broadened the dispute over slavery to matters of basic American liberties. It brought the conflict home to northerners who had little interest in abolition or westward migration. And it spread fear of an aggressive Slave Power. Abolitionists constantly warned of a threatening Slave Power; issues like slavery in the territories made the threat credible.

The Slave Power idea postulated a slaveholding oligarchy in control of the South and intent on controlling the nation. The evidence for such domination

Fear of a Slave Power

lay in the persecution of southern dissenters and the suppression of their ideas. Evidence for the oligarchy's desire to extend its control could be found in efforts to reopen the African slave trade and to acquire territory in the Caribbean, as well as in extreme proslavery arguments. A few slaveowners who wanted more slaves were saying that if Africans were unavailable, whites would do. Eventually, warned abolitionists, these southern oligarchs would consolidate their power, take over the government, deprive the middle and lower classes of their rights, and extend slavery nationwide.

The Slave Power's assault on northern liberties was said to have begun in 1836, when Congress passed the gag rule (see page 319). White northerners, even those who saw nothing wrong with slavery, interpreted John Quincy Adams's stand against the rule as a defense of their rights. Each subsequent demand for slave territory or protection of slaveholders' interests was seen in light of the Slave Power thesis.

Fear of the sinister Slave Power transformed the abolitionist impulse into a broader and more influential antislavery movement. It turned people who were not abolitionists—who were in fact often racists—into opponents of slavery. These northern whites were seeking to protect themselves, not southern blacks, from the Slave Power. As the prevailing issues shifted away from the morality of slavery, they excited larger numbers of people: more northerners cared about the Slave Power than about the extension of slavery, and more cared about slavery extension than about abolition. In the form of territorial controversies, issues that had at first alarmed only a few claimed the attention of many.

The sources of conflict

Meanwhile, northerners and southerners were developing ideologies—ways of viewing the world—that hardened the lines of conflict. Northerners looked at their own growing population, booming industries,

| Conflicting ideologies |

and increasing prosperity and thought they saw an explanation for it: the free labor system. Free labor and a free society seemed to be the key to progress. By contrast, the slave South appeared retrograde. Responding to this northern insult and a worldwide trend of opinion against slavery, southerners sprang to the defense of their society. They praised its traditions and stability, its order, and its devotion to the Constitution. The South, many of its leaders believed, was the true defender of constitutional principles, which runaway change in the North was subverting. On both sides, these increasingly influential ideologies lessened the possibility for compromise.

On top of all these conflicts came the unsettling impact of structural change in the political system. At a time when the nation most needed political institutions capable of handling a crisis, these institutions were themselves undergoing change. The second party system, which had blunted conflict successfully in the past, fell to pieces during the 1850s. Its collapse

| Demise of the second party system |

was only a symptom of the sectional crisis, but the system that replaced it made the crisis worse. Americans scrambled to form and adjust to new institutions, only to end up with a system that failed to promote unity. Indeed, the new system overstated sectional divisions and added momentum to the crisis.

This political restructuring was forced by the demise of the Whig party. Though blessed with influential congressional representatives, the Whigs had lacked commanding presidents in an era of strong leaders like Jackson and Polk. The deaths of President Taylor (1850), Webster (1852), and Clay (1852) deprived them of their most renowned figures just as sectional discord split the party into southern and northern wings. Unable to recover from these blows, the Whig party fell apart, never to field a national candidate after 1852. A variety of new parties—Free-Soilers, Know-Nothings, and then Republicans—vied to replace them.

Although the Whig party disappeared, former Whigs accounted for approximately half the elec-

torate, a magnificent prize for competing political organizations. The Whigs were emotionally unable to join the Democrats after fighting them vigorously for two decades, but they had to go somewhere. Thus the new parties stressed a variety of issues chosen to appeal to homeless Whigs. Immigration, temperance, homestead bills, the tariff, internal improvements—all played an important role in attracting voters during the 1850s. For many Americans it was these issues, not the controversy over slavery, that were the real stuff of politics.

But this process of party building had one crucial implication: if voters joined organizations that took strong sectional stands, they added to the sectional confrontation whether the issue of slavery seemed important to them or not. And that is exactly what happened. In the North, appeals to economic individualism and nativism brought into the Republican party many people who did not regard slavery as a primary issue. Nevertheless, they swelled the ranks of an organization whose stand was antislavery. In the South, Democratic leaders made a successful appeal to states' rights slaveholders, and the Democrats emerged as the only viable party in the region. The development of a one-party system in the South also magnified sectional divisions and obscured southern support for the Union.

Thus the interrelated problems of the 1850s reinforced each other and grew more dangerous and difficult. An examination of the decade's events will reveal how the issues shifted, intensified, and intertwined as the conflict escalated.

Sectional problems are compromised but re-emerge

The first sectional battle of the decade involved the territory of California. More than eighty thousand Americans flooded into California in 1849. President Taylor, seeing a simple solution to the challenge of governing lands acquired from Mexico, urged the settlers to apply for admission to the Union. They promptly did so, submitting a proposed state constitution that did not allow for slavery. But southern politicians wanted to make California slave territory, or at least to extend the Missouri Compromise line west through California. Representatives from nine southern states met in an unofficial convention in Nashville to assert the South's right to part of the territory.

Fourteen northern legislatures, on the other hand, were equally determined to keep slavery out of the new territories. They had endorsed the Wilmot Proviso, an amendment to a military appropriations bill

| Wilmot Proviso |

proposed by Representative David Wilmot of Pennsylvania in 1846. Wilmot's proviso stated simply that slavery should be prohibited from any territory won from Mexico. Though it did not pass Congress, it became the rallying cry for free-soilers and attracted considerable support in the North. Thus the issue was joined.

Sensing that the Union was in peril, the venerable Whig leader Henry Clay marshalled his energies once more. Twice before, in 1820 and 1833, the "Great Pacificator" had taken the lead in shaping sectional compromise; now he labored one last time to preserve the nation. To hushed Senate galleries Clay presented a series of compromise measures, balancing the issues of California and nearby territories, the Texan boundary claim, runaway slaves, and the slave trade in the District of Columbia. Over the weeks that followed, Clay and Senator Stephen A. Douglas of Illinois steered the proposals through debate and amendment, persisting despite serious reverses. Line by line, concerned and angry senators hammered out the final language of the bills.

The problems to be solved were thorny indeed. Would California or a part of it become a free state? How should the land acquired from Mexico be organized? Texas, which allowed slavery, claimed large portions of the new land as far west as Santa Fe, so that too had to be settled. And in addition to southern complaints about fugitive slaves and northern objections to the sale of human beings in the nation's capital, the lawmakers had to deal with competing theories of settlers' rights in the territories. It was these theories that proved most troublesome in the continuing debate over the territories.

In 1847 Lewis Cass (the Democratic candidate for president the following year) had introduced the idea of popular sovereignty. Though Congress had to ap-

| Popular sovereignty |

prove statehood for a territory, it should "in the meantime," Cass said, allow the people living there "to regulate their own concerns in their own way." These few words, seemingly clear, proved highly ambiguous, disagreement centering on the meaning of "meantime."

When could settlers bar slavery? Southerners claimed equal rights in the territories; therefore neither Congress nor a territorial legislature could bar slavery. Only when settlers framed a state constitution could they take that step. Northerners, meanwhile, argued that Americans living in a territory were entitled to local self-government, and thus could outlaw slavery at any time, if they allowed it at all. To avoid dissension within their party, northern and southern Democrats had explained Cass's statement to their constituents in these two incompatible ways. Their conflicting interpretations caused strong disagreement in the debate on Clay's proposals.

Despite bitter debate, the Compromise of 1850 finally passed (see map, 344). California was admitted

| Compromise of 1850 |

as a free state, and the Texan boundary was set at its present limits. The United States paid Texas $10 million in consideration of the boundary agreement. And the territories of New Mexico and Utah were organized with power to legislate on "all rightful subjects ... consistent with the Constitution." A stronger fugitive slave law and an act to suppress the slave trade in the District of Columbia completed the compromise.

Jubilation greeted passage of the Compromise of 1850; in Washington, crowds celebrated the happy news. "On one glorious night," records a contemporary historian, "the word went abroad that it was the duty of every patriot to get drunk. Before the next morning many a citizen had proved his patriotism," and several prominent senators "were reported stricken with a variety of implausible maladies—headaches, heat prostration, or overindulgence in fruit."

In reality, there was less cause for celebration than citizens thought. Fundamentally, the Compromise of 1850 was not a settlement of sectional disputes. It was at best an artful evasion. Though the compromise bought time for the nation, it did not create guidelines for the settlement of subsequent territorial questions. It merely put them off.

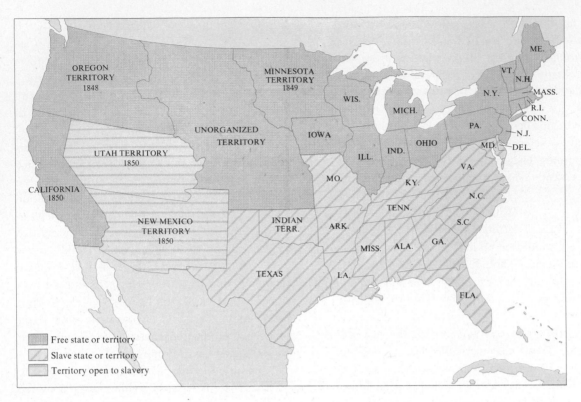

Free state or territory
Slave state or territory
Territory open to slavery

The Compromise of 1850

Furthermore, the compromise had two basic flaws. The first pertained to popular sovereignty. What were "rightful subjects of legislation, consistent with the Constitution"? During debate, southerners had defined them one way, northerners another. After passage of the compromise, legislators from the two sections went home and continued to define these words in two different ways, as if there were two different compromises. (In fact, the compromise admitted the disagreement by providing for the appeal of a territorial legislature's action to the Supreme Court. But no such case ever arose.) Thus, in the controversy over popular sovereignty, nothing had been settled. In one politician's words, the legislators seemed to have enacted a lawsuit instead of a law.

The second flaw lay in the Fugitive Slave Act, which stirred up controversy instead of laying it to rest. The new law empowered slaveowners to go into

Fugitive Slave Act court in their own states and present evidence that a slave who owed them service had escaped. The transcript of such a proceeding, including a de-

scription of the fugitive, was to be taken as conclusive proof of a person's slave status, even in free states and territories. Legal authorities had to decide only whether the black person brought before them was the person described, not whether he or she was indeed a slave. Fines and penalties encouraged U.S. marshals to assist in apprehending fugitives and discouraged citizens from harboring them. (Authorities were paid $10 if the alleged fugitive was turned over to the slaveowner, $5 if he was not.)

Abolitionist newspapers quickly attacked the fugitive slave law as a violation of the Bill of Rights. Why were alleged fugitives denied a trial by jury before being sent to bondage in a slave state? Why did suspected fugitives have no right to present evidence or cross-examine witnesses? Did not the law give authorities a financial incentive to turn prisoners over to slaveowners? These arguments convinced some northerners that free blacks could be sent into slavery, mistakenly or otherwise, with no means to defend themselves. Protest meetings were held in Massachusetts, New York, Pennsylvania, northern Ohio, northern Illinois, and elsewhere. In Boston in 1851, a mob grabbed a runaway slave from a U.S. marshal and sent him to safety in Canada.

At this point a novice writer dramatized the plight of the slave in a way that captured the sympathies of millions of northerners. Harriet Beecher Stowe, daughter of a religious New England family that had produced many prominent ministers, wrote *Uncle Tom's Cabin* out of deep moral conviction. Her book,

| Uncle Tom's Cabin |

published in March 1852, showed how slavery brutalized the men and women who suffered under it. Stowe also portrayed slavery's evil effects on slaveholders, indicting the institution itself more harshly than the southerners caught in its web. In nine months the book sold over 300,000 copies; by mid-1853, over a million. Countless people saw *Uncle Tom's Cabin* performed as a stage play or read similar novels inspired by it. Stowe had brought the issue of slavery home to many who had never before given it much thought.

At the same time, the policies of the newly elected Pierce administration revived sectional disputes. In 1852 Franklin Pierce, a Democrat from New Hampshire, won a smashing victory over the Whig presidential nominee, General Winfield Scott. Pierce backed the Compromise of 1850, believing that the defense of each section's rights was essential to the nation's unity. Scott was remembered as the conqueror of Mexico City but his views were unknown, and the Free-Soil candidate, John P. Hale of New Hampshire, openly repudiated the compromise. Thus Pierce's victory seemed to confirm most Americans' support for the Compromise of 1850.

But Pierce did not seem able to avoid sectional conflict. His proposal for a transcontinental railroad ran into congressional dispute over where it should be built, North or South. His attempts to acquire foreign territory stirred up more trouble. An annexation treaty with Hawaii failed because southern senators would not vote for another free state, and Pierce's efforts to annex Cuba angered antislavery northerners. Pierce tried to purchase Cuba from Spain in 1854. When publication of a government document revealed that three administration officials had rashly talked of "wresting" Cuba from Spain, some northerners concluded that Pierce was determined to acquire more slave territory.

CAUTION!!
COLORED PEOPLE
OF BOSTON, ONE & ALL,
You are hereby respectfully CAUTIONED and advised, to avoid conversing with the
Watchmen and Police Officers of Boston,
For since the recent ORDER OF THE MAYOR & ALDERMEN, they are empowered to act as
KIDNAPPERS
AND
Slave Catchers,
And they have already been actually employed in KIDNAPPING, CATCHING, AND KEEPING SLAVES. Therefore, if you value your LIBERTY, and the *Welfare of the Fugitives* among you, *Shun* them in every possible manner, as so many *HOUNDS* on the track of the most unfortunate of your race.
Keep a Sharp Look Out for KIDNAPPERS, and have TOP EYE open.
APRIL 24, 1851.

This broadside reveals northern outrage over the Fugitive Slave Act. The reference to kidnappers stems from the fear that free blacks would be transported into slavery under the law. Library of Congress.

But the shattering blow to sectional harmony originated in Congress, when Senator Stephen Douglas introduced a bill to organize the Kansas and Nebraska territories. Douglas, a rising Illinois Democrat and

| Kansas-Nebraska Act |

potential presidential candidate, hoped for a midwestern transcontinental railroad to boost Chicago's economy and encourage settlement on the Great Plains. A necessary precondition for a railroad was the organization of the territory it would cross. Thus it was probably in the interest of building such a railroad that Douglas introduced a bill that inflamed sectional passions, completed the destruction of the Whig party, damaged the northern wing of the Democratic party, gave birth to the Republican party, and injured his own national ambitions.

The Kansas-Nebraska bill exposed the first flaw of the Compromise of 1850, and conflict over popular

An advertisement for *Uncle Tom's Cabin* indicates the tremendous effect of the book on the general public. The New-York Historical Society.

sovereignty erupted once more. Douglas's bill clearly left "all questions pertaining to slavery in the Territories . . . to the people residing therein," but northerners and southerners still disagreed violently over what territorial settlers could constitutionally do. Moreover, the Kansas-Nebraska bill opened a new Pandora's box by explicitly repealing the Missouri Compromise. The new territories lay within the Louisiana Purchase, and under the compromise of 1820 all that land from 36°30′ north to the Canadian border was off-limits to slavery. Douglas believed that conditions of climate and soil would effectively keep slavery out of Kansas and Nebraska. But from a legal point of view his bill threw land open to slavery where it had been prohibited before.

Even Douglas sensed that his measure would raise "a hell of a storm," but he was able to obtain the endorsement of a careless President Pierce. After a titanic struggle lasting almost six months, the bill passed both houses and was signed into law in May 1854 (see map).

Unfortunately the storm—far more violent than Douglas had imagined—was only beginning. The Kansas-Nebraska Act inflamed fears and angers that had only simmered before. Abolitionists charged that the act was sinister aggression by the Slave Power, its

Chapter 13: The Union in crisis: the 1850s

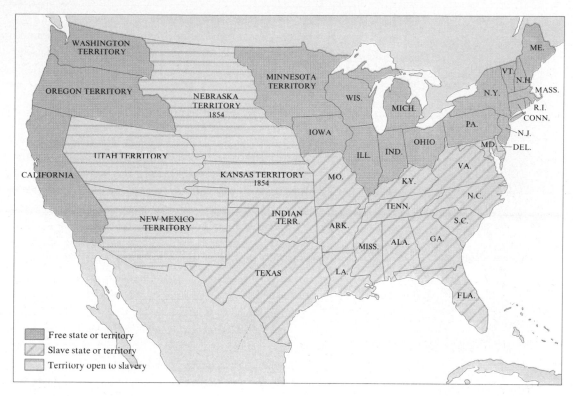

The Kansas-Nebraska Act, 1854

most brazen yet. Concern over the fugitive slave law deepened: between 1855 and 1859 Connecticut, Rhode Island, Massachusetts, Michigan, Maine, Ohio, and Wisconsin passed personal liberty laws designed to interfere with the swift action of the Fugitive Slave Act. These laws, which provided counsel for alleged fugitives and sought to guarantee trial by jury, revealed the strength of northern fear of the Slave Power. To the South, they were outrageous signs of bad faith. Even more important, however, was the devastating impact of the Kansas-Nebraska Act on political parties.

Political realignment

The Kansas-Nebraska Act divided the Whig party's northern and southern wings so irrevocably that it fell apart shortly thereafter. The Democrats survived, but they suffered at the polls in 1854 for their role in the legislation. Although southern Dem-

ocrats retained most of the offices they held, northern Democrats lost sixty-six of the ninety-one congressional seats they had won in free states in 1852. A Democrat, James Buchanan, was elected president in 1856, but he owed his victory to southern support. Eleven of sixteen free states voted against him, and Democrats did not regain power in those states for decades.

Moreover, anger over the territorial issue created a new political party. During debate on the Kansas-Nebraska bill, six congressmen had published an "Appeal of the Independent Democrats" attacking Douglas's legislation as "a gross violation of a sacred pledge" (the Missouri Compromise) and a "criminal betrayal of precious rights" that would make free territory a "dreary region of despotism." This appeal sparked other protests. In the summer and fall of 1854, antislavery Whigs and Democrats, free-soilers, and other reformers throughout the Northwest met to form a new Republican party, dedicated to keeping slavery out of the territories. The Republicans' influence rapidly spread to the East, and they won a stunning victory in the 1854 elections. In the party's

A Know-Nothing campaign ribbon. Note the pictures of Washington and the American eagle, references to the early days of the republic. The eagle holds a banner reading "Beware of foreign influence." Edmund B. Sullivan Collection, University of Hartford.

first appearance on the ballot, Republicans captured a majority of House seats in the North.

For the first time, a sectional party based on a sectional issue had gained significant power in the political system. In the second party system, the national base of support enjoyed by both Whigs and Democrats had moderated sectional conflict. The two parties had always patched up sectional differences in order to compete more effectively for national office. But the Whigs were gone, and politics in the 1850s would never be the same.

Nor were Republicans the only new party. An anti-immigrant organization, the American party, seemed likely for a few years to replace the Whigs. This party, also known as the Know-Nothings (because its members at first kept their purposes secret, answering all

Know-Nothings

queries with the words "I know nothing"), exploited nativist fear of foreigners. Between 1848 and 1860, nearly 3.5 million immigrants came to the United States—proportionally the heaviest influx of foreigners in American history (see pages 287–291). The Democratic party diligently ministered to the needs of these new citizens and relied on their votes in elections. But native Americans harbored serious misgivings about them. The temperance movement gained new strength early in these years, promising to stamp out the evils associated with liquor and immigrants. It was in this context that the Know-Nothings became prominent, campaigning to reinforce Protestant morality and restrict voting and officeholding to the native-born.

By the mid-1850s the American party was powerful and growing; in 1854 so many new congressmen won office with anti-immigrant as well as antislavery support that Know-Nothings could claim they outnumbered Republicans. In 1856 the Know-Nothing candidate for president, Millard Fillmore, won almost a million votes and ran a close third behind the Republican candidate, John C. Frémont, who garnered 1.3 million. The winner, Democrat James Buchanan, who benefited from superior party organization and a diplomatic assignment that had removed him from domestic controversy, captured fewer than 2 million votes. But like the Whigs, the Know-Nothings could not keep their northern and southern wings together, and they melted away after 1856. That left the field to the Republicans, who wooed nativists and in several states passed temperance ordinances and laws postponing suffrage for naturalized citizens (see table).

The Republicans also appealed to groups interested in the economic development of the West. Commercial agriculture was booming in the Ohio-Mississippi-

Republicans

Great Lakes area, but residents of that region needed more canals, roads, and river and harbor improvements to reap the full benefit of their labors. There was also widespread interest in a federal land-grant program: credit was

Chapter 13: The Union in crisis: the 1850s

Political Successors to the Whig Party

PARTY	PERIOD OF INFLUENCE	AREA OF INFLUENCE	OUTCOME
Free-Soil party	1848–1854	North	Merged with Republican party
Know-Nothings (American party)	1853–1856	Nationwide	Disappeared, freeing some northern voters to join Republican party
Republican party	1854–present	North (later nationwide)	Became rival of Democratic party in third party system

scarce, and proponents argued that western land should be made available free to whoever would use it. The Whigs had favored all these things before their party collapsed, but the Democrats resolutely opposed them. Following long-standing Democratic principles, presidents Pierce and Buchanan vetoed internal improvements bills, and Buchanan vetoed a homestead bill passed by Congress in 1859. Seizing their opportunity, the Republicans added internal-improvements and land-grant planks to their platform. They also backed higher tariffs as an enticement to industrialists and businessmen, whose interest in tariffs was quickened by a panic, or recession, in 1857.

Thus the Republican party picked up support from a variety of sources. Opposition to the extension of slavery had brought the party together, but party members carefully broadened their appeal by adopting the causes of other groups, whether or not those groups were alarmed by slavery. They were wise to do so. As the newspaper editor Horace Greeley wrote in 1856, "It is beaten into my bones that the American people are not yet anti-slavery." In 1860 Greeley observed again, "An Anti-Slavery man *per se* cannot be

elected." But, he added, "a Tariff, River-and-Harbor, Pacific Railroad, Free Homestead man, *may* succeed *although* he is Anti-Slavery."

Greeley's last remark was insightful. The Republican party was an amalgam of many interests, but functionally it had only one stand in the North-South controversy. Since a high proportion of the original activist Republicans were strongly opposed to slavery, the party's position on slavery and the territories was immune to change. Thus all Republicans, whatever their reasons for joining the coalition, weighed as antislavery voters in the minds of nervous southerners. Republican strength was antislavery strength.

A similar process was under way in the South. The disintegration of the Whig party had left many southerners at loose ends politically. Much of the support for Whigs had come from wealthy planters and small-town businessmen and slaveholders. Some of these people gravitated to the American party, but not for long. In the increasingly tense atmosphere of sectional crisis, they were highly susceptible to strong states' rights positions, which provided a handy defense for slavery. Democratic leaders markedly increased their

This Republican banner shows the party's effort to broaden its appeal through issues like the tariff and fear of the Slave Power. The man in the picture is the Republican presidential candidate of 1856, John C. Frémont.   Ontario County Historical Society.

Southern Democrats

use of such appeals during the 1850s, and managed to convert most of the formerly Whig slaveholders. Democrats spoke to the class interests of slaveholders, and the slaveholders responded.

Most Democrats south of the Mason-Dixon line, however, were not slaveholders. Yeomen had been the heart of the party since Andrew Jackson's day, and Democratic politicians, though often slaveowners themselves, had lauded the common man and appeared to champion his interests. Now the entry into the party of large numbers of anxious slaveholders threatened to change its character. But the yeomen did not immediately object to their strange bedfellows. Republican stands did not appeal to them. Their party loyalties were strong, and as long as political issues were not posed in a class-conscious way, they did not become restive.

Slaveholding Democrats were careful not to pursue their interests as class interests. On the contrary, they portrayed the sectional controversies as matters involving insult and injustice to all southerners. Their ultimate weapon—one they had been using in moments of danger for three decades—was the appeal to race prejudice. For years they had argued, as Jefferson Davis put it in 1851, that slavery elevated the status of the nonslaveholder and enabled the poor man to "*stand upon the broad-level of equality with the rich man.*" Now, as the sectional crisis heated up, slaveholders warned that the overriding issue was "shall negroes govern white men, or white men govern negroes?" The Montgomery *Mail* blatantly claimed that the aim of the Republicans was "to free the negroes and force amalgamation between them and the children of the poor men of the South. The rich will be able to keep out of the way of the contamination."

Chapter 13: The Union in crisis: the 1850s

These arguments had some effect, at least as long as nonslaveholders perceived outside forces as their greatest threat. The result was a one-party system in the South that emphasized sectional issues. Racial fears and traditional political loyalties kept this political alliance between yeomen and planters intact through the 1850s. The latent question—would nonslaveholders be willing to fight to protect slaveholders' property—was not openly expressed during the decade. Instead, in the South as in the North, political realignment obscured support for the Union and made sectional divisions seem sharper and deeper than they really were.

Free labor versus proslavery theory

While the new political parties were emerging, northerners and southerners were also developing opposing ideologies. The Republicans spoke to the image northerners had of themselves, their society, and their future when they preached "Free Soil, Free Labor, Free Men." These ideas resonated with the traditional American ideals of freedom, opportunity, and individualism, undercutting charges that the Republican party was radical and unreliable.

The Republican emphasis on individualism took root easily because in the 1850s the northern economy was energetic, expanding, and prosperous. Untold thousands of farmers had moved west to establish productive farms and growing communities. Midwestern farmers were using machines that multiplied their yields. Railroads were carrying their crops to market. And industry was beginning to perform wonders of production, making available goods that had hitherto been beyond the reach of the average person. To most northerners, the economic system seemed to be working spendidly.

The key element in this successful economy seemed, in the eyes of many, to be free labor. People believed in the dignity of labor. Any hard-working,

| Free labor |

virtuous person, it was thought, could improve his condition and gain economic independence by applying himself to any of the numerous opportunities the country had to offer. And to a great extent popular opinion was cor-

rect. The scale of most business operations was small, and abundant fertile land lay to the west. Monopolies and mammoth industrial firms were still things of the future. Economically it was a good age for the individual, and those who labored generally did make progress.

Republicans took advantage of this boom and formulated an ideology that captured much of the spirit of the age. They praised workers and encouraged their ambitions, holding up Abraham Lincoln as an example of a person of humble origins who had improved his lot. They portrayed their party as the guardian of economic opportunity, working to ensure that individuals could continue to apply their energies to the land's resources and attain success. In the words of an Iowa Republican, the United States was thriving because its "door is thrown open to all, and even the poorest and humblest in the land, may, by industry and application, gain a position which will entitle him to the respect and confidence of his fellow-men."

Republicans who declared their determination to help the independent entrepreneur saw no conflict between the interests of labor and capital. They relied on an old Whig idea, the harmony of economic interests, to justify the capitalistic system. According to this theory, farms and factories benefited each other, and the tariff safeguarded the jobs of American workers. "I rise to advocate the rights of labor," said a Pennsylvania representative speaking for the tariff in 1860, and his words were not wholly insincere. If free labor, economic individualism, and opportunity were protected, even propertyless workers could save money, buy property, and command the means of production.

Thus the fate of the territories was crucial to the nation's future. The North's free-labor economic system had to be extended to the territories if coming generations were to prosper. After all, the territories were the great reservoir of opportunity for decent people without means. To allow an aristocratic system of bondage and forced labor to enter the territories would be to poison the reservoir.

Thus Republican ideology encompassed an image of the South as well as the North. In fact, Republicans clarified their image of themselves by comparing their society to the slaveholding regions. For what they saw in the South was often the antithesis of what they valued in the North. The southern aristocracy, they felt,

An illustration from the *American Anti-Slavery Almanac* showing southern society as an unrelieved succession of slave torture, duels, lynchings, gambling, and cockfighting. Such blatant propaganda reinforced Republican fearmongering in the North.   Library of Congress.

defied equality and denied opportunity; proslavery theories posited a static, oppressive society rather than a developing and open one.

Southerners, meanwhile, had their own views. Abraham Lincoln clipped this description of northern society from a southern newspaper and put it into his political scrapbook:

Free society! We sicken of the name! What is it but a conglomeration of greasy mechanics, filthy operatives, small-fisted farmers, and moon-struck theorists? All the Northern and especially the New England states are devoid of society fitted for well bred gentlemen. The prevailing class one meets is that of mechanics struggling to be genteel, and small farmers who do their own drudgery; and yet are hardly fit for association with a southern gentleman's body servant.

Influential southerners were, in fact, developing an ideology of their own. At its heart this ideology did not depend on proslavery theories, though southerners often invoked such theories to defend their re-gion. Nor did it arise from territorial aspirations, though southerners insisted that they needed to expand west. Behind their ideology lay a deep fear that their way of life was about to collapse. Among southern representatives, state officials, and slaveholders generally, the feeling was growing that slavery was in jeopardy. The need to defend the institution became an obsession.

Slaveholders tended to see the world from the perspective of their plantations. Human bondage was so central to their world that life without slavery was almost unimaginable to them. They had built their fortunes and their society on the institution of slavery, and they wanted to keep the world they knew. But as intelligent men, southern leaders could not help but be aware of the worldwide movement away from slavery and the powerful forces gathering against it within the United States. Accordingly, they fought every battle in the sectional crisis with a white-hot intensity, for they knew what was ultimately at stake. In so doing they defended a whole range of propositions they did not truly believe in, all to protect the vital institution that supported their world.

By the 1850s virtually all southern representatives were familiar with the latest arguments in proslavery theory. At a moment's notice they could discuss the

| Proslavery theory |

anthropological evidence for the separate origin of the races; physicians' views on the inferiority of the black body; and sociological arguments for the superiority of the slave-labor system. But in private and in their hearts, most of these men fell back on two rationales: a belief that blacks were inferior and biblical accounts of slaveholding. Among friends, Jefferson Davis ignored all the latest racist theories and reverted to the eighteenth-century argument that southerners were doing the best they could with a situation they had inherited. "Is it well to denounce an evil for which there is no cure?" he asked. On another occasion, repeating the widespread belief that living with a sizeable free black population was impossible, he protested to a friend that Congress never discussed "any thing but that over which we have no control, slavery of the negro."

The South's defenders also developed a set of arguments to prove the necessity of expanding slavery into the territories. Expansion was essential to the welfare of the Negro, they declared, for prejudice lessened where the concentration of blacks decreased. It was necessary to the prosperity of the South, they argued, for rich opportunities lay waiting in the territories, while older areas of declining fertility had surplus slave populations. Yet there was a noticeable absence of huge migrations of slaveholders into the territories. A more likely cause of southern concern over the territories was the fear that if areas like Kansas became free soil, they would be used as a base from which to spread abolitionism into the slave states. Jefferson Davis voiced such a concern when he wrote in 1855 that "abolitionism would gain but little in excluding slavery from the territories, if it were never to disturb that institution in the States."

Southern leaders also spent a great deal of time commenting on the superior social values and practices of their region. Whereas the North was cold, materialistic, unstable, and polluted with radicalism and intellectual fads, the South was warm, caring (thanks to its practice of paternalism), and solidly devoted to home, family, and Christianity. The turmoil and change of northern life had evidently unhinged northern minds, these critics said. Even so, their arguments were primarily rebuttals of northern criticism. And many aspects of their thought—as well as the growing southern emphasis on woman's place in the home—were intended not so much to celebrate southern virtues as to suppress potential criticism from within.

But southern leaders' chief tool in defending slavery was constitutional theory. They developed an interpretation of the Constitution and the principles of American government that linked them to the founding fathers and the original purposes of the nation. Drawing on Thomas Jefferson's concept of strict construction, they emphasized that the nation arose from a compact among sovereign states; that the states were primary and the central government secondary; that the states retained all powers not expressly granted to the central government; and that the states were to be treated equally, and the rights of their citizens respected equally. Along with these theories went the philosophy that the power of the federal government should be kept to a minimum. By keeping government close to home, southerners hoped to keep slavery safe.

But as the 1850s advanced, a growing portion of slaveholders became convinced that slavery could not be protected within the Union. Such concern was not new. As early as 1838, the Louisiana planter Bennet Barrow had written in his diary, "Northern States medling with slavery . . . openly speaking of the sin of Slavery in the southern states . . . must eventually cause a separation of the Union." And in 1856, a calmer, more polished Georgian named Charles Colcock Jones, Jr., rejoiced at the Democrat James Buchanan's defeat of Republican John C. Frémont for the presidency. The result guaranteed four more years of peace and prosperity, wrote Jones, but "beyond that period . . . we scarce dare expect a continuance of our present relations." Increasingly slaveowners agreed with Jones and Barrow, accurately sensing that opposition to slavery was spreading in the North. Although Republicans disavowed any intention of disturbing slavery where it already existed, their ideology did portray slavery as a danger to the nation. Indeed, Jefferson Davis was not far wrong that hostility to slavery was the "vital element" in Republican strength.

Political impasse: slavery in the territories

Like successive hammer blows, events reinforced these sectional differences, driving North and South further apart. Controversy over Kansas did not subside; it grew. For among the settlers in the territory were partisans of both sides, each determined to make Kansas free or slave. Abolitionists and religious groups sent free-soil settlers to save the territory from slavery; southerners sent their own reinforcements, fearing that "northern hordes" were about to steal Kansas away. Clashes between the two groups led to violence, and soon the whole nation was talking about "Bleeding Kansas."

Indeed, political processes in the territory resembled war more than democracy. When elections for a territorial legislature were held in 1855, thousands of

| Bleeding Kansas |

proslavery Missourians invaded the polls and ran up a large but unlawful majority for slavery candidates. The legislature that resulted promptly legalized slavery, and in response free-soilers called an unauthorized convention and created their own government and constitution. A proslavery posse sent to arrest the free-soil leaders sacked the town of Lawrence; in revenge, John Brown, a fanatic who saw himself as God's instrument to destroy slavery, murdered five proslavery settlers. Soon armed bands of guerrillas roamed the state, battling over land claims as well as slavery.

The passion generated by this conflict erupted in the chamber of the United States Senate in May 1856, when Charles Sumner of Massachusetts denounced "the Crime against Kansas." Idealistic and radical in his antislavery views, Sumner attacked the president, the South, and Senator Andrew P. Butler of South Carolina. Soon thereafter Butler's nephew, Congressman Preston Brooks, approached Sumner at his Senate desk and beat him brutally with a cane. Voters in Massachusetts and South Carolina seethed; the country was becoming polarized.

But the agony of personal confrontation paled beside the consitutional issues raised by the Supreme Court's decision in *Dred Scott* v. *Sanford*. Scott, a Mis-

| Dred Scott *v.* Sanford |

souri slave, had sued his owner for his freedom, charging that he was free because he had resided in free territory (see page 292). After winding through the courts for eleven years, the case was decided in 1857, and the question of slavery in the territories was settled for good. Chief Justice Roger B. Taney wrote that Scott was not a citizen either of the United States or Missouri; that residence in free territory did not make Scott free; and most importantly, that Congress lacked the power to bar slavery from a territory, as it had done in the Missouri Compromise. This decision was not only controversial in content; it also had been reached in a manner that aroused sectional suspicions. The majority of the justices were southern; only one northerner had agreed with them. Three northern justices actively dissented or refused to concur in crucial parts of the decision.

A storm of angry reaction broke in the North. The decision alarmed a wide variety of northerners—abolitionists, would-be settlers in the West, even those who hated black people but feared the influence of the South. Every charge against the aggressive Slave Power seemed now to be confirmed. "There is such a thing as THE SLAVE POWER," warned the *Cincinnati Daily Commercial*. "It has marched over and annihilated the boundaries of the states. We are now one great homogenous slaveholding community." And the Cincinnati *Freeman* asked, "What security have the Germans and Irish that their children will not, within a hundred years, be reduced to slavery in this land of their adoption?" Echoed the *Atlantic Monthly,* "Where will it end? Is the success of this conspiracy to be final and eternal?" The poet James Russell Lowell both stimulated and expressed the anxieties of poor northern whites when he had his Yankee narrator, Ezekiel Biglow, say,

Wy, it's jest ez clear ez figgers,
    Clear ez one an' one make two,
Chaps thet make black slaves o' niggers,
    Want to make wite slaves o' you.

Republican politicians capitalized on these fears, using the threat of the Slave Power to build a coalition of abolitionists, who opposed slavery on moral grounds, and racists, who feared that slavery jeopardized their interests. Indeed, Abraham Lincoln's great-

Guerrilla warfare in Bleeding Kansas. Free staters fire on a pro-slavery settlement near Leavenworth (1856). Kansas State Historical Society.

est achievement in the 1850s, one historian has pointed out, was as a Republican political propagandist against slavery. Lincoln cloaked the crudest charges against the Slave Power in language of biblical majesty, chilling thousands of voters. The South threatened democracy, he argued, and slavery threatened all whites.

Abraham Lincoln on the Slave Power

At the crux of the matter was the self-interest of whites. Pointing to the southern obsession with the territories, Lincoln had declared as early as 1854 that "the whole nation is interested that the best use shall be made of these Territories. We want them for homes of free white people. This they cannot be, to any considerable extent, if slavery shall be planted within them." The territories must be reserved, he now insisted, "as an outlet for *free white people every-where*" so that immigrants could come to America and "find new homes and better their condition in life." After the Dred Scott decision, Lincoln charged that the next step in the unfolding Slave Power conspiracy would be a Supreme Court decision "declaring that the Constitution does not permit a State to exclude slavery from its limits. . . . We shall lie down pleasantly, dreaming that the people of Missouri are on the verge of making their State free; and we shall awake to the reality instead, that the Supreme Court has made Illinois a slave State." The proslavery argument's denigration of freedom and southerners' harping on the inferiority of blacks, Lincoln warned, were signs of a desire "to make *things* out of poor white men."

Lincoln's most eloquent statement against the Slave Power was his famous House Divided speech. In it Lincoln declared: "I do not expect the Union to be dissolved—I do not expect the House to fall—but I do expect it to cease to be divided. It will become all one thing or all the other. Either the opponents of slavery will arrest the further spread of it, and place it where the public mind shall rest in the belief that it is in the course of ultimate extinction; or its advocates will push it forward, till it shall become alike lawful in all the States, old as well as new, North as well as South. Have we no tendency to the latter condition?" The concluding question was the key element of the passage, for it drove home the idea that slaveholders were trying to extend bondage over the entire nation.

The brilliance of Republican tactics offset the difficulties the Dred Scott decision posed for them. By endorsing southern constitutional arguments, the Court had invalidated the central position of the Republican party: no extension of slavery. Republicans could only repudiate the decision, appealing to a "higher law," or hope to change the personnel of the Court.

Campaign medallions of Abraham Lincoln and Stephen Douglas, done two years after the famous Lincoln-Douglas debates. Edmund B. Sullivan Collection, University of Hartford.

For northern Democrats like Stephen Douglas, meanwhile, there was no escape. Douglas faced an awful dilemma. Northerners were alarmed by the prospect that the territories would be opened up to slavery. To retain support in the North, therefore, Douglas had to find some way to hedge, to reassure voters. Yet he had to do so without alienating southern Democrats. Douglas's task was problematic even at best; given the emotions of the time, it proved impossible.

Douglas chose to stand by his principle of popular sovereignty, which encountered a second test in Kansas in 1857. There, after free-soil settlers boycotted an election, proslavery forces met at Lecompton and wrote a constitution that permitted slavery. New elections to the territorial legislature, however, returned an antislavery majority, and the legislature promptly called for a popular vote on the new constitution, which was defeated by more than ten thousand votes. Despite this overwhelming evidence that Kansans did not want slavery, President Buchanan tried to force

the Lecompton constitution through Congress. Douglas threw his weight against a document the people had rejected; he gauged their feelings correctly, and in 1858 Kansas voters rejected the constitution a third time. But his action infuriated southern Democrats.

In his well-publicized debates with Abraham Lincoln in 1858, Douglas further alienated the southern wing of his party. Speaking at Freeport, Illinois, he attempted to revive the notion of popular sovereignty

> *Stephen Douglas proposes the Freeport Doctrine*

with some tortured extensions of his old arguments. Asserting that the Court had not ruled on the powers of a *territorial* legislature, Douglas claimed that a territorial legislature could bar slavery either by passing a law against it or by doing nothing. Without the patrol laws and police regulations that support slavery, he reasoned, the institution could not exist. This argument, called the Freeport Doctrine, temporarily shored up Douglas's crumbling position

Chapter 13: The Union in crisis: the 1850s

in the North. But it gave southern Democrats further evidence that Douglas was unreliable, and some turned viciously against him. A few southerners, like William L. Yancey of Alabama, studied the trend in northern opinion and concluded that southern rights would be safe only in a separate southern nation.

Thus the territorial issue continued to generate wider and more dangerous conflict. In itself it had diminishing practical significance. By 1858 even Jefferson Davis had given up on agricultural development in the Southwest and admitted his uncertainty that slavery could succeed in Kansas. In territories outside Kansas the number of settlers was small, and everywhere the number of blacks was negligible—less than 1 percent of the population in Kansas and New Mexico. Nevertheless, men like Davis and Douglas spent many hours attacking each other's theories on the floor of the Senate. And the general public, both North and South, moved from anxiety to alarm and anger. The situation had become explosive.

Violence inflamed passions further in October 1859, when John Brown led a small band in an attack on Harpers Ferry, Virginia, hoping to trigger a slave rebellion. Brown failed miserably, and was quickly captured, tried, and executed. It came to light, however, that Brown had had the financial backing of several prominent abolitionists, and northern intellectuals such as Emerson and Thoreau praised him as a hero and a martyr. Since slave rebellion excited the deepest fears in the white South, these disclosures multiplied southerners' fear and anger many times over. The unity of the nation was now in peril.

The election of 1860 and secession

Many observers feared that the election of 1860 would decide the fate of the Union. An ominous occurrence at the beginning of the campaign did nothing to reassure them. For several years, the Democratic party had been the only remaining organization that was truly national in scope. Even religious denominations had split into northern and southern wings during the 1840s and 1850s. "One after another," wrote a Mississippi newspaper editor, "the links which have bound the North and the South to-gether, have been severed . . . [but] the Democratic party looms gradually up, its nationality intact, and waves the olive branch over the troubled waters of politics." At the 1860 convention, however, the Democratic party broke in two.

Stephen A. Douglas wanted the party's presidential nomination, but could not afford to alienate northern opinion by accepting a strongly southern position on the territories. Southern Democrats like William L.

Splintering of the Democratic party

Yancey, on the other hand, were determined to have their rights recognized, and they moved to block Douglas's nomination. When Douglas nevertheless marshalled a majority for his version of the platform, delegates from the five Gulf states plus South Carolina, Georgia, and Arkansas walked out of the convention hall in Charleston. Efforts at compromise failed, so the Democrats presented two nominees: Douglas for the northern wing, John C. Breckinridge for the southern. The Republicans nominated Abraham Lincoln; a Constitutional Union party, formed to preserve the nation but strong only in Virginia and the upper South, nominated John Bell of Tennessee.

Bell and Douglas clearly preferred saving the Union to endangering it, and Breckinridge quickly backed away from any appearance of extremism; his supporters in several states declared that he was not a threat to the Union. But the New Orleans *Bee* charged that every disunionist in the land was enthusiastic for Breckinridge, and a Texas paper made an earthy reference to his association with radicals: "Mr. Breckinridge claims that he isn't a disunionist. An animal not willing to pass for a pig shouldn't stay in the stye." Frightened by such criticism, Breckinridge altered his plan to do no speaking during the campaign and delivered one address in which he flatly denied that his aim was secession. Thereafter his supporters stressed his loyalty and even went so far as to ridicule the possibility of secession in case of a Republican victory.

The results of the balloting were sectional in character, but they indicated clearly that most voters were satisfied in the Union. Breckinridge carried nine

Election of 1860

southern states, with his strength concentrated in the Deep South. Bell won pluralities in Virginia, Kentucky, and Tennessee. Lincoln defeated Douglas

Presidential Vote in 1860

	LINCOLN	OTHER CANDIDATES
Entire United States	1,866,452	2,815,617
North plus border and southern states that rejected secession prior to war[1]	1,866,452	2,421,752
North plus border states that fought for union[2]	1,864,523	1,960,842

Note the large vote for other candidates in the righthand column.

[1] Kentucky, Missouri, Maryland, Delaware, Virginia, North Carolina, Tennessee, Arkansas

[2] Kentucky, Missouri, Maryland, Delaware

Source: David Potter, *Lincoln and his Party in the Secession Crisis* (New Haven and London: Yale University Press, 1942, 1967), p. 189.

in the North, but in the states that ultimately remained loyal to the Union he won only a plurality, not a majority (see table). Lincoln's victory was won in the electoral college.

Thus the majority of voters cast their ballots against the extreme choices. And, given the heterogeneous nature of Republican voters, it is likely that most of even Lincoln's supporters did not view the issue of slavery in the territories as paramount. In such circumstances, partisan leaders had an opportunity either to work for compromise or to accentuate the conflict.

As it happened, Lincoln decided not to soften his party's position on the territories. In his inaugural address he spoke of the necessity of maintaining the bond of faith between voter and candidate, of declining to set "the minority over the majority." But Lincoln's party was *not* the majority. His refusal to compromise probably had more to do with the unity of the Republican party than with the integrity of the democratic process. For though many conservative Republicans—eastern businessmen and former Whigs

who did not feel strongly about slavery—hoped for a compromise, the original and strongest Republicans—antislavery voters and "conscience Whigs"—would not back away from the platform. To preserve the unity of his party, then, Lincoln had to take a position that endangered the Union.

Furthermore, political leaders in the North and the South tragically misjudged each other. As the historian David Potter has shown, Lincoln and other prominent Republicans believed that southerners were bluffing when they threatened secession; they expected a pro-Union majority in the South to assert itself. Therefore Lincoln determined not to yield to threats, but to call the southerners' bluff. On their side, southern leaders had become convinced that northerners were not taking them seriously, and that a posture of strength was necessary to win respect for their position. "To rally the men of the North, who would preserve the government as our fathers found it, we . . . should offer no doubtful or divided front," wrote Jefferson Davis. Thus southern leaders who hoped to avert disaster did not offer compromise, for

Chapter 13: The Union in crisis: the 1850s

fear of inviting aggression. Nor did northern leaders who loved the Union, believing it unnecessary and unwise. The misunderstanding was complete; the communication between the two groups nil.

Meanwhile the Union was being destroyed. On December 20, 1860, South Carolina passed an ordinance of secession amid jubilation and cheering. This

| Secession of South Carolina |

step marked the inauguration of a strategy known as separate-state secession. Despairing of persuading all the southern states to challenge the federal government simultaneously, foes of the Union had concentrated their hopes on the most extreme proslavery state. With South Carolina out of the Union, they hoped other states would follow suit and momentum would build toward disunion.

The strategy proved effective. By reclaiming its independence, South Carolina had raised the stakes in the sectional confrontation. No longer was secession an unthinkable step; the Union was broken. Now, argued extremists, other states should secede to support South Carolina. Those who wanted to compromise would surely be able to make a better deal outside the Union than in it. Moderates found it difficult to dismiss such arguments, since most of them—even those who felt deep affection for the Union—were committed to defending southern rights and the southern way of life.

Congress made last-minute efforts to save the Union. Both the Senate and the House established special committees to search for a satisfactory compromise. Their efforts focused on a series of proposals offered by Senator John J. Crittenden of Kentucky, who hoped to don the mantle of Henry Clay and avert disaster. Crittenden suggested that the two sections divide the territories between them at 36°30′. But his efforts came to grief when Lincoln indicated that Republicans would not make concessions on the territorial issue. Virginians called for a special convention in Washington, to which several states sent representatives. But this gathering, too, failed to find a magical formula or to reach unanimity on disputed questions.

In these circumstances, southern extremists soon got their way. Overwhelming their opposition, they quickly called conventions and passed secession ordinances in six other states: Mississippi, Florida, Ala-

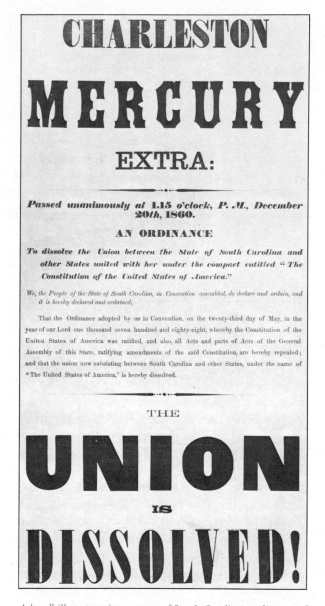

A handbill announcing passage of South Carolina's ordinance of secession.   Rare Book Division, The New York Public Library, Astor, Lenox and Tilden Foundations.

bama, Georgia, Louisiana, and Texas. By February 1861 these states had joined with South Carolina to form a new government in Montgomery, Alabama: the Confederate States of America. Choosing Jefferson Davis as their president, they began to function independently of the United States.

Yet this apparent unanimity of action was deceiving. Confused and dissatisfied with the alternatives,

Rival pro-Union and pro-Confederacy groups meet in the streets of Knoxville, Tennessee. In Kentucky, Missouri, and other parts of the upper South, sentiment was deeply divided. Corcoran Gallery of Art.

many voters who had cast a ballot for president stayed home rather than vote for delegates who would consider secession. In some conventions the vote to secede had been close, the balance tipped by the over-representation of plantation districts. Furthermore, the conventions were noticeably reluctant to seek ratification of their acts by the people. Four states in the upper South—Virginia, North Carolina, Tennessee, and Arkansas—flatly rejected secession, and did not join the Confederacy until after the fighting had started. In Kentucky and Missouri popular sentiment was too divided for decisive action; these states remained under Union control, along with Maryland and Delaware (see map).

Small wonder, since secession posed new and troubling issues for southerners, not the least of them the possibility of war and the question of who would be sacrificed. A careful look at election returns indicates that slaveholders and nonslaveholders were be-

ginning to part company politically. Heavy slave-holding counties drew together in strong support of secession, but many counties with few slaves took an antisecession position or were staunchly Unionist (see table, page 362). By sitting out the election, large numbers of yeomen refused to follow traditional Democratic party lines. In other words, non-slaveholders were beginning to act on class interests, as planters had been doing for some time. With the threat of war on the horizon, nonslaveholders began to ask themselves how far they would go to support slavery and the slaveowners.

Finally, there was still considerable love for the Union in the South. Some opposition to secession was fervently pro-Union, as is apparent in the comment of a northern Alabama delegate after his convention had approved secession: "Here I sit & from my window see the nasty little thing flaunting in the breeze which has taken the place of that glorious banner which has

Chapter 13: The Union in crisis: the 1850s

This Confederate ribbon was probably worn during the Con-
federacy's only presidential inauguration, on February 18, 1861.
Around the photograph of Jefferson Davis are the now ironic
words "The Right Man in the Right Place / Our First President /
Jeff Davis." Edmund B. Sullivan Collection, University of
Hartford.

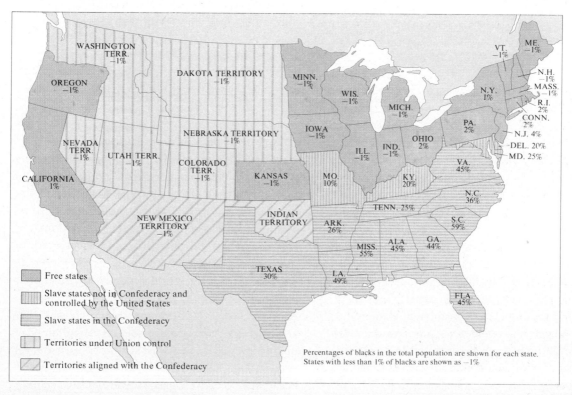

The divided nation—slave and free areas, 1861.

The election of 1860 and secession

Voting Returns of Counties with Few Slaveholders, Eight Southern States, 1860 and 1861

STATE	MEDIAN % OF ELIGIBLE VOTERS FOR BRECKINRIDGE, 1860	MEDIAN % OF ELIGIBLE VOTERS FOR SECESSION, 1861	% CHANGE
Alabama	42.0	28.3	–13.7
Georgia	44.8	34.1	–10.7
Louisiana	35.3	28.1	–7.2
Mississippi	50.3	26.8	–23.5
North Carolina	29.6	22.0	–7.6
Tennessee	34.7	11.1	–23.6
Texas	43.7	33.0	–10.7
Virginia	27.2	6.5	–20.7

been the pride of millions of Americans and the boast of freemen the wide world over." Such sentiments presented problems for the Confederacy, though they were not sufficiently developed to prevent secession.

The dilemma facing President Lincoln on inauguration day in March 1861 was how to maintain the authority of the federal government without provoking war in the states that had left the Union. He decided to proceed cautiously; by holding onto federal fortifications, he reasoned, he could assert federal sovereignty while waiting for a restoration of relations. But Jefferson Davis, who could not claim to lead a sovereign nation if its ports and military facilities were under foreign control, would not cooperate. A collision was inevitable.

It came in the early morning hours of April 12, 1861, at Fort Sumter in Charleston harbor. A federal garrison there was running low on food. Lincoln had decided to send a supply ship and had notified the South Carolinians of his intention. For the Montgomery government, the only alternative to an attack on the fort was submission to Lincoln's authority. Accordingly, orders were sent to obtain surrender or attack the fort. Under heavy bombardment for two days, the federal garrison finally surrendered. The Confederates permitted the soldiers to sail away on unarmed vessels while the residents of Charleston celebrated. Thus the bloodiest war in the nation's history began in a deceptively gala and gentlemanly spirit.

Attack on Fort Sumter

Blacks, who would play a crucial role in the Civil War, were involved in preparations for the first battle. In this contemporary drawing they mount cannon for the Confederate attack on Fort Sumter.   Library of Congress.

The war also began with its central issue shrouded in complexity and confusion. In the profoundest sense, slavery was tied up with the war. It had not been the single or direct cause of battle; the disagreement over the institution was complicated and unfocused. But indisputably the Civil War was, at bottom, about slavery. It arose from slavery in a multitude of ways, and it could hardly be conducted without affecting slavery. It addressed the questions of slavery's place in the law and black peoples' place in society. The answers to those questions, and the degree to which answers were sought, would be matters of fateful import.

Suggestions for further reading

Sources of conflict

Eugene H. Berwanger, *The Frontier Against Slavery* (1967); Ray Allen Billington, *The Protestant Crusade, 1800–1860* (1938 and 1964); Richard H. Brown, "The Missouri Crisis, Slavery, and the Politics of Jacksonianism," *South Atlantic Quarterly,* LXV (Winter 1966), 55–72; Louis Filler, *The Crusade Against Slavery, 1830–1860* (1960); Eric Foner, *Free Soil, Free Labor, Free Men* (1970); George M. Fredrickson, *The Black Image in the White Mind* (1971); Eugene D. Genovese, *The World the Slaveholders Made* (1969); Michael F.

Important events

1846	Wilmot Proviso
1847	Lewis Cass proposes idea of popular sovereignty
1848	Zachary Taylor elected president
1849	California applies for admission to Union as free state
1850	Nashville Convention Compromise of 1850 Vermont enacts personal liberty law
1851	Mob rescues fugitive slave in Boston
1852	Harriet Beecher Stowe, *Uncle Tom's Cabin* Franklin Pierce elected president
1854	Kansas-Nebraska bill "Appeal of the Independent Democrats" Free-Soil party promotes settlement of Kansas Republican party formed

	Pierce's effort to purchase Cuba fails Democrats lose ground in congressional elections
1856	Preston Brooks attacks Charles Sumner in Senate chamber Bleeding Kansas James Buchanan elected president
1857	*Dred Scott* v. *Sanford* Economic recession Lecompton Constitution
1858	Voters reject Lecompton Constitution Lincoln-Douglas debates Freeport Doctrine
1859	Buchanan vetoes homestead bill John Brown raids Harpers Ferry
1860	Democratic party splits in half Abraham Lincoln elected president Crittenden Compromise fails South Carolina secedes from Union
1861	Six more southern states secede Confederacy established Attack on Fort Sumter

Holt, *The Political Crisis of the 1850s* (1978); William Sumner Jenkins, *Pro-Slavery Thought in the Old South* (1935); Aileen S. Kraditor, *Means and Ends in American Abolitionism* (1969); Robert E. May, *The Southern Dream of a Caribbean Empire, 1854–1861* (1973); Roy F. Nichols, *The Disruption of American Democracy* (1948); Russell B. Nye, *Fettered Freedom* (1949); Lewis Perry and Michael Fellman, eds., *Antislavery Reconsidered* (1979); Joel H. Silbey, *The Transformation of American Politics, 1840–1860* (1967); Henry H. Simms, *A Decade of Sectional Controversy, 1851–1861* (1942); William R. Stanton, *The Leopard's Spots* (1960); Ronald G. Walters, *American Reformers, 1815–1860* (1978).

Political crises

Thomas B. Alexander, *Sectional Stress and Party Strength* (1967); William L. Barney, *The Secessionist Impulse* (1974); Stanley W. Campbell, *The Slave Catchers* (1968); Avery O. Craven, *The Coming of the Civil War* (1942); Don E. Fehrenbacher, *The Dred Scott Case* (1978); J. C. Furnas, *The Road to Harpers Ferry* (1959); Holman Hamilton, *Prologue to Conflict* (1964); Cleo Hearon, *Mississippi and the Compromise of 1850* (1913); Henry V. Jaffa, *Crisis of the House Divided* (1959); Paul D. Nagle, *One Nation Indivisible* (1964); Allan Nevins, *The Emergence of Lincoln,* 2 vols. (1950); Stephen B. Oates, *To Purge the Land with Blood* (1970); David M. Potter, *The Impending Crisis, 1848–1861* (1976); David M. Potter, *The South and the Sectional Conflict* (1968); Percy Lee Rainwater, *Mississippi: Storm Center of Secession, 1856–1861* (1938); James A. Rawley, *Race and Politics* (1969); Kenneth M. Stampp, *And the War Came* (1950); J. Mills Thornton III, *Politics and Power in a Slave Society* (1978); Alice Felt Tyler, *Freedom's Ferment* (1944); Gerald W. Wolff, *The Kansas-Nebraska Bill* (1977).

Secection and war

Steven A. Channing, *Crisis of Fear* (1970); Robert Gray Gunderson, *Old Gentlemen's Convention* (1961); Michael P. Johnson, *Toward a Patriarchal Republic* (1977); Seymour Martin Lipset, *Political Man* (1960); David M. Potter, *Lincoln and His Party in the Secession Crisis* (1942); Henry T. Shanks, *The Secession Movement in Virginia, 1847–1861* (1934); Joseph Carlyle Sitterson, *The Secession Movement in North Carolina* (1939); Ralph A. Wooster, *The Secession Conventions of the South* (1962).

Political leaders

Richard N. Current, *The Lincoln Nobody Knows* (1958); David Donald, *Charles Sumner and the Coming of the Civil War* (1960); David Donald, *Lincoln Reconsidered* (1956); Paul D. Escott, "Jefferson Davis and Slavery in the Territories," *Journal of Mississippi History,* 39 (May 1977), 97–116; Don E. Fehrenbacher, *Prelude to Greatness* (1962); George B. Forgie, *Patricide in the House Divided* (1979); Robert W. Johannsen, *Stephen A. Douglas* (1973); Roy F. Nichols, *Franklin Pierce* (1958); Philip Shriver Klein, *President James Buchanan* (1962).

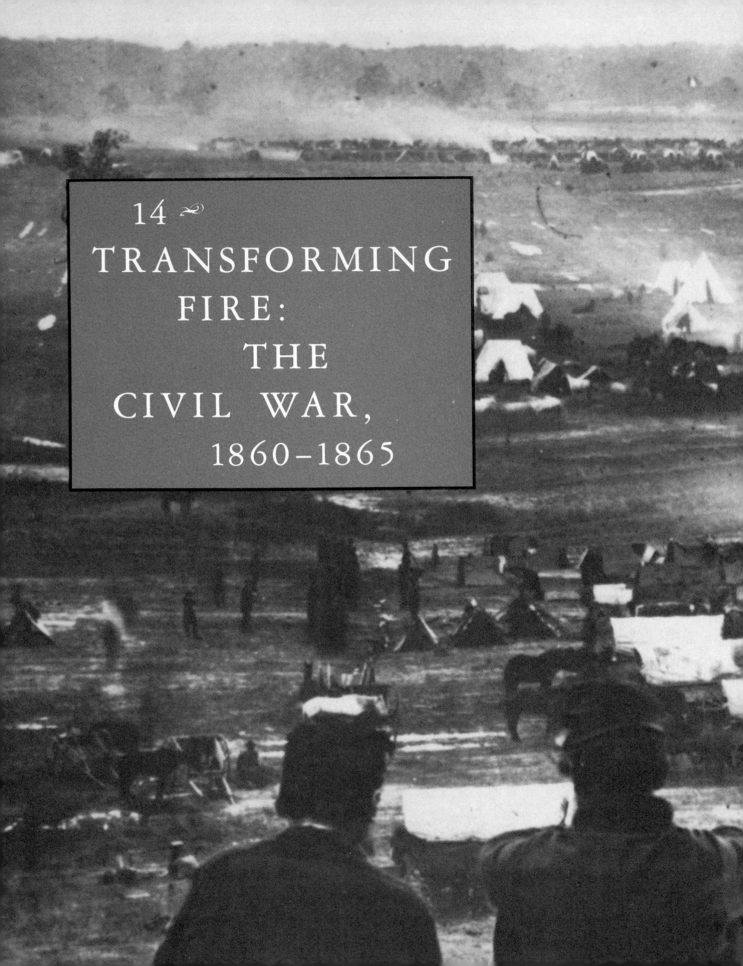

14 &

TRANSFORMING
FIRE:
THE
CIVIL WAR,
1860–1865

They came from many different places. They held many different points of view. Perhaps the only thing that united them was the fact that they were caught in a gigantic struggle. Each felt dwarfed by the immense force of the Civil War, a vast and complex event beyond any individual's control.

Moncure Conway, a Virginian who had converted to abolitionism and settled in New England, saw the Civil War as a momentous opportunity to bring justice to human affairs. The progress of reform in the North, Conway wrote in an earnest pamphlet, heralded the dawn of "Humanity's advancing day." Before this dawn, "Slavery, hoary tyrant of the ages," cried out " 'Back! back . . . into the chambers of Night!' " Conway urged northerners to accept slavery's challenge and defeat it, so that "the rays of Freedom and Justice" could shine throughout America. Then the United States would stand as a beacon not only of commercial power but of moral righteousness.

Conway's lofty idealism was far removed from the motives that drove most federal soldiers to march grimly to their death. Though slaves believed they were witnessing God's "Holy War for de liberation of de poor African slave people," Union troops took a different perspective. When a Yankee soldier ransacked a slave family's cabin and stole their best quilts, the mother exclaimed, "Why you nasty, stinkin' rascal. You say you come down here to fight for the niggers, and now you're stealin' from em." The soldier replied, "You're a G-- D--- liar, I'm fightin for $14 a month and the Union."

Southerners too acted on limited and pragmatic motives, fighting in self-defense or out of regional loyalty. A Union officer interrogating Confederate prisoners noticed the poverty of one captive. Clearly the man was no slaveholder, so the officer asked him why he was fighting. "Because y'all are down here," replied the Confederate.

The great suffering and frustration of the war were apparent in the bitter words of another southerner, a civilian. Impoverished by the conflict, this farmer had endured inflation, taxes, and shortages to support the Confederacy. Then an impressment agent arrived to take from him still more—grain and meat, horses and mules and wagons. In return the agent offered only a certificate promising repayment sometime in the future. Angry and fed up, the farmer bluntly declared,

"the sooner this damned Government falls to pieces, the better it will be for us."

In contrast, many northern businessmen looked to the economic effects of the war with optimism and anticipation. The conflict ensured vast government expenditures, a heavy demand for products, and lucrative government contracts. *Harper's Monthly* reported that an eminent financier expected a long war, the kind of war that would mean huge purchases, paper money, active speculation, and rising prices. "The battle of Bull Run," predicted the financier, "makes the fortune of every man in Wall Street who is not a natural idiot."

For each of these people and millions of others, the Civil War was a life-changing event. It obliterated the normal circumstances of life, sweeping millions of men into training camps and battle units. Armies numbering in the hundreds of thousands marched over the South, devastating once-peaceful countrysides. Families struggled to survive without their men; businesses tried to cope with the loss of workers. Women, North and South, faced added responsibilities in the home and moved into new jobs in the work force. Nothing seemed untouched.

Change was most drastic in the South, where the leaders of the secession movement had launched a revolution for the purpose of keeping things unchanged. Never were men more mistaken: their revolutionary means were fundamentally incompatible with their conservative purpose. Southerners had feared that a peacetime government of Republicans would interfere with slavery and upset the routine of plantation life. Instead their own actions led to a war that turned southern life upside down and imperiled the very existence of slavery. The Civil War forced drastic changes in every phase of southern society, and the leadership of Jefferson Davis resulted in policies more objectionable to the elite than any proposed by Lincoln. The Confederacy proved to be a shockingly unsouthern experience.

War altered the North as well, but not as deeply. Since the bulk of the fighting took place on southern soil, most northern farms and factories remained physically unscathed. The drafting of workers and the changing needs for products slowed the pace of industrialization somewhat, but factories and businesses remained busy. Though workers lost ground to inflation, the economy hummed. And a new probusiness

Optimistic and confident, these soldiers from a Virginia regiment vied for a place in the photographer's lens shortly before the war began.   Valentine Museum, Richmond, Virginia.

atmosphere dominated Congress, where southern representatives no longer filled their seats. To the discomfort of some, the powers of the federal government and the president increased during the emergency.

The war strained society, both North and South. Disaffection was strongest in the Confederacy, where the sufferings of ordinary citizens were greatest. There poverty and class resentment fed a lower-class antagonism to the war that threatened the Confederacy from within as federal armies assailed it from without. But dissent also flourished in the North, where antiwar sentiment occasionally erupted into violence.

Ultimately, the Civil War forced new social and racial arrangements on the nation. Its greatest effect was to compel leaders and citizens to deal with an issue they had often tried to avoid: slavery. This issue had, in complex and indirect ways, given rise to the war; now the scope and demands of the war forced reluctant Americans to deal with it.

The South goes to war

In the first bright days of the southern nation, few foresaw the changes that were in store. Lincoln's call for troops to put down the Confederate insurrection stimulated an outpouring of regional loyalty that unified the classes. Though four border slave states—Missouri, Kentucky, Maryland, and Delaware—and western Virginia refused to secede, the rest of the upper South promptly joined the Confederacy. From every quarter southerners flocked to defend their region against Yankee aggression. In the first few months of the war half a million men volunteered to fight; there were so many would-be soldiers that the government could not arm them all.

This groundswell of popular support for the Confederacy generated a mood of optimism and gaiety. Women sewed dashing, colorful uniforms for men who would before long be lucky to wear drab gray or butternut homespun. Confident recruits boasted of whipping the Yankees and returning home in time for dinner. And the first major battle of the war only increased such cockiness. On July 21, 1861, General Irvin McDowell and thirty thousand federal troops

| Battle of Bull Run |

attacked General P. G. T. Beauregard's twenty-two thousand southerners at a stream called Bull Run, near Manassas Junction, Virginia. Both armies were ill-trained, and confusion reigned on the battlefield. But nine thousand Confederate reinforcements and a timely stand by General Thomas Jackson (thereafter known as "Stonewall" Jackson) won the day for the South. Union troops fled back to Washington in disarray, and shocked northern picnickers who had expected to witness a victory suddenly feared their capital would be taken.

As 1861 faded into 1862, however, the North undertook a massive buildup of troops in northern Virginia. In the wake of Bull Run, Lincoln had given command of the army to General George B. McClellan, an officer who had always been better at organization and training than at fighting. McClellan devoted the fall and winter to readying a formidable force of a quarter-million men. "The vast preparation of the enemy," wrote one Confederate soldier, produced a "feeling of despondency" among southerners.

The North also moved to blockade southern ports in order to choke off the Confederacy's avenues of commerce and supply. At first the handful of available

| Union naval campaign |

steamers proved woefully inadequate to the task of patrolling 3,550 miles of coastline. But the Union navy substantially reduced southern maritime traffic in the first year of the war and eventually imposed a near-total blockade.

In the fall of 1861 Union naval power came ashore in the South. Federal squadrons captured Cape Hatteras and Hilton Head, part of the Sea Islands off Port Royal, South Carolina. A few months later, similar operations secured Albemarle and Pamlico sounds, Roanoke Island, and New Bern in North Carolina, as well as Fort Pulaski, which defended Savannah. Then in April 1862 ships commanded by Admiral David Farragut smashed through log booms on the Mississippi and fought their way upstream to capture New Orleans (see map).

The coastal victories off South Carolina foreshadowed another major development in the unraveling of the southern status quo. At the gunboats' approach, frightened planters abandoned their lands and fled. Their slaves, who thus became the first to escape slavery through military action, greeted what they hoped to be freedom with rejoicing and destruction of the cotton gins, symbols of their travail. Their jubilation and the constantly growing stream of runaways who poured into the Union lines removed any doubt about which side the slaves would support, given the opportunity. Ironically the federal government, unwilling at first to wage a war against slavery, did not acknowledge the slaves' freedom—though it did set to work finding ways to use them in the national cause.

With the approach of spring 1862, the military outlook for the Confederacy darkened again, this time in northern Tennessee. There a hard-drinking, hitherto unsuccessful general named Ulysses S. Grant rec-

| Grant's campaign in Tennessee |

ognized the strategic importance of forts Henry and Donelson, the Confederate outposts guarding the Tennessee and Cumberland rivers. Grant saw that if federal troops could capture these forts, two prime routes into the heartland of the Confederacy would lie open. In the space of ten days he seized the forts, using his forces so well that he was able to demand unconditional surrender of Fort Donelson's defenders. A path into Tennessee, Alabama, and Mississippi now lay open before the Union army.

But orders from General Henry Halleck, who coordinated federal operations from Washington, kept Grant from pressing the southern commander, Albert Sidney Johnston. On April 6, Johnston caught Grant's army in an undesirable position at Pittsburg Landing in southern Tennessee. The Confederates inflicted heavy damage in fierce fighting. Close to victory, however, General Johnston was struck by a ball that severed an artery in his thigh; within minutes he was dead. Deprived of their leader, southern troops faced a reinforced Union army the next day, and the tide of battle turned. After ten hours of heavy combat, Grant's men forced the Confederates to withdraw to Corinth, Mississippi. Though the Battle of Shiloh was a Union victory, it was hideously destructive on both sides. Northern troops lost 13,000 of 63,000 men; southerners sacrificed 11,000 out of 40,000.

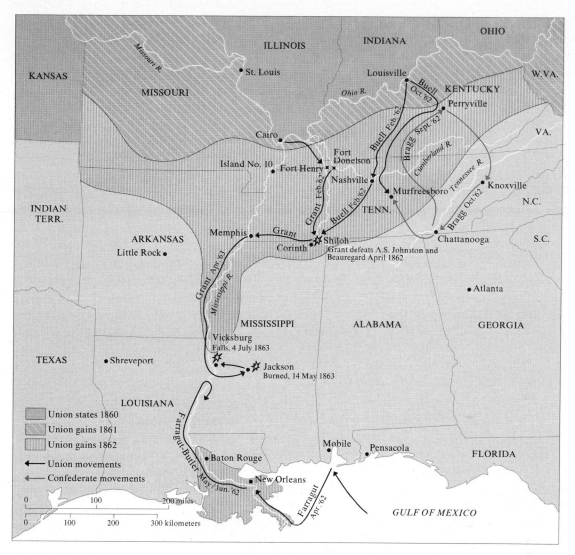

The war in the West, 1861–July 1863.   Source: Reprinted by permission of Alfred A. Knopf, Inc.

Both soldiers and civilians were beginning to recognize the enormous costs of this war. Never before in Europe or America had such massive forces pummeled each other with weapons of such destructive power. Many citizens, like soldier—later Supreme Court Justice—Oliver Wendell Holmes, wondered at "the butcher's bill." The improved range of modern rifles multiplied casualties; and, since medical knowledge was rudimentary, even minor wounds often led to death through infection. The slaughter was most vivid, of course, to the soldiers themselves, who saw the blasted bodies of their friends and comrades. "Any one who goes over a battlefield after a battle," wrote one Confederate, "never cares to go over another. . . . I for one don't care if I am never near another fight again. . . . It is a sad sight to see the dead, and if possible more sad to see the wounded—shot in every possible way you can imagine."

Troops learned the hard way that soldiering was far from glorious. "The dirt of a camp life knocks all its poetry into a cocked hat," wrote a North Carolina volunteer in 1862. One year later he marveled at his earlier innocence. Fighting had taught him "the realities of a soldier's life. We had no tents after the 6th August, but slept on the ground, in the woods or open fields, without regard to the weather. ... I learned to eat fat bacon raw, and to like it. . . . Without time to wash our clothes or our persons, and sleeping on the ground all huddled together, the whole army became lousy more or less with body lice. It was a necessary and unavoidable incident to our arduous campaign."

The scope and duration of the conflict had begun to have a visible effect on Confederate morale. As the spring of 1862 approached, southern officials worried about the strength of their armies. Tens of thousands of Confederate soldiers had volunteered for just one year's service, planning to return home in the spring to plant their crops. To keep southern armies in the field, the War Department offered bounties and furloughs to all who would re-enlist. Officials then called for new volunteers; but, as one admitted, "the spirit of volunteering had died out." Three states threatened or instituted a draft. Finally, still faced with a

Confederacy resorts to a draft

critical shortage of troops, the Confederate government enacted the first national conscription law in American history. The war had forced an unprecedented change on the states that had seceded for fear of change.

With their ranks swelled by conscripts, southern armies moved into heavier fighting. Early in 1862 most of the combat centered in Virginia. General McClellan sailed his troops to the York peninsula and advanced on Richmond from the east. By May and June the sheer size of the federal armies outside the South's capital was highly threatening. But when McClellan sent his legions into combat, generals Jackson and Lee managed to stave off his attacks. First Jackson maneuvered into the Shenandoah Valley, behind Union forces, and threatened Washington, drawing some of the federals away from Richmond to protect their own capital. Then, in a series of engagements culminating in the Seven Days' battles, Lee held McClellan off. On August 3 McClellan withdrew to the Potomac, and Richmond was safe for almost two more years.

Buoyed by these results, Jefferson Davis conceived an ambitious plan to turn the tide of the war and com-

pel the United States to recognize the Confederacy. He ordered a general offensive, sending Lee north to

Davis orders an offensive

Maryland and generals Kirby Smith and Braxton Bragg to Kentucky. The South would abandon the defensive and take the war north. Davis and his commanders issued a proclamation to the people of Maryland and Kentucky asserting that the Confederates sought only the right of self-government. Lincoln's refusal to grant them independence forced them to attack "those who persist in their refusal to make peace." Davis urged the invaded states to make a separate peace with his government and invited the Northwest, whose trade flowed down the Mississippi to New Orleans, to break with the Union.

The plan was promising, and Davis rejoiced that his outnumbered forces were at length ready to take the initiative. Every part of the offensive failed, however. In the bloodiest single day of fighting, September 17, 1862, McClellan turned Lee back in the Battle of Antietam near Sharpsburg, Maryland. Smith and Bragg had to withdraw from Kentucky just one day after Bragg had attended the inauguration of a provisional Confederate governor. The entire effort had collapsed.

But southern arms were not exhausted. Jeb Stuart executed a daring cavalry raid into Pennsylvania on October 10 through 12, and Lee decimated General Ambrose Burnside's soldiers as they charged his fortified positions at Fredericksburg, Virginia, on December 13. The Confederate Army of Northern Virginia performed so bravely and controlled the engagement so thoroughly that Lee, a restrained and humane man, was moved to say, "It is well that war is so terrible. We should grow too fond of it."

Nevertheless, the Confederacy had marshalled all its strength for a breakthrough and failed utterly. Outnumbered and disadvantaged in resources (see figure), the South could not continue its offensive. Meanwhile the North still had reserves of every kind on which to draw. Profoundly disappointed, Davis admitted to a committee of Confederate representatives that southerners had entered "the darkest and most dangerous period we have yet had." Tenacious defense and stoical endurance now seemed the South's only long-range hope. Perceptive southerners shared their president's despair.

Union States   Confederate States

Total Population 2.5 to 1	Naval Ship Tonnage 25 to 1	Farm Acreage 3 to 1
Free Male Population 18–60 Years 4.4 to 1	Factory Production Value 10 to 1	Draft Animals 1.8 to 1
Free Men in Military Service 1864 — 44% 90%	Textile Goods Production 14 to 1	Livestock 1.5 to 1
Wealth Produced 3 to 1	Iron Production 15 to 1	Wheat Production 4.2 to 1
Railroad Mileage 2.4 to 1	Coal Production 38 to 1	Corn Production 2 to 1
Merchant Ship Tonnage 9 to 1	Firearms Production 32 to 1	Cotton Production 1 to 24

Comparative resources, Union and Confederate states, 1861
Source: *Times Atlas of World History.* Times Books, London, 1978.

War transforms the South

Even more than the fighting itself, changes in civilian life robbed southerners of their gaiety and nonchalance. The war altered southern society beyond all expectations and with astonishing speed. One of the first traditions to fall was the southern preference for local government.

The South had been an area of little government. States' rights had been its motto, but even the state governments were weak and sketchy affairs by modern standards. To withstand the massive power of the North, however, the South had to centralize; like the colonial revolutionaries, southerners faced a choice of join or die. No one saw the necessity of centralization more clearly than Jefferson Davis. If the states insisted on fighting separately, said Davis, "we had better make terms as soon as we can."

From the outset, Davis pressed to bring all arms, supplies, and troops under his control. He advocated conscription when the states failed to enroll enough new soldiers. And he took a strong leadership role to-

Centralization of power in the South

ward the Confederate congress, which raised taxes and later passed a tax-in-kind—a levy not on money but on wheat, corn, oats, rye, cotton, peas, and other farm products. Almost three thousand agents dispersed to collect the tax, assisted by almost fifteen hundred appraisers. Where opposition arose, the government suspended the writ of habeas corpus and imposed martial law. In the face of a political opposition that cherished states' rights, Davis proved unyielding.

To replace the food that soldiers would have grown, Davis exhorted farmers to switch from cash crops to food crops; he encouraged the states to require that they do so. But the army was still short of food and labor. In emergencies the War Department resorted to impressing slaves for labor on fortifications, or took meat and grain in lieu of forced labor. After 1861, the government relied heavily on food impressment to feed the armies. Officers swooped down on farms in the line of march and carted away grain, meat, and other food, plus wagons and draft animals to carry it.

For her work in nursing the Confederate wounded, Sally Tompkins received a commission as a captain in the Confederate Army. Valentine Museum, Richmond, Virginia.

Soon the Richmond administration was taking virtually complete direction of the southern economy. Because it controlled the supply of labor through conscription, the administration could regulate industry, compelling factories to work on government contracts to supply government needs. In addition, the Confederate congress passed laws giving the central government almost full control of the railroads; and later shipping, too, came under extensive regulation. New statutes even limited corporate profits and dividends. A large bureaucracy sprang up to administer these operations: over seventy thousand civilians were needed to run the Confederate war machine. By the war's end the southern bureaucracy was proportionally larger than its northern counterpart.

The mushrooming bureaucracy expanded the cities. Clerks and subordinate officials, many of them women, crowded the towns and cities where Confederate departments had their offices. These sudden population booms stretched the existing housing supply and stimulated new construction. The pressure was especially great in Richmond, whose population increased two-and-a-half times. Before the war's end Confederate officials were planning the relocation of entire departments to diminish crowding in that city. Mobile's population jumped from 29,000 to 41,000; Atlanta began to grow; and 10,000 people poured into war industries in the little town of Selma, Alabama.

Effects of war on southern cities and industry

Another prime cause of urban growth was industrialization. Because of the Union blockade, which interrupted imports of manufactured products, the traditionally agricultural South became interested in industry. Davis exulted that southerners were manufacturing their own goods, thus "becoming more and more independent of the rest of the world." Many planters shared his expectations, remembering their battles against tariffs and hoping that their agrarian nation would industrialize enough to win "deliverance, full and unrestricted, from all commercial dependence" on the North. And indeed, though the Confederacy started from scratch, it achieved tremendous feats of industrial development. Chief of Ordnance Josiah Gorgas was able to increase the capacity of the Tredegar Iron Works and other factories to the point that his Ordnance Bureau was supplying all Confederate small arms and ammunition by 1865.

As a result of these changes southerners adopted new values. Women, sheltered in the patriarchal antebellum society, gained substantial new responsibilities. The wives and mothers of soldiers became heads of households and undertook what had previously been considered men's work. To them fell the added tasks of raising crops and tending animals. Though wives of nonslaveowners had a harder time cultivating their fields than women whose families owned slaves, the latter had to struggle with the management of field hands unused to feminine oversight. Only among the very rich were there enough servants to take up the slack and leave a woman's routine undisturbed. In the cities

Change in the southern woman's role

women found new and respectable roles (and paying jobs) in the workforce. "Government girls" who staffed the Confederate bureaucracy and female schoolteachers became a familiar sight. Such experiences undermined the image of the omnipotent male and gave thousands of women new confidence in their abilities.

One of those who acquired such confidence as a result of the war was a young North Carolinian named Janie Smith. Raised in a rural area by prosperous parents, she had faced few challenges or grim realities. Then suddenly the war reached her farm, and the troops turned her home into a hospital. "It makes me shudder when I think of the awful sights I witnessed that morning," she wrote to a friend. "Ambulance after ambulance drove up with our wounded. . . . Under every shed and tree, the tables were carried for amputating the limbs. . . . The blood lay in puddles in the grove; the groans of the dying and complaints of those undergoing amputation were horrible." But Janie Smith learned to cope with crisis. She helped to nurse the wounded and ended her account with the proud words "I can dress amputated limbs now and do most anything in the way of nursing wounded soldiers."

The Confederate experience introduced and sustained many other new values. Legislative bodies yielded power to the executive branch of government, which could act more decisively in time of war. The traditional emphasis on aristocratic lineage gave way to respect for achievement and bravery under fire. Thus many men of ordinary background, such as Josiah Gorgas, Stonewall Jackson, and General Nathan Bedford Forrest, gained distinction in industry and on the battlefield that would have been beyond their grasp in time of peace. Finally, sacrifice for the cause discouraged the pursuit of pleasure; hostesses gave "cold water parties" (at which water was the only refreshment) to demonstrate their patriotism.

For the elite such sacrifice was symbolic, but for millions of ordinary southerners it was terrifyingly real. Mass poverty descended on the South, afflicting for the first time a large minority of the white population. The crux of the problem was that many yeoman families had lost their breadwinners to the army. As a South Carolina newspaper put it, "The duties of war have called away from

Human suffering in the South

home the sole supports of many, many families. . . . Help must be given, or the poor will suffer." The poor sought such help from relatives, neighbors, friends, anyone. Sometimes they took their cases to the Confederate government, as did an elderly Virginian who pleaded, "If you dount send [my son] home I am bound to louse my crop and cum to suffer. I am eaighty one years of adge." One woman wrote: "I ask in the name of humanity to discharge my husband he is not able to do your government much good and he might do his children some good and thare is no use in keeping a man thare to kill and leave widows and poor little orphen children to suffer . . . my poor children have no home nor no Father."

Other factors aggravated the effect of the labor shortage. The South was in many places so sparsely populated that the conscription of one skilled craftsman could work a hardship on the people of an entire county. Often they begged in unison for the exemption or discharge of the local miller or the neighborhood tanner, wheelwright, or potter. Physicians were also in short supply. Most serious, however, was the loss of a blacksmith. As a petition from Alabama explained, "our Section of County [is] left entirely Destitute of any man that is able to keep in order any kind of Farming Tules, Such as the few aged Farmers and families of Those that is gone to defend there rites is Compeled to have to make a Support With."

The blockade created further shortages of common but important items—salt, sugar, coffee, nails—and speculation and hoarding made them worse. Avaricious businessmen moved to corner the supply of some commodities; prosperous citizens tried to stock up on food. The Richmond *Enquirer* criticized one man for hoarding seven hundred barrels of flour; another man, a planter, purchased so many wagonloads of supplies that his "lawn and paths looked like a wharf covered with a ship's loads." Some people bought up the entire stock of a store and held the goods to sell later at higher prices. "This disposition to speculate upon the yeomanry of the country," lamented the Richmond *Examiner,* "is the most mortifying feature of the war." North Carolina's Governor Zebulon Vance asked where it would all stop: "the cry of distress comes up from the poor wives and children of our soldiers. . . . What will become of them?"

Hoarding and runaway inflation in the South

Many prosperous southerners avoided military service by hiring a substitute. This advertisement for a substitute is graphic evidence of the lack of enthusiasm for the draft. Library of Congress.

Indeed, inflation raged out of control until prices had increased almost 7,000 percent. As early as 1861 and 1862, newspapers were reporting that "the poor of our . . . country will be unable to live at all" and that "want and starvation are staring thousands in the face." Officials warned of "great suffering next year," predicting that "women and children are bound to come to suffering if not starvation."

Some concerned citizens tried to help. "Free markets," which dispersed goods as charity, sprang up in various cities; some families came to the aid of their neighbors. But there were other citizens who would not cooperate: "It is folly for a poor mother to call on the rich people about here," raged one woman. "Their hearts are of steel they would sooner throw what they have to spare to their dogs than give it to a starving child." The need was so vast that it overwhelmed private charity. A rudimentary relief program organized by the Confederacy offered some hope, but was soon curtailed to avoid conflict with the task of supplying the armies. Millions of southern yeomen sank into poverty and suffering.

As their fortunes declined, these people of once-modest means looked around them and found abundant evidence that all classes were not sacrificing equally. They saw that the wealthy curtailed only their luxuries, while many poor families went without necessities. They saw that the government contributed to these inequities through policies that favored the upper class. Until the last year of the war, for example, prosperous southerners could avoid military

Inequities of the Confederate draft

service by furnishing a hired substitute. Prices for substitutes skyrocketed, until it was common for a man of means to pay $5,000 or $6,000 to send someone to the front. Well over fifty thousand upper-class southerners purchased such substitutes; Mary Boykin Chesnut knew of one young aristocrat who had "spent a fortune in substitutes. Two have been taken from him [when *they* were conscripted], and two he paid to change with him when he was ordered to the front. He is at the end of his row now, for all able-bodied men are ordered to the front. I hear he is going as some general's courier."

As Chesnut's last remark indicates, the rich also traded on their social connections to avoid danger. "It's a notorious fact," complained an angry Georgian, that "if a man has influential friends—or a little money to spare he will never be enrolled." The Confederate senator from Mississippi James Phelan informed Jefferson Davis that apparently "nine tenths of the youngsters of the land whose relatives are conspicuous in society, wealthy, or influential obtain some safe perch where they can doze with their heads under their wings."

Anger at such discrimination exploded when in October 1862 the Confederate congress exempted from military duty anyone who was supervising at least twenty slaves. The "twenty nigger law" became notorious. "Never did a law meet with more universal odium," observed one representative. "Its influence upon the poor is most calamitous." Immediately protests arose from every corner of the Confederacy, and North Carolina's legislators formally condemned the law. Its defenders argued, however, that the exemption preserved order and aided food production, and the statute remained on the books.

Dissension spread as growing numbers of citizens concluded that the struggle was "a rich man's war and a poor man's fight." Alert politicians and newspaper editors warned that class resentment was building to a dangerous level; letters to Confederate officials during this period contained a bitterness that suggested the depth of the people's anger. "If I and my little children suffer [and] die while there Father is in service," threatened one woman, "I invoke God Almighty that our blood rest upon the South." Another woman swore to the Secretary of War that

an allwise god . . . will send down his fury and judgment in a very grate manar [on] all those our leading men and those that are in power if thare is no more favors shone to . . . the wives and mothers of those who in poverty has with patrootism stood the fence Battles. . . . I tell you that with out some grate and speadly alterating in the conduckting of afares in this our little nation god will frown on it.

Trouble was brewing in the Confederacy.

The northern economy copes with war

With the onset of war, a tidal wave of change rolled over the North, just as it had over the South. Factories and citizens' associations geared up to support the war, and the federal government and its executive branch gained power they had never had before. Civil liberties were restricted, and social values were influenced by both personal sacrifice and wartime riches. Idealism and greed flourished side by side.

But there was an important difference between North and South: the war did not destroy the North's prosperity. Northern factories ran overtime, and unemployment was low. Furthermore, northern farms and factories came through the war unscathed, whereas most areas of the South suffered extensive destruction. To Union soldiers on the battlefield, sacrifice was a grim reality; but northern civilians experienced only the bustle and energy of wartime production.

Initially, the war was a shock to business. With the sudden closing of the southern market, firms could no longer predict the demand for their goods; many

Initial slump in northern business

companies had to redirect their activities in order to remain open. And southern debts became uncollectible, jeopardizing not only merchants but many western banks. In farming regions, families struggled with an aggravated shortage of labor. For reasons such as these, the war initially caused an economic slump.

A few enterprises never pulled out of the tailspin: cotton mills lacked cotton; construction declined; shoe manufacturers sold fewer of the cheap shoes planters had bought for their slaves. Overall the war slowed industrialization in the North. But historians have shown that the war's economic impact was not all negative. Certain entrepreneurs, such as wool producers, benefited from shortages of competing products, and soaring demand for war-related goods swept some businesses to new heights of production. To feed the voracious war machine the federal government pumped unprecedented amounts of money into the economy. The Treasury issued $3.2 billion in bonds and paper money called greenbacks, while the War Department spent over $360 million in tax revenues. Government contracts soon totaled more than $1 billion.

Secretary of War Edwin M. Stanton's list of supplies for the Ordnance Department indicates the scope of government demand: "7,892 cannon, 11,787 artillery carriages, 4,022,130 small-arms . . . 1,022,176,474 cartridges for small-arms, 1,220,555,435 percussion caps . . . 14,507,682 cannon primers and fuses, 12,875,294 pounds of artillery projectiles, 26,440,054 pounds of gunpowder, 6,395,152 pounds of niter, and 90,416,295 pounds of lead." Stanton's list covered only weapons; the government also purchased innumerable quantities of uniforms, boots, food, camp equipment, saddles, ships, and other necessaries.

War-related spending revived business in many northern states. In 1863, a merchants' magazine examined the effects of the war in Massachusetts: "Seldom, if ever, has the business of Massachusetts been more active or profitable than during the past year. . . . Labor has been in great demand . . . trade is again in a high state of prosperity. Wealth has flowed into the State in no stinted measure, despite war and heavy taxes. In every department of labor the government has been, directly or indirectly, the chief employer and paymaster." Government contracts had a particularly beneficial impact on the state's wool, metal, and ship-building industries, and saved shoe manufacturers there from ruin.

War production also promoted the development of heavy industry in the North. The output of coal rose substantially. Iron makers improved the quality of their product while boosting the production of pig iron from 920,000 tons in 1860 to 1,136,000 tons in 1864. And although new railroad construction slowed, the

Effects of war on northern industry and agriculture

manufacture of rails increased. Of considerable significance for the future were the railroad industry's adoption of a standard gauge for track, and foundries' development of new and less expensive ways to make steel.

Another strength of the northern economy was the complementary relationship between agriculture and industry. The mechanization of agriculture had begun well before the war. Now, though, wartime recruitment and conscription gave western farmers an added incentive to purchase labor-saving machinery. This shift from human labor to machines had a doubly beneficial effect, creating new markets for industry and expanding the food supply for the urban industrial workforce.

The boom in the sale of agricultural tools was tremendous. Cyrus and William McCormick built an industrial empire in Chicago from their sale of reapers. Between 1862 and 1864 the manufacture of mowers and reapers doubled to 70,000 yearly; manufacturers could not supply the demand. By the end of the war, there were 375,000 reapers in use, triple the number in 1861. Large-scale commercial agriculture had become a reality. As a result, farm families whose breadwinners had gone to war did not suffer as they did in the South. "We have seen," one magazine observed, "a stout matron whose sons are in the army, cutting hay with her team . . . and she cut seven acres with ease in a day, riding leisurely upon her cutter."

The northern workers who suffered most during the war were wage earners, particularly industrial and urban workers. Though jobs were plentiful following the initial slump, inflation took much of a worker's paycheck. By 1863 nine-cent-a-pound beef was selling for eighteen cents. The price of coffee had tripled; rice and sugar had doubled; and clothing, fuel, and rent had all climbed. Studies of the cost of living indicate that between 1860 and 1864 consumer prices rose at least 76 percent; meanwhile daily wages rose only 42 percent. To make up the difference, workers' families had to do without.

As their real wages shrank, industrial workers also lost job security. To increase production, some employers were replacing workers with labor-saving machines. Other employers urged the government to liberalize immigration procedures so they could import cheap labor. Workers responded by forming unions

Chapter 14: Transforming fire: the Civil War, 1860–1865

HARPER'S WEEKLY.

A JOURNAL OF CIVILIZATION.

VOL. V.—No. 238.]   NEW YORK, SATURDAY, JULY 20, 1861.   [SINGLE COPIES SIX CENTS.
[$2.50 PER YEAR IN ADVANCE.

Entered according to Act of Congress, in the Year 1861, by Harper & Brothers, in the Clerk's Office of the District Court for the Southern District of New York.

FILLING CARTRIDGES AT THE UNITED STATES ARSENAL AT WATERTOWN, MASSACHUSETTS.—[SEE NEXT PAGE.]

In both North and South women entered the factories to boost
wartime production. This *Harper's Weekly* cover shows women
filling cartridges in the United States arsenal at Watertown,
Massachusetts.   Library of Congress.

The northern economy copes with war

and sometimes by striking. Skilled craftsmen organ-

New militancy among northern workers

ized to combat the loss of their jobs and status to machines; women and unskilled workers, excluded by the craftsmen, formed their own unions. And in recognition of the increasingly national scope of business activity, thirteen occupational groups—including tailors, coalminers, and railway engineers—formed national unions during the Civil War. Because of the tight labor market, unions were able to win many of their demands without striking; but still the number of strikes rose steadily.

Employers reacted negatively to this new spirit among workers—a spirit that William H. Sylvis, leader of the iron molders, called a "feeling of manly independence." Manufacturers viewed labor activism as a threat to their property rights and freedom of action, and accordingly they too formed statewide or craft-based associations to cooperate and pool information. These employers compiled blacklists of union members and required new workers to sign "yellow dog" contracts, or promises not to join a union. To put down strikes, they hired strikebreakers from the ranks of the poor and desperate—blacks, immigrants, and women—and sometimes received additional help from federal troops.

Troublesome as unions were, they did not prevent many employers from making a profit. The biggest fortunes were made in profiteering on government contracts. Unscrupulous businessmen took advantage of the sudden immense demand for goods for the army by selling clothing and blankets made of "shoddy"—wool fibers reclaimed from rags or worn cloth. The goods often came apart in the rain; most of the shoes purchased in the early months of the war were worthless too. Contractors sold inferior guns for double the usual price and tainted meat for the price of good. Corruption was so widespread that it led to a year-long investigation by the House of Representatives. One group of contractors that had demanded $50 million for their products had to reduce their claims to $17 million as a result of the findings of the investigation.

Legitimate enterprises also turned a neat profit. The output of woolen mills increased so dramatically that dividends in the industry nearly tripled. Some cotton mills, though they reduced their output, made record profits on what they sold. Brokerage houses worked until midnight and earned unheard-of commissions. And railroads carried immense quantities of freight and passengers, increasing their business to the point that railroad stocks doubled or even tripled. Erie Railroad stock skyrocketed from $17 to $126 a share.

Wartime benefits to northern business

In fact, railroads were a leading beneficiary of government largesse. Congress had failed in the 1850s to resolve the question of a northern versus a southern route for the first transcontinental railroad. But with the South out of Congress, the northern route quickly prevailed. In 1862 and 1864 Congress chartered two corporations, the Union Pacific Railroad and the Central Pacific Railroad, and assisted them handsomely in connecting Omaha, Nebraska, with Sacramento, California. For each mile of track laid, the railroads received a loan of $16,000 to $48,000 plus twenty square miles of land along a free four-hundred-foot-wide right of way. Overall, the two corporations gained approximately 20 million acres of land and nearly $60 million in loans.

Other businessmen benefited handsomely from the Morrill Land Grant Act (1862). To promote public education in agriculture, engineering, and military science, Congress granted each state 30,000 acres of public land for each of its congressional representatives. The states were free to sell the land as they saw fit, as long as they used the income for the purposes Congress had intended. Though the law eventually fostered sixty-nine colleges and universities, one of its immediate effects was to enrich a few prominent speculators. Hard-pressed to meet wartime expenses, some states sold their land cheaply to wealthy entrepreneurs. Ezra Cornell, for example, purchased 500,000 acres in the Midwest.

Another measure that brought joy to the business community was the tariff. Northern businesses did not uniformly favor high import duties; some manufacturers desired cheap imported raw materials more than they feared foreign competition. But northeastern congressmen traditionally supported higher tariffs, and after southern lawmakers left Washington, they had their way: the tariff act of 1864 raised tariffs generously. According to one scholar, manufacturers had only to mention the rate they considered necessary and that rate was declared. And, as one would expect, some healthy industries made artificially high profits by raising their prices to a level just below that of the foreign competition. By the end of the war, tariff rates averaged 47 percent, more than double the rates of 1857.

The frantic wartime activity, the booming economy, and the Republican alliance with business combined to create a new atmosphere in Washington. The balance of opinion shifted against consumers and wage earners and toward large corporations; the notion spread that government should aid businessmen but not interfere with them. This was the golden hour of untrammeled capitalism, and railroad builders and industrialists—men such as Leland Stanford, Collis P. Huntington, John D. Rockefeller, John M. Forbes, and Jay Gould—took advantage of it. Their enterprises grew with the aid of government loans, grants, and tariffs.

As long as the war lasted, the powers of the federal government and the president continued to grow. Abraham Lincoln found, as had Jefferson Davis, that

Wartime powers of the U.S. executive

war required active presidential leadership. At the beginning of the conflict, Lincoln launched a major ship-building program without waiting for Congress to assemble. The lawmakers later approved his decision, and Lincoln continued to act in advance of Congress when he deemed it necessary. In one striking exercise of executive power, Lincoln suspended the writ of habeas corpus for all people living between Washington and Philadelphia. The justification for this action was practical rather than legal; Lincoln was ensuring the loyalty of Maryland. Later in the war, with congressional approval, Lincoln repeatedly suspended the writ and invoked martial law. Roughly ten to twenty thousand United States citizens were arrested on suspicion of disloyal acts.

On occasion Lincoln used his wartime authority to bolster his political power. He and his generals proved adept at arranging furloughs for soldiers who could vote in close elections. Needless to say, the citizens in arms whom Lincoln helped to vote usually voted Republican. In another instance, when the Republican governor of Indiana found himself short of funds be-

cause of Democratic opposition, Lincoln generously supplied eight times the amount of money the governor needed to get through the emergency.

Among the clearest examples of the wartime expansion of federal authority were the National Banking Acts of 1863, 1864, and 1865. Prior to the Civil War the nation did not have a uniform currency. Banks operating under a variety of state charters issued no fewer than seven thousand different kinds of notes, which had to be distinguished from a variety of forgeries. Now, acting on the recommendations of Secretary of the Treasury Salmon Chase, Congress established a national banking system empowered to issue a maximum number of national bank notes. At the close of the war in 1865, Congress laid a prohibitive tax on state bank notes and forced most major institutions to join the system. This process led to a sounder currency and a simpler monetary system, but also to an inflexibility in the money supply and an eastern-oriented financial structure.

Soldiers may have sensed the increasing scale of things better than anyone else. Most federal troops were young; eighteen was the most common age, followed by twenty-one. Many soldiers went straight from small towns and farms into large armies supplied by extensive bureaucracies. By December 1861 there were 640,000 volunteers in arms, a stupendous increase over the regular army of 20,000 men. The increase occurred so rapidly that it is remarkable the troops were supplied and organized as well as they were. But many soldiers' first experiences with large organizations were unfortunate.

Blankets, clothing, and arms were often inferior. Vermin were commonplace. Hospitals were badly managed at first. Rules of hygiene in large camps were badly written or unenforced; latrines were poorly made or carelessly used. One investigation turned up "an area of over three acres, encircling the camp as a broad belt, on which is deposited an almost perfect layer of human excrement." Water supplies were unsafe and typhoid fever epidemics common. About 57,000 army men died from dysentery and diarrhea.

The situation would have been much worse but for the U.S. Sanitary Commission. A voluntary civilian organization, the commission worked to improve conditions in camps and to aid sick and wounded soldiers. Still, 224,000 Union troops died from disease or

The U.S. Sanitary Commission, a voluntary civilian organization, did much to improve conditions in military camps. Here some of its members pose at Fredericksburg, Virginia, in 1864. Library of Congress.

accidents, far more than the 140,000 who died in battle.

Such conditions would hardly have predisposed the soldier to sympathize with changing social attitudes on the home front. Amid the excitement of money-making, a gaudy culture of vulgar display flourished

Self-indulgence versus sacrifice in the North

in the largest cities. A visitor to Chicago commented that "so far as lavish display is concerned, the South Side in some portions has no rival in Chicago, and perhaps not outside New York." Its new residences boasted "marble fronts and expensive ornamentation" that created "a glittering, heartless appearance." As William Cullen Bryant, the distinguished editor of the New York *Evening Post,* observed sadly, "Extravagance, luxury, these are the signs of the times. . . . What business have Americans at any time with such vain show, with such useless

magnificence? But especially how can they justify it . . . in this time of war?"

The newly rich did not bother to justify it. *Harper's Monthly* reported that "the suddenly enriched contractors, speculators, and stock-jobbers . . . are spending money with a profusion never before witnessed in our country, at no time remarkable for its frugality. . . . The ordinary sources of expenditure seem to have been exhausted, and these ingenious prodigals have invented new ones. The men button their waistcoats with diamonds . . . and the women powder their hair with gold and silver dust." The New York *Herald* summarized that city's atmosphere:

All our theatres are open . . . and they are all crowded nightly. . . . the most costly accommodations, in both hotels and theatres, are the first and most eagerly taken. . . . The richest silks, laces

Chapter 14: Transforming fire: the Civil War, 1860–1865

and jewelry are the soonest sold. . . . Not to keep a carriage, not to wear diamonds, not to be attired in a robe which cost a small fortune, is now equivalent to being a nobody. This war has entirely changed the American character. . . . The individual who makes the most money—no matter how—and spends the most—no matter for what—is considered the greatest man. . . .

The world has seen its iron age, its silver age, its golden age, and its brazen age. This is the age of shoddy.

Yet strong elements of idealism coexisted with ostentation. Abolitionists, after initial uncertainty over whether to fight the South or allow division of the Union to separate the North from slavery, campaigned to turn the war into a war against slavery. Free black communities and churches both black and white responded to the needs of slaves who flocked to the Union lines. They sent clothing, ministers, and teachers in generous measure to aid the runaways.

Northern women, like their southern counterparts, took on new roles. Those who stayed home organized over ten thousand soldiers' aid societies, rolled innumerable bandages, and raised $3 million. Thousands served as nurses in front-line hospitals, where they pressed for better care of the wounded. The professionalization of medicine since the Revolution had created a medical system dominated by men; thus dedicated and able female nurses had to fight both military regulations and professional hostility to win the chance to make their contribution. In the hospitals they quickly proved their worth, but only the wounded welcomed them. Even Clara Barton, the most famous female nurse, was ousted from her post during the winter of 1863.

The poet Walt Whitman, who became a daily visitor to wounded soldiers in Washington, D.C., left a record of his experiences as a volunteer nurse. As he dressed wounds and tried to comfort suffering and lonely men, Whitman found "the marrow of the tragedy concentrated in those Army Hospitals." But despite "indescribably horrid wounds . . . the groan that could not be repress'd . . . [the] emaciated face and glassy eye," he also found in the hospitals inspiration and a deepening faith in American democracy. Whitman admired the "incredible dauntlessness" and sacrifice of the common soldier who fought for the Union. "The genius of the United States is not

best or most in its executives or legislatures," he had written in the Preface to his great work *Leaves of Grass* (1855), "but always most in the common people." Whitman worked this idealization of the common man into his poetry, rejecting the lofty meter and rhyme characteristic of European verse and striving instead for a "genuineness" that would appeal to the masses.

Thus northern society embraced strangely contradictory tendencies. Materialism and greed flourished alongside idealism, religious conviction, and self-sacrifice. While wealthy men purchased 118,000 substitutes and almost 87,000 commutations at $300 each to avoid service in the Union army, other soldiers risked their lives out of a desire to preserve the Union or extend freedom. It was as if there were several different wars under way, serving several different motives.

The strange advent of emancipation

At the very highest levels of government there was a similar lack of clarity about the purpose of the war. Through the first several months of the struggle, both Davis and Lincoln studiously avoided references to slavery, the crux of the matter. For his part, Davis was intelligent enough to realize that emphasis on the issue might increase class conflict in the South. Earlier in his career he had struggled on occasion to convince nonslaveholders that defense of the planters' slaves was in their interest. Rather than face that challenge again, Davis articulated a conservative ideology. He told southerners they were fighting for constitutional liberty: northern betrayal of the founding fathers' legacy had necessitated secession. As long as Lincoln also avoided making slavery an issue, Davis's line seemed to work.

Lincoln had his own reasons for refraining from mention of slavery. For some time he clung to the hopeful but mistaken idea that a pro-Union majority would assert itself in the South. Perhaps it would be possible, he thought, to coax the South back into the Union and end the fighting. Raising the slavery issue would effectively end any such possibility of compromise.

Powerful political considerations also dictated that Lincoln remain silent. The Republican party was a young and unwieldy coalition. Some Republicans burned with moral outrage over slavery, while others were frankly racist, dedicated to protecting free whites from the Slave Power and the competition of cheap slave labor. Still others saw the tariff or immigration or some other issue as paramount. A forthright stand by Lincoln on the subject of slavery could split the party, pleasing some groups and alienating others. Until a consensus developed among the party's various wings, or until Lincoln found a way to appeal to all the elements of the party, silence was the best approach.

The president's hesitancy ran counter to some of his personal feelings. Lincoln was a sensitive and compassionate man whose self-awareness, humility, and moral anguish during the war were evident in his speeches and writings. But as a politician, Lincoln kept his moral convictions to himself. He distinguished between the personal and the official; he would not let his feelings determine his political acts. As a result, his political positions were studied and complex, calculated for maximum advantage. Frederick Douglass, the astute and courageous black protest leader, sensed that Lincoln the man was without prejudice toward black people. Yet Douglass judged him "preeminently the white man's president."

Lincoln first broached the subject of slavery in a major way in March 1862, when he proposed that the states consider emancipation on their own. He asked Congress to pass a resolution promising aid to any state that decided to emancipate, and he appealed to border-state representatives to give the idea of emancipation serious consideration. What Lincoln was talking about was gradual emancipation, with compensation for slaveholders and colonization of the freed slaves outside the United States. To a delegation of free Negroes he explained that "it is better for us both . . . to be separated." Until well into 1864 Lincoln steadfastly promoted an unpromising and in national terms wholly impractical scheme to colonize blacks in some region like Central America. Despite Secretary of State William H. Seward's care to insert phrases such as "with their consent," the word *deportation* crept into one of Lincoln's speeches in place of *colonization*. Thus his was as conservative a

Lincoln's plan for gradual emancipation

scheme as could be devised. Moreover, since the states would make the decision voluntarily, no responsibility for it would attach to Lincoln.

But others wanted to go much further. A group of congressional Republicans known as the Radicals had dedicated themselves to seeing that the war was prosecuted vigorously. They had been instrumental in creating a joint committee on the conduct of the war, which investigated Union reverses, sought to increase the efficiency of the war effort, and prodded the executive to take stronger measures. Early in the war these Radicals, with support from other representatives, turned their attention to slavery.

In August 1861, at the Radicals' instigation, Congress passed its first confiscation act. Designed to punish the Confederate rebels, the law confiscated all property used for "insurrectionary purposes." That is, if the South used slaves in a hostile action, those slaves

Confiscation Acts

were declared seized and liberated from their owners' possession. A second confiscation act (July 1862) was much more drastic: it confiscated the property of all those who supported the rebellion, even those who merely resided in the South and paid Confederate taxes. Their slaves were "forever free of their servitude, and not again [to be] held as slaves." The logic behind these acts was that the insurrection—as Lincoln always termed it—was a serious revolution requiring strong measures. Let the government use its full powers, free the slaves, and crush the revolution, urged the Radicals.

Lincoln chose not to go that far. He stood by his proposal of voluntary gradual emancipation by the states and made no effort to enforce the second confiscation act. His stance brought a public protest from Horace Greeley, editor of the powerful *New York Tribune*. In an open letter to the president entitled "The Prayer of Twenty Millions," Greeley wrote, "We require of you . . . that you execute the laws. . . . We think you are strangely and disastrously remiss . . . with regard to the emancipating provisions of the new Confiscation Act. . . . We complain that the Union cause has suffered from mistaken deference to Rebel Slavery." Reaching the nub of the issue, the influential editor went on, "On the face of this wide earth, Mr. President, there is not one disinterested, determined, intelligent champion of the Union cause who does not feel that all attempts to put down the

This photograph, taken four days before Lincoln's assassination, shows the effect of the burdens of war on the president. McLellan Lincoln Collection, Brown University Library.

Rebellion and at the same time uphold its inciting cause are preposterous and futile."

Lincoln's reply was an explicit statement of his complex and calculated approach to the question. He disagreed, he said, with all those who would make the saving or destroying of slavery the paramount issue of the war. "I would save the Union," announced Lincoln. "If I could save the Union without freeing *any* slave I would do it, and if I could save it by freeing *all* the slaves I would do it; and if I could save it by freeing some and leaving others alone I would also do that. What I do about slavery, and the colored race, I

do because I believe it helps to save the Union." Lincoln closed with a personal disclaimer: "I have here stated my purpose according to my view of *official* duty; and I intend no modification of my oft-expressed *personal* wish that all men every where could be free."

When he wrote those words, Lincoln had already decided to take a new step: issuance of the Emancipation Proclamation. On the advice of the cabinet, however, he was waiting for a major Union victory before announcing it, so the proclamation would not appear to be an act of desperation. Yet the letter to Greeley

The strange advent of emancipation

was not an effort to stall; it was an integral part of Lincoln's approach to the future of slavery, as the text of the Emancipation Proclamation would show.

On September 22, 1862, shortly after the Battle of Antietam, Lincoln issued the first part of his two-part proclamation. Invoking his powers as commander-in-chief of the armed forces, he announced that on January 1 he would emancipate the slaves in states whose people "shall then be in rebellion against the United States." The January proclamation would designate the areas in rebellion based on the presence or absence of bona fide representatives in Congress.

Emancipation proclamations

The September proclamation was not a declaration of the right of slaves to be free, but a threat to southerners to lay down their arms. "Knowing the value that was set on the slaves by the rebels," said Garrison Frazier, a black Georgian, "the President thought that his proclamation would stimulate them to lay down their arms . . . and their not doing so has now made the freedom of the slaves a part of the war." Lincoln may not actually have expected southerners to give up their effort, but he was careful to offer them the option, thus putting the onus of emancipation on them.

Lincoln's designation of the areas in rebellion on January 1 is worth noting. He excepted from his list every Confederate county or city that had fallen under Union control. Those areas, he declared, "are, for the present, left precisely as if this proclamation were not issued." And in a telling omission, Lincoln neglected to liberate slaves in the border slave states that remained in the Union.

"The President has purposely made the proclamation inoperative in all places where . . . the slaves [are] accessible," complained the anti-administration New York *World*. "He has proclaimed emancipation only where he has notoriously no power to execute it." The exceptions, said the paper, "render the proclamation not merely futile, but ridiculous." Partisanship aside, even Secretary of State Seward, a moderate Republican, said sarcastically, that "we show our sympathy with slavery by emancipating slaves where we cannot reach them and holding them in bondage where we can set them free." A British official, Lord Russell, commented on the "very strange nature" of the document, noting that it did not declare "a principle adverse to slavery."

Furthermore, by making the liberation of the slaves "a fit and necessary war measure," Lincoln raised a variety of legal questions. How long did a war measure have force? Did its power cease with the suppression of a rebellion? The proclamation did little to clarify the status or citizenship of the freed slaves. And a reference to garrison duty in one of the closing paragraphs suggested that slaves would have inferior duties and rank in the army. (For many months, in fact, their pay and treatment were inferior.)

Thus the Emancipation Proclamation was a puzzling and ambiguous document that said less than it seemed to say. Physically it freed no bondsmen, and major limitations were embedded in its language. But if as a moral and legal document it was wanting, as a political document it was nearly flawless. Because the proclamation defined the war as a war against slavery, liberals could applaud it. Yet at the same time it protected Lincoln's position with conservatives, leaving him room to retreat if he chose and forcing no immediate changes on the border slave states. The president had not gone as far as Congress had, and he had taken no position he could not change.

Lincoln seemed to take a stronger stand in June 1864. On the eve of the Republican national convention, he called the party's chairman to the White House and issued these instructions: "Mention in your speech, when you call the convention to order . . . to put into the platform as the keystone, the amendment of the Constitution abolishing and prohibiting slavery forever." It was done; the party called for a new constitutional amendment, the thirteenth. And though Republican delegates would probably have adopted such a plank without Lincoln's urging, still Lincoln worked diligently to win approval for the measure in Congress. He succeeded, and the proposed amendment went to the states for ratification.

But even this was not Lincoln's last word on the matter. In 1865 the newly re-elected president considered allowing the defeated southern states to re-enter the Union and delay or defeat the amendment. In February he and Secretary of State Seward met with three Confederate commissioners at Hampton Roads, Virginia. The end of the war was clearly in sight, and southern representatives angled vainly for an armistice that would allow southern independence. But Lincoln was doing some political maneuvering of his own, apparently contemplat-

Hampton Roads Conference

Chapter 14: Transforming fire: the Civil War, 1860–1865

Black troops, many of whom had been slaves, infused vital strength into the Union armies. The men above, members of Company E, Fourth U.S. Colored Infantry, were photographed at Fort Lincoln, Virginia.   Chicago Historical Society.

ing the creation of a new and broader party based on a postwar alliance with southern Whigs and moderates. The cement for the coalition would be concessions on the status of blacks.

Pointing out that the Emancipation Proclamation was only a war measure, Lincoln predicted that the courts would decide whether it had granted all, some, or none of the slaves their freedom. Seward observed that the Thirteenth Amendment, which constitutionally and definitively abolished slavery, was not yet ratified; re-entry into the Union would allow the southern states to vote against it and block it. Lincoln did not contradict him, but spoke in favor of "prospective" ratification—ratification with a five-year delay. He also promised to seek $400 million in compensation for slaveholders and to consider their position on such related questions as confiscation. Such financial aid would provide an economic incentive for planters to rejoin the Union, and capital to ease the transition to freedom for both races.

These were startling propositions from a president who was on the verge of military victory. Most north-

erners opposed them, and only the opposition of Jefferson Davis, who set himself against anything short of independence, prevented discussion of the proposals in the South. They indicated that even at the end of the war, Lincoln was keeping his options open, maintaining the line he had drawn between "*official* duty" and "*personal* wish." Contrary to legend, then, Lincoln did not attempt to lead public opinion on race, as did advocates of equality in one direction and racist Democrats in the other. Instead he moved cautiously, constructing complex and ambiguous positions. He avoided the great risks inherent in challenging, educating, or inspiring national conscience.

Before the war was over, the Confederacy too addressed the issue of emancipation. Ironically, a strong proposal in favor of liberation came from Jefferson Davis. Though emancipation was far less popular in the South than in the North, Davis did not flinch or conceal his purpose. He was dedicated to independence, and he was willing to sacrifice slavery to achieve that goal. After considering

Davis's plan for emancipation

the alternatives for some time, Davis concluded in the fall of 1864 that it was necessary to act.

Reasoning that the military situation of the Confederacy was desperate, and that independence with emancipation was preferable to defeat with emancipation, Davis proposed that the central government purchase and train forty thousand male Negro laborers. The men would work for the army under a promise of emancipation and future residence in the South. Later Davis upgraded his proposal, calling for the recruitment and arming of slave soldiers. The wives and children of these soldiers, he made plain, must also receive freedom from the states. Bitter debate resounded through the South, but Davis stood his ground. When the Confederate congress approved enlistments without the promise of freedom, Davis insisted on more. He issued an executive order to guarantee that owners would cooperate with the emancipation of slave soldiers, and his allies in the states started to work for emancipation of the soldiers' families.

Confederate emancipation began too late to revive southern armies or win diplomatic advantages with antislavery Europeans. But Lincoln's Emancipation Proclamation stimulated a vital infusion of manpower into the Union armies. Beginning in 1863 slaves shouldered arms for the North. Before the war was over, 150,000 of them had fought for freedom and the Union. Their participation was crucial to northern victory, and it discouraged recognition of the Confederacy by foreign governments. Lincoln's policy, despite its limitations and its lack of clarity, had much greater practical effect.

The disintegration of the Confederacy

During the final two years of fighting, both northern and southern governments waged the war in the face of increasing opposition at home. Dissatisfaction that had surfaced earlier grew more intense and sometimes even violent. The unrest was connected to the military stalemate: neither side was close to victory in 1863, though the war had become gigantic in scope and costly in lives. But protest also arose from fundamental stresses in the social structures of the North and the South.

The Confederacy's problems were both more serious and more deeply rooted than the North's. Vastly disadvantaged in terms of industrial capacity, natural resources, and labor, southerners felt the cost of the war more quickly, more directly, and more painfully than northerners. But even more fundamental were the Confederacy's internal problems; crises that were integrally connected with the southern class system threatened the Confederate cause.

One ominous development was the increasing opposition of planters to their own government, whose actions had had a negative effect on them. As a diplomatic weapon the South had withheld most of its cotton from world markets, hurting the planters' profits. Confederate military authorities had also impressed slaves to build fortifications. And when Union forces advanced on plantation areas, Confederate commanders had sent detachments through the countryside to burn stores of cotton that lay in the enemy's path. Such interference with plantation routines and financial interests was not what planters had expected of their government.

Planters' opposition to the Confederacy

Nor were the centralizing policies of the Davis administration popular. Many planters agreed with the Charleston *Mercury* that the southern states had seceded because the federal government had grown and "usurped powers not granted—progressively trenched upon State Rights." The increasing size and power of the Richmond administration therefore startled and alarmed them.

The Confederate constitution, drawn up by the leading political thinkers of the South, had in fact granted substantial powers to the central government, especially in time of war. But for many planters, states' rights had become virtually synonymous with complete state sovereignty. R. B. Rhett, editor of the Charleston *Mercury,* wishfully (and inaccurately) described the Confederate constitution: "[It] leaves the States untouched in their Sovereignty, and commits to the Confederate Government only a few simple objects, and a few simple powers to enforce them." Governor Joseph E. Brown of Georgia took a similarly exalted view of the importance of the states. During the brief interval between Georgia's secession from the Union and its admission to the Confederacy, Brown sent an ambassador to Europe to seek recognition for the sovereign republic of Georgia from Queen Victoria, Napoleon III, and the King of Belgium. His mentality harkened back to the 1770s and the Articles of Confederation, not to the Constitution of 1789 or the Confederate constitution.

In effect, years of opposition to the federal government within the Union had frozen southerners in a defensive posture. Now they erected the barrier of states' rights as a defense against change, hiding behind it while their capacity for creative statesmanship atrophied. Planters sought a guarantee that their plantations and their lives would remain untouched; they were deeply committed neither to building a southern nation nor to winning independence. If the Confederacy had been allowed to depart from the Union in peace and continue as a semideveloped cotton-growing region, they would have been content. When secession revolutionized their world, they could not or would not adjust to it.

Confused and embittered, southerners struck out instead at Jefferson Davis. Conscription, thundered Governor Brown, was "subversive of [Georgia's] sovereignty, and at war with all the principles for the support of which Georgia entered into this revolution." Searching for ways to frustrate the law, Brown bickered over draft exemptions and ordered local enrollment officials not to cooperate with the Confederacy. The Charleston *Mercury* told readers that "conscription . . . is . . . the very embodiment of Lincolnism, which our gallant armies are today fighting." And in a gesture of stubborn selfishness, planter Robert Toombs of Georgia, a former U.S. Senator, defied the government, the newspapers, and his neighbors' petitions by continuing to grow large amounts of cotton. His action bespoke the inflexibility and frustration of the southern elite at a crucial point in the Confederacy's struggle to survive.

The southern courts ultimately upheld Davis's power to conscript. He continued to provide strong leadership and drove through the legislature measures that gave the Confederacy a fighting chance. Despite his cold formality and inability to disarm critics, Davis possessed two important virtues: iron determination and total dedication to independence. These qualities kept the Confederacy afloat, for he implemented his measures and enforced them. But his actions earned him the hatred of most influential and elite citizens.

Meanwhile, at the bottom of southern society,

there were other difficulties. Food riots occurred in the spring of 1863 in Atlanta, Macon, Columbus, and Augusta, Georgia; and in Salisbury and High Point, North Carolina. On April 2, a crowd assembled in the Confederate capital of Richmond to demand relief from Governor Letcher. A passerby, noticing the excitement, asked a young girl, "Is there some celebration?" "There is," replied the girl. "We celebrate our right to live. We are starving. As soon as enough of us get together we are going to the bakeries and each of us will take a loaf of bread." Soon they did just that, sparking a riot that Davis himself had to quell at gunpoint. Later that fall, another group of angry rioters ransacked a street in Mobile, Alabama.

Food riots in southern cities

Throughout the rural South, ordinary people resisted more quietly—by refusing to cooperate with impressments of food, conscription, or tax collection. "In all the States impressments are evaded by every means which ingenuity can suggest, and in some openly resisted," wrote a high-ranking commissary officer. Farmers who did provide food refused to accept certificates of credit or government bonds in lieu of cash, as required by law. And conscription officers increasingly found no one to draft—men of draft age were hiding out in the forests. "The disposition to avoid military service," observed one of Georgia's senators in 1864, "is general." In some areas tax agents were killed in the line of duty.

Davis was ill-equipped to deal with such discontent. Austere and private by nature, he failed to communicate with the masses. For long stretches of time he buried himself in military affairs or administrative details, until a crisis forced him to rush off on a speaking tour to revive the spirit of resistance. His class perspective also distanced him from the sufferings of the common people. While his social circle in Richmond dined on duck and oysters, ordinary southerners leached salt from the smokehouse floor and went hungry. State governors who saw to the common people's needs won the public's loyalty, but Davis failed to reach out to them and thus lost the support of the plain folk.

Such civil discontent was certain to affect the Confederate armies. "What man is there that would stay in the army and no that his family is sufring at home?" an angry citizen wrote anonymously to the secretary of war. An upcountry South Carolina newspaper

A southern family flees its home as the battle lines draw near.
Photographed by Matthew Brady.   The Bettmann Archive.

agreed, asking, "What would sooner make our soldiers falter than the cry from their families?" Spurred
by concern for their loved ones and resentment of the
rich man's war, large numbers of men did indeed leave
the armies, supported by their friends and neighbors.

Desertions
from the
Confederate
army

Mary Boykin Chesnut observed a
man being dragged back to the
army as his wife looked on.
"Desert agin, Jake!" she cried
openly. "You desert agin, quick as
you kin. Come back to your wife and children."

Desertion did not become a serious problem for the
Confederacy until the summer of 1862, and stiffer po-
licing solved the problem that year. But from 1863
on, the number of men on duty fell rapidly as desertions soared. By the summer of 1863, John A. Campbell, a former justice of the Supreme Court, wondered
whether "so general a habit" as desertion could be

considered a crime. Campbell estimated that 40,000 to
50,000 troops were absent without leave and that
100,000 were evading duty in some way. Liberal furloughs, amnesty proclamations, and appeals to return
had little effect; by November 1863, Secretary of War
James Seddon admitted that one-third of the army
could not be accounted for. And the situation was to
worsen.

The gallantry of those who stayed on in Lee's army
and the daring of their commander made for a deceptively positive start to the 1863 campaign. On May
2 and 3 at Chancellorsville, Virginia, 130,000 mem-

*Battle of
Chancellorsville*

bers of the Union Army of the
Potomac bore down on fewer
than 60,000 Confederates. Acting
as if they enjoyed being outnumbered, Lee and Stonewall Jackson boldly divided their forces, ordering
50,000 men under Jackson on a day-long march west-

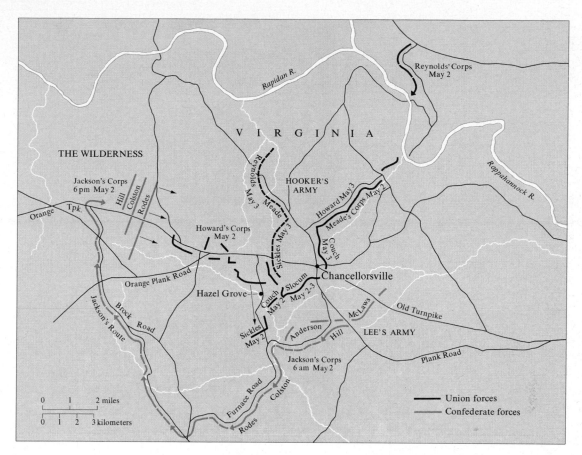

The Battle of Chancellorsville, May 2–3, 1863

ward and to the rear for a flank attack (see map). Jackson arrived at his position late in the afternoon to witness unprepared Union troops "laughing, smoking," playing cards, and waiting for dinner. "Push right ahead," Jackson said, and his weary but excited corps swooped down on the Federals and drove their right wing back in confusion. The Union forces left Chancellorsville the next day defeated. Though Stonewall Jackson had been fatally wounded, it was a remarkable southern victory.

But two critical battles in July 1863 brought crushing defeats to the Confederacy. General Ulysses S. Grant, after months of searching through swamps and bayous, had succeeded in finding an advantageous approach to Vicksburg, and promptly laid siege to that vital western fortification. If Vicksburg fell, U.S. forces would control the Mississippi, cutting the Confederacy in half and gaining an open path into the in-

terior. Meanwhile, with no serious threat to Richmond, General Robert E. Lee proposed a Confederate invasion of the North, to turn the tables on the Union and divert attention from Vicksburg. Both movements drew toward conclusion early in July.

In the North, Lee's troops streamed through Maryland and into Pennsylvania, where they threatened both Washington and Baltimore. The possibility of a major victory before the Union capital became more and more likely. But along the Mississippi, Confederate prospects darkened. Davis and Secretary of War Seddon repeatedly wired General Joseph E. Johnston to concentrate his forces and attack Grant's army. "Vicksburg must not be lost, at least without a struggle," they insisted. Johnston, however, either failed in imagination or did not understand the possibilities of his command. "I consider saving Vicksburg hopeless," he telegraphed at one point, and despite prodding he did nothing to relieve the garrison. In the meantime, Grant's men were supplying themselves by drawing on the agricultural riches of the Mississippi River valley. With such provisions, they could continue their siege indefinitely. In fact, their rich meat-and-vegetables diet had become so tiresome to them that one day, as Grant rode by, a private looked up and muttered, "Hardtack" (pilot biscuit). Soon a line of soldiers was shouting "Hardtack! Hardtack!" demanding respite from turkey and sweet potatoes.

In such circumstances the fall of Vicksburg was inevitable, and on July 4, 1863, its commander surrendered. That same day a battle that had been raging since July 1 concluded at Gettysburg, Pennsylvania.

| Battle of Gettysburg | On July 1 and 2, the Union and Confederate forces had both made gains in furious fighting. Then on |

July 3 Lee ordered a direct assault on Union fortifications atop Cemetery Ridge. Full of foreboding, General James Longstreet warned Lee that "no 15,000 men ever arrayed for battle can take that position." But Lee, hoping success might force the Union to accept peace with independence, stuck to his plan. His brave troops rushed the position, and a hundred momentarily breached the enemy's line. But most fell in heavy slaughter. On July 4 Lee had to withdraw, having suffered almost 4,000 killed and approximately 24,000 missing and wounded. The Confederate general reported to Jefferson Davis that "I am alone to blame," and tendered his resignation. Davis replied that to find a more capable commander was "an impossibility."

Though southern troops had displayed a courage and dedication that would never be forgotten, the results had been disastrous. Intelligent southerners could no longer deny that defeat lay ahead. Josiah Gorgas, the genius of Confederate ordnance operations, confided to his diary, "Today absolute ruin seems our portion. The Confederacy totters to its destruction." In desperation President Davis and several state governors resorted to threats and racial scare tactics to drive southern whites to further sacrifice. Defeat, Davis warned, would mean "extermination of yourselves, your wives, and children." Governor Charles Clark of Mississippi predicted "elevation of the black race to a position of equality—aye, of superiority, that will make them your masters and rulers." Abroad, English officials held back the delivery of

badly needed warships, and diplomats postponed any thought of recognizing the Confederate government.

From this point on, the internal disintegration of the Confederacy quickened. A few newspapers and a few bold politicians began to call openly for peace. "We are for peace," admitted the Raleigh, North Carolina, *Daily Progress,* "because there has been enough of blood and carnage, enough of widows and orphans." A neighboring journal, the North Carolina *Standard,* vowed to "tell the truth," tacitly admitted that defeat was inevitable, and called for negotiations. Similar proposals were made in several state legislatures, though they were presented as plans for independence on honorable terms. But more important, Confederate leaders had begun to realize that they were losing the support of the common people. A prominent Texan noted in his diary that secession had been the work of political leaders operating without the firm support of "the mass of the people without property." Governor Zebulon Vance of North Carolina, who agreed, wrote privately that independence would require more "blood and misery . . . and our people will not pay this price I am satisfied for their independence. . . . The great popular heart is not now & never has been in this war."

In North Carolina a peace movement grew under the leadership of William W. Holden, a popular Democratic politician and editor. In the summer of 1863 over one hundred public meetings took place in

| Southern peace movements | support of peace negotiations; many established figures believed that Holden had the majority of |

the people behind him. In Georgia early in 1864, Governor Brown and Alexander H. Stephens, vice president of the Confederacy, led a similar effort. Ultimately, however, these movements came to naught. The lack of a two-party system threw into question the legitimacy of any criticism of the government; even Holden and Brown could not entirely escape the taint of dishonor and disloyalty. That the movement existed despite the risks suggested deep disaffection.

The results of the 1863 congressional elections continued the tendency toward dissent. Everywhere secessionists and supporters of the administration lost seats to men who were not identified with the government. Many of the new representatives, who were often former Whigs, openly opposed the administration or publicly favored peace. In the last years of the war,

Davis depended heavily on support from Union-occupied districts to maintain a majority in the congress. Having secured the legislation he needed, he used the bureaucracy and the army to enforce his unpopular policies. Ironically, as the South's situation grew desperate, former critics such as the Charleston *Mercury* became supporters of the administration. They and a solid core of courageous and determined soldiers kept the Confederacy alive in the face of disintegrating popular support.

By 1864 much of the opposition to the war had moved entirely outside politics. Southerners were simply giving up the struggle, withdrawing their cooperation from the government, and forming a sort of counter-society. Deserters joined with ordinary citizens who were sick of the war to dominate whole towns and counties. Secret societies dedicated to reunion, such as the Heroes of America and the Red Strings, sprang up. Active dissent spread throughout the South but was particularly common in upland and mountain regions. "The condition of things in the mountain districts of North Carolina, South Carolina, Georgia, and Alabama," admitted Assistant Secretary of War John A. Campbell, "menaces the existence of the Confederacy as fatally as either of the armies of the United States." Confederate officials tried using the army to round up deserters and compel obedience, but this approach was only temporarily effective. The government was losing the support of its citizens.

Antiwar sentiment in the North

In the North opposition to the war was similar in many ways, but not as severe. There was concern over the growing centralization of government, and war-weariness was a frequent complaint. Discrimination and injustice in the draft sparked protest among poor citizens, just as they had in the South. But the Union was so much richer than the South in human resources that none of these problems ever threatened the stability of the government. Fresh recruits were always available, and food and other necessaries were not subject to severe shortages.

What was more, Lincoln possessed a talent that Davis lacked: he knew how to stay in touch with the ordinary citizen. Through letters to newspapers and to soldiers' families, he reached the common people and demonstrated that he had not forgotten them. Their grief was his also, for the war was his personal tragedy. After scrambling to the summit of political ambition, Lincoln had seen the glory of the presidency turn to horror. The daily carnage, the tortuous political problems, and the ceaseless criticism weighed heavily on him. In moving language, this president, with the demeanor of a self-educated man of humble origins was able to communicate his suffering. His words helped to contain northern discontent, though they could not remove it.

Much of this wartime protest sprang from politics. The Democratic party, though nudged from its dominant position by the Republican surge of the late 1850s, remained strong. Its leaders were determined to regain power, and they found much to criticize in Lincoln's policies: the carnage and length of the war, the expansion of federal powers, inflation and the high tariff, and the improved status of blacks. Accordingly, they attacked the continuation of the war, calling for reunion on the basis of "the Constitution as it is and the Union as it was." The Democrats denounced conscription and martial law, and defended states' rights and the interests of agriculture. They charged repeatedly that Republican policies were designed to flood the North with blacks, depriving white males of their status, jobs, and women. Their stand appealed to southerners who had settled north of the Ohio River, to conservatives, to many poor people, and to some eastern merchants who had lost profitable southern trade. In the 1862 elections, the Democrats made a strong comeback. And during the war, peace Democrats influenced New York state and won majorities in the legislatures of Illinois and Indiana.

Peace Democrats

Led by outspoken men like Clement L. Vallandigham of Ohio, the peace Democrats were highly visible. Vallandigham criticized Lincoln as a dictator who had suspended the writ of habeas corpus without congressional authority and arrested thousands of innocent citizens. Like other Democrats, he condemned both conscription and emancipation and urged voters to use their power at the polling place to depose "King Abraham." Vallandigham stayed carefully within legal bounds, but his attacks were so damaging

The New York City draft riot (July 1863), by far the most serious of northern riots against conscription. Library of Congress.

some saboteurs and Confederate agents were active in the North, they never effected any major demonstration of support for the Confederacy. Whether Lincoln overreacted in arresting his critics and suppressing opposition is still a matter of debate, but it is certain that he acted with a heavier hand and with less provocation than Jefferson Davis.

More violent opposition to the government came from ordinary citizens facing the draft, especially the urban poor. Conscription was a massive but poorly organized affair. Federal enrolling officers made up the list of eligibles, a procedure open to personal favoritism and ethnic or class prejudice. Lists of those conscripted reveal that poor men were called more often than rich, and that disproportionate numbers of immigrants were called. (Approximately 200,000 men born in Germany and 150,000 born in Ireland served in the Union army.) And rich men could furnish substitutes or pay a commutation to avoid service.

As a result, there were scores of disturbances and melees. Enrolling officers received rough treatment in many parts of the North, and riots occurred in Ohio, Indiana, Pennsylvania, Illinois, and Wisconsin, and in such cities as Troy, Albany, and Newark. By far the most serious outbreak of violence, however, occurred in New York City in July 1863. The war was unpopular in that Democratic stronghold,

New York City draft riot

and ethnic and class tensions ran high. Shippers had recently broken a longshoremen's strike by hiring black strikebreakers who worked under police protection. Working-class New Yorkers feared an influx of such black labor from the South and regarded blacks as the cause of an unpopular war. Irish workers, often recently arrived and poor themselves, resented being forced to serve in the place of others. And indeed, local draft lists certified that the poor foreign-born were going to have to bear the burden of service.

The provost marshal's office came under attack first. Then mobs crying "Down with the rich" looted wealthy homes and stores. But blacks proved to be the rioters' special target. Luckless blacks who happened to be in the rioters' path were beaten; soon the mob rampaged through black neighborhoods, destroying an orphans' asylum. At least seventy-four people died during the violence, which raged out of control for three days. Only the dispatch of army units fresh from Gettysburg ended the episode.

to the war effort that military authorities arrested him after Lincoln suspended habeas corpus. Fearing that Vallandigham might gain the stature of a martyr, the president decided against a jail term and exiled him to the Confederacy. Thus Lincoln rid himself of a troublesome critic, in the process saddling puzzled Confederates with a man who insisted on talking about "our country." Eventually Vallandigham returned to the North through Canada.

Lincoln believed that antiwar Democrats were linked to secret organizations, such as the Knights of the Golden Circle and the Order of American Knights, that harbored traitorous ideas. These societies, he feared, stimulated draft resistance, discouraged enlistment, sabotaged communications, and plotted to aid the Confederacy. Likening such groups to a poisonous snake striking at the government, Republicans sometimes branded them—and by extension the peace Democrats—as Copperheads. Though Democrats were connected with these organizations, most engaged in politics rather than treason. And though

Chapter 14: Transforming fire: the Civil War, 1860–1865

Once inducted, northern soldiers felt many of the same anxieties and grievances as their southern counterparts. Federal troops too had to cope with loneliness and concern for their loved ones, disease, and the tedium of camp life. Thousands of men slipped away from authorities. Given the problems plaguing the draft and the discouragement in the North over lack of progress in the war, it is not surprising that the Union army struggled with a desertion rate as high as the Confederates'.

Discouragement and war-weariness neared their peak during the summer of 1864. At that point the Democratic party nominated the popular General George B. McClellan for president and put a qualified peace plank into its platform. The plank, written by Vallandigham, condemned "four years of failure to restore the Union by the experiment of war" and called for an armistice. Lincoln concluded that it was "exceedingly probable that this Administration will not be re-elected."

Then, during a publicized interchange with Confederate emissaries in Canada, Lincoln insisted that the terms for peace include reunion and "the abandonment of slavery." A wave of protest rose in the North, for many voters were weary of war and unready to demand terms beyond preservation of the Union. Lincoln quickly backtracked, denying that his offer meant "that nothing *else* or *less* would be considered, if offered." He would insist on freedom only for those slaves (about 150,000) who had joined the Union cause under his promise of emancipation. Thus Lincoln in effect acknowledged the danger that he would not be re-elected. The fortunes of war, however, soon changed the electoral situation.

The northern vise closes

The year 1864 brought to fruition the North's long-term diplomatic strategy. From the outset, the North had pursued one paramount diplomatic goal:

| Northern diplomatic strategy |

to prevent recognition of the Confederacy by European nations. Foreign recognition would damage the North's claim that it was fighting an illegal rebellion, not a separate nation. But more important, recognition would open the way to the foreign military and financial aid that could assure Confederate victory. Among the British elite, there was considerable sympathy for southern planters, whose aristocratic values were similar to their own. And in terms of power politics, both England and France stood to benefit from a divided America, which would necessarily be a weaker rival. Thus Lincoln and Secretary of State Seward faced a difficult task. To achieve their goal, they needed to avoid both major military defeats and unnecessary controversies with the European powers.

Some southerners were supremely confident that England would recognize the Confederacy, in order to obtain cotton for its mills. But though cotton was a good card to play, it was not a trump. At the beginning of the war British mills had a 50-percent surplus of cotton on hand, and new sources of supply in India, Egypt, and Brazil helped to fill their needs later on. So the British government refused to be stampeded into recognition and kept its eye on the battlefield. France, though sympathetic to the South, was unwilling to act without the British. Confederate agents were able to purchase valuable arms and supplies in Europe and obtained some loans from continental financiers, but they never achieved a diplomatic breakthrough.

On three occasions the Union strategy nearly broke down. A major crisis occurred in 1861 when the overzealous commander of an American frigate stopped the British steamer *Trent* and abducted two Confederate ambassadors. The British reacted strongly, but Lincoln and Seward were able to delay until public opinion allowed them to back down and return the ambassadors. In another lengthy crisis, the United States protested but could not stop the sale of six warships to the Confederacy by British shipbuilders. And in the third crisis, the victories at Gettysburg and Vicksburg helped northern officials to block delivery to the Confederacy of British warships—the formidable Laird rams, whose pointed prows were designed to break the Union blockade.

The year 1864 also brought the military success the Union sought—a breakthrough in the West. After General George H. Thomas's inspired troops won the Battle of Chattanooga in November 1863 by ignoring orders and charging up Missionary Ridge, the heartland of the Confederacy lay open. In May Grant

"Our all depends on that army at Atlanta," wrote the southerner Mary Boykin Chesnut. But General Sherman's army occupied Atlanta on September 2, 1864, and demolished the railroad depot shown above.   Library of Congress.

Union
breakthrough
in the West moved to the Virginia theater, and General William Tecumseh Sherman, in command of 100,000 men, began an advance toward Atlanta. In Sherman's path the Confederacy placed the army of General Johnston. Popular with his men and a master of tactics, Johnston slowed Sherman down as he withdrew skillfully and with minimal losses toward Atlanta. From a purely military point of view, Johnston was conducting the defense shrewdly, if not with clear success.

But Jefferson Davis could not afford to take a purely military point of view. His entire political strategy for 1864 depended on the demonstration of Con-

federate military strength and a successful defense of Atlanta. With the federal elections of 1864 approaching, Davis hoped that a display of strength and resolution by the South would defeat Lincoln and elect a president who would sue for peace. Anxiously Davis pressed Johnston for news of his movements and assurances that Atlanta would be held. But the southern general was uninformative and continued to fall back. Finally Davis removed Johnston and replaced him with the one-legged General John Hood, who was ready to fight. "Our all depends on that army at Atlanta," wrote Mary Boykin Chesnut. "If that fails us, the game is up."

And the game was up. Hood attacked but was

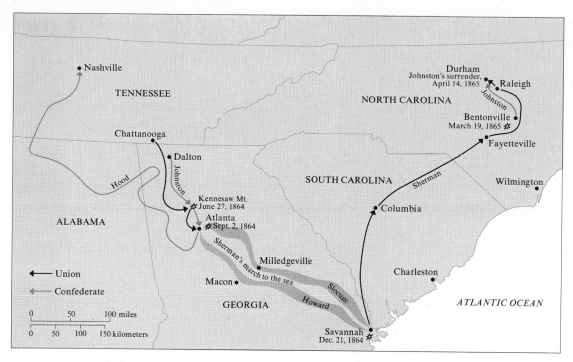

Sherman's march to the sea

beaten, and Sherman's army occupied Atlanta on September 2, 1864. The victory buoyed northern spirits and assured Lincoln's re-election. Mary Chesnut moaned, "There is no hope," and a government clerk in Richmond wrote, "Our fondly-cherished visions of peace have vanished like a mirage of the desert." Though Davis exhorted southerners to fight on and win new victories before the federal elections, he had to admit that "two-thirds of our men are absent . . . most of them absent without leave." Hood's army marched north to cut Sherman's supply lines and force him to retreat, but Sherman elected to live off the land and marched the greater part of his army straight to the sea, destroying Confederate resources as he went (see map).

The path Sherman cut across Georgia was fifty to sixty miles wide; the totality of the destruction was awesome. A Georgia woman described the "Burnt

Country" this way: "The fields were trampled down and the road was lined with carcasses of horses, hogs, and cattle that the invaders, unable either to consume or to carry away with them,

Sherman's march through Georgia

had wantonly shot down to starve our people and prevent them from making their crops. The stench in some places was unbearable." As many as nineteen thousand slaves gladly took the opportunity to escape bondage and join the Union army as it passed through the countryside. Others held back to await the end of the war on the plantations, either from an ingrained wariness of whites or from negative experiences with the soldiers. The destruction of food harmed them as well as white rebels; many blacks lost blankets, shoes, and other valuables to their liberators. In fact, the brutality of Sherman's troops shocked these veterans of the whip. "I'se seed dem cut de hams off 'n a live pig or ox and go off leavin' de animal groanin'," recalled one man. "De massa had 'em kilt den, but it wuz awful." Sherman reached Savannah in December, his mission accomplished.

In Virginia the preliminaries to victory were protracted and ghastly. Throughout the spring and summer Grant hurled his troops at Lee's army and suffered appalling losses: almost 18,000 casualties in the Battle of the Wilderness, more than 8,000 at Spotsylvania, and 12,000 in the space of a few hours at Cold

The northern vise closes

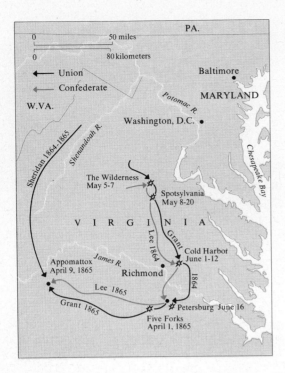

The war in Virginia, 1864–1865

and with fewer than 30,000 men left, Lee surrendered to Grant. At Appomattox Courthouse the Union general treated his rival with respect and paroled the defeated troops. Within weeks Jefferson Davis was captured, and the remaining Confederate forces laid down their arms. The war was over.

Lincoln did not live to see the last surrenders. On the evening of Good Friday, April 17, he went to Ford's Theatre in Washington, where an assassin named John Wilkes Booth shot him at point-blank range. Lincoln died the next day. The Union had lost its wartime leader, and to many, relief at the war's end was tempered by uncertainty about the future.

Costs and effects

The costs of the Civil War were enormous. Although precise figures on enlistments are impossible to obtain, it appears that during the course of the conflict the Confederate armies claimed the services of 700,000 to 800,000 men. Far more, possibly 2.3 million, served in the Union armies. Northern reserves were so great that more men were legally subject to the draft at the end of the war than at the beginning.

Statistics on casualties are more precise and more appalling. Approximately 364,222 federal soldiers died, 140,070 of them from wounds suffered in battle.

| *Casualties* | Another 275,175 Union soldiers were wounded but survived. On the Confederate side, an estimated 258,000 lost their lives, and even a conservative estimate of Confederate wounded brings the total number of casualties on both sides to more than 1 million—a frightful toll for a nation of 31 million people. More men died in the Civil War than in all other wars in American history combined.

Such carnage compels one to reflect on the choices that led to war. It is tempting to think of the Civil War as an unavoidable conflict, a necessary step in the elimination of an unjust and inhumane institution. But prewar election results clearly indicate that the majority in both North and South wanted peace. Their political system failed them, and other possibilities for compromise—such as a national convention—were never tried.

Harbor (see map). Before the last battle, Union troops pinned scraps of paper bearing their names and addresses to their backs, certain that they would be mowed down as they rushed Lee's trenches. In four weeks in May and June, Grant lost as many men as were enrolled in Lee's entire army. Undaunted, Grant remarked, "I propose to fight it out along this line if it takes all summer." And the heavy fighting did prepare the way for eventual victory: Lee's army shrank to the point that offensive action was no longer possible, while the Union army kept replenishing its forces with new recruits.

The end finally came in 1865. Sherman marched north, wreaking great destruction on South Carolina, and into North Carolina, where he moved against a small army commanded by General Johnston. In Virginia Grant kept battering at Lee, who tried but failed to break through the federal line east of Petersburg on March 25. With the numerical superiority of Grant's army now upwards of two-to-one, Confederate defeat

| *Heavy losses force Lee's surrender* | was inevitable. On April 2 Lee abandoned Richmond and Petersburg. On April 9, hemmed in by federal troops, short of rations,

Property damage and financial costs were also enormous, though difficult to tally. Federal loans and taxes during the conflict totaled almost $3 billion, and interest on the war debt was $2.8 billion. The Confederacy borrowed over $2 billion but lost far more in the destruction of homes, fences, crops, livestock, and other property. To give just one example of the wreckage that attended four years of conflict on southern soil, the number of hogs in South Carolina plummeted from 965,000 in 1860 to approximately 150,000 in 1865. Thoughtful scholars have noted that small farmers lost just as much, proportionally, as planters whose slaves were emancipated.

Financial cost of the war

Estimates of the total cost of the war exceed $20 billion—five times the total expenditure of the federal government from its creation to 1865. The northern government increased its spending by a factor of seven in the first full year of the war; by the last year its spending had soared to twenty times the prewar level. By 1865 the federal government accounted for over 26 percent of the gross national product.

These changes were more or less permanent. In the 1880s, interest on the war debt still accounted for approximately 40 percent of the federal budget, and soldiers' pensions for as much as 20 percent. Thus, although many southerners had hoped to separate government from the economy, the war made such separation an impossibility. And although federal expenditures shrank after the war, they stabilized at twice the prewar level, or 4 percent of the gross national product. Wartime emergency measures had brought the banking and transportation systems under federal control, and the government had put its power behind manufacturing and business interests through tariffs, loans, and subsidies. In political terms too, national power increased. Extreme forms of the states' rights controversy were dead, though Americans continued to favor a state-centered federalism.

Yet despite all these changes, one crucial question remained unanswered: what was the place of black men and women in American life? The Union victory provided a partial answer: slavery as it had existed before the war could not persist. But what would replace it? About 186,000 black soldiers had rallied to the Union cause, infusing it with new strength. Did their sacrifice entitle them to full citizenship? They and other former slaves eagerly awaited an answer, which would have to be found during Reconstruction.

Suggestions for further reading

Effects of the war on the South

Mary Boykin Chesnut, *A Diary from Dixie,* ed. Ben Ames Williams (1949); Beth G. Crabtree and James W. Patton, eds., *"Journal of a Secesh Lady": The Diary of Catherine Ann Devereux Edmondston, 1860–1866* (1979); Robert F. Durden, *The Gray and the Black* (1972); Clement Eaton, *A History of the Southern Confederacy* (1954); Paul D. Escott, *After Secession* (1978); Paul D. Escott, " 'The Cry of the Sufferers': The Problem of Poverty in the Confederacy," *Civil War History,* XXIII (September 1977), 228–240; Paul D. Escott, *Slavery Remembered* (1979); J. B. Jones, *A Rebel War Clerk's Diary,* 2 vols., ed. Howard Swiggett (1935); Ella Lonn, *Desertion During the Civil War* (1928); Charles W. Ramsdell, *Behind the Lines in the Southern Confederacy,* ed. Wendell H. Stephenson (1944); James L. Roark, *Masters Without Slaves* (1977); Georgia Lee Tatum, *Disloyalty in the Confederacy* (1934); Emory M. Thomas, *The Confederacy as a Revolutionary Experience* (1971); Emory M. Thomas, *The Confederate Nation* (1979); Emory M. Thomas, *The Confederate State of Richmond* (1971); Paul P. Van Riper and Harry N. Scheiber, "The Confederate Civil Service," *Journal of Southern History,* XXV (1959), 448–470; Bell Irvin Wiley, *The Life of Johnny Reb* (1943); Bell Irvin Wiley, *The Plain People of the Confederacy* (1943); W. Buck Yearns and John G. Barrett, *North Carolina Civil War Documentary* (1980).

Effects of the war on the North

Ralph Andreano, ed., *The Economic Impact of the American Civil War* (1962); Robert Cruden, *The War That Never Ended* (1973); Wood Gray, *The Hidden Civil War* (1942); Frank L. Klement, *The Copperheads in the Middle West* (1960); Susan Previant Lee and Peter Passell, *A New Economic View of American History* (1979); Benjamin Quarles, *The Negro in the Civil War* (1953); George Winston Smith and Charles Burnet Judah, *Life in the North during the Civil War* (1966); George Templeton Strong, *Diary,* 4 vols., ed. Allan Nevins and Milton Halsey Thomas (1952); Paul Studenski, *Financial History of the United States* (1952); Bell Irvin Wiley, *The Life of Billy Yank* (1952).

Military history

Bern Anderson, *By Sea and By River* (1962); Bruce Catton, *Grant Moves South* (1960); Bruce Catton, *Grant Takes Command* (1969); Bruce Catton, *This Hallowed Ground* (1956); Thomas L. Connelly and Archer Jones, *The Politics of Command* (1973); Burke Davis, *Sherman's March* (1980); Shelby Foote, *The Civil War, a Narrative,* 3 vols. (1958–1974); Douglas Southall Freeman, *R. E. Lee,* 4 vols. (1934–1935); Douglas Southall Freeman, *Lee's Lieutenants,* 3 vols. (1942–1944); Archer Jones, *Confederate Strategy from Shiloh to Vicksburg* (1961); J. B. Mitchell, *Decisive Battles of the Civil War* (1955); Thomas L. Livermore, *Numbers and Losses in the Civil War in America* (1957); Allan Nevins, *The War for the Union,* 4 vols. (1959–1972); Frank E. Vandiver, *Rebel Brass* (1956); T. Harry Williams, *Lincoln and His Generals* (1952).

Governmental policies during the war

Thomas B. Alexander and Richard E. Beringer, *The Anatomy of the Confederate Congress* (1972); Fawn Brodie, *Thaddeus Stevens* (1959); Dudley Cornish, *The Sable Arm* (1956); Richard N. Current, *The Lincoln Nobody Knows* (1958); David Donald, *Charles Sumner and the Rights of Man* (1970); Ludwell H. Johnson, "Lincoln's Solution to the Problem of Peace Terms, 1864–1865," *Journal of Southern History,* XXXIV (November 1968), 441–447; Peyton McCrary, *Abraham Lincoln and Reconstruction* (1978); James M. McPherson, *The Negro's Civil War* (1965); James M. McPherson, *The Struggle for Equality* (1964); Larry E. Nelson, *Bullets, Ballots, and Rhetoric* (1980); Frank L. Owsley, *State Rights in the Confederacy* (1925); James G. Randall, *Mr. Lincoln* (1957); Benjamin F. Thomas, *Abraham Lincoln* (1952); Hans L. Trefousse, *The Radical Republicans* (1969); Glyndon G. Van Deusen, *William Henry Seward* (1967); T. Harry Williams, *Lincoln and the Radicals* (1941).

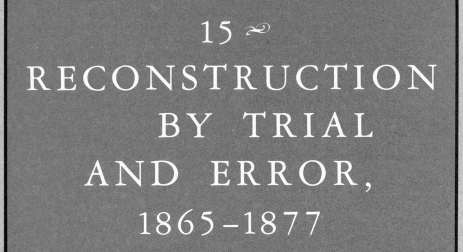

15 ✍
RECONSTRUCTION
BY TRIAL
AND ERROR,
1865–1877

Reconstruction of the Union held many promises. For Senator Benjamin Wade of Ohio, it began in a reassuring way. As a radical Republican who had demanded confiscation and emancipation early in the war, Wade had worried about the new president Andrew Johnson. How would he, a southerner and a former Democrat, deal with the planters and their newly freed slaves? Could he be relied on to check the aristocrats and promote equality? An interview at the White House in April 1865 seemed to suggest a favorable answer.

After speaking of the enormous costs of the war and the need to secure the Union victory, Wade suggested the exile or execution of ten or twelve leading traitors to set an example. President Johnson did not blanch at the idea. Instead he replied, "How are you going to pick out so small a number? Robbery is a crime; rape is a crime; murder is a crime; *treason* is a crime; and *crime* must be punished."

At the same time, black men and women in the South were preparing to seize the advantages of freedom. Their first opportunity came in the sea islands. During his last campaign, General Sherman had issued Special Field Order No. 15, which set aside for exclusive Negro settlement the sea islands and all abandoned coastal lands thirty miles to the interior, from Charleston to the Saint John's River in northern Florida. Negro refugees quickly poured into these lands; by the middle of 1865, forty thousand freedmen were living in their new home. One former slave-owner who visited his old plantation in Beaufort, South Carolina, received friendly and courteous treatment. His ex-slaves "firmly and respectfully" informed him, however, that "we own this land now. Put it out of your head that it will ever be yours again."

But neither Sherman's promise nor Johnson's was fulfilled. Although Jefferson Davis was imprisoned for two years, no Confederate leaders were executed. In fact, within a year southern aristocrats had come to view Johnson not as their enemy but as their friend and protector. And in the fall of 1865, the federal government began to confiscate the freedmen's land and return it to its original owners. "Why do you take away our lands?" the blacks protested. "You take them from us who have always been true, always true to the Government! You give them to our all-time enemies! That is not right!"

The cries of the freedmen did not go completely unheard. The unexpected turn of events led Congress to examine the president's policies and design new plans for Reconstruction. Out of negotiations in Congress and clashes between the president and the legislators, there emerged first one and then two new plans for Reconstruction. Before the process was over the nation had adopted the Fourteenth and Fifteenth amendments and impeached its president. But racism continued to thrive.

The nation's reluctance to treat the freedmen as equal citizens had first become evident during the war, when black volunteers and runaways from the Confederacy were discouraged from helping the Union. Even after black troops had entered federal service, they had faced persistent and galling discrimination. Eventually the Union's need for troops and the ideal of equality had made some headway against these attitudes, but differences over the proper status of blacks remained.

In Congress now politicians debated the future of black people. Democrats opposed efforts to defend the rights of freedmen, and Republicans were often divided among themselves. But a mixture of idealism and party purposes drove the Republicans forward. Ultimately, fear of losing the peace proved decisive with northern voters. The United States enfranchised the freedmen and gave them a role in reconstructing the South. The nation would force change on that recalcitrant section.

For black people themselves the benefits of freedom were often practical and ordinary. They moved out of slave quarters and built cabins of their own; they worked together in family units and worshipped in their own churches without white supervision. Blacks also took the risk of political participation, voting in large numbers and gaining some offices. But they knew their political success depended on the determination and support of the North.

In the South, opposition to Reconstruction grew steadily. By 1869 the Ku Klux Klan had added organized violence to southern whites' repertoire of resistance. Despite federal efforts to protect them, black people were intimidated at the polls, robbed of their earnings, beaten, or murdered. Prosecution of Klansmen rarely succeeded, and Republicans lost their offices in an increasing number of southern states. By the early 1870s the failure of Reconstruction was apparent; Republican leaders and northern voters had to decide how far they would persist in their efforts to reform the South.

As the 1870s advanced, other issues drew attention away from Reconstruction. Industrial growth accelerated, creating new opportunities and raising new problems. Political corruption became a nationwide scandal and bribery a way of doing business. North Carolina's Jonathan Worth, an old-line Whig who had opposed secession as strongly as he now fought Reconstruction, deplored the atmosphere of greed. "Money has become the God of this country," he wrote in disgust, "and men, otherwise good men, are almost compelled to worship at her shrine." Eventually these other forces triumphed, politics moved on to new concerns, and the courts turned their attention away from civil rights. Even northern Republicans gave up on racial reform in 1877. Reconstruction was over, and the position of black people remained inferior, North and South.

Equality: the unresolved issue

For America's former slaves, Reconstruction had one paramount meaning: a chance to explore freedom. A southern white woman admitted in her diary that the black people "showed a natural and exultant joy at being free." Former slaves remembered rejoicing and singing far into the night after federal troops reached their plantations. In Virginia one elderly woman spoke of freedom in an impromptu song:

Tain't no mo' sellin' today,
Tain't no mo' hirin' today,
Tain't no mo' pullin' off shirts today,
It's stomp down freedom today.
Stomp it down.

The slaves on one Texas plantation jumped up and down and clapped their hands as one man shouted, "We is free—no more whippings and beatings."

A few blacks gave in to the natural desire to do what had been impossible before. One grandmother who had long resented her treatment "dropped her hoe" and ran to confront the mistress. "I'se free!" she yelled at her. "Yes, I'se free! Ain't got to work fo' you

no mo! You can't put me in yo' pocket [sell me] now!" Another man recalled that he and others "started on the move" and left the plantation, either to search for family members or just to exercise their new-found freedom of movement. As he traveled, one man sang about being free as a frog, " 'cause a frog had freedom to git on a log and jump off when he pleases."

Most freedmen reacted more cautiously and shrewdly, taking care to test the boundaries of their new condition. "After the war was over," explained one man, "we was afraid to move. Jes' like tarpins or turtles after 'mancipation. Jes' stick our heads out to see how the land lay." As slaves they had learned to expect hostility from white people, and they did not presume it would instantly disappear. Life in freedom, they knew, might still be a matter of what was allowed, not what was right. " 'You got to say master?' " asked a freedman in Georgia. " 'Naw,' " answered his fellows, but "they said it all the same. They said it for a long time."

One sign of this shrewd caution was the way freedmen evaluated potential employers. "Most all de niggers dat had good owners stayed wid 'em, but de others lef'. Some of 'em come back an' some didn'," explained one man. If a white person had been relatively considerate to blacks in bondage, blacks reasoned that he might prove a desirable employer in freedom. Other blacks left their plantation all at once, for, as one put it, "that massa am sho' mean and if we doesn't have to stay we shouldn't, not with that massa."

Even more urgently than a fair employer, the freedmen wanted land of their own. Land represented their chance to farm for themselves, to have an independent life. It represented compensation for their generations of travail in bondage. A northern observer noted that freedmen made "plain, straight-forward" inquiries as they settled the land set aside for them by Sherman. They wanted to be sure the land "would be theirs after they had improved it." Not just in the sea island region but everywhere, blacks young and old thirsted for homes of their own. One southerner noted with surprise in her diary that

| Blacks' desire for land |

Uncle Lewis, the pious, the honored, the venerated, gets his poor old head turned with false notions of freedom and independence, runs off to the

Yankees with a pack of lies against his mistress, and sets up a claim to part of her land!

Lewis simply wanted a new beginning. Like millions of other freedmen, he hoped to leave slavery behind.

But no one could say how much of a chance the whites, who were in power, would give to blacks. During the war there had been much hesitation before black people were allowed to aid and defend the Union. As soon as the fighting began, black men volunteered as soldiers. But the government and the people of the North refused their offers, saying that the conflict was "a white man's war." "What upon earth is the matter with the American Government and people?" asked Frederick Douglass. "Colored men were good enough to fight under Washington," he pointed out, and "they were good enough to fight under Andrew Jackson." Denying them the chance to fight was like "fighting rebels with only one hand."

But many whites agreed with Corporal Felix Brannigan of the Seventy-fourth New York Regiment. "We don't want to fight side and side with the nigger," he said. "We think we are a too superior race for that." Other northerners believed that black people lacked the courage and will to fight. In September 1862 Abraham Lincoln said, "If we were to arm [the Negroes], I fear that in a few weeks the arms would be in the hands of the rebels." When a few Union generals raised companies of blacks, the War Department refused to accept them.

Necessity forced the United States to change its policy in the fall of 1862. Because the war was going badly, the administration authorized black enlistments. By spring 1863 black troops were proving their value. General David Hunter, Commander of

Black service in the military

the Department of the South, reported that his "colored regiments" possessed "remarkable aptitude for military training" and were "imbued with a burning faith that now is the time appointed by God . . . for the deliverance of their race." "They fight like fiends," said another observer, and Lincoln now looked to "the colored population" as "the great *available* and yet *unavailed of* force for restoring the Union." Recruitment of blacks proceeded rapidly.

Black leaders hoped that military service would secure equal rights for their people. As Frederick Douglass put it, "Once let the black man get upon his per-

son the brass letter, U.S., let him get an eagle on his button, and a musket on his shoulder and bullets in his pocket, and there is no power on earth which can deny that he has earned the right of citizenship in the United States." If black soldiers turned the tide, asked another man, "Would the nation refuse us our rights . . . ? Would it refuse us our vote?"

Wartime experience seemed to prove it would. Despite their valor, black soldiers faced persistent discrimination. In Ohio, for example, a mob shouting "Kill the nigger" attacked an off-duty soldier; on duty, blacks did most of the necessary manual labor. One Union general objected that black troops were used only as "diggers and drudges," and pointed out that "their equipments have been of the poorest kind." In June 1864, the War Department finally ordered that "colored troops . . . will only be required to take their fair share of fatigue duty [heavy labor]. . . ." But five months later General Lorenzo Thomas reported that "where white and black troops come together in the same command, the latter have to do all the work."

Most objectionable was the fact that black soldiers were expected to accept inferior pay as they risked their lives. The government paid white privates $13 per month plus a clothing allowance of $3.50. Black troops earned $10 per month less $3 deducted for clothing. Blacks resented this injustice so deeply that in protest two regiments in South Carolina refused to accept any pay. In June 1864 Congress finally made equal pay retroactive to the date of enlistment for those who had been free on April 19, 1861. Even this law was unfair to thousands of runaway slaves who had joined the army before 1864, and many commanders allowed such men to swear that they "owed no man unrequited labor" in order to receive full pay. When the paymaster visited black regiments following the legislation, "songs burst out everywhere" to celebrate the victory of principle.

Still, this was only a small victory over prejudice; the general attitude of northerners on racial questions was mixed. On the one hand, wartime idealism had promoted equality and weakened discrimination. Many abolitionists had worked vigorously to extend equal rights to black Americans, and a powerful element in the Republican party had committed itself to fighting racism. In 1864 their efforts brought about the acceptance of black testimony in federal courts and the desegregation of New York City's streetcars. Segregation on streetcars in the District of Columbia ended in 1865, and one state, Massachusetts, enacted a comprehensive public accommodations law.

On the other hand, there were many more signs of resistance to racial equality. The Democratic party adopted an explicit and vociferous stand against blacks, charging that Republicans favored race-mixing and were undermining the status of the white worker. Moreover, voters in three states—Connecticut, Minnesota, and Wisconsin—rejected black suffrage in 1865. The racial attitudes of northerners seemed to be in flux, the outcome uncertain.

Nowhere was the fundamental ambiguity of northern attitudes clearer than in the sea islands. Even before Sherman's special field order, these islands—

| *Sea-island blacks* |

which had a large slave population and had been captured early in the war—had become a kind of national laboratory of freedom. Abolitionists and missionaries had arrived to help the blacks, businessmen had investigated what the area could produce, and Union army recruiters had sought enlistments there. Free blacks had organized committees and Union Relief Associations to send clothes and blankets, ministers and teachers. Northerners of a variety of opinions had watched to see what former slaves could do.

The missionaries were delighted with the blacks' enthusiasm for education. Believing that "it was education which made us free [and] progressive," northern schoolteachers dispensed learning as the key to uplifting the slave. Along with literacy they stressed "industry and cleanliness" and the importance of work. The visiting businessmen believed that "the laws of labor, wages, competition, etc." would develop "habits of responsibility, industry, self-dependence, and manliness." Accordingly, they disapproved of charity and emphasized the values of competitive capitalism. "The danger to the Negro," wrote one worker in the sea islands, was "too high wages." It would be "most unwise and injurious," declared another, to give former slaves free land.

Sea-island blacks welcomed many of the missionaries' efforts, but they had some reservations. "The Yankees preach nothing but cotton, cotton!" complained one elderly man; most could not understand the capitalists' objection to free land. "We wants land," wrote one man, "dis bery land dat is rich

wid de sweat ob we face and de blood ob we back." Asking only for a chance to buy land, this man complained that "dey make de lots too big, and cut we out." Indeed, the government did sell thousands of acres in the sea islands for nonpayment of taxes, but when blacks pooled their earnings to buy almost 2,000 of the 16,749 acres sold in March 1863, 90 percent of the land went to wealthy investors from the North. Thus even among their northern supporters, the former slaves received only partial support. How much opportunity would freedom bring? That was a major question to be answered during Reconstruction, and the answer depended on the evolution of policy in Washington.

Johnson's reconstruction plan

Throughout 1865 the formation of reconstruction policy rested solely with Andrew Johnson, for shortly before he became president Congress recessed and did not reconvene until December. Thus Johnson had almost eight months to design and execute a plan of reconstruction on his own, unhindered by legislative suggestions. The new president undertook to restore the seceded states to the Union under his power to grant pardons.

Johnson had a few precedents to follow in Lincoln's wartime plans for Reconstruction. In December 1863 Lincoln had proposed a "10-percent" plan

| *Lincoln's reconstruction plan* |

for a government being organized in captured portions of Louisiana. According to this plan, a state government could be established as soon as 10 percent of those who had voted in 1860 took an oath of future loyalty. Only high-ranking Confederate officials would be denied a chance to take the oath, and Lincoln urged that at least a few well-qualified blacks be given the ballot. Radicals bristled, however, at such a mild plan, and a majority of Congress favored stiffer requirements and stronger proof of loyalty.

Later, in 1865, Lincoln suggested but then abandoned more lenient terms. At Hampton Roads, where he raised questions about the extent of emancipation (see page 386), Lincoln discussed restoration to

Andrew Johnson, a southern Unionist and an old foe of the planters.   Library of Congress.

Such views were a long-established part of the president's philosophy. Just as his past opinions on states' rights shaped this initial act, so Johnson's personal history influenced the rest of his program.

Johnson was not the average southern politician. He had built his entire career on championing the

> Andrew Johnson: his early life

cause of ordinary whites and attacking privileged planters. Born in humble circumstances, he started life as a tailor, uneducated and unable to read until taught by his wife. As he rose in Tennessee politics, he voiced his resentment of the pride and advantages of haughty aristocrats, who monopolized power and held the little man down. An outspoken Unionist, he refused to leave the Senate when Tennessee seceded, an action that commended him to Lincoln as a vice-presidential candidate in 1864.

Now as president, Johnson was able to define the terms on which southern states and rebellious planters would re-enter the Union. He laid out his program in a series of proclamations, beginning with two proclamations on North Carolina in May 1865. The first decreed amnesty for most southerners who would take an oath of loyalty to the United States. The second established a provisional military government and prescribed steps for the creation of new civilian governments. The key aspects of both proclamations lay in the details.

Certain classes of southerners were barred from taking the oath and gaining amnesty. Federal officials, elected or appointed, who had violated their oaths to

> Oaths of amnesty and new state governments

support the United States and aided the Confederacy could not take the oath. Nor could graduates of West Point or Annapolis who had resigned their commissions to fight for the South. The same was true for Confederate officers at the rank of colonel or above and for Confederate political leaders. Thus leaders of the rebellion and federal officeholders who had proved disloyal fell into an excepted category. To this category Johnson added southerners whose taxable property was worth more than $20,000. All such individuals had to apply personally to the president for pardon and restoration of political rights, or risk legal penalties, including confiscation of their land.

Under an appointed provisional governor, elections

the Union, with full rights, of the very state governments that had tried to leave it. Then in April he considered allowing the Virginia legislature to convene in order to withdraw its support from the Confederate war effort. Faced with strong opposition in his cabinet, however, Lincoln reversed himself, denying that he had intended to confer legitimacy on a rebel government. At the time of his death, Lincoln had given general approval to a plan drafted by Secretary of War Stanton that would have imposed military authority and provisional governors as steps toward new state governments. Beyond these general outlines, it is impossible to say what Lincoln would have done had he survived.

Johnson began with the plan Stanton had drafted for consideration by the cabinet. At a cabinet meeting on May 9, 1865, Johnson's advisors split evenly on the question of voting rights for freedmen in the South. Johnson said that he favored black suffrage, but only if the southern states adopted it voluntarily. A champion of states' rights, he regarded this decision as too important to be taken out of the hands of the states.

Chapter 15: Reconstruction by trial and error, 1865–1877

would be held for a state constitutional convention. The delegates chosen for the convention would draft a new constitution eliminating slavery and invalidating secession. After ratification of the constitution, new governments could be elected, and the state would be restored to the Union with full congressional representation. No southerner could participate in this process who had not taken the oath of amnesty or who had been ineligible to vote on the day the state seceded.

Thus freedmen could not participate in the new government, for although it was theoretically possible for the white constitutional conventions to enfranchise them, such action was at best unlikely. Nor could much of the former white leadership class, for the rich and powerful of prewar days needed Johnson's pardon first. To many observers, South and North, it appeared that the president meant to take his revenge on the haughty aristocrats whom he had always denounced, and to raise up a new leadership of deserving yeomen.

But the plan did not work as Johnson had hoped. The old white leadership proved resilient and influential; despite Johnson's regulations, prominent Confederates won election and turned up in appointive office. Moreover, Johnson himself had a hand in subverting his own plan. He pardoned first one and then another of the aristocrats and chief rebels. By fall 1865 the clerks at the pardon office were straining under the burden, and additional staff had to be hired to churn out the necessary documents.

| Confederates regain power |

Perhaps Johnson's vanity betrayed his judgment. Scores of gentlemen of the type who had previously scorned him now waited on him for an appointment. Too long a lonely outsider, Johnson may have succumbed to the attention and flattery of these pardon-seekers. Or perhaps he simply allowed himself too little time. It took months for the constitution-making and elections to run their course; by the time the process was complete and Confederate leaders had emerged in powerful positions, the reconvening of Congress was near. Johnson may have faced a choice between admitting failure and scrapping his entire effort or swallowing hard and supporting what had resulted. In either case, the president decided to stand behind his new governments and declare Reconstruction completed. Thus in December 1865 many Confederate congressmen traveled to Washington to claim seats in the United States Congress, and Alexander Stephens, vice-president of the Confederacy, returned to the capital as a senator.

The election of such prominent rebels was not the only result of Johnson's program that sparked negative comment in the North. Some of the state conventions were slow to repudiate secession; others only grudgingly admitted that slavery was dead. Two refused to take any action to repudiate the large Confederate debt. Northerners interpreted these actions as signs of defiance; subsequent legislation defining the status of freedmen confirmed their worst fears. Some legislatures merely revised large sections of the slave codes by substituting the word *freedman* for *slave*. In these black codes, former slaves who were supposed to be free were compelled to carry passes, observe a curfew, live in housing provided by a landowner, and give up hope of entering many desirable occupations. Finally, observers noted that the practice in state-supported institutions, such as schools and orphanages, was to exclude blacks altogether. To northerners, the South seemed intent on returning black people to a position of servility.

| Black codes |

Thus it was not surprising that a majority of northern congressmen decided to take a close look at the results of Johnson's plan. On reconvening, they voted not to admit the newly elected southern representatives, whose credentials were subject under the Constitution to congressional scrutiny. The House and Senate established a joint committee to examine Johnson's policies and advise on new ones. Reconstruction had entered a second phase, one in which Congress would play a strong role.

The congressional reconstruction plan

Northern congressmen disagreed on what to do, but they did not doubt their right to play a role in Reconstruction. The Constitution mentioned neither secession nor reunion, but it did assign a great many major responsibilities to Congress. Among them was the injunction to guarantee to each state a republican government. Under this provision, the legislators thought, they could devise policies for Reconstruction, just as Johnson had used his power to pardon for the same purpose.

They soon found that other constitutional questions had a direct bearing on the policies they followed. What, for example, had the fact of rebellion done to the relationship between southern states and the Union? Lincoln had always insisted that the Union remained unbroken; and not even Andrew Johnson could accept the southern view that the wartime state governments of the South could merely reenter the nation. Johnson argued that the Union had endured, though individuals had erred; thus the use of his power to grant or withhold pardons. But congressmen who favored vigorous reconstruction measures tended to argue that war *had* broken the Union. The southern states had committed legal suicide and reverted to the status of territories, they argued, or the South was a conquered nation subject to the victor's will. Moderate congressmen held that the states had forfeited their rights through rebellion, and had thus come under congressional supervision.

These diverse theories mirrored the diversity of Congress itself. Northern legislators fell into four major categories, no one of which held a majority: Democrats, conservative Republicans, moderate Republicans, and Radical Republicans. Overall, the Republican party had a majority, but there was considerable distance between conservative Republicans, who desired a limited federal role in Reconstruction and were fairly happy with Johnson's actions, and the Radicals. These men, led by Thaddeus Stevens, Charles Sumner, and George Julian, were a minority within their party, but they had the advantage of a clearly defined goal. They believed that it was essential to democratize the South, establish public education, and ensure the rights of freedmen. They favored black suffrage, often supported land confiscation and redistribution, and were willing to exclude the South from the Union for several years if necessary to achieve their goals. Between these two factions lay the moderates, who held the balance of power.

One overwhelming political reality forced these groups to unify: congressional elections were scheduled for the fall. Since Congress had questioned Johnson's program, they had to develop some modification or alternative program before the elections;

as politicians they knew better than to go before their constituents empty-handed. Thus they had to form a coalition among the various party factions.

What determined the kind of coalition that was formed and the direction of policy thereafter was the fact that Johnson and the Democrats refused to cooperate with conservative or moderate Republicans. The president and northern Democrats insisted, despite evidence of widespread concern, that Reconstruction was over, that the new state governments were legitimate, and that southern representatives should be admitted to Congress. This unrealistic, intransigent position blasted any possibility of bipartisan compromise. Republicans found themselves all lumped together by Democrats, and thus bargaining over changes in the Johnson program went on almost entirely within the party.

This development and subsequent events enhanced the influence of the Radicals. But in 1865, Republican congressmen were loath to break with the president; he was, for better or worse, the titular head of their party, so they tried to work with him. Early in 1866 many lawmakers thought a compromise had been reached. Under its terms Johnson would agree to two modifications of his program. The life of the Freedmen's Bureau, which fed the hungry, negotiated labor contracts, and started schools, would be extended; and a civil rights bill would be passed to counteract the black codes. This bill, drawn up by a conservative Republican, was designed to force southern courts to recognize equality before the law by giving federal judges the power to remove cases in which blacks were treated unfairly.

Congress struggles for a compromise

But in spring 1866, Johnson destroyed the compromise by vetoing both bills (they were later repassed). Denouncing any change in his program, the president condemned Congress's action in inflammatory language. In so doing he questioned the legitimacy of congressional involvement in policy making and revealed his own racism. Because the Civil Rights Bill defined United States citizens as native-born persons who were taxed, Johnson pronounced it discriminatory toward "large numbers of intelligent, worthy, and patriotic foreigners . . . in favor of the negro." The bill, he said, would "operate in favor of the colored and against the white race."

All hope of working with the president was now gone. But Republican congressmen sensed that their constituents remained dissatisfied with the results of Reconstruction. They therefore pushed on, and from bargaining among their various factions there emerged a plan. It took the form of a proposed amendment to the Constitution—the fourteenth—and it represented a compromise between radical and conservative elements of the party.

Of four points in the amendment, there was nearly universal agreement on one: the Confederate debt was declared null and void, the war debt of the United States guaranteed. Northerners uniformly rejected the notion of paying taxes to reimburse those who had financed a rebellion; and business groups agreed on the necessity of upholding the credit of the United States government. There was also fairly general support for altering the personnel of southern governments. In language that harkened back to Johnson's Amnesty Proclamation, the Fourteenth Amendment prohibited political power for prominent Confederates. Only at the discretion of Congress, by a two-thirds vote of each house, could these political penalties be removed.

Fourteenth Amendment

The section of the Fourteenth Amendment that would have the greatest legal significance in later years was the first (see Appendix). On its face, this section was an effort to strike down the black codes and guarantee basic rights to freedmen. It conferred citizenship on freedmen and prohibited states from abridging their constitutional "privileges and immunities." Similarly, the amendment barred any state from taking a person's life, liberty, or property "without due process of law" and from denying "equal protection of the laws." These clauses were phrased broadly enough to become powerful guarantees of black Americans' civil rights. In later decades they would take on added meaning with court rulings that corporations were legally "persons" (see page 476).

The second section of the amendment clearly revealed the compromises and political motives that had produced the document. Though many idealistic northerners favored voting rights for blacks, large portions of the electorate were just as adamantly opposed. Commenting on the ambivalent nature of northern opinion, a citizen of Indiana wrote that there was strong feeling in favor of "humane and liberal laws for the government and protection of the colored population." But he admitted to a southern relative that there was prejudice, too. "Although there is a great deal [of] profession among us for the relief of the darkey yet I think much of it is far from being sincere. I guess we want to compel you to do right by them while we are not willing ourselves to do so."

Republican congressmen shied away from confronting this ambivalence, but political reality required them to do something. Under the constitution, representation was based on population. During slavery each black slave had counted as three-fifths of a person for purposes of congressional representation. Republicans feared that emancipation, which made every former slave five-fifths of a person, might increase the South's power in Congress. If it did, and if blacks were not allowed to vote, the former secessionists would gain seats in Congress.

Republicans were determined not to hand over power to their political enemies, so they offered the South a choice. According to the second section of the Fourteenth Amendment, states did not have to give black men the right to vote. But if they did not do so, their representation would be reduced proportionally. If they did, it would be increased proportionally—but Republicans would be able to appeal to the new black voters.

The Fourteenth Amendment dealt with the voting rights of black men and ignored female citizens, black and white. Its proposal elicited a strong reaction from the women's rights movement. For decades advocates of equal rights for women had worked with abolitionists, often subordinating their cause to that of the slaves. During the drafting of the Fourteenth Amendment, however, female activists demanded to be heard. When legislators defined them as nonvoting citizens, prominent women's leaders such as Elizabeth Cady Stanton and Susan B. Anthony decided that it was time to end their alliance with abolitionists. Thus the independent women's rights movement grew.

In 1866, however, the major question in Reconstruction politics was how the public would respond to the amendment. Johnson did his best to see that the public would reject it. Condemning Congress's plan and its refusal to seat southern representatives, the president convinced state legislatures in the South to vote against ratification. Every southern legislature except Tennessee's rejected the amendment by a large margin. It did best in Alabama, where it failed by a vote of 69 to 8 in the assembly and 27 to 2 in the senate. In three states the amendment received no support at all.

To present his case to northerners, Johnson arranged a National Union convention to publicize his program. The chief executive also took to the stump himself. In an age when active personal campaigning was rare for a president, Johnson boarded a special train for a "swing around the circle" that carried his message far into the Midwest and then back to Washington. In cities such as Cleveland and St. Louis, Johnson castigated the Republicans in his old stump-speaker style. But increasingly audiences rejected his views and hooted and jeered at him.

The election was a resounding victory for Republicans in Congress. Men whom Johnson had denounced won re-election by large margins, and the Republican majority increased as some new candidates defeated incumbent Democrats. Everywhere Radical and moderate Republicans gained strength. The section of the country that had won the war had spoken clearly: Johnson's policies, people feared, were giving the advantage to rebels and traitors. Thus Republican congressional leaders received a mandate to continue with their reconstruction plan.

Congress, however, had reached an impasse. All but one of the southern governments created by Johnson had turned their backs on the Fourteenth Amendment, determined to resist. Nothing could be accomplished as long as those governments existed, and as long as the southern electorate was constituted as it was. To break the deadlock, Republicans had little choice but to form new governments and enfranchise the freedmen. They therefore decided to do both. The unavoidable logic of the situation had forced the majority toward the Radical plan.

The Radicals hoped Congress would do much more. Thaddeus Stevens, for example, argued that economic opportunity was essential to the freedmen. "If we do not furnish them with homesteads from forfeited and rebel property, and hedge them around with protective laws; if we leave them to the legislation of their late masters, we had better left them in bondage," Stevens declared. To provide that opportunity, Stevens drew up a plan for extensive confiscation and redistribution of land. Significantly, only one-tenth of the land affected by his plan was earmarked for freedmen, in 40-acre plots. All the rest was to be sold, to generate money for veterans' pensions, compensation for damaged property, and payment of the federal debt. By these means Stevens hoped to win support for a basically unpopular measure. But he failed; and in general the Radicals were not able to command the support of the majority of the public.

Instead, the Military Reconstruction Act of 1867 incorporated only the bare bones of the Radical program. The act called for new governments in the

South, with a return to military authority in the interim. It barred from political office those Confederate leaders listed in the Fourteenth Amendment. It guaranteed freedmen the right to vote in elections for state constitutional conventions and for subsequent state governments. In addition, each southern state was required to ratify the Fourteenth Amendment; to ratify its new constitution; and to submit the new constitution to Congress for approval. Thus black people gained an opportunity to fight for a better life through the political process. The only weapon put into their hands was the ballot, however. The law required no redistribution of land and guaranteed no basic changes in southern social structure. It did permit an early return to the Union.

Congress's role as the architect of Reconstruction was not quite over, for its quarrels with Andrew Johnson grew more bitter. To restrict Johnson's influence and safeguard its plan, Congress passed a number of controversial laws. First it set the date for its own reconvening—an unprecedented act, since the president had traditionally summoned the legislature to Washington. Then it limited Johnson's power over the army by requiring the president to issue military orders through the General of the Army, Ulysses S. Grant, who could not be sent from Washington without the Senate's consent. Finally, Congress passed the Tenure of Office Act, which gave the Senate power to interfere with changes in the president's cabinet. Designed to protect Secretary of War Stanton, who sympathized with the Radicals, this law violated the tradition that a president controlled his own cabinet.

The confrontation between Congress and Andrew Johnson culminated in the president's impeachment. Here the Senate sits in trial of Johnson, who ultimately escaped conviction and removal from office by a margin of one vote. Library of Congress.

Johnson took several belligerent steps of his own. He issued orders to military commanders in the South limiting their powers and increasing the powers of the civil governments he had created in 1865. Then he removed army officers who conscientiously enforced Congress's new law, preferring commanders who allowed disqualified Confederates to vote. Finally, in August 1867 he tried to remove Secretary of War Stanton. The confrontation had reached its climax.

Twice before, the House Judiciary Committee had considered impeachment, rejecting the idea once and then recommending it by only a five-to-four vote.

<table>
<tr><td>*Impeachment of President Johnson*</td><td>That recommendation had been decisively defeated by the House. After Johnson's last action, however, a third attempt to impeach</td></tr>
</table>

the president carried easily. In 1868, the House was so determined to indict Johnson that it voted before drawing up specific charges. The indictment concentrated on Johnson's violation of the Tenure of Office Act, though modern scholars regard his systematic efforts to impede enforcement of the Military Reconstruction Act as a far more serious offense.

Johnson's trial in the Senate lasted more than three months. The prosecution, led by such Radicals as Thaddeus Stevens and Benjamin Butler, argued that Johnson was guilty of "high crimes and misdemeanors." But they also advanced the novel idea that impeachment was a political matter, not a judicial trial of guilt or innocence. The Senate ultimately rejected such reasoning, which would have transformed impeachment into a political weapon against any chief executive who disagreed with Congress. Though a majority of senators voted to convict Johnson, the prosecution fell one vote short of the necessary two-thirds majority. Johnson remained in office for the few months left in his term, and his acquittal established the precedent that only serious misdeeds merited removal from office.

In 1869, in an effort to write democratic principles and color-blindness into the Constitution, the Radicals succeeded in presenting the Fifteenth Amendment for ratification. The measure forbade states to

| Fifteenth Amendment |

deny the right to vote "on account of race, color, or previous condition of servitude." Ironically, the votes of four uncooperative southern states—required by Congress to approve the amendment as an added condition to rejoining the Union—proved necessary to impose this principle on parts of the North. Although several states outside the South refused to ratify, the Fifteenth Amendment became law in 1870.

Thus Congress first tried to revise Johnson's program and then had to overturn it and start anew. And for black people in the South, the opportunities offered by Reconstruction did not fully come to pass until 1868. That year most of the state conventions met, and blacks participated in the democratic process for the first time. Blacks hoped to make a new life for themselves, but their task was formidable. According to Albion Tourgée, a northern soldier who became a Republican leader in postwar North Carolina, Congress had behaved toward the freedmen like a farmer who turns his livestock out in the middle of winter. The ex-slave had to fend for himself.

The response of the freedmen

Overjoyed as they were to be free, the freedmen also knew that their new status placed them in danger, for it infuriated some whites. When a Georgia planter heard a black woman singing about emancipation, he angrily knocked her down; another master threatened to "free" his servants with a shotgun. After announcing the end of the war, one slaveowner bitterly told his slaves, " 'you is free to live and free to die and free to go to de devil,' " as one of them later recalled. The idea of a freed slave wearing a starched shirt was intolerable to one planter, and a few southerners actually emigrated from the United States rather than stay, as one put it, "in a country with so many free Negroes."

Violence was directed at blacks from the first days of freedom. People took out their frustration on unlucky blacks, and often community mores did not challenge such abuses of the freedmen. In one North Carolina town a local magistrate clubbed a black man on a public street, and bands of "Regulators" terrorized blacks in parts of that state and Kentucky. Such incidents were predictable in a society in which many planters believed, as a South Carolinian put it, that blacks "can't be governed except with the whip."

The Union victory and emancipation changed this situation in principle but not always in reality. For the South remained a vast and sparsely settled region. Federal troops could not be everywhere at all times, even though they were theoretically in control. Sometimes racist northern troops and officials sided with local whites. Thus federal power often remained a distant or potential force, whereas the influence of local white people, who owned the land and controlled the jobs, was immediate and continuous.

Nevertheless, blacks took risks and reached out enthusiastically, hopefully, and prayerfully for freedom. As soon as Congress introduced black suffrage, freedmen seized the opportunity to participate in politics.

| Black suffrage |

They flocked to the polls and voted solidly Republican, for most agreed with one man who felt that he should "stick to de end wid de party dat freed me." Moreover, the freedmen had a shrewd sense of which party advocated their advancement. Although William Henry could read only "a little," he testified that he and his friends had no difficulty selecting the Republican ballot. "We stood around and watched," he explained. "We saw D. Sledge vote; he owned half the county. We knowed he voted Democratic so we voted the other ticket so it would be Republican."

The zeal for voting spread through the entire black community. Women, who could not vote, encouraged their husbands and sons, and preachers exhorted their congregations to use the franchise. Such urging could be an effective counter to white pressure tactics. Some preachers advised black women "to have nothin' to do wid deir husbands" if they gave in to white

Freed from slavery, blacks of all ages filled the schools to seek the education that had been denied them in bondage. Valentine Museum, Richmond, Virginia.

intimidation. One man who had succumbed to coercion lamented that "my wife wouldn't sleep wid me for six months."

Former slaves also hungered for education. Throughout bondage the knowledge that was in books had been denied them, but with freedom they filled the schools—young and old, day and night. On "log seats" or "a dirt flo'," many freedmen studied their letters in old almanacs, discarded dictionaries, or whatever was available. Young children brought infants to school with them, and adults attended at night or after "de crops was laid by." Many a teacher had "to make herself heard over three other classes reciting in concert" in a small room, but the scholars kept coming. The desire to escape slavery's ignorance was so great that many blacks paid tuition, typically $1.00 or $1.50 a month, despite their poverty. This seemingly small amount constituted one-tenth of many peoples' agricultural wage.

| Black education |

Blacks and their white allies also realized that higher education was essential—colleges and universities to train teachers and equip ministers and professionals for leadership. The American Missionary Association founded seven colleges, including Fisk and Atlanta universities, between 1866 and 1869. The Freedmen's Bureau helped to establish Howard University in Washington, D.C., and northern religious groups, such as Methodists, Baptists, and Congregationalists, supported dozens of seminaries, colleges, and teachers' colleges. By the late 1870s black churches had joined in the effort, founding numerous colleges despite their smaller financial resources. Though some of the new institutions did not survive, they brought knowledge to those who would educate others and laid a foundation for progress.

Some unlettered field hands managed to educate themselves and rise to positions of leadership. But most blacks who won public office during Reconstruction came from the educated prewar elite of free

| Black political leadership |

people of color. Better educated and less deprived, this group had benefited from its association with wealthy whites, who were often blood relatives. Some planters had given their mulatto children outstanding educations. Francis Cardozo, who served in South Carolina's constitutional convention and was later that state's secretary of the treasury and secretary of state, had attended universities in Scotland and England. P. B. S. Pinchback, who became lieutenant governor of Louisiana, was the son of a planter who had sent him to school in Cincinnati at age nine. And the two Negro senators from Mississippi, Blanche K. Bruce and Hiram Revels, were both privileged in their educations. Bruce was the son of a planter who had provided tutoring on his plantation; Revels was the son of free North Carolina mulattoes who had sent him to Knox College in Illinois. These men and others brought experience as artisans, businessmen, lawyers, teachers, and preachers to political office.

Black people used their new political power to seek opportunity and equality before the law. They concentrated their efforts on political and educational reform rather than sweeping economic or social change. In every southern state blacks led efforts to establish public schools. They did not press for integrated facilities; having a school to attend was the most important thing at the time, for the Johnson governments

had excluded blacks from schools and other state-supported institutions. As a result, virtually every public school organized during Reconstruction was racially segregated, and these separate schools established a precedent for segregation. By the 1870s segregation was becoming common in theaters, trains, and other public accommodations in the South.

A few black politicians did focus on civil rights and integration. Most were mulattoes from cities such as New Orleans or Mobile, where large populations of light-skinned free blacks had existed before the war. Their experience in such communities had made them sensitive to issues of status, and they spoke out for open and equal public accommodations. But they were a minority. Most elected black officials were intent rather on making crucial economic and educational gains in the face of enormous white hostility.

Economic progress was uppermost in the minds of many freedmen, especially politicians from agricultural districts. Land above all else had the potential to benefit the freedmen, but none of the black state legislators promoted confiscation; freedmen simply lacked the power to make that possible. Most black leaders sought instead to cooperate with whites. South Carolina established a land commission, but its purpose was to assist in the purchase of land. Any widespread redistribution of land had to arise from Congress, which never supported such action.

In most other areas as well, freedmen depended for support on three sets of allies—northern reformers and teachers, carpetbaggers, and scalawags. In its brief life

| Reformers, carpetbaggers, and scalawags |

the Freedmen's Bureau founded over four thousand schools, and idealistic men and women from the North established others and staffed them ably. The Yankee schoolmarm—dedicated, selfless, and religious—became an agent of progress in many southern communities. Thus, with the aid of religious and charitable organizations throughout the North, blacks began the nation's first assault on the problems created by slavery. The results included the beginnings of a public school system in each southern state and the enrollment of more than 600,000 blacks in elementary school by 1877.

A far more publicized ally of the freedman was the carpetbagger. Southerners opposed to Reconstruction used this derisive name to suggest an evil and greedy northern politician, recently arrived in the South with a carpetbag, into which he planned to stuff ill-gotten gains before fleeing. The stranger's carpetbag, a popular travel bag whose frame was covered with heavy carpet material, was presumably deep enough to hold all the loot stolen from southern treasuries and filched from hapless, trusting blacks. Immigrants from the North, who held the largest share of Republican offices, were all tarred with this brush.

There were a few northerners who deserved this unsavory description, along with a similar number of southerners who shared in the corruption and greed. But literally thousands of northerners settled in the South after the war, some because they liked the warm climate, others because they sought a new start in life and saw opportunities for success. Only a small portion of these migrants entered politics, and those who did generally shared an idealism bred of army service. They wanted to democratize the South and to introduce northern ways, such as industry, public education, and the spirit of enterprise. Though carpetbaggers supported black suffrage and educational opportunities, most opposed social equality and integration.

Scalawag was a term of contempt used to discredit any native white southerner who cooperated with the Republicans. A substantial number of southerners did so, including some wealthy and prominent men who saw that a new day had come and accepted it as a fact. In a few states, such as Mississippi, the scalawags were former Whig planters. Most scalawags, however, were men from mountain areas and small farming districts—average white southerners who saw that they could benefit from the education and opportunities promoted by Republicans. Banding together with the freedmen, they pursued common class interests and hoped to make headway against the power of the long-dominant planters. This black-white coalition, however, was always vulnerable to the issue of race, and scalawags shied away from support for racial equality. Except on issues of common interest, scalawags often deserted the other elements of the Republican party.

While elected officials wrestled with the political tasks of Reconstruction, millions of freedmen concentrated on improving life at home, on their farms, and in their neighborhoods. Given the eventual failure of Reconstruction, the small practical gains they made in their daily lives often proved the most enduring and

significant changes of the period. Living in official freedom but surrounded by an unfriendly white population, black men and women tried to gain some living space for themselves and their families. They sought to insulate themselves from white interference and to strengthen the bonds of their own community. Throughout the South they devoted themselves to reuniting their families, moving away from the slave quarters, and founding black churches.

The search for long-lost family members was awe-inspiring. With only shreds of information to guide them, thousands of black people embarked on odysseys in search of a husband, wife, child, or parent. By relying on the black community for help and information, many succeeded in their quest, sometimes almost miraculously. Others walked through several states and never found their loved ones.

Reunification of black families

Husbands and wives who had belonged to different masters established homes together for the first time. Husbands often took their wives out of the fields, and parents asserted the right to raise their own children. Saying "You took her away from me an' didn' pay no mind to my cryin', so now I'se takin' her back home," one mother reclaimed a child whom the mistress had been raising in her own house. Another woman bristled when her old master claimed a right to whip her children, promptly informing him that "he warn't gwine brush none of her chilluns no more." One girl recalled that her mistress had struck her soon after freedom. As if to clarify the new ground rules, this girl "grabbed her leg and would have broke her neck." The freedmen were too much at risk to act recklessly, but as one man put it, they were tired of punishment, and after freedom "dey sho' didn't tak no more foolishment off of white folks."

Black people frequently wanted to minimize all contact with whites. "There is a prejudice against us . . . that will take years to get over," the Reverend Garrison Frazier told General Sherman in January 1865. To avoid contact with intrusive whites, who were used to supervising and controlling them, blacks abandoned the slave quarters and fanned out into distant corners of the land they worked. Some moved away to build new homes in the woods. "After the war my stepfather come," recalled Annie Young, "and got my mother and we moved out in the piney

Given the eventual failure of Reconstruction, many blacks, like this elderly couple, probably benefited most from small gains in their daily lives—greater freedom from white supervision, and more living space for themselves and their families.   Valentine Museum, Richmond, Virginia.

woods." Others described moving "across de creek to [themselves]" or building a "saplin house . . . back in de woods" or " 'way off in de woods." Some rural dwellers established small all-black settlements that still exist today along the backroads of the South.

Even privileged slaves often shared this desire for independence and social separation. One man turned down the master's offer of the overseer's house as a residence and moved instead to a shack in "Freetown." He also declined to let the former owner grind his grain for free, because it "made him feel like a free man to pay fo' things jus' like anyone else." One couple, a carriage driver and trusted house servant during slavery, passed up the fine cooking of the "big house" so that they could move "in de colored settlement."

The other side of this distance from whites was closer communion within the black community. Freed from the restrictions and regulations of slavery, blacks could build their own institutions as they saw fit. The secret church of slavery now came out into the open; in countless communities throughout the South, "some of de niggers started a brush arbor." A brush arbor was merely "a sort of . . . shelter with leaves for a roof," but the freedmen worshiped in it enthusiastically. "Preachin' and shouting sometimes lasted all day," ex-slaves recalled, for there were "glorious times den" when black people could worship together in freedom. Within a few years independent black branches of the Methodist and Baptist churches had attracted the great majority of black Christians in the South.

This desire to gain as much independence as possible carried over into the freedmen's economic arrangements. Since most former slaves lacked money to buy land, they preferred the next best thing—renting the land they worked. But many whites would not consider renting land to blacks; there was strong social pressure against it. And few blacks had the means to rent a farm. Therefore other alternatives had to be tried.

Northerners and officials of the Freedmen's Bureau favored contracts between owners and laborers. To northerners who believed in "free soil, free labor, free men," contracts and wages seemed the key to progress. For a few years the Freedmen's Bureau helped to draw up and enforce such contracts, but they proved unpopular with both blacks and whites. Owners often filled the contracts with detailed requirements that reminded blacks of their circumscribed lives under slavery. Disputes frequently arose over efficiency, lost time, and other matters. Besides, cash was not readily available in the early years of Reconstruction; the region was devastated by war and hampered in some years by bad weather.

Black farmers and white landowners therefore turned to a system of sharecropping: in return for use of the land and "furnishing" (tools, mules, seed, a cabin, and food to last until harvest), the farmer paid the landowner a share of his crop. The cost of food and clothing was deducted from the crop before the owner took his share. Naturally, landowners tended to set their share at a high level, but blacks had some bargaining power. By holding out and refusing to make contracts at the end of the year, sharecroppers succeeded in lowering

the owners' share to around one-half during Reconstruction.

The sharecropping system originated as a desirable compromise. Blacks accepted it because it gave them a reasonable amount of freedom from daily supervision. Instead of working under a white overseer as in slavery, they were able to farm a plot of land on their own in family groups. But sharecropping later proved to be a disaster, both for blacks and for the South. Part of the problem lay in the fact that an unscrupulous owner in a discriminatory society had many opportunities to cheat a sharecropper. Owners and merchants frequently paid less for blacks' cotton than they paid for whites'. Greedy men could overcharge or manipulate records so that the sharecropper always stayed in debt. But the problem was even more fundamental than that.

Southern farmers were concentrating on cotton, a crop with a bright past and a dim future. During the Civil War, India, Brazil, and Egypt had begun to supply cotton to Britain; not until 1878 did the South recover its prewar share of British cotton purchases. This temporary loss of markets reduced per capita income, as did a decline in the amount of labor invested by the average southern farmer. Freed from the compulsion of slavery, black people tried, when possible, to keep their wives, daughters, and young children out of the fields. They valued human dignity more highly than the levels of production that had been achieved with the lash.

But even as southerners grew more cotton, matching and eventually surpassing prewar totals, their reward diminished. Cotton prices began a long decline whose causes merely coincided with the Civil War. From 1820 to 1860 world demand for cotton had grown at a rate of 5 percent per year; but from 1866 to 1895 the rate of growth was only 1.3 percent per year. By 1860 the English textile industry, world leader in production, had penetrated all the major new markets, and from that point on increases in demand were slight. As a result, when southern farmers planted more cotton they tended to depress the price.

In these circumstances overspecialization in cotton was a mistake. But most southern farmers had no choice. Landowners required sharecroppers to grow the prime cash crop, whose salability was sure. And due to the shortage of banks and credit in the South, white farmers often had to borrow from a local merchant, who insisted on cotton production to secure his loan. Thus southern agriculture slipped deeper and deeper into depression. Black sharecroppers struggled under a growing burden of debt that reduced their independence and bound them to landowners almost as oppressively as slavery had bound them to their masters. Many white farmers became debtors too and gradually lost their land.

Reconstruction in reality

From the start, many white southerners resisted Reconstruction. The former planter class proved especially unbending. In Georgia a landowning minister named John Jones expressed the common attitude when he voiced his dread of "the dark, dissolving, disquieting wave of emancipation" that would end his absolute control over the slaves. This unwillingness to accept black freedom received much encouragement from Andrew Johnson's policies, but it would have been a problem in any case.

Some planters attempted to postpone freedom by denying or misrepresenting events. Former slaves reported that their owners "didn't tell them it was freedom" or "wouldn't let [them] go." One ex-slave recalled that his mother "said us was gwine to be free." But "Marse Jeff said us warn't, and he didn't tell us no diffunt 'till 'bout Chris'mas atter de War was done over wid in April." Another tactic was to claim control over children or seize on guardianship and apprentice laws to bind black families to the plantation. Observing such actions, an agent of the Freedmen's Bureau reported that "there is an intention here [in North Carolina] to keep the freedmen in ignorance about their freedom, and it is widespread." Another agent in Georgia wrote, "I find the old system of slavery working with even more rigor than formerly at a few miles distant from any point where U.S. troops are stationed."

In some localities the Freedmen's Bureau put a stop to such practices. A former slave recalled, "I hears 'bout freedom in September [1865]," when a government agent rode up to the farm and asked "why ain't

White resistance to emancipation

massa turn the niggers loose." The bureau also issued regulations to support parents' control of their children and limit masters' abuse of guardianship laws. But at other times federal soldiers and agents of the Freedmen's Bureau were unsympathetic to blacks. The Reverend John Jones was elated when he called on the army to discipline his former bondsmen: the troops "whipped every Negro man reported to them . . . and punished by suspending by the thumbs."

Whites also blocked blacks from acquiring land. Freedmen knew they needed land and sought to own or rent it. Though a few planters divided up plots among their slaves, most condemned the idea of making blacks landowners. One planter in South Carolina refused to sell as little as an acre—even a half to each family, declaring that he would not take a hundred dollars an acre. Even a Georgian whose family was known for its concern for the slaves was outraged that two property owners planned to "rent their lands to the Negroes!" Such action was "injurious to the best interest of the community." On the other hand, a free black landowner in Virginia voluntarily sold nearly two hundred acres to former slaves whom he barely knew. "I don't reckon he got all his money," said the man's son, but "this was about the only land around here they could buy. . . . White folks wasn't lettin' Negroes have nothing."

Such adamant resistance by propertied whites soon manifested itself in other ways. After President Johnson encouraged southerners to resist congressional Reconstruction, many white conservatives worked hard to capture the new state governments. Elsewhere, large numbers of whites boycotted the polls in an attempt to defeat Congress's plans. Since the new constitutions had to be approved by a majority of registered voters, registered whites could defeat them by sitting out the elections. This tactic was tried in North Carolina and succeeded in Alabama, forcing Congress to readjust and base ratification on a majority of those voting. Opponents of Reconstruction also put economic and social pressure on Republicans. A black Republican complained that "my neighbors will not employ me, nor sell me a farthing's worth of anything." He wondered how his family would eat, and added, "My life has been freely threatened. . . ."

Sooner and later, white resistance to Reconstruction erupted in violence. Terrorism against blacks existed throughout Reconstruction—even in 1865 and

Chapter 15: Reconstruction by trial and error, 1865–1877

Terrorism against blacks became more organized and purposeful with the rise of the Ku Klux Klan.   Library of Congress.

1866, bands of armed men calling themselves Regulators attacked freedmen, and confrontations often escalated into violence. But after 1867 white violence became more organized and purposeful. The Ku

Ku Klux Klan

Klux Klan rose in a campaign to frustrate Reconstruction and keep the freedmen in subjection. Nighttime visits, whippings, beatings, and murder became common, and in some areas virtually open warfare developed despite the authorities' efforts to keep the peace.

The testimony of former slaves suggests that the earliest purpose of the nightriders may have been to control the source of plantation labor. A man from Virginia recalled that the Klan appeared "right after de war" and whipped "de slaves what leaves de plantations." Similarly, freedmen in other states recalled that the Klansmen concentrated on driving the freed-

men back to their old farms and "wouldn't let 'em roam none." "Doin' too much visitin' " or letting grass grow among the crops also brought trouble. At times freedmen were even able to identify their former owner or a neighboring planter by hearing his voice or recognizing his horse.

In time, however, the Klan's purpose became more openly political and social. Lawless nightriders made active Republicans the target of their attacks. Prominent white Republicans and black leaders were killed in several states. And after blacks who worked for a South Carolina scalawag started voting, terrorists promptly visited the plantation and "whipped every nigger man they could lay deir hands on." Like countless others, one black Republican was "given a warnin' . . . to watch my step and vote right." Klansmen also attacked Union League Clubs (Republican organizations that mobilized the Negro vote) and schoolteachers who were aiding the freedmen. No one who helped to raise blacks' status was safe.

Klan terror frightened many voters and weakened local party organization, but it did not stop Reconstruction. Throughout the South conventions met and drafted new constitutions in obedience to the mandate of Congress. Black voters exercised their newly acquired right of suffrage, electing some black delegates to participate for the first time in the processes of democracy. The conventions promptly completed their work, and new state governments came into being. In the first elections, Republicans won majorities everywhere except Georgia.

Southern white opponents of Reconstruction (who called themselves Conservatives and later Democrats) immediately denounced the new regimes. Cries of "Negro rule" and "black domination" filled the air. The South, they charged, had been turned over to ignorant blacks and predatory carpetbaggers. Such attacks were gross distortions. Blacks were a

| Reconstruction governments |

minority in eight out of ten state conventions; northerners were a minority in nine out of ten. In the new state legislatures only once—in the lower house in South Carolina—did blacks constitute a majority of either chamber; generally their numbers were far inferior to their proportion in the population. Sixteen blacks won seats in Congress before Reconstruction was over, but none was ever elected governor. Freedmen were participating in government, to be sure, but there was no justification for racist denunciations of "Ethiopian minstrelsy, Ham radicalism in its glory."

Nor were the constitutional conventions scenes of misrule. Indeed, they produced documents whose basic elements often lasted for generations, and they brought the South's fundamental law into line with progressive reforms that had been adopted in the rest of the nation. The new constitutions were, for example, more democratic; they eliminated property qualifications for voting and officeholding, and made state and local offices elective in cases where they had been appointive. They provided for public schools and institutions to care for the mentally ill, the blind, the deaf, the destitute, and the orphaned, and they ended imprisonment for debt and barbarous punishments such as branding. Women's rights in possession of property and divorce were broadened, al-

though white legislators ignored the call of black leaders for women's suffrage.

The Reconstruction governments also devoted themselves to stimulating industry. This policy reflected northern ideals, of course, but also sprang from a growing southern interest in industry. Confederates had learned how vital industry was to a nation, and many postwar southerners were eager to build up the manufacturing capacity of their region. Accordingly, Reconstruction legislatures designed many tempting inducements to local and northern investment. Loans, subsidies, and exemptions from taxation for periods up to ten years helped to bring new industries into the region. The southern railway system was rebuilt and expanded, coal and iron mining laid the basis for Birmingham's steel plants, and the number of manufacturing establishments nearly doubled between 1860 and 1880.

Despite these achievements, however, the Reconstruction governments were doomed to be unpopular. Struggling against powerful racial prejudice, they also faced major problems of taxation and public finance. Legislators wanted to continue prewar services and support such important new ventures as public schools. Rebuilding of bridges and transportation facilities devastated by the war was another obvious priority. But the Civil War had destroyed much of the South's tax base. One category of valuable property—slaves—was entirely gone. Hundreds of thousands of citizens had lost much of the rest of their real and personal property—money, livestock, fences, and buildings—to the war. Thus an increase in taxes was necessary even to maintain traditional services; new ventures required even higher taxes.

Southern Republicans were as aware as other politicians that raising taxes was unpopular, but they had no choice if they were to foster social progress. Some of the more radical legislators hoped that high taxes might lead to redistribution of land, though in practice few poor people could afford to buy the land sold for back taxes. Thus when taxes went up, Democrats could present themselves as guardians of the poor man's pocketbook. Charges of waste, extravagance, and exorbitant taxation became standard campaign rhetoric.

Corruption was another powerful charge levied against the Republicans. Unfortunately, it was true. Many carpetbaggers and black politicians sold their

A poster celebrating the election of blacks to Congress during
Reconstruction. From left to right, Senator Hiram R. Revels,
Representative Benjamin S. Turner, the Reverend Richard
Allen, Frederick Douglass, Representatives Josiah T. Walls
and Joseph H. Rainy, and the writer William Wells Brown.
Library of Congress.

votes and dipped their hands in the till. Corruption

Political corruption

was widespread in southern governments, and Republicans gained little from the efforts of some of their number to stop it, or from white Democrats' share in the guilt. Democrats convinced many voters that the scandal was the inevitable result of a foolish Reconstruction program based on blacks and carpetbaggers.

Historians have seen, more clearly than southern voters, that corruption was a national problem, not merely a southern one. During these years the nation confronted enormously tempting economic opportunities, and the greed for riches was contagious. Throughout the land railroads routinely bribed lawmakers, and the rapacious became confident enough to defend their activities openly. Public figures charged with stealing money or accepting bribes justified their behavior with cynicism. "The people [will] think I was a fool for not having taken twice as much," said Ben Butler of Massachusetts, when accused of stealing $8,000 from a New Orleans bank during his tenure as wartime military governor. Congressman John Bingham of Ohio, criticized for accepting stock in a lucrative but corrupt corporation benefiting from congressional legislation, reportedly answered that he "only wished he had ten times more."

But the most lasting failure of Reconstruction governments was neither fiscal nor venal but social. The new governments failed to alter the southern social structure or its distribution of wealth and power. Exploited as slaves, freedmen remained vulnerable to exploitation

Failure of Reconstruction

during Reconstruction. Without land of their own, they were dependent on white landowners, who could use their economic power to compromise blacks' political freedom. Armed only with the ballot, southern blacks had little chance to effect major changes.

To reform the southern social order, Congress would have had to redistribute land; and never did a majority of congressmen favor such a plan. Radical Republicans like Albion Tourgée condemned Congress's timidity. Turning the freedman out on his own without advantages, said Tourgée, constituted "cheap philanthropy." Indeed, freedmen who had to live

with the consequences of Reconstruction considered it a failure. The North should have "fixed some way for us," said former slaves, but instead it "threw all the Negroes on the world without any way of getting along."

Freedom had come, but blacks knew they "still had to depend on the southern white man for work, food, and clothing," and it was clear that most whites were hostile. Unless Congress exercised careful supervision over the South, the situation of the freedmen was sure to deteriorate. Whenever the North lost interest, Reconstruction would collapse.

The end of Reconstruction

The North's commitment to racial equality had never been total. And by the early 1870s it was evident that even its partial commitment was weakening. New issues were capturing people's attention, and soon voters began to look for reconciliation with southern whites. In the South Democrats won control of one state after another, and they threatened to defeat Republicans in the North as well. Before long the situation had returned to "normal" in the eyes of southern whites.

The Supreme Court, after first re-establishing its power, participated in the northern retreat from Reconstruction. During the Civil War the Court had been cautious and reluctant to assert itself. Reaction to the Dred Scott decision had been so violent, and the Union's wartime emergency so great, that the Court had refrained from blocking or interfering with government actions. The justices, for example, had breathed a collective sigh of relief when legal technicalities prevented them from reviewing the case of Clement Vallandigham, who had been convicted of aiding the enemy by a military court when regular civil courts were open (see pages 393–394).

But in 1866 a similar case, *Ex parte Milligan,* reached the Court through proper channels. Lambdin P. Milligan of Indiana had participated in a plot to free Confederate prisoners of war and overthrow state governments; for these acts a military court had sentenced him to death. In sweeping language the Court declared that military trials were illegal when civil

Supreme Court decisions on Reconstruction

courts were open and functioning, thus indicating that it intended to reassert itself as a major force in national affairs. This decision could have led to a direct clash with Congress, which in 1867 established military districts and military courts in the initial phase of its Reconstruction program. But Congress altered part of the Court's jurisdiction, as it was constitutionally empowered to do, and thus avoided a confrontation.

In 1873, however, an important group of cases, the *Slaughter-House* cases, tested the scope and meaning of the Fourteenth Amendment. In 1869 the Louisiana legislature had granted one company a monopoly on the slaughtering of livestock in New Orleans. Rival butchers in the city promptly sued. Their attorney, former Supreme Court justice John A. Campbell, argued that the Fourteenth Amendment had revolutionized the constitutional system by bringing individual rights under federal protection. Over the years his argument would win acceptance, offering shelter from government regulation to corporate "persons" in the nineteenth century and providing protection for blacks and other minorities in the twentieth.

The Court did not go that far, however, in the *Slaughter-House* decision. In a blow to the hopes of blacks, it refused to accept Campbell's argument. Neither the "privileges and immunities" clause nor the "due process" clause of the amendment guaranteed the great basic rights of the Bill of Rights against state action, the justices said. National citizenship involved only such things as the right to travel freely from state to state and to use the navigable waters of the nation. Thus the Court limited severely the amendment's potential for securing the rights of black citizens.

In 1876 the Court regressed even further, emasculating the enforcement clause of the Fourteenth Amendment and interpreting the Fifteenth in a narrow and negative fashion. In *United States* v. *Cruikshank* the Court dealt with Louisiana whites who were indicted for attacking a meeting of blacks and conspiring to deprive them of their rights. The justices ruled that the Fourteenth Amendment did not extend federal power to cover the misdeeds of private individuals against other citizens; only flagrant state discrimination was covered. And in *United States* v. *Reese* the

Court held that the Fifteenth Amendment did not guarantee a citizen's right to vote, but merely listed certain impermissible grounds for denying suffrage. Thus a path lay open for southern states to disfranchise blacks for supposedly nonracial reasons—lack of education, lack of property, or lack of descent from a grandfather qualified to vote before the Military Reconstruction Act. ("Grandfather clauses" became a popular way of excluding blacks from suffrage, since most blacks were slaves before Reconstruction and therefore could not vote.)

The retreat from Reconstruction continued steadily in politics as well. In 1868 Ulysses S. Grant defeated Horatio Seymour of New York in a presidential campaign that revived sectional divisions. Although he was not a Radical, Grant realized that Congress's program represented the wishes of northerners, and he supported a platform that praised congressional Reconstruction and endorsed Negro suffrage in the South. (The platform stopped short of endorsing black suffrage in the North.) The Democrats went in the opposite direction; their platform vigorously denounced Reconstruction. By associating themselves with rebellion and with Johnson's repudiated program, the Democrats went down to defeat in all but eight states, though the popular vote was fairly close.

In office Grant sometimes used force to support Reconstruction, but only when he had to. He hoped to avoid confrontation with the South, to erase the image of dictatorship that his military background summoned up. In fact, neither he nor Johnson had imposed anything approaching a military occupation on the South. Rapid demobilization had reduced a federal army of more than 1 million to 57,000 within a year of surrender. Thereafter the number of troops in the South continued to fall, until in 1874 there were only 4,082 in the southern states outside Texas. Throughout Reconstruction the strongest federal units were in Texas and the West, fighting Indians, not white southerners.

In 1870 and 1871 the violent campaigns of the Ku Klux Klan moved Congress to pass two Force Acts and an anti-Klan law. These acts permitted martial law and suspension of the writ of habeas corpus to combat murders, beatings, and threats by the Klan. Federal troops and prosecutors used them vigorously

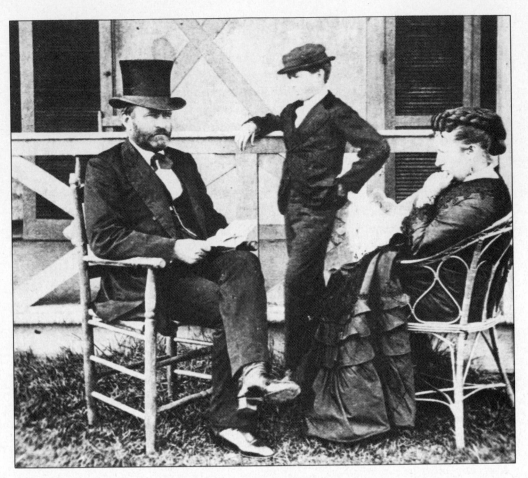

President Grant with his wife Julia and his youngest son Jessie. Photographed in 1872. Keystone-Mast Collection, University of California, Riverside.

but unsuccessfully, for a conspiracy of silence frustrated many prosecutions. Thereafter the Klan disbanded officially and went underground. Paramilitary organizations known as Rifle Clubs and Red Shirts often took the Klan's place.

In 1872 a revolt within the Republican ranks foreshadowed the end of Reconstruction. A group calling itself the Liberal Republicans bolted the party and

Liberal Republicans revolt	nominated Horace Greeley, the well-known editor of the New York *Tribune,* for president. The

Liberal Republicans were a varied group, including civil-service reformers, foes of corruption, and advocates of a lower tariff; they often spoke of a more lenient policy toward the South. That year the Democrats too gave their nomination to Greeley. Though the combination was not enough to

defeat Grant, it reinforced his desire to avoid confrontation with white southerners. Grant used troops very sparingly thereafter, and in 1875 refused a desperate request for troops from the governor of Mississippi.

The Liberal Republican challenge revealed the growing dissatisfaction with Grant's administration. Strong-willed but politically naive, Grant made a series of poor appointments. His secretary of war, his private secretary, and officials in the treasury and navy departments were all involved in bribery or tax-cheating scandals. Instead of exposing the corruption, Grant defended some of the culprits. As the clamor against dishonesty in government grew, Grant's popularity declined. So did his party's; in the 1874 elections Democrats recaptured the House of Representatives.

Chapter 15: Reconstruction by trial and error, 1865–1877

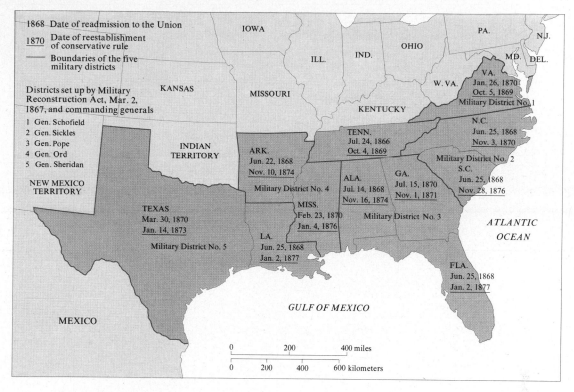

The Reconstruction

Congress's resolve on southern issues weakened steadily. By joint resolution it had already removed the political disabilities of the Fourteenth Amendment from many former Confederates. Then in 1872 it adopted a sweeping Amnesty Act, which pardoned most of the remaining rebels and left only five hundred excluded from political participation. A Civil Rights Act passed in 1875 purported to guarantee black people equal accommodations in public places, like inns and theaters. But it was weak and contained no effective provisions for enforcement. (The law was later struck down by the Supreme Court; see page 459.)

| Amnesty Act |

One by one, Democrats came to power in the southern states. Republican control ended in Virginia, North Carolina, and Georgia in 1870, in Texas in 1873, in Alabama and Arkansas in 1874, and in Mississippi in 1875. Thus by 1876 only Louisiana, South Carolina, and Florida remained "unredeemed" in the view of southern Democrats (see map).

In the North Republicans worried about their opponents' stress on the failure and scandals of Reconstruction governments. Many Republicans sensed that their constituents were tiring of the same old issues. In fact, a variety of new concerns were catching the public's eye. The Panic of 1873, which threw 3 million people out of work, focused attention on economic and monetary problems. Businessmen were disturbed by the strikes and industrial violence that accompanied the panic; debtors and unemployed sought easy-money policies to spur economic expansion.

The monetary issue aroused strong controversy. Civil War greenbacks had the potential to expand the money supply and lift prices, if they were kept in circulation. In 1872 Democratic farmers and debtors had urged such a policy, but they were overruled by "sound money" men. Now the depression swelled the ranks of "greenbackers"—voters who favored greenbacks and easy money. In 1874 Congress voted to increase the number of greenbacks in circulation, but Grant vetoed the bill in deference to the opinions of financial leaders. The next year sound money interests prevailed in Congress, winning passage of a law requiring that after 1878 greenbacks be convertible into gold. The law

| Greenbacks versus sound money |

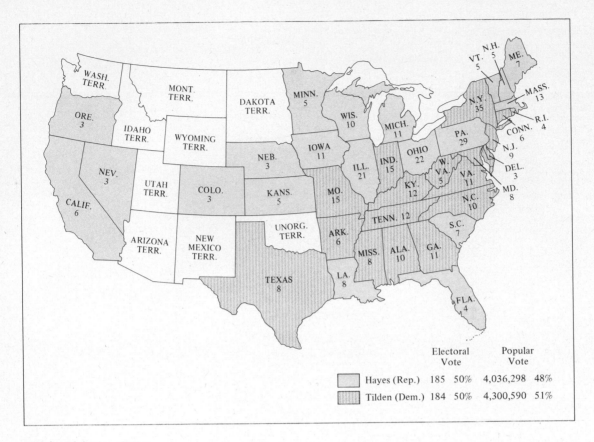

	Electoral Vote		Popular Vote	
Hayes (Rep.)	185	50%	4,036,298	48%
Tilden (Dem.)	184	50%	4,300,590	51%

Presidential election, 1876

limited the inflationary impact of the greenbacks and aided creditors, not debtors.

Indeed, the government's financial policies were almost perfectly tailored to revive and support industrial growth. Soon after the war Congress had shifted some of the government's tax revenues to pay off the interest-bearing war debt. The debt fell from $2.33 billion in 1866 to only $587 million in 1893, and every dollar repaid was a dollar injected into the economy for potential investment. Thus approximately 1 percent of the gross national product was pumped back into the economy from 1866 to 1872, and only slightly less than that during the rest of the 1870s. Low taxes on investment and high tariffs on manufactured goods also aided industrialists. With such help the northern economy quickly recovered the rate of growth it had enjoyed just before the war.

Another issue that claimed new attention in the 1870s was immigration. After the war the number of immigrants entering the United States began to rise again, along with the ingrained suspicions and hostil-

ities of native Americans. The Mormon question too–how Utah's growing Mormon community, which practiced polygamy, could be reconciled to American law–became prominent (see page 440).

Renewed pressure for expansion revived interest in international affairs. Secretary of State William H. Seward accomplished the only major addition of territory during these years in 1867. Through negotiation with the Russian government, he arranged the purchase of Alaska for $7.2 million dollars. Opponents ridiculed Seward's venture, calling Alaska Frigidia, the Polar Bear Garden, or Walrussia. But Seward convinced important congressmen of Alaska's economic potential, and other lawmakers favored the dawning of friendship with Russia. In the same year the United States took control of the Midway Islands, a thousand miles from Hawaii, which were scarcely mentioned again until the Second World War. Though in 1870 President Grant tried to annex the Dominican Republic, Senator Charles Sumner managed to block the attempt. Seward and his successor, Hamilton Fish,

Chapter 15: Reconstruction by trial and error, 1865–1877

All Colored People

THAT WANT TO

GO TO KANSAS,

On September 5th, 1877,

Can do so for $5.00

IMMIGRATION.

WHEREAS, We, the colored people of Lexington, Ky,. knowing that there is an abundance of choice lands now belonging to the Government, have assembled ourselves together for the purpose of locating on said lands. Therefore,

BE IT RESOLVED, That we do now organize ourselves into a Colony, as follows:— Any person wishing to become a member of this Colony can do so by paying the sum of one dollar ($1.00), and this money is to be paid by the first of September, 1877, in installments of twenty-five cents at a time, or otherwise as may be desired.

RESOLVED. That this Colony has agreed to consolidate itself with the Nicodemus Towns, Solomon Valley, Graham County, Kansas, and can only do so by entering the vacant lands now in their midst, which costs $5.00.

RESOLVED, That this Colony shall consist of seven officers—President, Vice-President, Secretary, Treasurer, and three Trustees. President—M. M. Bell; Vice-President —Isaac Talbott; Secretary—W. J. Niles; Treasurer—Daniel Clarke; Trustees—Jerry Lee, William Jones, and Abner Webster.

RESOLVED, That this Colony shall have from one to two hundred militia, more or less, as the case may require, to keep peace and order, and any member failing to pay in his dues, as aforesaid, or failing to comply with the above rules in any particular, will not be recognized or protected by the Colony.

Exodusters, southern blacks dismayed by the failure of Reconstruction, left the South by the thousands for Kansas in 1877. This handbill advertised the establishment of a black colony in Graham County, Kansas.   Kansas State Historical Society.

successfully used diplomacy to arrange a financial settlement of claims against Britain for permitting the sale of the *Alabama* and other Confederate cruisers.

By 1876 it was obvious to most political observers that the North was no longer willing to pursue the goals of Reconstruction. The results of a disputed presidential election confirmed this fact. Samuel J.

| Election of 1876 |

Tilden, Democratic governor of New York, ran strongly in the South and took a commanding lead in both the popular vote and the electoral college

over Rutherford B. Hayes, the Republican nominee. Tilden won 184 electoral votes and needed only one more for a majority. Nineteen votes from Louisiana, South Carolina, and Florida were disputed; both Democrats and Republicans claimed to have won in those states despite fraud on the part of their opponents. One vote from Oregon was undecided due to a technicality (see map).

To resolve this unprecedented situation, on which the Constitution gave no guidance, Congress established a fifteen-member electoral commission. In the

The end of Reconstruction

Important events

1865　Freedmen's Bureau established
President Andrew Johnson organizes new southern governments
Johnson permits election of prominent Confederates and passage of Black Codes
Congress refuses to seat southern representatives
Thirteenth Amendment ratified

1866　Congress passes Civil Rights Act over Johnson's veto
Congress approves Fourteenth Amendment
Freedmen's Bureau renewed by Congress over Johnson's veto
Most southern states reject Fourteenth Amendment
Tennessee readmitted to Union
Ex parte Milligan

1867　Military Reconstruction Act; Command of the Army Act; Tenure of Office Act
Purchase of Alaska
Constitutional conventions called in southern states

1868　Johnson impeached by House of Representatives, tried by Senate, and acquitted
Seven more southern states readmitted
Fourteenth Amendment ratified
Ulysses S. Grant elected president

1869　Congress approves Fifteenth Amendment

1870　Force Acts

Four more southern states readmitted
Attempt to annex Dominican Republic fails

1871　Ku Klux Klan Act
Treaty with England settles *Alabama* claims

1872　Amnesty Act
Liberal Republicans challenge party leadership
Debtors urge government to keep greenbacks in circulation
Grant re-elected

1873　*Slaughter-House* cases
Economic recession

1874　Grant vetoes increase in paper money
Democrats win control of House of Representatives

1875　Several Grant appointees indicted for corruption
Civil Rights Act

1876　Grant's secretary of war indicted for receiving bribes, resigns
Congress requires that after 1878 greenbacks be convertible into gold
U.S. v. Cruikshank
U.S. v. Reese
Results of presidential election disputed; Congress establishes commission to examine returns

1877　Congressional Democrats acquiesce in election of Rutherford B. Hayes
President Hayes withdraws troops from South; end of Reconstruction
Black Exodusters migrate to Kansas

interest of impartiality, membership on the commission was to be balanced between Democrats and Republicans. But one independent Republican, Supreme Court Justice David Davis, refused appointment in order to accept his election as a senator. A regular Republican took his place, and the Republican party prevailed 8-to-7 on every decision, a strict party vote. Hayes would then become the winner if Congress accepted the commission's findings.

Congressional acceptance, however, was not sure. Democrats controlled the House and had the power to filibuster to block action on the vote. Many citizens worried that the nation had entered a major constitutional crisis and was slipping once again into civil war. But the crisis was resolved when Democrats acquiesced in the election of Hayes. Scholars have found that negotiations went on between some of Hayes's supporters and southerners who were interested in federal aid to railroads, internal improvements, federal patronage, and removal of troops from southern states. But the most recent studies suggest that these negotiations did not have a deciding effect on the outcome. Neither party was well enough organized to implement and enforce a bargain between the sections. Northern and southern Democrats simply yielded to the pressure of events and failed to contest the election. Thus Hayes became president, and southerners looked forward to the withdrawal of federal troops from the South. Reconstruction was unmistakably over.

Southern Democrats rejoiced, but black Americans grieved over the betrayal of their hopes for equality. Tens of thousands of blacks pondered leaving the South, where freedom was no longer a real possibility.

| Black Exodusters |

"[We asked] whether it was possible we could stay under a people who had held us in bondage," said Henry Adams, who led a migration to Kansas. "[We] appealed to the President . . . and to Congress . . . to protect us in our rights and privileges," but "in 1877 we lost all hopes." Thereafter many southern blacks "wanted to go to a territory by ourselves." In South Carolina, Louisiana, Mississippi, and other southern states, thousands gathered up their possessions and migrated to Kansas. They were known as Exodusters, disappointed people still searching for their share in the American dream.

Thus the nation ended over fifteen years of bloody civil war and controversial reconstruction without establishing full freedom for black Americans. Their status would continue to be one of the major issues facing the nation. A host of other issues would arise from industrialization. How would the country develop its immense resources in a growing and increasingly integrated national economy? How would farmers, industrial workers, immigrants, and capitalists fit into the new social system? Industrialization promised not just a higher standard of living but also a different life style in both urban and rural areas. Moreover, it augmented the nation's power and laid the foundation for an increased American role in international affairs. As the United States entered its second hundred years of existence, it confronted these serious challenges. The experience of the 1860s and 1870s suggested that the solutions, if any, might not be clear or complete.

Suggestions for further reading

National policy and politics

Herman Belz, *A New Birth of Freedom* (1976); Herman Belz, *Emancipation and Equal Rights* (1978); Herman Belz, *Reconstructing the Union* (1969); Michael Les Benedict, *A Compromise of Principle* (1974); Michael Les Benedict, *The Impeachment and Trial of Andrew Johnson* (1973); Ellen Carol Dubois, *Feminism and Suffrage* (1978); W. E. B. Du Bois, *Black Reconstruction* (1935); John Hope Franklin, *Reconstruction* (1965); Harold M. Hyman, *A More Perfect Union* (1973); Eric L. McKitrick, *Andrew Johnson and Reconstruction* (1966); James M. McPherson, *The Abolitionist Legacy* (1975); William S. McFeely, *Grant* (1981); William S. McFeely, *Yankee Stepfather: General O. O. Howard and the Freedmen* (1968); Kenneth M. Stampp, *Era of Reconstruction* (1965).

Freedmen and Reconstruction in the South

Jonathan Daniels, *Prince of Carpetbaggers* (1958); Paul D. Escott, *Slavery Remembered* (1979); W. McKee Evans, *Ballots and Fence Rails* (1966); Eric Foner, "Reconstruction and the Crisis of Free Labor," in *Politics and Ideology in the Age of the Civil War,* ed. Eric Foner (1980); Herbert G. Gutman, *The Black Family in Slavery & Freedom, 1750–1925* (1976);

William C. Harris, *Day of the Carpetbagger* (1979); Thomas Holt, *Black Over White* (1977); Elizabeth Jacoway, *Yankee Missionaries in the South* (1979); Jacqueline Jones, *Soldiers of Light and Love* (1980); Peter Kolchin, *First Freedom* (1972); Leon Litwack, *Been In The Storm So Long* (1979); Robert Manson Myers, ed., *The Children of Pride* (1972); Lillian A. Pereyra, *James Lusk Alcorn* (1966); Michael Perman, *Reunion Without Compromise* (1973); Lawrence N. Powell, *New Masters* (1980); James Roark, *Masters Without Slaves* (1977); C. Peter Ripley, *Slaves and Freedmen in Civil War Louisiana* (1976); Willie Lee Rose, *Rehearsal for Reconstruction* (1964); Rebecca Scott, "The Battle Over the Child," *Prologue,* 10, No. 2 (Summer 1978), 101–113; James Sefton, *The United States Army and Reconstruction, 1865–1877* (1967); Emma Lou Thornbrough, ed., *Black Reconstructionists* (1972); Albion W. Tourgée, *A Fool's Errand by One of the Fools* (1879); Allen Trelease, *White Terror* (1967); Okon Uya, *From Slavery to Public Service* (1971); Sarah Woolfolk Wiggins, *The Scalawag in Alabama Politics, 1865–1881* (1977).

The end of Reconstruction

Robert G. Athearn, *In Search of Canaan* (1978); Michael Les Benedict, "Southern Democrats in the Crisis of 1876–1877," *Journal of Southern History,* XLVI, No. 4 (November 1980), 489–524; Norman L. Crockett, *The Black Towns* (1979); Stephen J. DeCanio, *Agriculture in the Postbellum South* (1974); William Gillette, *Retreat from Reconstruction, 1869–1879* (1980); William Gillette, *The Right to Vote* (1969); Susan Previant Lee and Peter Passell, *A New Economic View of American History* (1979); Jay R. Mandle, *The Roots of Black Poverty* (1978); Nell Irvin Painter, *Exodusters* (1977); Keith Ian Polakoff, *The Politics of Inertia* (1973); Howard Rabinowitz, *Race Relations in the Urban South, 1865–1890* (1978); Roger L. Ransom and Richard Sutch, *One Kind of Freedom* (1977); Jonathan M. Wiener, *Social Origins of the New South* (1978); C. Vann Woodward, *Origins of the New South* (1951); C. Vann Woodward, *Reunion and Reaction* (1951); Joel Williamson, *After Slavery* (1966).

APPENDIX

Historical reference books by subject

Encyclopedias, dictionaries, atlases, chronologies, and statistics

GENERAL AND BIOGRAPHICAL

Concise Dictionary of American Biography (1977); *Dictionary of American Biography* (1928–   ); *Dictionary of American History* (1976); *Encyclopedia of American History* (1981); *Family Encyclopedia of American History* (1975); George H. Gallup, *The Gallup Poll: Public Opinion, 1935–1971* (1972); George H. Gallup, *The Gallup Poll: Public Opinion, 1972–1977* (1978); John A. Garraty, ed., *Encyclopedia of American Biography* (1974); Bernard Grun, *The Timetables of History: A Horizontal Linkage of People and Events* (1975); Stanley Hochman, *Yesterday and Today: A Dictionary of Recent American History* (1979); *International Encyclopedia of the Social Sciences* (1968–   ); Thomas H. Johnson, *The Oxford Companion to American History* (1966); Richard B. Morris, *Encyclopedia of American History* (1976); *National Cyclopedia of American Biography* (1898–   ); U.S. Bureau of the Census, *Historical Statistics of the United States: Colonial Times to 1970* (1975); Charles Van Doren, ed., *Webster's American Biographies* (1974).

THE AMERICAN REVOLUTION

Mark M. Boatner, III, *Encyclopedia of the American Revolution* (1974).

ARCHITECTURE

William D. Hunt, Jr., ed., *Encyclopedia of American Architecture* (1980).

ATLASES

John L. Andriot, ed., *Township Atlas of the United States* (1979); Lester J. Cappon, ed., *Atlas of Early American History: The Revolutionary Era, 1760–1790* (1976); Edward W. Fox, *Atlas of American History* (1964); Edwin S. Gaustad, *Historical Atlas of Religion in America* (1976); *International Geographic Encyclopedia and Atlas* (1979); Kenneth T. Jackson and James T. Adams, *Atlas of American History*

(1978); Douglas W. Marshall and Howard H. Peckham, *Campaigns of the American Revolution* (1976); *Rand-McNally Atlas of the American Revolution* (1974); U.S. Department of the Interior, Geological Survey, *National Atlas of the United States of America* (1970); U.S. War Department, *The Official Atlas of the Civil War* (1958); U.S. Military Academy, *The West Point Atlas of American Wars, 1689–1953* (1959).

BLACKS

Peter M. Bergman, *The Chronological History of the Negro in America* (1969); W. A. Low and Virgil A. Clift, eds., *Encyclopedia of Black America* (1981); Harry A. Ploski and William Marr, eds., *The Negro Almanac* (1976); Erwin A. Salk, ed., *A Layman's Guide to Negro History* (1967); Mabel M. Smythe, ed., *The Black American Reference Book* (1976); Edgar A. Toppin, *A Biographical History of Blacks in America* (1971).

THE CIVIL WAR

Mark M. Boatner, III, *The Civil War Dictionary* (1959); E. B. Long, *The Civil War Day by Day: An Almanac, 1861–1865* (1971); Jon L. Wakelyn, ed., *Biographical Dictionary of the Confederacy* (1977); Ezra J. Warner and W. Buck Yearns, *Biographical Register of the Confederate Congress* (1975).

CONSTITUTIONAL HISTORY

Congressional Quarterly, *Guide to the Supreme Court* (1979); Leon Friedman and Fred I. Israel, eds., *The Justices of the United States Supreme Court, 1789–1978: Their Lives and Major Opinions* (1980); *Judges of the United States* (1980).

ECONOMIC HISTORY

Glenn Porter, *Encyclopedia of American Economic History* (1980).

EDUCATION

Lee C. Deighton, ed., *The Encyclopedia of Education* (1971); John F. Ohles, ed., *Biographical Dictionary of American Educators* (1978).

ENTERTAINMENT

Tim Brooks and Earle Marsh, *The Complete Directory to Prime Time Network TV Shows, 1946–present* (1979); John Chilton, *Who's Who of Jazz* (1972); John Dunning, *Tune in Yesterday* [radio] (1976); *Notable Names in the American Theater* (1976); *New York Times Encyclopedia of Television* (1977); Andrew Sarris, *The American Cinema: Directors and Directions, 1929–1968* (1968); Evelyn M. Truitt, *Who Was Who on Screen* (1977).

FOREIGN POLICY

Alexander DeConde, ed., *Encyclopedia of American Foreign Policy* (1978); John E. Findling, *Dictionary of American Diplomatic History* (1980); Richard B. Morris and Graham W. Irwin, eds., *Harper Encyclopedia of the Modern World* (1970); Jack E. Vincent, *A Handbook of International Relations* (1969).

IMMIGRATION AND ETHNIC GROUPS

Stephen Thernstrom, ed., *Harvard Encyclopedia of American Ethnic Groups* (1980).

INDIANS

Frederick J. Dockstader, *Great North American Indians: Profiles in Life and Leadership* (1977); Barry Klein, ed., *Reference Encyclopedia of the American Indian* (1978).

LABOR

Gary M. Fink, ed., *Biographical Dictionary of American Labor Leaders* (1974); Gary M. Fink, ed., *Labor Unions* (1977).

POLITICS AND GOVERNMENT

Congressional Quarterly, *Congress and the Nation, 1945–1976* (1965–1977); Congressional Quarterly, *Guide to U.S. Elections* (1975); Roy R. Glashan, comp., *American Governors and Gubernatorial Elections, 1775–1978* (1979); Joseph E. Kallenbach and Jessamine S. Kallenbach, *American State Governors, 1776–1976* (1977); Svend Peterson, *A Statistical History of the American Presidential Elections* (1963); *Political Profiles, Truman Years to . . .* (1978); John W. Raimo, *Biographical Directory of American Colonial and Revolutionary Governors, 1607–1789* (1980); William Safire, *Safire's Political Dictionary* (1978); Richard M. Scammon, ed., *America at the Polls: Handbook of Presidential Election Statistics* (1965); Arthur M. Schlesinger, Jr., and Fred I. Israel, eds., *History of American Presidential Elections, 1789–1968* (1971); Robert Sobel, ed., *Biographical Directory of the United States Executive Branch, 1774–1977 (1977)*; U.S. Congress, Senate, *Biographical Directory of the American Congress, 1774–1971* (1971); Robert Vexler, *The Vice-Presidents and Cabinet Members: Biographies Arranged Chronologically by Administration* (1975).

REGIONS AND STATES

Robert Bain, *et al.,* eds., *Southern Writers: A Biographical Dictionary* (1979); John Clayton, ed., *The Illinois Fact Book and Historical Almanac, 1673–1968* (1970); Howard R. Lamar, ed., *The Reader's Encyclopedia of the American West* (1977); David C. Roller and Robert W. Twyman, eds., *The Encyclopedia of Southern History* (1979); Walter Prescott Webb, H. Bailey Carroll, and Eldon S. Branda, eds. *The Handbook of Texas* (1952, 1976).

RELIGION

Henry Bowden, *Dictionary of American Religious Biography* (1977); J. Gordon Melton, *The Encyclopedia of American Religions* (1978); Arthur C. Piepkorn, *Profiles in Belief: The Religious Bodies of the United States and Canada* (1977–1979).

SCIENCE

Charles C. Gillispie, ed., *Dictionary of Scientific Biography* (1970–   ); National Academy of Sciences, *Biographical Memoirs* (1877–   ).

SPORTS

Ralph Hickok, *New Encyclopedia of Sports* (1977); Ralph Hickok, *Who Was Who in American Sports* (1971); Frank G. Menke and Suzanne Treat, *The Encyclopedia of Sports* (1977); Paul Soderberg, *et al., The Big Book of Halls of Fame in the United States and Canada* (1977).

WARS AND THE MILITARY

R. Ernest Dupuy and Trevor N. Dupuy, *The Encyclopedia of Military History* (1977); Robert Goralski, *World War II Almanac, 1931–1945* (1981); Thomas Parrish, ed., *The Simon and Schuster Encyclopedia of World War II* (1978); *Webster's American Military Biographies* (1978).

WOMEN

Edward T. James, Janet W. James, and Paul S. Boyer, eds., *Notable American Women, 1607–1950* (1971); Barbara Sicherman and Carol Hurd Green, eds., *Notable American Women: The Modern Period* (1980).

Declaration of Independence in Congress, July 4, 1776

The unanimous declaration of the thirteen United States of America

When, in the course of human events, it becomes necessary for one people to dissolve the political bonds which have connected them with another, and to assume, among the powers of the earth, the separate and equal station to which the laws of nature and of nature's God entitle them, a decent respect to the opinions of mankind requires that they should declare the causes which impel them to the separation.

We hold these truths to be self-evident: That all men are created equal; that they are endowed by their Creator with certain unalienable rights; that among these are life, liberty, and the pursuit of happiness; that, to secure these rights, governments are instituted among men, deriving their just powers from the consent of the governed; that whenever any form of government becomes destructive of these ends, it is the right of the people to alter or to abolish it, and to institute new government, laying its foundation on such principles, and organizing its powers in such form, as to them shall seem most likely to effect their safety and happiness. Prudence, indeed, will dictate that governments long established should not be changed for light and transient causes; and accordingly all experience hath shown that mankind are more disposed to suffer, while evils are sufferable, than to right themselves by abolishing the forms to which they are accustomed. But when a long train of abuses and usurpations, pursuing invariably the same object, evinces a design to reduce them under absolute despotism, it is their right, it is their duty, to throw off such government, and to provide new guards for their future security. Such has been the patient sufferance of these colonies; and such is now the necessity which constrains them to alter their former systems of government. The history of the present King of Great Britain is a history of repeated injuries and usurpations, all having in direct object the establishment of an absolute tyranny over these states. To prove this, let facts be submitted to a candid world.

He has refused his assent to laws, the most wholesome and necessary for the public good.

He has forbidden his governors to pass laws of immediate and pressing importance, unless suspended in their operation till his assent should be obtained; and, when so suspended, he has utterly neglected to attend to them.

He has refused to pass other laws for the accommodation of large districts of people, unless those people would relinquish the right of representation in the legislature, a right inestimable to them, and formidable to tyrants only.

He has called together legislative bodies at places unusual, uncomfortable, and distant from the depository of their public records, for the sole purpose of fatiguing them into compliance with his measures.

He has dissolved representative houses repeatedly, for opposing, with manly firmness, his invasions on the rights of the people.

He has refused for a long time, after such dissolutions, to cause others to be elected; whereby the legislative powers, incapable of annihilation, have returned to the people at large for their exercise; the state remaining, in the mean time, exposed to all the dangers of invasions from without and convulsions within.

He has endeavored to prevent the population of these states; for that purpose obstructing the laws for naturalization of foreigners; refusing to pass others to encourage their migration hither, and raising the conditions of new appropriations of lands.

He has obstructed the administration of justice, by refusing his assent to laws for establishing judiciary powers.

He has made judges dependent on his will alone, for the tenure of their offices, and the amount and payment of their salaries.

He has erected a multitude of new offices, and sent hither swarms of officers to harass our people and eat out their substance.

He has kept among us, in times of peace, standing armies, without the consent of our legislatures.

He has affected to render the military independent of, and superior to, the civil power.

He has combined with others to subject us to a jurisdiction foreign to our constitution, and unacknowledged by our laws, giving his assent to their acts of pretended legislation:

For quartering large bodies of armed troops among us;

For protecting them, by a mock trial, from punishment for any murders which they should commit on the inhabitants of these states;

For cutting off our trade with all parts of the world;

For imposing taxes on us without our consent;

For depriving us, in many cases, of the benefits of trial by jury;

For transporting us beyond seas, to be tried for pretended offenses;

For abolishing the free system of English laws in a neighboring province, establishing therein an arbitrary government, and enlarging its boundaries, so as to render it at once an example and fit instrument for introducing the same absolute rule into these colonies;

For taking away our charters, abolishing our most valuable laws, and altering fundamentally the forms of our governments;

For suspending our own legislatures, and declaring themselves invested with power to legislate for us in all cases whatsoever.

He has abdicated government here, by declaring us out of his protection and waging war against us.

He has plundered our seas, ravaged our coasts, burned our towns, and destroyed the lives of our people.

He is at this time transporting large armies of foreign mercenaries to complete the works of death, desolation, and tyranny already begun with circumstances of cruelty and perfidy scarcely paralleled in the most barbarous ages, and totally unworthy the head of a civilized nation.

He has constrained our fellow-citizens, taken captive on the high seas, to bear arms against their country, to become the executioners of their friends and brethren, or to fall themselves by their hands.

He has excited domestic insurrection among us, and has endeavored to bring on the inhabitants of our frontiers the merciless Indian savages, whose known rule of warfare is an undistinguished destruction of all ages, sexes, and conditions.

In every stage of these oppressions we have petitioned for redress in the most humble terms; our repeated petitions have been answered only by repeated injury. A prince, whose character is thus marked by every act which may define a tyrant, is unfit to be the ruler of a free people.

Nor have we been wanting in our attentions to our British brethren. We have warned them, from time to time, of attempts by their legislature to extend an unwarrantable jurisdiction over us. We have reminded them of the circumstances of our emigration and settlement here. We have appealed to their native justice and magnanimity; and we have conjured them, by the ties of our common kindred, to disavow these usurpations, which would inevitably interrupt our connections and correspondence. They, too, have been deaf to the voice of justice and of consanguinity. We must, therefore, acquiesce in the necessity which denounces our separation, and hold them, as we hold the rest of mankind, enemies in war, in peace friends.

We, therefore, the representatives of the United States of America, in General Congress assembled, appealing to the Supreme Judge of the world for the rectitude of our intentions, do, in the name and by the authority of the good people of these colonies, solemnly publish and declare, that these United Colonies are, and of right ought to be, FREE AND INDEPENDENT STATES; that they are absolved from all allegiance to the British crown, and that all political connection between them and the state of Great Britain is, and ought to be, totally dissolved; and that, as free and independent states, they have full power to levy war, conclude peace, contract alliances, establish commerce, and do all other acts and things which independent states may of right do. And for the support of this declaration, with a firm reliance on the protection of Divine Providence, we mutually pledge to each other our lives, our fortunes, and our sacred honor.

JOHN HANCOCK
and fifty-five others

Constitution of the United States of America, Amendments, and Proposed Amendments

PREAMBLE

We the people of the United States, in order to form a more perfect union, establish justice, insure domestic tranquillity, provide for the common defense, promote the general welfare, and secure the blessings of liberty to ourselves and our posterity, do ordain and establish this Constitution for the United States of America.

ARTICLE I

Section 1 All legislative powers herein granted shall be vested in a Congress of the United States, which shall consist of a Senate and a House of Representatives.

Section 2 The House of Representatives shall be composed of members chosen every second year by the people of the several States, and the electors in each State shall have the qualifications requisite for electors of the most numerous branch of the State Legislature.

No person shall be a Representative who shall not have attained to the age of twenty-five years, and been seven years a citizen of the United States, and who shall not, when elected, be an inhabitant of that State in which he shall be chosen.

Passages no longer in effect are printed in italic type.

Representatives and direct taxes shall be apportioned among the several States which may be included within this Union, according to their respective numbers, *which shall be determined by adding to the whole number of free persons, including those bound to service for a term of years and excluding Indians not taxed, three-fifths of all other persons.* The actual enumeration shall be made within three years after the first meeting of the Congress of the United States, and within every subsequent term of ten years, in such manner as they shall by law direct. The number of Representatives shall not exceed one for every thirty thousand, but each State shall have at least one Representative; *and until such enumeration shall be made, the State of New Hampshire shall be entitled to choose three, Massachusetts eight, Rhode Island and Providence Plantations one, Connecticut five, New York six, New Jersey four, Pennsylvania eight, Delaware one, Maryland six, Virginia ten, North Carolina five, South Carolina five, and Georgia three.*

When vacancies happen in the representation from any State, the Executive authority thereof shall issue writs of election to fill such vacancies.

The House of Representatives shall choose their Speaker and other officers; and shall have the sole power of impeachment.

Section 3 The Senate of the United States shall be composed of two Senators from each State, *chosen by the legislature thereof,* for six years; and each Senator shall have one vote.

Immediately after they shall be assembled in consequence of the first election, they shall be divided as equally as may be into three classes. The seats of the Senators of the first class shall be vacated at the expiration of the second year, of the second class at the expiration of the fourth year, and of the third class at the expiration of the sixth year, so that one-third may be chosen every second year; *and if vacancies happen by resignation or otherwise, during the recess of the legislature of any State, the Executive thereof may make temporary appointments until the next meeting of the legislature, which shall then fill such vacancies.*

No person shall be a Senator who shall not have attained to the age of thirty years, and been nine years a citizen of the United States, and who shall not, when elected, be an inhabitant of that State for which he shall be chosen.

The Vice-President of the United States shall be President of the Senate, but shall have no vote, unless they be equally divided.

The Senate shall choose their other officers, and also a President *pro tempore,* in the absence of the Vice-President, or when he shall exercise the office of President of the United States.

The Senate shall have the sole power to try all impeachments. When sitting for that purpose, they shall be on oath or affirmation. When the President of the United States is tried, the Chief Justice shall preside: and no person shall be convicted without the concurrence of two-thirds of the members present.

Judgment in cases of impeachment shall not extend further than to removal from the office, and disqualification to hold and enjoy any office of honor, trust or profit under the United States: but the party convicted shall nevertheless be liable and subject to indictment, trial, judgment and punishment, according to law.

Section 4 The times, places and manner of holding elections for Senators and Representatives shall be prescribed in each State by the legislature thereof; but the Congress may at any time by law make or alter such regulations, except as to the places of choosing Senators.

The Congress shall assemble at least once in every year, and such meeting *shall be on the first Monday in December, unless they shall by law appoint a different day.*

Section 5 Each house shall be the judge of the elections, returns and qualifications of its own members, and a majority of each shall constitute a quorum to do business; but a smaller number may adjourn from day to day, and may be authorized to compel the attendance of absent members, in such manner, and under such penalties, as each house may provide.

Each house may determine the rules of its proceedings, punish its members for disorderly behavior, and with the concurrence of two-thirds, expel a member.

Each house shall keep a journal of its proceedings, and from time to time publish the same, excepting such parts as may in their judgment require secrecy; and the yeas and nays of the members of either house on any question shall, at the desire of one-fifth of those present, be entered on the journal.

Neither house, during the session of Congress, shall, without the consent of the other, adjourn for more than three days, nor to any other place than that in which the two houses shall be sitting.

Section 6 The Senators and Representatives shall receive a compensation for their services, to be ascertained by law and paid out of the treasury of the United States. They shall in all cases except treason, felony and breach of the peace, be privileged from arrest during their attendance at the session of their respective houses, and in going to and returning from the same; and for any speech or debate in either house, they shall not be questioned in any other place.

No Senator or Representative shall, during the time for which he was elected, be appointed to any civil office under the authority of the United States, which shall have been created, or the emoluments whereof shall have been increased, during such time; and no person holding any office under the United States shall be a member of either house during his continuance in office.

Section 7 All bills for raising revenue shall originate in the House of Representatives; but the Senate may propose or concur with amendments as on other bills.

Every bill which shall have passed the House of Representatives and the Senate, shall, before it become a law, be presented to the President of the United States; if he approve he shall sign it, but if not he shall return it with objections to that house in which it originated, who shall enter the objections at large on their journal, and proceed to reconsider it. If after such reconsideration two-thirds of that house shall agree to pass the bill, it shall be sent, together with the objections, to the other house, by which it shall likewise be reconsidered, and, if approved by two-thirds of that house, it shall become a law. But in all such cases the votes of both houses shall be determined by yeas and nays, and the names of the persons voting for and against the bill shall be entered on the journal of each house respectively. If any bill shall not be returned by the President within ten days (Sundays excepted) after it shall have been presented to him, the same shall be a law, in like manner as if he had signed it, unless the Congress by their adjournment prevent its return, in which case it shall not be a law.

Every order, resolution, or vote to which the concurrence of the Senate and House of Representatives may be necessary (except on a question of adjournment) shall be presented to the President of the United States; and before the same shall take effect, shall be approved by him, or being disapproved by him, shall be repassed by two-thirds of the Senate and House of Representatives, according to the rules and limitations prescribed in the case of a bill.

Section 8 The Congress shall have power

To lay and collect taxes, duties, imposts, and excises, to pay the debts and provide for the common defense and general welfare of the United States; but all duties, imposts and excises shall be uniform throughout the United States;

To borrow money on the credit of the United States;

To regulate commerce with foreign nations, and among the several States, and with the Indian tribes;

To establish an uniform rule of naturalization, and uniform laws on the subject of bankruptcies throughout the United States;

To coin money, regulate the value thereof, and of foreign coin, and fix the standard of weights and measures;

To provide for the punishment of counterfeiting the securities and current coin of the United States;

To establish post offices and post roads;

To promote the progress of science and useful arts by securing for limited times to authors and inventors the exclusive right to their respective writings and discoveries;

To constitute tribunals inferior to the Supreme Court;

To define and punish piracies and felonies committed on the high seas and offenses against the law of nations;

To declare war, grant letters of marque and reprisal, and make rules concerning captures on land and water;

To raise and support armies, but no appropriation of money to that use shall be for a longer term than two years;

To provide and maintain a navy;

To make rules for the government and regulation of the land and naval forces;

To provide for calling forth the militia to execute the laws of the Union, suppress insurrections, and repel invasions;

To provide for organizing, arming, and disciplining the militia, and for governing such part of them as may be employed in the service of the United States, reserving to the States respectively the appointment of the officers, and the authority of training the militia according to the discipline prescribed by Congress;

To exercise exclusive legislation in all cases whatsoever, over such district (not exceeding ten miles square) as may, by cession of particular States, and the acceptance of Congress, become the seat of government of the United States, and to exercise like authority over all places purchased by the consent of the legislature of the State, in which the same shall be, for erection of forts, magazines, arsenals, dock-yards, and other needful buildings;—and

To make all laws which shall be necessary and proper for carrying into execution the foregoing powers, and all other powers vested by this Constitution in the government of the United States, or in any department or officer thereof.

Section 9 *The migration or importation of such persons as any of the States now existing shall think proper to admit shall not be prohibited by the Congress prior to the year 1808; but a tax or duty may be imposed on such importation, not exceeding $10 for each person.*

The privilege of the writ of habeas corpus shall not be suspended, unless when in cases of rebellion or invasion the public safety may require it.

No bill of attainder or ex post facto law shall be passed.

No capitation, or other direct, tax shall be laid, unless in proportion to the census or enumeration herein before directed to be taken.

No tax or duty shall be laid on articles exported from any State.

No preference shall be given by any regulation of commerce or revenue to the ports of one State over those of another; nor shall vessels bound to, or from, one State, be obliged to enter, clear, or pay duties in another.

No money shall be drawn from the treasury, but in consequence of appropriations made by law; and a regular statement and account of the receipts and expenditures of all public money shall be published from time to time.

No title of nobility shall be granted by the United States: and no person holding any office of profit or trust under them, shall, without the consent of the Congress, accept of any present, emolument, office, or title, of any kind whatever, from any king, prince, or foreign state.

Section 10   No State shall enter into any treaty, alliance, or confederation; grant letters of marque and reprisal; coin money; emit bills of credit; make anything but gold and silver coin a tender in payment of debts; pass any bill of attainder, ex post facto law, or law impairing the obligation of contracts, or grant any title of nobility.

No State shall, without the consent of Congress, lay any imposts or duties on imports or exports, except what may be absolutely necessary for executing its inspection laws: and the net produce of all duties and imposts, laid by any State on imports or exports, shall be for the use of the treasury of the United States; and all such laws shall be subject to the revision and control of the Congress.

No State shall, without the consent of Congress, lay any duty of tonnage, keep troops or ships of war in time of peace, enter into any agreement or compact with another State, or with a foreign power, or engage in war, unless actually invaded, or in such imminent danger as will not admit of delay.

ARTICLE II

Section 1   The executive power shall be vested in a President of the United States of America. He shall hold his office during the term of four years, and, together with the Vice-President, chosen for the same term, be elected as follows:

Each State shall appoint, in such manner as the legislature thereof may direct, a number of electors, equal to the whole number of Senators and Representatives to which the State may be entitled in the Congress; but no Senator or Representative, or person holding an office of trust or profit under the United States, shall be appointed an elector.

The electors shall meet in their respective States, and vote by ballot for two persons, of whom one at least shall not be an inhabitant of the same State with themselves. And they shall make a list of all the persons voted for, and of the number of votes for each; which list they shall sign and certify, and transmit sealed to the seat of government of the United States, directed to the President of the Senate. The President of the Senate shall, in the presence of the Senate and House of Representatives, open all the certificates, and the votes shall then be counted. The person having the greatest number of votes shall be the President, if such number be a majority of the whole number of electors appointed; and if there be more than one who have such majority, and have an equal number of votes, then the House of Representatives shall immediately choose by ballot one of them for President; and if no person have a majority, then from the five highest on the list said house shall in like manner choose the President. But in choosing the President the votes shall be taken by States, the representation from each State having one vote; a quorum for this purpose shall consist of a member or members from two-thirds of the States, and a majority of all the States shall be necessary to a choice. In every case, after the choice of the President, the person having the greatest number of votes of the electors shall be the Vice-President. But if there should remain two or more who have equal votes, the Senate shall choose from them by ballot the Vice-President.

The Congress may determine the time of choosing the electors and the day on which they shall give their votes; which day shall be the same throughout the United States.

No person except a natural-born citizen, *or a citizen of the United States at the time of the adoption of this Constitution,* shall be eligible to the office of President; neither shall any person be eligible to that office who shall not have attained to the age of thirty-five years, and been fourteen years a resident within the United States.

In case of the removal of the President from office or of his death, resignation, or inability to discharge the powers and duties of the said office, the same shall devolve on the Vice-President, and the Congress may by law provide for the case of removal, death, resignation, or inability, both of the President and Vice-President, declaring what officer shall then act as President, and such officer shall act accordingly, until the disability be removed, or a President shall be elected.

The President shall, at stated times, receive for his services a compensation, which shall neither be increased nor diminished during the period for which he shall have been elected, and he shall not receive within that period any other emolument from the United States, or any of them.

Before he enter on the execution of his office, he shall take the following oath or affirmation:—"I do solemnly swear (or affirm) that I will faithfully execute the office of the President of the United States, and will to the best of my ability preserve, protect and defend the Constitution of the United States."

Section 2 The President shall be commander in chief of the army and navy of the United States, and of the militia of the several States, when called into the actual service of the United States; he may require the opinion, in writing, of the principal officer in each of the executive departments, upon any subject relating to the duties of their respective offices, and he shall have power to grant reprieves and pardons for offenses against the United States, except in cases of impeachment.

He shall have power, by and with the advice and consent of the Senate, to make treaties, provided two-thirds of the Senators present concur; and he shall nominate, and by and with the advice and consent of the Senate, shall appoint ambassadors, other public ministers and consuls, judges of the Supreme Court, and all other officers of the United States, whose appointments are not herein otherwise provided for, and which shall be established by law: but Congress may by law vest the appointment of such inferior officers, as they think proper, in the President alone, in the courts of law, or in the heads of departments.

The President shall have power to fill up all vacancies that may happen during the recess of the Senate, by granting commissions which shall expire at the end of their next session.

Section 3 He shall from time to time give to the Congress information of the state of the Union, and recommend to their consideration such measures as he shall judge necessary and expedient; he may, on extraordinary occasions, convene both houses, or either of them, and in case of disagreement between them, with respect to the time of adjournment, he may adjourn them to such time as he shall think proper; he shall receive ambassadors and other public ministers; he shall take care that the laws be faithfully executed, and shall commission all the officers of the United States.

Section 4 The President, Vice-President and all civil officers of the United States shall be removed from office on impeachment for, and on conviction of, treason, bribery, or other high crimes and misdemeanors.

ARTICLE III

Section 1 The judicial power of the United States shall be vested in one Supreme Court, and in such inferior courts as the Congress may from time to time ordain and establish. The judges, both of the Supreme and inferior courts, shall hold their offices during good behavior, and shall, at stated times, receive for their services a compensation which shall not be diminished during their continuance in office.

Section 2 The judicial power shall extend to all cases, in law and equity, arising under this Constitution, the laws of the United States, and treaties made, or which shall be made, under their authority;—to all cases affecting ambassadors, other public ministers and consuls;—to all cases of admiralty and maritime jurisdiction;—to controversies to which the United States shall be a party;—to controversies between two or more States;—*between a State and citizens of another State;*—between citizens of different States;—between citizens of the same State claiming lands under grants of different States, and between a State, or the citizens thereof, and foreign states, citizens or subjects.

In all cases affecting ambassadors, other public ministers and consuls, and those in which a State shall be party, the Supreme Court shall have original jurisdiction. In all the other cases before mentioned, the Supreme Court shall have appellate jurisdiction, both as to law and fact, with such exceptions, and under such regulations, as the Congress shall make.

The trial of all crimes, except in cases of impeachment, shall be by jury; and such trial shall be held in the State where said crimes shall have been committed; but when not committed within any State, the trial shall be at such place or places as the Congress may by law have directed.

Section 3 Treason against the United States shall consist only in levying war against them, or in adhering to their enemies, giving them aid and comfort. No person shall be convicted of treason unless on the testimony of two witnesses to the same overt act, or on confession in open court.

The Congress shall have power to declare the punishment of treason, but no attainder of treason shall work corruption of blood, or forfeiture except during the life of the person attainted.

ARTICLE IV

Section 1 Full faith and credit shall be given in each State to the public acts, records, and judicial proceedings of every other State. And the Congress may by general laws prescribe the manner in which such acts, records, and proceedings shall be proved, and the effect thereof.

Section 2 The citizens of each State shall be entitled to all privileges and immunities of citizens in the several States.

A person charged in any State with treason, felony, or other crime, who shall flee from justice, and be found in another State, shall on demand of the executive authority of the State from which he fled, be delivered up, to be removed to the State having jurisdiction of the crime.

No person held to service or labor in one State, under the laws thereof, escaping into another, shall, in consequence of any law or regulation therein, be discharged from such service or labor, but shall be delivered up on claim of the party to whom such service or labor may be due.

Section 3   New States may be admitted by the Congress into this Union; but no new State shall be formed or erected within the jurisdiction of any other State; nor any State be formed by the junction of two or more States, or parts of States, without the consent of the legislatures of the States concerned as well as of the Congress.

The Congress shall have power to dispose of and make all needful rules and regulations respecting the territory or other property belonging to the United States; and nothing in this Constitution shall be so construed as to prejudice any claims of the United States, or of any particular State.

Section 4   The United States shall guarantee to every State in this Union a republican form of government, and shall protect each of them against invasion; and on application of the legislature, or of the executive (when the legislature cannot be convened), against domestic violence.

ARTICLE V

The Congress, whenever two-thirds of both houses shall deem it necessary, shall propose amendments to this Constitution, or, on the application of the legislatures of two-thirds of the several States, shall call a convention for proposing amendments, which, in either case, shall be valid to all intents and purposes, as part of this Constitution, when ratified by the legislatures of three-fourths of the several States, or by conventions in three-fourths thereof, as the one or the other mode of ratification may be proposed by the Congress; provided *that no amendments which may be made prior to the year one thousand eight hundred and eight shall in any manner affect the first and fourth clauses in the ninth section of the first article;* and that no State, without its consent, shall be deprived of its equal suffrage in the Senate.

ARTICLE VI

All debts contracted and engagements entered into, before the adoption of this Constitution, shall be as valid against the United States under this Constitution, as under the Confederation.

This Constitution, and the laws of the United States which shall be made in pursuance thereof; and all treaties made, or which shall be made, under the authority of the United States, shall be the supreme law of the land; and the judges in every State shall be bound thereby, anything in the Constitution or laws of any State to the contrary notwithstanding.

The Senators and Representatives before mentioned,

and the members of the several State legislatures, and all executive and judicial officers, both of the United States and of the several States, shall be bound by oath or affirmation to support this Constitution; but no religious test shall ever be required as a qualification to any office or public trust under the United States.

ARTICLE VII

The ratification of the conventions of nine States shall be sufficient for the establishment of this Constitution between the States so ratifying the same.

Done in Convention by the unanimous consent of the States present, the seventeenth day of September in the year of our Lord one thousand seven hundred and eighty-seven and of the Independence of the United States of America the twelfth. In witness whereof we have hereunto subscribed our names.

GEORGE WASHINGTON
and thirty-seven others

*Amendments to the Constitution**

AMENDMENT I

Congress shall make no law respecting an establishment of religion, or prohibiting the free exercise thereof; or abridging the freedom of speech, or of the press; or the right of the people peaceably to assemble, and to petition the government for a redress of grievances.

AMENDMENT II

A well-regulated militia being necessary to the security of a free State, the right of the people to keep and bear arms shall not be infringed.

AMENDMENT III

No soldier shall, in time of peace, be quartered in any house without the consent of the owner, nor in time of war, but in a manner to be prescribed by law.

AMENDMENT IV

The right of the people to be secure in their persons, houses, papers, and effects, against unreasonable searches and seizures, shall not be violated, and no warrants shall issue but upon probable cause, supported by oath or affirmation, and particularly describing the place to be searched, and the persons or things to be seized.

*The first ten Amendments (the Bill of Rights) were adopted in 1791.

AMENDMENT V

No person shall be held to answer for a capital, or otherwise infamous crime, unless on a presentment or indictment of a grand jury, except in cases arising in the land or naval forces, or in the militia, when in actual service in time of war or public danger; nor shall any person be subject for the same offense to be twice put in jeopardy of life or limb; nor shall be compelled in any criminal case to be a witness against himself, nor be deprived of life, liberty, or property, without due process of law; nor shall private property be taken for public use without just compensation.

AMENDMENT VI

In all criminal prosecutions, the accused shall enjoy the right to a speedy and public trial, by an impartial jury of the State and district wherein the crime shall have been committed, which district shall have been previously ascertained by law, and to be informed of the nature and cause of the accusation; to be confronted with the witnesses against him; to have compulsory process for obtaining witnesses in his favor, and to have the assistance of counsel for his defense.

AMENDMENT VII

In suits at common law, where the value in controversy shall exceed twenty dollars, the right of trial by jury shall be preserved, and no fact tried by a jury shall be otherwise reexamined in any court of the United States, than according to the rules of the common law.

AMENDMENT VIII

Excessive bail shall not be required, nor excessive fines imposed, nor cruel and unusual punishments inflicted.

AMENDMENT IX

The enumeration in the Constitution, of certain rights, shall not be construed to deny or disparage others retained by the people.

AMENDMENT X

The powers not delegated to the United States by the Constitution, nor prohibited by it to the States, are reserved to the States respectively, or to the people.

AMENDMENT XI
[Adopted 1798]

The judicial power of the United States shall not be construed to extend to any suit in law or equity, commenced or prosecuted against one of the United States by citizens of another State, or by citizens or subjects of any foreign state.

AMENDMENT XII
[Adopted 1804]

The electors shall meet in their respective States, and vote by ballot for President and Vice-President, one of whom, at least, shall not be an inhabitant of the same State with themselves; they shall name in their ballots the person voted for as President, and in distinct ballots the person voted for as Vice-President, and they shall make distinct lists of all persons voted for as President, and of all persons voted for as Vice-President, and of the number of votes for each, which lists they shall sign and certify, and transmit sealed to the seat of government of the United States, directed to the President of the Senate;—the President of the Senate shall, in the presence of the Senate and House of Representatives, open all the certificates and the votes shall then be counted;—the person having the greatest number of votes for President shall be the President, if such number be a majority of the whole number of electors appointed; and if no person have such majority, then from the persons having the highest numbers not exceeding three on the list of those voted for as President, the House of Representatives shall choose immediately, by ballot, the President. But in choosing the President, the votes shall be taken by States, the representation from each State having one vote; a quorum for this purpose shall consist of a member or members from two-thirds of the States, and a majority of all the States shall be necessary to a choice. And if the House of Representatives shall not choose a President whenever the right of choice shall devolve upon them, before *the fourth day of March* next following, then the Vice-President shall act as President, as in the case of the death or other constitutional disability of the President.

The person having the greatest number of votes as Vice-President shall be the Vice-President, if such number be a majority of the whole number of electors appointed; and if no person have a majority, then from the two highest numbers on the list the Senate shall choose the Vice-President; a quorum for the purpose shall consist of two-thirds of the whole number of Senators, and a majority of the whole number shall be necessary to a choice. But no person constitutionally ineligible to the office of President shall be eligible to that of Vice-President of the United States.

AMENDMENT XIII
[Adopted 1865]

Section 1 Neither slavery nor involuntary servitude, except as a punishment for crime whereof the party shall have been duly convicted, shall exist within the United States, or any place subject to their jurisdiction.

Section 2 Congress shall have power to enforce this article by appropriate legislation.

AMENDMENT XIV
[Adopted 1868]

Section 1 All persons born or naturalized in the United States, and subject to the jurisdiction thereof, are citizens of the United States and of the State wherein they reside. No State shall make or enforce any law which shall abridge the privileges or immunities of citizens of the United States; nor shall any State deprive any person of life, liberty, or property, without due process of law; nor deny to any person within its jurisdiction the equal protection of the laws.

Section 2 Representatives shall be apportioned among the several States according to their respective numbers, counting the whole number of persons in each State, excluding Indians not taxed. But when the right to vote at any election for the choice of Electors for President and Vice-President of the United States, Representatives in Congress, the executive and judicial officers of a State, or the members of the legislature thereof, is denied to any of the male inhabitants of such State, being twenty-one years of age and citizens of the United States, or in any way abridged, except for participation in rebellion, or other crime, the basis of representation therein shall be reduced in the proportion which the number of such male citizens shall bear to the whole number of male citizens twenty-one years of age in such State.

Section 3 No person shall be a Senator or Representative in Congress, or Elector of President and Vice-President, or hold any office, civil or military, under the United States, or under any State, who, having previously taken an oath, as a member of Congress, or as an officer of the United States, or as a member of any State legislature, or as an executive or judicial officer of any State, to support the Constitution of the United States, shall have engaged in insurrection or rebellion against the same, or given aid or comfort to the enemies thereof. Congress may, by a vote of two-thirds of each house, remove such disability.

Section 4 The validity of the public debt of the United States, authorized by law, including debts incurred for payment of pensions and bounties for services in suppressing insurrection or rebellion, shall not be questioned. But neither the United States nor any State shall assume or pay any debt or obligation incurred in aid of insurrection or rebellion against the United States, or any claim for the loss of emancipation of any slave; but all such debts, obligations, and claims shall be held illegal and void.

Section 5 The Congress shall have power to enforce, by appropriate legislation, the provisions of this article.

AMENDMENT XV
[Adopted 1870]

Section 1 The right of citizens of the United States to vote shall not be denied or abridged by the United States or by any State on account of race, color, or previous condition of servitude.

Section 2 The Congress shall have power to enforce this article by appropriate legislation.

AMENDMENT XVI
[Adopted 1913]

The Congress shall have power to lay and collect taxes on incomes, from whatever source derived, without apportionment among the several States, and without regard to any census or enumeration.

AMENDMENT XVII
[Adopted 1913]

Section 1 The Senate of the United States shall be composed of two Senators from each State, elected by the people thereof, for six years; and each Senator shall have one vote. The electors in each State shall have the qualifications requisite for electors of [voters for] the most numerous branch of the State legislatures.

Section 2 When vacancies happen in the representation of any State in the Senate, the executive authority of such State shall issue writs of election to fill such vacancies: Provided, that the Legislature of any State may empower the executive thereof to make temporary appointments until the people fill the vacancies by election as the Legislature may direct.

Section 3 This amendment shall not be so construed as to affect the election or term of any Senator chosen before it becomes valid as part of the Constitution.

AMENDMENT XVIII
[Adopted 1919; Repealed 1933]

Section 1   After one year from the ratification of this article the manufacture, sale, or transportation of intoxicating liquors within, the importation thereof into, or the exportation thereof from the United States and all territory subject to the jurisdiction thereof, for beverage purposes, is hereby prohibited.

Section 2   The Congress and the several States shall have concurrent power to enforce this article by appropriate legislation.

Section 3   This article shall be inoperative unless it shall have been ratified as an amendment to the Constitution by the legislatures of the several States, as provided by the Constitution, within seven years from the date of the submission thereof to the States by the Congress.

AMENDMENT XIX
[Adopted 1920]

Section 1   The right of citizens of the United States to vote shall not be denied or abridged by the United States or by any State on account of sex.

Section 2   The Congress shall have power to enforce this article by appropriate legislation.

AMENDMENT XX
[Adopted 1933]

Section 1   The terms of the President and Vice-President shall end at noon on the 20th day of January, and the terms of Senators and Representatives at noon on the 3d day of January, of the years in which such terms would have ended if this article had not been ratified; and the terms of their successors shall then begin.

Section 2   The Congress shall assemble at least once in every year, and such meeting shall begin at noon on the 3d day of January, unless they shall by law appoint a different day.

Section 3   If, at the time fixed for the beginning of the term of the President, the President-elect shall have died, the Vice-President-elect shall become President. If a President shall not have been chosen before the time fixed for the beginning of his term, or if the President-elect shall have failed to qualify, then the Vice-President-elect shall act as President until a President shall have qualified; and the Congress may by law provide for the case wherein neither a President-elect nor a Vice-President-elect shall have qualified, declaring who shall then act as President, or the manner in which one who is to act shall be selected, and such persons shall act accordingly until a President or Vice-President shall have qualified.

Section 4   The Congress may by law provide for the case of the death of any of the persons from whom the House of Representatives may choose a President whenever the right of choice shall have devolved upon them, and for the case of the death of any of the persons from whom the Senate may choose a Vice-President whenever the right of choice shall have devolved upon them.

Section 5   Sections 1 and 2 shall take effect on the 15th day of October following the ratification of this article.

Section 6   This article shall be inoperative unless it shall have been ratified as an amendment to the Constitution by the Legislatures of three-fourths of the several States within seven years from the date of its submission.

AMENDMENT XXI
[Adopted 1933]

Section 1   The eighteenth article of amendment to the Constitution of the United States is hereby repealed.

Section 2   The transportation or importation into any State, Territory, or Possession of the United States for delivery or use therein of intoxicating liquors, in violation of the laws thereof, is hereby prohibited.

Section 3   This article shall be inoperative unless it shall have been ratified as an amendment to the Constitution by conventions in the several States, as provided in the Constitution, within seven years from the date of submission thereof to the States by the Congress.

AMENDMENT XXII
[Adopted 1951]

Section 1   No person shall be elected to the office of President more than twice, and no person who has held the office of President, or acted as President, for more than two years of a term to which some other person was elected President shall be elected to the office of President more than once. But this article shall not apply to any person holding the office of President when this article was proposed by the Congress, and shall not prevent any person who may be holding the office of President, or acting as President, during the term within which this article becomes operative from holding the office of President or acting as President during the remainder of such term.

Section 2   This article shall be inoperative unless it shall have been ratified as an amendment to the Constitution by the legislatures of three-fourths of the several States within seven years from the date of its submission to the States by the Congress.

AMENDMENT XXIII
[Adopted 1961]

Section 1 The District constituting the seat of Government of the United States shall appoint in such manner as the Congress may direct:

A number of electors of President and Vice-President equal to the whole number of Senators and Representatives in Congress to which the District would be entitled if it were a State, but in no event more than the least populous State; they shall be in addition to those appointed by the States, but they shall be considered for the purposes of the election of President and Vice-President, to be electors appointed by a State; and they shall meet in the District and perform such duties as provided by the twelfth article of amendment.

Section 2 The Congress shall have the power to enforce this article by appropriate legislation.

AMENDMENT XXIV
[Adopted 1964]

Section 1 The right of citizens of the United States to vote in any primary or other election for President or Vice-President, for electors for President or Vice-President, or for Senator or Representative in Congress, shall not be denied or abridged by the United States or any State by reason of failure to pay any poll tax or other tax.

Section 2 The Congress shall have the power to enforce this article by appropriate legislation.

AMENDMENT XXV
[Adopted 1967]

Section 1 In case of the removal of the President from office or of his death or resignation, the Vice President shall become President.

Section 2 Whenever there is a vacancy in the office of the Vice President, the President shall nominate a Vice President who shall take office upon confirmation by a majority vote of both Houses of Congress.

Section 3 Whenever the President transmits to the President pro tempore of the Senate and the Speaker of the House of Representatives his written declaration that he is unable to discharge the powers and duties of his office, and until he transmits to them a written declaration to the contrary, such powers and duties shall be discharged by the Vice President as Acting President.

Section 4 Whenever the Vice President and a majority of either the principal officers of the executive departments or of such other body as Congress may by law provide, transmit to the President pro tempore of the Senate and the Speaker of the House of Representatives their written declaration that the President is unable to discharge the powers and duties of his office, the Vice President shall immediately assume the powers and duties of the office as Acting President.

Thereafter, when the President transmits to the President pro tempore of the Senate and the Speaker of the House of Representatives his written declaration that no inability exists, he shall resume the powers and duties of his office unless the Vice President and a majority of either the principal officers of the executive department[s] or of such other body as Congress may by law provide, transmit within four days to the President pro tempore of the Senate and the Speaker of the House of Representatives their written declaration that the President is unable to discharge the powers and duties of his office. Thereupon Congress shall decide the issue, assembling within forty-eight hours for that purpose if not in session. If the Congress, within twenty-one days after receipt of the latter written declaration, or, if Congress is not in session, within twenty-one days after Congress is required to assemble, determines by two-thirds vote of both Houses that the President is unable to discharge the powers and duties of his office, the Vice President shall continue to discharge the same as Acting President; otherwise, the President shall resume the powers and duties of his office.

AMENDMENT XXVI
[Adopted 1971]

Section 1 The right of citizens of the United States, who are eighteen years of age or older, to vote shall not be denied or abridged by the United States or by any State on account of age.

Section 2 The Congress shall have power to enforce this article by appropriate legislation.

PROPOSED AMENDMENT
[Sent to the states, 1972]

Section 1 Equality of rights under the law shall not be denied or abridged by the United States or by any State on account of sex.

Section 2 The Congress shall have the power to enforce, by appropriate legislation, the provisions of this article.

Section 3 This amendment shall take effect two years after the date of ratification.

PROPOSED AMENDMENT

[Sent to the states, 1978]

Section 1   For purposes of representation in the Congress, election of the President and Vice President, and article V of this Constitution, the District constituting the seat of government of the United States shall be treated as though it were a State.

Section 2   The exercise of the rights and powers conferred under this article shall be by the people of the District constituting the seat of government, and as shall be provided by the Congress.

Section 3   The twenty-third article of amendment to the Constitution of the United States is hereby repealed.

Section 4   This article shall be inoperative, unless it shall have been ratified as an amendment to the Constitution by the legislatures of three-fourths of the several States within seven years from the date of its submission.

The American people: A statistical profile

Population of the United States

YEAR	NUMBER OF STATES	POPULATION	PERCENT INCREASE	POPULATION PER SQUARE MILE	PERCENT URBAN/ RURAL	PERCENT MALE/ FEMALE	PERCENT WHITE/ NONWHITE
1790	13	3,929,214		4.5	5.1/94.9	NA/NA	80.7/19.3
1800	16	5,308,483	35.1	6.1	6.1/93.9	NA/NA	81.1/18.9
1810	17	7,239,881	36.4	4.3	7.3/92.7	NA/NA	81.0/19.0
1820	23	9,638,453	33.1	5.5	7.2/92.8	50.8/49.2	81.6/18.4
1830	24	12,866,020	33.5	7.4	8.8/91.2	50.8/49.2	81.9/18.1
1840	26	17,069,453	32.7	9.8	10.8/89.2	50.9/49.1	83.2/16.8
1850	31	23,191,876	35.9	7.9	15.3/84.7	51.0/49.0	84.3/15.7
1860	33	31,443,321	35.6	10.6	19.8/80.2	51.2/48.8	85.6/14.4
1870	37	39,818,449	26.6	13.4	25.7/74.3	50.6/49.4	86.2/13.8
1880	38	50,155,783	26.0	16.9	28.2/71.8	50.9/49.1	86.5/13.5
1890	44	62,947,714	25.5	21.2	35.1/64.9	51.2/48.8	87.5/12.5
1900	45	75,994,575	20.7	25.6	39.6/60.4	51.1/48.9	87.9/12.1
1910	46	91,972,266	21.0	31.0	45.6/54.4	51.5/48.5	88.9/11.1
1920	48	105,710,620	14.9	35.6	51.2/48.8	51.0/49.0	89.7/10.3
1930	48	122,775,046	16.1	41.2	56.1/43.9	50.6/49.4	89.8/10.2
1940	48	131,669,275	7.2	44.2	56.5/43.5	50.2/49.8	89.8/10.2
1950	48	150,697,361	14.5	50.7	64.0/36.0	49.7/50.3	89.5/10.5
1960	50	179,323,175	19.0	50.6	69.9/30.1	49.3/50.7	88.6/11.4
1970	50	203,235,298	13.3	57.5	73.5/26.5	48.7/51.3	87.6/12.4
1980	50	226,504,825	11.4	64.0	NA/NA	48.6/51.4	83.2/16.8

NA = Not available.
*1979 figures

IMMIGRATION TOTALS BY DECADE

YEARS	NUMBER	YEARS	NUMBER
1820	8,385	1901–1910	8,795,386
1821–1830	143,439	1911–1920	5,735,811
1831–1840	599,125	1921–1930	4,107,209
1841–1850	1,713,251	1931–1940	528,431
1851–1860	2,598,214	1941–1950	1,035,039
1861–1870	2,314,824	1951–1960	2,515,479
1871–1880	2,812,191	1961–1970	3,321,677
1881–1890	5,246,613	Total	45,162,638
1891–1900	3,687,546		

REGIONAL ORIGINS OF IMMIGRANTS (in percentages)

PERIOD	TOTAL EUROPE	NORTH AND WEST[a]	EAST AND CENTRAL[b]	SOUTH AND OTHER[c]	WESTERN HEMISPHERE	ASIA	ALL OTHER
1821–1830	69.2	67.1	–	2.1	8.4	–	22.4
1831–1840	82.8	81.8	–	1.0	5.5	–	11.7
1841–1850	93.3	92.9	0.1	0.3	3.6	–	3.1
1851–1860	94.4	93.6	0.1	0.8	2.9	1.6	1.1
1861–1870	89.2	87.8	0.5	0.9	7.2	2.8	0.8
1871–1880	80.8	73.6	4.5	2.7	14.4	4.4	0.4
1881–1890	90.3	72.0	11.9	6.3	8.1	1.3	0.3
1891–1900	96.5	44.5	32.8	19.1	1.1	1.9	0.5
1901–1910	92.5	21.7	44.5	26.3	4.1	2.8	0.6
1911–1920	76.3	17.4	33.4	25.5	19.9	3.4	0.4
1921–1930	60.3	31.7	14.4	14.3	36.9	2.4	0.4
1931–1940	65.9	38.8	11.0	16.1	30.3	2.8	0.9
1941–1950	60.1	47.5	4.6	7.9	34.3	3.1	2.5
1951–1960	52.8	17.7	24.3	10.8	39.6	6.0	1.6
1961–1970	34.0	11.7	9.4	12.9	51.7	12.7	1.7

[a] Great Britain, Ireland, Norway, Sweden, Denmark, Iceland, Netherlands, Belgium, Luxembourg, Switzerland, France.
[b] Germany (Austria included, 1938–1945), Poland, Czechoslovakia (since 1920), Yugoslavia (since 1920), Hungary (since 1861), Austria (since 1861, except 1938–1945), U.S.S.R. (excludes Asian U.S.S.R. between 1931 and 1963), Latvia, Estonia, Lithuania, Finland, Romania, Bulgaria, Turkey (in Europe).
[c] Italy, Spain, Portugal, Greece, and other European countries not classified elsewhere.

Source: Stephen Thernstrom, ed., *Harvard Encyclopedia of American Ethnic Groups* (1980), p. 480.

MAJOR SOURCES OF IMMIGRANTS BY COUNTRY (in thousands)

PERIOD	GERMANY	ITALY	GREAT BRITAIN	IRELAND	AUSTRIA-HUNGARY	RUSSIA	CANADA	DENMARK, NORWAY, SWEDEN	MEXICO	WEST INDIES
1821–1830	7	–	25	51	–	–	–	–	–	–
1831–1840	152	2	76	207	–	–	–	2	–	–
1841–1850	435	2	267	781	–	–	–	14	–	–
1851–1860	952	9	424	914	–	–	–	25	–	–
1861–1870	787	12	607	436	8	3	–	126	–	–
1871–1880	718	56	548	437	73	39	–	243	–	–
1881–1890	1,453	307	807	655	354	213	–	656	–	–
1891–1900	505	652	272	388	593	505	–	372	–	–
1901–1910	341	2,046	526	339	2,145	1,597	179	505	50	108
1911–1920	144	1,110	341	146	896	921	742	203	219	123
1921–1930	412	455	330	221	64	62	925	198	459	75
1931–1940	114	68	29	13	11	1	109	11	22	16
1941–1950	226	57	132	27	28	1	172	26	61	50
1951–1960	478	185	192	57	–	6	378	57	300	123
1961–1970	191	214	206	40	–	8	413	43	454	470
Total	6,915	5,175	4,782	4,712	4,172	3,356	2,918	2,481	1,565	965

Source: Stephen Thernstrom, ed., *Harvard Encyclopedia of American Ethnic Groups* (1980), p. 480.

The American Farm

YEAR	FARM POPULATION (IN THOUSANDS)	PERCENT OF TOTAL POPULATION	NUMBER OF FARMS (IN THOUSANDS)	TOTAL ACRES (IN THOUSANDS)	AVERAGE ACREAGE PER FARM
1850	NA	NA	1,449	293,561	203
1860	NA	NA	2,044	407,213	199
1870	NA	NA	2,660	407,735	153
1880	21,973	43.8	4,009	536,082	134
1890	24,771	42.3	4,565	623,219	137
1900	29,875	41.9	5,740	841,202	147
1910	32,077	34.9	6,366	881,431	139
1920	31,974	30.1	6,454	958,677	149
1930	30,529	24.9	6,295	990,112	157
1940	30,547	23.2	6,102	1,065,114	175
1950	23,048	15.3	5,388	1,161,420	216
1960	15,635	8.7	3,962	1,176,946	297
1970	9,712	4.8	2,949	1,102,769	374
1979	6,241	2.8	2,333	1,049,000	450

NA = Not available.

YEAR	TOTAL NUMBER OF WORKERS*	MALE WORKERS		FEMALE WORKERS		PERCENT OF CIVILIAN LABOR FORCE UNEMPLOYED	PERCENT OF WORKERS IN LABOR UNIONS*
		NUMBER*	PERCENT OF TOTAL WORKERS*	NUMBER*	PERCENT OF TOTAL WORKERS*		
1870	12,506,000	10,670,000	85	1,836,000	15	NA	NA
1880	17,392,000	14,745,000	85	2,647,000	15	NA	NA
1890	23,318,000	19,313,000	83	4,006,000	17	4 (1894 = 18%)	NA
1900	29,073,000	23,754,000	82	5,319,000	18	5	3
1910	38,167,000	30,092,000	79	8,076,000	21	6	6
1920	41,614,000	33,065,000	79	8,550,000	21	5 (1921 = 12%)	12
1930	48,830,000	38,078,000	78	10,752,000	22	9 (1933 = 25%)	7
1940	52,705,000	39,818,000	76	12,887,000	24	15 (1944 = 1%)	17
1950	58,646,000	42,126,000	72	16,520,000	28	5	22
1960	68,144,000	45,763,000	67	22,381,000	33	6	24
1970	82,715,000	51,195,000	62	31,520,000	38	5	23
1980	104,400,000	60,100,000	58	44,300,000	42	7	20[†]

*Figures for 1870–1930 are for all workers, civilian and military; figures for 1940–1980 are for civilian workers only.
[†]1978 figure.
NA = Not available.

Territorial Expansion of the United States

TERRITORY	DATE ACQUIRED	SQUARE MILES	HOW ACQUIRED
Original states and territories	1783	888,685	Treaty with Great Britain
Louisiana Purchase	1803	827,192	Purchase from France
Florida	1819	72,003	Treaty with Spain
Texas	1845	390,143	Annexation of independent nation
Oregon	1846	285,580	Treaty with Great Britain
Mexican Cession	1848	529,017	Conquest from Mexico
Gadsden Purchase	1853	29,640	Purchase from Mexico
Alaska	1867	589,757	Purchase from Russia
Hawaii	1898	6,450	Annexation of independent nation
The Philippines	1899	115,600	Conquest from Spain (granted independence in 1946)
Puerto Rico	1899	3,435	Conquest from Spain
Guam	1899	212	Conquest from Spain
American Samoa	1900	76	Treaty with Germany and Great Britain
Panama Canal Zone	1904	553	Treaty with Panama (returned to Panama by treaty in 1978)
Corn Islands	1914	4	Treaty with Nicaragua (returned to Nicaragua by treaty in 1971)
Virgin Islands	1917	133	Purchase from Denmark
Pacific Islands Trust (Micronesia)	1947	8,489	Trusteeship under United Nations (some granted independence)
All others (Midway, Wake, and other islands)		42	

YEAR	NUMBER OF STATES	CANDIDATES	PARTIES	POPULAR VOTE	% OF POPULAR VOTE	ELEC- TORAL VOTE	% VOTER PARTICI- PATION
1789	11	**GEORGE WASHINGTON**	No party			69	
		John Adams	designations			34	
		Other candidates				35	
1792	15	**GEORGE WASHINGTON**	No party			132	
		John Adams	designations			77	
		George Clinton				50	
		Other candidates				5	
1796	16	**JOHN ADAMS**	Federalist			71	
		Thomas Jefferson	Democratic-Republican			68	
		Thomas Pinckney	Federalist			59	
		Aaron Burr	Democratic-Republican			30	
		Other candidates				48	
1800	16	**THOMAS JEFFERSON**	Democratic-Republican			73	
		Aaron Burr	Democratic-Republican			73	
		John Adams	Federalist			65	
		Charles C. Pinckney	Federalist			64	
		John Jay	Federalist			1	
1804	17	**THOMAS JEFFERSON**	Democratic-Republican			162	
		Charles C. Pinckney	Federalist			14	
1808	17	**JAMES MADISON**	Democratic-Republican			122	
		Charles C. Pinckney	Federalist			47	
		George Clinton	Democratic-Republican			6	
1812	18	**JAMES MADISON**	Democratic-Republican			128	
		DeWitt Clinton	Federalist			89	
1816	19	**JAMES MONROE**	Democratic-Republican			183	
		Rufus King	Federalist			34	
1820	24	**JAMES MONROE**	Democratic-Republican			231	
		John Quincy Adams	Independent Republican			1	
1824	24	**JOHN QUINCY ADAMS**	Democratic-Republican	108,740	30.5	84	26.9
		Andrew Jackson	Democratic-Republican	153,544	43.1	99	
		Henry Clay	Democratic-Republican	47,136	13.2	37	
		William H. Crawford	Democratic-Republican	46,618	13.1	41	

YEAR	NUMBER OF STATES	CANDIDATES	PARTIES	POPULAR VOTE	% OF POPULAR VOTE	ELECTORAL VOTE	% VOTER PARTICIPATION
1828	24	**ANDREW JACKSON**	Democratic	647,286	56.0	178	57.6
		John Quincy Adams	National Republican	508,064	44.0	83	
1832	24	**ANDREW JACKSON**	Democratic	688,242	54.5	219	55.4
		Henry Clay	National Republican	473,462	37.5	49	
		William Wirt	Anti-Masonic	101,051	8.0	7	
		John Floyd	Democratic			11	
1836	26	**MARTIN VAN BUREN**	Democratic	765,483	50.9	170	57.8
		William H. Harrison	Whig			73	
		Hugh L. White	Whig	739,795	49.1	26	
		Daniel Webster	Whig			14	
		W. P. Mangum	Whig			11	
1840	26	**WILLIAM H. HARRISON**	Whig	1,274,624	53.1	234	80.2
		Martin Van Buren	Democratic	1,127,781	46.9	60	
1844	26	**JAMES K. POLK**	Democratic	1,338,464	49.6	170	78.9
		Henry Clay	Whig	1,300,097	48.1	105	
		James G. Birney	Liberty	62,300	2.3		
1848	30	**ZACHARY TAYLOR**	Whig	1,360,967	47.4	163	72.7
		Lewis Cass	Democratic	1,222,342	42.5	127	
		Martin Van Buren	Free Soil	291,263	10.1		
1852	31	**FRANKLIN PIERCE**	Democratic	1,601,117	50.9	254	69.6
		Winfield Scott	Whig	1,385,453	44.1	42	
		John P. Hale	Free Soil	155,825	5.0		
1856	31	**JAMES BUCHANAN**	Democratic	1,832,955	45.3	174	78.9
		John C. Frémont	Republican	1,339,932	33.1	114	
		Millard Fillmore	American	871,731	21.6	8	
1860	33	**ABRAHAM LINCOLN**	Republican	1,865,593	39.8	180	81.2
		Stephen A. Douglas	Democratic	1,382,713	29.5	12	
		John C. Breckinridge	Democratic	848,356	18.1	72	
		John Bell	Constitutional Union	592,906	12.6	39	
1864	36	**ABRAHAM LINCOLN**	Republican	2,206,938	55.0	212	73.8
		George B. McClellan	Democratic	1,803,787	45.0	21	
1868	37	**ULYSSES S. GRANT**	Republican	3,013,421	52.7	214	78.1
		Horatio Seymour	Democratic	2,706,829	47.3	80	
1872	37	**ULYSSES S. GRANT**	Republican	3,596,745	55.6	286	71.3
		Horace Greeley	Democratic	2,843,446	43.9	*	
1876	38	**RUTHERFORD B. HAYES**	Republican	4,036,572	48.0	185	81.8
		Samuel J. Tilden	Democratic	4,284,020	51.0	184	
1880	38	**JAMES A. GARFIELD**	Republican	4,453,295	48.5	214	79.4
		Winfield S. Hancock	Democratic	4,414,082	48.1	155	
		James B. Weaver	Greenback-Labor	308,578	3.4		

YEAR	NUMBER OF STATES	CANDIDATES	PARTIES	POPULAR VOTE	% OF POPULAR VOTE	ELEC- TORAL VOTE	% VOTER PARTICI- PATION
1884	38	GROVER CLEVELAND	Democratic	4,879,507	48.5	219	77.5
		James G. Blaine	Republican	4,850,293	48.2	182	
		Benjamin F. Butler	Greenback- Labor	175,370	1.8		
		John P. St. John	Prohibition	150,369	1.5		
1888	38	BENJAMIN HARRISON	Republican	5,477,129	47.9	233	79.3
		Grover Cleveland	Democratic	5,537,857	48.6	168	
		Clinton B. Fisk	Prohibition	249,506	2.2		
		Anson J. Streeter	Union Labor	146,935	1.3		
1892	44	GROVER CLEVELAND	Democratic	5,555,426	46.1	277	74.7
		Benjamin Harrison	Republican	5,182,690	43.0	145	
		James B. Weaver	People's	1,029,846	8.5	22	
		John Bidwell	Prohibition	264,133	2.2		
1896	45	WILLIAM McKINLEY	Republican	7,102,246	51.1	271	79.3
		William J. Bryan	Democratic	6,492,559	47.7	176	
1900	45	WILLIAM McKINLEY	Republican	7,218,491	51.7	292	73.2
		William J. Bryan	Democratic; Populist	6,356,734	45.5	155	
		John C. Wooley	Prohibition	208,914	1.5		
1904	45	THEODORE ROOSEVELT	Republican	7,628,461	57.4	336	65.2
		Alton B. Parker	Democratic	5,084,223	37.6	140	
		Eugene V. Debs	Socialist	402,283	3.0		
		Silas C. Swallow	Prohibition	258,536	1.9		
1908	46	WILLIAM H. TAFT	Republican	7,675,320	51.6	321	65.4
		William J. Bryan	Democratic	6,412,294	43.1	162	
		Eugene V. Debs	Socialist	420,793	2.8		
		Eugene W. Chafin	Prohibition	253,840	1.7		
1912	48	WOODROW WILSON	Democratic	6,296,547	41.9	435	58.8
		Theodore Roosevelt	Progressive	4,118,571	27.4	88	
		William H. Taft	Republican	3,486,720	23.2	8	
		Eugene V. Debs	Socialist	900,672	6.0		
		Eugene W. Chafin	Prohibition	206,275	1.4		
1916	48	WOODROW WILSON	Democratic	9,127,695	49.4	277	61.6
		Charles E. Hughes	Republican	8,533,507	46.2	254	
		A. L. Benson	Socialist	585,113	3.2		
		J. Frank Hanly	Prohibition	220,506	1.2		
1920	48	WARREN G. HARDING	Republican	16,143,407	60.4	404	49.2
		James M. Cox	Democratic	9,130,328	34.2	127	
		Eugene V. Debs	Socialist	919,799	3.4		
		P. P. Christensen	Farmer- Labor	265,411	1.0		
1924	48	CALVIN COOLIDGE	Republican	15,718,211	54.0	382	48.9
		John W. Davis	Democratic	8,385,283	28.8	136	
		Robert M. La Follette	Progressive	4,831,289	16.6	13	
1928	48	HERBERT C. HOOVER	Republican	21,391,993	58.2	444	56.9
		Alfred E. Smith	Democratic	15,016,169	40.9	87	
1932	48	FRANKLIN D. ROOSEVELT	Democratic	22,809,638	57.4	472	56.9
		Herbert C. Hoover	Republican	15,758,901	39.7	59	
		Norman Thomas	Socialist	881,951	2.2		

YEAR	NUMBER OF STATES	CANDIDATES	PARTIES	POPULAR VOTE	% OF POPULAR VOTE	ELEC-TORAL VOTE	% VOTER PARTICI-PATION
1936	48	FRANKLIN D. ROOSEVELT	Democratic	27,752,869	60.8	523	61.0
		Alfred M. Landon	Republican	16,674,665	36.5	8	
		William Lemke	Union	882,479	1.9		
1940	48	FRANKLIN D. ROOSEVELT	Democratic	27,307,819	54.8	449	62.5
		Wendell L. Wilkie	Republican	22,321,018	44.8	82	
1944	48	FRANKLIN D. ROOSEVELT	Democratic	25,606,585	53.5	432	55.9
		Thomas E. Dewey	Republican	22,014,745	46.0	99	
1948	48	HARRY S TRUMAN	Democratic	24,179,345	49.6	303	53.0
		Thomas E. Dewey	Republican	21,991,291	45.1	189	
		J. Strom Thurmond	States' Rights	1,176,125	2.4	39	
		Henry A. Wallace	Progressive	1,157,326	2.4		
1952	48	DWIGHT D. EISENHOWER	Republican	33,936,234	55.1	442	63.3
		Adlai E. Stevenson	Democratic	27,314,992	44.4	89	
1956	48	DWIGHT D. EISENHOWER	Republican	35,590,472	57.6	457	60.6
		Adlai E. Stevenson	Democratic	26,022,752	42.1	73	
1960	50	JOHN F. KENNEDY	Democratic	34,226,731	49.7	303	64.0
		Richard M. Nixon	Republican	34,108,157	49.5	219	
1964	50	LYNDON B. JOHNSON	Democratic	43,129,566	61.1	486	61.7
		Barry M. Goldwater	Republican	27,178,188	38.5	52	
1968	50	RICHARD M. NIXON	Republican	31,785,480	43.4	301	60.6
		Hubert H. Humphrey	Democratic	31,275,166	42.7	191	
		George C. Wallace	American Independent	9,906,473	13.5	46	
1972	50	RICHARD M. NIXON	Republican	47,169,911	60.7	520	55.5
		George S. McGovern	Democratic	29,170,383	37.5	17	
		John G. Schmitz	American	1,099,482	1.4		
1976	50	JIMMY CARTER	Democratic	40,830,763	50.1	297	54.3
		Gerald R. Ford	Republican	39,147,793	48.0	240	
1980	50	RONALD REAGAN	Republican	43,901,812	50.7	489	53.0
		Jimmy Carter	Democratic	35,483,820	41.0	49	
		John B. Anderson	Independent	5,719,722	6.6	0	
		Ed Clark	Libertarian	921,188	1.1	0	

Candidates receiving less than 1 percent of the popular vote have been omitted. Thus the percentage of popular vote given for any election year may not total 100 percent.

Before the passage of the Twelfth Amendment in 1804, the Electoral College voted for two presidential candidates; the runner-up became vice president.

Before 1824, most presidential electors were chosen by state legislatures, not by popular vote.

*Greeley died shortly after the election; the electors supporting him then divided their votes among minor candidates.

THE WASHINGTON ADMINISTRATION

President	George Washington	1789–1797
Vice President	John Adams	1789–1797
Secretary of State	Thomas Jefferson	1789–1793
	Edmund Randolph	1794–1795
	Timothy Pickering	1795–1797
Secretary of Treasury	Alexander Hamilton	1789–1795
	Oliver Wolcott	1795–1797
Secretary of War	Henry Knox	1789–1794
	Timothy Pickering	1795–1796
	James McHenry	1796–1797
Attorney General	Edmund Randolph	1789–1793
	William Bradford	1794–1795
	Charles Lee	1795–1797
Postmaster General	Samuel Osgood	1789–1791
	Timothy Pickering	1791–1794
	Joseph Habersham	1795–1797

THE JOHN ADAMS ADMINISTRATION

President	John Adams	1797–1801
Vice President	Thomas Jefferson	1797–1801
Secretary of State	Timothy Pickering	1797–1800
	John Marshall	1800–1801
Secretary of Treasury	Oliver Wolcott	1797–1800
	Samuel Dexter	1800–1801
Secretary of War	James McHenry	1797–1800
	Samuel Dexter	1800–1801
Attorney General	Charles Lee	1797–1801
Postmaster General	Joseph Habersham	1797–1801
Secretary of Navy	Benjamin Stoddert	1798–1801

THE JEFFERSON ADMINISTRATION

President	Thomas Jefferson	1801–1809
Vice President	Aaron Burr	1801–1805
	George Clinton	1805–1809
Secretary of State	James Madison	1801–1809
Secretary of Treasury	Samuel Dexter	1801
	Albert Gallatin	1801–1809
Secretary of War	Henry Dearborn	1801–1809
Attorney General	Levi Lincoln	1801–1805
	Robert Smith	1805
	John Breckinridge	1805–1806
	Caesar Rodney	1807–1809

Postmaster General	Joseph Habersham	1801
	Gideon Granger	1801–1809
Secretary of Navy	Robert Smith	1801–1809

THE MADISON ADMINISTRATION

President	James Madison	1809–1817
Vice President	George Clinton	1809–1813
	Elbridge Gerry	1813–1817
Secretary of State	Robert Smith	1809–1811
	James Monroe	1811–1817
Secretary of Treasury	Albert Gallatin	1809–1813
	George Campbell	1814
	Alexander Dallas	1814–1816
	William Crawford	1816–1817
Secretary of War	William Eustis	1809–1812
	John Armstrong	1813–1814
	James Monroe	1814–1815
	William Crawford	1815–1817
Attorney General	Caesar Rodney	1809–1811
	William Pinkney	1811–1814
	Richard Rush	1814–1817
Postmaster General	Gideon Granger	1809–1814
	Return Meigs	1814–1817
Secretary of Navy	Paul Hamilton	1809–1813
	William Jones	1813–1814
	Benjamin Crowninshield	1814–1817

THE MONROE ADMINISTRATION

President	James Monroe	1817–1825
Vice President	Daniel Tompkins	1817–1825
Secretary of State	John Quincy Adams	1817–1825
Secretary of Treasury	William Crawford	1817–1825
Secretary of War	George Graham	1817
	John C. Calhoun	1817–1825
Attorney General	Richard Rush	1817
	William Wirt	1817–1825
Postmaster General	Return Meigs	1817–1823
	John McLean	1823–1825
Secretary of Navy	Benjamin Crowninshield	1817–1818
	Smith Thompson	1818–1823
	Samuel Southard	1823–1825

THE JOHN QUINCY ADAMS ADMINISTRATION

President	John Quincy Adams	1825–1829
Vice President	John C. Calhoun	1825–1829
Secretary of State	Henry Clay	1825–1829
Secretary of Treasury	Richard Rush	1825–1829
Secretary of War	James Barbour	1825–1828
	Peter Porter	1828–1829
Attorney General	William Wirt	1825–1829
Postmaster General	John McLean	1825–1829
Secretary of Navy	Samuel Southard	1825–1829

THE JACKSON ADMINISTRATION

President	Andrew Jackson	1829–1837
Vice President	John C. Calhoun	1829–1833
	Martin Van Buren	1833–1837
Secretary of State	Martin Van Buren	1829–1831
	Edward Livingston	1831–1833
	Louis McLane	1833–1834
	John Forsyth	1834–1837
Secretary of Treasury	Samuel Ingham	1829–1831
	Louis McLane	1831–1833
	William Duane	1833
	Roger B. Taney	1833–1834
	Levi Woodbury	1834–1837
Secretary of War	John H. Eaton	1829–1831
	Lewis Cass	1831–1837
	Benjamin Butler	1837
Attorney General	John M. Berrien	1829–1831
	Roger B. Taney	1831–1833
	Benjamin Butler	1833–1837
Postmaster General	William Barry	1829–1835
	Amos Kendall	1835–1837
Secretary of Navy	John Branch	1829–1831
	Levi Woodbury	1831–1834
	Mahlon Dickerson	1834–1837

THE VAN BUREN ADMINISTRATION

President	Martin Van Buren	1837–1841
Vice President	Richard M. Johnson	1837–1841
Secretary of State	John Forsyth	1837–1841
Secretary of Treasury	Levi Woodbury	1837–1841
Secretary of War	Joel Poinsett	1837–1841
Attorney General	Benjamin Butler	1837–1838
	Felix Grundy	1838–1840
	Henry D. Gilpin	1840–1841
Postmaster General	Amos Kendall	1837–1840
	John M. Niles	1840–1841
Secretary of Navy	Mahlon Dickerson	1837–1838
	James Paulding	1838–1841

THE WILLIAM HARRISON ADMINISTRATION

President	William H. Harrison	1841
Vice President	John Tyler	1841
Secretary of State	Daniel Webster	1841
Secretary of Treasury	Thomas Ewing	1841
Secretary of War	John Bell	1841
Attorney General	John J. Crittenden	1841
Postmaster General	Francis Granger	1841
Secretary of Navy	George Badger	1841

THE TYLER ADMINISTRATION

President	John Tyler	1841–1845
Vice President	None	
Secretary of State	Daniel Webster	1841–1843
	Hugh S. Legaré	1843
	Abel P. Upshur	1843–1844
	John C. Calhoun	1844–1845
Secretary of Treasury	Thomas Ewing	1841
	Walter Forward	1841–1843
	John C. Spencer	1843–1844
	George Bibb	1844–1845
Secretary of War	John Bell	1841
	John C. Spencer	1841–1843
	James M. Porter	1843–1844
	William Wilkins	1844–1845
Attorney General	John J. Crittenden	1841
	Hugh S. Legaré	1841–1843
	John Nelson	1843–1845
Postmaster General	Francis Granger	1841
	Charles Wickliffe	1841
Secretary of Navy	George Badger	1841
	Abel P. Upshur	1841
	David Henshaw	1843–1844
	Thomas Gilmer	1844
	John Y. Mason	1844–1845

THE POLK ADMINISTRATION

President	James K. Polk	1845–1849
Vice President	George M. Dallas	1845–1849
Secretary of State	James Buchanan	1845–1849
Secretary of Treasury	Robert J. Walker	1845–1849
Secretary of War	William L. Marcy	1845–1849
Attorney General	John Y. Mason	1845–1846
	Nathan Clifford	1846–1848
	Isaac Toucey	1848–1849
Postmaster General	Cave Johnson	1845–1849
Secretary of Navy	George Bancroft	1845–1846
	John Y. Mason	1846–1849

THE TAYLOR ADMINISTRATION

President	Zachary Taylor	1849–1850
Vice President	Millard Fillmore	1849–1850
Secretary of State	John M. Clayton	1849–1850
Secretary of Treasury	William Meredith	1849–1850
Secretary of War	George Crawford	1849–1850
Attorney General	Reverdy Johnson	1849–1850
Postmaster General	Jacob Collamer	1849–1850
Secretary of Navy	William Preston	1849–1850
Secretary of Interior	Thomas Ewing	1849–1850

THE FILLMORE ADMINISTRATION

President	Millard Fillmore	1850–1853
Vice President	None	
Secretary of State	Daniel Webster	1850–1852
	Edward Everett	1852–1853
Secretary of Treasury	Thomas Corwin	1850–1853
Secretary of War	Charles Conrad	1850–1853
Attorney General	John J. Crittenden	1850–1853
Postmaster General	Nathan Hall	1850–1852
	Sam D. Hubbard	1852–1853
Secretary of Navy	William A. Graham	1850–1852
	John P. Kennedy	1852–1853
Secretary of Interior	Thomas McKennan	1850
	Alexander Stuart	1850–1853

THE PIERCE ADMINISTRATION

President	Franklin Pierce	1853–1857
Vice President	William R. King	1853–1857
Secretary of State	William L. Marcy	1853–1857
Secretary of Treasury	James Guthrie	1853–1857
Secretary of War	Jefferson Davis	1853–1857
Attorney General	Caleb Cushing	1853–1857
Postmaster General	James Campbell	1853–1857
Secretary of Navy	James C. Dobbin	1853–1857
Secretary of Interior	Robert McClelland	1853–1857

THE BUCHANAN ADMINISTRATION

President	James Buchanan	1857–1861
Vice President	John C. Breckinridge	1857–1861
Secretary of State	Lewis Cass	1857–1860
	Jeremiah S. Black	1860–1861
Secretary of Treasury	Howell Cobb	1857–1860
	Philip Thomas	1860–1861
	John A. Dix	1861
Secretary of War	John B. Floyd	1857–1861
	Joseph Holt	1861
Attorney General	Jeremiah S. Black	1857–1860
	Edwin M. Stanton	1860–1861
Postmaster General	Aaron V. Brown	1857–1859
	Joseph Holt	1859–1861
	Horatio King	1861
Secretary of Navy	Isaac Toucey	1857–1861
Secretary of Interior	Jacob Thompson	1857–1861

THE LINCOLN ADMINISTRATION

President	Abraham Lincoln	1861–1865
Vice President	Hannibal Hamlin	1861–1865
	Andrew Johnson	1865
Secretary of State	William H. Seward	1861–1865

Secretary of Treasury	Samuel P. Chase	1861–1864
	William P. Fessenden	1864–1865
	Hugh McCulloch	1865
Secretary of War	Simon Cameron	1861–1862
	Edwin M. Stanton	1862–1865
Attorney General	Edward Bates	1861–1864
	James Speed	1864–1865
Postmaster General	Horatio King	1861
	Montgomery Blair	1861–1864
	William Dennison	1864–1865
Secretary of Navy	Gideon Welles	1861–1865
Secretary of Interior	Caleb B. Smith	1861–1863
	John P. Usher	1863–1865

THE ANDREW JOHNSON ADMINISTRATION

President	Andrew Johnson	1865–1869
Vice President	None	
Secretary of State	William H. Seward	1865–1869
Secretary of Treasury	Hugh McCulloch	1865–1869
Secretary of War	Edwin M. Stanton	1865–1867
	Ulysses S. Grant	1867–1868
	Lorenzo Thomas	1868
	John M. Schofield	1868–1869
Attorney General	James Speed	1865–1866
	Henry Stanbery	1866–1868
	William M. Evarts	1868–1869
Postmaster General	William Dennison	1865–1866
	Alexander Randall	1866–1869
Secretary of Navy	Gideon Welles	1865–1869
Secretary of Interior	John P. Usher	1865
	James Harlan	1865–1866
	Orville H. Browning	1866–1869

THE GRANT ADMINISTRATION

President	Ulysses S. Grant	1869–1877
Vice President	Schuyler Colfax	1869–1873
	Henry Wilson	1873–1877
Secretary of State	Elihu B. Washburne	1869
	Hamilton Fish	1869–1877
Secretary of Treasury	George S. Boutwell	1869–1873
	William Richardson	1873–1874
	Benjamin Bristow	1874–1876
	Lot M. Morrill	1876–1877
Secretary of War	John A. Rawlins	1869
	William T. Sherman	1869
	William W. Belknap	1869 1876
	Alphonso Taft	1876
	James D. Cameron	1876–1877

Attorney General	Ebenezer Hoar	1869–1870
	Amos T. Ackerman	1870–1871
	G. H. Williams	1871–1875
	Edwards Pierrepont	1875–1876
	Alphonso Taft	1876–1877
Postmaster General	John A. J. Creswell	1869–1874
	James W. Marshall	1874
	Marshall Jewell	1874–1876
	James N. Tyner	1876–1877
Secretary of Navy	Adolph E. Borie	1869
	George M. Robeson	1869–1877
Secretary of Interior	Jacob D. Cox	1869–1870
	Columbus Delano	1870–1875
	Zachariah Chandler	1875–1877

THE HAYES ADMINISTRATION

President	Rutherford B. Hayes	1877–1881
Vice President	William A. Wheeler	1877–1881
Secretary of State	William B. Evarts	1877–1881
Secretary of Treasury	John Sherman	1877–1881
Secretary of War	George W. McCrary	1877–1879
	Alex Ramsey	1879–1881
Attorney General	Charles Devens	1877–1881
Postmaster General	David M. Key	1877–1880
	Horace Maynard	1880–1881
Secretary of Navy	Richard W. Thompson	1877–1880
	Nathan Goff, Jr.	1881
Secretary of Interior	Carl Schurz	1877–1881

THE GARFIELD ADMINISTRATION

President	James A. Garfield	1881
Vice President	Chester A. Arthur	1881
Secretary of State	James G. Blaine	1881
Secretary of Treasury	William Windom	1881
Secretary of War	Robert T. Lincoln	1881
Attorney General	Wayne MacVeagh	1881
Postmaster General	Thomas L. James	1881
Secretary of Navy	William H. Hunt	1881
Secretary of Interior	Samuel J. Kirkwood	1881

THE ARTHUR ADMINISTRATION

President	Chester A. Arthur	1881–1885
Vice President	None	
Secretary of State	F. T. Frelinghuysen	1881–1885
Secretary of Treasury	Charles J. Folger	1881–1884
	Walter Q. Gresham	1884
	Hugh McCulloch	1884–1885
Secretary of War	Robert T. Lincoln	1881–1885
Attorney General	Benjamin H. Brewster	1881–1885
Postmaster General	Timothy O. Howe	1881–1883
	Walter Q. Gresham	1883–1884
	Frank Hatton	1884–1885
Secretary of Navy	William H. Hunt	1881–1882
	William E. Chandler	1882–1885
Secretary of Interior	Samuel J. Kirkwood	1881–1882
	Henry M. Teller	1882–1885

THE CLEVELAND ADMINISTRATION

President	Grover Cleveland	1885–1889
Vice President	Thomas A. Hendricks	1885–1889
Secretary of State	Thomas F. Bayard	1885–1889
Secretary of Treasury	Daniel Manning	1885–1887
	Charles S. Fairchild	1887–1889
Secretary of War	William C. Endicott	1885–1889
Attorney General	Augustus H. Garland	1885–1889
Postmaster General	William F. Vilas	1885–1888
	Don M. Dickinson	1888–1889
Secretary of Navy	William C. Whitney	1885–1889
Secretary of Interior	Lucius Q. C. Lamar	1885–1888
	William F. Vilas	1888–1889
Secretary of Agriculture	Norman J. Colman	1889

THE BENJAMIN HARRISON ADMINISTRATION

President	Benjamin Harrison	1889–1893
Vice President	Levi P. Morton	1889–1893
Secretary of State	James G. Blaine	1889–1892
	John W. Foster	1892–1893
Secretary of Treasury	William Windom	1889–1891
	Charles Foster	1891–1893
Secretary of War	Redfield Proctor	1889–1891
	Stephen B. Elkins	1891–1893
Attorney General	William H. H. Miller	1889–1891

Postmaster General	John Wanamaker	1889–1893
Secretary of Navy	Benjamin F. Tracy	1889–1893
Secretary of Interior	John W. Noble	1889–1893
Secretary of Agriculture	Jeremiah M. Rusk	1889–1893

THE CLEVELAND ADMINISTRATION

President	Grover Cleveland	1893–1897
Vice President	Adlai E. Stevenson	1893–1897
Secretary of State	Walter Q. Gresham	1893–1895
	Richard Olney	1895–1897
Secretary of Treasury	John G. Carlisle	1893–1897
Secretary of War	Daniel S. Lamont	1893–1897
Attorney General	Richard Olney	1893–1895
	James Harmon	1895–1897
Postmaster General	Wilson S. Bissell	1893–1895
	William L. Wilson	1895–1897
Secretary of Navy	Hilary A. Herbert	1893–1897
Secretary of Interior	Hoke Smith	1893–1896
	David R. Francis	1896–1897
Secretary of Agriculture	Julius S. Morton	1893–1897

THE McKINLEY ADMINISTRATION

President	William McKinley	1897–1901
Vice President	Garret A. Hobart	1897–1901
	Theodore Roosevelt	1901
Secretary of State	John Sherman	1897–1898
	William R. Day	1898
	John Hay	1898–1901
Secretary of Treasury	Lyman J. Gage	1897–1901
Secretary of War	Russell A. Alger	1897–1899
	Elihu Root	1899–1901
Attorney General	Joseph McKenna	1897–1898
	John W. Griggs	1898–1901
	Philander C. Knox	1901
Postmaster General	James A. Gary	1897–1898
	Charles E. Smith	1898–1901
Secretary of Navy	John D. Long	1897–1901
Secretary of Interior	Cornelius N. Bliss	1897–1899
	Ethan A. Hitchcock	1899–1901
Secretary of Agriculture	James Wilson	1897–1901

THE THEODORE ROOSEVELT ADMINISTRATION

President	Theodore Roosevelt	1901–1909
Vice President	Charles Fairbanks	1905–1909
Secretary of State	John Hay	1901–1905
	Elihu Root	1905–1909
	Robert Bacon	1909
Secretary of Treasury	Lyman J. Gage	1901–1902
	Leslie M. Shaw	1902–1907
	George B. Cortelyou	1907–1909
Secretary of War	Elihu Root	1901–1904
	William H. Taft	1904–1908
	Luke E. Wright	1908–1909
Attorney General	Philander C. Knox	1901–1904
	William H. Moody	1904–1906
	Charles J. Bonaparte	1906–1909
Postmaster General	Charles E. Smith	1901–1902
	Henry C. Payne	1902–1904
	Robert J. Wynne	1904–1905
	George B. Cortelyou	1905–1907
	George von L. Meyer	1907–1909
Secretary of Navy	John D. Long	1901–1902
	William H. Moody	1902–1904
	Paul Morton	1904–1905
	Charles J. Bonaparte	1905–1906
	Victor H. Metcalf	1906–1908
	Truman H. Newberry	1908–1909
Secretary of Interior	Ethan A. Hitchcock	1901–1907
	James R. Garfield	1907–1909
Secretary of Agriculture	James Wilson	1901–1909
Secretary of Labor and Commerce	George B. Cortelyou	1903–1904
	Victor H. Metcalf	1904–1906
	Oscar S. Straus	1906–1909
	Charles Nagel	1909

THE TAFT ADMINISTRATION

President	William H. Taft	1909–1913
Vice President	James S. Sherman	1909–1913
Secretary of State	Philander C. Knox	1909–1913
Secretary of Treasury	Franklin MacVeagh	1909–1913
Secretary of War	Jacob M. Dickinson	1909–1911
	Henry L. Stimson	1911–1913
Attorney General	George W. Wickersham	1909–1913
Postmaster General	Frank H. Hitchcock	1909–1913
Secretary of Navy	George von L. Meyer	1909–1913
Secretary of Interior	Richard A. Ballinger	1909–1911
	Walter L. Fisher	1911–1913

Secretary of Agriculture	James Wilson	1909–1913
Secretary of Labor and Commerce	Charles Nagel	1909–1913

THE WILSON ADMINISTRATION

President	Woodrow Wilson	1913–1921
Vice President	Thomas R. Marshall	1913–1921
Secretary of State	William J. Bryan	1913–1915
	Robert Lansing	1915–1920
	Bainbridge Colby	1920–1921
Secretary of Treasury	William G. McAdoo	1913–1918
	Carter Glass	1918–1920
	David F. Houston	1920–1921
Secretary of War	Lindley M. Garrison	1913–1916
	Newton D. Baker	1916–1921
Attorney General	James C. McReynolds	1913–1914
	Thomas W. Gregory	1914–1919
	A. Mitchell Palmer	1919–1921
Postmaster General	Albert S. Burleson	1913–1921
Secretary of Navy	Josephus Daniels	1913–1921
Secretary of Interior	Franklin K. Lane	1913–1920
	John B. Payne	1920–1921
Secretary of Agriculture	David F. Houston	1913–1920
	Edwin T. Meredith	1920–1921
Secretary of Commerce	William C. Redfield	1913–1919
	Joshua W. Alexander	1919–1921
Secretary of Labor	William B. Wilson	1913–1921

THE HARDING ADMINISTRATION

President	Warren G. Harding	1921–1923
Vice President	Calvin Coolidge	1921–1923
Secretary of State	Charles E. Hughes	1921–1923
Secretary of Treasury	Andrew Mellon	1921–1923
Secretary of War	John W. Weeks	1921–1923
Attorney General	Harry M. Daugherty	1921–1923
Postmaster General	Will H. Hays	1921–1922
	Hubert Work	1922–1923
	Harry S. New	1923
Secretary of Navy	Edwin Denby	1921–1923
Secretary of Interior	Albert B. Fall	1921–1923
	Hubert Work	1923

Secretary of Agriculture	Henry C. Wallace	1921–1923
Secretary of Commerce	Herbert C. Hoover	1921–1923
Secretary of Labor	James J. Davis	1921–1923

THE COOLIDGE ADMINISTRATION

President	Calvin Coolidge	1923–1929
Vice President	Charles G. Dawes	1925–1929
Secretary of State	Charles E. Hughes	1923–1925
	Frank B. Kellogg	1925–1929
Secretary of Treasury	Andrew Mellon	1923–1929
Secretary of War	John W. Weeks	1923–1925
	Dwight F. Davis	1925–1929
Attorney General	Henry M. Daugherty	1923–1924
	Harlan F. Stone	1924–1925
	John G. Sargent	1925–1929
Postmaster General	Harry S. New	1923–1929
Secretary of Navy	Edwin Derby	1923–1924
	Curtis D. Wilbur	1924–1929
Secretary of Interior	Hubert Work	1923–1928
	Roy O. West	1928–1929
Secretary of Agriculture	Henry C. Wallace	1923–1924
	Howard M. Gore	1924–1925
	William M. Jardine	1925–1929
Secretary of Commerce	Herbert C. Hoover	1923–1928
	William F. Whiting	1928–1929
Secretary of Labor	James J. Davis	1923–1929

THE HOOVER ADMINISTRATION

President	Herbert C. Hoover	1929–1933
Vice President	Charles Curtis	1929–1933
Secretary of State	Henry L. Stimson	1929–1933
Secretary of Treasury	Andrew Mellon	1929–1932
	Ogden L. Mills	1932–1933
Secretary of War	James W. Good	1929
	Patrick J. Hurley	1929–1933
Attorney General	William D. Mitchell	1929–1933
Postmaster General	Walter F. Brown	1929–1933
Secretary of Navy	Charles F. Adams	1929–1933
Secretary of Interior	Ray L. Wilbur	1929–1933
Secretary of Agriculture	Arthur M. Hyde	1929–1933

Secretary of Commerce	Robert P. Lamont	1929–1932
	Roy D. Chapin	1932–1933
Secretary of Labor	James J. Davis	1929–1930
	William N. Doak	1930–1933

THE FRANKLIN D. ROOSEVELT ADMINISTRATION

President	Franklin D. Roosevelt	1933–1945
Vice President	John Nance Garner	1933–1941
	Henry A. Wallace	1941–1945
	Harry S Truman	1945
Secretary of State	Cordell Hull	1933–1944
	E. R. Stettinius, Jr.	1944–1945
Secretary of Treasury	William H. Woodin	1933–1934
	Henry Morgenthau, Jr.	1934–1945
Secretary of War	George H. Dern	1933–1936
	Henry A. Woodring	1936–1940
	Henry L. Stimson	1940–1945
Attorney General	Homer S. Cummings	1933–1939
	Frank Murphy	1939–1940
	Robert H. Jackson	1940–1941
	Francis Biddle	1941–1945
Postmaster General	James A. Farley	1933–1940
	Frank C. Walker	1940–1945
Secretary of Navy	Claude A. Swanson	1933–1940
	Charles Edison	1940
	Frank Knox	1940–1944
	James V. Forrestal	1944–1945
Secretary of Interior	Harold L. Ickes	1933–1945
Secretary of Agriculture	Henry A. Wallace	1933–1940
	Claude R. Wickard	1940–1945
Secretary of Commerce	Daniel C. Roper	1933–1939
	Harry L. Hopkins	1939–1940
	Jesse Jones	1940–1945
	Henry A. Wallace	1945
Secretary of Labor	Frances Perkins	1933–1945

THE TRUMAN ADMINISTRATION

President	Harry S Truman	1945–1953
Vice President	Alben W. Barkley	1949–1953
Secretary of State	James F. Byrnes	1945–1947
	George C. Marshall	1947–1949
	Dean G. Acheson	1949–1953
Secretary of Treasury	Fred M. Vinson	1945–1946
	John W. Snyder	1946–1953
Secretary of War	Robert P. Patterson	1945–1947
	Kenneth C. Royall	1947
Attorney General	Tom C. Clark	1945–1949
	J. Howard McGrath	1949–1952
	James P. McGranery	1952–1953

Postmaster General	Frank C. Walker	1945
	Robert E. Hannegan	1945–1947
	Jesse M. Donaldson	1947–1953
Secretary of Navy	James V. Forrestal	1945–1947
Secretary of Interior	Harold L. Ickes	1945–1946
	Julius A. Krug	1946–1949
	Oscar L. Chapman	1949–1953
Secretary of Agriculture	Clinton P. Anderson	1945–1948
	Charles F. Brannan	1948–1953
Secretary of Commerce	Henry A. Wallace	1945–1946
	W. Averell Harriman	1946–1948
	Charles W. Sawyer	1948–1953
Secretary of Labor	Lewis B. Schwellenbach	1945–1948
	Maurice J. Tobin	1948–1953
Secretary of Defense	James V. Forrestal	1947–1949
	Louis A. Johnson	1949–1950
	George C. Marshall	1950–1951
	Robert A. Lovett	1951–1953

THE EISENHOWER ADMINISTRATION

President	Dwight D. Eisenhower	1953–1961
Vice President	Richard M. Nixon	1953–1961
Secretary of State	John Foster Dulles	1953–1959
	Christian A. Herter	1959–1961
Secretary of Treasury	George M. Humphrey	1953–1957
	Robert B. Anderson	1957–1961
Attorney General	Herbert Brownell, Jr.	1953–1858
	William P. Rogers	1958–1961
Postmaster General	Arthur E. Summerfield	1953–1961
Secretary of Interior	Douglas McKay	1953–1956
	Fred A. Seaton	1956–1961
Secretary of Agriculture	Ezra T. Benson	1953–1961
Secretary of Commerce	Sinclair Weeks	1953–1958
	Lewis L. Strauss	1958–1959
	Frederick H. Mueller	1959–1961
Secretary of Labor	Martin P. Durkin	1953
	James P. Mitchell	1953–1961
Secretary of Defense	Charles E. Wilson	1953–1957
	Neil H. McElroy	1957–1959
	Thomas S. Gates, Jr.	1959–1961
Secretary of Health, Education, and Welfare	Oveta Culp Hobby	1953–1955
	Marion B. Folsom	1955–1958
	Arthur S. Flemming	1958–1961

THE KENNEDY ADMINISTRATION

President	John F. Kennedy	1961–1963
Vice President	Lyndon B. Johnson	1961–1963
Secretary of State	Dean Rusk	1961–1963
Secretary of Treasury	C. Douglas Dillon	1961–1963
Attorney General	Robert F. Kennedy	1961–1963
Postmaster General	J. Edward Day	1961–1963
	John A. Gronouski	1963
Secretary of Interior	Stewart L. Udall	1961–1963
Secretary of Agriculture	Orville L. Freeman	1961–1963
Secretary of Commerce	Luther H. Hodges	1961–1963
Secretary of Labor	Arthur J. Goldberg	1961–1962
	W. Willard Wirtz	1962–1963
Secretary of Defense	Robert S. McNamara	1961–1963
Secretary of Health, Education, and Welfare	Abraham A. Ribicoff	1961–1962
	Anthony J. Celebrezze	1962–1963

THE LYNDON JOHNSON ADMINISTRATION

President	Lyndon B. Johnson	1963–1969
Vice President	Hubert H. Humphrey	1965–1969
Secretary of State	Dean Rusk	1963–1969
Secretary of Treasury	C. Douglas Dillon	1963–1965
	Henry H. Fowler	1965–1969
Attorney General	Robert F. Kennedy	1963–1964
	Nicholas Katzenbach	1965–1966
	Ramsey Clark	1967–1969
Postmaster General	John A. Gronouski	1963–1965
	Lawrence F. O'Brien	1965–1968
	Marvin Watson	1968–1969
Secretary of Interior	Stewart L. Udall	1963–1969
Secretary of Agriculture	Orville L. Freeman	1963–1969
Secretary of Commerce	Luther H. Hodges	1963–1964
	John T. Connor	1964–1967
	Alexander B. Trowbridge	1967–1968
	Cyrus R. Smith	1968–1969
Secretary of Labor	W. Willard Wirtz	1963–1969
Secretary of Defense	Robert F. McNamara	1963–1968
	Clark Clifford	1968–1969
Secretary of Health, Education, and Welfare	Anthony J. Celebrezze	1963–1965
	John W. Gardner	1965–1968
	Wilbur J. Cohen	1968–1969

Secretary of Housing and Urban Development	Robert C. Weaver	1966–1969
	Robert C. Wood	1969
Secretary of Transportation	Alan S. Boyd	1967–1969

THE NIXON ADMINISTRATION

President	Richard M. Nixon	1969–1974
Vice President	Spiro T. Agnew	1969–1973
	Gerald R. Ford	1973–1974
Secretary of State	William P. Rogers	1969–1973
	Henry A. Kissinger	1973–1974
Secretary of Treasury	David M. Kennedy	1969–1970
	John B. Connally	1971–1972
	George P. Shultz	1972–1974
	William E. Simon	1974
Attorney General	John N. Mitchell	1969–1972
	Richard G. Kleindienst	1972–1973
	Elliot L. Richardson	1973
	William B. Saxbe	1973–1974
Postmaster General	Winton M. Blount	1969–1971
Secretary of Interior	Walter J. Hickel	1969–1970
	Rogers Morton	1971–1974
Secretary of Agriculture	Clifford M. Hardin	1969–1971
	Earl L. Butz	1971–1974
Secretary of Commerce	Maurice H. Stans	1969–1972
	Peter G. Peterson	1972–1973
	Frederick B. Dent	1973–1974
Secretary of Labor	George P. Shultz	1969–1970
	James D. Hodgson	1970–1973
	Peter J. Brennan	1973–1974
Secretary of Defense	Melvin R. Laird	1969–1973
	Elliot L. Richardson	1973
	James R. Schlesinger	1973–1974
Secretary of Health, Education, and Welfare	Robert H. Finch	1969–1970
	Elliot L. Richardson	1970–1973
	Casper W. Weinberger	1973–1974
Secretary of Housing and Urban Development	George Romney	1969–1973
	James T. Lynn	1973–1974
Secretary of Transportation	John A. Volpe	1969–1973
	Claude S. Brinegar	1973–1974

THE FORD ADMINISTRATION

President	Gerald R. Ford	1974–1977
Vice President	Nelson A. Rockefeller	1974–1977
Secretary of State	Henry A. Kissinger	1974–1977
Secretary of Treasury	William E. Simon	1974–1977
Attorney General	William Saxbe	1974–1975
	Edward Levi	1975–1977
Secretary of Interior	Rogers Morton	1974–1975
	Stanley K. Hathaway	1975
	Thomas Kleppe	1975–1977
Secretary of Agriculture	Earl L. Butz	1974–1976
	John A. Knebel	1976–1977
Secretary of Commerce	Frederick B. Dent	1974–1975
	Rogers Morton	1975–1976
	Elliot L. Richardson	1976–1977
Secretary of Labor	Peter J. Brennan	1974–1975
	John T. Dunlop	1975–1976
	W. J. Usery	1976–1977
Secretary of Defense	James R. Schlesinger	1974–1975
	Donald Rumsfeld	1975–1977
Secretary of Health, Education, and Welfare	Casper Weinberger	1974–1975
	Forrest D. Mathews	1975–1977
Secretary of Housing and Urban Development	James T. Lynn	1974–1975
	Carla A. Hills	1975–1977
Secretary of Transportation	Claude Brinegar	1974–1975
	William T. Coleman	1975–1977

THE CARTER ADMINISTRATION

President	Jimmy Carter	1977–1981
Vice President	Walter F. Mondale	1977–1981
Secretary of State	Cyrus R. Vance	1977–1980
	Edmund Muskie	1980–1981
Secretary of Treasury	W. Michael Blumenthal	1977–1979
	G. William Miller	1979–1981
Attorney General	Griffin Bell	1977–1979
	Benjamin R. Civiletti	1979–1981
Secretary of Interior	Cecil D. Andrus	1977–1981
Secretary of Agriculture	Robert Bergland	1977–1981
Secretary of Commerce	Juanita M. Kreps	1977–1979
	Philip M. Klutznick	1979–1981
Secretary of Labor	F. Ray Marshall	1977–1981
Secretary of Defense	Harold Brown	1977–1981
Secretary of Health, Education, and Welfare	Joseph A. Califano	1977–1979
	Patricia R. Harris	1979

Secretary of Health and Human Services	Patricia R. Harris	1979–1981
Secretary of Education	Shirley M. Hufstedler	1979–1981
Secretary of Housing and Urban Development	Patricia R. Harris Moon Landrieu	1977–1979 1979–1981
Secretary of Transportation	Brock Adams Neil E. Goldschmidt	1977–1979 1979–1981
Secretary of Energy	James R. Schlesinger Charles W. Duncan	1977–1979 1979–1981

THE REAGAN ADMINISTRATION

President	Ronald Reagan	1981–
Vice President	George Bush	1981–
Secretary of State	Alexander M. Haig	1981–
Secretary of Treasury	Donald Regan	1981–
Attorney General	William Smith	1981–

Secretary of Interior	James Watt	1981–
Secretary of Agriculture	John Block	1981–
Secretary of Commerce	Malcolm Baldrige	1981–
Secretary of Labor	Raymond Donovan	1981–
Secretary of Defense	Casper Weinberger	1981–
Secretary of Health and Human Services	Richard Schweiker	1981–
Secretary of Education	Terrel Bell	1981–
Secretary of Housing and Urban Development	Samuel Pierce	1981–
Secretary of Transportation	Drew Lewis	1981–
Secretary of Energy	James Edwards	1981–

Party Strength in Congress

		HOUSE				SENATE				
PERIOD	CONGRESS	MAJORITY PARTY		MINORITY PARTY		OTH-ERS	MAJORITY PARTY		MINORITY PARTY		OTH-ERS	PARTY OF PRESIDENT

PERIOD	CONGRESS	MAJORITY PARTY		MINORITY PARTY		OTH-ERS	MAJORITY PARTY		MINORITY PARTY		OTH-ERS	PARTY OF PRESIDENT
1789–91	1st	Ad	38	Op	26		Ad	17	Op	9		F	Washington
1791–93	2nd	F	37	DR	33		F	16	DR	13		F	Washington
1793–95	3rd	DR	57	F	48		F	17	DR	13		F	Washington
1795–97	4th	F	54	DR	52		F	19	DR	13		F	Washington
1797–99	5th	F	58	DR	48		F	20	DR	12		F	J. Adams
1799–1801	6th	F	64	DR	42		F	19	DR	13		F	J. Adams
1801–03	7th	DR	69	F	36		DR	18	F	13		DR	Jefferson
1803–05	8th	DR	102	F	39		DR	25	F	9		DR	Jefferson
1805–07	9th	DR	116	F	25		DR	27	F	7		DR	Jefferson
1807–09	10th	DR	118	F	24		DR	28	F	6		DR	Jefferson
1809–11	11th	DR	94	F	48		DR	28	F	6		DR	Madison
1811–13	12th	DR	108	F	36		DR	30	F	6		DR	Madison
1813–15	13th	DR	112	F	68		DR	27	F	9		DR	Madison
1815–17	14th	DR	117	F	65		DR	25	F	11		DR	Madison

		HOUSE			SENATE			PARTY OF
PERIOD	CONGRESS	MAJORITY PARTY	MINORITY PARTY	OTHERS	MAJORITY PARTY	MINORITY PARTY	OTHERS	PARTY OF PRESIDENT
1817–19	15th	DR 141	F 42		DR 34	F 10		DR Monroe
1819–21	16th	DR 156	F 27		DR 35	F 7		DR Monroe
1821–23	17th	DR 158	F 25		DR 44	F 4		DR Monroe
1823–25	18th	DR 187	F 26		DR 44	F 4		DR Monroe
1825–27	19th	Ad 105	J 97		Ad 26	J 20		C J. Q. Adams
1827–29	20th	J 119	Ad 94		J 28	Ad 20		C J. Q. Adams
1829–31	21st	D 139	NR 74		D 26	NR 22		D Jackson
1831–33	22nd	D 141	NR 58	14	D 25	NR 21	2	D Jackson
1833–35	23rd	D 147	AM 53	60	D 20	NR 20	8	D Jackson
1835–37	24th	D 145	W 98		D 27	W 25		D Jackson
1837–39	25th	D 108	W 107	24	D 30	W 18	4	D Van Buren
1839–41	26th	D 124	W 118		D 28	W 22		D Van Buren
1841–43	27th	W 133	D 102	6	W 28	D 22	2	W W. Harrison
								W Tyler
1843–45	28th	D 142	W 79	1	W 28	D 25	1	W Tyler
1845–47	29th	D 143	W 77	6	D 31	W 25		D Polk
1847–49	30th	W 115	D 108	4	D 36	W 21	1	D Polk
1849–51	31st	D 112	W 109	9	D 35	W 25	2	W Taylor
								W Fillmore
1851–53	32nd	D 140	W 88	5	D 35	W 24	3	W Fillmore
1853–55	33rd	D 159	W 71	4	D 38	W 22	2	D Pierce
1855–57	34th	R 108	D 83	43	D 40	R 15	5	D Pierce
1857–59	35th	D 118	R 92	26	D 36	R 20	8	D Buchanan
1859–61	36th	R 114	D 92	31	D 36	R 26	4	D Buchanan
1861–63	37th	R 105	D 43	30	R 31	D 10	8	R Lincoln
1863–65	38th	R 102	D 75	9	R 36	D 9	5	R Lincoln
1865–67	39th	U 149	D 42		U 42	D 10		R Lincoln
								R Johnson
1867–69	40th	R 143	D 49		R 42	D 11		R Johnson
1869–71	41st	R 149	D 63		R 56	D 11		R Grant
1871–73	42nd	R 134	D 104	5	R 52	D 17	5	R Grant
1873–75	43rd	R 194	D 92	14	R 49	D 19	5	R Grant
1875–77	44th	D 169	R 109	14	R 45	D 29	2	R Grant
1877–79	45th	D 153	R 140		R 39	D 36	1	R Hayes
1879–81	46th	D 149	R 130	14	D 42	R 33	1	R Hayes
1881–83	47th	D 147	R 135	11	R 37	D 37	1	R Garfield
								R Arthur
1883–85	48th	D 197	R 118	10	R 38	D 36	2	R Arthur
1885–87	49th	D 183	R 140	2	R 43	D 34		D Cleveland
1887–89	50th	D 169	R 152	4	R 39	D 37		D Cleveland
1889–91	51st	R 166	D 159		R 39	D 37		R B. Harrison
1891–93	52nd	D 235	R 88	9	R 47	D 39	2	R B. Harrison
1893–95	53rd	D 218	R 127	11	D 44	R 38	3	D Cleveland
1895–97	54th	R 244	D 105	7	R 43	D 39	6	D Cleveland
1897–99	55th	R 204	D 113	40	R 47	D 34	7	R McKinley
1899–1901	56th	R 185	D 163	9	R 53	D 26	8	R McKinley
1901–03	57th	R 197	D 151	9	R 55	D 31	4	R McKinley
								R T. Roosevelt

PERIOD	CONGRESS	HOUSE MAJORITY PARTY		MINORITY PARTY		OTH-ERS	SENATE MAJORITY PARTY		MINORITY PARTY		OTH-ERS	PARTY OF PRESIDENT	
1903–05	58th	R	208	D	178		R	57	D	33		R	T. Roosevelt
1905–07	59th	R	250	D	136		R	57	D	33		R	T. Roosevelt
1907–09	60th	R	222	D	164		R	61	D	31		R	T. Roosevelt
1909–11	61st	R	219	D	172		R	61	D	32		R	Taft
1911–13	62nd	D	228	R	161	1	R	51	D	41		R	Taft
1913–15	63rd	D	291	R	127	17	D	51	R	44	1	D	Wilson
1915–17	64th	D	230	R	196	9	D	56	R	40		D	Wilson
1917–19	65th	D	216	R	210	6	D	53	R	42		D	Wilson
1919–21	66th	R	240	D	190	3	R	49	D	47		D	Wilson
1921–23	67th	R	301	D	131	1	R	59	D	37		R	Harding
1923–25	68th	R	225	D	205	5	R	51	D	43	2	R	Coolidge
1925–27	69th	R	247	D	183	4	R	56	D	39	1	R	Coolidge
1927–29	70th	R	237	D	195	3	R	49	D	46	1	R	Coolidge
1929–31	71st	R	267	D	167	1	R	56	D	39	1	R	Hoover
1931–33	72nd	D	220	R	214	1	R	48	D	47	1	R	Hoover
1933–35	73rd	D	310	R	117	5	D	60	R	35	1	D	F. Roosevelt
1935–37	74th	D	319	R	103	10	D	69	R	25	2	D	F. Roosevelt
1937–39	75th	D	331	R	89	13	D	76	R	16	4	D	F. Roosevelt
1939–41	76th	D	261	R	164	4	D	69	R	23	4	D	F. Roosevelt
1941–43	77th	D	268	R	162	5	D	66	R	28	2	D	F. Roosevelt
1943–45	78th	D	218	R	208	4	D	58	R	37	1	D	F. Roosevelt
1945–47	79th	D	242	R	190	2	D	56	R	38	1	D	Truman
1947–49	80th	R	245	D	188	1	R	51	D	45		D	Truman
1949–51	81st	D	263	R	171	1	D	54	R	42		D	Truman
1951–53	82nd	D	234	R	199	1	D	49	R	47		D	Truman
1953–55	83rd	R	221	D	211	1	R	48	D	47	1	R	Eisenhower
1955–57	84th	D	232	R	203		D	48	R	47	1	R	Eisenhower
1957–59	85th	D	233	R	200		D	49	R	47		R	Eisenhower
1959–61	86th	D	284	R	153		D	65	R	35		R	Eisenhower
1961–63	87th	D	263	R	174		D	65	R	35		D	Kennedy
1963–65	88th	D	258	R	177		D	67	R	33		D	Kennedy
												D	Johnson
1965–67	89th	D	295	R	140		D	68	R	32		D	Johnson
1967–69	90th	D	247	R	187		D	64	R	36		D	Johnson
1969–71	91st	D	243	R	192		D	57	R	43		R	Nixon
1971–73	92nd	D	254	R	180		D	54	R	44	2	R	Nixon
1973–75	93rd	D	239	R	192	1	D	56	R	42	2	R	Nixon
1975–77	94th	D	291	R	144		D	60	R	37	3	R	Ford
1977–79	95th	D	292	R	143		D	61	R	38	1	D	Carter
1979–81	96th	D	276	R	157		D	58	R	41	1	D	Carter
1981–83	97th	D	243	R	192		R	53	D	46	1	R	Reagan

Ad = Administration; AM = Anti-Masonic; C = Coalition; D = Democratic; DR = Democratic-Republican; F = Federalist; J = Jacksonian; NR = National Republican; Op = Opposition; R = Republican; U = Unionist; W = Whig. Figures are for the beginning of first session of each Congress, except the 93rd, which are for the beginning of the second session.

	TERM OF SERVICE	YEARS OF SERVICE	LIFE SPAN		TERM OF SERVICE	YEARS OF SERVICE	LIFE SPAN
John Jay	1789–1795	5	1745–1829	Howell E. Jackson	1893–1895	2	1832–1895
John Rutledge	1789–1791	1	1739–1800	Edward D. White	1894–1910	16	1845–1921
William Cushing	1789–1810	20	1732–1810	Rufus W. Peckham	1895–1909	14	1838–1909
James Wilson	1789–1798	8	1742–1798	Joseph McKenna	1898–1925	26	1843–1926
John Blair	1789–1796	6	1732–1800	Oliver W. Holmes	1902–1932	30	1841–1935
Robert H. Harrison	1789–1790	–	1745–1790	William R. Day	1903–1922	19	1849–1923
James Iredell	1790–1799	9	1751–1799	William H. Moody	1906–1910	3	1853–1917
Thomas Johnson	1791–1793	1	1732–1819	Horace H. Lurton	1910–1914	4	1844–1914
William Paterson	1793–1806	13	1745–1806	Charles E. Hughes	1910–1916	5	1862–1948
*John Rutledge**	1795	–	1739–1800	Willis Van Devanter	1911–1937	26	1859–1941
Samuel Chase	1796–1811	15	1741–1811	Joseph R. Lamar	1911–1916	5	1857–1916
Oliver Ellsworth	1796–1800	4	1745–1807	*Edward D. White*	1910–1921	11	1845–1921
Bushrod Washington	1798–1829	31	1762–1829	Mahlon Pitney	1912–1922	10	1858–1924
Alfred Moore	1799–1804	4	1755–1810	James C. McReynolds	1914–1941	26	1862–1946
John Marshall	1801–1835	34	1755–1835	Louis D. Brandeis	1916–1939	22	1856–1941
William Johnson	1804–1834	30	1771–1834	John H. Clarke	1916–1922	6	1857–1945
H. Brockholst Livingston	1806–1823	16	1757–1823	William H. Taft	1921–1930	8	1857–1930
Thomas Todd	1807–1826	18	1765–1826	George Sutherland	1922–1938	15	1862–1942
Joseph Story	1811–1845	33	1779–1845	Pierce Butler	1922–1939	16	1866–1939
Gabriel Duval	1811–1835	24	1752–1844	Edward T. Sanford	1923–1930	7	1865–1930
Smith Thompson	1823–1843	20	1768–1843	Harlan F. Stone	1925–1941	16	1872–1946
Robert Trimble	1826–1828	2	1777–1828	*Charles E. Hughes*	1930–1941	11	1862–1948
John McLean	1829–1861	32	1785–1861	Owen J. Roberts	1930–1945	15	1875–1955
Henry Baldwin	1830–1844	14	1780–1844	Benjamin N. Cardozo	1932–1938	6	1870–1938
James M. Wayne	1835–1867	32	1790–1867	Hugo L. Black	1937–1971	34	1886–1971
Roger B. Taney	1836–1864	28	1777–1864	Stanley F. Reed	1938–1957	19	1884–1980
Philip P. Barbour	1836–1841	4	1783–1841	Felix Frankfurter	1939–1962	23	1882–1965
John Catron	1837–1865	28	1786–1865	William O. Douglas	1939–1975	36	1898–1980
John McKinley	1837–1852	15	1780–1852	Frank Murphy	1940–1949	9	1890–1949
Peter V. Daniel	1841–1860	19	1784–1860	*Harlan F. Stone*	1941–1946	5	1872–1946
Samuel Nelson	1845–1872	27	1792–1873	James F. Byrnes	1941–1942	1	1879–1972
Levi Woodbury	1845–1851	5	1789–1851	Robert H. Jackson	1941–1954	13	1892–1954
Robert C. Grier	1846–1870	23	1794–1870	Wiley B. Rutledge	1943–1949	6	1894–1949
Benjamin R. Curtis	1851–1857	6	1809–1874	Harold H. Burton	1945–1958	13	1888–1964
John A. Campbell	1853–1861	8	1811–1889	*Fred M. Vinson*	1946–1953	7	1890–1953
Nathan Clifford	1858–1881	23	1803–1881	Tom C. Clark	1949–1967	18	1899–1977
Noah H. Swayne	1862–1881	18	1804–1884	Sherman Minton	1949–1956	7	1890–1965
Samuel F. Miller	1862–1890	28	1816–1890	*Earl Warren*	1953–1969	16	1891–1974
David Davis	1862–1877	14	1815–1886	John Marshall Harlan	1955–1971	16	1899–1971
Stephen J. Field	1863–1897	34	1816–1899	William J. Brennan, Jr.	1956–	–	1906–
Salmon P. Chase	1864–1873	8	1808–1873	Charles E. Whittaker	1957–1962	5	1901–1973
William Strong	1870–1880	10	1808–1895	Potter Stewart	1958–1981	23	1915–
Joseph P. Bradley	1870–1892	22	1813–1892	Byron R. White	1962–	–	1917–
Ward Hunt	1873–1882	9	1810–1886	Arthur J. Goldberg	1962–1965	3	1908–
Morrison R. Waite	1874–1888	14	1816–1888	Abe Fortas	1965–1969	4	1910–
John M. Harlan	1877–1911	34	1833–1911	Thurgood Marshall	1967–	–	1908–
William B. Woods	1880–1887	7	1824–1887	*Warren C. Burger*	1969–	–	1907–
Stanley Matthews	1881–1889	7	1824–1889	Harry A. Blackmun	1970–	–	1908–
Horace Gray	1882–1902	20	1828–1902	Lewis F. Powell, Jr.	1972–	–	1907–
Samuel Blatchford	1882–1893	11	1820–1893	William H. Rehnquist	1972–	–	1924–
Lucius Q. C. Lamar	1888–1893	5	1825–1893	John P. Stevens, III	1975–	–	1920–
Melville W. Fuller	1888–1910	21	1833–1910	Sandra Day O'Connor	1981–	–	1930–
David J. Brewer	1890–1910	20	1837–1910				
Henry B. Brown	1890–1906	16	1836–1913				
George Shiras, Jr.	1892–1903	10	1832–1924				

*Appointed and served one term, but not confirmed by the Senate.   NOTE: Chief justices are in italics.

INDEX